COLLECTED WORKS OF ERASMUS

VOLUME 35

COLLECTED WORKS OF
ERASMUS

ADAGES

III iv 1 to IV ii 100

translated and annotated by Denis L. Drysdall

edited by John N. Grant

University of Toronto Press
Toronto / Buffalo / London

The research and publication costs of the
Collected Works of Erasmus are supported by
University of Toronto Press.

© University of Toronto Press Incorporated 2005
Toronto / Buffalo / London
Printed in Canada

ISBN 0-8020-3643-0

Printed on acid-free paper

Canadian Cataloguing in Publication Data

Erasmus, Desiderius, d. 1536
[Works]
Collected works of Erasmus

Translation of Adagia Des. Erasmi Roterdami
Includes bibliographical references.
Contents: v. 35. Adages III iv 1 to IV ii 100 /
translated and annotated by Denis Drysdall ; edited by John N. Grant.
ISBN 0-8020-3643-0 (v. 35)

1. Erasmus, Desiderius, d. 1536 – Collected works.   I. Title.

PA8500 1974   199'.492   C74-006326-x rev

University of Toronto Press acknowledges the financial assistance to its
publishing program of the Canada Council and the Ontario Arts Council.

University of Toronto Press acknowledges the financial support
for its publishing activities of the Government of Canada
through the Book Publishing Industry Development Program (BPIDP).

Collected Works of Erasmus

The aim of the Collected Works of Erasmus
is to make available an accurate, readable English text
of Erasmus' correspondence and his
other principal writings. The edition is planned
and directed by an Editorial Board, an Executive Committee,
and an Advisory Committee.

Contents

Editor's Preface

The first volume of translation and annotation of the *Adagia* (CWE 31), covering the first five hundred adages of the first chiliad, was published in 1982. In that volume Margaret Mann Phillips was the translator and Sir Roger Mynors was responsible for the annotation. For the next three volumes Sir Roger was both translator and annotator, but he saw only the first of these (CWE 32) in print. This appeared in 1989, only a short time before his death in October of that year. He had virtually completed, however, the translation and annotation of CWE 33 and CWE 34, and these two volumes were published in quick succession in 1991 and 1992. The delay in completing the translation and annotation of the remainder of the *Adagia* (III iv 1 to v ii 51) is testimony to the debt CWE owes to Sir Roger and to the reluctance of others to attempt to complete the labours of Hercules. As Erasmus himself remarked:

> Since the work knows no limits and aims at being generally useful, is there any reason why we should not share the labour and by our joint efforts finish it? I have completed my task; let me have a successor who is ready to take his turn. I have supplied a mass of material on an, I think, not wholly ungenerous scale; now for men who will hew it to shape and polish it and inlay it.[1]

Sir Roger's successors in the final two volumes of translation and annotation in this series will try to do justice to their distinguished predecessor.

This volume covers III iv 1 to IV ii 100. Both the translation and annotation are the work of Denis L. Drysdall, of the University of Waikato in New Zealand until his retirement. Although Sir Roger had not begun the translation of these adages, he left among his papers annotated photocopies

* * * * *

1 *Adagia* III i 1 CWE 34 180

of the relevant pages of the Leiden edition (1703–6) of Erasmus' *Opera*, on which he had identified most of the references. These have proved most helpful. A considerable debt is also owed to the work of the editors of the new critical Amsterdam edition of the Erasmian corpus (ASD). One benefit of the delay in completing the *Adagia* volumes has been the recent appearance of volumes II-7 and II-8 in that series. A critical text with apparatus and commentary is now available for all the adages that appear in this and the succeeding volume.

JNG

Translator's Preface

This volume of the *Adages* contains the last seven centuries of chiliad III and the first two of chiliad IV. It includes two of Erasmus' more important essays on power and its abuse: 'A dung-beetle hunting an eagle' and 'War is a treat for those who have not tried it.' These constitute a major part of that enrichment which, as Erasmus boasted in several letters (Epp 307, 313, 322, 333, and 334), made the edition of 1515 virtually a new book. A second feature of special interest is the series of some two hundred and seventy adages derived from Homer in centuries III viii–x, where, as explained in the introductory note (281 below), both the selection and the form differ from Erasmus' usual practice.

The aims of this translation and the purposes of the notes remain the same as those of the preceding volumes. The task was rendered considerably easier by the notes on Erasmus' sources and references which Sir Roger Mynors had made on these centuries before his death. The timely appearance of the corresponding volumes of ASD provided a convenient and accurate textual apparatus to work with in place of the less reliable text of LB, whose occasional errors have for the most part been corrected silently. In regard to the many quotations in Greek it should be remembered that Erasmus' verse renderings of the originals are often rather loose, that the policy has been, in general, to translate his Latin, and that only obvious errors or extreme divergences from the original have been noted. ASD was also helpful in compiling the notes; it was felt necessary to add to these in some cases, though, it is hoped, without making them too weighty.

The practice of referring to the *Suda* as 'Suidas' has been maintained in Erasmus' text for the reason explained in CWE 31 12 n41; '*Suda*' is used in the notes. Notes on Erasmus' use of the names 'Zenodotus,' 'Eudemus,' and

'Plutarch' will be found in III v 1 n1, III v 1 n48, and III v 30n respectively (59, 66, 83 below).

I could not have completed this work without help. It is my pleasure to record here my special gratitude to Professor John N. Grant of Toronto, who has suggested many corrections and has given generous guidance at every stage.

DLD

ADAGES

III iv 1 to IV ii 100

1 Chamaeleonte mutabilior
As changeable as a chameleon

Χαμαιλέοντος εὐμεταβολώτερος, As changeable as a chameleon. The chameleon is recorded among animals that change their colour. Aristotle describes its appearance carefully in the second book of his *Nature of Animals*. As far as the changing of colour is concerned, he reports as follows:

> Its colour changes when it is breathed on. This becomes at one time black, not unlike the colour of crocodiles, at another pale, like lizards', at yet another a spotted black such as that of leopards. This sort of change of colour occurs over the whole body. Even the eyes and tail end up becoming the same colour as the rest of the body. The animal's movement is sluggish, very much like that of the tortoise. It turns pale when it is dying. This same colour persists after death.[1]

That is what Aristotle has to say. Quite compatible with these remarks is what Pliny reports in book 8 chapter 33, with the addition that this animal imitates with its whole body whatever colour it is near, except red and white.[2] The adage therefore can be applied to the man who is a turncoat,[3] or who is inconstant and adopts any appearance to suit the time. Plato says in the *Ion*: 'But you change into every possible shape, absolutely like Proteus, as you twist back and forth.'[4] In the first book of the *Nicomachean Ethics*, Aristotle uses the word 'chameleon' to describe the vice of inconstancy.[5]

* * * * *

1 Apostolius 18.9. Tilley C 221 As changeable as a chameleon. In *1508* the first part, with the quotation from Aristotle's *Historia animalium*, appeared where III iv 35 is now; it was moved here and the sentence suggesting the application was added in *1515*. The reference to Pliny was inserted in *1517/18* and the rest added in *1528* and *1533*. For an opposite, approbatory use of the same set of images of the chameleon, the polyp (see n5 below), and Proteus (see n4 below) applied to the figures of Christ and the apostle Paul see Erasmus *Ratio verae theologiae* (LB V 94B, 98F, and 111D).
1 Aristotle *Historia animalium* 2.11 (503b)
2 Pliny *Naturalis historia* 8.121–2. Cf Erasmus *Parabolae* CWE 23 144 / LB I 565A, Tilley C 222 The chameleon can change to all colours save white, and Otto 381.
3 The Latin *versipellis* means 'one who changes his skin,' sometimes a werewolf.
4 Plato *Ion* 541E; added in *1523* to *Adagia* II ii 74 As many shapes as Proteus
5 Aristotle *Ethica Nicomachea* 1.10.8 (1100b6); a rather loose interpretation. In *Adagia* I i 93 Adopt the outlook of the polyp, and IV viii 35 A four-square man, Erasmus quotes Aristotle more precisely as saying that if the definition

2 Suus cuique crepitus bene olet
Everyone thinks his own fart smells sweet

Ἕκαστος αὑτοῦ τὸ βδέμα μήλου γλύκιον ἡγεῖται, Everyone thinks his own fart smells as sweet as apples; there is no one, in other words, to whom his own faults do not seem to be his best qualities. In the *Nicomachean Ethics* book 9, Aristotle says: 'For most things are not reckoned at the same price by those who possess them and by those who wish to acquire them. For to everyone his own goods, and what he gives, seem to be of great value.'[1] This passage was better suited to the proverb 'What is one's own is beautiful,'[2] but that page has already passed out of my hands. I suspect this proverb about the fart was drawn by Apostolius from the dregs of the common herd,[3] for I have never yet heard of anyone to whom his own fart smelled sweet. It is true that men shrink from other men's excrement and farts more violently than from their own.

3 E poculo perforato bibere
To drink from a cup with a hole in it

Ἐκ τετριμμένης κύλικος πιεῖν, To drink from a cup with a hole in it. This is said of those who cannot contain anything and who cannot manage to keep to themselves the secrets entrusted to them. This one smacks of the common herd too.[1]

* * * * *

of happiness depends on fortune we should have to suppose the happy man to be a sort of chameleon.

2 Apostolius 6.98. Suringar 219. Tilley F 65 Everyone thinks his own fart smells sweet. The quotation from the *Ethica Nicomachea* and the remarks evoked by the reference to Apostolius were added in *1533*.
1 Aristotle *Ethica Nicomachea* 9.1.9 (1164b16)
2 *Adagia* I ii 15
3 Apostolius himself adds the word δημώδης 'popular.' For Erasmus' attitude to Apostolius see the notes to *Adagia* III iii 31 and 37. There are several other examples of this judgment in the following adages. The remark replaced a phrase that had stood here from *1508* 'This is recounted by Apostolius and borrowed from the common people, as I guess,' to which was added from *1515* 'for he seems to have included several things of this sort.'

3 Apostolius 6.93D. *Suda* E 643. Zenobius (Aldus) column 78
1 The last sentence was added in *1533*.

4 In pulicis morsu Deum invocat
He calls on God for a flea bite

Ἐν ψύλλας δήξει θεὸν ἐπικαλεῖται, He calls on God for a flea bite. Said of
those who are as seriously upset by any small thing as they are in a very
important matter. It is drawn from a fable found among those of Aesop.[1] A
certain individual, distressed by the pain of a flea biting his foot, sat down
and called upon Hercules 'defender against evil.'[2] The flea soon hopped
off, and he cursed Hercules, who, not having helped when called in such a
small peril, seemed unlikely to come for more serious ones. This is similar
to what Aristotle says in book 7 of the *Nicomachean Ethics* concerning those
who are excessively timid: 'Like[3] someone who is afraid of everything, even
if a mouse makes a noise.' He calls such timidity that 'of a wild animal.'[4]

5 Κίβδηλος, id est Adulterinus
Adulterated

Anything that is not untainted and not pure the Greeks refer to by the
widely used word κίβδηλος, a word derived from the fact that people
may do one thing openly and conceal another, from τὸ κεύθειν τὸ δῆλον
'to conceal what is manifest.' Or from τὸ τοὺς Χίους βδελύττειν 'to abominate the Chians,'[1] because the Athenians with their extreme hatred of the
Chians, if they wish someone ill, have the custom of inscribing his name
on a coin, with the letter *Chi* added; they throw these on the ground and

* * * * *

4 Apostolius 7.38. At this point Erasmus leaves Apostolius, but returns to him
   at no 13.
1 Aesop 231 Perry
2 Given in Greek: ἀλεξίκακος
3 Henri Estienne pointed out Erasmus' error here (LB II 806n): 'Οἷος does not
   mean *veluti* 'like' [adverb]. It means 'such' [adjective] . . .' As J.A.K. Thompson
   translates in the Loeb edition, 'A man so constituted that he is scared by
   anything . . .'
4 Aristotle *Ethica Nicomachea* 7.5.6 (1149a7): 'of a wild animal' is θηριώδης (given
   in Greek). The passage is already in *Adagia* I v 66 He is afraid of the very flies
   fluttering past. The last two sentences were added in *1533*.

5 The *Suda* and the *Etymologicum magnum* (see n1 below). In *1508* this adage
   began with the quotation from Plato's *Laws*; new material was added at the
   beginning in *1515*.
1 *Suda* K 1575; *Etymologicum magnum* 512.44. For the problems of the Greek texts
   and etymologies see ASD II-5 243:54–6n.

pronounce fearful curses. But the first meaning of κίβδηλος is 'a coin which has copper in it,' and κιβδηλία is 'debasement' or 'means of corruption,' as in Aristophanes: 'He took away much corruption from life.'[2] Also, κιβ-δηλεύειν is 'to pass something off deceitfully,' and those who lose their natural colour are said to be κιβδηλιῶντες, because there seems to be beneath the skin some sickness or defect, in the same way that the colour sometimes betrays an alloy in coins. So the word will be appropriate for insincere and feigned friendship, or for the man with smiling face but poisonous heart, or for the man who puts on a show of sanctimoniousness when he lives an impious life. As Pisides, quoted by Suidas, says: 'Anyone who is the author of two entirely different things is insincere,'[3] as the saying goes.[4]

Or it will be appropriate for insincere speech, as Plato says in book 5 of his *Laws*: 'Again we must consider titles, and which of these is true and which are false.'[5] And again in the same book: 'So that he too should not at times seem false to anyone, but always plain and truthful.'[6] So this word, derived from coins, will acquire proverbial force if applied metaphorically to quite different things. But we mentioned this subject in the proverb Πονηροῦ κόμματος 'Of a bad stamp.'[7]

6 Nemo malus hoc sciet
Nobody who is wicked shall know this

Οὐδεὶς κακὸς εἴσεται τοῦτο, No wicked person shall know this. Said whenever we mean something that is extraordinary and worth knowing. In the fifth

* * * * *

2 Aristophanes *Birds* 158: κιβδηλία; also in the *Suda* K 1573. B.B. Rogers (Loeb) translates 'There goes a grand corrupter of our life!'
3 Latin *insincerus*. ASD remarks that the prose translation which followed here from 1515 to 1523, *Rerum omnino duarum adulterinus est autor unus* 'One author of two quite different ideas is not genuine,' is better than this verse, which replaced it in 1526.
4 *Pisida* fragment 112 PG 92 1745B: Πραγμάτων πάντως δύο / Κίβδηλός ἐστιν ἐργάτης εἷς, ὡς λόγος; *Suda* K 1575
5 Plato *Laws* 5.728D; the word for 'false' is κίβδηλοι.
6 Plato *Laws* 5.738E; 'false' is κίβδηλος.
7 *Adagia* III ii 6. The subject in question is 'metaphors [from coins] that are virtually proverbial.'

6 *Collectanea* no 785

book of the *Laws* Plato says: 'How good is what is ordained now, bringing
order and its trappings to all states, if only they conform; "no one in any
way ignorant or wicked will get to know them," as the ancient proverb
says, but only one who is experienced, and endowed with virtuous habits.'[1]
Similar to this is what the same author writes in the *Laches*: 'Not every
pig will get to know this.'[2] It appears to have arisen from the mysteries
of the pagan gods, which only the initiated and the pure were allowed to
know.[3]

7 Moenia ferrea, non terrea
Walls of iron, not earth

Plato, in the sixth book of the *Laws*: 'But as to the walls, Megillus, I indeed
would agree with Sparta that we should allow walls that have been razed
to the ground to sleep and not wake them up, and for this reason. There
is a poetic saying about these matters which is rightly celebrated: "Walls
should be of bronze and iron rather than of earth."'[1] It seems to have been
used as a proverb, and it has something of the appearance of a riddle. It
suggests, however, that it is not in walls that the safety of a city should
be placed but in armed men, whose unity, serving as unassailable walls,
protects it best of all. Plato, however, is alluding to the Spartan saying that
Plutarch mentions.[2] I think, for myself, that Horace too hinted at this when
he says:

> Be this our wall of bronze.[3]

* * * * *

1 Plato *Laws* 5.741D: οὐδεὶς εἴσεταί ποτε κακὸς ὤν (given in Greek)
2 Erasmus gives in Greek Οὐ πᾶσα ὗς τοῦτο εἴσεται. Plato *Laches* 196D: Κατὰ τὴν
   παροιμίαν ἄρα τῷ ὄντι οὐκ ἂν πᾶσα ὗς γνοίη ... W.R.M. Lamb translates (Loeb)
   'And so in fact this is not a thing which, as the proverb says, "any pig would
   know."'
3 The last sentence was added in *1517/18*.

7 Plato *Laws* 6.778D
1 The author is unknown. The corresponding Greek in the passage from Plato
   is τὸ χαλκᾶ καὶ σιδηρᾶ δεῖν εἶναι τὰ τείχη μᾶλλον ἢ γήϊνα.
2 Plutarch *Moralia* 210E–F *Apophthegmata Laconica* nos 29 and 30; *Lycurgus* 19.4:
   'A city will be well fortified that is surrounded by brave men and not by
   bricks.'
3 Horace *Epistles* 1.1.60, translated by H. Rushton Fairclough (Loeb); also quoted
   in *Adagia* II x 25 A wall of bronze, and I vii 44 Hard as iron, Tough as bronze

8 Nemo nos insequitur
Nobody is chasing us

Plato in book 10 of the *Laws*: 'For at present there is no reason why we should prefer brevity to prolixity. Οὐδεὶς γὰρ ἡμᾶς τὸ λεγόμενον ἐπείγων διώκει "because nobody is chasing us and forcing us to hurry," as the saying goes.' This proverb remains common even today; when people indicate that one is free to spend longer on any matter, they say, 'Nobody is pushing us.'[1]

9 Mare proluit omnia mortalium mala
The sea washes away all mortal ills

Θάλασσα κλύζει πάντα τἀνθρώπων κακά, The sea washes away all the ills of men. This is mentioned by Eustathius, commenting on the first book of Homer's *Iliad*.[1] But it is also found in Euripides' *Iphigenia in Tauris*.[2] It arose from some such incident as the following: Diogenes Laertius relates that Euripides was a travelling companion of Plato when he went to Egypt. There he was seized by his sickness, epilepsy, if I am not mistaken, and the Egyptian priests cured the man by immersion in the sea. Hence he subsequently composed this verse: 'The sea doth wash away all human ills,'[3] as if the water of the sea cured all ills.[4] Better still, it is thought nowadays

* * * * *

8 Plato *Laws* 10.887B (from *1508* to *1523* 'book 7,' corrected in *1526*)
1 Suringar 137

9 The source for adages 9 to 12 is Eustathius (see n1 below) whose commentaries on Homer Erasmus could have seen in manuscript in Venice in 1508. Suringar 260
1 Eustathius 108.30 on *Iliad* 1.314: 'And they purified themselves, and cast the defilement into the sea' (translation by A.T. Murray [Loeb])
2 Euripides *Iphigenia Taurica* 1193; added in *1526*
   In *1508* the text from here to the end read: 'This leaves it to us to divine the meaning and use. For myself I think it can be adapted to this sense: we should understand that in a large and dense population vices are hidden and crime is not noticed because of the crowding. But perhaps some will like this meaning more, understanding that from a well-established state all evil men are gradually washed away. For the sea casts up on the shore all the bodies of the dead.' The present text dates from *1515*.
3 Given in Greek: Κλύζει θάλασσα πάντα τἀνθρώπων κακά. Erasmus does not provide a translation of the verse.
4 Diogenes Laertius 3.6 ('Plato'); translation by R.D. Hicks (Loeb)

that those bitten by a mad dog are relieved of rabies if they are immersed nine times in the sea.

10 Canere de Telamone
Sing the song of Telamon

Ἄιδειν τὰ Τελαμῶνος, To sing the song of Telamon. A proverb said about words of lamentation, because Telamon wept uncontrollably for his son Ajax, who perished at Troy, and particularly for the way he died.[1] Eustathius, commenting on the verse of Homer which is in the catalogue of ships, 'And Ajax led from Salamis twelve ships,'[2] calls this proverb to mind: 'And what is said in the proverb, "To sing the song of Telamon," from the "slanting" song,[3] which begins: "O son of Telamon, warlike Ajax."'[4] It is very similar to something we have recorded elsewhere: Ἀδμήτου μέλος 'Admetus' dirge'[5] and Ἁρμοδίου μέλος 'The Harmodius song.'[6]

11 Argiva calumnia
Argive accusation

Ἀργεία φορά, Argive persecution.[1] Usually said of libellers and informers, because the ancients branded the Argives as informers and avid litigants. Eustathius' commentary on the catalogue of ships bears witness to this,[2]

* * * * *

10 Eustathius (see n4 below)
1 'because Telamon ... died' was added in 1517/18.
2 Given in Greek (untranslated): Αἴας δ' ἐκ Σαλαμῖνος ἄγεν δύο καὶ δέκα νῆας.
3 ab obliquo cantu translates the Greek word σκόλιον 'indirect, riddling' used for a drinking song, but see Erasmus' explanation of this word in Adagia II vi 22. Erasmus' source for this and the two other adages mentioned here was probably Athenaeus 15.694B–695C.
4 Eustathius 285.3–4 on Iliad 2.557; PMG fragment 898. The song of Telamon is also mentioned in Aristophanes Lysistrata 1237 and by the scholiast on Plato Gorgias 451E.
5 Adagia II vi 22
6 Adagia II x 93; last sentence added in 1515

11 Collectanea no 143. Zenobius (Aldus) column 43. Cf Adagia IV i 3 Argive thieves.
1 Latin insectatio; both of Erasmus' translations of φορά seem a little loose, but it is clear that he has the idea of 'false attack' in mind, perhaps understanding the Greek word here in the sense of 'rush,' 'onset.'
2 Eustathius 286.19 on Iliad 2.559. Cf PCG 8 adespota 183.

quoting the proverb from Pausanias,[3] as does Diogenianus in his *Collected Proverbs*.[4]

12 Initio confidens, in facto timidus
Bold at the start, timid in the act

Commenting on the seventh book of the *Iliad* Eustathius gives a proverb like this: Θρασὺς πρὸ ἔργου ἐκ πολλοῦ κακός 'One who is bold before action is most often a coward.' The same author quotes from Epicharmus: 'The coward is completely confident in himself at first, but then flees.'[1] We see it commonly happens that people are very brave and boastful before the danger appears, but when the business demands a man then they have no courage.

13 Γοργὸν βλέπειν
Having a Gorgon's eyes

Γοργὸν βλέπειν. Sometimes found in Lucian for 'looking with keen eyes.'[1] Taken from the legend of Perseus and the Gorgon. It is thought the word 'Gorgon' comes παρὰ τῆς ὀργῆς 'from anger,' because angry people have a fierce look.[2] Likewise Homer, in the *Iliad* book 8, speaking of Hector: 'With Gorgon eyes like those of cruel Mars.'[3] Μανικὸν βλέπειν 'To look mad,' we have mentioned elsewhere.[4]

* * * * *

3 Pausanias Atticista, the lexicographer, fragment α 142 Erbse; see *Adagia* I i 4 5n (CWE 31 53).
4 Diogenianus 2.79 = Apostolius 3.76

12 Eustathius 667.41 on *Iliad* 7.93 (Menelaus' reproach to the Achaeans)
1 Epicharmus fragment 217 Kaibel, adespota 449 Nauck

13 Apostolius 5.57. Zenobius (Aldus) column 61
1 Lucian *Hermotimus* 1: γοργὸν ἀποβλέπῇ; see also *Alexander* 3, *Asinus* 8, *Dialogues of the Gods* 23 (19). The exact expression is found in Aelianus *Varia historia* 2.44.
2 *Etymologicum magnum* 238.31; added in *1533*
3 Homer *Iliad* 8.349: Γοργοῦς ὄμματ᾽ ἔχων ἠδὲ βροτολοιγοῦ Ἄρηος (given in Greek)
4 Quoted in *1508* in what became *Adagia* IV ii 7 (506 below) Born of the Furies, and added to IV i 2 You are seeing Argives (440 below) in *1515*. The source of this expression is given there as Aristophanes [*Plutus* 424]; it was added here in *1533*.

14 Tolle digitum
Raise your finger

Αἶρε δάκτυλον, Raise your finger. Confess yourself beaten. Because with this signal the one who had been overcome in a fight acknowledged his defeat.[1] Persius in Satire 5: 'Not one point has reason granted you; hold out your finger, and you cannot do it right.'[2]

Related to what is mentioned elsewhere: 'Yield the palm.'[3] It was to this, if I am not mistaken, that St Jerome alluded in the *Dialogue between a Luciferian and an Orthodox Christian*, when he says: 'There! I raise my hand. I yield. You have won.'[4] Athenaeus, in book 6, quotes these verses from Antiphanes about tragic poets:

> When they are at a loss for something more to say,
> But are completely perplexed about how to continue the play,
> They suddenly raise a crane[5] instead of raising their finger.[6]

Cicero seems to have a slightly different usage from this in book 6 of the *Verrines*: 'The guardians hasten up; uncle Junius raises his finger.'[7] For this appears to be a gesture of approval or the way in which someone declares himself to be a buyer or a hirer. Votes were cast this way, and in auctions whoever wished to be a buyer or a hirer showed it in the same manner.

* * * * *

14 Apostolius 1.75. *Suda* Αι 281. Otto 554
1 Given in Greek: τὴν ἧτταν
2 Persius 5.119. The next line begins: *Et quid tam parvum est?* 'And what can be a slighter thing than that [ie, holding out your finger]?'
3 *Adagia* I ix 78
4 Jerome *Dialogus contra Luciferianos* 14.5 PL 23 168B; added in *1515*
5 Latin *machina*, the stage machine; that is, they introduce some stage trick or *deus ex machina*.
6 Athenaeus 6.222B–C, citing PCG 2 Antiphanes fragment 189:13–15; added in *1528*. Erasmus gives the Greek: "Οταν μηθὲν δύνωντ᾽ εἰπεῖν ἔτι, / Κομιδῇ δ᾽ ἀπειρήκασιν ἐν τοῖς δράμασιν, / Αἴρουσιν ὥσπερ δάκτυλον τὴν μηχανήν. The Loeb edition has ἀπειρήκωσιν; C.B. Gulick translates 'And then, when the poets can say no more, and their dramatic resources have completely given out, they raise "the machine" like a beaten athlete's finger ...'
7 Cicero *Verrines* 2.1.54.141; added in *1533*. The numbering Erasmus gives for books of the *Verrines* is erratic; he appears to have used two or more editions at different times and counts *In Q. Caecilium* as book 1. See also *Adagia* III ix 36 n2 (332 below) and III ix 65 n2 (343 below).

15 **Videberis me videns plane Martem videre**
   You will seem, when you see me, to see Mars himself

Βλέπειν γὰρ ἄντικρυς δόξεις μ᾽ Ἄρην, It will seem plain to you that in me you are looking at Mars. Said of those who offer promptly and vigorously to be helpful, and to be ready to play the role of a Mars. It is in Aristophanes somewhere, but the place escapes me at the moment.[1]

16 **Bos in civitate**
   An ox in the city

Βοῦς ἐν πόλει, An ox in the city. Said when someone is appointed to a new office. Lysias placed a bronze image of an ox in the citadel in Athens, and this became a joke among the common people, for oxen are useful in the country, not in towns.[1] So it will be applied to those who are elevated beyond their deserts to the highest honours, as when some ignorant fornicator is made a bishop or an abbot.[2]

17 **Brasidas quidem vir bonus**
   Brasidas indeed is a good man

Βρασίδας μὲν ἀνὴρ ἀγαθός, ἁ δὲ Λακεδαίμων πολλοὺς ἔχει κάρρονας, This Brasidas is indeed a good man, but Sparta has a lot who are better. Against those who reckon that they are not only very distinguished, but the only ones. It comes from an apophthegm, as Plutarch tells us in his 'Sayings of Spartans,'[1]

* * * * *

15 Apostolius 4.98 (from whom Erasmus takes the form Ἄρην; the Attic form is Ἄρη). *Suda* B 329
 1 Aristophanes *Plutus* 328

16 Diogenianus 3.67. Apostolius 5.15. Zenobius (Aldus) column 57. PCG 5 Heniochus fragment 2, adespota 820 Kock
 1 From Apostolius; the same in Zenobius (Aldus) column 57. The details that the image was bronze and in Athens were added in *1528* from Hesychius B 76.
 2 Last sentence added in *1528*

17 Apostolius 5.16
 1 Plutarch *Moralia* 219D *Apophthegmata Laconica*; cf 190C *Regum et imperatorum apophthegmata*, and 240C *Lacaenarum apophthegmata*; 'as Plutarch tells us' to the end was added in *1526*.

and again in his life of Lycurgus.[2] Very similar to another one, 'Many men called Manius at Aricia.'[3]

18 Hedera post Anthisteria
Ivy after the Anthisteria

Ἀ κισσὸς μετ' Ἀνθιστήρια, Ivy after the Anthisteria.[1] When something happens too late. The reason for the name is that in that month many things blossom from the earth.[2] It seems it was the custom in these games to be crowned with ivy. We have spoken of the Anthisteria, that is the Festival of Flora, in the proverb Κᾶρες θύραζε 'Carians out!'[3] It seems to be what the Romans called the Bacchanalia.[4] The ivy was sacred to Bacchus, whence those who won the ivy in those games were called 'ivy-wearers.'[5] This proverb goes with one we have noted elsewhere: Μετὰ τήν ἑορτήν 'After the feast.'[6]

19 Ex Academia venis
You come straight out of the Academy

Ἀκαδημίηθεν ἥκεις, You come straight out of the Academy. Said of a grave and impassive or learned individual, with reference to the school of Plato – although it could also be turned ironically against someone playing the

* * * * *

2 Plutarch *Lycurgus* 25.5
3 *Adagia* II x 24

18 Apostolius 2.4
1 Usually spelled Anthesteria; the three-day festival of flowers at Athens held in the month of Anthesterion (end of February and beginning of March). From 173 BC games were held at Rome on 28 April, dedication day of the temple of Flora.
2 Erasmus relates the name to ἀνθεῖν 'to blossom.' The sentence was added in 1533 from the *Suda* A 2500.
3 *Adagia* I ii 65. For the variants 'Kares' and 'Keres,' 'evils,' see the article 'Anthesteria' in the *Oxford Classical Dictionary*.
4 The Anthesteria was only one of the several festivals of Dionysius or Bacchus held in the course of a year. This sentence and the following ones were added in 1533.
5 Given in Greek: κιττοφόροι
6 *Adagia* I ix 52

19 Apostolius 2.1. Zenobius (Aldus) column 16

disdainful philosopher with sombre face. Athenaeus in book 12 indicates
rather that it is said of refined people, of excessive elegance, because Plato
delighted in such refinements.[1] Similarly, when Antiphanes portrayed the
most elegantly dressed philosopher, this same author says: 'But what need
is there to say more? It seems to me I see the Academy itself.'[2]

20 Senem erigere
Correcting an old man

Γέροντα δ' ὀρθοῦν φλαῦρον, ὃς νέος πέσοι, It is hard to raise up an old man
who fell as a youth.[1] It is not at all easy for old men to unlearn the vices
that they learned as boys and that have become ingrained in their whole
way of life. Yet in old age too we have to try to be without vices, however
ingrained they may be.

21 Terra defossum habes
You are keeping something hidden in the ground

Γῇ κρύψας ἔχεις, You are keeping something hidden in the ground. Said of
someone who does not share or show his gifts.[1] Derived from misers who
bury their treasure in the ground. This is what Euclio does in Plautus.[2]
Horace has the same in the *Epodes*:

> I shall have saved nothing
> That either like miserly Chremes I can bury in the earth,
> Or that I can lose like a reckless prodigal.[3]

* * * * *

1 Athenaeus 12.545F citing PCG 2 Antiphanes *Antaeus* fragment 35. Everything
  from the beginning of this sentence to the end of the adage was added in
  1517/18.
2 Athenaeus 12.545A: Τί μακρὰ δεῖ λέγειν; ὅλως / αὐτήν ὁρᾶν γὰρ τήν Ἀκαδημίαν
  δοκῶ (given in Greek)

20 Apostolius 5.39. Suringar 206
1 Sophocles *Oedipus Coloneus* 395, translated by Hugh Lloyd-Jones (Loeb) 'But
  it is a poor thing to uplift when he is old a man who has fallen when he was
  young.' This is Oedipus' response to Ismene: 'For now the gods are lifting
  you up, though earlier they destroyed you.'

21 Apostolius 5.41G
1 Following Apostolius
2 Plautus *Aulularia* 7–8, 60–6, 465–9; added in *1517/18*
3 Horace *Epodes* 1.32–4; added in *1517/18*; Chremes seems to have been a stock

22 Senescit bos
The ox is getting old

Γηρᾷ ὁ βοῦς, τὰ δ᾽ ἔργα πολλὰ τοῦ βοός, The ox is getting old, but there
is much work for the ox. Said when someone becomes unfit to do his job
because of the weakness of old age. For the ordinary run of wealthy people
treat their servants as if they were no more than horses and dogs, or even
rather more inhumanely. While they are of some use, they curry favour
with them; when they have become old, they reject them. This is why it was
considered wise for everyone to procure for himself the means to provide
for and support his old age in some comfort, so that he would not be obliged
to depend on someone else's generosity, for this is despised by everyone.
And he should remember that Diogenes, when he was asked what was the
greatest calamity in this life, answered: 'An old man destitute.'[1]

23 Sus acina dependes
You are a pig who will pay for the grapes

Ἀποτίσεις χοῖρε γίγαρτα, You are a greedy pig who will pay for the grapes.
You will pay a penalty for what you have done; you will pay back what
you have taken away, and with interest.[1] It will be applicable when some
trifling gain is paid for with a great evil. It arose probably when some rustic
threatened his pig with these words as it feasted on bunches of grapes.[2]

24 Dum cessat Boreas
Until the north wind stops

In his *Problems* section 26 problem 47, according to the numbering of
Theodorus, Aristotle declares this verse was well known as a proverb:

* * * * *

name for an old man in New Comedy (as in Terence's *Andria* and *Heautontimorumenos*).

22 Apostolius 5.43. Diogenianus 3.86
  1 Diogenes Laertius 6.51 ('Diogenes'), given in Greek Γέρων ἄπορος

23 Apostolius 3.69. Diogenianus 3.32. *Suda* A 3600. Zenobius (Aldus) column 42
  1 Following Apostolius or Diogenianus
  2 The last sentence was added in *1515*.

24 Apostolius 3.72. In *1508* the title was *Incipiente noto et desinente Borea*, from
   1515 to *1533 Cum cessat Boreas*.

Ἀρχομένου τε νότου καὶ λήγοντος Βορέαο 'When the south wind begins to rise, and the north wind dies down.'[1] This meant weather suitable for favourable navigation. For there is understood δεῖ πλεῖν 'it is time to set sail' or εὖ πλεῖν 'good sailing,'[2] because the south wind is less violent when it comes up, but very violent as it ends. The opposite happens with the north wind. And the Philosopher gives the most probable cause of this saying: 'For we lie further towards the north than to the south, and Aquilo blows from the north, Auster from the south. Hence it comes about that the former assails the nearest regions more violently, then moves its violence on to more remote places becoming milder in those closer to its origin. The former, on the contrary, first bears hard on places towards the south, and afterwards, when it has passed on, is more gentle when it reaches us.' One may stretch the proverb further, and quite aptly, when we want to indicate that the time is convenient and right for doing something, so that it fits in with the one which is published somewhere else: 'When it is raining, get on with the grinding.'[3]

25 Invulnerabilis ut Caeneus
Invulnerable like Caeneus

Ἄτρωτος ὑπάρχεις ὡς Καινεύς, You are invulnerable like Caeneus. Said of those who cannot be hurt. It is stated in the poets' tales that Caeneus, by Neptune's help, could not be injured by any missile.[1] But according to history Caeneus was a certain Thessalian, among the most skilled in fighting, and so skilled that, though he was involved in many battles, he never received a wound. Finally, when he went to the help of the Lapiths against the Centaurs he was taken alone by surprise, overwhelmed by a multitude of enemies, and killed without any bodily wound. And so the Lapiths, finding the

* * * * *

1 Aristotle *Problems* 26.45 (47 in the edition by Theodorus Gaza, Venice 1504) (945a29).
2 The explanation *id est Navigandum est. Apto tempore quaeque res faciunda* 'It is time to set sail. Do things at the right time,' present in *1508*, was deleted in *1515*.
3 Erasmus' Latin is *Cum pluit, molendum.* 'Somewhere else' means in the collection of Polydore Vergil *Adagiorum liber*, first published in Venice 1498; in the Basle 1521 edition *Dum pluit molendum esse* is no 189 folio 31[v].

25 Apostolius 4.19. Zenobius (Aldus) column 47. For a different account of Caeneus' death see *Adagia* iv i 80 (490 below).
1 Ovid *Metamorphoses* 12.169–209 and 459–535

unwounded body, spread the rumour that Caeneus had been invulnerable throughout his whole life.² It will be quite a graceful comparison to make.

26 Sale perunctus hic adiuvabitur
A rub with salt will do this man good

Ἁλσὶν διασμηχθεὶς ὄναιτ᾽ ἂν οὑτοσί, This man will benefit if he is rubbed with bitter salt. This used to be said of those who were out of their senses, either because of age or because of wine. Some think the metaphorical use is derived from leather bottles, because their condition is improved if they are washed with salt; the corrosiveness of salt improves the consistency of the hide. In the same way it was the custom to smear people who were ill through drunkenness with salt and oil; this was thought to be a remedy for inebriety. Some prefer to think it is derived from earthenware jars which are impregnated with salt and so contain better the liquid put in them. And indeed the proverb is found in Aristophanes' *Clouds*.¹

27 Haec iustitia
This is justice

Αὕτη τοι δίκη ἐστὶ θεῶν οἳ Ὄλυμπον ἔχουσι, This is the justice of the gods, whom great Olympus encloses.¹ Customarily said whenever criminals were punished, as if by the avenging gods themselves. It comes from Homer.

28 Atqui non est apud aram consultandum
But the place for deliberation is not before the altar

Ἀλλ᾽ οὐδὲν δεῖ περὶ τὸν βωμὸν τὰς ἐπινοίας, But there must be no deliberation before the altar. You should deliberate before you start; discussion during

* * * * *

2 From 'But according to history' to here follows Apostolius.

26 Apostolius 2.34. *Suda* A 1409
1 Aristophanes *Clouds* 1237

27 Homer *Odyssey* 19.43. Apostolius 4.43. Diogenianus 3.20
1 Erasmus' Latin is *magnus quos claudit Olympus*; the Greek says 'who hold Olympos' not 'whom Olympos holds.'

28 Apostolius 2.44 (but see Zenobius 1.66, Diogenianus 2.14, and Zenobius [Aldus] column 24)

the business itself is too late. Derived from priests who prepare everything for the ritual of sacred observances before they approach the altar. For it was thought to be dangerous if, during the actual ceremony, anything was said or done not according to the rite by priests with a living parent. Cicero explains this in his speech *On the Responses of the Augurs*: 'What? If the celebration[1] has come to a stop, or if the flute-player has suddenly fallen silent, or if that boy or girl whose mother is alive has not kept their place,[2] or has not kept hold of the chariot, or has dropped the reins, or if the aedile[3] has made a mistake in word or gesture;[4] are the celebrations not done according to the rite?'[5]

29 Mars haud concutit sua ipsius arma
Mars never shuffles his own weapons about

Ἄρης τὰ αὑτοῦ ὅπλα οὐ σαλεύει, Mars does not fret about his own arms. Things we have become accustomed to and which suit us are easily borne, even if they are very heavy.[1] We fret under things which we find hard to

* * * * *

1 Latin *ludus*; the accepted reading is *ludius* 'dancer.'
2 Latin *puer ille matrimus et matrima*. The accepted text has *puer ille patrimus et matrimus* 'that boy whose father and mother are alive,' and does not have the words translated here as 'their place, or kept.' A person whose father and mother were still alive was considered pure for ritual purposes because he or she had not been polluted by contact with the dead. The Greek word was ἀμφιθαλής 'blooming on both sides,' 'flourishing'; cf *Adagia* IV ii 15 Ἀμφιθαλής ἔρως, Love blossoming on both sides (509 below).
3 A minor Roman magistrate, one of whose responsibilities was the superintendence of games
4 Latin *nutu*; the accepted text has *simpuvio*, the sacred vessel, and the final phrase is not a question.
5 Cicero *De haruspicum responsis* 23. This reference and quotation were added in 1533, being drawn from the Aldine edition of 1519.

29 Mantissa 1.27. Ultimately from Plutarch *Fabius Maximus* 2.3–4; possibly related to the converse expression found in Livy 22.1.11–12: 'Mavors brandishes his spear.'
1 Estienne (LB II 810) correctly points out that the Greek means 'Mars does not brandish his own arms' and thinks this proverb means that armed men who moved about in a great mass and brandished their arms for the sake of show were met with this criticism. Erasmus has either misunderstood the Greek or is trying to drag it towards another meaning by taking *concutio* and *iacto* (translated here as 'fret about/under') in the sense of 'try to cast off.'

bear. Hence Juvenal says: 'Life has taught them not to fret under the yoke.'
So the labour of study, which would kill an athlete, does not trouble the
scholar.[2]

30 Smaragdus in luce obscurus
An emerald, dark in the light

Ἀρίγνωτος σμάραγδος ἐν μὲν τῷ φάει σκοτεινός, A notable emerald, dark even
in daylight. A rebuke customarily hurled at those who absurdly hide themselves just when they should most give an example of virtue. Pliny mentions among the varieties of emeralds some that are said to be 'blind,' because they are rather dark in colour.[1] This fault can be seen most in sunlight, since that intense, delightfully green colour is not changed by the sun,
or by shade, or by lamps, or even by liquids. Pliny tells us the same in book
37 chapter 6.[2]

31 Martis pullus
A fledgling of Mars

One who is much inclined to fighting battles is called Ἄρεος νεοττός, A
fledgling of Mars. Aristophanes in the *Birds* says: Ἄρεος νεοττός. – Ὦ νεοττὲ
δέσποτα 'Fledgling of Gradivus. – O fledgling ruler and master.'[1] But he is
referring to the cockerel, which is the most pugnacious and warlike of all
birds and therefore, being equipped with both crest and claws, sacred to
Mars. Or because this bird was formerly a young man who was a favourite
of Mars, and who kept watch, when Mars lay with Venus, lest any of the
gods should intrude. Then, when the sun rose and the youth was sleeping,
Mars was caught in disgrace and in his anger changed the young Gallus
into a bird, which still keeps traces of its original nature. Lucian tells this

* * * * *

2 Juvenal 13.22; cf *Adagia* III vii 78 (268 below).

30 Apostolius 4.5. Zenobius (Aldus) column 44
  1 Pliny *Naturalis historia* 37.68; added in 1517/18
  2 Pliny *Naturalis historia* 37.63; added in 1517/18

31 Apostolius 4.7. Cf *Adagia* II vii 42 The field of Mars.
  1 Aristophanes *Birds* 835; B.B. Rogers (Loeb) translates 'Armipotent cockerel. –
    O, Prince Cockerel ...' Gradivus is a title of Mars. See Virgil *Aeneid* 3.35 and
    10.542, Ovid *Metamorphoses* 6.427, and Juvenal 2.128, quoted in *Adagia* III vi
    10 (130 below).

tale in his *Cockerel*.[2] Diogenes Laertius too recalls the proverb in his life of Diogenes the Cynic.[3]

32 Utrem mergis vento plenum
You are trying to sink a bladder full of air

Ἀσκὸν βαπτίζεις πνεύματος πλήρη, You are trying to sink a bladder full of air. Suitable for one who makes vain efforts, like someone who rebukes the incorrigible, because an inflated bladder, however hard you push it under, springs up again. Derived, it seems, from an oracle pronounced by the Sybil concerning the city of Athens: 'You may have wet the bladder, but no one will be strong enough to sink it.'[1]

33 Durus alloquiis
Deaf to entreaty

Ἄτηκτος[1] ἄνθρωπος προσηγορήμασιν, Immovable or unbending to entreaty. Derived from wax, which becomes soft when it is handled. What cannot be liquefied is said to be ἄτηκτος, so this fits a man who is inexorable.

34 Profectus ad Apaturia
Gone to the Apaturia

Ἀπιών ἐς Ἀπατούρια ἐπανῆκ· ἐς θαργηλιῶνα, Having set out for the Apaturia, he returns in May. Usually said of those who lingered excessively[1] over some business. In Athens there was a festival called the Apaturia which

* * * * *

2 Lucian *Gallus* 3. Ares' watchman is called Alectryon, ie, *Gallus* 'cock.'
3 Diogenes Laertius 6.61 ('Diogenes'); added in 1526

32 Apostolius 4.11
1 Plutarch *Theseus* 24.5: Ἀσκὸς βαπτίσῃ, δῦναι δέ τοι οὐ θέμις ἔσται (given in Greek); an addition of 1526

33 Apostolius 4.16
1 ἄτηκτος replaced ἄτεκτος, found in Apostolius, in 1528. Probably the equivalent of ἄτεγκτος (*Suda* A 4329) meaning 'not softened by water.' The last sentence was added in 1515.

34 Apostolius 3.31
1 *licentius* 'excessively' in 1520 to 1536, *lentius* 'too slowly' in 1508 to 1517/18

lasted three days. They called the first day Δόρπεια,[2] because the members of the phratry assembled just before nightfall for a banquet. The second day they called Ἀνάρρυσις,[3] because in it they performed sacred rites for Jove, protector of the Phratrae and Minerva. The third was Κουρεῶτις,[4] because the young boys and girls were enrolled in the clan. Suidas recalls rather a lot things about this festival, but they do not have much to do with the explanation of the proverb.[5]

35 Ego tibi de alliis loquor, tu respondes de cepis
I talk to you about garlic, and you answer about onions

Ἐγὼ σκόροδά σοι λέγω, σὺ δὲ κρόμμυ· ἀποκρίνεις, I talk to you about garlic, and you answer with onions. This is very similar to another: Ἅμας ἀπῄτουν 'Sickles I asked for.'[1] Said when some answer is given that was unrelated to a question, or, on the other hand, when a silly answer is given to a silly question. Garlic and onions are related to each other.

36 Aurificem te futurum credebas
You thought you were going to strike gold

Χρυσοχοήσειν ᾤου, You thought you were going to be a goldsmith. It is said this was derived from some such occurrence as this. At one time a rumour had become rife among the common people of Athens that on Mount Hymettus were to be seen large pieces of gold which were guarded by the fighting ants they have there. So certain credulous people seized their arms and went out to conquer them. When these people came back to the city, without accomplishing anything and

* * * * *

2 From δόρπον 'the evening meal'
3 From ἀνάρρυμα 'victim'
4 From κούρειον 'the victim offered at the feast'; also linked with κοῦρος 'boy'
5 *Suda* A 2940; Erasmus commits the fault for which he criticizes the *Suda*. It would have been more pertinent to say that the Apaturia were held in the month of Pyanopsion (October–November) and the Thargelia in the month of Thargelion (May–June). The comment was added in *1515*.

35 Apostolius 18.8 under the word Χαίρος; also in 6.48A. This is the first of a series of seven proverbs taken from Apostolius' sections X, Ψ, and Ω.
1 *Adagia* II ii 49; also used in III ii 96 I twine my ivy clusters

36 Apostolius 18.39. Story in *Suda* X 586

doing all the work for nothing, they were laughed at by the rest of the citizens, who jeered at them: Σὺ δὲ ᾤου χρυσοχοήσειν 'You thought you would be smelting gold.' Eubulus recalls this in a play entitled *Glaucus*:

> We once persuaded some Athenian men
> To take arms, assault Mount Hymettos
> And bear rations for three days against the ants,
> In the belief that small fragments of melted gold
> Had appeared.[1]

In the penultimate line there is either an error or something missing; perhaps we should read σῖτον 'provisions' for σὺ 'you.' In this way the verse will scan properly: Καὶ σῖτον ἐπὶ μύρμηκας ἡμερῶν τριῶν.[2]

In Plato, book 5 of the *Republic*, we have: 'But what was your Thrasymachus, if he had come as a goldsmith to those who are here now, and not as someone willing to listen to arguments?'[3] And in Aeschines: 'When he withdrew here, it is very clear that he learned to smelt gold rather than do or suffer what was intended for him.'[4] The proverb will be appropriate when someone has conceived great expectations but is disappointed in the outcome. This nearly always happens to those who send men to explore unknown lands, or who pour all they have into alchemical furnaces.[5]

* * * * *

1 Given in Greek as Ἡμεῖς ποτ' ἄνδρας Κεκροπίδας ἐπείσαμεν, / Λαβόντες εἰς Ὑμηττὸν ἐξελθεῖν ὅπλα. / Καὶ σὺ ἐπὶ μύρμηκας ἡμερῶν τριῶν / Ὡς χρυσοτεύκτου ψήγματος πεφηνότος. PCG 5 Eubulus fragment 19 cited by Harpocration X 14 (*Lexeis of the Ten Orators* ed John J. Keaney [Amsterdam 1991]).

2 This speculation was added in *1533*; according to ASD, modern editors since Valesius (1682) read σιτί(α).

3 Plato *Republic* 5.450B. Paul Shorey (Loeb) translates ' "Well," said Thrasymachus, "do you suppose this company has come here to prospect for gold and not to listen to discussion?" ' For Thrasymachus see Diels-Kranz 85 (II.319–26).

4 Dinarchus fragment 6.13 = 3.4 Burtt (*Minor Attic Orators* II Loeb) from Harpocration X 14. The attribution to Aeschines is an error caused by a reference to him immediately before this in the text, which Burtt translates, 'Again, he left this master and resorted to Aeschines, under whom he clearly learnt to melt gold ...'

5 The last sentence was added in *1517/18*. The editors of ASD remark that here Erasmus is criticizing contemporary voyages of discovery and exploitation – especially of the Portuguese to South America and India – and alchemy,

37 Seiuncta sunt Merrhae ac Siloam fluenta
The waters of Merrha and Siloam are far apart

Χωρὶς τὰ Μερρᾶ καὶ Σιλωὰμ ῥεύματα, The rivers of Merrha and Siloam are far apart. About things that are extremely remote from each other. As someone might say, 'There is a big difference between a friend and a flatterer.' Very similar to that other one: Χωρὶς τὰ τῶν Μυσῶν καὶ Φρυγῶν 'The lands of the Mysians and the Phrygians are far apart.'[1] It seems the proverb is modern, and I rather think it was added by Apostolius from patristic literature,[2] since Merrha is the name of the place where Moses made the pestilent and bitter waters fresh and healthy by throwing in wood.[3] But it was to the pool of Siloam that the blind man in the Gospel was sent by Jesus, to recover his sight.[4] From this it appears that salutary waters were very different from the waters of Merrha.

38 Ψευδόπυρα
False fires

Ψευδόπυρα οἷον τὰ σά, For yours are false fires. Said of deterrents and scarecrows, or when the appearance of danger is created artificially, there being none in reality. The metaphor is derived from a military ruse in which, in order to frighten the enemy, fires are lit in a number of places at night, so that it is thought there is a very large army present; these counterfeit fires they call ψευδόπυρα. It will not have the charm of a proverb unless you apply it metaphorically to people who use a smokescreen of words to frighten

* * * * *

which he attacked somewhat later (1524) in the Colloquy *Alcumistica* CWE 39 545–56.

37 Apostolius 18.45. Also in *Suda* X 445
 1 *Adagia* II iv 50; Erasmus does not always use quite the same Latin words: here he has *possessiones* for *termini* and *separatae* for *discreti*. See also *Adagia* I vi 77 Lowest of the Mysians. The Latin translation and all that follows were added in *1515*.
 2 Gregorius Nazianzenus *Carmina* 2.1.12.662–3 PG 37 1214
 3 Exod 15:22–3
 4 John 9:7

38 Apostolius 18.53. Erasmus does not give a translation of the title or the initial phrase. The last two sentences were added in *1528*.

someone or trap them in a fraud. Even sailors can sometimes be deceived in this way.[1]

39 Psyra Bacchum
Bacchus to Psyra

Ψύρα τὸν Διόνυσον, Bacchus to Psyra. Stephanus[1] and Suidas quote from Cratinus: 'Taking Bacchus to Psyra,' and again in his *Nemesis*: 'And you are taking Sparta to Psyra.'[2] This proverb is noted by Ermolao Barbaro too.[3] The adage was used frequently when no one liked the wine set out at a banquet, or of mean preparations. Psyra is a tiny island not far from Chios, on which wine cannot be produced. Strabo too recalls it in book 14.[4] This is the island Homer calls Psyria in book 3 of the *Odyssey*.[5] In Greek commentaries I have sometimes seen Ψυρᾷ, with a circumflex on the final syllable, but this is incorrect if I am not mistaken.

40 Caput vacuum cerebro
A head devoid of brains

Ὦ οἵα κεφαλή, καὶ ἐγκέφαλον οὐκ ἔχει, O what a head, and it has no brains! Said of those who have a splendid physical appearance but lack intelligence. Derived from a fable which is included in those of Aesop.[1] In the vernacular too they say to stupid and silly people that their heads are devoid of brains.

* * * * *

1 Possibly an allusion to the story of Nauplius, in Euripides *Helena* 767 and 1126–31, who set fires to lure the Greek ships on their return from Troy in order to avenge the death of his son Palamedes

39 Apostolius 18.55. *Suda* Ψ 155. Zenobius (Aldus) column 171
1 Stephanus Byzantinus page 704 Meineke; see *Adagia* I vi 53 n9 (CWE 32 297).
2 PCG 4 Cratinus fragments 347: Ψύρα τὸν Διόνυσον ἄγοντες (given in Greek), and 119: Ψύρα τε τὴν Σπάρτην ἄγεις (given in Greek); both proverbs are mentioned in *Adagia* I x 94 As they do in Psyra. Added in *1515*
3 *Castigationes Plinianae* ed G. Pozzi 2 (Padua 1974) 421 on Pliny *Naturalis historia* 5.134 (Pserema)
4 Strabo *Geographica* 14.1.35; this sentence to the end was added in *1528*.
5 Homer *Odyssey* 3.171

40 Apostolius 18.60. Suringar 38
1 Aesop 27 Perry

41 Crudelis Bacchus
Bacchus is cruel

Ὠμηστὴς Διόνυσος, Bacchus is cruel. It was the custom at one time that men were sacrificed live to Bacchus.[1] So the saying is applicable to people who are cruel, or it is appropriate because drunkenness makes people fierce and harsh.

42 Hoc calciamentum consuit Histiaeus, Aristagoras induit
This shoe was stitched by Histiaeus, Aristagoras put it on

Τοῦτο ὑπόδημα ἔρραψε μὲν Ἱστιαῖος, ὑπεδύσατο δὲ Ἀρισταγόρας, This shoe was stitched by Histiaeus certainly, but Aristagoras put it on. Diogenianus informs us that this used to be said to rebuke those who craftily shift the blame for their misdeeds onto others.[1] The adage derives from the following story: Histiaeus, an individual from Samos and a friend of Darius, was sent by him to Persia. Staying there for some time, he was seized by a desire to see his homeland again. But finding he could not obtain free passage from the king he wrote to Aristagoras, a nephew by his brother, asking him to induce the Ionians to revolt, the purpose being of course that this would be the occasion for him to be sent away. However, he devised a novel way of sending his letter, which Aulus Gellius recalls in book 17 chapter 9 of the *Attic Nights*:[2] He shaved off all the hair from the head of a well-trusted slave who had suffered for a long time with an infection of the eyes, as if to cure him, and covered[3] his smooth scalp with writing. In this way he wrote what he wanted. He then kept the man at home until the hair grew back. When the hair had regrown, he sent him to Aristagoras, saying, 'When you reach him, say

* * * * *

41 Apostolius 18.59
1 Following Apostolius, but see also Plutarch *Themistocles* 13.2.

42 Apostolius 16.81
1 Diogenianus 8.49
2 Aulus Gellius *Noctes Atticae* 17.9.20–27. Of what follows, only the passage *Servo cuidam ... frustra ratus* 'He shaved ... without reason' is quoted, somewhat loosely, from Aulus Gellius; the rest is probably paraphrased from Diogenianus.
3 *compingit* (found in the Venice edition of 1496); the accepted reading is *compungit* 'tattooed.'

that my message was that he should shave your head, as I have just done.'
The slave went to Aristagoras, according to his orders, and gave him his
master's message. Aristagoras, thinking that this was not without reason,
shaved the slave's head, read the letter, and, recognizing Histiaeus' intention, drew almost the whole of Ionia into a rebellion. When Darius learned
the news that the Ionians had revolted, he summoned Histiaeus to ask
whom it was most appropriate to send to Asia Minor to settle matters.
The latter persuaded him to send himself as being most suitable for settling the Ionians' revolt. And so, after he had reached Asia Minor and
had then fallen under suspicion of the prefect of the Sardians as having
been the author of this insurrection, he heard the prefect say this: 'This
is the truth of this matter, Histiaeus: it was you who stitched this shoe,
and Aristagoras that put it on.' Herodotus recalls the story too in his fifth
and sixth books, reporting it as I have told it.[4] And indeed he made it
clear that Histiaeus was the source and author of this counsel and that
Aristagoras was the one who put it into effect. Then this expression, as often happens, became known to ordinary people because of the novelty of
the lie, and it passed into a popular story. It seems to be most applicable
whenever one person supports another in crafty and dishonest deliberations and they bring mutual assistance to each other. For giving advice is
like stitching the shoe, and making use of the advice and carrying it out is
like wearing it.

43 Quae non posuisti, ne tollas
Do not take away what you did not put in place

"Α μὴ κατέθου, μὴ ἀνέλῃ, Do not take away what you did not put in place.
This is quoted by Plato in book 11 of the *Laws*, apparently from some poet.[1]
Laertius reports it among the laws of Solon,[2] having in mind, I think, the
prohibition on moving field boundaries fixed by ancestors. It is applicable to
thievish people, and to those who ask for repayment of what they have not
lent, and likewise to those who demand to be given credit for undertakings
they have not fulfilled.

* * * * *

4 Herodotus 5.35 and 106–7, 6.1

43 Plato *Laws* 11.913C. Appendix 1.25
1 The author is Solon; see n2.
2 Diogenes Laertius 1.57 ('Solon')

44 Bulbos quaerit
He's looking for onions

Βολβοὺς ζητεῖ, He's looking for onions. A proverbial joke against those who, according to Persius, 'keep their heads down and their eyes fixed on the ground.'[1]

In his 'Table-talk' Plutarch has: 'For this much ridiculed and now proverbial bulb, he says, is protected from lightning not because it is very small, but because it has a power to resist lightning, like the fig tree and the skin of the sea-cow.'[2] Further the proverbial joke which Plutarch alludes to is taken, I think, from the *Clouds* of Aristophanes, when Strepsiades, entering Socrates' school, expresses wonder at the disciples of Socrates who are all looking at the ground with bent heads. And to someone who answers, 'They seek things beneath the earth,' Strepsiades says:

> Then it's onions[3]
> They are looking for. But don't let anything of that sort
> Trouble you, for I have discovered where there are fine big ones.[4]

If anyone wants to link this with what is in the *Plutus* by the same writer, 'You who have eaten the same onions with me,'[5] I would certainly not have had any great objection. But it refers to needy friends who, as Terence says, 'have born great poverty together.'[6] And there is Persius in his fourth *Satire* about a mean person, one sparing of expenditure and frugal [who grumbles]: ' "I hope it will be all right," as he salts and gnaws on an onion / Still in its skin, while the slaves celebrate a full jar.'[7]

* * * * *

44 Aristophanes (see n4 below)
1 Persius 3.80
2 Plutarch *Moralia* 664C *Symposiaca* 4.2; *vituli marini pellis* 'skin of the sea-cow,' but *1508* to *1526* has *hyenae* 'of the hyena.' The Greek continues ὥς φασι καὶ τὸ τῆς ὑαίνης, translated by Herbert B. Hoffleit (Loeb) 'and the pelt of the hyena.'
3 B.B. Rogers (Loeb) translates βολβοὺς 'truffles.'
4 Aristophanes *Clouds* 188–90: Ζητοῦσιν οὗτοι τὰ κατὰ γῆς. βολβοὺς ἄρα / Ζητοῦσι; μὴ νῦν τοῦτό γε φροντίζετε, / Ἐγὼ γὰρ οἶδ᾽ ἵν᾽ εἰσὶ μεγάλοι καὶ καλοί.
5 Aristophanes *Plutus* 253: Ταὐτὸν θύμον φαγόντες (given in Greek); see *Adagia* III i 8 8n (CWE 34 375), which explains Erasmus' conviction that θύμος 'thyme' was a sort of onion.
6 Terence *Adelphoe* 496
7 Persius 4.30–1. Cf *Adagia* I vi 53 and III vi 100 (178 below).

There is another joke of this sort about the onion also in Aristophanes, in the *Women in Parliament*: 'Having devoured a pot of onions.'[8] These are words spoken by an old woman to a young man who was refusing to have intercourse, because he could not take on two women on his own. She says: 'You will, when you have eaten a pot of onions ...'[9] For Martial too claims that onions are an aphrodisiac: 'You can do nothing but satisfy your hunger with onions.'[10] And Columella in his verse: 'Now from Megara let the fruitful seeds of the hyacinth come.'[11] However, there are many species of bulb, but according to Dioscorides book 2, 'all have a pungency of taste and incite sexual desire with their heat, like the rocket lettuce.'[12] Columella says of this: 'It may, like rocket, rouse sluggish husbands to make love.'[13]

Suidas passes on two adages about onions: Κρόμμυα ἐσθίειν 'To eat onions,' and Κρομμύων ὀσφραίνεσθαι 'To sniff onions.' We have given these their own place.[14]

45 Exacta via viaticum quaerere
To seek money for the journey already completed

In his *De moribus* Seneca says: 'For, as they say, what is sillier than seeking or accumulating the money for a journey when there is no further to go?' The adage suits greedy old people. This age group generally labours under this vice, that the less time they have to live, the more they become worried

* * * * *

8 Given in Greek as Καταφαγὼν βολβῶν χύτραν with Latin translation
  From *1508* to *1528* there followed here *Quo quidem libidinosum et immodice mulierosum hominem innuit* 'By which he meant a lustful man, excessively fond of women.' This was replaced by what follows in *1533*.
9 Aristophanes *Ecclesiazusae* 1092: Καλῶς, ἐπειδὰν καταφάγῃς βολβῶν χύτραν (given in Greek; not translated)
10 Martial *Epigrams* 13.34.2; cf *Adagia* IV ii 42 An onion would be no good at all (525 below).
11 Columella *De re rustica* 10.106; added in *1528*
12 Dioscorides *De materia medica* 2.170; 'rocket lettuce' is *brassica eruca*.
13 Columella *De re rustica* 10.109
14 *Suda* K 2464; *Adagia* III ii 38 To eat, or to sniff, onions. For Columella see *Adagia* II i 4n.

45 Pseudo-Seneca *De moribus* 18. The work is not by Seneca but by St Martin, archbishop of Braga in the sixth century. Together with another work called *De formula honestae vitae* or *De quattuor virtutibus*, by the same author and apparently based on Seneca's lost *De officiis*, it formed part of all early editions of Seneca including that of Erasmus published by Froben in 1515. Otto 1890

about their livelihood. On the other hand, young people are as careless as can be about this concern. In the *Elder Cato* Cicero says: 'But as for the avarice of old people, I cannot understand what purpose it has. For can there be anything more absurd than to seek more and more provision when less and less of the journey remains?'[1]

46 Ventis tradere
To cast to the winds

To cast to the winds is used to mean 'to forget,' 'to cast out of one's mind.' Servius informs us that it is a proverbial expression.[1] Virgil says in the tenth book of the *Aeneid*: 'and sees not that the winds carry off his joys.'[2] And elsewhere: 'but the winds scatter all things,'[3] and again: 'Part he granted in his heart, and part he scattered to the flying winds.'[4] Horace, in the *Odes*, has:

> Sadness and fears
> I shall confide to wild winds
> To carry away to the Cretan sea.[5]

And Ovid:

> Have all these things blown away in vain in the wind from the sea?
> Are they all born away drowned in the waters of Lethe?[6]

And again:

> Know what things you must do, and do not give my words
> To the east wind nor to the warm southerly to be borne away.[7]

* * * * *

1 Cicero *De senectute* 65–6 (*Cato Maior* is an alternative title)

46 Servius (see n1 below). Otto 1864
1 Servius on Virgil *Aeneid* 10.652; citing all three Virgil passages (nn2–4 below), he gives *Venti ferunt gaudia* as the form of the proverb.
2 Virgil *Aeneid* 10.652
3 Virgil *Aeneid* 9.312–13, 'commands scattered on the breezes,' quoted in *Adagia* I iv 85
4 Virgil *Aeneid* 11.794–5
5 Horace *Odes* 1.26.1–3
6 Ovid *Tristia* 1.8.35–6; added in 1536
7 Ovid *Amores* 1.4.11–12; added in 1536

47 Os infrene
An unbridled mouth

'Αχάλινον στόμα, An unbridled mouth, is said of one who speaks impudently
and abusively. The figure comes from horses unrestrained by any bridle.
In book 3 of the *Laws* Plato speaks of 'unbridled mouths,'[1] imitating Euripides I think, who writes in the *Bacchanals*: 'Of unbridled mouths and wicked
folly, the end is disaster,'[2] as we have recalled elsewhere.[3] Plutarch, in 'On
the Education of Children,' said 'needing a janitor,' as it were.[4] Aristophanes in the *Frogs* has '[A man] of shameless speech / Having an unbridled, intemperate mouth without a gate.'[5] Julius Pollux informs us that this
sort of man is said to be ἀθυρόγλωττος,[6] a term that Euripides uses in the
Orestes:

> About this time, up comes some man whose mouth
> Lacked a door. Mighty in his audacity,
> This Argive no Argive was so outrageous
> In his compliance to the crowd and his clumsy impudence,
> That he threatened with the eloquence of his speech
> To topple princes themselves.[7]

This is how Euripides portrays the foolish orator. If only this description
did not fit so many preachers – I don't mean the evangelistic ones, but the
sycophants and pure flatterers.

* * * * *

47 Plato (see n1 below)
1 Given in Greek: ἀχάλινα στόματα (not translated); Plato *Laws* 3.701C (Loeb): καὶ
μή καθάπερ ἀχάλινον κεκτημένον τὸ στόμα; quoted with context in *Adagia* I vii
31A
2 Euripides *Bacchae* 386–8: Τῶν ἀχαλίνων στομάτων ἀνόμου τε ἀφροσύνας τέλος
δυστυχίαν (given in Greek); cf Apostolius 4.63A but without the source.
3 *Adagia* I i 27:46–8
4 Given in Greek: ἀθύρωτον στόμα 'a mouth without a door'; Plutarch *Moralia*
11C *De liberis educandis* (Loeb): τῆς ἀθυροστομίας ταύτης
5 Aristophanes *Frogs* 837–8: Αὐθαδόστομον, / Ἔχοντ᾿ ἀχάλινον, ἀκρατὲς, ἀπύλωτον
στόμα (given in Greek)
6 Pollux *Onomasticon* 2.109 (mentioning the *Orestes* passage) and 6.119 (ἀθυρόγλωττος); for Pollux see *Adagia* I i 4 31n (CWE 31 53). This sentence to the end
was added in 1526.
7 Euripides *Orestes* 902–6

48 Ego ac tu idem trahimus iugum
You and I bear the same yoke

'Εγώ τε καὶ σὺ τὸν αὐτὸν ἕλκομεν ζυγόν, Both you and I bear the same yoke
equally. Said of those who are prone to similar vices or evils. Not unlike
'You are in the same boat,'[1] although this refers more to a common danger.
Pliny, somewhere in his *Letters*, said, 'to bear the yoke equally,' meaning
to bear the ups and downs of business equally,[2] a figure drawn from oxen
ploughing. Horace seems to be alluding to this in the first book of the *Odes*:

> When the wine-jars
> Are drained to the dregs friends scatter,
> Too crafty to bear the yoke equally.[3]

49 Res indicabit
The facts will show

Αὐτὸ δείξει, with ἔργον understood, The facts themselves will show. When
we mean that the truth of what is said is ascertained in the experience
and the outcome. Plato uses it in the *Theaetetus*, for there Socrates says:
'Theaetetus, the fellow who led the way into the river said δείξει αὐτό
"The outcome will show." And so if we pursue this inquiry perhaps the
nature of our problem will become apparent; but if we stay here, nothing will be clear.'[1] This seems to be derived from a particular incident.

* * * * *

48 Zenobius 3.43. Zenobius (Aldus) column 73 (where Erasmus may have found
  the incorrect τὸν αὐτὸν ... ζυγόν). Apostolius 6.47. *Suda* E 151. Adespota 524
  Kock. Otto 876
1 *Adagia* II i 10
2 Pliny *Letters* 3.9.8: *uterque pari iugo ... niteretur*, but Erasmus has obviously
  quoted from memory (*ex aequo iugum ducere*). Cf *Adagia* I vi 8 Matched in
  double harness.
3 Horace *Odes* 1.35.26–8; added in 1526

49 Apostolius 4.49. *Suda* A 4490. Quoted in *Adagia* I v 17. Cf Otto 1522.
1 Plato *Theaetetus* 200E
  From 1520 to 1528 this was followed by: 'But the translator Marsilio, following
  some unknown author, thinks we should understand the word ὕδωρ, water,
  because this was the answer usually given by those who waded into the water
  and asked how deep it was.' On Marsilio see n2 below.

Someone about to wade into a river, to show the way to others who are to follow, is asked if the water is deep, and answers αὐτὸ δείξει 'Experience will show.' Marsilio[2] translates this passage of Plato as though the word ὕδωρ 'water' is to be understood, because the word ποταμός 'river' comes just before it. Suidas thinks ἔργον, the fact itself, is to be understood.[3] Aristophanes used the expression in the *Lysistrata*: 'The facts will soon prove it.'[4] And Pindar in the *Nemeans*: 'But experience finally shows which of the others he excels.'[5] Close to this is: 'The facts talk' in Lucian's *Toxaris*.[6] Then there is Aristophanes' expression in the *Wasps*: 'The fact is manifest, since it shouts aloud for itself.'[7] Imitating this, Marcus Tullius said in one of his orations: 'The whole appearance of the man shouted his malice.'[8]

50 Omissa hypera pedem insequeris
You let go the brace and run after the sheet

Ἀφεὶς τὴν ὑπέραν τὸν πόδα διώκει, He lets go the brace and runs after the footrope. This applies when someone passes over what matters most and worries about some minor things. The braces are ropes on ships by which the ends of the yardarms are brought round. The 'foot' is what they call the bottom of the rudder.[1] In fact the braces are what are most used in sailing. Suidas[2] quotes the proverb from Hyperides,[3] as does the author of

* * * * *

2 Marsilio Ficino in his Latin edition of Plato, Venice 1491, folio 57[v].
3 *Suda* A 4490
4 Aristophanes *Lysistrata* 375: Τοὔργον τάχ' αὐτὸ δείξει (given in Greek)
5 Pindar *Nemeans* 3.70–1: Ἐν δὲ πείρᾳ τέλος / διαφαίνεται, ὧν τις ἐξοχώτερος γένηται (given in Greek)
6 Lucian *Toxaris* 35: τὰ ἔργα ὑπερφθέγγηται τοὺς λόγους. But Erasmus gives Τὸ πρᾶγμα λέγει, his own back translation of *Res ipsa loquitur*.
7 Aristophanes *Wasps* 921: Τὸ πρᾶγμα φανερόν ἐστιν, αὐτὸ γὰρ βοᾷ (given in Greek)
8 Cicero *Pro Q. Roscio comoedo* 20, quoted from memory

50 Apostolius 4.52. *Suda* A 4599
1 In Latin *imam clavi partem*; this may be correct, but πούς and *pes* 'foot' are also the sheet or footrope of a sail. It is much more likely that the adage refers to this, which is of small use if the yardarm has not been brought round with the brace.
2 *Suda* A 4599, following the scholia on Demosthenes (see n4 below)
3 Hyperides fragment 181 Blass-Jensen = 34 Burtt (*Minor Attic Orators* II Loeb) from Harpocration A 277

the scholia on Demosthenes, from book 1 of *In defence of Chaerephilus on the salt fish*.[4]

51 Becceselenus
Moonstruck

Βεκκεσέληνος, a proverbial expression for one who is senseless or deranged, possessed, or completely senile. *Beccus* in the ancient Phrygian language means 'bread,' according to Herodotus book 2,[1] and σελήνη means 'moon.' Hence the Arcadians, who wish to be thought the most ancient of all mortals, are said to be προσέληνοι 'pre-selenian,' as if they were older than the moon itself. Apollonius notes this in book 4 of the *Argonautica*: 'Arcadians who are said to have lived before the moon.'[2] But King Psammitichus claims, using this word as proof, that the Phrygians were the most ancient of all, because some children, who had never heard a human voice, reportedly made the sound 'beccus.' Suidas[3] jokes about this and says there should be no cause for wonder if those fed by a goat imitated the sound of goats, for Herodotus reports this as a fact.[4] Plutarch uses the expression in book 1 of 'On the Lives of Philosophers': 'For when loud-talking Plato says "God made the world in his own image," he smacks of the "Becceselenian" madness, as the writers of the old comedy say.'[5] The proverb comes from Aristophanes' *Clouds*: 'How, you Cronos-reeking dotard, can it be old when the moon was young?'[6] The scholiast reports several things about this expression, if more is perhaps wanted.[7]

* * * * *

4 Actually Harpocration, which was published as an appendix to Ulpian's scholia on Demosthenes by Aldus in 1503; added in *1528*

51 Apostolius 4.89. *Suda* B 228, 229
1 Herodotus 2.2, who gives the form βεκός. Erasmus found Βεκκεσέληνος in the 1499 edition of the *Suda*.
2 Apollonius *Argonautica* 4.264: Ἀρκάδεες, οἳ καὶ πρόσθε σεληναίης ὑδέονται (given in Greek). Erasmus gives no translation, and omits the infinitive ζώειν 'to live' in his quotation.
3 *Suda* B 229
4 Herodotus 2.2. This and the quotation attributed to Plutarch replaced the words *nam id quidam existimant* 'for some think so,' in *1526*.
5 Plutarch *Moralia* 881A *Placita philosophorum* (see Teubner v.2, 1). This work is now attributed to Aëtius and does not appear in the Loeb edition.
6 Aristophanes *Clouds* 398: Καὶ πῶς, ὦ μῶρε σὺ καὶ Κρονίων ὄζων καὶ Βεκκεσέληνε (given in Greek), translated as in *Adagia* II i 75
7 Dübner page 101–2

As for me, I have mentioned what I judged to be enough to explain the adage.

52 Imperitus anaxyride indutus omnibus id ostentat
The ignorant man who has just put on trousers shows them off to everyone

Ἀμαθὴς ἀναξυρίδα περιθέμενος πᾶσι ταύτην ἐδείκνυ, The ignorant man who has just put on pants or breeches shows them off to everyone. This is applicable to the man who, because of his inexperience, is entranced by even the most absurd things. For to people inexperienced in the world anything foreign or new seems smart. Some scholars think that *anaxyris* is the Greek for what in Latin is called *bracchae* 'breeches' or *feminalia*, which covered the middle part of the body and the thighs. *Bracchae* then were a type of barbarian clothing, but particularly of certain Gallic tribes. Hence Gaul is sometimes called *Gallia bracchata*. But *anaxyris* was used by the Persians, according to Strabo.[1] And we have seen young patricians from Venice, when they are abroad, who delight in wearing French breeches without any upper garment – which they do not do at home. And it will suit those who fancy themselves because they speak French among Germans, or who show off by using obsolete, obscure, or unusual words. This adage has an air of being added by Apostolius from among modern ones.

53 Minervae suffragium
Minerva's vote

Ἡ Ἀθηνᾶς ψῆφος, Minerva's vote.[1] Said of a careful judgment, and the

* * * * *

52 Apostolius 2.75. Zenobius (Aldus) column 29. All editions of Erasmus have ἐνδύκνει; ASD corrects to ἐδείκνυ following Apostolius (and Zenobius [Aldus]). In 1533 the word *anaxyride* replaced *subligaculo* in the title and the passage 'For to people ... unusual words' was added after Erasmus read Lazare de Baïf's *De re vestiaria* (Basle 1526 and 1531). See ASD II-5 267:602–7n, and nn5 and 6 to Ep 1479 by James M. Estes (CWE 10 339). In this letter Erasmus remarks, 'I am surprised that anyone today can be dogmatic about the correct language for ancient garments, since in my own lifetime I have witnessed so many changes of fashion' (translation by Alexander Dalzell).
1 Strabo *Geographica* 15.3.19

53 This adage occurs in Philostratus *Vitae sophistarum* 2.3.568 and in Lucian *Harmonides* 3; it is alluded to in Lucian *Piscator* 21. Neither this nor the opposite proverb quoted here is found in the collections of the paroemiographers.
1 Latin *suffragium*; ψῆφος Ἀθηνᾶς, usually *calculus Minervae* in Latin, was a proverbial phrase signifying an acquittal when votes were even, because

opposite of 'A pig gave judgment.'[2] But it will be more wittily applied if it is said ironically of a man who is stupid and of no judgment.[3]

54 Per parietem loqui
Talking through a wall

Διὰ τοῦ τοίχου λαλεῖν, To talk through a wall. Said of anyone who does something absurd, either because neither hears the other when there is a wall between, or because this is how lovers talk, as Ovid testifies of Pyramus and Thisbe.[1]

55 Intervallo perit fames et optime perditur
Time kills hunger and is the best way to overcome it

Διὰ μέσου καὶ λιμὸς ἔρρει καὶ κάλλιστ᾽ ἀπόλλυται, Time is the best way to kill hunger. A pause brings a cure for many things, and most of all for anger. We even find this interpreted as if the meaning were: 'When the starving man is dead, hunger must necessarily die with him.'[1]

56 Statuam faucibus colas
You are trying to drink a statue

Ἀνδριάντα γαργαλίζεις,[1] You are trying to pour a statue down your throat. Said of some particularly absurd undertaking, which cannot possibly be

* * * * *

Minerva intervened to procure the acquittal of Orestes (Aeschylus *Eumenides* 752–3).
2 Given in Greek: Ὗς ἔκρινεν. Cf *Adagia* I i 40 The sow (teaches) Minerva.
3 The last sentence was added in 1517/18.

54 Apostolius 6.28. Diogenianus 4.31. *Suda* Δ 795. Zenobius (Aldus) column 69
1 Ovid *Metamorphoses* 4.55–70; from 'either because' to the end was added in 1515.

55 Apostolius 6.31
1 'When ... him': following Apostolius

56 Apostolius 2.84. *Suda* A 2169. This is the first of a series from Apostolius letter A which continues to number 64.
1 The only meaning given for this verb is 'to tickle.' It seems Erasmus may have misunderstood the Greek, possibly thinking of γαργαρίζειν 'to gurgle.' In *Adagia* III x 91 Straining at a gnat (393 below), he describes that adage as not inconsistent with this one.

fulfilled, like trying vainly to crush a very powerful and invincible man. A statue, of course, does not turn to liquid.

57 Insperabilem vitam vivis
You live a life one could not hope for

Ἀνέλπιστον βίον ζῆς, You lead an unhoped-for life. This is an Attic expression meaning a wonderful life such as one would not even dare to hope for, or in which the spirit is not kept alive by hope, but what is hoped for is really present. It is found in Pindar.[1]

58 Amens longus
Big and foolish

Ἄνους ὁ μακρός, The big man is a fool, or, as the popular saying has it: 'Tall people lack brains, little ones have too much confidence.'[1] It seems to come from Sophocles, who has these lines in his *Ajax the Whipbearer*:

> For it is not on those
> Who present a vast mass of a body,
> And a broad back, that one should chiefly depend,
> But rather on those who are pre-eminent in wisdom.[2]

It seems that Homer was of the same mind, when he portrayed Tydeus as small in body but energetic, for this is what he says in book 5 of the *Iliad*: 'Tydeus, aggressive in battle, though small of body.'[3] The same is to be found in an obscene poem: 'More effective was Tydeus who, if you give Homer any credence, / Was a battler by temperament though

* * * * *

57 Apostolius 2.91. *Suda* A 2252. Zenobius (Aldus) column 33
  1 ASD suggests Pindar *Isthmians* 5.12, where the manuscripts give ἀνέλπιστον, but the modern reading, supported by the scholiast, is ἄλπνιστον 'sweetest,' 'loveliest.'

58 Apostolius 3.4. Zenobius (Aldus) column 35. Suringar 10. It is also mentioned in *Adagia* III v 43 (94 below).
  1 The editors of ASD refer to Heinrich Bebel's *Proverbia Germanica* (1508) 36 and quote *Longos et procerae statuae raro esse sapientes, breves autem raro demissos et humiles*, which is not so far from Erasmus' version.
  2 Sophocles *Ajax* 1250–2
  3 Homer *Iliad* 5.801

small of body.'[4] And in Statius: 'Greater valour reigned in a meagre body.'[5]

59 Antiopae luctus
Antiope's sorrow

Ἀντιόπης θρῆνος, Antiope's sorrow. This used to be said when someone was undeservedly afflicted by misfortunes and was then rescued from their troubles. The adage is drawn from the legend of Antiope who, according to the story, was the daughter of Nycteus. She was defiled by a certain citizen,[1] and her father in great anger sent an order to his brother Lycus to punish her; but he, seeing she was pregnant, took pity on her and spared her. And so she bore Zethus and Amphion, whom Lycus exposed on a mountain. Lycus, however, had a wife called Dirce, who, as soon as she perceived that her husband was in love with Antiope, had her abducted to a mountain and tied to the neck of a bull, with burning torches hanging from the horns, intending to put an end to her with this sort of torture. But people came running at Antiope's cries, peasants in the vicinity and in particular Amphion and Zethus; they recognized their mother, rescued her, and took revenge on Dirce.[2]

60 Fuge procul a viro maiore
Run a long way from a bigger man

Ἄλευ᾽ ἀπὸ μείζονος ἀνδρός, If someone is stronger than you, remember you and he should not meet. Beware of dealing with the powerful; have your

* * * * *

4 *Priapea* 80.5–6. The manuscript tradition ascribed the *Priapea* to Virgil and the poems were included in the early editions of his work. Most humanists, including apparently Erasmus, rejected this as unthinkable for a poet they regarded as a model of virtue and believed the poems were of multiple authorship, though Poliziano thought they were all by Ovid. Erasmus ignores the fact that in the priapic poem, of course, Tydeus' ability is spoken of in a sexual context.
5 Statius *Thebaid* 1.417

59 Apostolius 3.1. *Suda* A 2689. Zenobius (Aldus) column 36
1 A tongue-in-cheek reference to Zeus by the *Suda*, repeated by Apostolius
2 Apostolius seems to follow the second account given by Hyginus *Fabulae* 8. See Euripides *Antiope* in Nauck pages 410–1.

60 Apostolius 3.15. Diogenianus 2.56. *Suda* A 1149

dealings with equals. Familiarity with the upper class either makes you slavish and base, or, if you do not know how to flatter, puts you in danger. Life with one's equals is both much more pleasant and much more safe. Pindar says in the *Nemeans*: 'Beware of joining battle with more powerful men.'[1] This coincides with what we have said elsewhere, 'Away from Jove and from the thunderbolt' and 'Kings have long hands.'[2] Herodotus in the 'Urania' says: 'And kings have power indeed over men and very long arms.'[3] This was more appropriate for the latter proverb, but when the passage in Herodotus came to my notice, the printer had already finished the earlier pages.[4]

61 Absque baculo ne ingreditor
Never walk without a staff

Ἄνευ ξύλου μὴ βάδιζε, Don't walk without a stick. Do not be unarmed, but always have to hand the means to beat off anyone who may try to harm you. Said to have originated with a certain Cleomenes, a leader of the Athenians. This man went mad, because he was hated by everyone, and would walk about carrying a staff with which to drive off attackers.[1]

62 Omnem facultatem indutus est
He is wearing all his wealth

Ἄπασαν τὴν οὐσίαν ἠμφίασται, He is dressed with all his wealth. Said of a pauper who, apart from what he wears, has no possessions. In another form, 'homeless and luckless.'[1] This is expressed nowadays too in a popular

* * * * *

1 Pindar *Nemeans* 10.72; added in *1526*. The correct sense is, 'It is difficult for mortals to fight with those who are more powerful,' ie the gods.
2 *Adagia* I iii 96 and I ii 3; 'This coincides' to the end added in *1528*
3 Herodotus 8.140.6. The title 'Urania' derives from the apocryphal division of the work under the names of the nine Muses. Cf 'Terpsichore' in *Adagia* IV ii 27 (518 below). Erasmus' copy of the Aldine Herodotus of 1502 is in the British Library.
4 Erasmus is referring to *Adagia* I ii 3; cf Suringar 107.

61 Apostolius 3.16. *Suda* A 2345. Zenobius (Aldus) column 32
1 Erasmus takes this from Apostolius or the *Suda*. Aristophanes *Frogs* 715 describes a certain Cleigenes in a similar way.

62 Apostolius 3.44. *Suda* A 2932. Zenobius (Aldus) column 38. Suringar 159
1 Given only in Greek: ἀνέστιος καὶ ἀνόλβιος. Not found in this form exactly, but cf Lucian *De sacrificiis* 11: μὴ ἄοικοι μηδὲ ἀνέστιοι, translated by A.M. Harmon

jest, like this: 'When I jump, all my possessions go up with me.' The saying of Bias the philosopher is well known: 'I carry all my possessions with me.'[2] And Plautus in the *Rope* has: 'What I am wearing is the sum of my resources.'[3]

63 Hostis non hostis
No enemy, but still an enemy

Ἀπόλεμος πολέμιος, An enemy when there is no war. Said of someone who is not provoked by any injury but behaves like an enemy, or who commits hostilities under cover of peace. It will suit particularly those who, without discussing a complaint[1] about an injury with a friend, immediately make an unfriendly attack.

64 Nefasti dies
Unpropitious days

Ἀποφράδες ἡμέραι, Unpropitious days. These used to be called 'days without auspices,' on which no public business could be done. Hence the habit of calling people who were hated and deserved to be abominated ἀποφράδες.[1] Lucian is witness to this in his essay against the mistaken critic on the topic of ἀποφράς.[2] Among the Athenians there were seven such days, on which sacrifices were made to the shades of the dead, and which were held for that reason to be inauspicious. Further, the superstition of the ancients led them to believe that certain days of the lunar cycle were of sinister omen, such as the fourth, the fifth and the

* * * * *

(Loeb) as 'not houseless and hearthless.' Cf also *Adagia* III x 38 Home is best (370 below).
2 Cicero *Paradoxa Stoicorum* 1.8; also in *Adagia* IV v 9 The wise man carries his possessions with him. Otto 1293. The name, Bias, was added in *1526*.
3 Plautus *Rudens* 207; added in *1526*. Erasmus gives the title at this point in the plural as 'in *Rudentibus*,' a title that is found in early editions.

63 Cf Apostolius 3.49. *Suda* A 338. Zenobius (Aldus) column 41 – all without the word πολέμιος, which ASD suggests Erasmus himself added
1 'Discussing a complaint' = *expostulaverint*; for this meaning see ASD II-5 271:694n

64 Apostolius 3.51. *Suda* A 3642. Zenobius (Aldus) column 42
1 Literally 'not to be spoken of'; not translated by Erasmus
2 Lucian *Pseudologista* especially 16–23

second[3] of the waning moon, which they also called ἀπεικάδες.[4] And again, days on which people were condemned to loss of civil rights were ἀποφράδες. Finally the days on which some exceptional calamity was mourned were said to be ἀποφράδες. Horace says: 'The man who planted you did it on an ill-omened day.'[5] Plato recalls these days in book 7 of the *Laws* when he says that they are not καθαροί 'pure,' but calls them ἀποφράδες, being days of mourning and sacred to the burial of the dead.[6] The term was then used figuratively of men who were to be cursed, men of abominable evil, as this verse shows: 'A man ill-starred, and looking malice from his eyes.'[7] The etymology of the Greek word is the same as the Latin, from φράζω.[8] Suidas, Hesychius[9] and the Etymologist[10] all explain it more or less in this way. Further, we say that contemptible men are *sacri* 'accursed,' as Horace does: 'The accursed shall be disqualified from giving evidence.'[11] Virgil even uses it figuratively of a mental state: 'The accursed hunger for gold.'[12]

65 Anus cothonissat
The old woman is in her cups

Γρᾶες κωθωνιζόμεναι, Old women in their cups. Said of old women who are being indecently wanton. For κώθων means 'drunk'; from this is formed the verb κωθωνίζειν.[1] In book 11, Athenaeus shows that in several authors *cothon*

* * * * *

3 *Quartam, quintam et secundam*; the editors of ASD, following the *Etymologicum magnum* (see n10 below), suggest that *quintam* 'fifth' should be *tertiam* 'third.'

4 'Unrepresented' (Greek untranslated); ASD suggests that for ἀπεικάδας (accusative) we should read ἐπεικάδας, the intercalated days following the twentieth of the month.

5 Horace *Odes* 2.13.1 (on a fallen tree)

6 Plato *Laws* 7.800D

7 PCG 5 Eupolis fragment 332: Ἄνθρωπος ἀποφρὰς καὶ βλέπων ἀπιστίαν (given in Greek)

8 'Declare, pronounce'; the Latin *fas* is derived from the same root as *fari* 'to speak,' and as the Greek φάς, participle of φημί 'say.'

9 Hesychius A 6792

10 *Etymologicum magnum* 131.13

11 Horace *Satires* 2.3.181: *uter aedilis fueritve / vestrum praetor, is intestabilis et sacer esto*, translated by H. Rushton Fairclough (Loeb) as 'whichever of you becomes aedile or praetor, let him be outlawed and accursed'

12 Virgil *Aeneid* 3.57; cf Otto 221.

65 Apostolius 5.62. See also *Adagia* IV vi 69 To be in one's cups.

1 'To become drunk'; *Suda* K 2228

is a type of cup;[2] thence may be derived κωθωνίζεσθαι, for 'to get drunk,' and κωθωνισμός, the state of drunkenness. Hesychius informs us that the Greeks called a drunken man a *cothon*, just as the Romans say *lagena* 'a flagon' or *uter* 'a wineskin.'[3] In the *Odes*, Horace says of the old woman who was the wife of the poor man Ibycus:

> Wool shorn near noble Luceria
> Is fit for you, not the music of a cithara,
> Nor the purple flower of the rose,
> And not for you, old woman, wine jars drained to the dregs.[4]

An old woman dancing has been described elsewhere.[5]

66 Anus hircum olet
The old woman smells like a goat

Γραῦς ἀναθυᾷ, The old woman smells like a goat. Said of an old woman who is indulging in debauchery, because armpits and other parts smell strongly in those aroused to lust.[1] Horace speaks of the old woman thus:

> For I can smell out for myself whether a polyp
> Or a great goat lies in your hairy armpits more shrewdly
> Than a keen-nosed hound can smell where a sow is hidden.[2]

67 Nudo capite
Barefaced

Γυμνῇ κεφαλῇ, Barefaced. People are said to do things barefaced when they do them openly and without any sense of shame. Those who did something

* * * * *

2 Athenaeus 11.483B–F; added in *1526*
3 Hesychius K 3219–20 and 4790–1; added in *1526*
4 Horace *Odes* 3.15.13–16
5 *Adagia* II viii 11; added in *1528*

66 Apostolius 5.66. Diogenianus 4.10
1 ASD observes that the explanation is based to all appearances on Aristotle *Problemata* 4.12 (877b20–40).
2 Horace *Epodes* 12.4–6

67 Apostolius 5.69. Appendix 1.85. Otto 346

shameful were customarily made to cover their heads with rags. Plautus in the *Two Captives*: 'These men go from the forum to the pimps barefaced, with their heads uncovered just as they do in court when they pronounce the accused guilty.'[1] And it does not matter whether you read *aperto* 'uncovered' here or, ironically, *operto* 'covered,' for the two readings come to the same thing. Cyril used this proverbial tag too, in his commentary on the Gospel of John,[2] and St Chrysostom in his *Praise of Babyla the martyr*.[3] And in Plato's *Phaedrus*, Socrates covers his face when he is about to pronounce his invective on love.[4]

68 In re mala, animo si bono utare, adiuvat
In an evil pass it helps if you face it with courage

This verse from Plautus' *Two Captives* certainly deserves to be counted as an adage: 'In an evil pass it helps if you face it with courage.'[1] Evil that cannot be avoided is defeated by bearing it with courage. He expresses the same sentiment slightly differently in the *Pseudolus*: 'Courage in an evil pass halves the evil.'[2]

69 Mulieris oculus
A woman's eye

Γυναικὸς ὄμμα τοῖς ἀκμάζουσιν βέλος, A woman's eye is an arrow to youth in its prime. Virgil says: 'The sight of the female sets him on fire.'[1] And

* * * * *

1 Plautus *Captivi* 475–6. *Duo captivi* 'Two Captives' is a title found in early editions.
2 Cyrillus Alexandrinus *In Iohannis evangelium* is in PG 73–4, but the expression has not been found there; see ASD II-5 273:744n; added in *1517/18*
3 Chrysostom *Liber in sanctum martyrem Babylam* 1 PG 50 533; added in *1526*
4 Plato *Phaedrus* 237A; added in *1515*

68 Tilley E 136 He that endures is not overcome, and H 305 A good heart conquers ill fortune. Otto 1027
1 Plautus *Captivi* 202, corrected in *1526* from *Asinaria*. The verse is also used in *Adagia* III vii 78 (268 below).
2 Plautus *Pseudolus* 452; added in *1526*

69 Apostolius 5.78K
1 Virgil *Georgics* 3.215–16

the same author: 'I saw, I was lost, the wild delusion seized me!'[2] We have recorded elsewhere this other one: 'Love is born of a look.'[3]

70 Decempes umbra
The ten-foot shadow

Δεκάπους σκιά ἐστι, There is a ten-foot shadow, or 'It's time for dinner.' The ancients reckoned the time of day by the length of the shadow. Lucian in the *Cockerel* says: 'Observing carefully how many feet long the shadow was.'[1] Formerly those who issued invitations to a meal specified the shadow-length on the sundial at which they wanted the guests to arrive. Likewise those who were invited, to avoid coming too early, asked 'at what mark' people were supposed to come. Moreover the ten-foot shadow was the one most welcome to parasites, creating the hope of a meal, like the abundant smoke spreading from the kitchen. I can see no use for this adage, unless someone wanting to indicate that a man was excessively greedy should say that he particularly likes the ten-foot shadow,[2] or that someone does nothing but watch for the ten-foot shadow, as Aristophanes uses it in the *Women in Parliament*:

> But this would be your concern
> When the shadow reached the ten-foot line
> To hasten to your rich evening meal.[3]

In book 23 Ammianus reports that among the Persians there was no fixed time for taking food, except for the kings, but that everyone's belly was his own sundial.[4] And in Plautus, if I remember correctly, a certain parasite vents his spleen at those who invented the clock, when the stomach is the best clock.[5] The adage is recorded by Suidas.[6]

* * * * *

2 Virgil *Eclogues* 8.41
3 *Adagia* I ii 79: Ἐκ τοῦ ὁρᾶν γίγνεται τὸ ἐρᾶν (given in Greek); this also uses both quotations from Virgil.

70 Apostolius 5.92. *Suda* Δ 177 and 178
1 Lucian *Gallus* 9: συνεχὲς ἐπισκοπῶν ὁποσάπουν τὸ στοιχεῖον εἴη (given in Greek)
2 From 'I can see' to here was added in 1517/18.
3 Aristophanes *Ecclesiazusae* 651–2; added in 1526
4 Ammianus Marcellinus 23.6.77; this sentence to the end added in 1528
5 Plautus *Boeotia* fragment (Loeb 5.356), from Aulus Gellius *Noctes Atticae* 3.3.5
6 See headnote.

71 Altera navigatio
The next best way to sail

Δεύτερος πλοῦς, The next best way to sail. This is what they said when
the wind failed and they drove the ship with the oars. For, according to
Pausanias, there is a saying 'When you can go with following winds, that is
the best way';[1] he is quoted by Eustathius in his commentary on the *Odyssey*
book 2, where he also mentions the proverb.[2] Aristotle says in book 2 of the
Nicomachean Ethics: 'And so when it is difficult to follow the middle path
exactly, you will incur the least trouble along the next best way, as they
say.'[3] The Philosopher holds that virtue is located in the middle path, but
advises us, since this is sometimes difficult to achieve, to move away from
it as little as possible. Aristophanes' remark in the *Women in Parliament* is
pertinent here: 'For now we are not driven either by wind or by oar.'[4] The
scholiast tells us that sailors resort to oars when they are forsaken by the
wind.[5] It is appropriate that, whenever the means which would be most
effective are not to hand, we should resort to the nearest means of help.

There is a related proverb, which we have recorded elsewhere: 'Second thoughts are better.'[6] John Chrysostom used this in his first homily
on Matthew: 'But after we have cast out this state of grace, let us embrace the next best way.'[7] And here the translator Anianus[8] was imme-

* * * * *

71 Menander fragment 205 Körte-Thierfelder in Stobaeus (see n11 below). *Suda*
    Δ 295. Apostolius 5.98
1 Pausanias Atticista fragment δ 9 Erbse: Ὁ ἐξ οὐρίας πλοῦς πρῶτος (given in
    Greek).
2 Eustathius 1453.19 on *Odyssey* 2.434
3 Aristotle *Ethica Nicomachea* 2.9.4 (1109a35): 'next best way' is κατὰ τὸν δεύτερον
    ... πλοῦν. The passage is translated by H. Rackham (Loeb) 'Hence, inasmuch
    as to hit the mean extremely well is difficult, the second best way to sail, as
    the saying goes, is to take the least of the evils.' This sentence is an addition
    of *1533*.
4 Aristophanes *Ecclesiazusae* 109; originally used in *1508* in the adage that be-
    came I iv 18; added here and made an independent adage, IV viii 47 Neither
    running nor rowing, in *1533*
5 Dübner page 316
6 Given only in Greek: Δευτέρων φροντίδων ἀμεινόνων, *Adagia* I iii 38 Better luck
    next time, where the Greek has the form Δευτέρων ἀμεινόνων and is translated
    'Better the second time.' Cf Zenobius (Aldus) column 68.
7 Chrysostom *In sanctum Evangelium secundum Mattaeum Homiliae* 1.1.1 PG 57 13:
    τὸν δεύτερον ἀσπασώμεθα πλοῦν (given in Greek)
8 Author of the first Latin translation of St John Chrysostom's homilies, identi-
    fied with the Pelagian An(n)ianus attacked by St Jerome in his *Letters* 143.3;

diately shipwrecked, as they say, in the harbour itself,[9] when he translated this passage thus: 'But because we drove away this grace from ourselves, let us wish at least for favourable prosperity' – even if, in the copies
published by the printers, *excusamus* is found for *excussimus*, and *expecta-
mus* for *expetamus*. Chrysostom is maintaining at this point that the first
and best choice is not to make use of scripture, but that, having fallen
from what was best, we should follow the example of sailors, who, when
they cannot reach the point they want by a straight course, try nevertheless to continue in that direction either by rowing or by tacking. But ignorance of the proverb led the translator astray, and so for πλοῦν 'way,'
'course,' he read πλοῦτον 'wealth.' I indicate these points not to expose
Anianus, to whose work scholars are indebted, but in order to remove an
error.[10]

     There is extant a poem by Naumachius, a Christian poet I suspect,
in which he commends virginity first, and calls marriage the next best
way:

> But if the common love of life holds you, let me add
> What I have learned to practise, how you should
> Prudently pursue, as they say, this other way.[11]

Cicero alludes to this in the *Perfect Orator*: 'But if perhaps someone lacks
physical endowment, or outstanding intellectual ability, or if he is less well
instructed in cultural studies, let him nevertheless follow the path that he
can. For one who is striving for the first place it is no disgrace to stop
with the second or third alternatives.'[12] When he wanted an expression for
'maximum speed,' he put the two together in the first *Philippic*: 'But at that
moment I was inflamed with such desire to return that no oars nor any
winds could satisfy me.'[13]

          * * * * *

     see ASD II-5 277:813n. This whole addition reflects a paragraph in Ep 1558 of
     1525 to Willibald Pirckheimer.
   9 *Adagia* I v 76; that is, to make a blunder almost before starting
  10 From 'There is a related proverb' to here was an addition of *1526*.
  11 Naumachius, perhaps as early as the second century AD, is known only in a
     few fragments preserved by Stobaeus; this passage is in the latter's *Eclogae*
     4.17.9 in the edition by Otto Hense (Weidmann 1974) IV 402–3. Added in
     1533
  12 Cicero *Orator* 1.4; an addition of *1526*
  13 Cicero *Philippics* 1.4.9; added here in *1533* but already used in *Adagia* I iv 18;
     quoted by Otto 1521 note

72 Diagoras Melius
Diagoras of Melos

Διαγόρας ὁ Μήλιος, Diagoras of Melos. A name for the wicked, perfidious, and impious. After the capture of Melos, this man lived in Athens and expressed such contempt for the rites of Athenian sacred observances that he turned many against religion and discouraged them from wanting to be initiated. Worse than this, in his impiety he divulged publicly the occult mysteries that it is sacrilegious to reveal to the uninitiated, mocking them in all sorts of ways. For these acts he was proscribed by the Athenians, who posted the proscription in public on a bronze column, a talent being offered in addition as a reward if anyone killed the man, two talents if anyone brought him back alive. Aristophanes recalls this in the *Birds*:

> If any one of you should kill Diagoras the Melian,
> He will carry off a reward of one talent – so too anyone
> Who does away with one of the dead tyrants.[1]

73 Sedecim pedibus superavit
He was the best by sixteen feet

There is an expression in Aristides' *Pericles* that is nothing short of a proverbial figure – namely, that Pericles as an orator excelled everyone else by sixteen feet. He says: 'Saying this man had beaten the Rhetoricians in speaking by sixteen feet, and in his mouth alone dwelt this sort of persuasiveness; everything else was trifling beside this.'[1] So 'sixteen feet' is an expression for 'the greatest distance.' The figure is derived from the race track, and indeed this passage about Pericles is to be found in Eupolis the comic writer, in a comedy entitled *Demoi*:

* * * * *

72 Apostolius 6.4 (Μιλήσιος). *Suda* Δ 524 = scholion on Aristophanes *Birds* 1073 (Dübner page 234). Zenobius (Aldus) column 69
1 Aristophanes *Birds* 1073–5; 1075 is used in *Adagia* I ii 54

73 Publius Aelius Aristides (see n1 below); on Aristides, see *Adagia* I i 13 6n (CWE 31 63). See ASD II-5 277:852n for Erasmus' use of a note by Poliziano in *Miscellanea* 91.
1 Aristides *Orationes* 46 *De quattuor* ed Dindorf II 174 and note; 'had beaten by sixteen feet' is ἐκκαίδεκα μὲν ποδῶν ᾕρει.

This man alone had the mastery by far among men
In rhetoric, outstripping them every time;[2] like a good
And agile runner, sixteen feet of space
He left between himself and other orators.
He was fluent in speaking, and with this fluency
A certain persuasiveness dwelt naturally in his speech.[3]

Aristophanes too alludes to these lines and the next two from Eupolis'
Demoi in his *Acharnians*:

He was so moving, and alone among rhetoricians
He left a deep impression in the minds of his hearers.[4]

Cicero in his *Brutus* says Eupolis wrote that it was as if the goddess[5] sat
upon the lips of Pericles.[6] Aristophanes reproached Pericles for excessive
eloquence in the same comedy: 'But Olympian Pericles, indignant at this, /
Thunders, shakes, stirs up the whole of Greece.'[7] One more point in connection with *suadela* 'persuasiveness': Ennius, as reported by Cicero in his
Elder Cato,[8] repeated the remark that Marcus Cethegus was *Suadae medulla*
'the marrow, essence of Suadela.'[9] The form of this proverb is not unlike
Aristophanes' expression in the *Clouds*: 'I shall be said to surpass the men
of Greece by a hundred miles.'[10] The adage will sound even more witty if,
instead of 'feet,' you say 'parasangs.'[11]

* * * * *

2 Estienne (LB II 820) points out that ὁπότε παρέλθοι, translated as *quoties prae-
teribat*, does not mean 'outstripping them every time,' but 'as often as he rose
to speak.'
3 PCG 5 Eupolis fragment 102; 'sixteen feet of space' is ἐκκαίδεκα ποδῶν.
4 Erasmus is referring to the scholion on Aristophanes *Acharnians* 530 (Dübner
page 16); added in *1526*.
5 That is, Suadela or Peitho, personification of persuasion
6 Cicero *Brutus* 59; added in *1526*
7 Aristophanes *Acharnians* 530–1. From *1508* to *1526* *Etiam Aristophanes*; from
1528 *idem* 'the same [writer],' referring back to Aristophanes beyond the quotation from Cicero
8 Cicero *De senectute* 50. The statement is also in the *Brutus*, in the passage
referred to above.
9 Ennius *Annales* 305–8 Skutsch; for Suadela see n5 above.
10 Aristophanes *Clouds* 430: 'a hundred miles' is ἑκατὸν σταδίοισιν.
11 For Greek uses of 'parasang,' a measure of Persian origin of about 5000 metres,
see *Adagia* II iii 82; this comment was added in *1517/18*.

74 **Saxum volutum non obducitur musco**
   A rolling stone gathers no moss

Λίθος κυλινδόμενος τὸ φῦκος οὐ ποιεῖ, A rolling stone gathers no moss.[1] Someone who cannot stay in the same place rarely prospers. Even today it is still
said in almost as many words. Very similar is that expression of Fabius: 'A
plant often moved does not take root.'[2]

75 **Lityersam cantionem canis**
   You are singing the Lityerses

Λιτυέρσαν ᾠδὴν ᾄδεις, You are singing the Lityerses. Lityerses was a bastard son of king Midas who, when he was living in Celaenae and guests
happened to arrive, forced them to reap corn with him, then cut off their
heads and wrapped the rest of the body in the sheaves. This same man instituted the singing of a *thericos*, a summer or harvest song, in honour of
Midas,[1] from which we get the proverb that says, Those who do not sing
willingly or are forced to sing, sing Lityerses' song. Menander in the *Chal-
cedon*: 'Singing the Lityerses from lunch on.'[2] Julius Pollux recalls this legend in his *Vocabulary* book 4, in the chapter 'On national songs.'[3] But he
invented the idea that Lityerses used to strangle those whom he defeated in
reaping duels, and that he was slain when he encountered a reaper stronger
than himself. According to him too there are certain authors who say he

* * * * *

74 Apostolius 10.72. This is the first of another series taken from Apostolius
   beginning with the letters Λ and M. Suringar 202. Tilley s 885 A rolling stone
   gathers no moss
   1 Φῦκος, which Erasmus translates *muscus*, is more strictly *fucus*, a red lichen.
   2 Quoted from memory – not Quintilian (= Fabius), but Seneca *Letters* 2.3: *Non
   convalescit planta, quae saepe transfertur*; Otto 1435

75 Apostolius 10.74. *Suda* Λ 626. The 'Lityerses' was said to be a traditional reaping song; see J.M. Edmonds' introduction to Theocritus 10 'The Reapers' in
   The Greek Bucolic Poets (Loeb) 129.
   1 Erasmus misunderstands Apostolius' sentence: '[After Lityerses' death] a harvest song about him was composed in honour of his father Midas.'
   2 Menander fragment 230 Körte-Thierfelder, quoted by the *Suda* and Apostolius from the play properly called *Carchedonios* 'The Carthaginian': Ἄδοντα
   Λιτυέρσην ἀπ᾽ ἀρίστου τέως (given in Greek, not translated). I have used the
   translation by J.M. Edmonds in *The Fragments of Attic Comedy* ... (Leiden, 1957–
   61) IIIB 643. See also W.G. Arnott *Menander* (Loeb) II 104–5.
   3 Pollux *Onomasticon* 4.54

died at the hands of Hercules, and therefore that this song was invented to assuage his father's grief. Lityerses is also mentioned by Theocritus.[4]

76 Lydum in planiciem provocas
You are calling a Lydian onto the plain

Λυδὸν εἰς πεδίον προκαλεῖς, You are calling a Lydian onto the plain. Applicable to a man who provokes someone to something he has long been willing and ready for. The Lydians were particularly noted for their excessive willingness to engage in battle. Herodotus tells us in book 1 that the Lydians were superior in their horsemanship; accordingly Croesus wants the Ionians to attack the Lydians with cavalry.[1] This is closely related to one we have described elsewhere: Τὸν ἵππον εἰς πεδίον 'The horse to the plain.'[2]

77 Sublata lucerna nihil interest inter mulieres
When the lamp is removed there's no difference between women

Λύχνου ἀρθέντος γυνὴ πᾶσα ἡ αὐτή, When the lamp is removed there's no difference between women. The adage implies there are no women who are not immodest if there is an opportunity for sin without a witness. It is recorded by Apostolius, and used by Plutarch in his 'Precepts on Marriage.'[1]

* * * * *

4 Theocritus 10.41; added in *1515*. See also the scholiast, quoted in the 'Folk-Songs: Introduction' (*Lyra Graeca* ed J.M. Edmonds III 504–5).

76 Apostolius 10.81, where Leutsch suggests the source is Libanius *Epistolae* 532 Wolf = 617 Foerster
1 Herodotus 1.29; added in *1528*
2 *Adagia* I viii 82

77 Apostolius 10.90. Cf Otto 1244; Tilley J 57 Joan is as good as my lady in the dark. As Estienne (LB II 821) points out, Erasmus is mistaken in his reading of this proverb: 'Putting the worst interpretation on this adage, he deserves the worst from women. It does not imply that every woman is shameless if there is no witness, but, as he should have learned from Plutarch [see n1 below], a man who looks only for superficial beauty could be satisfied with any woman in the dark. This is why Plutarch adds: "This is well said as an answer to adulterous and licentious men."' Erasmus' mistaken interpretation is taken from Apostolius. See ASD II-5 281:913–14n and, for a general account of Erasmus' attitude to women, Erika Rummel *Erasmus on Women* (Toronto 1996).
1 Plutarch *Moralia* 144E–F *Coniugalia praecepta*; added in *1520*

78 Lysicrates alter
A second Lysicrates

Λυσικράτης ἕτερος, A second Lysicrates. A certain Lysicrates became a popular legend because he tinted his greying hair with black, so that he would seem still young. Ollus, in Martial, is mocked in this way, because he tints his hair when he cannot tint his beard.[1]

79 Lysistrati divitias habes
You have the wealth of Lysistratus

Λυσιστράτου πλοῦτον πλουτεῖς, You are rich with the riches of Lysistratus. A proverb used ironically about people who are exceedingly poor. It originates with some Lysistratus who was a man of extreme poverty.[1]

80 Expecta bos aliquando herbam
You can expect grass sometime, ox

Μένε, βοῦς, ποτε βοτάνην, Expect grass sometime, ox. To be said when something comes late. For the ox labours in the field, but in the hope of tasting fresh grass sometime. Very closely related to: 'And your harvest is still in the green.'[1]

81 Expecta anus
Old woman, wait

Μένε, γραῦ, ἐμόν σε παῖδα φιλήσοντα, Old woman, wait for my son who will love you. For before the boy grows up, she will have died. Related to the preceding one, when hope comes late.[1]

*****

78 Apostolius 10.97. *Suda* Λ 860
1 Martial *Epigrams* 4.36

79 Apostolius 10.98
1 Erasmus evidently did not look for this in the *Suda* which refers (Λ 868) to Lysistratus and Thumantis in Aristophanes' *Knights* 1267–8; there is also a Lysistratus in the *Acharnians* 855–9.

80 Apostolius 11.11
1 Ovid *Heroides* 17.263; cf *Adagia* II ii 89 To be in the blade. Otto 798

81 Apostolius 11.12
1 From Apostolius, where the two proverbs are also adjacent

82 Magnus versator in re pusilla
A big mover in a little affair

Μέγας κυληκτής[1] ἐν μικρῷ γε πράγματι, A mighty mover in a trifling business (for with the addition of the particle the Greek verse will scan).[2] This is appropriate to use against those who acquire wealth for themselves by less than honest means. It derives from a saying of Eudamidas; he was the son of Archidamus and brother of Agis.[3] When a certain musician appeared to have sung well, someone among those present asked Eudamidas what he thought of it and he replied: Μέγας κηληκτὰς ἐν μικρῷ πράγματι 'He's a big charmer in a small affair' – because he reckoned his knowledge of the art was thorough but produced nothing useful. The story is recorded by the paroemiographers, and related by Plutarch in his 'Sayings of Spartans,'[4] except that in the latter we read κηληκτής, because this is the orators' power to charm and move. Not unlike this is what Musonius says in Aulus Gellius book 5 chapter 1 of those who, by the modulation of their voice and the meretricious charm of words excite the fatuous applause of their hearers: 'Know,' he says, 'that it's not a philosopher speaking but a flute player piping.'[5]

83 Surdaster cum surdastro litigabat
Hard-of-hearing vs Nearly deaf

Δύσκωφος δυσκώφῳ ἐκρίνετο, ὁ δὲ κριτὴς ἦν κωφότερος, A nearly deaf man had a case against another equally deaf, but the judge was deafer than both – used when there is a dispute between people in every way ridiculous and stupid. There survives a Greek epigram of Nicarchus on this maxim,[1] which Thomas More, in his youth, translated cleverly thus:

The case is on, the defendant was deaf and the plaintiff was deaf,

* * * * *

82 Apostolius 11.14, slightly emended by Erasmus (see nn1 and 2 below)
  1 Erasmus offers κυληκτής, presumably from κυλίνδω, corresponding to the Latin *versari*; hence his *versator*; κηληκτής, as in Apostolius and Plutarch (see n4 below), is from κηλέω 'to charm.'
  2 The particle γε was introduced by Erasmus to make an iambic trimeter.
  3 Archidamus and Agis were kings of Sparta 467(?)–427 and 427–circa 399 BC; the names were added in 1526.
  4 Plutarch *Moralia* 220F *Apophthegmata Laconica*; added in 1526
  5 Aulus Gellius *Noctes Atticae* 5.1.1; added in 1528

83 Apostolius 6.39. From here to the end of the century we have another series from Apostolius, letters Δ and E, except numbers 85–7.
  1 Nicarchus *Anthologia palatina* 11.251

But the judge himself was more deaf than both.
The plaintiff demands the rent for the house, these five months past;
The defendant claims 'All night my mill-stone has been grinding.'
The judge looks at them and asks 'Why are you disputing?
Is she not the mother of both of you? Look after her both of you.'[2]

84 Docui te urinandi artem
I taught you how to dive

Ἐδίδαξά σε κυβιστᾶν καὶ σὺ βυθίσαι με ζητεῖς, I taught you to dive and you try to drown me.[1] Applicable to those who pay back good deeds with bad, and turn a benefit received into harm for the very one from whom they received it. It smacks of the dregs.

85 Pro eleganti medico malus poeta
Instead of an exclusive physician, a bad poet

Ἀντὶ χαρίεντος ἰατροῦ κακὸς ποιητὴς καλεῖσθαι ἐπιθυμεῖς, Instead of a fashionable physician, you want to be called a bad poet. Customarily said of one who, not content with the skills of his own profession in which he had a moderate standing, persists in making a profession of other matters in which he is not so practised and therefore not likely to win an equal reputation. A certain Periander, a physician of wide reputation and as learned as the best in this art, turned his attention to poetry and began to write some inept verse. From this a popular joke became a proverb. In his 'Sayings of Spartans' Plutarch attributed this saying to Archidamus son of Agesilaus.[1]

* * * * *

2 The epigram and More's translation were added in 1517/18, when Erasmus must have used the manuscript of More's epigrams and the *Utopia* in his possession since 1516 (Ep 461:20). The epigrams were first printed as a whole in the *Utopia* edited by Erasmus for Froben in 1518. It is no 52 in the Yale edition of the *Complete Works of St Thomas More*, volume 3 part II.

84 Apostolius 6.49
1 In 1508 this was mistranslated as *Docui te tesseris ludere et tu mihi vis imponere* 'I taught you to play κύβοι "dice" and you try to cheat me.' It was corrected in 1515.

85 Apostolius 2.80
1 Plutarch *Moralia* 218F *Apophthegmata Laconica*; added in 1526. Archidamus was another king of Sparta, who reigned 361–338 BC.

86 A remo ad tribunal
From the oar to the bench

'Ἀπὸ κώπης ἐς τὸ βῆμα, From a galley oar to the magistrate's bench. Usually said when someone rises suddenly from the lowest condition to holding an honourable office. I don't think this could be applied to anyone more aptly than to Julius II. For tradition has it that as a youth this man used to row a boat to earn a penny, and yet he was raised from the tow-rope not only to the bench but to the highest summit of mortal affairs. And not content with this summit he expanded greatly the bounds of papal authority, and would have extended them still further if unmerciful death had allowed him to extend his life.[1] Syrianus the commentator of Hermogenes reproaches Demades the orator because, without any knowledge of the art, he rushed into pleading cases: 'He dashes, "With unwashed hands,"[2] as they say, from the oar to the bench.'[3]

87 In coelum expuis
You are spitting against heaven

'Ἐς οὐρανὸν πτύεις, You are spitting at the sky. That is, what you are doing may fall back on your own head. Or, you are speaking against those who can easily harm you. Because anyone who spits against heaven seems in the first place to be showing contempt for the gods themselves; then it happens most often that the spit falls back in his own face. It is quite similar to Πρὸς κέντρα λακτίζειν 'To kick against the goad.'[1]

* * * * *

86 Apostolius 3.65. Diogenianus 1.98
1 Cf *Adagia* III iii 1 The Sileni of Alcibiades. The passage about Julius was added in *1515* and should be compared for the irony probably implied with the *Julius exclusus* (CWE 27 171), composed, perhaps by Erasmus, in 1513.
2 *Adagia* I ix 55
3 'Syriani, Sopatri et Marcellini scholia ad Hermogenis *Status*' in Christianus Walz ed *Rhetores graeci* (Stuttgart and Tübingen 1832–36) IV 40:3–4. Erasmus' text in *1508* corresponds to that of the Aldine edition of 1509 (page 16), which he must have seen before it was published.

87 Apostolius 6.57. Tilley H 355–6 To spit against heaven, Who spits against heaven it falls in his face; cf *Collectanea* no 373 *In expuentem recidit quod in coelum expuitur* and *Adagia* I iv 92 You are shooting at heaven.
1 *Adagia* I iii 46

88 Unus Deus et plures amici
One God and many friends

Εἷς θεὸς καὶ πολλοὶ φίλοι, One God and many friends. A proverb that counsels providing oneself with as many friends as possible, because they can
be the greatest help after God. Hesiod, however, did not approve of multiplicity of friends or, on the other hand, of inhospitality.[1] I suppose this one
too is borrowed from common speech, not from writers.

89 Si caseum haberem, non desiderarem opsonium
If I had cheese, I wouldn't want meat

Εἰ τυρὸν εἶχον, οὐκ ἂν ἐδεόμην ὄψου, If I had cheese, I wouldn't need meat.
To be said when someone is content with the least and meanest things.
There is a story in Plutarch's 'Sayings of Spartans,' that when a certain
Lacedemonian gave an innkeeper some meat to cook and the latter asked
for cheese and oil to flavour it, the Lacedemonian said, 'There would be
no need for meat if I had cheese.'[1] If anyone prefers *butyrum* 'butter' in
this passage instead of *caseum* 'cheese,' I shall not dispute with him; for it
seems 'butter' is more consistent with 'oil,' even if, with the Italians, even
the driest cheese is a condiment.

90 In antrum haud legitimum stimulum impingis
To push the goad into an unlawful hole

Εἰς τρυμαλιὴν οὐχ ὁσίην τὸ κέντρον ὠθεῖς, You are sticking the goad into an
illicit hole. A sarcasm of Sotades against Philadelphus, who, following the
example of Jove, married his sister Arsinoë.[1] The king took offence at this

* * * * *

88 Apostolius 6.63. Tilley G 242 One God, no more, but friends, good store
1 Hesiod *Works and Days* 715 (πολυφιλία 'multiplicity of friends' and ἀξενία
  'inhospitality' in Greek); see *Adagia* III vi 37 Be not a friend to none, nor to
  many (143 below).

89 Apostolius 6.76
1 Plutarch *Moralia* 234E *Apophthegmata Laconica*; 'There is a story' to the end was
  added in 1526 to replace the remark 'This one too seems to be of the same
  sort as the one above,' which had appeared in 1515.

90 Apostolius 6.53. Athenaeus 14.620F–621A
1 Sotades fragment 1 Diehl. Iambic poet of the time of Ptolemy II Philadelphus;
  Ptolemy married Arsinoë c 276–5 BC.

remark and inflicted capital punishment on the author. Plutarch recalls this in his treatise 'On the Education of Children.'[2]

91 Quamquam non dixeris, tamen apparet e pelle
You may say nothing, but it shows from your face

Εἰ μὴ λέγεις, ἀπὸ τοῦ δέρματος φαίνῃ, Even if you say nothing you show it by your appearance. The truth and the look on the face confute the liar. Whence that sally of Cicero: 'If you were not lying, you would not speak so.'[1] It seems to have originated from a fable.[2]

92 Decipula murem cepit
The net catches the mouse

Εἴληφεν ἡ παγὶς τὸν μῦν, The net catches the mouse. Said of those who are rightly and deservedly caught and worthy of punishment. As if you were to say 'The wolf falls into the trap' or 'A boar in a net.'[1]

93 Iisdem e literis comoedia ac tragoedia componitur
Comedy and Tragedy are written with the same letters

Ἐκ τῶν αὐτῶν τραγῳδία γίνεται καὶ κωμῳδία γραμμάτων, It is with the same letters that both comedy and tragedy are written. This suits those who know how to make different things from the same material,[1] or those who can vary products that are the same.

* * * * *

2 Plutarch *Moralia* 11A *De liberis educandis*; added in 1526

91 Apostolius 6.77
 1 Cicero *Brutus* 278, from memory: *Nisi fingeres, sic ageres?* 'If you were not lying, would you act like this?' This is cited in the *Brutus* from the lost speech *Pro Quinto Gallio*. In Quintilian 11.3.155 it is quoted as *An ista si vera essent, sic a te dicerentur?* Valerius Maximus 8.10.3 follows the *Brutus*.
 2 Aesop 20 Perry; added in 1533

92 Apostolius 6.86. Also found in *Suda* Eι 118.
 1 These expressions, added in 1533, are not found as independent proverbs in Erasmus, nor in Otto *Nachträge*, Suringar, or Tilley.

93 Apostolius 6.92. The source is Aristotle *De generatione et corruptione* 1.2 (315b14–15).
 1 In 'This suits ... material' Erasmus is following Apostolius.

94 A fronte praecipitium, a tergo lupi
An abyss in front, and wolves behind

Ἔμπροσθεν κρημνὸς, ὄπισθεν λύκοι, An abyss in front, and wolves behind. When someone is hard pressed on both sides by two great evils, so that whichever he falls into, he is bound to be lost.

95 Oscitante uno deinde oscitat et alter
When one yawns another yawns too

Ἑνὸς χανόντος μετέσχηκεν ἕτερος, When one yawns, immediately another yawns too. Applicable whenever, by an example of sin, someone is provoked to a similar deed. This happens by some obscure power of nature, so that anyone who sees someone yawning is forced to yawn himself. The philosophers even try to give an explanation of this.[1] Some emotions are communicated in a similar way. Socrates, in Plato's *Charmides*, says, 'When Critias heard these things, and had seen me perplexed, just like those who, seeing someone opposite yawning, are seized by the same impulse, so he seemed to me to be constrained by my doubt, so that he too was seized by doubt.'[2] However, the Romans used the word *oscitantia* for torpor and laziness.[3] Anyone who lives with the idle easily becomes like them. 'We all have a natural inclination away from work' as the comic writer says.[4] The torpedo[5] fish makes people torpid at once by its touch. Plato says, in the *Meno*: 'You seem to me to be very like the flat torpedo fish, for this always makes anyone who approaches and touches it torpid, and you seem to have done something like this to me so that I am sluggish.'[6]

* * * * *

94 Apostolius 7.15. Cf Otto 986.

95 Apostolius 7.20
  1 Aristotle *Problemata* 7.1–2 and 6 (886a24, 31 and 887a4). ASD also gives Alexander of Aphrodisias *Problemata* 1.34, of which Theodore Gaza's translation appeared in print in 1488.
  2 Plato *Charmides* 169C; added in *1533*
  3 The dictionaries record *oscitatio* in this sense but not *oscitantia*. However the participle *oscitans* is used by Terence *Andria* 181, Cicero *De natura deorum* 1.72, *Brutus* 200, *De oratore* 2.144, and Valerius Maximus 9.1.4. This final passage is an addition of *1528*.
  4 Terence *Andria* 77–8; from memory. Erasmus has *Omnes enim proclives sumus a labore ad libidinem*. The accepted text (Loeb) is *ita ut ingeniumst omnium / hominum ab labore proclive ad libidinem*.
  5 Like 'torpor,' Latin *torpedo* is an abstract noun derived from *torpeo*, to be sluggish.
  6 Plato *Meno* 80A

96 Inter caecos regnat strabus
Among the blind the cross-eyed man is king

Ἐν τοῖς τόποις τῶν τυφλῶν λάμων βασιλεύει, In the kingdom of the blind the one-eyed man is king.[1] Among the uneducated, one who is half-educated is considered very learned. Among beggars, one who has a few pennies is a Croesus. It smacks of the common dregs.

97 In area latitas
Hiding on a threshing floor

Ἐν ἅλῳ δρασκάζεις, You are hiding on a threshing floor. Said of one who is involved in business such that he cannot be inconspicuous. Or of one who hides in such a way that he can be seen by everyone, for on a threshing floor there is nowhere to hide.

98 Cum licet fugere, ne quaere litem
When you can run away, don't look for a quarrel

Ἐξὸν φυγεῖν μή ζήτει δίκην, When there is the possibility of fleeing, do not seek a quarrel. Derived from a saying of Alcibiades. When he was summoned from Sicily by the Athenians to answer charges, he refused to go, saying there was no need to go to law if by some means he could get away. To others who suggested, 'Do you not trust your country to judge you?' he replied, 'On the contrary, I would not trust my mother. For I should be afraid that she might in ignorance put a black stone in place of a white one,[1] or that anyone experienced in lawsuits would subscribe to Alcibiades' view [of the law].'[2] The Greeks have the one word φυγοδικεῖν 'to shun a lawsuit' for those who refuse litigation.

* * * * *

96 Apostolius 7.23. Suringar 96. Tilley E 240 He that has one eye is a king among the blind
  1 Cf Adagia II ii 92 In tuneless company the lark can sing.

97 Apostolius 7.44 (= Zenobius 3.74, Zenobius [Aldus] column 80)

98 Apostolius 7.53
  1 In Greek city-states resolutions of the Assembly concerning individuals and sentences by juries were decided by a secret ballot in which voters cast black or white stones.
  2 Erasmus follows Apostolius, but the anecdote comes from Plutarch Moralia 186E–F Regum ac imperatorum apophthegmata; cf Erasmus' Apophthegmata V Alcibiades 3.

99 **In tergore bovis desedit**
Seated on the ox's hide

Ἐπὶ βύρσης ἐκαθέζετο, He sat on the ox's hide, that is, as a suppliant asking for help. An adage originating from a custom native to the
Scythians, as Lucian records in the *Toxaris*.[1] For among those people, if
someone was by chance harmed, and had insufficient power to take revenge, he killed an ox, cut the flesh into small pieces and cooked it.
He himself sat on the hide of the animal, which was spread out on the
ground, with his hands behind his back. This was considered among
them to be the strongest sort of supplication. Anyone who wished to
give help approached, tasted a portion of the meat, placed his right
foot on the animal's hide, and promised that he would do all he could
to help. Among the Scythians, such a covenant was held to be most
sacred.

100 **Hospes indigenam**
The foreigner drove out the native

Ἔπηλυς τὸν ἔνοικον, The newcomer drove out the local;[1] the word ἐξέβαλεν
'drove out' is understood.[2] It would have been used when someone of
a different profession beats another in his own skill, such as when a
theologian shows himself better in grammar than a teacher of grammar.
Or when a child who has been taken in or adopted displaces the son
from a family, or if some outsider of a soldier[3] should drive out native
farmers.[4]

* * * * *

99 Apostolius 7.75. *Suda* E 2255
  1 Lucian *Toxaris* 48

100 Apostolius 7.76
  1 The Latin word *inquilinus* 'the local' is derived from *in-colo* 'inhabit' (cf the use
    of *coloni*, n4 below). The usual sense is 'one who inhabits a place not his own,
    tenant, lodger' and the word seems less appropriate here than the *indigena* of
    the title.
  2 Following Apostolius
  3 Latin *miles ascititius*; the latter word is not classical. The *Dictionary of Medieval
    Latin* gives the meaning 'adventitious,' but see also *Adagia* IV ii 33 (520 below)
    where it means an 'adopted' child.
  4 Latin *coloni*; the whole phrase is a reminiscence of Virgil *Eclogues* 1.70 and
    9.4.

1 Risus Sardonius
A sardonic laugh

Σαρδώνιος γέλως, A sardonic laugh. Said of a pretended, bitter, or mad laugh.
Both the meaning and the source of the proverb are so variously described
by authors that I fear this account of a 'sardonic laugh' cannot be read
without arousing laughter, but we shall brace ourselves to relate a few
points.

Zenodotus in his *Collected Proverbs*[1] quotes Aeschylus, who reported
roughly as follows in his work *On Proverbs:*[2] 'There is a people who inhabit the area of Sardon,[3] a colony of the Carthaginians; it is their custom

* * * * *

1 *Collectanea* no 2, where it consisted of some sixteen lines based on Cicero's
   Ad familiares 7.25.1. The major part of the expansion was made in *1508*, using
   Zenobius 5.85 or Zenobius (Aldus) column 148–9 down to the end of the story
   of Talus. See also *Suda* Σ 120 and 123–7. Otto 1586

1 That is, Zenobius. The incorrect name appears in the scholia to Aristophanes'
   Clouds line 133 (Dübner page 423) and is an emendation of Marcus Musurus, who edited the first edition of Aristophanes, published by Aldus in 1498
   (see the Introduction of CWE 31 10–11 and 10:21n). In the same year Musurus also edited Angelo Poliziano's *Opera omnia*. In chapter 16 of the *Miscellanea* (see *Adagia* I iv 8, CWE 31 325:15–18) Musurus arbitrarily replaced
   Poliziano's reference to Apostolius with one to 'Zenodotus.' Erasmus uses
   'Zenodotus' when referring both to the de Giunta edition of Zenobius' epitome of Tarrhaeus and Didymus of 1497 and to the Aldine Aesop of 1505,
   where the proverbs appear under the names of Tarrhaeus, Didymus, and
   Suidas, and 'Zenobius' or 'Zenodotus' is not mentioned. See W. Buehler
   Zenobii Athoi proverbia I (Göttingen 1987) 102 n52 and ASD II-6 363:361n.
   For Erasmus' general view of the paroemiographers see *Adagia* III i 1 (CWE
   34 173).
2 Aeschylus (not the fifth-century dramatist) fragment 455 Nauck. Erasmus follows Zenobius, but there is some doubt as to whether a work *On Proverbs*
   should be ascribed to an Alexandrian Aeschylus or to a paroemiographer Demon of the third century BC; see Jacoby's commentary on Demon *FGrHist* 327
   F 18 and Crusius *Analecta* 148 n1.
3 *Sardonem regionem*; the Greek *Sardo* or *Sardon* is usually treated as invariable.
   According to ASD, Erasmus distinguishes this region from the island of Sardinia, which first comes into question in the next paragraph (*Sardorum insula*).
   If this is so, there is an inconsistency at the end of the essay where *Sardo*, or
   Sardon, is said explicitly to be the island of Sardon or Ichnusa, which is another name for Sardinia. In *1526*, however, *Sardonem* does replace the forms
   Sardorum (*1508–1517/18*) and *Sardonum* (*1520–1523*) and Erasmus does specu-
   late in his last paragraph that, in an epigram referring to Sardinian grass, the
   island should be described as 'mother of Illyrians' not 'mother of Iberians.'

to sacrifice to Saturn old men who have exceeded the age of seventy, and to laugh and embrace each other while doing so. For they believed it was unseemly to utter lamentations at a funeral or to shed tears. This is how a feigned laugh came to be called "sardonic."' According to the same Zenodotus, Timaeus says that it was the custom of the Sardinians for sons to set parents who had reached a great age on the edge of a precipice or a pit in which they were to be buried, and then, felling them with cudgels, to knock them headlong into it. But the parents laughed as they died, reckoning this was a happy and noble death because their children, in killing them, had lost respect for them.[4]

There are some who say that a certain herb is found on the island of the Sards, called 'Sardinian grass,' rather like wild parsley.[5] It has a sweet taste, but after it is swallowed it twists men's mouths in a grimace of pain, so that they die apparently laughing. This is what Solinus seems to have meant,[6] and Servius the grammarian too when he was explaining this line from the *Thyrsis* of Virgil: 'Now let me seem to you more bitter than Sardinian herbs.'[7] And the commentator of Lycophron, talking about the sardonic laugh, reports something quite similar, following Servius.[8] Latinus Drepanus says in his *Panegyric*: 'So we put on calm faces, and, after the manner of those who have tasted the juice of Sardinian herbs and are said to laugh in death, feigned joys as we mourned.'[9]

And there are also some who think that a 'sardonic' laugh is so called 'because it opens and uncovers the teeth,'[10] as the laugh of those who laugh insincerely usually does. And this is the source of that joke by the parasite

* * * * *

This in turn, however, would scarcely fit with his knowing that 'Sardon' was a Carthaginian colony.

4 Timaeus *FGrHist* 566 F 64

5 'Sardinian grass' is *herbam ... cui Sardoae cognomen sit*, that is, crowfoot, *ranunculus alpestris*; 'wild parsley' translates *apiastrum*.

6 Solinus *Collectanea rerum memorabilium* 4.4; Solinus, like Servius, reproduces other information found in Pliny (n22 below) and Sallust (n7 below).

7 Servius on Virgil *Eclogues* 7.41. The previous two sentences are in fact adapted from Servius, who gives Sallust as his source (*Sallustii Historiarum fragmenta* II 10 Maurenbrecher). Cf also Isidore *Etymologiae* 14.6.40.

8 Tzetzes *Lycophronis Alexandra Scholia* ed Scheer (Berlin 1958) II 250–1 on line 796

9 Latinus Pacatus Drepanius *Panegyricus Pacati Theodosio dictus* 1.25 PL 13 501. Erasmus has omitted the words *nubilis mentibus*: 'So, with gloomy minds, we put on calm faces ...' Drepanus [sic] is an error.

10 *Scholia Platonis* 1 c (Leipzig 1892) VI: ἀπὸ τοῦ σεσηρέναι τοὺς ὀδόντας (given in Greek); σεσηρέναι is a part of the verb σαίρω, to bare the teeth like a dog. This is the accepted etymology of the word.

of Plautus who complained that young people never laughed at what he said and would not even imitate dogs and show their teeth.[11] And there is Apuleius: 'If you laugh perhaps with distended lips.'[12] Homer described this sort of laugh speaking of Juno in the *Iliad* book 15: 'She was laughing indeed with her lips, but her clouded face shone not at all.'[13] Consistent with this is what Aristophanes writes in the *Peace*: '[When your allies saw] you growing angry with each other and baring your teeth.'[14] The image is taken from dogs for whom it is a sign of anger to bare the teeth. This is a habit, they say, in horses too, whenever they are about to bite: whence in common language nowadays they call this sort of laugh a 'horse laugh.' On the other hand, others[15] consider it was the custom among the Sardinians that they should offer to Saturn all the handsomest of their captives and all the oldest who had passed their seventieth year, and that these should laugh as they died because this seemed strong and manly. The writer Clitarchus is quoted as saying it was a solemn custom at Carthage, when great vows were made, to place a child in Saturn's hands. A bronze statue would be made of this god, with hands outstretched. Beneath it was a furnace; this was kindled from below, and so the child, made to wriggle and twist by the heat of the fire, had the appearance of one who was laughing.[16]

Finally Zenodotus names Simonides too as the source of a strange story. For he says that Talus, a figure of a man made of bronze, before he arrived in Crete, landed in Sardinia, where he put not a few mortals to death. Since these showed their teeth as they died with an appearance of laughter, they gave rise to the proverbial expression.[17] Several add that, being prevented from leaving Sardinia for Crete, he leapt into a fire, for he had a body of bronze, then held the Sardinians close to his chest and killed them. They died as it were in his embrace, and with lips distended by the heat of the fire, like men laughing.[18] A ridiculous tale is told of this Talus. They say that he was fashioned out of bronze by Vulcan and sent as a gift for Minos to guard the island of Crete. However he had

* * * * *

11 Ergasilus in the *Captivi* 484–6
12 Apuleius *Apologia* 6
13 Homer *Iliad* 15.101–2
14 Aristophanes *Peace* 620
15 Demon (see n2 above), also quoted in Zenobius (Aldus) column 149
16 Following the *Suda* which quotes from the scholiast of Plato *Republic* 337A (see n31 below); *FGrHist* 137 F 9. 'Cletarchus' in *1508*; 'Clearchus' [sic] in all subsequent editions including LB.
17 Simonides PMG fragment 63, in Zenobius 5.85 (CPG 1 155) = Zenobius (Aldus) column 148
18 Eustathius 1893.6 on Homer *Odyssey* 20.301–2

a single blood-vessel, and this extended from the top of his head to his heels. He travelled three times each day around the island, keeping watch. It was thus that he prevented the ship Argo from putting into a Cretan port when it was returning from Colchis with Jason. But he was deceived by Medea and perished, as some say, by the poison she gave him, which caused insanity; according to others, she promised she would make him immortal and pulled out the nail fixed in the extremity of the blood-vessel. So he died as the blood and all the humours of the body consequently flowed away.[19] Yet again, others report that he died when shot in the heel by Poias.[20]

Dioscorides stated in book 6, speaking of poisons, that there was a species of grass which some call *ranunculus* in Latin and *batrachion* in Greek; it is called Sardoan, or Sardonian, from the region in which it grows most abundantly. When eaten or drunk, it can cause madness, and gives the appearance of a smile by compressing the lips. This, he says, is how that proverb of sinister omen about the 'sardonic laugh' was born.[21] Pliny too mentions this herb in book 25 near the end.[22] Strabo, in book 11 of his *Geography*, writes that in Cambysena, which lies along the river Alazon, a certain species of spider is found which can drive some to death from laughing and others from weeping for the loss of their loved ones.[23] Certain authors mention besides the *tarcotella*,[24] whose bite is followed by death with laughing. And does not Aristotle say, in book 3 of *On the Parts of Animals*, it is recorded that in fighting the piercing of the diaphragm by a thrust appeared to cause laughter and that this happens because of the heat that the wound can produce.[25] Zeuxis the painter[26] and Chrysippus[27] both died from laughing, the former when he was unable to stop laughing at the old woman he had painted, and the latter when he saw an ass eating figs.

* * * * *

19 Erasmus has taken all this from Zenobius (see n1 above). A similar account is to be found in Apollodorus *Bibliotheca* 1.9.26.
20 Father of Philoctetes (*Odyssey* 3.190), who lit Herakles' funeral pyre; for this detail see Apollodorus (n19 above).
21 Dioscorides *Alexipharmaca* 14
22 Pliny *Naturalis historia* 25.172–4
23 Strabo *Geographica* 11.4.5–6; Strabo's word is *phalangia* of which H.L. Jones (Loeb), in a note, says 'here, apparently, tarantulas.'
24 Possibly also the tarantula. In the *Collectanea* no 2 Erasmus refers to commentators of Cicero's *Ad familiares* 7.25.1 who state that people bitten by the *tarcotella* or *tarcontella* die with laughing. See ASD II-5 293:78n.
25 Aristotle *De partibus animalium* 3.10 (673a10)
26 In Pompeius Festus page 228 Lindsay; see *Adagia* I i 28 13n (CWE 31 77)
27 Diogenes Laertius 7.185 ('Chrysippus')

Cicero says in book 7 of his *Letters to Friends*, writing to Fabius Gallius: 'You seem to me to be afraid that, if we have him, we may have to laugh "with a sardonic laugh,"'[28] meaning that, if Caesar were to gain power, they would be obliged to smile on and applaud many things of which they strongly disapproved. Lucian, in the *Ass*, has: 'Thus they spoke, laughing sardonically,'[29] meaning an insolent and mocking laugh. In another place the same author says: 'But Damis, laughing with a sardonic laugh, caused even more irritation.'[30] The expression seems to be used in the same sense by Plato too in book 1 of the *Republic*, when he writes that Thrasymachus, whom he portrays everywhere as very bitter and arrogant, 'laughed sardonically': 'When he heard these words, he spoke with a loud and very sardonic laugh.'[31]

Homer too makes mention of this laugh in some passages in book 20 of the *Odyssey*.[32] He tells how one of the suitors, namely Ctesippus, attacked Ulysses, who was sitting in his house disguised as a beggar, with the hoof of an ox snatched out of the provision basket, and how Ulysses, turning his head away in good time, deflected the blow: 'And in his heart he smiled a right grim and bitter smile ...' The commentator Eustathius here points out that one who laughs a 'sardonic laugh' laughs only with distended lips and inwardly is tormented with anger or disgust.[33] For the ancients called it a sardonic laugh every time someone not only laughed with contempt but also jeered; the expression comes 'from the distending of the lips.'[34] This is more or less how people laugh who are planning among themselves to kill someone, like Ulysses when he was just about to murder the suitors, and as he decided on this in his mind, he laughed a certain, somewhat bitter laugh. In Hesiod, Jupiter laughs with a similar laugh when he is enraged with Prometheus because of the theft of fire. I have appended the verses, which are in the first book of the work entitled *Works and Days*:

> He who gathers the clouds said to him in anger:
> Son of Iapetus, by far in cunning and deceit

* * * * *

28 Cicero *Ad familiares* 7.25.1. The name of the addressee is Fadius, not Fabius, Gallus. The reference is not to Caesar directly, but to Tigellius, the subject of the previous letter, who is described as one of his intimate friends (and who was born in Sardinia).
29 Lucian *Asinus* 24
30 Lucian *Jupiter tragoedus* 16
31 Plato *Republic* 1.337A
32 See n18 above and n37 below.
33 See n18 above.
34 In Greek: παρὰ τὸ σεσηρέναι τὰ χείλη. On σεσηρέναι see n10 above.

The one most skilled among all mortals,
You rejoice to have cheated me and to have stolen the fire;
Truly this shall be a great and cruel plague both to you and to posterity,
To whom I shall give as the price for the theft of fire an evil in which all
Will rejoice, at the same time embracing it to their own destruction.
Thus spoke the father of men and gods, and laughed.[35]

The commentators understand a laugh as fateful in this way whenever a calamity determined by the fates threatens. Such was the laugh of the suitors that Homer describes in the same book that we referred to shortly before and quoted for support in another place:[36]

The divine Tritonia roused loud laughter,
And numbed their barely constrained wits; and they
Laughed demently now with alien lips.
The pieces of meat they devoured were raw and bleeding.
Meanwhile their eyes were filled with tears, and lamentation
Overwhelmed their very spirits.[37]

I believe we should take as 'sardonic' the laugh that Homer attributes to Ajax as he is about to fight in single combat in the *Iliad*, book VII: 'Just so huge Ajax sprang up, the bulwark of the Achaians, / With a smile on his grim face ...'[38]

In certain very old commentaries on Hesiod, I have found an epigram, in which the saying about the 'sardonic laugh' is quite elegantly explained. This too, as is my practice for the less learned, I have rendered roughly into Latin:

There is a certain island called Iberian Sardinia,
Where a noxious weed grows.
It is called Sardinian, looks like the wild parsley,[39]
But when it is eaten by imprudent people
The mouth is presently twisted and shows the likeness of a laugh,

* * * * *

35 Hesiod *Works and Days* 53–9. In some early editions the work is indeed split into two books.
36 *Adagia* I vii 46 To laugh like Ajax
37 Homer *Odyssey* 20.345–9
38 Homer *Iliad* 7.211–12
39 Latin *apiastrum*, Greek σέλινον; cf n5 above.

Then death lays hold straightway,
With a simulacrum of a laugh. But there are those who say
There is a barbarous tribe of Sardinians
Who abduct their age-stricken parents,
Carry them off to rocky places and there put them to death
With stones and with clubs; these wretched folk
They thereupon throw down from steep rocks.
While this goes on, they laugh with godless jokes,
And heedlessly play at parricidal games.
This phrase is thought by others to mean rather
That those who are thus put to death laugh, because
They observe the folly of their children,
And the swift and fretful changes of the world.[40]

According to Pausanias in his *Phocians* the island of Sardinia breeds snakes that are harmless. Further it is entirely free of plant poisons, except that it supports one fatal one which looks like parsley and which, though it grows near springs, does not infect the water of the springs; any who eat it die laughing. And this, he says, is where Homer and others after Homer derived the adage whereby they could say 'they laugh a sardonic laugh,' for those who gave a laugh 'in no healthy manner,'[41] that is, one that was completely senseless.[42] So, not unreasonably, the expression 'sardonic laugh' seems to be usable for the mindless laugh which occurs whenever someone laughs stupidly as evil threatens. For we read indeed that when Caius Gracchus, canvassing for the magistracy, had been defeated, he shouted to some enemies who were laughing most insolently, that they were laughing a sardonic laugh, not knowing into what great darkness they would be plunged by the measures he had taken. This story is told by Plutarch in his lives of the Gracchi, and in his essay 'On Superstition' also: 'Note therefore on these occasions that the man who believes there are no gods laughs with a mad, sardonic laugh.'[43]

* * * * *

40 Tzetzes on *Works and Days* 59. Erasmus must have seen a manuscript since the scholia of Hesiod were first published in 1537. In the edition by Daniel Heinsius of 1603, *Hesiodi Ascraei ... cum scholis Procli, Moschopuli, Tzetzae ...* the epigram appears in the scholion of Tzetzes on page 26 column 2.

41 Erasmus' Greek τὸν ἐπὶ οὐδενὶ ὑγιῆ is corrected from Pausanias in a note by Estienne (LB II 827–8): τὸν ἐπὶ οὐδενὶ ὑγιεῖ.

42 Pausanias 10.17.12–13

43 Plutarch *Caius Gracchus* 12.4–5, *Moralia* 169D *De superstitione*: Σαρδώνιον γέλωτα 'sardonic laugh' (given in Greek)

One commentator of Hesiod[44] interprets a sardonic laugh as 'broad,' that is, a full laugh, where someone laughs with his mouth broadly distended; I think they mean the same by 'jarring laughter,' that is, a discordant laugh.[45] This interpretation is supported indeed by the etymology of the word itself, which I showed just above is because it opens and uncovers the teeth.[46] Finally it will not seem entirely inappropriate that the expression 'sardonic laugh' could be applied to a sad and mournful laugh such as Homer attributes, in the *Iliad* book VI, to Andromache, as if it were the sign of a mind foreseeing the death of Hector: 'She clasped him to her fragrant bosom, / Laughing through her tears.'[47] Eudemus the rhetorician, in his *Miscellany of Rhetorical Sayings*, says several authors agree that it may be used of an insolent laugh in which someone laughs disdainfully and contemptuously;[48] whence indeed the proverb is derived: 'You mock me from your lofty height.'[49] The same author adds that there is a kind of stone called the 'sardonic laugh.'[50] Suidas writes that there is even a verb derived from the proverb, so that those who laugh sardonically are said to σαρδάζειν.[51]

Now I want to stop talking about the sardonic laugh, but before I do, I shall add that this adjective 'sardonic' is found in various forms in the classical writers. In Lucian and Cicero we read Σαρδώνιος, in Homer Σαρδάνιος, in Virgil *sardous*, in the commentator of Lycophron Σάρδιος γέλως,[52] in Plutarch Σαρδιανός: 'If there is such a thing as a sardonic laugh in the mind.'[53]

* * * * *

44 Manuel Moschopulus (page 23 column 2) on *Works and Days* 59. See n40 above.
45 Zenobius 2.100; Diogenianus 3.76; Apostolius 5.28. The terms πλατύς 'broad' and γέλως συγκρούσιος 'jarring laughter' are given in Greek. Cf *Adagia* II vi 39 *Risus syncrusius* Shaking with laughter.
46 Given in Greek ἀπὸ τοῦ σεσηρέναι τοὺς ὀδόντας; see n10 above.
47 Homer *Iliad* 6.483–4. The sense of a despairing laugh is also seen in the *Greek Anthology* 16.86.
48 Eudemus *Lexeis rhetoricae*, which Erasmus calls here his *Collectanea dictionum rhetoricarum*. See *Adagia* II vi 38 and III i 61; according to ASD II-5 75:323n Erasmus had his own copy. It has never been printed as a whole, but K. Rupprecht gives selections from the letters A and Π from Paris BN graecus 2635 in 'Apostolis, Eudem und Suidas' *Philologus* Supplementband XV Heft 1 (1922). See also *Die Neue Pauly* IV column 220.
49 All editions of Erasmus give the Greek here as Ἀφ' ὕψους καταγελᾶς μου, though *Adagia* I ii 80, from Diogenianus 3.24 or Apostolius 4.62, reads Ἀφ' ὑψηλοῦ μου καταγελᾶς.
50 Here and in the next sentence the form *risus Sardonius* is used.
51 *Suda* Σ 120 and Σ 127
52 On Lucian, Cicero, Homer, Virgil, and Lycophron, see notes 29, 24, 32, 7 and 8.
53 Plutarch *Moralia* 1097F *Non posse suaviter vivi secundum Epicurum*: εἰ τίς ἐστι τῆς ψυχῆς Σαρδιανὸς γέλως (given in Greek)

Stephanus showed that Σαρδωνικός, and Σαρδιανικόν were used: 'However, not all these forms come from the same word. For it is from the island of Sardo or Sardon, which formerly had the name Ichnusa,[54] that *Sardonius*, *Sardous*, and *Sardonicus* are derived. It is from Sardos, a city in Illyria, that Σαρδηνοί originates' – whence, I suppose, with a change of η to α, we have Σαρδάνιοι – 'From Sardis, a town in Lydia, we have *Sardianos* and *Sardianicus*.'[55] From these points a conjecture comes to mind: in the Greek epigram which I have just quoted, we should read perhaps not Ἰβηροτρόφος 'mother of Iberians,' but Ἰλλυροτρόφος 'mother of Illyrians.'[56] Salvianus used the adage in his seventh book: 'You would think the whole Roman nation was sated somehow with Sardinian grass: it is dying and it laughs.'[57]

2 Facta iuvenum, consilia mediocrium, vota senum
Deeds of the young, advice of the middle-aged, prayers of the old

This line of moralizing verse is famous among the Greeks: Ἔργα νέων, βουλαὶ δὲ μέσων, εὐχαὶ δὲ γερόντων 'Prayers of the old, advice of men, deeds of youth.'[1] Aristophanes the grammarian recalls this adage.[2] Hyperides quotes it from Hesiod in his speech against Autocles, because the verse is thought to be by him.[3] The meaning is clear enough in itself, that young people should of course be employed in action, because that age excels in physical strength. Men of middle age should be admitted in counsel because

* * * * *

54 Pliny *Naturalis historia* 3.85
55 Stephanus Byzantinus pages 556–7 Meineke. The phrase 'whence . . . Σαρδάνιοι' was inserted by Erasmus.
56 The epigram from Tzetzes' commentary on Hesiod (see n40 above) where Ἰβηροτρόφος was translated as *Sardo Hiberiae* 'Iberian Sardinia.'
57 Salvian of Marseille *De gubernatione Dei* 7.1.6 CSEL 8 156; added in 1533

 2 Apostolius 7.90, first of a series from Apostolius (letters E to K) continuing to *Adagia* III v 14. For Erasmus' own use of this proverb, including an occasion when he declined Melanchthon's invitation to support the reformers, see the introduction to Ep 1034 (CWE 8 116).
 1 From 1508 to 1523 Erasmus translated here as in the title, which closely follows the Greek and is in prose; from 1526 he revised this translation to make a hexameter: *Vota senum, consulta virorum, et facta iuventae.*
 2 Aristophanes Byzantinus (Grammaticus) Παροιμίαι fragment 4 page 237 Nauck. Erasmus is following Apostolius who in turn is following Harpocration E 130.
 3 Hyperides fragment 57 Blass-Jensen = 14.2 Burtt (*Minor Attic Orators* II Loeb); Hesiod fragment 220 Rzach² = 18 Evelyn-White (Loeb); the source for both is the same passage in Harpocration (n2 above).

in their case, although their physical energy is somewhat lessened, their increased wisdom in the practice of affairs is valuable. Old people, being religious, are accustomed to pray for the best from the gods, and moreover no longer have either useful strength or sufficient constancy of mind through the weakness of age. In Euripides' *Melanippus* as quoted by Stobaeus: 'It's an old saying, deeds are the province of youth, / But mature people give the best advice.'[4] The same is implied by Pindar when he says: 'The daring needed for cruel battles goes with youth.'[5] And Homer, in the *Iliad* book 16, tells us that strength is needed in battle and in deliberations ability to speak:

> Battles depend upon hands, but deliberations upon words.
> There it is a matter of fighting, and harsh words are of no avail.[6]

In Homer too Nestor is foremost in councils, but useless in battle.[7] Plutarch, in the essay entitled 'Whether an Older Man Should Engage in Public Affairs,' says: 'And the state is best preserved when the advice of the aged and the spears of the young have supremacy.'[8] In the speech against Ctesiphon, Aeschines affirms that it was provided in Solon's laws that the oldest should be the first to speak in deliberations.[9] And it was formerly the custom among the Athenians that the public crier, when opening a debate to the floor, should pronounce these words: 'Who wishes to address the assembly from among those who have passed their fiftieth year?'[10]

3 Silentii tutum praemium
Safety is silence's reward

Σιγῆς ἀκίνδυνον γέρας, The reward of silence is safety. Aristides quotes this in his defence of Pericles from some poet from Cios.[1] Plutarch, in his 'Sayings of Romans' attributes it to Augustus Caesar, who approved some advice

* * * * *

4 Euripides fragment 508 Nauck; Stobaeus *Eclogae* 4.50.12 Hense v 1023
5 Pindar *Pythians* 2.63–4
6 Homer *Iliad* 16.630–1
7 Homer *Iliad* 4.317–25
8 Plutarch *Moralia* 789E *An seni respublica gerenda sit*, quoting Pindar fragment 182 Bergk (also quoted in *Lycurgus* 100.21); added in 1515
9 Aeschines 3.2; added in 1528
10 Plutarch, in the same essay, *Moralia* 784C–D

3 Apostolius 7.97 (the whole phrase as quoted from Plutarch; see n3 below)
1 Aristides *Orationes* 46 *De quattuor* ed Dindorf II 192; the 'poet from Cios' is Simonides PMG fragment 582.

of Athenodorus and added: 'The value of silence is that it brings no risk.'[2]
The complete verse seems to go like this: 'The reward of silence is the
absence of risk.'[3] Horace uses it in book 3 of the *Odes*: 'There is a sure
reward for faithful silence too.'[4] Nobody sins by keeping silent, but often
by speaking. And this noble saying of Simonides was already a proverb
long before it also became well known as a proverb among the Romans:[5]
'For to keep silent does no harm; what harms is talking.'[6] However Valerius
Maximus, in book 7 chapter 2, attributed this saying to Xenocrates. He says:
'What of Xenocrates' most praiseworthy answer? When he responded with
complete silence to the abuse of certain people and someone asked him
why he alone restrained his tongue, he said, "Because I have sometimes
regretted speaking, but never keeping silence."'[7]

4 Felicitas multos habet amicos
Good fortune has many friends

Εὐτυχία πολύφιλος, Good fortune has many friends. Very similar to one
we have noted elsewhere: Τῶν εὐτυχούντων πάντες εἰσὶ συγγενεῖς 'To those
who prosper all men are akin';[1] the meaning is too well known to need
an interpreter. On the other hand, in adversity friends are few or none at
all; Pindar in the tenth *Nemean*, says: 'The respect of friends is lost when
a man falls into misfortune,[2] and when things go wrong few mortals are
loyal enough to be companions in trouble.'[3]

* * * * *

2 Given in Greek: Ἔστι καὶ σιγῆς ἀκίνδυνον γέρας (translation here by J.M. Edmonds in *Lyra graeca* [Loeb] III fragment 69)
3 Plutarch *Moralia* 207D *Romanorum apophthegmata*: Ἀκίνδυνον γάρ ἐστι τῆς σιγῆς
 γέρας (translated by Erasmus); attributed to Simonides. The reference to
 Plutarch was added in *1526* and the quotations in *1528*.
4 Horace *Odes* 3.2.25; added in *1526*
5 See the *Disticha Catonis* 1.12.2.
6 See n1 above. Both references to Simonides are from *1508*; the failure to correct
 the first circumlocution, which Erasmus copied from Aristides, is probably
 evidence of haste in preparing the Venice edition.
7 Valerius Maximus 7.2 ext 6; added in *1526*. Xenocrates was a disciple and
 successor of Plato.

4 Apostolius 8.7. Otto 93. Cf *Adagia* I iii 16 (Menander *Sententiae* 748 Jäkel).
1 *Adagia* III i 88 The fortunate have many kinsmen
2 Erasmus mistranslates the Greek which means here 'Honour is lost when a
 man loses his friends.'
3 Pindar *Nemeans* 10.78–9 (already used in *Adagia* II viii 81 and III i 88); added
 in *1533*

5 Stulto ne permittas digitum
Don't let a fool have your finger

Εὐήθει δάκτυλον μὴ δείξης, ἵνα μὴ καὶ τὴν παλάμην καταπίῃ, You should not show your finger to a fool, lest he devour your whole hand. No licence, however small, should be given to the foolhardy.[1] They can harm you even in the most important affairs, if you entrust the least thing to them. This one too smacks of the common herd.

6 Opta vicino ut habeat, magis autem ollae
Wish for something for the neighbour, but more for the pot

Εὔχου τῷ πλησίον ἔχειν, ἐπὶ πλέον δὲ τῇ χύτρᾳ, Wish that the neighbour has something, but that the pot has more. The most important is for you yourself to possess what is necessary. The next most important is to have a wealthy neighbour, from whom you can beg.[1] It seems to be drawn from the common dregs.

7 Habet et musca splenem
Even a fly has a spleen

Ἔχει καὶ ἡ μυῖα σπλῆνα, Even a fly has a spleen. Very like that other one: 'And children have the nose of a rhinoceros.'[1] Or again: 'There is gall even in an ant.'[2] It smacks of the dregs.[3]

8 Camelus desiderans cornua etiam aures perdidit
The camel asked for horns and lost his ears too

Ἡ κάμηλος ἐπιθυμήσασα κεράτων καὶ τὰ ὦτα προσαπώλεσεν, While the camel was coveting horns, he lost his ears as well. This is suitable for people who

* * * * *

5 Apostolius 8.10
1 From Apostolius, whom Erasmus condemns in his usual way at the end

6 Apostolius 8.11
1 Following Apostolius; the final dig at Apostolius was added in 1528.

7 Apostolius 8.25
1 Martial *Epigrams* 1.3.6; also quoted in *Adagia* I viii 22
2 *Adagia* II v 31 Even ant and gnat have their gall
3 Again the concluding condemnation was added later, in 1533.

8 Apostolius 9.59B (abbreviated in 8.43)

run after exotic things and do not protect their own.[1] Derived from the fable
of the camels, who, through a spokesman, demanded horns from Jove. The
god was offended by the silly demand and deprived them of ears too.[2] This
one it seems is also from Apostolius.[3]

9 Hercules et simia
Hercules and an ape

Ἡρακλῆς καὶ πίθηκος, Hercules and an ape.[1] Said of those who are completely
incompatible.[2] The ape's power lies in deceit, Hercules excels in strength.
Very close to 'A camel to an ant.'[3] There is a well-known story about the
brothers Perperi, whom Hercules tied together and hung up from his club.[4]
It is said they were turned into apes.[5]

10 Aut manenti vincendum aut moriendum
He must stay and conquer or die

Ἢ μένοντα ἀποθανεῖν ἢ νικᾶν, He must stay and conquer, or he must die.
Usually said when it is felt for certain either that some business must be
resolved or that one must die in the attempt. A figure of speech derived
from the tradition of the Spartans, who went into battle with the intention
of returning home conquerors or dying in defeat. There is a famous saying
pronounced by a Spartan mother as she gave her son his shield: 'With this,
or on this,' meaning, in the laconic Spartan way, you must bring the shield
back or you must be brought back dead on it.[1]

* * * * *

1 Following Apostolius 9.59B
2 Aesop 117 Perry
3 Added in 1533

9 Apostolius 8.65
1 'Ape' is *simia*; at this point Erasmus uses the feminine form, the usual one in
   Latin, though the Greek is masculine, but in the final sentence, referring to
   the Cercopians (see n4 below), he uses the masculine.
2 Following Apostolius
3 *Adagia* I v 47
4 The story is in fact about the Cercopians; cf *Adagia* II i 43, II vii 35, II vii 37. The
   mistaken name 'Perperi' is explained by the editors of ASD as resulting from
   Suda M 449, where the Cercopians are not named but described as πέρπεροι
   'cheats.' Added in 1533
5 Xenagoras *FGrHist* 240 F 28; *Suda* K 1405; Ovid *Metamorphoses* 14.91–100

10 Apostolius 8.55. Plutarch *Moralia* 222F *Apophthegmata Laconica*
1 Plutarch *Moralia* 241F *Lacaenarum apophthegmata*

11 Maritimus cum sis, ne velis fieri terrestris
Since you are a seaman, don't try to become a landsman

Θαλάττιος δ᾽ ὢν μήποτε χερσαῖος γενοῦ, If you are a seaman keep away from
landsmen's affairs. This adage advises us not to change our condition, not
even into something better. Indeed each one should maintain the kind of
life into which he either seems to have been placed by nature, or has fallen
by chance. The adage was borrowed from a fable of Aesop, which goes like
this. A certain crab left the sea and began to feed in a field. There by chance
he was spotted by a fox, and immediately seized and eaten. And so, on the
point of death, he deplored too late his folly because, when he was a sea
creature, he wanted to defect and join the party of the land animals.[1] There
is a similar fable about a wolf playing the flute and then, when attacked by
dogs, bewailing the fact that from a butcher he had become a flute-player.[2]
Ermolao Barbaro, writing to Pico, reversed the proverb elegantly:[3] 'When
you are a landsman, you should not look to go to sea.'[4]

12 Thynni more
Squinting like a tunny fish

Θύννου δίκην, Like a tunny fish. People are said to be looking like a tunny
when they squint or peer sideways with one eye. Aeschylus is quoted by
Athenaeus in book 7: 'Casting awry his left eye upon it, like a tunny'[1] – for
Aristotle states that tunny only look with the left eye, as Athenaeus quotes
him here,[2] although just before that,[3] quoting the same author, he has said
that it sees with the right eye and is half blind in the left. Pliny says, in book

* * * * *

11 Apostolius 8.83. Cf *Adagia* IV ix 34 The horseman should not take to singing.
1 Aesop 116 Perry
2 Aesop 97 Perry; added in 1515
3 *Non ineleganter*; LB *non eleganter*
4 Ermolao Barbaro *Epistolae* 81.38 Branca I 109 (on whom see *Adagia* III iii 37 n3
  [CWE 34 414]); added in 1528

12 Apostolius 8.96 who quotes Aeschylus (fragment 308 Nauck)
1 Athenaeus 7.303C: θύννου δίκην (given in Greek)
2 Aristotle *Historia animalium* 7(8).13 (598b18–22): '. . . they see more sharply with
  the right eye, not having sharp sight by nature.' Athenaeus' words, immediately after the quotation, are: 'For the tunny cannot see with the left eye, as
  Aristotle says.' The references to Aristotle was added in 1528.
3 Athenaeus 7.301E; Erasmus appears to have misunderstood the first passage
  quoted from Athenaeus, who, like Aristotle, is quite consistent in saying that
  the tunny sees better with the right eye.

9 chapter 15, that they have weak sight in both eyes, but see more with the right.[4] The same verse is repeated from the same author[5] by Plutarch in his dialogue 'On Comparing Land and Sea Animals.' He adds that these fish have such poor sight in the one eye, that as they swim towards the sea they hug the right bank, and as they come back the reverse.[6] The adage can also be applied to those who scrutinize keenly and carefully. Persius says: 'As straight as if he is setting a ruddle cord with one eye.'[7] And Aristotle says in Problems 3 and 4 of section 31 that he thinks this happens 'because the eyes arise from the same point' [in the brain].[8] The result is that, when one eye is closed, the force that drove both is bestowed on one, the more keen because the more concentrated.

13 Canis reversus ad vomitum
A dog goes back to his vomit

Κύων ἐπὶ τὸ ἴδιον ἐξέραμα, A dog to his own vomit. This fits those who fall back into the same crimes, crimes for which they have already paid the penalty. There is a passage in the Epistle of St Peter in these words: 'For them the proverb has proved true: "The dog turns back to his own vomit,[1] and the sow is washed only to wallow in the mire."'[2] The figure appears to be taken from dogs who swallow again what they have vomited up, and pigs who run straight from the stream to the mud. The Hebrew author of Proverbs expresses the same idea: 'Like a dog that returns to his vomit is a fool that repeats his folly.'[3] Peter was alluding to this passage, if I am not mistaken.[4]

* * * * *

4 Pliny *Naturalis historia* 9.50; added in *1528*
5 That is, the verse of Aeschylus quoted by Athenaeus; see n1 above.
6 Plutarch *Moralia* 979E *Terrestriane an aquatilia animalia sint callidiora*. Plutarch is referring to the Black Sea though he claims to be repeating Aristotle, who refers to the Adriatic. Added in *1515*
7 Persius 1.66; translation by G.G. Ramsey (Loeb)
8 Aristotle *Problemata* 31.2 (not 3) and 4 (957b5 and 18–23). This reference quotes the translation of Theodore Gaza (*quod oculorum initia ab eodem dependeant*) and was added in *1515*.

13 *Collectanea* no 750. Apostolius 10.30 (Κύων εἰς τὸν ἴδιον ἔμετον). Erasmus has preferred the biblical version.
1 Given in Greek: Κύων ἐπιστρέψας ἐπὶ τὸ ἴδιον ἐξέραμα.
2 2 Peter 2:22; the quotation of the actual words was added in *1515*.
3 Proverbs 26:11
4 Last sentence added in *1517/18*

14 Cani das paleas, asino ossa
You are giving chaff to the dog and bones to the ass

Κυνὶ δίδως ἄχυρα, ὄνῳ δὲ ὀστέα, You are giving chaff to the dog but bones to the ass. Said when things are distributed the wrong way. For example if someone sends a gift of a literary work to someone who is uneducated, flowers or a sword or a belt to a scholar, a book to a soldier, or hunting dogs to a bishop. Such gifts are unwelcome for the good reason that they are not suitable. Sometimes they are given in order to insult.[1]

15 Praemovere venatum
To disturb the prey

Προσοβεῖν τὴν θήραν, To scare away the prey. Aristides, in his *Pericles*, quotes from Plato 'And so in this way, as he himself says, he disturbed the game.'[1] Further, there is a passage of Plato in his *Lysis* as follows: 'What sort of hunter would he seem to you to be if, during the hunt, he disturbed the beast and made the capture more difficult?'[2] It seems to be said usually when someone does not conceal sufficiently what he is plotting. In this way the animal, disturbed by the turmoil, usually becomes aware of the trap and escapes.

16 Rectam ingredi viam
To walk a straight path

Τὴν ὀρθὴν βαδίζειν ὁδόν, To walk a straight path. This is said of someone who never deviates from the honest path. Aristides in his *Pericles*: 'To pro-

* * * * *

14 Apostolius 10.31
  1 'a book ... insult' added in *1528*. Erasmus undoubtedly remembers the occasion in 1503 when he was given a sword by the gunsmith to whom he had given a copy of the *Enchiridion*. See Epp 858:16–23, 1556:48–51 and the introduction to Ep 164 CWE 2 51.

15 Aristides (see n1 below)
  1 Aristides *Orationes* 46 *De quattuor* ed Dindorf II 158 and scholia (Dindorf III 443 scholion no 117,8): ἀνεσόβει τὴν θήραν, παροιμία. ASD believes Erasmus formed the related compound προσοβεῖν himself, and is unlikely to have taken it from Synesius *De regno* (*Opuscula* 8 line 13 Terzaghi PG 66 1057A) who has προσοβῆσαι τὴν θήραν. This work was first published in 1553.
  2 Plato *Lysis* 206A: ἀνασοβοῖ θηρεύων 'disturbed the beast' (given in Greek); added in *1520*

16 Cf Apostolius 12.31. Otto 1886

ceed in an orderly manner, and keep to the right road, as the proverb says.'[1] Philo in his 'On Humanity': 'For the public way, which leads to justice, this he had learned.'[2] Plautus in the *Casina*: 'Now I'm on the right road at last,'[3] and a little later: 'You are leaving the highway for the by-path deliberately.'[4] The servant-girl is telling him, after he had imprudently blurted out the truth, to go back to the lie that he had started with.

17 Αὐτόθεν κατάβαλλε
Lay it down on the spot

Αὐτόθεν κατάβαλλε, Lay it down on the spot.[1] Aristides in the *Pericles*: 'Drop this talk straightway now about the chatterers, the idle, and the faint-hearted, O Plato, lest perchance some other god should raise up the Trojans.'[2] The scholiast indicates this is a proverb taken from victors who prevent the conquered opponent from escaping by any means, but demand that he offer grass[3] on the spot, acknowledge the victor, and pay for the prize of victory.[4] It will be used whenever we order something to be shown immediately and without delay, either proof of what someone has said, or a promise, or a sample of craft in which someone boasts of his ability. It is used in Plato too.[5]

* * * * *

1 Aristides *Orationes* 46 *De quattuor* ed Dindorf II 159. Estienne in a long note (LB II 831) seeks to show that the passage from Aristides is inappropriate, because the expression in question is not used metaphorically there.
2 Philo *De virtutibus* 51 'On humanity'
3 Plautus *Casina* 469
4 Plautus *Casina* 675

17 Apostolius 4.42. This saying was added in 1528 to the end of *Adagia* III iii 28, where Erasmus appears to accept the meaning later suggested by Estienne (see n1 below) without looking for a more general application.
1 *Hoc ipso depone loco*; Estienne (LB II 831 n2): 'I do not see what must or can be understood by these words, "Lay it down on the spot," nor in what sense *depone* ["put down"] can be taken absolutely. I think therefore it is to be translated "Pay up in the present business," or "Pay on the spot" or "immediately."'
2 Aristides *Orationes* 46 *De quattuor* ed Dindorf II 169: Αὐτόθεν κατάβαλλε 'Drop this talk straightway.' On 'raise up the Trojans' Estienne (LB II 832) comments: 'Here ἐγείρῃσι does not stand for *erigat* ["raise up"], but for *expergefaciat, excitet à somno* ["waken, raise from sleep"]. It is a verse from the *Iliad* book 10 [line 511].'
3 That is, 'yield the palm'; cf Pliny *Naturalis historia* 22.8 and *Adagia* I ix 78.
4 Dindorf III 465 line 29
5 The editors of ASD suggest *Laws* 5.742B and 11.932D.

18 Ostium obdite prophani
Shut the door, ye profane

Θύρας ἐπίθεσθε βέβηλοι, Close tight your doors, any who are unconsecrated. The allusion is to Orpheus, from whom this verse is quoted: Φθέγξομαι οἷς θέμις ἐστί, θύρας ἐπίθεσθε βέβηλοι 'I shall speak to those for whom it is lawful to hear; you, the unconsecrated crowd, / Close your doors ...' He commands that profane people should put a door on their ears, so that none of the secret words may enter. Aristides in his *Pericles*: 'I speak these things among those for whom it is lawful to hear, for the profane are of no account at all.'[1] It will be appropriate to use at times when we want to indicate that we are about to speak of difficult and arcane matters. This is what Horace was thinking of when he wrote in his *Odes*:

> I hate the vulgar crowd and hold aloof;
> Take care what you say, for I, priest of the Muses,
> Sing songs not heard before
> To virgins and young boys.[2]

And Ovid:

> Let a propitious tongue speak which thinks no more of my labours,
> For mine, I think, has forgotten how to utter auspicious words.[3]

Before a sacrifice the public crier would order the populace to 'be favourable with your tongues,' that is, to speak words of good omen, whence *faventia* is also said for 'good prognostication.' Then there is Seneca, speaking of Philosophy: 'Worship her too like the gods, and her teachers like priests, and speak favourably whenever mention of sacred scriptures occurs. This word *favete* is not, as many think, derived from *favor* "good-will," but commands silence, so that a sacred rite can be carried through without being hindered by any ill-omened voice.'[4] However, it will appear rather more witty if it is used

* * * * *

18 Erasmus' source is almost certainly the scholion (Dindorf III 471) of the quotation from Aristides (see n1 below), though the fragment was very well known and could be seen in Clement of Alexandria and Eusebius of Caesarea. *Orphicorum fragmenta* ed Otto Kern (Berlin 1922) fragment 245 line 1.
1 Aristides *Orationes* 46 *De quattuor* ed Dindorf II 173
2 Horace *Odes* 3.1.1–4
3 Ovid *Tristia* 5.5.5–6
4 Seneca *De vita beata* 26.7

ironically, as for example if someone who is about to recite some sophistic Scotist quibblings announces them thus: 'Close tight your doors, any who are unconsecrated.'[5] Lucian used the expression in this way more than once.[6]

19 **Ad restim funiculum**
   Cord to rope

Ἐπὶ σπείρᾳ σχοινίον, Cord to rope. 'You are joining' is understood, or 'You are rendering cord for rope'; said when someone repeats the same things or makes self-evident comparisons. It is related to 'You join thread with thread,'[1] as when someone adds lie to lie, fraud to fraud, triviality to triviality.

20 **Salem et fabam**
   Salt and a bean

Ἅλα καὶ κύαμον, Salt and a bean, understanding *proposuerunt* 'they set out' or any other word more appropriate to the context. Diogenianus informs us that it was said of those who pretended to know something that they did not know, and the proverb arises from the fact that formerly soothsayers set out salt and a bean. Because I was in some doubt whether or not this was different from the one which I noted in the first chiliad,[1] I thought it should be repeated here, for I find it quoted in this form in some old copies of the Greek writers.[2]

21 **Ἐκπερδικίσαι**
   To fly away

Ἐκπερδικίσαι is what the Greeks say, in a proverbial metaphor, for 'to slip out,' or 'evade.' Aristophanes in the *Birds*: 'To be sure, among us there is no shame in evading snares.'[1] It is derived from birds who often escape from

* * * * *

5 Given in Greek: Θύρας ἐπίθεσθε βέβηλοι.
6 Lucian *De sacrificiis* 14

19 Apostolius 7.84
1 *Adagia* I viii 59 Λίνον λίνῳ συνάπτεις (given here in Greek)

20 *Collectanea* no 719. Diogenianus 1.50. Apostolius 2.41
1 *Adagia* I i 12 Around salt and beans
2 Diogenianus 1.50; see also Zenobius 1.25.

21 Apostolius 6.96
1 Aristophanes *Birds* 768

nets or snares; for they say the *perdix* 'partridge' is particularly clever at escaping from the hands of the fowlers. On this subject it is well to set out here the words of Aristotle himself which are in book 9 of the *Nature of Animals*:

> And they do not lay their eggs and incubate them in the same place, lest anyone should notice that they have been sitting for a rather long time in the same place. Further, when someone comes upon a nest during a hunt, the partridge throws herself at the feet of the hunter, just as if she intended to be caught, and in this way attracts him towards herself, making him think he can capture her, until the chicks can escape in the interval one by one. When this is achieved, she flies away and calls the chicks to herself.[2]

That is what Aristotle has to say. And I shall be happy to add to this passage what Plutarch writes along just the same lines in the book he entitled 'Whether Land or Sea Animals Are Cleverer':

> But another kind of cleverness is shown, along with love of their young, by partridges. For they accustom their young, while they are still flightless, to lie flat on their backs holding a lump of earth or some covering of straw over their bodies, and thus covered to remain hidden, whilst they themselves draw the hunter off somewhere else by the following deception. They attract him towards themselves, flying in front of his feet and continually keeping a little ahead of him, offering hope of being caught only until they draw him away from the chicks.[3]

From these words, I think, it is clear enough what is meant by ἐκπερδικίσαι: truly, to escape by the art of the partridge. At the same time, there is an allusion to a certain notably dishonest shopkeeper, who was given the name Partridge because he limped. Aristophanes recalls him in the *Birds*.[4]

22 Munus Levidensae
A threadbare present

A 'threadbare present' is what Cicero, using a doubtless proverbial figure,

* * * * *

2 Aristotle *Historia animalium* 8(9).8 (613b15–22)
3 Plutarch *Moralia* 971C–D *Utra animalia sunt prudentiora, terrestria an marina?*
4 Aristophanes *Birds* 1292; added in 1533

22 *Collectanea* no 295. Cicero (see n1 below). *Levidensa*, which Erasmus takes to be a noun meaning a garment, is taken from the Aldine editions of 1490, 1493, or 1502.

called a mean present, the cheapest sort, such as rich people were accustomed to send often to their plebeian friends. This is what he writes to Dolabella in book 9 of his *Letters to Friends*: 'The little speech on behalf of Deiotarus, that you were asking for, I had with me – though I did not think I had – and so I have sent it to you. I would like you to read it as a meagre, poor example, not really worth the writing. But to an old guest and friend I wanted to send a threadbare little present, of coarse material, such as his own presents are wont to be.'[1] Servius shows that the 'levidensa' is a poor kind of garment, of loose thin weave.[2] At one time garments were among the principal presents given to guests. Hence in Juvenal too someone complains that he is sometimes given garments of coarse hair and bad colour: 'And ill combed by the Gallic weaver.'[3] In like manner Marcus Tullius calls his undeveloped, unpolished speech a 'present of a threadbare garment.' This can be applied nicely to the small present or trivial service, offered quite unwillingly and thoughtlessly, to some plebeian friend. This is quite different from Πελληναῖος χιτών 'A tunic Pellene-style,' and Συλοσῶντος χλαμύς 'Syloson's cloak.'[4]

23 Multi discipuli praestantiores magistris
Many pupils surpass their teachers

Marcus Tullius in book 9 of his *Letters to Friends*, writing to Varro, quotes a verse – from which poet I do not yet know. Even nowadays his aphorism is very commonly repeated among ordinary people. He says: 'Dolabella is coming. I think he will be my teacher: Πολλοὶ μαθηταὶ κρείσσονες διδασκάλων "Many pupils excel their teachers."'[1] This can be adapted to various uses; perhaps in the plain sense, for example that it quite often happens that the pupil surpasses in learning the one from whom he learnt his letters or some skill. Or jokingly when we want to imply that someone who was a teacher of deceit is the victim of dishonesty; for example, if someone is cheated by the person to whom he had once demonstrated ways and means of deception. Or when someone of lower class and

* * * * *

1 Cicero *Ad familiares* 9.12.2, quoted by Otto 1119 in relation to the expression *crasso filo* 'of coarse material'
2 Not Servius but Isidore of Seville *Etymologiae* 19.22.19
3 Juvenal 9.30
4 *Adagia* III iii 17 and I x 84

23 Cicero (see n1 below). Suringar 123
1 Cicero *Ad familiares* 9.7.2 quoting Menander *Sententiae* 651 (Jäkel = adespota 107 Nauck). In Ep 962, dating from the first half of May 1519, Erasmus ascribed the verse tentatively to Euripides.

condition has more power than one who is thought to be the master not the servant.

24 Ad Herculis columnas
To the pillars of Hercules

Ἡράκλειαι στῆλαι, The pillars of Hercules. They were proverbial in former times, as the scholiast of Pindar shows, for it used to be said popularly, 'The regions beyond Gades are inaccessible.'[1] By this they meant that beyond the pillars of Hercules there was nowhere further to go. Hercules is said to have placed these pillars there when he was seeking the cattle of Geryon, as if that point was the extreme end of the world. Pindar in the *Nemeans*: 'There is nowhere to go further west beyond Gades.'[2] And in another passage: 'But if the son of Aristophanes, being fair to look upon and doing deeds that befit the fairness of his form, embarked on the highest achievement of manly prowess, he cannot easily sail further across the trackless sea beyond the pillars of Heracles, which that hero and god set up [as far-famed witnesses] of the furthest limit of voyaging.'[3] He means that the son of Aristophanes, having joined illustrious deeds to exceptional beauty, has achieved the highest glory, which he cannot surpass. For if anyone should seek further glory, it would be as if someone should try to go beyond the pillars set up by Hercules. Again, in the third *Olympian*: 'Now reaching by his deeds of courage right to the extreme limits, Theron arrives from his home at the pillars of Hercules. What is beyond, to the wise as to the foolish, is inaccessible.'[4] In an exactly similar way Gregory of Nazianzus used it in his *Monodia*,[5] meaning that Basil had reached such a point of perfection that human nature was debarred from going further. Heraclides Ponticus, in his *Allegories of Homer*, thinks that bad interpreters of the poems

* * * * *

24 Scholiast of Pindar (see n2 below). Otto *Nachträge* page 167 Gades
1 ASD points out that the quotation, in Greek, reproduces Apostolius 16.19 Τὰ γὰρ Γαδείρων οὐ περατά, not the scholiast of Pindar.
2 Pindar *Nemeans* 4.69
3 *Nemeans* 3.19–22: Εἰ δ᾽ ὢν καλὸς ἔρδων τ᾽ ἐοικότα μορφᾷ / Ἀνορέαις ὑπερτάταις ἐπέβα / Παῖς Ἀριστοφάνευς, οὐκέτι πρόσω / Ἀβάταν ἅλα κιόνων ὑπὲρ Ἡρακλέους περᾶν εὐμαρές, / Ἥρως θεὸς ἃς ἔθηκε ναυτιλίαις ἐσχάτας; given in Greek not translated by Erasmus; this translation by Sir J.E. Sandys (Loeb)
4 *Olympians* 3.43–45: Νῦν γε πρὸς ἐσχατίαν / Θήρων ἀρεταῖσιν ἱκάνων ἅπτεται / Οἴκοθεν Ἡρακλέος / Στηλᾶν. τὸ πόρσω δ᾽ ἐστὶ σοφοῖς ἄβατον / Κἀσόφοις. Given in Greek, translated by Erasmus
5 Gregory of Nazianzus *Orationes* 43.24 PG 36 528C

of Homer should be thrust 'beyond the outermost pillars of Hercules and the inaccessible sea of Oceanus.'[6]

25 Ariolari
Crystal-gazing

A person was said proverbially to be 'crystal-gazing' if he offered nothing certain, brought no immediate gain, but only kept making promises day after day. Thus, in Terence's *Phormio*, when the young man, Phaedria, promises Dorio, the pimp, that he will give him money and says, 'Don't you believe me?' Dorio replies, 'Crystal-gazing!'[1] Sannio too in the *Adelphoe*: 'But I am talking like a crystal-gazer.'[2] The word is derived from soothsayers who predict what will happen. But of future things there is no certain knowledge, as is elegantly stated by Pindar:

> Knowledge of future things is wrapped in darkness,
> But for mortals many things will come to pass beyond their hopes.[3]

26 Ciceris emptor
A buyer of chickpeas

For my part I think this expression too, used by Horace in his *Art of Poetry*, is to be counted as a proverb, 'A buyer of chickpeas and nuts,' meaning the most humble sort of man, someone of the lowest class: 'For people with horses, fathers, and substance take offence and do not greet with equanimity, or reward with a crown, anything the buyer of cracked[1] chickpeas and chestnuts recommends.'[2]

* * * * *

6 Heraclides Ponticus *Quaestiones homericae* 21: ὑπὲρ Ἡρακλέους ἐσχάτας στήλας 'beyond the outermost pillars of Hercules' (given in Greek); published by Aldus with his *Aesop* in 1505. The reference is to *Iliad* 1.399–404.

25 Terence *Phormio* 492
1 Dorio's reply is a sarcastic one. J. Sargeaunt (Loeb) translates 'Moonshine.'
2 *Adelphoe* 202; added in *1517/18*
3 Pindar *Olympians* 12.9–10

26 Horace (see n2 below)
1 Erasmus' text has *fracti* 'cracked'; the accepted reading is *fricti* 'roasted.'
2 Horace *Ars poetica* 248–250; *Ars poetica* is a usual title for *Epistles* 2.3 *Ad Pisones*.

27 Nemo quenquam ire prohibet publica via
No one stops anyone from walking on the public road

Plautus' expression in the *Curculio* looks like a proverb too: 'No one stops anyone from walking on the public road.' By this they mean that public property is for the use of everyone equally, and that what the public law allows is not to be imputed to anyone as a crime. Plautus gave a somewhat disgusting turn to it, namely to using the services of a prostitute selling herself in public. It seems to have been formed in imitation of the Pythagorean precept which commands us Τῆς λεωφόρου βαδίζειν 'To walk by the public way,' or the opposite, Τῆς λεωφόρου μὴ βαδίζειν 'Not to walk in the public highway.'[1] Flaccus seems to me to be harking back to this when he says in his *Art of poetry*:

> You will gain private rights on public property if
> You do not linger on the banal and beaten path
> Or try to translate word for word ...[2]

28 Hinc belli initium
This is where the war begins

Among the proverbs which are taken from writers' allusions, I think I should not pass over in silence one from Thucydides that Lucian used in his *False Prophet*: 'And in the words of Thucydides "Here beginneth the war."'[1] This can be adapted to various uses, either when we mean girding ourselves to begin some business, or when we imply that something has generated dissension and unrest has broken out. It was to the same passage in Thucydides, no doubt, that Aristophanes alluded in the *Acharnians*: 'And hence the beginning of the war.'[2] And he repeats this word κἀντεῦθεν

* * * * *

27 *Collectanea* no 65a. Plautus *Curculio* 35
  1 See *Adagia* I i 2:280 and 308 (CWE 31 41–2). Erasmus gives no Latin here for the second precept. In the case of the first, he has not quoted it in the form he gave earlier: Ἐκτὸς λεωφόρου μὴ βαδίζειν 'Do not walk outside the public highway.'
  2 Horace *Ars poetica* 131–3, echoing Callimachus *Aetia* 1 fragment 1.25–8 Pfeiffer.

28 Lucian (see n1 below). Cf Diogenianus 3.5 and Apostolius 3.86. An inadvertent duplication of *Adagia* II x 75
  1 Lucian *Alexander* 8; Thucydides 2.1
  2 Aristophanes *Acharnians* 528: Κἀντεῦθεν 'And hence.' But, as the editors of ASD point out, the *Acharnians* antedates Thucydides' work by some twenty years.

in this passage quite often to make it clearer that he has made the allusion for a joke.[3]

29 Inanium inania consilia
Futile advice from futile people

Κενοὶ κενὰ βουλεύονται, Futile advice from futile people, and Κενοὶ κενὰ λογίζονται, Useless ideas of useless people.[1] Said when someone is foiled in his hopes; related to Μωρὰ μωρὸς λέγει 'A fool says foolish things.'[2] It is said to have arisen from an actual event: Archias demanded from Demetrius[3] a promise of five hundred talents to betray Cyprus; when the affair was discovered, he snatched a rope from those who were pitching tents and hanged himself. To be found in the Greek Collections.[4]

30 Nutricum more male
Badly, like foster mothers

Καθώσπερ αἱ τίτθαι γε σιτίζεις κακῶς, You are a poor provider, after the manner of foster mothers indeed. I found this in some very ancient *Collected*

* * * * *

3 *Acharnians* 530, 535, and 539

29 Apostolius 9.66. Diogenianus 5.100
1 Zenobius (Aldus) column 103
2 *Adagia* I i 98 from *Suda* K 1346, which Erasmus follows for the story of Archias
3 Demetrius I of Macedonia, called Poliorcetes, took Cyprus in 306.
4 *Graecorum Collectanea.* Erasmus occasionally uses this title to refer either to Apostolius (*Adagia* IV ii 23, 62, 64, 73; 514, 533, 534, 539 below), of which he possessed a manuscript, or to Zenobius (*Adagia* IV i 15, 45; 450, 468 below), first published in 1497.

30 Pseudo-Plutarch (see n1 below). Erasmus makes frequent use of a collection found in a manuscript which is either that now known as Laurentianus 80.13 or one very like it (see *Adagia* II vii 21 and ASD II-6 473 note on III vii 83). The Laurentian manuscript contains five selections of proverbs corresponding largely to Zenobius (Athous), with some differences and not in the same order (see Otto Crusius *Plutarchi de proverbiis Alexandrinorum libellus ineditus* in *Supplementum* IIIA viii and Crusius *Analecta* pages 5–7). The first selection of the five bears the name Plutarch in the title, abbreviated here as *Alexandrian Proverbs*, and is published in CPG 1.321–42, the others by H. Jungblut in *Supplementum* VI pages 395–420. Erasmus makes more extensive use of this source in *Adagia* III vii, III x, IV i, and IV ii.

Proverbs that some attribute to Plutarch.[1] It can be found, however, in the *Knights* of Aristophanes who, in addition, explains the metaphorical sense with these lines:

> You are a poor provider, after the manner of foster mothers indeed.
> For you chew it and put a little in his mouth,
> But you yourself gobble at least three times more food than he does.[2]

So this will be suitable for people who give a small share of their profit to their associates; or those who administer other people's property and so divert the greatest part to their own uses, which is what the common run of guardians do nowadays too.[3]

31 Amphictyonum consessus
An assembly of Amphictyons

Ἀμφικτυονικὸν συνέδριον, An Amphictyonian assembly. Said of crowded meetings of important people. Derived from the meeting of the Greeks, which was formerly very famous, called the Council of the Amphictyons. Either it was named after Amphictyon son of Deucalion, who is said, when he came to power, to have called the Greek peoples together; the authority for this is Theopompus in his *Histories* book 8,[1] supported by Pausanias in his *Phocians*.[2] The peoples who used to meet in this council, I may add, were twelve in number: the Ionians, Dorians, Perrhaebians, Boeotians, Magnetes, Achaeans, Phthians, Malians, Dolopians, Aeneans, Delphians,[3] and Phocians. Or the name Amphictyons, 'surrounding peoples,' was given because they came to this council from all parts of Greece, as Anaximenes and Androtion say in Pausanias' *Description of Greece* in the passage I have

* * * * *

1 This proverb is to be found now only in a late recension under the name of Gregorius Cyprius in CPG 1.365 and CPG 2.73 and in Apostolius 9.55. This case suggests that Erasmus' source was a manuscript other than Laurentianus 80.13.
2 Aristophanes *Knights* 716–18: Καθώσπερ αἱ τίτθαι γε σιτίζεις κακῶς, / Μασώμενος γὰρ τῷ μὲν ὀλίγον ἐντιθεῖς, / Αὐτὸς δ᾽ ἐκείνου τριπλάσιον κατέσπακας.
3 See Suringar 265.

31 Apostolius 2.70. *Suda* A 1736. For a modern account of the Council of the Amphictyons see the *Oxford Classical Dictionary*.
1 Erasmus is following Harpocration A 98. See *FGrHist* 115 F 63.
2 Pausanias 10.8.1
3 In modern accounts, the Delphians are replaced by the Locrians.

just pointed out.[4] Here in fact many other things worth reading on this subject are related, if anyone perchance should seek them. I think this is sufficient for the explanation of the proverb. The adage would be wittier if turned ironically to apply to an assembly of ignoramuses who think nevertheless that they are Solons.

32 Etiam capillus unus
Even a single hair

The mime Publianus too, if I am not mistaken, is well known for an image which is certainly proverbial: 'Even a single hair has its shadow.'[1] The smallest thing can give pleasure, the slightest fault can do harm.

33 Xenocratis caseolus
Xenocrates' scrap of cheese

Ξενοκράτους τυρίον, Xenocrates' scrap of cheese. Said of food which lasts a long time before it is finished. However nothing prevents us from transposing it to other things too, such as clothing, a book, small change, or anything like this which someone uses so sparingly and carefully that it lasts as long as possible. The adage is derived from the astonishing frugality of the philosopher Xenocrates.[1] It is told that he often threw out food because it had already gone rancid, and it happened not infrequently, when he wished to open a wine-jar, that he would find the wine had already turned sour. Therefore the proverb will be used appropriately of certain mean types who have this habit of keeping every sort of food until it is rotten, as if it is a crime to enjoy pure and wholesome things. The adage is recorded in Stobaeus' *Collectanea*.

* * * * *

4 See n2 above. For Anaximenes see *FGrHist* 72 F 2; he is not mentioned by Pausanias but by Apostolius. For Androtion see *FGrHist* 324 F 58.

32 Publilius Syrus (see n1 below). Otto 341
1 Publilius Syrus line 186 in *Minor Latin Poets* (Loeb). The name Publianus (Erasmus also refers to him as Publius) was added in *1517/18* after Erasmus had published an edition of Publilius' *dicta* with his *Cato: Opuscula aliquot Erasmo Roterodamo castigatore et interprete* ... *Mimi Publiani* [sic] ... (Cologne, in aedibus Martini Werdenensis [1514]). See *Adagia* I ii 4 30n (CWE 31 149) and II 1 68 n1 (CWE 33 358).

33 Stobaeus *Eclogae* 3.17.24 Hense III 495–6
1 See *Adagia* III v 3 (69 above).

34 Aperto pectore
Open-heartedly

We say 'With open breast' of anything which comes passionately, from the heart, with no pretence, as if the inmost parts of the soul were open to view. Marcus Tullius in his book *On Friendship*: 'In this, unless you see, as they say, an open breast, and show your own, there is no trust.'[1] And the younger Pliny writing to Fabatus: 'The letters that you have written to me, as you say, with open breast, you command me to forget. But there are none that I remember with greater pleasure.'[2] The phrase is an allusion to the words of Momus, who is said to have wanted to make openings in men's breasts so that what was hidden in those cavities could be examined.[3] Persius in his fifth *Satire*: 'So that I may proclaim with a clear voice how firmly I have planted you in the depths of my heart, and so that these words may reveal everything that lies hidden and ineffable in my soul.'[4] Likewise Phoebus in Naso:

> Behold, look at
> My face, would that with your eyes you could pierce my breast,
> And understand the father's cares that are within.[5]

35 Ad calcem pervenire
To reach the chalk mark

'To reach the chalk mark' is said for reaching a goal, and an end. This has a proverbial quality when it is turned to something other than the human body.[1] Marcus Tullius *On Friendship*: 'As you may be able to live with your

* * * * *

34 Cicero (see n1 below). Otto 1366
1 Cicero *De amicitia* 97
2 Pliny *Letters* 6.12.3; added in *1533*
3 See Lucian *Hermotimus* 20.
4 Persius 5.27–9
5 Ovid *Metamorphoses* 2.92–4

35 Cicero (see n3 below). Otto 308. Cf also *Adagia* III vii 56 We have come to the final line (249 below).
1 This remark is difficult to understand unless Erasmus takes this word *calx* 'pebble, chalk' to be the same word as that meaning 'heel' (also *calx*), but seems pointless if, as ASD implies, he clearly distinguishes the two. Cf *Adagia* I ii 37 *A capite usque ad calcem*.

equals, having been, as it were, sent off from the starting boxes[2] with them, so you may be able with these same people, as the saying is, *ad calcem ... pervenire* "to reach the goal."'[3] And the same author *On Old Age*: 'Nor would I wish, having as it were run the whole course, to be called back to the starting boxes from the line.'[4] To this kind are related the following: 'Right up to the call for applause,' that is, 'Up to the very end.' The same author in the same speech: 'Let him win approval for whatever part of the play he appears in; and it is not for the wise man to continue right up to the call for applause.'[5] Again, in another passage: 'Those who have put these to noble use seem to me to have played through the drama of life and to have avoided collapsing in the final scene like inexperienced actors.'[6] Yet again elsewhere in the same work: 'The final act is neglected, as if it were by a careless poet.'[7] However, I have noted this sort in another place.[8]

36 Bellum omnium pater
War is the father of all things

Ὁ πόλεμος ἁπάντων πατήρ, War is the father of all things. Lucian tells us in his essay *How History Should be Written* that this was uttered by way of a proverb: 'Better still, they are all a Thucydides, a Herodotus, a Xenophon to us. So much so that the saying would seem to be true that Πόλεμος ἁπάντων πατήρ "War is the father of all things" since it produced so many writers at a single stroke.'[1] It was spoken as a proverb therefore, because war is the cause of the renewal of all things, so that every thing seems to be born from it. But some may prefer to relate it to the statement of certain philosophers who said that everything is generated by strife.[2]

* * * * *

2 *ad carceres revocari*; see *Adagia* I vi 58.
3 Cicero *De amicitia* 101
4 Cicero *De senectute* 83
5 *De senectute* 19.70; *usque ad plaudite* is listed in the index of LB with reference to this adage but not treated by Erasmus as a separate proverb.
6 *De senectute* 18.64
7 *De senectute* 2.5
8 *Adagia* I ii 35 To add a last act to the play

36 Lucian (see n1 below)
1 Lucian *Quomodo historia conscribenda sit* 2 quoting Heraclitus 22 B 53 Diels-Kranz; also quoted by Plutarch *Moralia* 370D *De Iside et Osiride*
2 Heraclitus 22 B 8 and 22 B 80 Diels-Kranz, quoted by Aristotle *Ethica Nicomachea* 8.1.6 (1155b5): Πάντα κατ᾽ ἔριν γίνεσθαι.

37 Phaniae ianua
The doors of Phanias

Φανίου θύρα, The doors of Phanias. Eustathius, on the *Odyssey* book 24, shows that this was said of those who pretend they have accumulations of wealth which do not exist. Derived from a certain Phanias who created a false reputation for himself as having great store of wealth hidden in his house. I have mentioned 'The doors of Phanias' elsewhere in the proverb 'Phanus' front door.'[1] Scholars will decide whether that is the same as this one or not.

38 Ἐκλινίσαι
To slip through the net

Ἐκλινίσαι, To slip through the net. Eustathius, writing on the third book of the *Iliad*, shows that this was used as a proverbial figure.[1] The metaphor is based on fish which escape from the nets, or slip off the hook. For nets are called *lina* by the Romans too, as in Maro: *Humida lina trahunt* 'They drag their wet nets.'[2] Some fish have a real innate ability to slip out of the mesh of nets, as Oppian tells us in his stylish account of the grey mullet. But since the author has not been published at all so far, it is better to give the text of the poem:

> When the grey mullet is caught in the rippling mesh,
> It is well aware of the skill and guile by which it may escape;
> It shoots upward, striving with all its might
> To rise straight up with a rapid leap,
> Its whole body flashing up to the tops of the waves.
> And luck favours skill, for often, jumping over the corks
> To which the topmost strings are tied and the cords of the net,

* * * * *

37 Eustathius 1959.14 on *Odyssey* 24.304 (cf *Adagia* IV i 37 Gifts of an Alybantian host, 463 below). Cf Zenobius 4.24, Diogenianus 5.5, *Suda* H 655.
1 *Adagia* II vii 70

38 Eustathius (see n1 below)
1 Eustathius 574.30 on *Iliad* 5.487 (not book 3): ὡς ἀψῖσι λίνοι ἀλόντε πανάγρου 'As if caught in the meshes of all-ensnaring flax'
2 Virgil *Georgics* 1.142

The impudent fish slips away escaping its dark fate.
But if from its first upward leap it falls back again into the nets,
In anguish it makes no further effort to fight,
No more vain leaps, but learning from its trials
It ceases to torment itself and rises up no more.[3]

He records in the same way the tricks by which many other fish escape
when caught; but it would take too long to set forth all the rest. The poet
Claudian's account of the *torpedo* 'electric ray' is amusing to know: how,
when caught on the bait, it can get away by the power of the poison that
it sends through the line and the rod all the way to the fisherman's hand.
The poem goes like this – and why should I not set it out, since it is so neat
and so witty?

If incautiously it takes a bait that hides the bronze hook
And feels the pull of the curved barbs,
It does not swim away nor try to pluck it out with vain biting;
But cunningly moves closer to the dark line and, though a prisoner,
Remembers its power and emits from its poisonous veins
A deadening shock which spreads far through the water.
The power of the poison creeps up the line and leaves the sea,
To overcome the fisherman despite his distance. The fearful horror
Rises from the deep waters and climbing up the hanging line,
Jumps over the knots of the cane rod with its mysterious coldness,
And in the very moment of victory congeals the blood in the captor's
    hand.
The fisherman casts away the dangerous burden
And throws away his rebel prey, returning home disarmed without his rod.[4]

The scholiast of Aristophanes believes the expression is derived from birds.[5]
Persius' fifth *Satire* has a very similar figure: 'So that you do not want to
thrash about or gnaw at the tight-drawn nets.'[6]

* * * * *

3 Oppian *Halieutica* 3.98–107; the first edition of Oppian appeared in 1515; this
  adage was first published in 1508.
4 Claudian *Carmina minora* 49.13–25
5 The scholiast of Aristophanes *Birds* 768; Erasmus appears to be confusing
  ἐκλινίσαι with ἐκπερδικίσαι (Dübner page 227); cf *Adagia* III v 21 (77 above).
6 Persius 5.170

39 Αἰγυπτιάζειν
To talk Egyptian

Αἰγυπτιάζειν, To talk Egyptian is what astute liars were said to do. It comes from the customs of that people. Theocritus in the *Syracusan Women*: 'No villain wounds / Or harms, creeping up with Egyptian cunning.'[1] On Egyptian habits we also have this witness from Aeschylus that I have noted elsewhere:[2] 'The Egyptians are astonishing at heaping up contrivances.'[3] This proverb is referred to by Synesius in his *Eulogy of Baldness*.[4] However, αἰγυπτιάζειν is sometimes taken to mean 'to set fire to,' as in this poem: 'Burning Phoebus sets your complexion afire / With his fiery flames.'[5]

40 Ne bolus quidem relictus
Not one bite left

Οὐδ᾽ ἔγκαφος λέλειπται, Not one bite left; that is, not even a small amount. Eustathius, in his commentary on the third book of the *Odyssey*, quotes this line by Eupolis: Οὐχὶ λέλειπται τῶν ἐμῶν οὐδ᾽ ἔγκαφος 'Not a morsel is left of my possessions.'[1] For ἔγκαφος means in Greek what we call, in the vernacular more than in Latin, a morsel; it comes from the verb κάπτω, which is 'to eat greedily.'[2]

* * * * *

39 The word is used and noted as proverbial by Eustathius 1484.27 commenting on *Odyssey* 4.83 and 1494.11 on *Odyssey* 4.231. Cf also Zenobius (Aldus) column 10.
  1 Theocritus 15.47–8, quoted from the scholiast of Aristophanes *Clouds* 1130 (Dübner page 125). Theocritus' poem has the title 'The Syracusan Women at the Adonis Festival.'
  2 *Adagia* II vi 57 The Egyptians have a wonderful gift for weaving webs
  3 Aeschylus fragment 373 Nauck, from the same place in the scholiast of Aristophanes; see n1 above.
  4 Synesius *Encomium calvitii* 7 PG 66 1180D; see *Adagia* III iii 29 n1 (CWE 34 413) and III v 67 (105 below).
  5 Author unknown: adespota 161 Nauck; 'sets afire' is αἰγυπτιάσει; also cited by Eustathius 1484.34 on *Odyssey* 4.83

40 Eustathius on the *Odyssey* (see n1 below)
  1 PCG 5 Eupolis fragment 360, quoted by Eustathius 1481.34 on *Odyssey* 4.40 (not book 3)
  2 Etymology from the *Etymologicum magnum* 310.21 ἔγκαφος

41 Rex aut asinus
A king or an ass

Βασιλεὺς ἢ ὄνος, A king or an ass. That is, either victor or vanquished. Similar to ῍Η τρὶς ἕξ, ἢ τρεῖς κύβοι 'Either three sixes or three ones.'[1] Eustathius, commenting on book 6 of the *Odyssey*, shows that the metaphor is drawn from people playing with a ball; they called the winner the king and the loser was dubbed the ass.[2] Plato in the *Theaetetus*: 'Anyone who makes a mistake will sit idle, the ass, as they say in a ball game; but the one who makes no mistake and wins, let him be our king.'[3] Julius Pollux, in book 9 of his *Vocabulary*, mentions four types of ball game: the first is called ἐπίσκυρος, the second φανίδα or φανίδου, the third ἀπόρραξις, and the fourth οὐρανία. The last of these, the one relevant to the proverb, he describes in these terms:

> But the game of Urania is played like this. One person, bending backwards, sends the ball skywards. For the others, it was a competition to snatch it away before it fell back to the ground, which is what Homer seems to mean when he refers to the Phaeacians. Clearly, however, when they threw the ball against the wall, they counted the number of bounces. The one who lost was called the Ass and did whatever was commanded. On the other hand the winner was the King and gave the commands.[4]

This is what Pollux has to say. I add the passage which he quotes from Homer's *Odyssey* book 8, as follows:

> This with a whirl he sent from his stout hand, and the stone hummed as it

* * * * *

41 Mantissa 1.34
1 *Aut ter sex aut tres tali*, following Mantissa. The κύβοι, or *tesserae*, were six-sided dice, the *tali* were four-sided. Since the Greeks threw three *tesserae*, three sixes was the maximum score. Neither term is given as meaning a one, which seems to be required if the second phrase is to mean to make the minimum score. In *Adagia* II iii 66 this Greek proverb is rendered in Latin as *Aut ter sex aut tres tesserae*, which Mynors translated 'Either three times six dice or three'; his note admits it would be clearer to say 'three ones.' See also *Adagia* I ii 13 17n (CWE 31 154).
2 Eustathius 1601.45 on *Odyssey* 8 (not 6) 376
3 Plato *Theaetetus* 146A, also quoted from Mantissa 1.34
4 Pollux *Onomasticon* 9.105–6. Presumably the winner was the person who caught the ball with the least number of bounces.

flew; and down they crouched to the earth, the Phaeacians of the long oars, men famed for their ships, beneath the rush of the stone. Past the marks of all it flew . . .[5]

Not unlike this form of the proverb, seemingly, is another which is in Plautus' *Carthaginian*: 'I am king, if I can entice that man to me today.'[6] It will be appropriate to use it when we mean taking a risk which makes us winners or losers.

42 Stellis signare
To go by the stars

Ἄστροις σημειοῦσθαι τὴν ὁδόν, To plot a journey by the stars. Said of those who inquire into something that is difficult to investigate in other ways, using certain small signs and conjectures. Eustathius, expounding the fifth book of the *Odyssey*, tells us that it fits those who are setting out on a long and remote journey.[1] The figure is borrowed from sailors who estimate their course on night voyages by observing the stars, just like Ulysses in Homer's *Odyssey*, book 5:

> He sat and guided his ship skilfully with the steering oar,
> Sleep never overcame his tired eyes.
> But he watches the Pleiads, and late-setting Bootes,
> And the Bear, which is also called the Plough . . .[2]

Marcus Tullius alluded neatly to this in book 4 of the *Academic Questions* when he says the completely wise man is not led by opinions, but holds firmly to the truth, and does so led and guided by the Little Bear. This

* * * * *

5 Homer *Odyssey* 8.189–92; translation by A.T. Murray (Loeb). The editors of ASD point out that Erasmus is mistaken about this passage, which is about Odysseus throwing the discus – the passage Pollux intended to refer to, the Phaeacians' ball game, is 8.372.
6 Plautus *Poenulus* 671; added in 1533. Otto 1533

42 Eustathius (see n1 below). Cf Diogenianus 2.66. Apostolius 4.12
1 Eustathius 1535.59 on *Odyssey* 5.276–7: 'For this star Calypso, the beautiful goddess, had bidden him to keep on the left hand as he sailed over the sea.'
2 Homer *Odyssey* 5.270–3. Also quoted in *Adagia* I v 57 To mark with stars. To brand with an obelus, which deals with the same expression

constellation, being carried round in a smaller orbit since it is closer to the pole, shows the way more surely, even if it is less bright. But the man who has not yet achieved complete wisdom and who, meanwhile, embraces at every moment what seems probable as he wanders, follows the Great Bear, which, although brighter and easier to see, is yet not such a certain indicator of the way because it follows a wider orbit and goes further away from the pole or axis of the world. These are Cicero's words:

> Nor am I such that I never accept anything false, never agree, never have an opinion. But we are asking about the wise man. I myself on the other hand am very inclined to conjecture; for I am not a wise man, and I direct my thoughts, not by the Little Bear – 'In whom up in the heavens the Phoenicians put their trust as a night-time guide,' as Aratus says, and steer the more straightly because they hold to her 'Who goes around the inner course and the short orbit'[3] – but by the Great Bear and the brightest northern stars, that is, by arguments of the broader sort, not worn thin by filing down. This is why I may make mistakes and wander rather far from the point.[4]

I know I have mentioned this proverb elsewhere,[5] but since I have found some passages worth knowing, it seemed right to come back to it here.

43 Sambucam citius
Sooner tune a harp

There is a verse of Persius which has the appearance of an adage: 'You could sooner tune a harp for a lanky horse-boy.'[1] This will serve when we want to indicate that someone is too unsuited to learning a subject or doing a job. For a *sambuca* is a musical instrument, which is in no way appropriate for a horse-boy. However Athenaeus, in book 14, points out that there is a military device also called a *sambuca* which was moved

* * * * *

3 Aratus *Phaenomena* 39 and 43
4 Cicero *Academica* 2.66. The Latin name for the Little Bear is *Cynosura*, in Greek 'the dog's tail,' and for the Great Bear *Helice*, from the name of one of the Danaïds, or *Currus* 'plough.'
5 *Adagia* I v 57, which quotes the whole passage from Aratus (36–44)

43 *Collectanea* no 271. Persius (see n1 below). Otto 1576
1 Persius 5.95

up to enemy walls like a siege machine,[2] and *calones* was the word for military auxiliaries who carried timbers for fortifications and firewood – grammarians assert this was the origin of their name.[3] On the other hand, soldiers are unskilled as musicians, and auxiliaries even more so. However, there is no inconsistency if the proverb is taken to mean the *sambuca* as military machine, which is prepared for use, like the musical instrument, by tightening a number of cords. Auxiliaries are not at all fitted for preparing this machine, because they are unintelligent, and confined to the meanest tasks for this very reason that they are altogether untrained and untrainable in military science. So Persius strengthened the idea of the proverb, when he added *alto* 'lanky,' because exceptionally tall men are also branded proverbially for their foolishness – Ἄνους ὁ μακρός 'Big and foolish'![4]

44 Nostrae farinae
Same flour as we are

People are said to be of the same flour when they are indistinguishable. 'Like as two bags of flour' means the same as 'Like as two puddles of water.'[1] Persius in his fifth *Satire*: 'You keep the same old skin / Though you were of the same flour as I a while ago.'[2] Exactly as he might say 'same flock as I am,'[3] 'same sort as I am.' It belongs to a group which I have already mentioned: 'The same wax,'[4] 'The same dust.'[5] Using a similar figure, 'of the same stamp' Seneca said in book 3, letter 24: 'To these you can add this, which is of the same stamp: "The foolishness, even madness, of men is such that some are driven to death by the fear of death." '[6]

* * * * *

2 Athenaeus 14.634A, added in *1528*; a good example of how Erasmus would make an addition without really integrating it with the earlier version
3 *Calo*, dative *caloni*, was linked by ancient writers to *cala* 'wood, log.' Servius on Virgil *Aeneid* 6.1. Pompeius Festus page 54 Lindsay. Nonius Marcellus 62M (see *Adagia* I i 97 9n [CWE 31 139])
4 *Adagia* III iv 58 (36 above) Big and foolish

44 *Collectanea* no 396. Otto 643. Erasmus follows Poliziano *Epistolae* 12.13.
1 *Adagia* I v 12 As like as water to water
2 Persius 5.115–16
3 *Adagia* III vi 86 He is from that flock (168 below)
4 *Adagia* II viii 57 One and the same wax, which already refers to this adage
5 *Adagia* I vii 27 All is the same dust, which also refers to *Nostrae farinae*
6 Seneca *Letters* 24.23; added in *1533*. *Eiusdem notae* 'of the same stamp' is not treated separately as an adage. See Otto *Nachträge* pages 88 *nota* and 160 *farina*.

45 Nullo scopo iaculari
Shooting aimlessly

Ἄσκοπα τοξεύειν, Shooting without a target, is said of those who have no certain objectives to pursue or nothing by which they can justify the arguments for what they undertake and deliberate. Lucian in the *Toxaris*: 'Because in the present matter ἄσκοπα τετοξεύκαμεν 'we have shot aimlessly,' let us once again accept a judge and refer other pairs of friends to him.'[1] Persius in his third *Satire*:

Is there anything you are heading for, at which you aim your bow?
Or do you follow the crows hither and thither, with bricks or mud
Not caring where your foot may fall?[2]

46 De pulmone revellere
To pluck from the lung

There is no doubt that this expression too from Persius belongs in the category of proverbs, 'To pluck from the lung,' meaning to remove a silly and arrogant opinion from the mind: 'While I pluck these old prejudices from your lung.'[1] Excitement and pride are located in the lungs. Hence μέγα πνέειν 'to be high spirited' in Greek.[2] And the same occurs elsewhere in Persius: 'Something great, which an exceptionally capacious lung may breathe in.'[3]

47 Quos non tollerent centum Aegyptii
They wouldn't be lifted by a hundred Egyptians

Οὖς οὐκ ἄραιντ᾽ ἂν οὐδ᾽ ἑκατὸν Αἰγύπτιοι, Whom not a hundred Egyptians would be able to lift. Used to be said of those with disgusting and un-

* * * * *

45 Lucian (see n1 below)
 1 Lucian *Toxaris* 62
 2 Persius 3.60–62; quoted by Otto 160

46 Persius (see n1 below)
 1 Persius 5.92
 2 Pollux *Onomasticon* 4.72; ASD suggests Euripides *Bacchae* 640 and *Andromache* 189.
 3 Persius 1.14

47 *Suda* A 4703. Zenobius (Aldus) column 138 (misnumbered 146)

bearable habits, or those who were swollen with arrogance. It came about
because most Egyptians were accustomed to earn a rather disreputable living transporting loads, whence the so-called ἀχθόφόροι 'load carriers' became a proverbial joke. The adage is mentioned by Eudemus in his *Miscellany of Rhetorical Sayings*,[1] and by Suidas too.[2] But it is found in Aristophanes' *Frogs*, as follows: 'He threw in two wagons and two corpses, / That
a hundred Egyptians would not be able to carry.'[3] The same in the *Birds*:
'No Egyptian carrying bricks ...'[4] In a very similar figure Lucilius, quoted
by Nonius: 'Whom not even bulls born in the Lucanian hills / Can pull by
the yoke on their powerful backs.'[5] And the same author elsewhere: 'This
one a hundred teams of mules yoked together could not drag.'[6]

48 Aegyptius laterifer
An Egyptian brick-carrier

Αἰγύπτιος πλινθοφόρος, An Egyptian carrier of bricks. Suidas mentions this
explicitly as a proverb. It occurs in Aristophanes' *Birds*, where someone
asks who could have placed the horse Durius a hundred cubits high on the
fortress of Pallas. The answer given is: 'The birds, and no other, no Egyptian
/ Brick-carrier, or stone worker.'[1] The expression seems to be suitable for a
mean man, one of the lowest sort, a sense for which 'cheap as Carians'[2] is
also used; or for someone who is besieged by troublesome business. We have
just noted[3] that the Egyptians became the subject of popular tales and jokes
because they earned their living carrying loads on their backs like asses. In
such work they were more experienced for this reason, I suppose, that this
sort of labourer was absolutely necessary in Egypt for digging out ponds and

* * * * *

1 See n48 on *Adagia* III v 1 (66 above).
2 *Suda* A 4703
3 Aristophanes *Frogs* 1405–6
4 Aristophanes *Birds* 1133–4; cf the next proverb.
5 Lucilius 247–8 Marx; Nonius Marcellus 363M; added in *1515*
6 Lucilius 435–6 Marx; Nonius Marcellus 363M; added in *1515*

48 *Suda* Αι 75 (from whom Erasmus takes the word πλινθοφόρος)
   1 Aristophanes *Birds* 1133–4; the horse's name is a mistaken interpretation of ὁ
     δούρειος 'the Trojan horse' in line 1128; cf *Adagia* IV ii 1 A wooden horse (502
     below). Added in *1533*
   2 See *Adagia* I vi 14 for Carians as cheap mercenaries, I ii 65 for Carians as cheap
     hired servants, II x 38 for Carians more wicked than Lydians or Egyptians.
   3 In the previous adage

carrying away mud and clay bricks because of the mud brought down by the Nile. There, I believe, sparrows and swallows showed them the art of building walls from mud.[4] The proof of this is that the Hebrews, when they lived among the Egyptians, were forced to do slave labour for the Pharaoh by carrying mud and bricks.[5] You will find something on Marian mules elsewhere.[6]

49 Coenare me doce
Teach me to eat

Δειπνεῖν με δίδασκε, Teach me to eat. This was used as a proverbial figure by Aristophanes in his *Frogs*. It can be used opportunely whenever a person unskilled in a matter about which there is dispute tries to teach or command or even refute someone. They are the words of Bacchus to Hercules when he was making judgments about tragedies, because he was more practised in devouring bulls than in evaluating the verses of poets.

50 Rhamnusius
Rhamnusius

'Ραμνούσιος, Rhamnusius. Eudemus in his *Rhetorical Sayings*[1] tells us this name used to be given as a sort of proverbial nickname to wise and moderate men. But he does not explain how it became proverbial. We may suppose therefore, either that the term comes from the customs of that people,[2] or from the goddess Rhamnusia, who commends us to show moderation in all affairs. We have discussed this at greater length elsewhere.[3]

* * * * *

4 'because ... from mud' was added in *1533*.
5 Cf Exod 1:11–14.
6 *Adagia* IV iv 79 Marian mules

49 Aristophanes *Frogs* 107

50 Eudemus (see n1 below). Cf *Suda* P 33 who specifically mentions at the end the proverbial expression 'Ραμνούσιος. Mantissa 2.77
1 See n48 on *Adagia* III v 1 (66 above).
2 That is, the people of Rhamnus, a town in Attica, celebrated for the cult of Nemesis. See Pausanias 1.32.2–8 and Pliny *Naturalis historia* 4.24, 36.17.
3 *Adagia* II vi 38, where he gives Rhamnusia as an alternative name for Nemesis and quotes Eudemus for another point. The goddess is not described there as commending moderation in all affairs, though her province is said to be to 'forbid excessive hopes.' In the *Moria* (CWE 27 141) she is described, ironically of course, as the bitterest enemy of the wise.

51 Papae Myxus!
Blow-me-down Myxus!

Βαβαὶ Μύξος, Blow-me-down Myxus! Used to be said with reference to swaggerers and boasters. Βαβαί is an exclamation of stupefaction and wonder,[1] and Myxus was some pretentious, pompous priest of Diana, who pretended to be astonished at everything. It is recorded by Suidas and Zenodotus.[2]

52 Lenticulam angulo tenes
You've got hold of the lentil by the point

Φακοῦ γωνίας κρατεῖς, You've got hold of the lentil by the point. Said of business which simply cannot be done, because this type of legume has no points. It is recorded by Suidas, in case anyone thinks it should not be considered.[1]

53 Patrocli occasio
The opportunity of Patroclus

Πατροκλέους πρόφασις, The opportunity or 'pretext' of Patroclus. Diogenianus shows that this is customarily said of those who do not dare because of fear to lament their own misfortunes but weep for them under pretext of mourning for someone else. In the essay entitled 'On Inoffensive Self-praise,' Plutarch says: 'And so that we do not appear to be using Πάτροκλον πρόφασιν "Patroclus as a pretext," and actually praising ourselves through them ...'[1] For he is talking about those who imply praise of themselves as they praise others. Derived I think from the character of Patroclus whom Aristophanes jokes about several times.[2]

* * * * *

51 *Suda* B 6
  1 Βαβαί is the form found in the *Suda* and the paroemiographers (see n2 below). The dictionaries give Παπαί. For Latin examples see Plautus *Rudens* 1320, Terence *Eunuchus* 229 and 317, Persius 5.79.
  2 Zenobius (Aldus) column 50 (= Diogenianus 3.65; Apostolius 4.79)

52 *Suda* Φ 23
  1 'in case ... considered' was added in 1533.

53 Diogenianus 7.47 (Πατρόκλειος). Apostolius 14.8
  1 Plutarch *Moralia* 546F *Quomodo quis se citra invidiam laudare possit*
  2 Aristophanes *Frogs* 1041. Having noted the appearance of Patroclus in Homer (*Iliad* 19.301–2), to whom Diogenianus refers, ASD points out that the Patro-

54 Exiguum oboli precium
Small value even for an obol

Μικρὸν τοῦ ὀβολοῦ τίμιον, Small value even for an obol. Suidas, quoting from the *Maricas* of Eupolis, says that this can be used of worthless and good-for-nothing men.[1] But there is nothing to prevent it being used figuratively of a thing which is despised. Eudemus recalls it too.[2] We have noted many expressions of this sort before: a penny-ha'penny man,[3] a three-farthing man,[4] a fourpenny-ha'penny man,[5] a man scarcely worth two farthings.[6] Justinian wanted to call young men just entering on the study of law 'two-farthing types,'[7] as being of the lowest class. Those who had already made some progress he called *prolytae* and *lytae* 'discharged,' as it were.[8]

55 Pedum visa est via
That path has been looked at

Τῶν ποδῶν ἑώραται ὁδός,[1] That path has been looked at, of an undertaking which you have already tried; derived from travellers. Terence in the *Phormio*: 'Ah, not like that. It has been tried. That path has been looked at.'[2]

* * * * *

clus mentioned in Aristophanes *Plutus* 84 is not the Homeric character but an Athenian. In fact Erasmus does not seem to link this Patroclus with the Homeric one at all.

54 *Suda* M 1050 = Apostolius 11.70
1 PCG 5 Eupolis fragment 198
2 See n48 on *Adagia* III v i (66 above).
3 *Obolaris homo*; cf *Adagia* IV ix 33 Twopenny fellows.
4 *Adagia* I viii 11 A threepenny man
5 *Adagia* I viii 10 A three-ha'penny fellow
6 Jerome *Adversus Helvidium* 16 PL 23 200B; cf *Adagia* I viii 11 A threepenny man.
7 Erasmus' memory appears to be at fault concerning *dupondii* 'two-farthing types,' or perhaps a printing error (*voluit* 'wanted' for *noluit* 'did not want') has been perpetuated in subsequent editions, including LB. Justinian declares (*Digest* preface 2) that he does not wish first-year law students to be called by this nickname. The passage is quoted correctly in *Adagia* I viii 11, where it was added in *1533*; this example and the four previous ones were added here also in *1533*.
8 Justinian *Digest* preface 5 προλύται from λύω 'loosen, discharge'

55 *Collectanea* no 564. Terence (see n2 below). Otto 1891, who doubts whether the expression is really proverbial, or simply metaphorical
1 Erasmus has formed the Greek version himself.
2 Terence *Phormio* 326

56 **Phoenicum pacta**
Phoenicians' bargains

Φοινίκων συνθῆκαι, Contracts of Phoenicians. The Phoenicians who took possession of Carthage, on first landing in that region, asked the people who inhabited Libya at that time to be allowed to enjoy the hospitality of the land for a day and a night. Having obtained this, and having been ordered after the allowed time had passed to move beyond the frontiers, they declined asserting they had made an agreement that it was their right to stay there both night and day. Clearly, they misused the ambiguity of the words to their own advantage. From this, it is agreed, was derived the proverbial expression about treacherous and cunning bargains. The authorities are Suidas and Diogenianus. What is more, Phoenician is in general a term for everyone who is greedy for profit. Hence Pindar, in the second *Pythian Ode*, said 'Phoenician business.'[1] And the scholiast quotes from some comic writer: 'Straightway I become Phoenix.'[2] And this from Sophocles: 'As a man, Phoenix began[3] to buy and sell.'[4] Finally Plato, in the third book of the *Republic*, talking of those who think that lying is proper for magistrates, says: 'There is nothing noble[5] in this, but rather something Phoenician.'[6]

57 **Pusillus quantus Molon**
Short as Molon

Μικρὸς ἡλίκος Μόλων, Short as Molon. Said of little men of extremely small stature. Suidas states there were two persons called Molon, whose shortness was, I suppose, notorious; one of them was an actor, the other

* * * * *

56 *Collectanea* no 692. Diogenianus 8.67. Apostolius 17.87. *Suda* Φ 796. Zenobius (Aldus) column 167. Cf *Adagia* I viii 28 Punic faith. Otto 1490
 1 Pindar *Pythians* 2.67. The passage from 'What is more' to 'buy and sell' is an addition of *1526*.
 2 Scholiast of Pindar at the passage quoted (n1 above). PCG 3.2 Aristophanes fragment 957, adespota 397 Kock. Phoenix was the son of Agenor, eponymous founder of Carthage.
 3 The Latin is *coepit*. Estienne (LB II 841) points out that the Greek verb is second person. The line should therefore read: 'As a man, Phoenix, you began to buy and sell.'
 4 Sophocles fragment 823 Nauck
 5 Erasmus has *pulcher* for Greek καλός. The accepted reading in Plato is καινός 'new, unprecedented.'
 6 Plato *Republic* 3.414C; added in *1528*

57 *Suda* M 1053. Cf Apostolius 11.69 and Zenobius (Aldus) column 121. The source is Aristophanes *Frogs* 55.

a thief, clearly both honourable professions.[1]

58 Per antiquum diem
In olden time

Διὰ παλαιᾶς ἡμέρας, Going back to ancient days. Said of something completely worn out, ancient; recorded by Diogenianus. It is very close to one which is tossed around nowadays, not inappropriately, in the schools of philosophy: 'In the great year of Plato.'[1]

59 Perierunt bona
It is the end of good things

Ἔρρει τὰ καλά, It is the end of worthy things. Hippocrates was secretary to Mindarus, leader of the Spartans. When the latter was killed by the Athenians, he wrote a letter to Sparta along these lines: Ἔρρει τὰ καλά, Μίνδαρος δ' ἀπέσσυται, meaning that the cause was lost with the death of the leader. The adage is recorded by Diogenianus; the story is recounted by Xenophon in the *Paralipomena* book 1.[1] The Greek words above make a senarius: 'It is the end of worthy things, Mindarus is gone.'[2]

60 Qui nimium properat, serius absolvit
More haste less speed

Plato in his dialogue entitled *The Statesman* says:

* * * * *

1 The comment is by Erasmus.

58 Diogenianus 4.38. Cf Apostolius 6.30.
   1 Cf *Adagia* I v 84 and Plato *Timaeus* 39D.

59 Diogenianus 4.89 (= Apostolius 7.85). From *1508* to *1523* Erasmus' understanding of this text was completely wrong, but he was able to correct himself when he received a copy of the Aldine Xenophon of 1525. See ASD II-5 327:973n and also the textual apparatus to this adage.
   1 Xenophon *Hellenica* 1.1.18 and 23, but the accepted emendation for καλά is κᾶλα 'timbers,' 'ships': Ἔρρει τὰ κᾶλα, Μίνδαρος ἀπεσσύα 'The ships are gone. Mindarus is dead.' Erasmus also misunderstands Xenophon in *Adagia* I i 23 where Hippocrates is described as ἐπιστολεύς which can mean 'secretary' but was also the name given in Sparta to the second-in-command.
   2 Erasmus ends by giving a Latin translation in the form of an iambic senarius.

   60 Cf *Adagia* II i 1 Make haste slowly, and IV ii 75 Take a long time to think (540 below). Tilley H 198

– For that has even now resulted in our experiencing what is said proverbially.

– What is that?

– By making incorrect distinctions too hastily, we have taken longer to finish.[1]

The same author alludes to the proverb in the seventh book of the *Republic*: 'In my haste, he said,[2] to run over everything quickly, I am slower.'[3] And in the *Cratylus* he has something similar: 'Lest it happen to us, like night wanderers on Aegina[4] who complete their journey too late, that we too appear to reach the point in very truth later than we should.'[5] Well known too is what St Augustine says in *Against Petilianus*, that it often happens to those who are in a hurry because of some disturbance 'that they put their clothes or their shoes on the wrong way,'[6] which later causes delay. The same happens to those who try to do many things at once and achieve none of them. Plato, book 3 of the *Republic*, says: 'Let each one pursue one study properly, never many; for if someone tries, having tackled many, he will be frustrated in all.'[7] In the same work, book 10, he tells us the same happens to those who rush to gain honour not by truth but by pretences and deceits: 'And do not some dishonest craftsmen do the same as certain runners, who run well from the starting point, but not at all well after the turn. At first indeed they shoot out in front rapidly, but then at the end of the race they are laughable, and drag themselves off uncrowned with their heads between their shoulders.'[8] The adage warns us that something should be undertaken not with speed but with care, lest later it should be delayed because there was a mistake at the beginning of the task. This proverb applies to those who for the sake of economy pass by Greek literature and plunge straight into the study of philosophy, but as they foolishly economize, they run into the greatest expense. For it turns out that while these people are eager to become instant philosophers they never achieve a knowledge of philosophy, and when they think they have already reached the finishing line, they have to go back again to the starting boxes,[9] and, as the Greeks say, begin again

* * * * *

1 Plato *Statesman* 264B
2 Erasmus has mistakenly translated ἔφην 'I said' as *inquit* 'he said.'
3 Plato *Republic* 7.528D; added in *1526*
4 The reference is unknown.
5 Plato *Cratylus* 433A; added in *1528*
6 Augustine *Contra literas Petiliani* 2.62.140 PL 43 305
7 Plato *Republic* 3.394E; added in *1528*
8 Plato *Republic* 10.613B–C; added in *1528*
9 Cf *Adagia* I vi 58 From the start and III v 35 To reach the chalk mark (86 above).

from scratch.[10] In military matters, too, more was achieved by the delays of Fabius than by the hasty temerity of Marcus Minutius.[11] For the former alone overcame Hannibal, undefeated at that time in many battles, not by force but by delaying methods. This is admirably narrated by Ennius[12] as quoted by Marcus Tullius in his *Elder Cato*:

> One man, by delay, restored the situation for us,
> For he did not put popular reputation before salvation.[13]

61 Ultra catalogum
Beyond the count

Ὑπὲρ τὸν κατάλογον ζῇ, He is living beyond the count. Used to be said of one who lived to a great age, as if he were considered to have exceeded the prescribed number of years. It is to be found, if I am not mistaken, in Lucian.[1] Reported by Suidas.

62 Ultra peram sapere
To have tastes beyond one's wallet

Ὑπὲρ τὴν πήραν φρονεῖν, To be desirous of things beyond one's wallet. Said by way of a proverbial figure in Lucian's *Timon*: 'It is essential for the philosopher to be content with few things and to be frugal, and not "To have wants beyond his wallet."'[1] It will be fitting for a philosopher or a

* * * * *

10 *Adagia* I vi 57 To start from scratch
11 Livy 22.23–31. Fabius is, of course, Quintus Fabius Maximus Verrucosus 'Cunctator' ('the Delayer').
12 Ennius *Annales* 363–4 Skutsch. Otto 479. Also quoted in *Adagia* II i 1 (CWE 33 4–5).
13 Cicero *De senectute* 10

61 *Suda* Υ 373. Apostolius 17.55. Zenobius (Aldus) column 166. It is Erasmus who adds ζῇ 'he is living.'
 1 The editors of ASD suggest Lucian *Timon* 51, and *Navigium* 33, where the word κατάλογος means the 'muster-roll' or the 'ranks'; in neither case does the phrase have any proverbial meaning. Demosthenes 13.4, uses the phrase to mean 'beyond the age limit' for military service.

62 Lucian (see n1 below)
 1 Lucian *Timon* 57. According to Estienne (LB II 842) the expression does not mean 'to have tastes or wants beyond one's wallet,' but 'to have concerns

poor person, but especially for a Christian, whom Jesus forbids to think of the morrow.[2] Very close to 'Life in a tub.'[3]

63 Virgo primum
Like a virgin the first time

Παρθένος τὰ πρῶτα,[1] Like a virgin the first time. Said of those who have squandered their patrimony. Probably it arose because virgins are so inexperienced and ignorant of how harlots make their living that they give themselves away easily. Later, in order to receive more, they prove difficult. Likewise young people, who have recently been given allowances and before they understand what money is, spend too lavishly. And the earliest part of life, which is indeed the best, we waste in gross stupidity.

64 Vir videbatur navis supplicans scopulo
The man looked like a ship beseeching a rock

Ἀνὴρ ἔοικε ναῦς ἱκετεύειν πέτραν, The man looked like a ship beseeching a rock. Suidas indicates this was said of stupid, obtuse people who mistake one thing for another, the figure being derived from a ship striking a rock.

65 Viro esurienti necesse[1] furari
A hungry man must needs be a thief

Πεινῶντι κλέπτειν ἐστ᾽ ἀναγκαίως ἔχον, A starving man is forced to be a thief. Suidas classifies this as a proverb suited to those who are driven by

* * * * *

beyond those of men' (ὑπὲρ ἄνθρωπον φρονεῖν) and Lucian uses the proverbial expression jokingly when he intends the more philosophical meaning.
2 Matt 6:34
3 *Adagia* I viii 61

63 Diogenianus 7.88
1 CPG 1.302 5n records this reading from the Palatine manuscript (p) but corrects it to Παρθένος τὰ πατρῷα 'As a virgin [wastes] her inheritance'; cf Mantissa 2.52.

64 *Suda* A 2430. Cf Diogenianus 6.79 Ναῦς ἱκετεύει πέτρας, Apostolius 11.95, and Zenobius (Aldus) column 34.

65 *Suda* A 2173, where the adage is Ἀνδρὶ πεινῶντι ... ἔχον. Cf Mantissa 1.16. According to the editors of ASD, by omitting the word Ἀνδρί Erasmus makes an iambic trimeter.
1 1508 to 1517/18 and LB have *necesse est*.

extreme necessity to do something. For example, someone who confesses
he has lied, may say, 'What was I to do? Either I had to lie or descend to
the worst disgrace. A hungry man must steal.' Or someone greedy for fame
may publish other people's work as his, because he can produce nothing
outstanding of his own.

66 Vixit, dum vixit, bene
While he lived, he lived well

As long as he lived, he lived well. This is in Terence's *Mother-in-law*. Some
old man indicates that it was proverbial when he asks someone whether he
had brought anything other than this one aphorism. It suits those who live
at ease and pleasantly, or spend freely so that they give no great pleasure
to their heir. However, there is an ambiguity in the verb *vivere*, which is
sometimes simply 'to live' and sometimes 'to enjoy life' as in Catullus: 'Let
us live, Lesbia mine, and let us love.'[1]

67 Fumantem nasum ursi ne tentaveris
Do not touch the nose of a bear when it is fuming

This is a line in Martial which has the appearance of a proverb:

> Wretch with foaming mouth, do not
> Touch the fuming nose of a living bear.
> Allow him to be quiet, let him lick fingers and hands.
> If grief and pain, or just anger compel him,
> He will be a bear. You should exercise your teeth on an empty skin.[1]

It warns us that those who can harm us are not to be tempted. In exactly
the same way, Synesius wrote in his *Praise of Baldness*: 'To take a dog by the
nose,'[2] meaning to provoke one who would bite and will injure. Bears are
particularly enraged when struck on this part of the body, so the bestiaries
tell us.

* * * * *

66 Terence *Hecyra* 461. Cf Otto 1925n.
1 Catullus 5.1

67 *Collectanea* no 662. Martial (see n1 below). Otto 1837
1 Martial *Epigrams* 6.64.27–31
2 Synesius *Encomium calvitii* (see n4 on *Adagia* III v 39, 90 above); added in *1515*.
According to ASD the expression is not found in this work or in any ancient
literature.

68 Muris in morem
Mouse fashion

Plautus in the *Two Captives*: 'Like mice, we are always eating someone else's food.'[1] Said of parasites, whose delight is 'to live at another person's table.'[2] Freedom and eating another person's food do not go together, nor are they to be found in the same place, as is neatly shown in Aesop's fable of the country mouse and the town mouse.[3] Further, the Greeks have a proverbial word μυσπολεῖν 'to scurry around like a mouse,' for those who walk up and down and wander around like mice in search of food. It was indicated as such by Hesychius.[4]

69 E tribus malis unum
One of three penalties

Τῶν τριῶν κακῶν ἕν, One of three penalties. Suidas states that the proverb survived in Menander.[1] However it derives from Theramenes, who imposed on a certain person one of three penalties, from which he might choose which he wanted.[2] This is the source too for Aristophanes in the *Triphales*, as quoted by the same Suidas: 'For I was made to fear τὰ τρία ταῦτα "these three things" by Theramenes.'[3] What these three things may be, you may seek in the proverb Τὰ τρία τῶν εἰς θάνατον 'Three ways to die.'[4] Alexander

* * * * *

68 Plautus (see n1 below). Otto 1170
  1 Plautus *Captivi* 77: *quasi mures*
  2 Juvenal 5.2: *aliena vivere quadra*
  3 Aesop 352 Perry; Erasmus' source is perhaps Horace *Satires* 2.6.79–117. The fable is also found in *Suda* E 3268.
  4 Hesychius M 1961, from Aristophanes *Wasps* 140; added in 1528

69 *Suda* T 871
  1 Menander fragment 735 Körte-Thierfelder, with a reference to Athenaeus 4.157D where there is an allusion to the three ways of committing suicide. See also the scholiast of Pindar on *Olympians* 1.97 in *Scholia vetera in Pindari carmina* ed A.B. Drachmann (Leipzig 1903) 1.40–1.
  2 The story is not in Xenophon nor in Diodorus Siculus and is probably based on the line from Aristophanes (n3 below). In Aristophanes *Frogs* 967–8 there is a reference to Theramenes' involvement in the battle of Arginusae (see *Adagia* III vii 89, 275 below).
  3 PCG 3.2 Aristophanes *Triphales* fragment 563
  4 *Suda* T 154; cf Zenobius 6.11 (= Zenobius [Aldus] column 156)

used this in his *Goatherds*.[5] Aristides says that an oracle used to be given under seal, and if anyone opened it before the right time, one of three penalties awaited him, removal of his eyes, or of a hand, or loss of his tongue.[6] Some say that those who were sentenced to capital punishment were offered three means, the sword, the noose, or poison.

70 **Quam facile vulpes pyrum comest**
As easily as a fox eats a pear

Plautus in his *Haunted House*: 'You will win, as easily as a fox eats a pear.' Said of something easy to do. For it is no work at all for a well-toothed fox to eat a pear.

71 **Contrahere supercilium, inflare buccas**
Contracting the brow, inflating the cheeks

Ὀφρῦς ἀνασπῶντες καὶ γνάθους φυσῶντες, With knitted brow and puffed out cheeks. Used of pompous and bombastic individuals, Suidas tells us. For it is in the brow, as we have shown elsewhere,[1] that the seat of arrogance is found. Horace took puffed-out cheeks as a sign of anger: 'That Jupiter should not / Puff out both cheeks in anger.'[2] St Augustine, in his *Confessions*, has 'cheeks bursting with *typhus* "arrogance."'[3] Some people wrongly read *typus* 'mark of a blow' here. But it is surprising that Augustine should have been so pleased with a Greek word that, when he could have said *fastus* 'haughtiness,' 'arrogance' he preferred to say *typhus*, unless it was because it

* * * * *

5 The *Suda* also mentions this but gives what is probably the correct name for the author, Alexis, although no play of this name (*Aipoloi*) by him is otherwise attested. PCG 2 Alexis fragment 8; added in 1526, following Zenobius
6 Aristides Milesius fragment 33 *FHG* IV 327; added in 1526

70 Plautus *Mostellaria* 559. Otto 1941

71 *Suda* O 1027. Zenobius (Aldus) column 139. Otto 274 and Otto *Nachträge* pages 97 *bucca* and 141 *bucca*
1 *Adagia* I viii 49 To raise the brows, to relax the brows. There is some inconsistency here with III v 46 To pluck from the lung (95 above) where *animi fastus*, very close to *arrogantia* as is shown by the presence of the adjective *arrogans*, is said to reside in the lungs.
2 Horace *Satires* 1.1.20–1
3 Augustine *Confessions* 4.16.28 PL 32 704

appeared to be already accepted as Latin usage. The figure is derived from frogs, which blow themselves up with anger. There is a well-known fable of Aesop about a frog which burst with arrogance.[4] And Horace writes: 'Inflate the swelling bag with pompous utterances.'[5]

72 Sus comessatur
A swine revelling

 Ὗς ἐκώμασεν, A swine danced, or A swine revelling. Diogenianus declares this was said of those who committed some impropriety and who, when the objection is made that things have turned out better than they deserve, are all the more insolently proud of themselves. Both Suidas and Zenodotus mention it. For the Greeks κωμάζειν 'to revel' is to disport oneself like young lovers with wreaths, songs, dances, and all the other juvenile nonsense, and to burst into other people's houses. Swine burst in too. Hence Theocritus in the *Syracusan Women*: 'A dense crowd all together like swine bursting in.'[1] But it is wonderful how little those of rather rustic nature are suited to these things. There will be a place for this adage when someone who is savage and coarse by nature tries to seem witty.

73 Dat veniam corvis, vexat censura columbas
The laws absolve ravens and harass doves

There is a line in Juvenal which bears a closer resemblance to a proverb than one egg to another:[1] 'The laws absolve ravens and harass doves.' The penalty of the laws is employed against some humble folk, from whom, because of their gentleness of character, some gain can be extracted. The greedy are forgiven. The adage comes from a maxim of Anacharsis who said this in mockery of Solon's care in writing his laws, as Plutarch relates

*****

4 Aesop Phaedrus 1.24, 376A Perry; cf Horace *Satires* 2.3.314–320 and Otto 1504.
5 Horace *Satires* 2.5.98

72 Cf *Collectanea* no 688. Diogenianus 8.60. *Suda* K 2258. Zenobius (Aldus) column 166
1 Theocritus 15.72–3. See *Adagia* III v 39 n1 (90 above). 'For the Greeks' to here added in 1533

73 *Collectanea* nos 149 and 565. Juvenal 2.63. Otto 446
1 *Adagia* I v 10

in his life of Solon: 'He used to say that the laws are like the webs of spiders, because if anything lightweight or feeble runs into them, it sticks, but if it is something larger, it cuts through and gets away.'[2] The same meaning is contained in what Terence says in his *Phormio*:

> Because a net is not spread for a kite or a hawk,
> Birds which are harmful, it is spread for harmless ones.
> The latter are profitable, the former are a waste of labour.[3]

74 Sutorium atramentum
Cobbler's blacking

Marcus Tullius to Paetus in book 9 of his *Letters to Friends*: 'Now his father has been accused by Marcus Antonius: it is thought he was acquitted with the use of some cobbler's blacking.'[1] There seems to be a proverb underlying this. He means, I think, that the man was acquitted, not without scandal, by bribing the judges. For cobbler's blacking is such that it does not make an excessively black mark, nor on the other hand does it leave no blemish at all. So scandal is symbolized in the poets by blacking; Horace, for example: 'This is the juice of the black cuttle-fish, this is / Pure venom.'[2] This juice is of a type that is to be found in many sorts of soft fish, especially cuttle-fish, according to Aristotle in book 4 of *On the Parts of Animals*: 'It is contained in an inner bag of skin and emitted through a tube; they squirt it out when afraid, and darken the water so that they cannot be caught.'[3] Horace again:

> But as inks when handled leave a mark and a stain,
> So writers often besmirch the splendid achievements of others
> With shameful verse.[4]

* * * * *

2 Plutarch *Solon* 5.2 tells this story, but Erasmus had quoted from Diogenes Laertius 1.58 ('Solon') in *1508*; this was added, with the correct attribution to Anacharsis, in *1526*.
3 Terence *Phormio* 330–2

74 *Collectanea* no 36. Cicero *Ad familiares* (see n1 below)
1 Cicero *Ad familiares* 9.21.3
2 Horace *Satires* 1.4.100–1
3 Aristotle *De partibus animalium* 4.5 (679a1–7)
4 Horace *Epistles* 2.1.235–7; from 'Horace again' to the end of the commentary consists of additions made between *1526* and *1533*.

Finally, what the Greeks call *chalcanthum* Cornelius Celsus translates roughly as *sutorium atramentum* 'cobbler's blacking,' which he recalls frequently among his treatments, especially in book 5.[5] It is gathered from bronze. Whence the Greek term χάλκανθος, in other words 'flower of bronze.'[6] Which makes me suspect that 'cobbler's blacking' means rather a stain which is removed with difficulty. For the black called 'writers' black' is more easily washed off and does not adhere to the skin. Pliny used a similar figure in one of his letters: 'Marked with a Vitellian scar.'[7]

75 Surda testimonia
Deaf testimonies

Κωφαὶ μαρτυρίαι, Deaf testimonies, so-called, are those which are given on tablets, because, if a question is addressed to them, they give no answer, so that this adage does not differ from 'Silent teachers.'[1] This is why people are said proverbially to 'plead a case on deaf testimonies' when they quote only those who are far away or those who are dead, so that they cannot be apprehended.

76 Perdere naulum
To throw away the fare

In the *Satire* of Juvenal which begins 'What can pedigrees do?'

> Look round for an auctioneer, Charippus, for your rags,

* * * * *

5 Celsus *Medicina* 5.1, 6, 7, 8, 20.3. According to Celsus, *atramentum sutorium* is made from *chalcitis*, carbonate and sulphate of copper; *chalcamentum* or 'flower of bronze' is red oxide of copper.
6 Celsus *Medicina* 5.7, 9, 20.1
7 Pliny *Letters* 1.5.2. The 'Vitellian scar' was literally the scar of a wound inflicted by one of Vespasian's soldiers on L. Junius Arulenus Rusticus, but one which branded him as a partisan of Vitellius, under whom he had been a praetor. For another reference to the same passage in Pliny and to Rusticus see *Adagia* III v 79 n4 (113 below)

75 *Collectanea* no 481, from Poliziano's *Miscellanea* 23. According to ASD the Greek form seems to have been created by Erasmus.
1 *Adagia* I ii 18

76 Juvenal (see n1 below). Otto 1204

Since Pansa snatches away whatever Natta left you,
And keep quiet now, it is madness to throw away the fare after
   everything else.[1]

Domizio Calderini, by no means a bad authority among the moderns, tells us this is a proverb directed against someone who has lost a great deal and wants to throw away even what is left.[2] The figure is derived from traders, who, if they have been able to make less profit on their voyages than they want, strive to recuperate from the goods they retail at least enough to pay off the cost of the sea transport. When Aristippus was asked by someone whether he was ubiquitous, he said with a laugh, 'Well then, I do not lose my fare,' he said, 'if indeed I am ubiquitous.' The story is told by Plutarch in his essay entitled 'Whether Virtue Can Be Taught.'[3]

77 Siculissare
To behave like a Sicilian

Σικελίζειν, To behave like a Sicilian. Eudemus[1] indicates this was used in antiquity for strict, harsh behaviour, and that Epicharmus indeed used it in this way.[2] But in fact others hold it should be used rather of dishonest and crafty individuals. There is no doubt but that it arose from the character of that nation. But Athenaeus, in the first book of the *Doctors at Dinner*, says that the adage arose from a Sicilian called Andron who introduced the fashion of dancing and pantomiming to the flute.[3]

* * * * *

1 Juvenal 8.95–7; Pansa and Natta are fictitious names for plundering officials.
2 Domizio Calderini *Commentarii in Satyras Iuvenalis* (Venice 1475) on the passage in question
3 Plutarch *Moralia* 439E *An virtus doceri possit*: Οὐκοῦν . . . παραπόλλυμι τὸ ναῦλον, εἴ γε πανταχοῦ εἰμι. Added in 1515

77 *Suda* Σ 389
1 For Eudemus, see n48 on *Adagia* III v 1 (66 above). Erasmus read this text in the *Suda*.
2 Epicharmus fragment 206 Kaibel
3 Athenaeus 1.22C; added in *1517/18*. Athenaeus attributes the account of Andron to Theophrastus (fragment 92 Wimmer) and says the word meant 'to dance.'

78 **Sedens columba**
   A sitting dove

Ἡμένη πελειάς, A sitting dove. Suidas records this explicitly as a proverbial expression and indicates that it was said of excessively mild and guileless people. For when doves fly off, they outstrip all others with the speed of their flight, but when they are sitting, there is nothing gentler or sweeter. Nor do they have any means of defence against kites and hawks apart from the speed of their wings. It seems to me it can also be said of those who pretend to be guileless in order to be more successful in their deceitfulness, because it is the habit of bird-catchers to put in the net a blinded dove, which flutters up and down and attracts other doves. This bird is called by the Greeks παλεύτρια, a decoy, from the verb παλεύειν 'to catch by decoy-birds,' that is 'to lead astray' or 'to entice into the net.' Aristophanes, talking of doves, in the *Birds*: Καὶ ἐπαναγκάζει παλεύειν δεδεμένας ἐν δικτύῳ 'And makes them act as decoys entangled in the net.'[1] The reader may consider whether one should read ἠμμένη 'enmeshed' here, because this makes sense, whereas there would be none otherwise.[2]

79 **Simia barbata seu caudata**
   A monkey with a beard, or with a tail

Πίθηκος πώγων᾽ ἔχων, A monkey with a beard. Aristophanes in the *Acharnians*: Ὦ πίθηκε, τὸν πώγων᾽ ἔχων 'Oh monkey, what a beard!'[1] From the scholiast I learned that this is an allusion to the saying of Archilochus: 'O monkey, what a tail[2] you have!'[3] Used to be said of absurd people. Regulus called Rusticus the 'Stoics' monkey' as an insult, as Pliny relates in his *Letters*, I think because he acted the Stoic more with his beard and his

* * * * *

78 *Suda* H 290. Cf Apostolius 8.54.
 1 Aristophanes *Birds* 1083
 2 Erasmus is suggesting the proverb should be 'A dove in a net,' rather than 'A sitting dove.'

79 Aristophanes (see n1 below)
 1 Aristophanes *Acharnians* 120 (given in Greek only)
 2 Erasmus has *cauda*; Estienne (LB II 846) corrects him: πυγή is not *cauda* but *nates* 'buttocks' or even by synecdoche *podex* 'anus.'
 3 Archilochus fragment 187 West; scholiast of Aristophanes *Acharnians* 120 (Dübner page 6): Τοιήνδ᾽, ὦ πίθηκε, τὴν πυγήν ἔχων (given in Greek)

cloak than in his morals.⁴ Aristophanes again, in another passage, calls certain people δημοπίθηκοι 'monkeys of the people,' as it were.⁵ This animal is by nature γελωτοποιός⁶ 'a buffoon,' and seems to have been created for no other purpose, for it is of no use for eating like sheep, nor for guarding the house like dogs, nor for carrying burdens like horses. Athenaeus in book 14 tells a story about the philosopher Anacharsis, a Scythian by race, who was the only one, when skilled comedians were brought in at a banquet, not to laugh. Later, when some monkeys were brought in, he began to laugh, and when asked the reason he said, 'These are funny by nature, the others are feigning it.'⁷

80 Sibi canere
Singing your own song

Ἑαυτῷ ψάλλειν, Singing for oneself. People are said to sing for themselves if they do something, not at another person's behest, but following their own will. In Plato's *Banquet* they order the flute-girl to pipe for herself.¹ And a certain singer, Antigenidas I think, because his pupil was not sufficiently popular with the audience, orders him to sing for him and for the Muses. Marcus Tullius in the *Brutus*: 'For it is the mark of the greatest orator to be recognized as the greatest by the people. Thus while the flute-player Antigenidas may very well have said to his pupil, when he was coldly received by the audience, "Sing for me and for the Muses," to the man, my dear Brutus, who usually addresses a large crowd,

* * * * *

4 Pliny *Letters* 1.5.2; added in *1533*. Cf Otto *Nachträge* page 248. M. Aquilius Regulus was a notorious informer under Nero and, according to Pliny, under Domitian, but was also a noted orator and advocate. L. Junius Arulenus Rusticus defended Thrasea Paetus, who was executed by Nero, and was finally executed himself under Domitian for publishing a panegyric of Thrasea and because his Stoicism caused him to be suspected of revolutionary views.
5 Aristophanes *Frogs* 1085
6 Erasmus has taken the word from the passage in Athenaeus quoted below. It is also used as an adjective, meaning 'inclined to excite laughter,' by Aeschylus (fragment 180 Nauck). The section from 'This animal' to the end was added in *1528*.
7 Athenaeus 14.613D

80 *Collectanea* no 348. Reminiscent of Jerome *Letters* 50.2.3 PL 22 513–14 *qui sibi tantum caneret et Musis.* Otto 1178
1 Plato *Symposium* 176E

I would say, "Sing for me and for the people."'[2] St Jerome identifies the pupil of Antigenidas, if I am not mistaken, as Ismenias. And the latter is not ordered to 'sing for himself' but for his teacher, so that he can judge him.[3]

81 Si leonina pellis non satis est, vulpina addenda
If the lion's skin is not enough, a fox's must be added

Ἂν ἡ λεοντῆ μὴ ἐξίκηται, τὴν ἀλωπεκῆν πρόσαψον, If a lion's skin is not enough, add a fox's. When something cannot be gained by force, guile is called for. The proverb arose from a saying of Lysander. For, as Plutarch recalls in the life of Lysander, he used to ridicule those who, as if they were descendants of Hercules, thought they should wage war by frank use of force and without deceit, whereas he held that it was more the duty of a good leader, where the lion's skin would not reach, to patch it out with a fox's.[1] This is almost the same idea as Maro alludes to as well when he says: 'Cunning or courage, which is desirable in an enemy?'[2] The adage is recorded by Zenodotus. It is similar to something which Plutarch recalls Carbo saying in the life of Sulla. Because Sulla carried on the war not only with open force but also by cunning, he says: 'He waged war both as a fox and as a lion, for his mind was of the nature of both, but he was more strongly affected by the fox's.'[3] In Aristophanes someone is said to be κυναλώπηξ 'a fox-dog,' because he combined the shamelessness of the dog and the cunning of the fox.[4]

* * * * *

2 Cicero *Brutus* 186–7; added in 1526. Erasmus' text is faulty; the sense of the accepted text after 'Sing for me and for the Muses' is 'to Brutus here ... I would say, "Sing for me and for the people, my dear Brutus."' In Epp 731, 784, 785, 826, and 1053 Erasmus uses the expression to describe the way he intends to spend his retirement.

3 Jerome *Adversus Rufinum* 2.27 PL 23 472D; *In Ieremiam* 3 preface PL 24 757B; *Paralipomena* preface PL 28 1394B. See Erasmus' commentary on Jerome's *Adversus Rufinum* 2.27.

81 Zenobius 1.93 (= Diogenianus 1.83, Apostolius 3.24). Cf *Suda* A 2411, Zenobius (Aldus) column 35. Otto 932 quotes the title of a fable by Phaedrus (Appendix 23) which is also an exact translation of Zenobius.

1 Plutarch *Lysander* 7.4; cf *Moralia* 229B *Apophthegmata Laconica*.

2 Virgil *Aeneid* 2.390

3 Plutarch *Sulla* 28.3; added in 1533

4 Aristophanes *Lysistrata* 957; *Knights* 1067 and 1069

82 Siculus miles
A Sicilian soldier

Σικελὸς στρατιώτης, A Sicilian soldier. This was said by way of proverbial banter against a foreign mercenary soldier because in the time of Hiero the Sicilians commonly made use of foreign infantry, as Zenodotus tells us. Appropriate for a man who is willing to undertake any sort of service for love of gain. It is close to what we have said elsewhere about the Carian.[1]

83 Pro bonis glomi
Reels for good deeds

'Αντ' ἀγαθῶν ἀγαθίδες, Reels for good deeds. This was customarily said whenever someone was rewarded abundantly and with interest for a benefit he had conferred on someone else. For *agathides* is the Greek word for *glomi*[1] 'reels,' but there is an ornament of word-play in the Greek expression which cannot be rendered in Latin. Suidas records it.

84 Sine pennis volare haud facile est
It is not easy to fly without feathers

Still well known popularly these days[1] is this proverb from Plautus' *Carthaginian*: 'It is not easy to fly without feathers.'[2] We find the same in the *Comedy of Asses*: 'Would I cheat you? Come on, please! Fly without feathers!'[3] It comes in appropriately when we say that certain aids are missing without

* * * * *

82 Zenobius 5.89 (= Apostolius 15.47, Zenobius [Aldus] column 150)
  1 *Adagia* I vi 14 Risk it on a Carian

83 *Suda* A 2601. Cf Apostolius 1.14, Zenobius (Aldus) column 35. A variant of *Adagia* II iv 92 Reels of good things; also mentioned in III iii 88 Of ultimate disasters the ultimate
  1 The plural of *glomus* is *glomera*. Erasmus appears to have thought of *globus*, which Lewis and Short describe as kindred in origin. The Greek expression is described as proverbial by LSJ and translated as 'quantities of goods,' with an example in PCG 8 adespota fragment 796, 827 Kock.

84 *Collectanea* no 210. Plautus (see n2 below). Otto 1424
  1 On 'these days,' see ASD II-5 339:246n and Suringar 210.
  2 Plautus *Poenulus* 871
  3 Plautus *Asinaria* 93

which some business cannot be completed. Among respectable authors we find *accidere alas*[4] 'to cut off the wings' as an expression for taking away the material or the means to undertake anything, and *addere alas* 'to add wings.'[5] Horace, using a similar expression, said *decidere pennas* 'to clip the wings':

> As soon as the battle of Philippi discharged me,
>> Brought down with my wings clipped ...[6]

And Cicero says in the *Letters to Atticus*, book 4: 'Those who had cut off my wings do not want them to grow again.'[7] In the *Academic Questions* the same author said 'to cut the sinews' for taking away one's strength.[8]

This[9] is similar to an expression we have noted elsewhere, Εἰς πῦρ ξαίνειν 'To divide fire,'[10] which Plato used in the *Laws* book 6 to mean the impossible: 'With the result that the maker of laws does precisely what those people do who make a game of thrashing at a fire,'[11] that is, he wastes his labour, because fire immediately runs together again. Another expression of the same sort is found in Plato's *Eryxias*: 'Then I recognized that the man's mind was such that persuading him would be no different from cooking a stone.'[12] I confess these passages could have been quoted more opportunely in other places,[13] but they do not all come to mind on all occasions.

* * * * *

4 The verb *accidere* has no authority in this phrase; the sentence is taken without correction from the *Collectanea* where the passages from Cicero containing the correct *incidere* had not appeared.

5 Virgil *Aeneid* 8.224; cf *Adagia* IV viii 86 Lend wings.

6 Horace *Epistles* 2.2.49–50; added in *1526*. Otto 1422

7 Cicero *Ad Atticum* 4.2.5

8 Cicero *Academica* 1.10.35: *nervos virtutis inciderit* 'to hamstring virtue'

9 The reference appears to be not to Cicero's expressions but to Plautus' 'Fly without feathers!' The text from here to the end is from *1533*; the whole addition belongs properly in *Adagia* I iv 55, but at this stage the first chiliad of this edition had already been printed.

10 *Adagia* I iv 55. The correct translation is *Lanam in ignem carminare* 'To card wool into the fire'; cf Schneidewin on Zenobius 5.27. Erasmus has allowed himself to be misled by fire as a Pythagorean symbol; cf *Adagia* I i 2:134 (CWE 31 36) *Ignem ne gladio fodito* Stir not the fire with the sword. Cf also *Adagia* III vi 38 To divide the clouds.

11 Plato *Laws* 6.780C. The passage is translated by R.G. Bury 'and so causes the lawgiver (if he tries) to be practically carding his wool (as the proverb has it) into the fire.'

12 Pseudo-Plato *Eryxias* 405B

13 See n9 above.

85 Siphniassare
To give a Siphnian wave

Σιφνιάζειν, To give a Siphnian wave. Suidas indicates this is a proverbial expression for waving the hand towards the backside, and that it was derived from a custom of the Siphnians, who used to do it as a lewd gesture. Siphnos is an island not far from Crete, one of the Cyclades, whose name at one time was apparently Merope,[1] and was well known for this expression.[2] Pliny mentions it too in book 4, chapter 12.[3] Stephanus also mentions the proverb.[4]

86 Iuxta melam
With a probe

Κατὰ μήλην, With a probe.[1] Suidas shows this is a proverbial expression used when someone pursues uncertain ideas by guessing. The metaphor is derived from doctors examining an internal sore by inserting an instrument into the throat. This instrument is called a μήλη, and μηλῶσαι is to probe in this way.[2]

87 Non idem sunt scriptura et Leucaeus
Leucaeus and his writings are not the same

Γραφή τε καὶ Λευκαῖος οὐ ταὐτόν, Leucaeus and his writings are not the same, or do not agree. Said when someone writes one thing and does or says another. This would be justly uttered in reproach of those who will

* * * * *

85 *Suda* Σ 510. The *Suda* compares this word to λεσβιάζειν (*Adagia* III vii 70, 260 below). Cf Appendix 4.73.
 1 Erasmus is following Stephanus Byzantinus (see n4 below).
 2 PCG 3.2 Aristophanes fragment 930; Pollux *Onomasticon* 4.65; Hesychius Σ 783 and X 449 χιάζειν καὶ σιφνιάζειν
 3 Pliny *Naturalis historia* 4.66 (Meropia)
 4 Stephanus Byzantinus page 573 Meineke

86 *Suda* K 652. Zenobius (Aldus) column 103
 1 Latin *melam*; Erasmus seems to prefer to latinize the Greek word rather than to use the common Latin word for a medical probe *specillum* (Pliny *Naturalis historia* 7.183, Celsus *Medicina* 5.28.12c).
 2 *Suda* K 649 and Zenobius (Aldus) column 103

87 *Suda* Γ 434 and Zenobius (Aldus) column 65. Cf Appendix 1.83, where according to ASD it is a matter of a drawing and Leucaeus is the person portrayed.

not stand by agreements, for these often consist of written bonds, or against those whose lives do not match up to their published books. The Greek will make a line of verse if you add λέγει 'say.' We may suppose that Leucaeus was some dishonest scribe.

88 Bellicum canere. Receptui canere
To give the signal for war. To sound the retreat

Elsewhere[1] I have pointed out how close to proverbs are metaphors taken from war, such as 'To give the signal for war,' for 'to encourage,' 'to exhort.' Marcus Tullius, in his *Philippics* book 7, says 'They say I gave the signal for war.'[2] And someone who is said to 'Sound the trumpet,' is stirring up dissension.[3] 'To sound the retreat,' for 'to finish,' is found in Marcus Tullius *Philippics* book 12: 'For who can hasten to war when the senate sounds the recall and the retreat?'[4] Quintilian, book 12 in the chapter 'What studies after the end,' says: 'Wherefore, before he comes to these snares of age, let him sound the retreat and enter port with his ship entire.'[5] 'Let the trumpets sound,' in Martial, means 'Now let us make love together.'[6] In Plautus we have *Collatis signis depugnare* 'To close standards and fight it out,' and in the same author *Versis gladiis depugnare* 'To fight it out at the point of our swords.'[7] Moreover, this same expression, *collatis signis*, has unquestionably the appearance of a proverb when we mean a serious and precise debate about something, as Marcus Tullius does in his *Letters to Atticus*: 'So that [I may settle it] with Maphrago in a pitched battle.'[8] In Juvenal 'this trumpet of discord' is 'this beginning of the war.'[9]

* * * * *

88 *Collectanea* no 769. Cicero (see nn2 and 4 below). Otto 1510
1 See section XIII 'On proverbial metaphors' of Erasmus' introduction (CWE 31 21), where he mentions these two examples among others.
2 Cicero *Philippics* 7.3
3 Erasmus is giving the expression a very broad sense; it is commonly used literally (Caesar *De bello civil* 3.82, Livy 28.27.15); in Virgil *Georgics* 2.539 more poetically.
4 Cicero *Philippics* 12.8 (only this is quoted by Otto 1510). The accepted text has *Quid enim . . .?* 'Why hasten . . .?'
5 Quintilian 12.11.4
6 Martial *Epigrams* 11.20.8
7 Plautus *Casina* 352 and 344. From this point Erasmus mentions expressions other than those in the title.
8 Cicero *Ad Atticum* 5.15.3 ('Moeragenes' is the name in modern editions, 'Mophrago' [sic] in the editions by Badius, Paris 1511 and Aldus 1513)
9 Juvenal 15.52

89 Pithon formosus
Pretty monkey

Πίθων καλός, Pretty monkey. This will be appropriate when someone is praised falsely through flattery. In Pindar's second *Pythian Ode*:

The monkey is 'pretty,' always 'pretty,' in the eyes of children.[1]

The scholiast shows that this is taken from children who repeatedly say 'Pretty monkey' when they are petting a monkey.[2] And it is apparent that *pithon* is a diminutive of the word πίθηκος – 'little ape,' as it were. Pindar is criticizing someone indirectly, either because he put on airs[3] when flattered by ignorant people, or because he himself was flattering Hiero, praising the unpraiseworthy. But these animals have a particular φιλαυτία 'self-love,'[4] so that they are sensitive to praise, and take pleasure in mirrors, and enjoy allowing their young to be touched, and themselves tire their young with their embraces.[5] For 'speaking to please' the ancients said 'to talk pleasantly,' a word which Aeschylus used in his *Prometheus* according to Athenaeus book 4.[6] According to the same source, those who were more concerned to be witty than truthful were said to 'speak sweetly.'[7]

90 Semel rubidus ac decies pallidus
Once flushed, but ten times pale

Ἅπαξ πυρρὸς καὶ δέκατον χλωρός, Once flushed and ten times pale. Suidas tells us this is said of those who obtain a loan, and who of necessity must in

* * * * *

89 Pindar (see n1 below)
1 Pindar *Pythians* 2.72
2 Drachmann 1.131–3 (see *Adagia* III v 69 n1, 106 above)
3 Cf *Adagia* I viii 69 To raise one's crest.
4 Cf *Adagia* I iii 92 Self-lovers.
5 Cf Pliny *Naturalis historia* 8.216. The passage from 'And indeed it is apparent' to this point was added in 1526.
6 The word is given in Greek as χαριγλωττεῖν; Athenaeus 4.165C (χαριτογλωσσεῖν) citing Aeschylus *Prometheus* 296; added in 1528
7 Given in Greek: ἡδυγλωττεῖν; Athenaeus, six lines before the passage cited in n6, quotes the comic poet Phrynichus (PCG 7 Phrynichus fragment 3; the word there is ἡδυλογοῦσιν); added in 1536

90 *Suda* A 2907. Zenobius (Aldus) column 37

quick succession first blush with shame, then go pale with fear. They blush as they ask for the loan; they go pale while they are insolvent and fear to be taken to court or to prison.[1]

91 Semper seni iuvenculam subiice
To an old man always join a young girl

Ἀεὶ γέροντι νέαν ἐπιβάλλειν κόρην, To an old man always join a young virgin. A proverbial senarius[1] counselling that men of more advanced age should marry a girl rather than an old woman, lest, frigidity being added to frigidity, Venus languish and the marriage prove sterile. But it may be applied aptly in other ways too, whenever we want to indicate that the association of things should be adjusted in such a way that what may be diminished on the one hand may be increased on the other. So that, for example, a young companion might be associated with an old man and the gaiety of the former would limit the melancholy of old age, or contrariwise the sternness of age would temper the liveliness of youth. Or again, a chatterer might be joined to one who is too taciturn, a rash man to a timid one, a poor person to a rich one. The proverb is recalled by Diogenianus.

92 Semper superioris anni proventus melior
Last year's harvest was always the best

Ἀεὶ τὰ πέρυσι βελτίω, The previous year was always better. Said when present affairs are not pleasing and past ones are preferred. Diogenianus tells us this was the cry of the Athenians under Macedonian government. The figure is borrowed from farmers, who always complain to their landlords about the present year's harvest. There is a phrase of Horace that is pertinent here: 'An apologist of times past / When he was a boy.'[1]

* * * * *

1 From 'who of necessity' to the end is an amplification by Erasmus, not the *Suda*.

91 Diogenianus 2.72. Cf Apostolius 1.89 and *Suda* Αι 102.
1 The Greek is unmetrical; Erasmus either is referring to his Latin translation or thought the Greek verse was an iambic trimeter.

92 Diogenianus 2.54. Cf Apostolius 1.67A, 2.73, and 16.12.
1 Horace *Ars poetica* 173–4

93 Sacra nihil sunt
The sacrifices are nothing

Τὰ θύματα οὐδέν ἐστιν πλὴν γένεια καὶ κέρατα, The sacrifices are nothing but jawbones and horns. Said of lean victims. It may be applied quite aptly to food which is inedible. It is reported by Suidas.

94 Scytharum solitudo
The wilderness of the Scythians

Σκυθῶν ἐρημία, The wilderness of the Scythians. There is an expression in Aristophanes' *Acharnians* for the greatest disasters and ruin:

> To perish trapped in the Scythian wilderness.

At this point the scholiast indicates that the proverb was usually used of some vast desert.[1] It is derived from the fact that the Scythians used no fixed abodes, but travelled about in wagons, and for this reason the country abounds in wild animals.[2] Quintus Curtius also recalls the adage in book 7 of the *Deeds of Alexander*. An ambassador of the Scythians speaks in these words:

> I hear that Scythian deserts are mocked by the Greeks even in proverbs. We seek out empty places devoid of human cultivation rather than cities and rich fields.[3]

Plutarch uses the expression too in his book 'On the Contradictions of the Stoics,'[4] as we noted in the proverb 'To be pitched head foremost.'[5]

* * * * *

93 *Suda* Θ 550 citing Aristophanes *Birds* 901–2

94 Aristophanes (see n1 below). Cf Apostolius 15.54. Otto 1617
 1 Aristophanes *Acharnians* 704: Σκυθῶν ἐρημία, and the scholiast on the passage (Dübner page 20 – the scholia for lines 704 and 705 are in the wrong order).
 2 Following the scholiast (see n1 above)
 3 Curtius *Historia Alexandri* 7.8.23; added in 1517/18. See *Adagia* I i 11:15n (CWE 31 60).
 4 Plutarch *Moralia* 1043E *De Stoicorum repugnantiis*; added in 1526
 5 *Adagia* III iii 83

95 Scindere glaciem
To break the ice

To break the ice is to open the way and to be the first in beginning a task.
A figure derived from boatmen, who send one of their number ahead to
break up the ice on a frozen river and open the way for the others.

96 Vivus fueris vel cepe solum accipiens
You would be alive if only you had accepted the onion

Ζωὸς γενήσῃ κρομμύου μόνον λαβών,[1] If only you had taken the onion, you
would be alive now. Zenodotus and Suidas declare that this used to be said
about those who form a great expectation from some trifling thing. It seems
to have arisen from the case of a sick man who was restored to health when
the doctor offered an onion, a rather vulgar plant and not one particularly
healthy for the body.

97 Sapientes tyranni sapientum congressu
Kings become wise through association with the wise

Σοφοὶ τύραννοι τῶν σοφῶν συνουσίᾳ, The prince acquires wisdom by dealing
with the wise.[1] Zenodotus quotes this from *Ajax the Locrian*,[2] adding that
the same line of verse was quoted by Plato under the name of Euripides,
and in fact I have found it mentioned under his name in the *Republic* book
8: 'Kings are wise through conversation with the wise.'[3] I am all the more

* * * * *

95 *Collectanea* no 374; the source given there is Francesco Filelfo, probably, accord-
ing to ASD, one of his published letters (*Epistolae* 12.45), which has *glaciem fregi*
'I have broken the ice.' Erasmus uses it in Ep 20, which is dated 15 May 1489.
The expression is not found in classical literature. Tilley I 3 To break the ice.

96 Zenobius 4.15. Cf Diogenianus 4.99. Apostolius 8.37. *Suda* Z 148. Zenobius
(Aldus) column 91
1 According to ASD the Greek phrase is a trimeter, probably from comedy; cf
Strömberg *Greek Proverbs* (Göteborg 1954) 95

97 Zenobius 5.98 (= Apostolius 15.58). *Suda* Σ 823. Zenobius (Aldus) column 151
1 Erasmus has presumably translated with a singular subject and explicit verb
for the sake of a different metre.
2 Sophocles fragment 13 Nauck = 14 Pearson; in the edition by Hugh Lloyd-
Jones (Loeb) 3.14. Aulus Gellius (see n5 below) claims to have seen this.
3 Plato *Republic* 8.568A

surprised that Aulus Gellius refers to the *Theaetetus* of Plato, unless through an error of the scribes '*Theages*' has been corrupted to '*Theaetetus*,' for it is also reported in the *Theages*.[4] Aulus Gellius declares in book 13 that this same proverb was in both authors, in Sophocles in a play of the same name, and in Euripides, just as several other lines of verse are found in Euripides which are also to be found in Sophocles and Aeschylus. Moreover Gellius says the line that we have just quoted is 'of known antiquity,'[5] so that you can deduce that it had become a proverb. And if only it were as welcome to the princes of our age as it is weighty and elegant, for of them you could quite well say: Μωροὶ τύραννοι τῶν κολάκων συνουσίᾳ 'Kings become foolish through conversation with flatterers.'[6]

98 Leonis exuvium super crocoton
A lion's skin over a saffron dress

Λεοντῆ ἐπὶ κροκωτῷ, A lion's skin over a saffron dress. Said when two entirely unsuited things are brought together. It is derived from Bacchus who, in Aristophanes, goes down into Hades attired thus: he put on a charming woman's dress and over this garb he draped a lion's skin so that, if you please, he would be believed in Hades to be the fearful Hercules. Adorned in this way, he is also mocked in the *Frogs* by Hercules:

> I can hardly restrain my laughter
> Seeing the dress worn with the lion's skin.'[1]

It will be aptly quoted against certain monks or scholastics who in public wear the insignia of their rule and in private act like soldiers, or those who are severe of face and effeminate in their ways.[2]

* * * * *

4 Plato *Theages* 125B
5 Aulus Gellius *Noctes Atticae* 13.19.1–2; added in 1526. Erasmus is mocking Aulus Gellius who says that he is surprised that Plato attributes the line to Euripides in his *Theaetetus*; the section from here to the end was added in 1515.
6 The recasting of the Sophoclean verse is Erasmus' own; he gives no Latin version. For his satire of princes, cf especially *Adagia* III vii 1 A dung-beetle hunting an eagle (178 below).

98 Aristophanes (see n1 below). *Suda* K 2460 and O 991
 1 Aristophanes *Frogs* 46 and scholiast to line 46 (Dübner page 276)
 2 Cf *Adagia* III iii 1 The Sileni of Alcibiades, especially CWE 34 267–7 and 277.

99 Quod scis, nescis
What you know, you do not know

What you know, you do not know. Terence, in the *Eunuchus*: 'You, if you
are wise by heaven, what you know, you do not know.'[1] The same author in
the *Heautontimorumenos*: 'You will ignore what you know, if you are wise.'[2]
Donatus informs us that this is a proverb derived from the games of the
dialecticians, in which riddles like this are propounded: 'I do and do not,
I am a friend and not a friend, I hear and do not hear.'[3] We mentioned
this type right at the beginning of this work pointing out that all figures
of this sort which are formed by linking opposites belong to the family of
proverbs.[4] Such is this one from Plautus: 'Where I am, I am not.'[5] This, on
the face of it,[6] as they say, seems to be a riddle. But its meaning is: 'I am not
where my mind is.' So by this proverb we signify a promise to keep silence,
when someone keeps back and hides what he knows as if he does not know.

100 Nec aures habeo nec tango
I neither hear nor touch

'Having no hearing or touch,' was said proverbially of a person who was
caught red-handed, and was the object of protests from everyone. In the
preface of his declamation about reconciling a mother and a daughter (for
why should I not call this a declamation, when he himself indicates at one
point explicitly that this material was put together by himself as an exercise?)[1] Jerome says: 'Because I tried to convict crime I have myself been
made out a criminal. It is like the popular proverb: "As all the world disputes it and denies it, I believe it too that I have no ears, and do not touch
them." '[2] that is, 'I must keep silence and what I hear and touch must be as

* * * * *

99 *Collectanea* no 538. Terence (see n1 below). Otto 1605
   1 Terence *Eunuchus* 721–2
   2 Terence *Heautontimorumenos* 748
   3 Donatus on Terence *Eunuchus* 722
   4 CWE 31 Introduction XIII On proverbial metaphors, lines 49–92
   5 Plautus *Cistellaria* 211
   6 *Adagia* 1 ix 88 At first sight. On the face of it

100 Jerome (see n3 below). Otto 216
   1 Jerome *Letters* 117.12
   2 Erasmus' text has *iurgantibus et negantibus cunctis, Nec aures me credo habere, nec
   tango* in all editions, which varies slightly from the accepted text, translated by
   F.A. Wright (Loeb) as 'As all the world declares on oath that I have no ears, I
   believe it too and do not touch them.' Wright has a note: 'This proverb has not
   been identified, nor has any satisfactory explanation of its nature been given.'

if I do not know.'[3] This may come from Aristophanes' *Thesmophoriazusae*: 'I neither hear nor see.'[4]

1 Priusquam sortiaris, communia devoras
You devour the commons even before you get your share

Πρὶν λαχεῖν, τὰ κοινὰ κατεσθίεις, You devour the commons even before the distribution is made. This is appropriate for one who plunges into an affair without waiting for a part to be allocated. Suidas informs us it is a figure derived from banquets at which it was the custom in ancient times to distribute a share to each person, as we may deduce from several passages in Homer. He has this very frequently: 'And none missed the equally shared feast.'[1] We also learn from several authors that food was put out for all without any apportioning and each person took as much as he wanted. This is shown by Plautus: 'He piles up heaps of dishes.'[2] Plutarch mentions this fact too in his 'Table-talk,' discussing which of the two customs might be more commendable.[3] However, the proverb is taken from the *Knights* of Aristophanes:

When, before you get your share, you devour the commons.'[4]

2 Res in foro nostro vertitur
There is activity in our market

Plautus' Tranio in the *Haunted House* says: 'When I see there is activity in our market.'[1] This is a proverbial expression for 'After I see that our fortunes are turning around entirely' – a figure taken from the markets where the

* * * * *

3 Jerome *Letters* 117.1 (Praefatio) PL 22 954
4 Aristophanes *Thesmophoriazusae* 19

1 *Suda* Π 2293
1 An inexact recollection of a common phrase in Homer: *Iliad* 1.468, 602. The Homeric sort of feast is fully described by Plutarch in the passage quoted below.
2 Plautus *Menaechmi* 102; also quoted in *Adagia* III ii 37
3 Plutarch *Moralia* 642F–644D *Symposiaca* 10
4 Aristophanes *Knights* 258

2 *Collectanea* no 186. Otto 712
1 Plautus *Mostellaria* 1051. Erasmus has *Ubi egomet video rem verti in meo foro*; the accepted reading is *Ubi ego me video venire in meo foro*, translated by P. Nixon (Loeb) as 'Seeing they're selling me out in my own market.'

price of goods changes very often according to the circumstances. Or, of course, from the formulae of judgments or of legal explanations. It is the opposite of 'To plead in a strange court,'[2] but it is related to 'Taking the market as you find it,' which is dealt with elsewhere.[3]

3 Quodcunque in solum venit
Whatever falls on the ground

Whatever falls on the ground, Whatever is created by nature. Marcus Tullius in book 1 of *On the Nature of the Gods*: 'From these you form and produce "whatever falls on the ground," as they say.'[1] He is ridiculing the Epicureans' atoms, from which they believe all things are engendered, whatever is born anywhere in the universe.

4 Quando id fieri non potest
When it cannot be done

There is no saying more elegant or more useful than this aphorism which is to be found in Terence's *Andria*: *Quoniam id fieri quod vis non potest, / Id velis quod possit* 'Since what you want cannot be done, you should wish for what can be done' Οὐ δυνάμενος ὃ θέλεις θέλης ὃ δύνασαι.[1] This *conversio* 'repetition and interchange of words' is very ornamental, for example in this phrase: 'You should not live to eat, but eat to live.'[2] And indeed this adage is very close to Δεῖ τὸ παρὸν εὖ ποιεῖν 'Accept things as they are in good part.'[3] And

* * * * *

2 *Adagia* II ii 90; Martial *Epigrams* 12 preface
3 *Adagia* I i 92

3 *Collectanea* no 573; Cicero (see n1 below). Otto 1671
1 Cicero *De natura deorum* 1.65; see also *Ad familiares* 9.26.2 (omitting *venit*). The expression also means 'Whatever comes into your head.'

4 *Collectanea* no 283; Terence (see n1 below). Otto 1456
1 Terence *Andria* 305–6; cf *Adagia* I viii 43 As best we can, since as we would we may not. According to the editors of ASD the Greek translation is Erasmus' own.
2 Ascribed by many authors to Socrates. See for example Plutarch *Moralia* 21E; Stobaeus *Eclogae* 3.17.21 Hense III 495; Aulus Gellius 19.2.7; Athenaeus 4.158F; Diogenes Laertius ('Socrates') 2.34. See also Quintilian 9.3.85, who calls this figure *antimetabolē*, and the *Rhetorica ad Herennium* 4.28.39 (*commutatio*); see Otto 588.
3 *Adagia* III x 34 (369 below); cf also *Adagia* II ix 33 Take your present fortune in good part; and *Adagia* IV ii 43 What is given (525 below)

Martial counts among his considerations of happiness 'Be content with what you are.'[4]

5 Quantum non milvus oberret
More than a hawk could fly around

So much that a hawk could not fly around it. This is a proverbial hyperbole about the excessively wealthy man who has so much land that not even a hawk can fly around it. Persius: 'At Cures there is a rich man who / Farms more than a hawk can fly around.'[1] Juvenal imitated this in Satire 9: 'Within your pastures so many exhausted hawks.'[2] So too some writer of tragedies[3] quoted in Plutarch: 'I farm a field twice six days / Journey round, the Berecynthian land.'[4] In book 18 Pliny speaks of the *latifundia*, large estates which he says were the beginning of the ruin of Italy. Accordingly the ancients thought 'it is more satisfactory to sow less and to plough better.'[5]

6 Caedimus inque vicem praebemus crura sagittis
Now we strike, and now expose our shins to arrows

Persius in his fourth *Satire*: 'Now we strike, and now expose our shins to arrows.' Alternately we criticize and are criticized, we are mocked and we mock, we bite and are bitten, we wound and are wounded. Derived from warfare. Likewise Horace: 'We are struck, and wear out our enemy with just as many wounds.'[1] In his essay on 'Progress in Virtue' Plutarch introduces a similar metaphor of a ball thrown back and forth: Καὶ πεπαύμεθα τοὺς λόγους ὥσπερ ἱμάντας ἢ σφαίρας ἐπιδούμενοι πρὸς ἀλλήλους 'And have ceased

* * * * *

4 Martial *Epigrams* 10.47.12; also quoted in *Adagia* IV v 4 He is not happy who does not know it

5 *Collectanea* no 266; Persius (see n1 below). Otto 1116
1 Persius 4.26; Erasmus follows the fifteenth century edition.
2 Juvenal 9.55; Erasmus follows the Venice 1483 or 1494 edition.
3 Aeschylus fragment 158 Nauck = 278 C Mette
4 Plutarch *Moralia* 603A *De exilio* 'On Exile' and 778B *Maxime cum principibus philosopho esse disserendum* 'Philosophers and Men in Power'; this and what follows were added in *1515*.
5 Pliny *Naturalis historia* 18.35

6 *Collectanea* no 267; Persius 4.42. Otto 279
1 Horace *Epistles* 2.2.97

to equip ourselves with arguments as if they were thongs or spheres to use against one another'[2] as in the proverb we have noted elsewhere, 'To throw the ball from one to another.'[3]

7 Ptolemaica lis
Ptolemaic dispute

Πτολεμαῒς ἡ δίκη, Ptolemaic dispute. Diogenianus informs us this was said to reproach those who are eager for quarrels. Ptolemaïs was some old woman who, during her whole life, was engaged in disputes and never stopped pleading cases.[1]

8 Provolvitur ad milvios
He kneels to the kites

Προκυλινδεῖται ἰκτῖνος, He worships the kite. At the beginning of spring the kites reappear, an event at which poor people, released from winter, kneel and rejoice, and as it were worship them. This can be adapted to describe those who are made happy by a new hope. Suidas recalls it as a proverb. And Juvenal has 'Endure, and wait for the cicadas.'[1] In fact it comes from the Birds of Aristophanes: προκυλινδεῖσθαι τοῖς ἰκτίνοις 'to prostrate oneself to the kites.'[2] The scholiast traces the origin to the same circumstances,

* * * * *

2 Plutarch Moralia 80B Quomodo quis suos in virtute sentiat profectus. Erasmus, who does not give a translation here, has misunderstood σφαῖραι which in this case are knuckledusters not spheres or balls. See Adagia III i 99 n1 (CWE 34 388).
3 Adagia III i 99

7 Diogenianus 7.53 (= Apostolius 15.3; Laurentianus 2.25; Suda Π 3031). This is the beginning of a series of some seventy proverbs taken in reverse alphabetical order from the Suda (P–M), with occasional items from other authors. For the significance of this as evidence for Erasmus' progress in gathering material for a larger collection than the Collectanea before his stay in Italy, see ASD II-6 349–51 note to III vi 7.
1 Following Diogenianus

8 Suda I 283
1 Juvenal 9.69
2 Aristophanes Birds 501. In Greek only; translation by B.B. Rogers (Loeb). At this point it is said that people knelt to a kite because it was formerly held to be the monarch of Hellas. It is in line 713 that the kite is described as announcing the advent of spring.

explaining that the four seasons of the year are announced to men through birds, and he attributes the spring to hawks.[3]

9 Prienensis iustitia
Prienian justice

Πριήνη δίκη, Prienian justice. Suidas declares that this is appropriate when we want to say that someone is the most outstanding in judgment. It originated with Bias of Priene whose integrity in judging and pleading cases became proverbial, so that one can say, 'In judgment more eminent than Bias of Priene.'[1] It is quoted from Hipponax, the iambic poet, by Strabo in book 14 of his *Geography*, and in the life of Bias by Diogenes Laertius.[2] Likewise the trochaic line of Demodicus Lerius: 'If you plead any case, make sure you plead in the manner of Priene.'[3] The scazon[4] of Hipponax goes like this: 'Whenever you make a judgment, make sure you surpass Bias of Priene.' I have talked elsewhere about the judgment of Bochoris and of Rhadamanthys.[5]

10 Primum Mars in filiis laudatus est
Mars was honoured initially in his sons

Τὰ πρῶτα Ἄρης εἰς τοὺς παῖδας ἐπῃνεῖτο, At first Mars was praised because of his sons. Said of those who set an example of exceptional nature at first, then gradually slip into other habits. This is what happened to the Romans. Once they were vigorous and showed by their courage that Mars was the

* * * * *

3 Dübner pages 222 and 226. The scholiast does not appear to give the explanation that Erasmus attributes to him.

9 *Suda* Δ 1055
1 *Suda* B 270
2 Hipponax of Ephesus fragment 123 West; Strabo *Geographica* 14.1.12; Diogenes Laertius 1.84 ('Bias'); added in *1526*
3 Given in Greek: Εἰ τύχῃς τίνων, δικάζευ τὴν Πριηνήων δίκην, and translated by Erasmus. See *Greek Elegy and Iambus* (Loeb) 1.167; Demodicus of Lerius fragment 6 West. This and the remainder were added in *1533*.
4 The scazon, an iambic trimeter, or, as here, a trochaic tetrameter whose second last element is long rather than short, was said to have been invented by Hipponax.
5 *Adagia* II vii 65 Bocchyris, and II ix 30 The verdict of Rhadamanthys

10 *Suda* T 108; cf Diogenianus 8.38.

founder of their race; later they slipped into unmartial softness, so that Juvenal was right to thunder: 'But whence, O Gradivus,[1] this lust that has infected your grandsons?'[2] The proverb is recorded by Suidas.

11 Phrynichi lucta
Fighting like Phrynichus

Τὸ Φρυνίχου πάλαισμα, Fighting like Phrynichus. Diogenianus declares this was commonly said of people who do business by cunning and tricks. This Phrynichus[1] betrayed the Spartans and got a black mark[2] in old comedy.[3]

12 Pro malo cane suem reposcis
You demand a sow for a sick dog

Ἀντὶ κακῆς κυνὸς σῦν ἀπαιτεῖς, You demand a sow for a sick dog, that is, something valuable for something worthless, for the pig is food, but dogs are never edible.[1] Recorded by Diogenianus.

13 Prudens in flammam mittere manum
To put one's hand in the flame intentionally

St Jerome uses a proverb like this somewhere: 'I insert my hand into the flame intentionally,' meaning 'I expose myself knowingly to danger and face evils.'[1] It seems it may be derived from the story of Mutius Scaevola.[2] It is to be found in Cicero too.[3]

* * * * *

1 A title of Mars also used by Virgil; cf *Adagia* III iv 31 (19 above).
2 Juvenal 2.127–8. 'But' is added by Erasmus.

11 Diogenianus 8.29 (= Apostolius 17.16)
1 On Phrynichus, see Thucydides 8.27, 50–1, 68.
2 Cf *Adagia* I v 54 To mark with chalk, with coal.
3 Cf *Suda* Φ 766: Φρυνίχου πάλαισμα, citing Aristophanes *Frogs* 689.

12 Apostolius 3.22; Diogenianus 1.89; cf Zenobius (Aldus) column 36, *Suda* A 2666.
1 *Vescus* 'consuming' or 'poor in nourishment' is rare; the editors of ASD suggest Erasmus takes it in the sense of 'edible' following Servius' commentary on Virgil *Georgics* 4.131.

13 *Collectanea* no 529; Jerome (see n1 below). Otto 671
1 Jerome *Adversus Rufinum* 2.32 PL 23 475C; cf *Letters* 54.2 PL 22 550.
2 Livy 2.12; Valerius Maximus 3.3.1
3 Perhaps a somewhat vague memory, added in *1515*; ASD suggests *Ad Atticum* 16.15.6 contaminated by *Ad familiares* 6.6.6 or 8.16.5.

14 **Proba est materia, si probum adhibeas artificem**
The material is good, if only you engage a good workman

Used by Plautus in the *Carthaginian* with the appearance of a proverb: 'The
material is good, if only you engage a good workman.'[1] A talent is exceptional if only it is taught well, a mind is productive if a suitable teacher
is found, or a business is rewarding if only it is negotiated skilfully. The
figure is too well known to need to be pointed out.

15 **Illo respiciens, sed hic remitte bona**
You may look back that way, but pass the goods this way

Aeschylus, in Aristophanes' *Frogs*, wishing to return to the upper world,
says: 'I shall speak there, for I do not wish to speak out here.' And Bacchus answers him thus: 'Not a bit of it, why not rather tell us the good
news here.'[1] The scholiast informs us this is an allusion to the proverb Ἐκεῖ
βλέπουσα δεῦρ' ἀνίει τἀγαθά 'You may be looking that way, but pass the
goods this way.'[2] This will be appropriate when we hold out the promise
of one thing and do something else, or when we flatter some people and
give a benefit in fact to others. Certain authors say this is borrowed from
the Graces, one of whom looks over her shoulder, offers a gift to the second,
and smiles at the third.[3]

16 **Ranae aquam**
Water to a frog

Βατράχῳ ὕδωρ, You are offering water to a frog. When something is presented which particularly pleases the recipient. For example if you challenge
someone who is a drinker by nature to a drinking competition, or if you offer

* * * * *

14 *Collectanea* no 213
 1 Plautus *Poenulus* 915. See also Otto 701.

15 Scholiast of Aristophanes (see n1 below).
 1 Aristophanes *Frogs* 1461–62 (Bacchus' reply is given in Greek: Μή δῆτα σύ γ',
   ἀλλ' ἐνθαδὶ ἀνίει τἀγαθά), and the scholiast on 1462 (Dübner page 312); not in CPG
 2 Here Erasmus translates *Illuc tuens, at huc remitte commoda*.
 3 On the asymmetrical disposition of the three Graces, see Edgar Wind *Pagan
   Mysteries of the Renaissance* (London 1968) 44; where Erasmus got this subver-
   sive idea about them is unclear.

16 *Collectanea* no 308. Zenobius 2.79; Diogenianus 3.58; Apostolius 4.8. Zenobius
   (Aldus) column 53

a talkative man the matter and the chance to tell a story. It is the opposite of Βατράχῳ οἰνοχοεῖς 'You are offering wine to a frog.'[1] It will be properly applied when someone is given what he has in abundance,[2] for frogs have water in abundance. In Athenaeus there is recorded this verse about Syracusans: 'Who live without food drinking like frogs.'[3] Theocritus in the *Reapers*:

> Boys, the life of a frog is desirable, because
> He has no fear of drinking himself dry; for ample
> Supplies lie below him.[4]

The shepherd is criticizing the meanness of a contractor, because he offered a miserly drink to sweating men when frogs living in idleness may drink as much as they like. There are some drunkards today who think they will die of thirst if they cannot live in the very barrels. This is different from 'The horse to the plain,'[5] and the opposite of Ἀσπάλακα εἰς Κορώνιαν 'A mole to Coronea.' Coronea is a town in Boeotia, where there are no moles, and if one is brought in from somewhere else, it dies. This is what Stephanus says,[6] and it is rather like the dung-beetle at a place near Olynthus in Thrace according to Pliny.[7]

17 Post bellum auxilium
Help when the war is over

Μετὰ τὸν πόλεμον ἡ συμμαχία, Support when the war is over. Said whenever a remedy comes too late. It is recorded by Suidas. It originated with, or

* * * * *

1 *Adagia* II iii 20 You are offering wine to frogs. Also cited in Zenobius (Aldus)
2 This sentence, and the rest of the essay, were added in *1515* or later and Erasmus seems to have shifted his idea of the meaning slightly from what he had said in *1508*.
3 Athenaeus 3.101C–D
4 Theocritus *Idylls* 10.52–3; added in *1515*, with the following explanation in *1526*. In the second line J.M. Edmonds (Loeb) translates: 'He needs no drawer to his drink'; cf the note by Estienne (LB II 852) whose Latin may be translated 'he does not care who pours his drink.' Erasmus corrected himself in the following sentence, added in *1526*, but without correcting his translation of the verse.
5 *Adagia* I viii 82; added in *1528*
6 Stephanus Byzantinus page 377 Meineke, but the proverbial expression about the mole appears to be Erasmus' own invention; cf *Adagia* III vii 1 (213 with n213 below).
7 Pliny *Naturalis historia* 11.99. Cf *Adagia* III vii 1 (213 with n214 below).

17 *Suda* M 739

at least was used by Diogenes the Cynic. Laertius tells a story about him like this. A young man was being rather boastful about the wife he had recently taken and put the following inscription on his house: 'The son of Jupiter, victorious Hercules, lives here. Here let no evil enter.' Diogenes wrote after this: 'Help when the war is over,' meaning, that is, that evil had already been received into the house, when the man, who was evil himself, moved in.[1] This belongs with that expression of Plato which I have recorded elsewhere: 'To arrive after the war is over.'[2] Brutus in the letter to the Lycians: 'Your machines have been brought in, as the proverb has it, when the war is over.'[3] Likewise in the letter to the Myrians: 'For delay in war is the same as doing nothing at all; what is done late is done in vain.'[4] In his 'Declamation on Feeding a Dead Body,' Quintilian has two phrases rather like this proverb: 'Is not medicine for the dead too late? Does anyone pour water onto ashes?'[5] This is how he denotes a remedy that comes too late, since for the mortally sick a doctor comes too late, and it is too late to pour water on a building reduced to ashes.

18 Pinguis venter non gignit sensum tenuem
Fat stomach never bore fine feeling

In one of his letters St Jerome quotes a proverb well known among the Greeks which goes like this: 'Fat stomach never bore fine feeling.' But one must admit that it runs more neatly in Greek than in Latin. And a Greek senarius survives in the Greek writers which goes like this: Παχεῖα γαστὴρ λεπτὸν οὐ τίκτει νόον 'A gross stomach never bears a subtle heart.'[1] Galen too records in *Against Thrasybulus* that this was commonly repeated: 'And this is chanted by almost everyone, for it is one of the truest of all things, that a fat stomach does not bear a subtle mind.'[2] By the Spartans it was held

* * * * *

1 Diogenes Laertius 6.50 ('Diogenes')
2 This remark was made in *1508*; the anecdote was in fact added in *1526* to *Adagia* II ix 52 That's the way to take part in a battle, when it's all over (Plato *Gorgias* 447A).
3 *Bruti epistolae* 23 (*Epistolographi graeci*, ed R. Hercher page 181), the subject of *Adagia* III i 17; added in *1533*
4 *Bruti epistolae* 45 (Hercher page 185); added in *1533*
5 Pseudo-Quintilian *Declamationes maiores* 12.23

18 Jerome *Letters* 52.11 PL 22 557. Otto 1860
1 Gregorius Nazianzenus *Carmina* De virtute 1.10.589 PG 37 723A; Antonius Melissa *Loci communes* 1.29 PG 136 911D
2 Galen *Thrasybulus* 37 in *Galeni scripta minora* ed G. Helmreich (Leipzig 1893) III 85. This citation and the following two from Athenaeus were added in *1526*.

to be disgraceful if someone was excessively fat. Agatharchides, as reported in book 12 of Athenaeus, says that Anclides, having become extraordinarily corpulent through luxurious living, was summoned to the council and there sharply reprimanded by Lysander; he was very close to being sent into exile, and the Spartans threatened him with this if he did not live more frugally.[3] In the same passage Menander says of some obese person: 'For a fat pig all but hid the man's mouth.'[4] The adage warns us that the keenness of the mind grows dull through indulgence of the body. As Horace writes too: 'For a heavy body / Also weighs down the mind itself with yesterday's excesses, / And traps the wisp of divine spirit in earth.'[5] Plutarch, quoted in Gellius, declares that heavy feeding produces children who are quite dull and slow of mind.[6]

19 Piscem natare doces
You are teaching a fish to swim

'Ιχθὺν νήχεσθαι διδάσκεις, You are teaching a fish to swim. This is just as if you were to say, 'You are teaching the learned.' Very close to one we have recorded elsewhere: 'You teach a dolphin to swim.'[1] Which is also expressed thus: 'You are giving advice to a dolphin on how to swim.' The authority is Diogenianus.

20 Pitana sum
I am Pitana

Πιτάνη εἰμί, I am Pitana. Zenodotus declares this used to be said of people

* * * * *

3 Athenaeus 12.550D (Naucleides, not Anclides); Agatharchides FGrHist 85 F 11
4 Athenaeus 12.549C; Menander fragment 21 Körte-Thierfelder. C.B. Gulick (Loeb) translates 'Indeed he was a fat hog lying upon his snout.' Erasmus has premebat os viri, literally 'pressed the face of a man.'
5 Horace Satires 2.2.77–79
6 Aulus Gellius Noctes Atticae 4.19; not Plutarch, but Marcus Terentius Varro in his Logistoricus, of which only fragments survive (this is fragment 17 Riese). Varro's treatise might have been confused with Plutarch's life of Cato because of its subtitle Catus sive de liberis educandis.

19 Diogenianus 5.33; Apostolius 9.19; Suda I 780. Cf Collectanea no 499 Aquilam volare doces. Tilley F 323 Teach fish to swim
1 Adagia I iv 97

20 Zenobius 5.61; Zenobius (Aldus) column 142; Alcaeus fragment 439 Lobel-Page

who had been reduced to extreme misfortune and restored again to their former happiness. For this is what happened once to Pitana, a town in Aetolia.[1] It was reduced to servitude by the Pelasgians and freed to enjoy its former liberty by the Erythraeans.[2]

21 Pistillo retusius
As blunt as a pestle

There is a proverbial hyperbole which St Jerome used in his *Letters*: 'As blunt as a pestle,' for something which is far from sharp. Timon[1] the misanthropist calls Cleanthes 'an idle pestle' or 'mortar,' because of his slowness of wit. And 'the sharpness of Chrysippus' is used ironically in the same author for a stupid person[2] – and 'a syllogism with horns' for a ridiculous and frivolous argument.[3]

22 Partitio, non praefocatio
Don't choke, share

Μερὶς οὐ πνίξ, A casting of lots,[1] not a throttling. Formerly, because those who were strongest laid hands on the weaker ones and snatched food from them, a scheme was devised so that food should be divided equally by lots and immediately it became accepted to shout: Μερὶς οὐ πνίξ 'Don't strangle,[2] share.' The expression became proverbial, and we can use it when we want to say that there is no place for violence, but that the business must be dealt with equitably and legally. Plutarch, in the *Collected Proverbs*, if indeed they

* * * * *

1 Pomponius Mela *De chorographia* 1.18.1. Stephanus Byzantinus page 524 Meineke
2 Hellanicus *FGrHist* 4 F 93, from Zenobius

21 *Collectanea* no 709. Jerome *Epistolae* 69.4 PL 22 657. Otto 1431
1 Timon fragment 41 Diels (*Poetarum philosophorum fragmenta* in *Poetarum graecorum fragmenta* vol III fasc 1) quoted by Diogenes Laertius 7.170 ('Cleanthes')
2 Jerome *Letters* 57.12 PL 22 579; 'the same author' refers back to Jerome over the reference to Timon inserted in *1533*.
3 Jerome *Letters* 69.2 PL 22 655. This sentence dates from *1508*; in *1515*, Erasmus added the example to *Adagia* III iii 12, but gave as its meaning a dilemma from which there is no escape.

22 *Suda* M 630 (= Apostolius 11.26)
1 Erasmus has *sortitio* here.
2 Here he has *strangulatio*.

are his, quotes it in these words: Μερὶς οὐ μὴ πνίγει 'It is a sharing, there's no strangulation.'[3] Suidas too tells us that the proverb usually has this form.

23 Paries dealbatus
A whited wall

Τοῖχος κεκονιαμένος, A whitewashed or plastered wall. The apostle Paul, in the Acts of the Apostles, calls the false and pretentiously dressed high priest Ananias a 'whited wall,'[1] because inwardly he was far different from what he appeared to be outwardly by his dress and bearing. Likewise Christ in the gospels calls those who make a pretence of holiness 'whited sepulchres' for though these sparkle on the outside, on the inside they are full of the bones of the dead. This is what is found in Matthew: 'Woe unto you, Scribes and Pharisees, for such as you are like[2] τάφοις κεκονιαμένοις 'whited sepulchres,' which outwardly appear beautiful but inwardly are full of the bones of the dead and every sort of filth.'[3] Lucian brings in the colossi of Myron and Praxiteles as a simile of this sort in his *Cockerel*, because outwardly they gleamed with much ivory, flashed with much gold, and were bright with diverse colours, and because, moreover, they were images of Jupiter and Neptune holding the lightning bolt or the trident in the right hand so that they seem to be in truth something divine, when inside there was nothing but pitch, nails, spiders, mice and other such rubbish which corresponded not at all to the exterior image. And such is the life of Princes, he declares: if you reckon by the noise and pomp, there is nothing more happy, more like the life of the gods than theirs; but if you consider the anxieties, the suspicions, the hatreds with which they are secretly tormented, there is no life more wretched.[4] Seneca wrote that philosophers who teach virtue yet live scandalously are like the little caskets of certain physicians whose labels promise cure though they conceal poison

* * * * *

3 On the *Collected Proverbs* of the Pseudo-Plutarch, see *Adagia* III v 30 n1 (83 above). This second form of the proverb is Laurentianus 2.16 Jungblut page 404, Zenobius 5.23, and Zenobius (Aldus) column 118, though none of these sources has the particle μή.

23 Acts of the Apostles (see n1 below)
1 Acts 23:3
2 Erasmus' Greek text has παρομοιάζεσθε for παρομοιάζετε – he has translated with a subjunctive (*similes sitis*) – and omits the word ὑποκριταί 'hypocrites.'
3 Matt 23:27
4 Lucian *Gallus* 24–5

within.[5] On the other hand, those who are better within than they show by
their speech, by the immediate appearance of their lives, by their exterior,
as it were, these Plato likens to *sileni*[6] of which we have spoken elsewhere.[7]

24 Ollam alere
To keep the pot full

Χύτραν τρέφειν, To keep the pot full, was said of those who made a show of
fear so that they could discourage someone – for example if someone places
defences somewhere so that the neighbours are less likely to commit acts
of aggression. This originates with the custom of the city of Athens, where
they used to place pots on the roofs to deter screech-owls which were very
numerous there. For birds of every sort shun the noise made by [the wind
in] these pots.[1] The adage is recorded both by Suidas and by Diogenianus.[2]
It comes from the comedy of Aristophanes called the *Birds*:

> – We must fight and have pots to hand at the same time.
> – But what good is a pot?
> – The screech owl won't come to bother us then.[3]

25 Oleum et salem oporteret emere
Buy both oil and salt

Τοὔλαιον καὶ τὸν ἅλα δεῖ ὠνεῖσθαι, It is essential to buy both oil and salt.
Aristotle records this adage in book 2 of his *Rhetoric* when he is dealing
with topoi and enthymemes. He offers this example of the antistrephon: 'A

* * * * *

5 Seneca fragment 18 Haase, quoted by Lactantius *Institutiones* 3.15.11 ('Seneca
  in his *Exhortations*')
6 Plato *Symposium* 215A–B
7 *Adagia* III iii 1

24 *Suda* X 611. Zenobius (Aldus) column 171.
 1 Scholiast of Aristophanes *Birds* 357–8 (Dübner page 219)
 2 Not found; perhaps Erasmus confused this with the previous item in the *Suda*,
   Χύτραν ποικίλλεις or Zenobius (Aldus) column 171 Χύτραν ποικίλλειν You are
   embellishing the pot, which is Diogenianus 1.45.
 3 Aristophanes *Birds* 357–8

25 The Greek form given by Erasmus is based on the Latin translation of Aristotle
   of both Ermolao Barbaro and George of Trebizond; see n1 below.

priestess was advising her son against speaking in public at any time. "For
if you recommend something unjust," she says, "you will have the gods
angry with you; but if something just, then men will be angry." This the
son ἀντιστρέφει "turns round" like this: "No rather, it is an advantage to
speak in public. Because if I say just things, the gods will love me, if unjust,
then men will love me."'[1] Aristotle thinks this sort of argumentation[2] is very
similar to this proverb, in which we are commanded to buy both oil and salt:
'But this is the same as the common expression τὸ ἔλαιον πρίασθαι καὶ τοὺς
ἅλας "Buy both oil and salt"' meaning that sometimes opposite remedies are
necessary, now sharp, now mild. For salt is biting and drying; oil soothes
and moistens. Thus physicians add oil to salt, lest it be too corrosive, and
wise people soften the sharpness of rebuke with kind words.[3] I am aware
that in the Aldine edition[4] you will read ἔλκος[5] 'wound' for ἔλαιον 'oil,' as
if to say the evil and the cure for the evil can be gathered from the same
place. But who normally buys a wound?

26 Tanquam suber
Like cork

'Ὡς φελλός, Like cork. Said of those who do not know how to dissimulate,
or of those who cannot be sunk by the storms of fortune. It occurs in Pindar
and is derived from the nature of this wood, which not only does not sink
itself, but when tied to other things holds them up so that they do not sink.
So it is threaded onto nets[1] and is used to support swimmers.

* * * * *

1 Aristotle *Rhetoric* 2.23.15 (1399a25). The correct reading – τὸ ἔλος πρίασθαι καὶ
τοὺς ἅλας 'To buy the swamp with the salt,' that is, to take the bad with the
good – was unknown to Erasmus. See E.M. Cope *The Rhetoric of Aristotle* ed
J.E. Sandys II 272–3 and n5 below.
2 For the antistrephon as a form of fallacious argument see Aulus Gellius *Noctes
Atticae* 5.10.3.
3 'For salt . . . kind words' added in *1528*
4 The 1508 edition of Greek rhetoricians containing Aphthonius, Hermogenes,
and Aristotle. This was added in *1533*.
5 According to ASD ἔλκος is found in all editions of Aristotle available to
Erasmus.

26 Pindar *Pythians* 2.80; cf Pliny *Naturalis historia* 16.34.
1 Following the scholiast of Pindar ad loc. Cf the poem of Oppian translated in
Adagia III v 38 (88 above).

27 Obtrudere palpum
To smother with caresses

To smother with caresses, in Plautus, is to deceive by skill and trickery. He says: 'I am a master of handing that to others; you can't smother me with caresses.'[1] Hence we also say *palpari* for 'to flatter,' and *palpones* for 'flatterers'[2] by a similar figure. The metaphor is drawn from grooms, who try to calm down fiery horses by a pat of the hand, as we have explained elsewhere.[3]

28 Ne quis unquam Megarensibus
Never anyone more than the Megarians

Μηδέποτε μηδεὶς Μεγαρέων γένοιτο σοφώτερος, Never let anyone be wiser than the Megarians. A proverbial joke customarily uttered against stupid people. But it was said to flatter the Megarians according to Diogenianus.[1]

29 Nulla candidorum virorum utilitas
White-skinned men are no use

Οὐδὲν λευκῶν ἀνδρῶν ὄφελος ἢ σκυτοτομεῖν. White-skinned men are no use except as cobblers. A jibe at soft and effeminate men, and those born to luxury.[1] This is what is implied, I think, by *cerdonica* 'shoemaking,'[2] as in

* * * * *

27 *Collectanea* no 234. Plautus (see n1 below). Otto 1327
1 Plautus *Pseudolus* 945
2 Cf Persius 5.176.
3 *Adagia* IV i 35 Piercing with a caress (462 below), where he refers for this to Virgil *Georgics* 3.186 and Horace *Satires* 2.1.20

28 Diogenianus 6.57 (= Apostolius 11.54)
1 ASD points out that Erasmus appears to misunderstand Diogenianus who says in fact 'as a joke about the Megarians.' Cf *Adagia* II i 79 The Megarians are neither third nor fourth.

29 *Suda* O 801; cf Apostolius 13.35, Zenobius (Aldus) column 133, and Appendix 4.35.
1 Erasmus' interpretation is not based on the *Suda*, which says only that it is a jibe 'about those who are useful for nothing.'
2 The word *cerdonica*, based on *cerdo* 'cobbler' (Martial *Epigrams* 3.16.1 and 3.59.1), is not ancient; the adjective *cerdonicus* is attested in the thirteenth century.

Martial: 'What is it to you what this one or that may do with his own leather?'[3] In any case, such people are useless in managing affairs. On the other hand, those who are dark-skinned and hairy are better choices for governing the nation. Hence even Hercules was called μελάμπυγος 'black-bottom,' as someone energetic and by no means effeminate, as is explained elsewhere in the adage 'Mind you don't fall in with Blackbottom.'[4]

30 Nox humida
A damp night

Νὺξ ὑγρά, A damp night. Customarily said when misfortunes befall, according to Diogenianus. In the same way, in happier circumstances, we say 'Dawn is breaking.'[1] In the same author we find νὺξ δασεῖα 'a thick night,' for a winter night.[2] And if anyone thinks these should not be classed as adages, he can blame Diogenianus, if he wishes.

31 Quid ad farinas?
How does that help with daily bread?

Τί πρὸς τἄλφιτα, How does that help with daily bread? That is, How does this help to make a living? For the poets commonly say ἄλφιτα for daily bread, and for household goods. Aristophanes in the Clouds: Τί δέ μ' ὠφελήσουσ' οἱ ῥυθμοὶ πρὸς τἄλφιτα; 'How would tunes help me gain my daily bread?'[1] This can be applied appropriately to unpractical arts, like poetry: οὐδὲν πρὸς τἄλφιτα 'nothing to do with daily bread,' or as the common people say 'with earning bread,' an expression which is more well known than learned.[2]

* * * * *

3 Martial *Epigrams* 7.10.1–2. The passage, in which the expression *de cute ... sua* is better translated as 'with his own hide,' has nothing to do with shoemaking – *curare cutem* means 'to look after one's own skin.' Cf *Adagia* II iv 75 To cultivate one's dainty skin and Otto 494 who quotes Juvenal 2.105. Erasmus uses the latter himself in III ix 58 Relax (340 below).
4 *Adagia* II i 43

30 Diogenianus (see n2 below); Apostolius 17.48; also in *Suda* N 613
1 Perhaps recalling *Adagia* II vii 77 Light has dawned
2 Diogenianus 6.89; cf also Apostolius 5.81.

31 Aristophanes (see n1 below). Suringar 186
1 Aristophanes *Clouds* 649
2 'or as ... learned' was added in *1515*; cf Suringar page 343.

32 Numeris Platonicis obscurius
As obscure as Plato's maths

Apparently a proverbial hyperbole used by Marcus Tullius in book 7 of his *Letters to Atticus*: 'I could not understand at all the riddle of the Oppii from Velia; it is more obscure than Plato's maths.'[1] This is said because Plato obscures his philosophy with Pythagorean numbers and covers it as with clouds, especially in the *Timaeus*.[2] For Pythagoras brought almost all philosophical reasoning back to numbers. Macrobius wrote a great deal on this in the commentaries he published on the *Dream of Scipio*.[3]

33 Nihil ex agro dicis
Your words are never rustic

Οὐδὲν ἐξ ἀγροῦ λέγεις, Your words are never from the fields; that is, never base or common. For anything inelegant or unpolished is said to have come 'from the fields.' On the other hand anything witty or graceful is called urbane or city talk. Recalled by Suidas.

34 Nihil grave passus es, nisi etc.
You have not been badly hurt, unless ...

Οὐδὲν πέπονθας δεινόν, εἰ μὴ προσποιεῖ, There is no serious harm except what you do to yourself. Recalled by Diogenianus. No one is hurt, except by himself. There is no insult to anyone if he believes it does not concern him.

* * * * *

32 Cicero (see n1 below)
  1 Cicero *Ad Atticum* 7.13.5
  2 The editors of ASD suggest that Erasmus is thinking of passages like *Timaeus* 35B–C and 43D. Cicero however is referring to the Platonic 'perfect' number in *Republic* 8.546B–C. In *De Finibus* 2.5.15 Cicero describes the *Timaeus* as obscure because of its abstruse subject matter and he is echoed by Jerome, in his preface to *On Isaiah* 12 PL 24 409D and *On Amos* 2 chapter 5 verse 3 PL 25 1038A.
  3 Macrobius *Commentarii in Ciceronis somnium Scipionis* 1.6.2–4, 2.2.15–16; added in *1515*

33 *Suda* O 788; cf Apostolius 13.43.

34 Diogenianus 7.38. Menander *Sententiae* 594 Jäkel; *Epitrepontes* fragment 9 Körte-Thierfelder; also quoted by Plutarch *Moralia* 599C *De exilio* and by Stobaeus 4.34.57 Hense v 972.

35 **Ne spina quidem vulnerabit bonos**
   Not even a thorn will harm the good

Μηδ᾽ ἄκανθα ἀμύξῃ τοὺς ἀγαθούς, Not even a thorn will harm the good. No
one will be troublesome to the innocent. Although the thorn by its nature
pricks everyone, innocence and purity of life are always safe.[1]

36 **Naaera et Charmione**
   Naaera and Charmione

Νάαιρα καὶ Χαρμιόνη, Naaera and Charmione. Zenodotus wrote that this used
to be said of faithful friends who did not hesitate to keep company with
their friends even in death. This type of friendship was highly thought of
among the Egyptians; they called it συναποθνῃσκόντων 'of those who die together.' Those who found satisfaction in this sort of intimacy bound themselves together by this rule, that if some fatal accident happened to one, the
other would join him in death.[1] Antony and Cleopatra bound themselves to
each other by such a covenant. Horace speaks in poem 17 of the second book
of *Odes* of some such alliance with Maecenas: 'That day will bring the doom
of both. / I am not one to have pronounced a faithless oath. / We shall both
go, we shall both go, / Wherever you lead, companions / Ready to hasten
on the final journey.'[2] And again, in another passage: 'What of us? to whom
life while you survive may be / Enjoyable, grievous if not.'[3] But let me come
back to this proverb. Naaera and Charmione were two waiting women of
queen Cleopatra who copied her in her voluntary death, and they were seen,
when they were still half-alive, putting back the crown which had fallen
from the head of their already dead mistress. A story worthy to be remembered especially, and pleasant to know, but if anyone perchance questions
it, he can find it in Plutarch's life of Antony.[4] I would not have included
this adage, if I had not been afraid that, since it appears more than once in

* * * * *

35 *Suda* A 1683; Zenobius (Aldus) column 119; cf Diogenianus 6.69.
 1 'Although the thorn ... safe' was added in *1515*.

36 Zenobius 5.24. Zenobius (Aldus) column 123 (Ναήρα, καὶ Χαρμίνη)
 1 From Plutarch *Antony* 71.3, where 'partners in death' are called συναποθανού-
    μενοι. In the prologue of Terence's *Adelphoe* (6) there is reference to a Greek
    comedy by Diphilus called the *Synapothnescontes*, translated under this name
    by Plautus.
 2 Horace *Odes* 2.17.8–12
 3 Horace *Epodes* 1.5
 4 Plutarch *Antony* 85, where the two women are named as Iras and Charmion

the printed editions of Zenodotus' *Collectanea*,[5] some uneducated individual would accuse me of having overlooked it. For to me, if my nose does not betray me, this adage smells as if it were not produced by antiquity at all but were born in Zenodotus' study.

37 Neque nulli sis amicus neque multis
Be not a friend to none, nor to many

This verse of Hesiod, like many others became a proverb: Μηδὲ πολύξεινον μηδ' ἄξεινον καλέεσθαι 'Be not a friend to many, but not to none either.'[1] In book 9 of his *Ethics* Aristotle cites this as a proverb,[2] and appears to approve what it says, because it seems to be uncivilized and joyless to live without the society of any friends at all. On the other hand we cannot love many deeply at the same time or please a lot. And does not Lucian tell us in the *Toxaris* that among the Scythians *polyphilia*, that is, friendship with many, was just as shameful as it is among other peoples for one woman to have intercourse with many men?[3] But Marcus Tullius has the opposite opinion in his book *On Friendship*.[4] And Plutarch in his essay 'On Multiple Friendships.'[5]

38 Nebulas diverberare
To divide the clouds

Νεφέλας ξαίνειν, To card clouds.[1] This is said of someone who vainly strives to do something stupid or impossible. It is recalled by Diogenianus. Suidas suspects that it originated with the person who said that the clouds were

* * * * *

5 Zenobius (Junta 1497) and Zenobius (Aldus 1505) (see *Adagia* III v 1 n1, 59 above). For a similar suspicion about the source of an adage see *Adagia* III vi 88 (170 below).

37 Hesiod (see n1 below). Referred to in *Adagia* III iv 88 (54 above). From *1520* on the title was *Neque nullis ...*; cf Ep 999 (CWE 7 18:99–100).
1 Hesiod *Works and Days* 715
2 Aristotle *Ethica Nicomachea* 9.10.1 (1170b22)
3 Lucian *Toxaris* 37; cf Ep 756.
4 Cicero *De amicitia* 44–51
5 Plutarch *Moralia* 94A *De amicorum multitudine*; the addition, made in *1515*, is slightly misplaced: Plutarch is of the same opinion as Lucian's Scythians.

38 *Collectanea* no 647; Diogenianus 6.83 (= Apostolius 12.5, Zenobius [Aldus] column 124)
1 The Latin for 'card' is *diverberare* 'to divide, split.' In the last phrase, where he is following the *Suda*, Erasmus uses *carminari*, suggesting that he intended

stretched out like fleeces.[2] The image suggests that they had to be carded in the same way.

39 Myconius vicinus
A Myconian neighbour

Μυκόνιος γείτων, A Myconian neighbour. A jibe at someone who comes to a banquet uninvited. For the Myconians had a reputation in ancient times for being gourmandisers and for greedily seeking out other peoples' tables.[1] This is what Suidas says. Zenodotus however says that it suits mean, base men, because the island of Myconos was among the most despised by reason of its infertility, which made its people rather miserly and covetous of others' goods. Athenaeus asserts almost the same thing in the first conversation of the *Doctors at Dinner* where he quotes this verse of Archilochus who criticized someone called Pericles: 'For bursting uninvited into banquets like a Myconian.'[2] The same author adds that the Myconians were known 'for their stinginess and their covetousness' because they were poor, inhabiting as they did an infertile island. For extreme poverty makes people greedy of others' possessions; hence Cratinus called a certain Ischomachus, who was a slave to greed, a Myconian.[3]

40 Mortuos videns
Seeing the dead

Νεκροὺς ὁρῶν νέκρωσιν ἕξεις πραγμάτων, Your business will fail,[1] if you dream of the dead. This is recorded by Suidas as something commonly uttered

* * * * *

diverberare to be taken in this sense. Cf Adagia III v 84 It is not easy to fly without feathers (115 above).
2 *Suda* N 274, is alluding, without mentioning the name, to Aristophanes *Clouds* 343. Added in *1528*.

39 *Suda* M 1400; Zenobius 5.21. Zenobius (Aldus) column 122
1 Cf *Adagia* II 1 7 Myconian baldpate and IV viii 24 Like the Myconians.
2 Athenaeus 1.7F, alluding to Archilochus fragment 124 West
3 PCG 4 Cratinus fragment 365, quoted from Athenaeus 1.8A

40 *Suda* N 142; Astrampsychus *Oneirocriticon* ed Joseph Scaliger in *Oracula metrica ... a Ioanne Opsopoeo collecta* (Paris 1607) 94; cf Apostolius 12.4B.
1 Erasmus' translation here is *tibi occident res*. In his article νέκρωσις in the *Thesaurus linguae graecae* Estienne cites Erasmus with approval on this and para-

from divination based on dreams, the most vain by far of all superstitions.[2] But this is said in such a way as to suggest that death is the end of all the evils of this life.

41 Mortui non mordent
Dead men do not bite

Οἱ τεθνηκότες οὐ δάκνουσιν, Dead men do not bite. This is still commonly said these days. I believe it originated with the saying of Theodore[1] of Chios who was king Ptolemy's teacher of rhetoric. Being co-opted to the council when it was discussing whether Pompey should be driven away from Egypt or admitted, he expressed the opinion that he should be received and then killed, adding this saying: 'Dead men do not bite.' Plutarch tells the story in the life of Pompey.

42 Ascisce ad extremum scientiam
Use knowledge in the last resort

Πέμπε εἰς ἔσχατον τὴν ἐπιστήμην, Call on knowledge in the last resort. You should not use immediately the ultimate powers of your mind, but when extreme peril presses, then you should resort to your skills.[1]

* * * * *

phrases: 'If you see the dead, the desire to complete what you have undertaken will languish and die' (see the note in CPG 2 on Apostolius 12.4[b]). The meaning that Erasmus gives to πράγματα in his final sentence ('toil, troubles') is also quite possible.
2 Cf *Adagia* III vi 58 (154 below).

41 Plutarch *Pompey* 77.4. Cf Apostolius 12.4A. According to ASD, in the Latin Plutarch of Venice 1478 and 1496 the expression is singular; the plural form was invented by Erasmus influenced perhaps by the Dutch form (Suringar 120 page 218). He uses it in Ep 29 of 1489.
1 Erasmus corrects 'Theodore' to 'Theodotus' in *Apophthegmata* VI *Varia mixta* 40 LB IV 290D.

42 Diogenianus 7.85
1 An incorrect interpretation. Apostolius 14.23 adds: παραινετικὴ πρὸς τὸ σπου-δάζειν ἀεί '[the proverb] urges one to work / study hard all the time.' The sense of the Greek seems to be 'Use, or direct, your knowledge to the utmost,' but Erasmus has misunderstood the prepositional phrase and seems to have read πέμπε 'send' as equivalent to the middle 'send for, summon.'

43 Miserrimum fame mori
Nothing worse than death by starvation

According to Plato it was a saying repeated even in songs among the ancients that the most wretched sort of death was to die by starvation. However, it comes from book 12 of Homer's *Odyssey*: 'Any death is hard indeed for wretched mortals. / But to perish of hunger is by far the most wretched thing of all.'[1] Plato quotes these lines in book 3 of the *Republic* as unhealthy for the morals of young people, since no death is wretched which is encountered in a noble cause.[2] It could be used against miserly people who deprive themselves of pleasure[3] in order to save their money, or those who die without knowledge of the truth, because the mind of man is nourished by the word of God no less than the body by food.[4] Death by such hunger is indeed the most wretched of all.[5]

44 I modo venare leporem, nunc Itym tenes
Go hunt for a hare, now you have a pheasant

Plautus said in the *Two Captives* by way of a proverbial figure: 'Go hunt for a hare, now you have *itys* "a pheasant"';[1] that is, 'You have this meal here which is safe, however modest it may be; go seek another, bigger if you can.' The pheasant is a bird so called from 'Phasis' a river in Scythia.[2] Therefore when we want to order someone who has found something good to take on something else, we can use this adage quite opportunely.

But I think this passage in Plautus, like many others, is corrupt.[3] The

* * * * *

43 Plato (see n2 below)
1 Homer *Odyssey* 12.341–2
2 Plato *Republic* 3.390B
3 The Latin is *defraudant genium suum*; cf Plautus *Aulularia* 725, Terence *Phormio* 44.
4 Deut 8:3, Matt 4:4, Luke 4:4: Man shall not live by bread alone but by every word that proceeds from the mouth of God
5 From 'or those who die' to the end added in 1528

44 Plautus (see n1 below). Otto 940
1 Plautus *Captivi* 184
2 The word for 'pheasant' here is *phasianus*; according to ASD the identification of *itys* with *phasianus* comes from Giambattista Pio's commentary on this passage; Erasmus owned a copy of the Milan 1500 edition. The etymology comes from the scholiast on Juvenal 11.139 (*Scythicae volucres*) which says *Fasianus* ἀπὸ τῆς Φάσιδος 'from the [river] Phasis [in Colchis].'
3 This whole textual gloss was added in 1515.

reading should be, not *itym*, as the codices have,[4] nor *ichthyn*, an erroneous change I see one editor has made,[5] since neither a bird nor a fish have anything to do with the hunting of a hare, but *ictin* 'ferret.' For this is an animal belonging to the family of the weasels[6] which is put into rabbit-warrens to chase out the prey. The Romans call it *viverra*.[7] Suidas declares that the same animal traps fish.[8] Aristotle recalls this in book 9 chapter 6 of his *Nature of Animals*, although he does not state that it traps hares, but birds and bees.[9] If there is general agreement that *ictis* is the *viverra*, Pliny in book 8 states that this was particularly prized for hunting hares and rabbits. He says: 'They introduce them into the warrens which have many surface openings, whence the name of the animal,[10] and thus they catch them above as they are forced out.'[11]

45 Minimo provocare
To challenge with the little finger

'To challenge with the little finger' is to challenge to a contest contemptuously. It comes from the gesture of those who challenge to a fight by raising the little finger. Horace in his *Satires*:

> Behold,
> Crispinus challenges me with his little finger: 'Take these, if you wish,
> Take these tablets now; let's have a place, a time,
> Judges; let's see who can write the most.'[1]

* * * * *

4 The editors of ASD think Erasmus must mean the printed editions, since the manuscript reading *irim* 'hedgehog' is unknown to him.
5 Pio (see n2 above), who says: 'Since the *itys*, that is, the pheasant, may not be considered second to the hare in either taste or price, I am persuaded to write *hichtim* [sic] for "fish," that is.'
6 Pliny *Naturalis historia* 29.60 gives *ictys* as equivalent of *mustela* 'weasel.'
7 Pliny *Naturalis historia* 8.218
8 *Suda* I 281
9 Aristotle *Historia animalium* 8(9).6 (612b10–14)
10 The word *cuniculus* 'rabbit-warren' means both 'rabbit' and 'underground passage.' The confusion of hare and rabbit seems to come from Pliny 8.217: 'The animals in Spain called *cuniculi* "rabbits" also belong to the genus of *lepores* "hares."' Erasmus' interpretation 'Go hunt for a hare, now you have a ferret' ignores a vital difference: hares do not live in warrens, so ferrets would be of no use in hunting them.
11 See n6 above.

45 *Collectanea* no 704; Horace (see n1 below). Otto 547
1 Horace *Satires* 1.4.13–16. Erasmus here follows the interpretation given by the

It can be most wittily applied to intellectual situations; for example, 'This grammar teacher on his own challenges all theologians with his little finger.'[2]

46 Minore finire pomoerio et his similia
To enclose with a smaller pomoerium, and sayings like these

There is a flavour of the nature of the proverb in almost all metaphors of this sort: 'To enclose in a pomoerium,' 'To prescribe the goal,'[1] 'To surround with barriers,'[2] and any that are similar. Varro in *On Agriculture*: 'It was all the better done by certain people who confined the subject in narrower limits, excluding those areas which are not pertinent.'[3] And again in book 1 of the same work: 'Whether it is an art or not, and from what starting points it evolves towards its goal.'[4] Cicero in book 1 of *On the Orator*: 'You have constrained the whole profession of the orator within rather narrow boundaries.'[5]

47 Mens peregrina
A mind elsewhere

Νοῦν τὸν ξένον. People are said to have their mind elsewhere when they are lost in thought and so not attentive enough to what is being done in front of them. Aristophanes has a joke in the *Acharnians* against Euripides for using dialectical quibblings (something which even Fabius Quintilian notes in the *Institutes*)[1] in these lines:

* * * * *

commentator Porphyrion. Another commentator, Acron (see *Adagia* III vii 11 n4, 221 below), gives the interpretation followed by H. Rushton Fairclough who translates 'challenges me at long odds.'

2 The grammar teacher was, of course, the elementary teacher at the bottom of the educational ladder; the theologian was at the top.

46 Varro (see n3 below). The pomoerium was the space inside and outside a city's walls left open and uncultivated for defence purposes (Livy 1.44.4).
1 Both expressions from Varro (see n3 below)
2 From Cicero *De oratore* 1.52
3 Varro *De re rustica* 1.2.13
4 Varro *De re rustica* 1.3
5 Cicero *De oratore* 1.264; added in *1526*

47 Diogenianus 6.85; Apostolius 12.14; Zenobius (Aldus) column 125
1 Quintilian 10.1.68

– The same man is in there, and he is not in there, if you know what I mean.
– How can anyone be in there and not in there?
– Perfectly well, old man. For his mind is outside, far away, collecting little scraps of poetry, not inside, but he himself is inside, composing a tragedy, flat on his back.[2]

He calls his little poems *epyllia*, making a diminutive from *epos*. The same author in the *Knights*: 'You are always gaping at the speaker, but for all that you are present your own mind is far away.'[3] And Terence with the same meaning: 'When you are with him, be as if you are not with him.'[4]

48 Mitior columba
As gentle as a dove

Πρᾳότερος περιστερᾶς, As gentle as a dove. The guilelessness and gentleness of the dove is praised even in sacred scriptures.[1] For the dove is among birds what the sheep is among quadrupeds. She contemplates no harm to any living thing and has no other defence against the hawk but the speed of her flight.[2] The adage is recalled by Diogenianus.

49 Ad porcellum da mihi mutuo tres drachmas
Give me a loan of three drachmas to buy a piglet

Εἰς χοιρίδιόν μοι νῦν δάνεισον τρεῖς δραχμάς, Now, give me a loan of three drachmas to buy a piglet. This was said by one who was resolved on dying or who wanted to be initiated. For initiates used to sacrifice a pig. Suidas quotes Aristophanes. It is in the *Peace*: 'Lend me now three drachmas with which I may buy a pig; / I am to be initiated, before I go to meet with death.'[1]

* * * * *

2 Aristophanes *Acharnians* 396–9
3 Aristophanes *Knights* 1118–20. This and the following are quoted by Otto 1464.
4 Terence *Eunuchus* 192. Cf *Adagia* II vii 84 Though present he is far away.

48 Diogenianus 7.64 (= Apostolius 14.97). Cf Otto 413.
1 Matt 10:16 'Behold I send you forth as sheep in the midst of wolves; be ye therefore wise as serpents, and harmless as doves'
2 This sentence added in *1528*; cf *Adagia* III v 78 (112 above) A sitting dove.

49 *Suda* Δ 1516; cf Apostolius 8.5c.
1 Aristophanes *Peace* 374–5

50 Mulieris podex
A woman's rump

Γυναικὸς πυγή, A woman's rump. This used to be said of a slothful and idle person. Woman is an idle creature and the less intelligence she has, the more she is given to ignoble pleasures. She is fond of idleness and like the drone, as Hesiod says, she takes for herself what is gained by the labour of men.[1] This is what is meant by the proverb 'Ocnus the ass.'[2] France has many such women, and yet Holland has uncounted numbers of women who support lazy and pleasure-loving men with their labour.[3]

51 Mulieris animus
Heart of a woman

Γυναικὸς φρένες, A womanish nature. Diogenianus states that this was said of stupid people. But it seems to apply better to those who are cowardly and changeable. Hence the remark of Ennius: 'For you young men have womanish hearts, / And that virgin has a man's.'[1] And Terence: 'I have learned what a woman's nature is. When you will, they won't; when you won't, they want.'[2]

52 Perendinum ventum praediscere
To learn what the wind will be the day after tomorrow

Τὸν τριταῖον ἄνεμον προγινώσκειν, To know what the wind will be the day after tomorrow. This is said of people who guess what is going to happen at a much later time. It originates with sailors or merchants. Pindar says:

* * * * *

50 *Suda* Γ 499; cf Zenobius (Aldus) column 66.
 1 Hesiod *Theogony* 590–9
 2 *Adagia* I iv 83 The sluggard twists the rope
 3 The last sentence was added in *1528*.

51 Diogenianus 4.3 (= Apostolius 5.75)
 1 Ennius tragic fragment *Ex incertis incertorum fabulis* 210 TRF, quoted in Cicero *De Officiis* 1.61. The attribution to Ennius comes from the edition of the *De Officiis* with commentary by Petrus Marsus (Venice 1481).
 2 Terence *Eunuchus* 812–13

52 For the title cf Virgil *Georgics* 1.51.
 1 The 1528 to 1536 editions and LB have *praedicere* 'foretell,' for *praediscere* 'learn beforehand.'

'Wise men know what the wind will be the day after tomorrow.'[2] For this is wisdom, to see not only what is in front of your feet[3] but to foresee what is further away.

53 Caute loquacior
As garrulous as a reef

Ῥαχίας λαλίστερος, As garrulous as a reef. A proverbial hyperbole applied to an intemperate man who is unbearably talkative. The figure is derived from reefs that, continuously beaten by the waves, make a great roaring noise.[1]

54 Lepori esurienti etiam placentae fici
To a starving hare even cakes are figs

Λαγῷ πεινῶντι καὶ πλακοῦντες εἰς σῦκα, To a starving hare even cakes serve for figs. According to Suidas this was said of those who, when driven by necessity, consumed even their most precious possessions.[1] Probably derived from the sort of story which Apuleius tells of himself, that driven by hunger he first learned to lick the cakes then to consume them.[2]

55 Lex et regio
Law and country

Νόμος καὶ χώρα, Custom, or law, and country. A proverb which tells us, as

* * * * *

2 Pindar *Nemeans* 7.17; J.E. Sandys (Loeb) translates: 'But mariners wise knew well of a blast that is bound to blow on the third day after.'
3 The phrase 'to see ... feet,' added in *1515*, echoes Terence *Adelphoe* 386–7, and is also quoted in *Adagia* III vii 17 Before your feet (226 below). The final phrase was added in *1517/18*.

53 Diogenianus 7.99; Apostolius 15.21; *Suda* P 60; Zenobius (Aldus) column 147: λαλέστερος
1 Erasmus reproduces Diogenianus, as do Apostolius and the *Suda*.

54 *Suda* Λ 28
1 Erasmus misunderstands the *Suda*: πρὸς τοὺς τὰ ἐν ἀνάγκῃ πολυτελῆ λογιζομένους 'of those who weigh up what is most valuable in times of need,' that is, things that would not normally be thought of as valuable.
2 Apuleius *Metamorphoses* 10.13–14

55 Zenobius 5.25; Zenobius (Aldus) columns 124–5. Cf Laurentianus 2.10 Jungblut page 403. Tilley L 100 Law and country

I have shown elsewhere with other illustrations,[1] that you must follow and obey the customs of the region into which you go.

Zenodotus writes that all peoples have their own laws and principles for living. It is the custom of the Persians for one thing to take counsel in their cups when they are drunk, and to worship their kings as gods. For another, equals kiss each other; lower class folk only touch the knee of higher class people. They set eyes upon their male children only after four years. The Gordians crown as king the one who is the most corpulent among them. The Syrraci grant the crown to the one who is slimmest in body, and, according to some, the one who has the longest head. The Stymphali honour a woman who consorts with many men. The mountain Massagetae copulate in the streets. The Sauromatae sell their daughters when they are drunk. The Mazusian refrains from intercourse with women unless it is one he has captured in battle. The Tabareni, after their wives have given birth, lie with their heads bound just as if they themselves have given birth. Among the Cecertaei artisans carry their work around until someone approaches to buy it. The Sidones eat their parents, except the head, which they cover with gold. The Caesiae, or according to others the Heniochi, weep for the new-born and rejoice for the dead. The Bachiri, if they have recovered from an illness, present themselves to dogs. The Orgenipei have no houses and do not eat flesh; but they are hairless, not only the men but the women too, and they say this happens because of the nature of the water they drink. The Thysetae sacrifice bones to their gods and themselves eat the meat (and these, in my opinion, are really the most sensible). Tauroscythians make human sacrifice. Mediterranean Byzoni live on cow's milk and never eat any other food. Iberians, instead of sheep, keep herds of dogs. The Africans who are called Colcenses have hyenas.[2] And the differences in our cultures and customs nowadays are no smaller than these. To adapt ourselves to them as far as possible, imitating the octopus,[3] is no small part of wisdom.

56 Aegis venit
There's a storm coming

Αἰγὶς ἔρχεται, There's a storm coming. Suidas states this was customarily said of those who acted wantonly and shamelessly, and takes it from Phere-

* * * * *

1 *Adagia* I i 93 Adopt the outlook of the polyp
2 Erasmus takes all his material from 'Zenodotus writes' down to here from Zenobius.
3 Cf the adage quoted in n1 above.

56 *Suda* Αι 61

crates: 'Alas, woe is me, a storm is coming.'[1] *Aegis* means several things to the Greeks: the shield made of hide that is carried by Africans;[2] then the waves of a rising sea and hurricanes, and this latter in Doric,[3] whence we find ἐπαιγίζειν for 'to blow hard.'[4] Others prefer to say it means what is woven from wreaths or a net woven from creepers. He[5] says this is how it is used in book 4 of Herodotus,[6] and in Lycurgus.[7] And there are some who believe that it means the priestess who carries the sacred *aegis* at Athens, and goes with it into the homes of those who have recently taken a wife. It seems that in these rites there was much licence, just as even among Christians marriages are celebrated with much foolery, with allusions to hurricanes at the same time.

57 Multam sylvam gestis
You're carrying a lot of undergrowth

Λόχμην πολλὴν φορεῖς, You're carrying a lot of undergrowth. A jibe at Phormio, a soldier who was apparently shaggy and covered with a thick forest of hair.[1] We have mentioned him elsewhere.[2] It would apply to someone rustic and stupid, such as almost all soldiers are. It is recorded by Suidas.

* * * * *

1 PCG 7 Pherecrates *Myrmekanthropoi* 'Ant-Men' fragment 118: Οἴμοι κακοδαίμων, αἰγὶς ἔρχεται.
2 *Afri; Suda* Αι 59: 'Libyans'
3 Based ultimately on Aeschylus *Choephori* 593; *Suda* Αι 61 gives καταιγίς, which *Suda* Κ 890 defines as 'violent wind storms.'
4 *Suda* Ε 2006
5 'He' is 'Suidas,' that is, *Suda* Αι 60, which is the source for everything from 'Others prefer' to 'wife.'
6 Herodotus 4.189, who in fact describes tasselled goatskin corselets worn by Libyan women
7 Lycurgus fragment 23 Baiter-Sauppe

57 *Suda* Λ 715, following Aristophanes (see n1 below)
1 Aristophanes *Lysistrata* 800 and 804 and the scholion on the passage (Dübner page 258). Phormio was a successful Athenian admiral of the second half of the fifth century. According to the scholiast of Aristophanes' *Peace* 347 (Dübner page 181) he was convicted in 428 for embezzlement. Erasmus clearly has no information about him except what he finds in Aristophanes and the scholiast. Estienne (LB II 860) remarks: 'Perhaps to be understood as referring to the beard. [The emperor] Julian was certainly speaking of his own, which was long, when he said Ταῦτά τοι διαθεούντων [sic] ἀνέχομαι τῶν φθειροῦν [sic] ὥσπερ ἐν λόχμῃ τῶν θηρίων "For the same reason I put up with the lice that scamper about in it as though it were a thicket for wild beasts" in the *Misopogon* "Beard-hater."' The passage comes from Julian *Misopogon* 338C.
2 *Adagia* II ix 66 Phormio's camp beds

58 Leonem videre hostium praelia portendit
To see a lion portends battles with the enemy

Λέοντας ἰδεῖν δυσμενῶν δηλοῖ μάχας, To see lions indicates a battle with the enemy. A metaphor taken either from the interpretation of dreams or from the observation of omens. It is recalled by Suidas. I notice that verses like these saying what every dream foretells are carefully recorded by Suidas and Hesychius, though there is nothing more vain. Yet it is likely that both were monks.[1]

59 Larus in paludibus
A gull in the swamps

Λάρος ἐν ἕλεσι, A gull in the swamps. Suidas writes that this was commonly said of those who are easily enticed into giving something. It is derived from the bird, the gull, which is also thought to be called κέπφος 'the petrel,'[1] although Theodorus of Gaza translates the latter as *fulica* 'coot' and the former as *gavia* 'gull.'[2] This bird is easily deceived and enticed, and gave rise to the proverb because of this characteristic.[3]

60 Issa
Issa!

Ἴσσα, Issa! was a proverbial taunt shouted at those to whom the letter 'Z'

* * * * *

58 *Suda* Λ 250 (from Astrampsychus *Oneirocriticon* page 98; cf *Adagia* III vi 40, 144–5 above). LB II 860 has an unsigned note: 'Scholars have been left in some doubt whether these words of Astrampsychus in the *Oneirocriticon* are a proverb. Erasmus passed off similar interpretations of dreams as proverbs elsewhere too.'
  1 'I notice ... monks' was added in *1528*; the last sentence seems to be a quite gratuitous supposition introduced simply as a jibe at monks.

59 *Suda* Λ 128; Apostolius 10.48. Zenobius (Aldus) column 110
  1 Following the scholiast of Aristophanes *Plutus* 912 (Dübner page 372)
  2 Theodorus Gaza in his translation of Aristotle *Historia animalium* 7(8).3 (593b4 and 14)
  3 This sentence is from the same passage of the scholiast of Aristophanes (n1 above).

60 *Suda* I 605. In *1508*, but not in later editions, an additional adage, based on *Collectanea* no 217, stood between the previous one and this one. It read, '*Laterna punica* A Carthaginian lamp. In Plautus, referring to someone who is talkative

fell when lots were drawn,[1] and at those who were in any way unfortunate. This according to Suidas, who quotes the proverb from the *Messenia* of Menander,[2] and who states that it is used by writers in other places. We may suppose that this letter was inauspicious in the drawing of lots. Martianus Capella, in the *Marriage of Philology and Mercury*, tells us this letter was hated by Appius Claudius because, when it is pronounced, it sounds like the grinding of a dead man's teeth.[3]

61 Ipso horreo
By the granaryful

When anything is given abundantly and sufficiently it is said to be given 'By the granaryful'; it is just like 'By the basketful,' because more can be supplied from the granary than from a *choenix*.[1] It is similar to 'You draw from the cask.'[2]

62 In tua ipsius arena
In your own arena

In your own arena,[1] that is, 'In your own craft.' Derived from the gladiators who used to fight in the arena. And it was a matter of no small importance to them, whether they fought in a familiar or a strange arena.

* * * * *

and too indiscreet, we find: "He lets out light like a Carthaginian lamp." Terence took his metaphor from a cracked vase: "I am full of cracks, I leak from every side."' The quotations from Plautus (*Aulularia* 566) and Terence (*Eunuchus* 105) are both cited by Otto (1490 and 1543n).
1 Erasmus is using the Milan 1499 edition of the *Suda*: ἐπὶ τῶν ζ λαχόν-των 'about those who drew a "Z"'; later editions change this, following Photius (ἴσσα), to ἐπὶ τῶν ἀπολαχόντων 'about those who failed to draw a lot.'
2 Menander fragment 273 Körte-Thierfelder; the reference was added in 1515. The *Suda* is still reproducing Photius.
3 Martianus Capella *De nuptiis Philologiae et Mercurii* 3.261; added in 1515

61 Plautus *Menaechmi* 15
1 A *choenix* is a measure that holds one day's ration; see *Adagia* I i 2 line 56.
2 *Adagia* II i 87

62 *Collectanea* no 387, which gives Poliziano (*Epistolae* 12.5) as its source.
1 Cf Pliny *Letters* 6.12.2 'in my own arena, that is, in the centumviral court,' quoted in *Adagia* I ix 83 To descend into the arena.

63 **In saltu uno duos apros capere**
   To capture two boars in one copse

To capture two boars in one copse, means to catch two people in the same
way in the same action. Plautus in the *Casina*:

> Now I shall capture two boars neatly in one copse.[1]

64 **Ignis ad torrem**
   Fire to a torch

Πῦρ ἐπὶ δαλὸν ἐλθόν, Fire meeting a torch. Said of a deal which is speedily
and easily completed, like fire jumping spontaneously to a torch because
of the dryness of the materials. Recalled by Diogenianus. It would be the
same as saying 'Fire to naphtha,'[1] for naphtha is a type of pitch to which
fire jumps, even across a wide gap.

65 **Hippolytum imitabor**
   I shall imitate Hippolytus

Ἱππόλυτον μιμήσομαι, I shall imitate Hippolytus. In his collections of
proverbs Diogenianus says this was customarily said of those who had resolved to live pure and chaste lives. The legend is well known from Euripides or Seneca[1] of how this youth, out of hatred for the female sex, devoted
himself entirely to the service of Diana, despising the power of Venus. This
is how he speaks in Euripides:

> I declare that I shall take no pleasure in your Venus for a long time.[2]

*****

63 *Collectanea* no 74; Plautus (see n1 below). Otto 124; cf Tilley в 400 To hit two
   birds with one stone.
 1 Plautus *Casina* 476

64 Diogenianus 7.82
 1 Erasmus may have got this idea from Pliny *Naturalis historia* 2.235.

65 Diogenianus 5.32
 1 Seneca *Hippolytus* or *Phaedra*, especially lines 525–64
 2 Euripides *Hippolytus* 113

66 Nihil agere
To achieve nothing

Suidas quotes this line from a play by Cratinus called *Horae*: 'And someone doing these things says he is achieving nothing.'[1] Suidas informs us
that underlying this there is a proverb which can be applied to people who
labour in vain. Among Latin speakers, likewise, people who undertake useless labour are 'doing nothing,' as in Terence: 'Besides, this achieves nothing.'[2] And the remark of Attilius is famous: 'It is more satisfying to be idle
than to achieve nothing.'[3]

67 Herculis cothurnos aptare infanti
To put Hercules' boots on a baby

To put Hercules' mask or boots on a baby is to treat very small matters with
very weighty means that are entirely inappropriate or unbecoming, as for
example if someone speaks of a trivial subject in the tragic style. In book
6, on the peroration, Quintilian says:

> For adopting these tragic tones in petty cases is like wanting to fit Hercules'
> mask and boots on babies.[1]

Plutarch recalls a saying of Agesilaus which is not very different from this.
When some sophist was being commended to him because he made the
smallest matters seem important by his oratorical skill, he said he did not

* * * * *

66 *Suda* T 173. In *Adagia* v ii 21 A man is not free unless he sometimes does nothing, Erasmus quotes Cicero *De oratore* 2.24 'When will you be doing nothing?'
   and refers to the current adage as demonstrating a different meaning.
1 PCG 4 Cratinus fragment 272; the Greek as now restored is ταῦτ᾽ αὐτὰ πράσσω
   φάσκ᾽ ἀνὴρ οὐδὲν ποιῶν ' "I am doing these very things," said a man who was
   doing nothing.'
2 *Caeterum hoc nihil agit*; probably from Terence *Adelphoe* 167: *Ceterum hoc nihil
   facis*, which J. Sargeaunt (Loeb) translates: 'What? No regard for what I say?'
   Erasmus' alteration brings the text closer to the well-known *Nihil agis* 'It's no
   use,' as in Horace *Satires* 1.9.15.
3 Pliny *Letters* 1.9.8; cf Erasmus *Apophthegmata* VIII Attilius 25 LB IV 358 AB; Tilley
   N 281 It is better to be idle than to work for nothing

67 *Collectanea* no 781 To fit big shoes on a small foot. Otto 1387; and cf 297.
1 Quintilian 6.1.36

think a cobbler was good if he put a big shoe on a small foot,[2] meaning that speech should be adapted to the subject, just as clothes should be fitted to the body.

68 Grues lapidem deglutientes
Cranes that swallow a stone

Αἱ γέρανοι λίθους καταπεπωκυῖαι, Cranes that swallow stones. Suidas quotes this from Aristophanes stating that it was said of those who conduct their business with the greatest forethought, and that it entered into popular speech because cranes, since they fly at a great height and at great speed and cannot look downwards, have the habit of carrying stones which they drop, if they begin to get tired as they fly; by this means apparently they can tell from the noise of the falling stones whether they are flying over land or over the sea. If the stone falls into the sea they carry on their way, but if on land they stop to rest.[1] Pliny relates things very like this in book 10 chapter 23. He says: 'They agree when they will set out. They fly at a great height so that they can see far ahead; they choose a leader whom they can follow. At the end of the line they post birds by turns who utter cries and keep the flock together. At night time they have sentries who hold a stone in their claw; this betrays their inattention by the noise of its fall if they relax in sleep. The others sleep with their heads under their wings and standing first on one foot then on the other. The leader, with head raised, keeps watch and gives warning.'[2] Shortly after Pliny says: 'It is known that when they are about to cross the Black Sea they seek first of all the narrowest point, between the two promontories of Criumetopon [Cape Sarich] and Carambis [Cape Inca], then take on a ballast of sand. When they have passed the mid-point of the sea, they drop the stones, and

* * * * *

2 Plutarch *Moralia* 208c *Apophthegmata laconica*; cf Erasmus *Apophthegmata* 1 Agesilaus 5 LB IV 94B.

68 *Suda* Γ 184, whom Erasmus follows for everything down to the reference to Pliny (and accepting apparently the nonsense about the sound of the falling stones)
1 Aristophanes *Birds* 1137, but the *Suda* is also quoting the scholiast (Dübner pages 235–6).
2 Pliny *Naturalis historia* 10.58–59. For a different (and incorrectly derived) reason for the cranes' alleged habit see *Adagia* III vii 1 A dung beetle hunting an eagle (194 with n92 below).

when they reach the continent the sand from their throats as well.'[3] This
is what Pliny says. The passage which Suidas quotes is in Aristophanes'
Birds:

> There came some thirty thousand cranes
> From the shores of Africa, having swallowed huge
> Stones ...[4]

The scholiast has the same to say on this passage as Suidas.

69 Fortuna aestuaria
Fortune is like a tidal channel

Τύχη Εὔριπος, Fortune is Euripus,[1] or changeable, because she is accustomed
to favour now this one now that in turn. About her Boethius says: 'Carried
like the boiling tide of Euripus.'[2] We have spoken of the sea of Euripus
elsewhere.[3] Just as the sea has its tidal flows and ebbs, so nothing in human
affairs is permanent. No sea, however, changes its flow more frequently
or more swiftly than Euripus. Pindar in the third Pythian ode took his
metaphor from the winds: 'It is right, when it happens, to accept benefits
from the gods. For the rest, at other times the winds blow other ways. The
happiness of mortals does not come to stay for long.'[4] The scholiast quotes
some lines of Euripides: 'Nay rather, even disasters can be eclipsed for
men, / And blasts of wind do not always keep their force.'[5]

* * * * *

3 Pliny *Naturalis historia* 10.60; added in 1526
4 Aristophanes *Birds* 1136–7

69 *Suda* T 1234; cf Apostolius 3.18, Zenobius (Aldus) column 34 (under Ἄνθρωπος
  Εὔριπος).
1 Any tidal channel, but particularly the narrow strait between Boeotia and
  Euboea, notorious for its frequent and unpredictable changes of tidal currents.
  See *Adagia* I ix 62 Man's a Euripus.
2 Boethius *Consolation of Philosophy* 2 metrum 1.2
3 *Adagia* I ix 62 Man's a Euripus, where Τύχη Εὔριπος and the verse from
  Boethius are mentioned. The whole of the remainder is an addition of 1526,
  which was possibly inspired by the extended use Erasmus made of the image
  in a letter of 1524 to Archbishop Warham (Ep 1504).
4 Pindar *Pythians* 3.103–5
5 Euripides *Hercules Furens* 101–2

70 Fores aperire
To open doors

Ἀνοίγειν τὴν θύραν. Someone was said 'To open doors' if he revealed the way into some matter or its beginning. The elder Pliny in book 2 chapter 8: 'Anaximander of Miletus is said to have understood its obliquity,[1] that is, to have opened the doors of this science.'[2] Plutarch indicated this was a proverb in the second decade of his 'Table-talk': 'Unwisely, Firmus, instead of the proverbial door you have opened up the world to your own undoing.'[3] 'To open a window' is found in this particular sense in Terence.[4]

71 Tua res agitur, cum proximus ardet paries
It is your concern when next door's wall is burning

Nowadays[1] too this is commonly heard from ordinary people, that it is time for us to beware when the neighbour's house is burning. The proverb warns us to learn from the example of another's misfortune, and to take thought for our own concerns when others are in danger. It comes from Horace's *Epistles*: 'Do you feel any danger about to come upon you soon? / For it is your concern when next door's wall is burning.'[2] And Virgil: 'Even now his neighbour Ucalegon blazes.'[3]

72 Fontibus apros, floribus austrum
Pigs to springs, the south wind to flowers

There is no doubt that this, which is in Virgil's *Eclogues*, belongs to the

* * * * *

70 *Collectanea* no 160. Pliny (n2 below) and the Greek from Plutarch (n3 below)
  1 That is, the obliquity of the zodiac or of the earth's axis
  2 Pliny *Naturalis historia* 2.31 = Anaximander 12 Diels-Kranz A 5
  3 Plutarch *Moralia* 636F *Symposiaca*
  4 Terence *Heautontimorumenos* 481. In *Adagia* I iv 3 To open a window, Erasmus states that this is always used in a bad sense; Terence's full expression is 'What a window onto wickedness you will have opened'; quoted by Otto page 133n.

71 *Collectanea* no 156. Horace (see n2 below). Otto 1343
  1 Latin *hodiernis temporibus*; cf S. Singer *Sprichwörter des Mittelalters* II (Bern 1946) no 109.
  2 Horace *Epistles* 1.18.82–4
  3 Virgil *Aeneid* 2.311–12; translation by H. Rushton Fairclough (Loeb)

72 *Collectanea* nos 812 and 811. Virgil (see n1 below). Cf *Adagia* IV ii 19 To allow boars in springs (512 below).

category of proverbs: 'Alas, alas! what wish, poor wretch, has been mine? Madman, I have let in the south wind to my flowers, and boars to my crystal springs!'[1] Used when someone makes choices that will be harmful. For the wind is the greatest enemy of flowers, especially the south wind because of its violence.

73 Ollaris Deus
An earthenware god

Χυτρεοῦς θεός, An earthenware god. A jibe at a poor man of despised condition. Aristophanes says in the *Clouds*: 'When I thought you too, a piece of earthenware, were a god.'[1] The great gods were sculptured in ivory, gold, and silver. But the ordinary gods, the petty ones, such as Silenus and Priapus, were portrayed in any sort of material – wood, sometimes, and clay – the same costly material[2] as pots are made of. Hence it can be applied quite aptly to one who seeks to be accepted among the greatest courtiers but has no power through wealth nor influence with the prince through authority. It is akin to this one: 'Blue pimpernel too is a vegetable';[3] or this one: 'Nothing sacred.'[4] It is recorded in the *Collectanea* of Zenodotus.[5]

74 Oetaeus genius
The Oetaean spirit

Οἰταῖος δαίμων, The Oetaean spirit. Diogenianus says that this spirit had a passionate hatred of brutality and arrogance and would not allow them

* * * * *

1 Virgil *Eclogues* 2.58–9; translation by H. Rushton Fairclough (Loeb)

73 Apostolius 18.44; *Suda* X 617 who follows the scholiast of Aristophanes (Dübner page 134)
1 Aristophanes *Clouds* 1474; added in 1526 from the *Suda*; remainder from 1515.
2 Literally silver: *quo ... argento* is an imitation of a similar ironical use of the phrase *eodem argento* in Ovid *Metamorphoses* 8.668–9.
3 *Adagia* I vii 21
4 *Adagia* I viii 37 You're nothing sacred
5 The reference of this sentence is confused; since Χυτρεοῦς θεός is not in Zenobius, it could be either of the two adages just mentioned (Zenobius 4.57 and 5.47). At this point Erasmus has omitted the verb of the second one and translated *Nihil sacri*, giving a rather different meaning to that which he gave in *Adagia* I viii 37.

74 Diogenianus 7.23 (= Apostolius 12.42); appeared twice in editions from 1508 to 1528 as *Adagia* III i 5 and III vi 74. It does not seem to occur to Erasmus that

to go unavenged. Hence haughty and impetuous people were threatened with the Oetaean spirit. The published *Collectanea*[1] attribute the proverb to the writer Clearchus.[2] However, Oeta is a mountain close to Trachis,[3] and there is a city of the Melienses[4] of the same name. So the application of this proverb will be similar to 'The Temessian spirit will be there.'[5]

75 Vel hosti miserandus
To be pitied even by an enemy

Suidas quotes the following words from an unnamed author: 'As the proverb has it, even an enemy would have taken pity, if he had seen the present state of the man.' This is a hyperbole, for an enemy is not easily moved to pity. Virgil in book 12: 'A hand to be pitied even by Priam.'[1] And in book 2: 'What Myrmidon or Dolopian or soldier of stern Ulysses could in telling such a tale refrain from tears?'[2] Very similar to 'What even Momus himself would approve.'[3]

76 Aequales calculi
Votes equal

Ἴσαι ψῆφοι, Votes equal, said whenever someone is close to being condemned and yet is acquitted, or when the mind wavers and hesitates about which way to turn for reasons which persuade and dissuade equally one

* * * * *

this expression might be linked with *Oetaeus deus* 'the Oetaean god,' that is, Hercules (see n3 below and Propertius 4.1.32, Ovid *Ibis* 347, Seneca *Hercules Oetaeus*).
1 That is, Zenobius (Aldus) column 128 (= Zenobius 5.44 and Zenobius [Athous] 3.100)
2 Clearchus fragment 65 Wehrli
3 Trachis in Thessaly; Hercules built his funeral pyre on Mount Oeta, now Mt Kumayta.
4 Stephanus Byzantinus page 487 Meineke; Melis or Malis is the district in Thessaly in which Mt Oeta stands. There was a second Trachis in Phocis on Mt Helicon.
5 *Adagia* I i 88, which Erasmus interprets as meaning that whatever is taken by illegal means will have to be repaid with interest

75 *Suda* Π 1242; quoted as a proverb by Polybius 38.16.7
1 Virgil *Aeneid* 11.259 (not book 12)
2 Virgil *Aeneid* 2.6–8; translation by H. Rushton Fairclough (Loeb)
3 *Adagia* I v 74 To satisfy Momus, and the like

76 *Suda* I 623

way or the other. Such as in Terence: 'When the mind is in doubt, a small impulse pushes it one way or the other.'[1] Suidas declares that the metaphor is taken from the ancient custom of the courts whereby an accused man was acquitted if the judges' votes were equal, but was still at risk.[2] In one of his *Problems* Aristotle gives many reasons why the ancients thought that an accused should be acquitted rather than condemned when the votes were equal.[3] For it seemed appropriate for many reasons that, all other things being equal, the accused should be favoured rather than the accuser. In the first place the accuser comes prepared and with forethought, while the accused is obliged to answer many unforeseen questions. Then it is generally agreed that the accused, being the one who is at greater risk in speaking, is more likely to leave certain things out through fear than the accuser. Then again in an uncertain matter it is important to lean towards the solution where, if there is a mistake, there is less wrong. It is a lesser evil to acquit the guilty than to condemn the innocent, especially in capital cases where, if it happens that the judge errs, there is no way in which he can mend his mistake for the future, once the man has been executed. On the other hand, if a guilty man is released, he can be punished in another trial. Finally an accusation is more liable to the suspicion of malice than a defence, so that, since in other respects there is no apparent means of discrimination, we judge harshly of the accuser rather than of the accused. This, with a few other such things, is what Aristotle has to say. Therefore, just as the one absolutely sure to be released from the accusation is the one who is acquitted by unanimous vote, so the closest to danger seems to have been the one who is released by a sort of special favour because the votes were equal.

77 Lusciniae deest cantio
A nightingale without a song

A nightingale without a song. A proverbial allegory, just the same as if you say, 'A woman without words,' 'A poet without verses,' 'An orator without ornaments,' 'A sophist without quibbles.' For no bird equals it in

* * * * *

1 Terence *Andria* 266
2 'Still at risk' (*at non citra periculum*) seems to contradict what precedes. Erasmus may have been misled by a following item in the *Suda* (I 625, also headed Ἴσαι ψῆφοι): 'There is a hyperbolic expression "may he be done for (or, perish) even if the votes are equal." For when the votes were equal, the accused was acquitted.' If he read this quickly with the preceding, he may have thought there was still some danger even when a man was acquitted by equal votes.
3 Aristotle *Problemata* 29.13 (951a20–35)

77 *Collectanea* no 85 from Plautus (see n3 below). Otto 991

melodiousness; even the female nightingale is more melodious than any other bird, as Pliny attests in book 10 chapter 29. But it would not be at all inappropriate to set out here his own words:

> The nightingale – not, after all, a bird of notable appearance – sings its chattering song for fifteen successive days and nights as the leaf-buds thicken. On the one hand there comes such a powerful voice from such a tiny body, such a long breath; on the other a sound modulated and uttered in complete mastery of music. Now it is drawn out in length in one continuous breath, now varied with inflections, now marked off staccato, linked with a turn; it is prolonged, withheld, unexpectedly hushed. Sometimes she[1] murmurs, or is full, deep, high, rapid, slow; trilling notes, when this seems right, high, middle, low. And in short, in these tiny throats everything that the art of men has devised with the elaborately wound pipes of the flute.[2]

Plautus in the *Bacchis Sisters*: 'In truth, I too am afraid the nightingale may lose its song.'[3]

78 Ego ex bono in bonum traductus sum
I have been led from one good to another

Ἐγὼ μὲν ἐκ τοῦ καλοῦ εἰς καλὸν μετήνεγκα, I have indeed gone[1] from one good to another. Suidas tells us this used to be said of those who exchange one good occupation for another. He implies that it arose from someone who was a good cithara-player and then became a tragic poet. Poetry is very akin to the art of music, which is why Terence called poetry music.[2] The source of the adage is Aristophanes' *Frogs*.[3]

* * * * *

1 Erasmus' text has *ipsa* 'she,' as is consistent with the text of Pliny he was using, but the accepted reading is now *ipse* (masculine to agree with *sonus* 'sound').
2 Pliny *Naturalis historia* 10.81–2; added in 1515
3 Plautus *Bacchides* 38

78 *Suda* E 154, Zenobius (Aldus) columns 73–4, from the scholiast of Aristophanes *Frogs* 1298–9 (Dübner page 309)
1 Latin *transii*; Estienne (LB II 864) remarks: μετήνεγκα does not mean *transii* 'I have gone' or *traductus sum* 'I have been led' ... but *traduxi* 'I have brought, or led across.' ASD comments that Erasmus often understands the transitive μετήνεγκα as intransitive.
2 Terence *Phormio* 17
3 Aristophanes *Frogs* 1298–9, where B.B. Rogers (Loeb) translates 'From noblest source for noblest ends I brought them'

79 Anguillas captare
To hunt eels

Ἐγχέλεις θηρᾶσθαι. People are said 'To hunt eels' when they stir up trouble
for the sake of a private advantage. The metaphor arises from the fact that
those who hunt eels catch nothing if the water remains still, only when they
stir the water up and down and thoroughly muddy it do they catch them.
It will be suitable for those for whom there is no profit when the nation is
in a peaceful state. Therefore they are glad if rebellions arise whereby they
can turn the state's public disaster to their private advantage. The proverb
is found in Aristophanes' *Knights*:

> For your case is like those who hunt for eels[1]
> When the fen remains still, they come away with no fish,
> But if they stir the mud up and down,
> They make catches; thus you yourself make catches when you make public
>   trouble.[2]

This art, alas, is understood only too well by certain princes,[3] who, because
of their desire for power, sow discord between states or stir up war on some
pretext so that they can more freely tax the wretched common people and
satisfy their greed by starving absolutely innocent citizens.

80 Ego faciam omnia more Nicostrati
I shall do everything as Nicostratus did

Ἐγὼ ποιήσω πάντα κατὰ Νικόστρατον, I shall do everything as Nicostratus
did. Said of whatever is extraordinary. For this Nicostratus is said to have

* * * * *

79 *Suda* E 174, from the scholiast of Aristophanes *Knights* 865 (Dübner page 65);
cf Zenobius (Aldus) column 73 Ἐγχέλεις θηρώμενος 'hunting eels.'
1 In Greek: ἐγχέλεις θηρώμενοι
2 Aristophanes *Knights* 864–7
3 This passage, added in *1517/18*, is to be compared with *Adagia* III iii 1 The
Sileni of Alcibiades, with I ix 12 To exact tribute from the dead, and with
III vii 1 A dung-beetle hunting an eagle (178 below). Erasmus replaced the
expression 'certain princes' with 'princes of these times' in *1533*; this may
be put alongside other cases of progressive watering-down of particular references (see the introductory note to III vii 1 by the editors of ASD II-6
395–7).

80 *Suda* E 155 and N 405; Zenobius (Aldus) column 74

been a comic actor with the sort of reputation Roscius[1] had among the Romans. So he became proverbial in popular language because of his fame as an artist.[2] It is Suidas who describes it as a proverb.

81 Duplex cappa
Double kappa

Διπλοῦν κάππα, Double kappa, that is, a riddle by which some evil is signified, for κακά 'evils' is written as two kappas. Using a similar figure Plautus called a thief 'a three-letter man.'[1]

82 Tria cappa pessima
Nothing worse than three 'C's

Τρία κάππα κάκιστα, Nothing worse than three 'C's. This too was formerly spoken as a riddle in which the customs of three peoples were censured, the Cappadocians, the Cretans and the Cilicians.[1] In his *Rules of Grammar* Augustine tells us it was shifted to mean Cornelius Sulla, Cornelius Cinna and Cornelius Lentulus.[2] And it was believed that in the Sybilline books the names of these three men were designated by these three letters.[3] The Greek forms the ending of a heroic verse.

* * * * *

1 For Roscius' artistry and popularity see Cicero *Brutus* 290, *De oratore* 1.130 and 1.258, *Pro Archia* 8.17. Cf *Adagia* IV vii 69 Roscius, and Otto 1553.
2 Following the *Suda*, but with the reference to Roscius inserted by Erasmus. There were two comic poets named Nicostratus, not distinguished in the *Suda*, neither of whom survives in anything but recorded titles or appears otherwise to be known as an actor.

81 *Suda* Δ 1261 and K 324; cf Apostolius 6.25A.
1 Plautus *Aulularia* 325–6: the word for 'thief' is *fur*; also quoted in *Adagia* II viii 89 A three-letter man, where the expression is initially described as meaning someone with unjustified pretensions.

82 *Suda* Δ 1262 and K 324. Otto 888
1 Following the *Suda*. The translation adopted here is that of Sir Roger Mynors and D.F.S. Thomson in Ep 903.
2 Augustine *Regulae*; see H. Keil *Grammatici Latini* v page 501 line 27.
3 Following Augustine. Cf Cicero *In Catilinam* 3.9; Sallust *Catilinae coniuratio* 47.2.

83 Temulentus dormiens non est excitandus
Let a sleeping drunk lie

Proverbial in appearance is this advice given by Theognis, that a sleeping
drunk should not be woken from his sleep. It is very similar to 'Do not disturb a well concealed evil.'[1] You should not reawaken the hatred of someone whom time has already persuaded to forget. You should not reopen a
wound in the mind which a scar has already begun to cover. Theognis' ode
goes like this:

> Do not drive away slumber from any one of us, Simonides,
>   Whom deep[2] Sleep holds stifled with wine.[3]

84 Utroque nutans sententia
Wavering both ways in his opinion

Δίσχωλοι γνῶμαι, Swaying both ways in his opinion, or, A mind turning
this way and that. This is how I think it must be read: δίσχωλος with an
omega (ω), so that it means 'swaying both ways.'[1] In the published editions[2]
I find it spelled with an *omicron* (o).[3] It will be applicable then to a man
of slippery faith and uncertain allegiances, one whom this line of Homer
fits: 'He has a wavering gait and he totters on both feet.'[4] It is reported by
Zenodotus.

* * * * *

83 Theognis (see n3 below)
1 *Adagia* I i 62
2 The Greek is μαλθακός 'soft,' 'gentle,' which Erasmus has translated *altus*
  'deep.'
3 Theognis 469–70

84 Zenobius 3.25; cf Diogenianus 4.32, Apostolius 6.18
1 Erasmus invented the word δίσχωλοι in *1515* from δισ 'twice,' 'double,' and
  χωλός 'lame,' 'limping.' Zenobius has δίχολοι (Zenobius [Aldus] column 71
  δίσχολοι) which was reproduced by Erasmus in *1508* with the translation
  Utroque versatilis sententia 'Opinion turning both ways.'
2 Ie Zenobius (Junta 1497) and Zenobius (Aldus 1505)
3 'This ... omicron (o)' was added in *1515*.
4 Homer *Iliad* 13.281; added in *1528*. The description applies in Homer to the behaviour of a coward. The translation of A.T. Murray (Loeb) reads: 'He shifteth
  from knee to knee and resteth on either foot.'

85 Dictum ac factum
Said and done

Ῥεχθὲν καὶ πραχθέν, Said and done. A proverbial figure which signifies that nothing has been omitted in taking care of an affair. Terence: 'I have carried it out, said and done.' Donatus, in his commentary on the *Andria* asserts this is a proverb for speed: 'He will have found some cause, no sooner said than done.'[1] Again in the *Self-Tormentor*: 'Clitipho went in there, no sooner said than done.'[2]

And how familiar is this figure of speech in the Greek poets: 'Neither said nor done,' for what is in no way true.[3] In the *Iliad* book 1 Homer has: 'Neither a good word nor a deed has ever come from you.'[4] Euripides in the *Hecuba*: 'As for you, do not stand in my way / Either by word or by deed . . .'[5] In the opposite sense, those who are skilful and energetic in every respect, are said to avail 'in words and deeds.' According to Homer Phoenix taught Achilles thus: 'To be both a speaker of words and a doer of deeds.'[6] Likewise Pindar[7] in the first *Nemean Ode*: 'But your character has the use of one and the other.' This was preceded by: 'For strength displays itself in action, but intelligence in counsel.'[8]

86 De grege illo est
He is from that flock

He is from that flock, He belongs to that party or group. Terence in the

* * * * *

85 *Collectanea* no 559. Otto 529. According to ASD the Greek version is by Erasmus who wrote ῥεχθέν 'done' instead of ῥηθέν or ῥεθέν 'said.'
 1 Donatus on Terence *Andria* 382, ed Wessner (Teubner) I 139; added in *1515*
 2 Terence *Heautontimorumenos* 760 and 904. Although he distinguishes the idea of full completion from that of speed, Erasmus uses the same construction with *ac* as Terence, whose three examples of *dictum ac factum* would seem to be more appropriate for *Adagia* II ix 72 *Simul et dictum et factum*, No sooner said than done.
 3 Homer *Odyssey* 15.375
 4 Homer *Iliad* 1.108
 5 Euripides *Hecuba* 372–3
 6 Homer *Iliad* 9.443; translation by A.T. Murray (Loeb); Erasmus gives no Latin at this point.
 7 Pindar *Nemeans* 1.29–30 and 1.26–7
 8 'In the opposite sense . . . counsel' was all added in *1526*.

86 Terence *Adelphoe* 362; used as an example in *Adagia* III v 44 Of the same flour (94 above), and quoted by Otto 643

Adelphoe says: 'But this one, by Hercules, is from that flock'; and in the
Eunuchus: 'So that you will accept me into your flock.'[1] Marcus Tullius
in his *Letters to Atticus* has: 'But I wish you had returned to your old
flock';[2] and in the first speech against Verres: 'Whom he will find as the
fourth one I cannot see, unless perhaps it is one of that herd of orators,[3] who demanded to support the prosecution ...'[4] In the fourth action against the same man he used *de illo conventu* 'from that gang' in the
same sense: 'A certain Turpio, his scout and spy, was the basest man of
all the informers from that gang.'[5] He was alluding[6] to what we have described elsewhere as ἀτιμαγελεῖν.[7] Flaccus, too, says: 'Enrol him in your circle, and believe him brave and good.'[8] But this expression is often used
in a good sense too.[9] St Jerome says in his second book *Against Jovinian*:
'They are from your herd. Yes, they go around grunting among your citizens.'[10] Marcus Tullius calls friends and those belonging to the same society 'members of the herd,' as in the speech to the pontiffs in defence of
his house: 'What you used to say about me to the members[11] of Catilina's
herd.'[12]

* * * * *

1 Terence *Eunuchus* 1084
2 Cicero *Ad Atticum* 6.1.10
3 Latin *oratorum*; the modern reading is *moratorum* 'people who delay,' 'obstruc-
   tionists.'
4 Cicero *In Q. Caecilium* 49 (not called *Verrines* 1 in modern editions); added in
   1533
5 Cicero *Verrines* 2.2.7.22. L.H.G. Greenwood (Loeb) translates *conventu* as 'district.'
6 This refers to the quotation from Cicero *Ad Atticum* above (see n2), but it
   has become separated from it by the addition in 1533 of everything in between.
7 See *Adagia* I i 43 lines 30–45 where Erasmus explains Theodorus of Gaza's
   translation of the word (*coarmentari*) as referring to the social behaviour of
   bulls out of the mating season when away from the females.
8 Horace *Epistles* 1.9.13; translation by H. Rushton Fairclough (Loeb); added in
   1520
9 This sentence and the next are also additions of 1533. 'This expression' therefore refers to *ex illo conventu* in the extract from Cicero *Verrines* 2 (n5 above).
   One may suppose with ASD that the quotation from Horace introduced by *Sic
   et Flaccus*, being the only example of use in a good sense, should follow this
   sentence.
10 Jerome *Adversus Iovinianum* 2.36 PL 23 334A
11 Erasmus' text has *Quod vos ad Catilinae gregales de me dicere solebatis*. The ac-
    cepted reading is *Quod vos, Catilinae gregales, de me dicere solebatis* 'What you,
    the cronies of Catiline, used to say about me.'
12 Cicero *De domo sua* 75; added in 1536

87 Dentata charta
A document with teeth

Language is said to 'have teeth' when it is biting and witty. Marcus Tullius in the second book of letters to his brother:

> I shall deal with the matter with a good pen and well-mixed ink, and in a document that has teeth.[1]

Seneca does not want jokes to be cutting.[2] On the other hand things that are 'toothless'[3] are things which lack bite.

88 Daulia cornix
A Daulian crow

Δαυλία κορώνη, A Daulian crow, is what the poets call a nightingale, either because Tereus lived with Philomena in Phocian Daulis or because it was there that she was changed into the bird.[1] I cannot see what the adage might mean, unless perhaps it is used of talkative people or those given to singing. I am more inclined to suspect that Zenodotus (whether this is Zenobius or someone else) pretended this was a proverb[2] so that he could

* * * * *

87 Cicero (see n1 below)
1 Cicero *Ad Quintum fratrem* 2.15B.1. Erasmus was apparently unaware (as was Estienne judging by the absence of a note) that here the expression means 'polished papyrus' (polished with a boar's tooth; see *Thesaurus linguae latinae*: *dentatus* 2); cf Epp 821 and 824.
2 *De formula honestae vitae* 4.8; also called *De quattuor virtutibus*. Not by Seneca, but by St Martin archbishop of Braga in the sixth century. See the note to *Adagia* III iv 45 (28 above).
3 Latin *edentula*, used of people by Plautus: *Mostellaria* 275, *Casina* 550, and, figuratively of wine, *Poenulus* 700; cf Jerome, source of *Adagia* III i 7 The toothless man looks askance at those who have teeth to eat with. Added in *1517/18*

88 Zenobius 3.14; Zenobius (Aldus) columns 66–7
1 Following Zenobius; in the older version of the legend, Philomela (it is Erasmus who has changed this to Philomena; LB corrects to Philomela) became a swallow and Procne, her sister, a nightingale; a reversal took place in the Latin tradition represented, for example, by Virgil *Georgics* 4.511 and Ovid *Metamorphoses* 6.424–674 where it is Procne who is Tereus' wife and becomes a swallow, and Philomela who becomes a nightingale. For fuller references see the note by Sir James Frazer in the Loeb edition of Apollodorus 3.14.8, who is the principal source of Zenobius.
2 In fact the expression goes back to a fragment of Aristophanes (PCG 3.2 Aristophanes fragment 936) quoted in the *Etymologicum magnum* 250.7–9.

introduce a story, something which I have a notion he did in several other cases.[3]

89 Cum Musis
With the Muses

Μετὰ Μουσῶν, With the Muses, that is with the favour of the Muses. Said of learned people or anything expressed in a learned manner, or, as Suidas asserts, of an illiterate man living among scholars, as an ironical expression.[1]

90 Amicos tragoedos aemulatur
He's imitating his tragic friends

Τοὺς ἑταίρους τραγῳδοὺς ἀγωνιεῖται, He's imitating his tragic friends. Suidas quotes this from Didymus, adding that it was said of people who were compliant and adopted stern morals in imitation of others. Derived from tragic actors who may be shallow good-for-nothings, but when they are taking the part of a god or a king in a play, they put on an appearance of majesty by means of dress, voice and gesture.[1]

91 Aesopicus graculus
Aesop's jackdaw

Αἰσώπειος κολοιός, Aesop's jackdaw.[1] This is said of someone who appropriates other people's goods for himself, or promotes himself with other

* * * * *

3 For a similar remark about 'Zenodotus' see *Adagia* III vi 36 (143 above).

89 *Suda* M 711. Cf Diogenianus 6.50, Zenobius (Aldus) column 119 and Apostolius 11.28 (μετὰ Μουσῶν κόρυδος 'A lark among the Muses').
1 Cf *Adagia* II ii 92 In tuneless company the lark can sing.

90 *Suda* T 833; cf Zenobius (Aldus) column 162. In *1508* Erasmus had ἑτέρους 'the others,' probably the correct reading from Harpocration T 19, and translated *Cum reliquis tragoedis decertat* 'He's competing with the other tragedians.' In *1533* he used the expression from Harpocration a second time as *Adagia* IV ix 64 He challenges the other tragedians, without suppressing this one.
1 The last sentence was added in *1515*.

91 *Collectanea* no 593. Lucian (see n2 below). Cf Otto 64 who, in addition to Lucian and Horace, cites uses by Jerome, Eusebius, and Tertullian surprisingly omitted by Erasmus.
1 Estienne has a long note (LB II 866) on whether κολοιός should not be translated *monedula* (modern dictionaries translate both this and *graculus* as 'jackdaw').

people's virtues. Lucian makes use of it in the *Pretended Critic*.[2] Horace has:

> The little crow inspires laughter
> When deprived of his stolen colours.[3]

The fable circulates among the others under Aesop's name.[4] Pindar in the third *Nemean Ode*: 'And it is no better for a man to foster greed for other people's goods; seek from your own resources.'[5] The poet is blaming himself for digressing and orders himself to praise the person he undertook to celebrate for his own virtues rather than for others.[6]

92 Aries cornibus lasciviens
A ram frisking with its horns

Κριὸς ἀσελγόκερως, A ram frisking with its horns. Diogenianus states that this is suitably used against wealthy and lustful people. The horns of well-fed rams itch, and the same happens to oxen. Virgil describing a bull calf being frisky:

> Already one who attacks with his horn and scatters the sand with his hooves.[1]

Hesychius indicates the origin of the proverb. In the temple of Pallas there was kept an immense bronze ram, which Plato the comic writer[2] said was 'frisking with its horns,' not so much because it was lascivious but because of its immense size, for it is comparable to the Wooden Horse. He says the ancients used ἀσελγές 'licentious,' 'extravagant' not only of what was frisky

* * * * *

Pliny *Naturalis historia* 10.77 makes a distinction which Estienne is inclined to maintain.
2 Lucian *Pseudologista* 5 ('his speech was after the fashion of Aesop's jackdaw, cobbled up out of motley feathers from others')
3 Horace *Epistles* 1.3.19–20
4 Aesop 101 Perry; Phaedrus 1.3. In the Aldine edition of 1505 it is among the verse fables ascribed to 'Gabrias' for whom see *Adagia* III ii 98 note.
5 Pindar *Nemeans* 3.30–1; added in 1526
6 Following the scholiast of Pindar on lines 51 and 53

92 Diogenianus 5.61 (= Apostolius 10.9)
1 Virgil *Aeneid* 9.629
2 PCG 7 Plato fragment 232

and untamed but of what was extraordinarily large, just as Eupolis said
ἄνεμος ἀσελγής[3] for 'a strong wind.'[4] These are torments for grammarians
who do not want to admit that this bronze ram might be formidable because
its horns were large. But what prevents us from saying even that the wind
is frisky and unrestrained, because it plays as it will, where it will? To me it
seems that the adage could also be suitably used about stupid people raised
to offices beyond their merits.

93 Ductus per phratores canis
A dog among the phratry members

Ἀγόμενος διὰ φρατόρων ὁ κύων, A dog among the phratry members. Said
when someone falls among those by whom he may be punished; for a dog
in these meetings is immediately killed. Among the Athenians the people
were divided into tribes, a third part of each tribe was called a *phratria* and
the leader of this the *phratriarchos*.[1] If a dog ran into their meetings, it was
at once attacked by the people.

94 Calabri hospitis xenia
Gifts of a Calabrian host

There appears to be a proverb underlying these lines of Horace in his
Epistles:

> 'Twas not in the way a Calabrian host invites you to eat his pears
> That you have made me rich.' 'Eat some, pray.'
> 'I've had enough.' 'Well take away all you please.' 'No, thanks.'
> 'Your tiny tots will love the little gifts you take them.'
> 'I'm as much obliged for your offer as if you sent me away loaded down.'
> 'As you please; you'll be leaving them for the swine to gobble up today.'[1]

* * * * *

3 PCG 5 Eupolis fragment 345
4 Hesychius K 4141 provides from 'In the temple' to here. All the rest was added
in *1528*.

93 *Collectanea* no 584. Diogenianus 2.45 (= Apostolius 1.20)
1 This sentence was added in *1515* from Harpocration Φ 26 or *Suda* Φ 693–4.

94 *Collectanea* no 421. Horace (see n1 below)
1 Horace *Epistles* 1.7.14–19; translation by H. Rushton Fairclough (Loeb)

So you could rightly call 'gifts of a Calabrian host' rustic and naïve things and things which are more of a burden than a pleasure to the receiver, or are despicable gifts. The Calabrians, having plenty of pears, were in the habit of setting them before their guests, then when they were sated they invited them to take them home as dessert. If you refused, they were thrown to the pigs. However this is not the giving of a gift but a throwing away of waste. The true giver is one who is aware of the value of the gift he is offering and of the merit of the person he gratifies with it. In Athenaeus, Antiochus is accorded the title of 'Illustrious,' because he used not so much to give away any surplus of money as to pour it away. Sometimes, standing in the public streets, he would say, 'This is for the one that chance gives it to'; then he would throw the money away and leave.[2]

95 In ostio formosus
'Good-looking' on the doorpost

Ἐν θύρᾳ καλός, 'Good-looking' on the doorpost. Said of those who are beloved and popular with the common people. Derived from the ancients' custom of writing the names of handsome men or lovers on trees, leaves or walls: 'So-and-so is good-looking.' Aristophanes alludes to this in the *Wasps*:

> But if, by Jupiter, Pyrilampus sees
> 'Demus is good-looking' written anywhere in a doorway,
> He hastens up and writes 'Cemus is good-looking'
> Next to it.[1]

And the same author in the *Acharnians*:

> Ὑμῶν ἐραστὴς ἦν ἀληθῶς, ὥστε καὶ
> Ἐν τοῖσι τοίχοις ἔγραφον, Ἀθηναῖοι καλοί

* * * * *

2 Athenaeus 10.438E, quoting the *Commentaries* of Ptolemy Euergetes, *FGrHist* 234 F 3; added in *1528*. Antiochus is Antiochus IV Epiphanes, Seleucid king 175–64 BC.

95 Aristophanes (see n1 below); not in CPG
1 Aristophanes *Wasps* 97–9. The editors of ASD remark that Erasmus' text is corrupt. Moreover he added his translation, in *1526*, without the help of the scholion (Dübner page 138) which would have told him that Demos is the son of Pyrilampes and that κημός means the funnel-shaped top of the voting urn in Athenian law-courts. Cf also Plato *Gorgias* 481D.

This man was never a false lover to you, for he had written[2]
'The Athenians are good-looking' on the walls of your buildings.[3]

There is one syllable too many in the second line of the Greek, but this is
what the Aldine edition[4] has. I suspect the order of the words should be
changed. It will be correct if you read it thus: Ἐν τοῖς ἔγραφον τοίχοις· Ἀθ-
ηναῖοι καλοί 'On the walls they wrote: "The Athenians are good-looking."'
Unless we prefer to read: Ἐν τοῖσι τοίχοις ἐγραφον· Ἀθῆναι καλαί 'On the
walls they wrote: "Athens is beautiful,"' as if it was to flatter the city that
they had written this on its walls. In Athenaeus book 6 it is related from
some unnamed author that those who governed the Athenian state flattered
the people by saying that everything else was the common property of the
Greeks but that this was peculiar to the Athenians that they knew the way
which led to heaven.[5] Anyone who has read the eulogies of Aeschines and
Meno in Plato[6] understands how handsome they made the Athenians out
to be, flattering them with marvellous oratorical skill. The scholiast quotes
this distichon from Callimachus:

> Inscribe here on these fronds as many letters
> As are necessary to recall that Cydippe is beautiful.[7]

Maro imitated this with:

> and carve my love on the young
> Trees. They will grow; thou too, my love, wilt grow.[8]

This adage could also be turned against those who are falsely praised for
flattery's sake, or against the thoroughly mendacious titles given to certain

* * * * *

2 Latin *scripserat*. Erasmus interprets the lines correctly though without guessing
the correct reading of the Greek (ἔγραφ· 'he wrote' singular). Both of the
following emendations, added in *1528*, are consequently mistaken.
3 Aristophanes *Acharnians* 143–4
4 The 1498 *editio princeps* by Marcus Musurus with the scholia but lacking the
Lysistrata and the *Thesmophoriazusae*
5 Athenaeus 6.250F, which in fact names Hegesander (fragment 9 *FHG* IV 415)
6 In Plato's *Meno* the eponymous figure is 'handsome' but not an Athenian. For
suggestions about whom Erasmus had in mind see ASD II-6:962–3n.
7 The scholiast of Aristophanes *Acharnians* 144 (Dübner page 7). Callimachus
Aetia 3 fragment 73 Pfeiffer
8 Virgil *Eclogues* 10.53–4; translation by H. Rushton Fairclough (Loeb)

princes, such as Father of his country, Delight of the earth, Beloved of the world, Most serene Highness, Renowned, Most merciful, when they are really just plunderers of the public estate.[9]

96 Caput scabere et consimilia
To scratch one's head, and similar phrases

Scratching one's head, gnawing one's nails, these are the gestures of one who is thoughtful and one who is thinking about making a change which he may regret. From gestures they become proverbial expressions, as in Horace's tenth satire, book 1: 'Yet, if fate had dropped him into our times, he would smooth away much of his work, would prune off all that trailed beyond the proper limit, and as he wrought his verse he would often scratch his head and gnaw his nails to the quick. Often you must turn your stilus to erase, if you hope to write something worth a second reading.'[1] Persius imitated this when he said: 'He does not thump his desk nor taste his torn nails.'[2] And the same author elsewhere: 'Choerestratus gnawing his nails to the quick says this.'[3] In the first passage he is criticizing poets' lack of care in writing; in the second he is describing a young man thinking of changing his past way of life.

97 Caricus hircus
A Carian goat

Καρικὸς τράγος, A Carian goat. Diogenianus indicates that this was applied to base and despicable people. Hesychius tells us it was used by Sophocles.[1] Because the Carian people commonly served as mercenary troops in wars and held life to be cheap, they became a byword of contempt. Hence Plato too said, 'Carian midget,' for someone who is worthless and of no account,

* * * * *

9 'This adage could' to the end added in 1517/18. Cf especially *Adagia* III vii 1 A dung-beetle hunting an eagle (178 below).

96 *Collectanea* no 240
1 Horace *Satires* 1.10.67–71; translation by H. Rushton Fairclough (Loeb), with slight modification
2 Persius 1.106
3 Persius 5.162–3

97 Diogenianus 5.48 (= Apostolius 9.52)
1 Hesychius K 821; Sophocles fragment 497 Nauck = 540 Pearson; added in 1528

as we have said elsewhere.[2] It is possible that the proverb derives from the fact that the Carians used to sacrifice a dog in place of a goat, as explained in the proverb 'A Carian victim.'[3]

98 Bullatae nugae
Trifles and bubbles

Language that is windy and senseless is said to be *bullata*, full of bubbles. The source of the metaphor is πομφόλυγοι 'bubbles in water,' which we have described elsewhere in the proverb 'Man is but a bubble.'[1] Persius says: 'that my page should swell with trifles and bubbles'[2] – what he calls 'trifles and bubbles' being a meaningless mass of noisy utterances in which there is no trace of solid sense. Horace used the expression 'melodious trifles' in his *Art of Poetry*:

> Than verses void of thought, melodious trifles.[3]

99 Bolus ereptus e faucibus
The morsel snatched from one's throat

We say 'The morsel snatched from one's throat' whenever some gain which was almost within our grasp is suddenly and unexpectedly snatched away. Terence in the *Self-Tormentor*: 'I am enraged that such a morsel is suddenly snatched from my jaws.'[1] He used *bolus* for what the Greeks call βλωμός 'a morsel of bread.'[2] The metaphor is clear enough.

* * * * *

2 *Adagia* I vi 14 Risk it on a Carian, where Erasmus refers to Plato's *Euthydemus* (285C) and translates ὥσπερ ἐν Καρί by *velut in homuncione Care* As in a Carian midget. Erasmus gives 'Carian midget' here in Greek: Καρικὸν ἀνθρώπιον; according to ASD Plato nowhere used this expression.
3 *Adagia* III ii 31. The sentence was added in *1528*.

98 *Collectanea* no 269. Persius (see n2 below)
1 *Adagia* II iii 48; Erasmus seems to be referring particularly to the third sentence for the physical description of a bubble: 'that round swollen empty thing which we watch in water as it grows and vanishes in a moment of time' (CWE 33 156).
2 Persius 5.19–20
3 Horace *Ars poetica* 322

99 *Collectanea* no 557. Otto 257
1 Terence *Heautontimorumenos* 673
2 Erasmus does not translate the Greek; cf *Adagia* III vii 50 (246 below).

100 Bene sit
May it be for the best

Καλῶς ἔστω, May it be for the best. A word of omen uttered when someone begins some new and difficult undertaking, as they used to say at the
beginning of wills:[1] Τοῦτο καλῶς ἔσται 'This will be for the best.' 'But if human nature takes its course ...'[2] Likewise in speeches: 'Let my words be
propitious and fortunate.'[3] The expression is likely to be more piquant if
used ironically about something ridiculous and of no moment as if it were
of the greatest importance, like Persius' rich miser about to open a wine-
jar: 'May this be for the best.'[4] Often found in literature is 'May this turn
out well' or 'May it turn out badly.' Virgil says in the *Bucolics*: 'We send
him these kids – our curse go with them!'[5] And 'May the gods bring good
fortune to what you do.'[6] Servius the grammarian thinks this figure is borrowed from Hector and Ajax, whose gifts brought ruin to each other.[7]

1 Scarabaeus aquilam quaerit
A dung-beetle hunting an eagle

Κάνθαρος ἀετὸν μαίεται, A dung-beetle hunting an eagle. Said when a weaker
and less powerful person seeks to do harm to a far more powerful enemy

* * * * *

100 Cf Suetonius *Domitian* 23.2 and *Adagia* III ii 79.
  1 For the testamentary formula, Ἔσται μὲν εὖ, see Diogenes Laertius 5.11 'Aris-
    totle' and 5.51 'Theophrastus.'
  2 Latin *Sed si quid acciderit humanitus*; a further example of a 'word of omen.'
    Cf Cicero *Philippics* 1.10 (*si quid mihi humanitas accidisset* translated by Walter
    C.A. Ker (Loeb): 'if anything that may befall humanity had happened to me')
    and Diogenes Laertius 10.21 'Epicurus' (Ἐὰν δέ τῶν ἀνθρωπίνων περὶ Ἑρμαρχον
    γένηται 'If anything to which humans are liable should happen to Hermarchus').
  3 Livy 1.17.10, 3.34.2, 3.54.8, 10.8.12, 24.16.9 (*Quod bonum, faustum felixque sit*);
    8.25.10 (*Quod bonum, faustum, felix ... esset*). Cicero *De divinatione* 1.102 (*Quod
    bonum, faustum, felix, fortunatumque esset*)
  4 Persius 4.30
  5 Virgil *Eclogues* 9.6; translation by H. Rushton Fairclough (Loeb)
  6 Terence *Phormio* 552, *Hecyra* 196–7
  7 Servius on Virgil *Eclogues* 9.6; according to Servius Hector gives Ajax the sword
    with which he will commit suicide (cf Sophocles *Ajax* 659–66), and Ajax gives
    Hector the belt by which his body will be dragged behind Achilles' chariot –
    only the exchange of gifts is in Homer (*Iliad* 7.303–5). Cf *Adagia* I iii 35 Gifts
    of enemies are no gifts.

  1 *Collectanea* no 581; Zenobius 1.20, Diogenianus 2.44. In *1508* the adage
    amounted to only 32 lines; the first part, corresponding to the twenty lines
    ending with the words 'heaven together,' was somewhat different from what

and lays an ambush for him. There is another reading, one that in my

* * * * *

is found after *1515*; the second part, consisting of the final quotation from
Aristophanes' *Peace* and the following paragraph, was almost the same as the
present conclusion.

The beginning of the 1508 version read: Κάνθαρος ἀετὸν μαιεύεται, A dung-
beetle hunting [see n1 below] an eagle. Said when a weaker and less powerful person seeks to do harm to a far more powerful enemy and lays an
ambush for him. For there is mutual hostility between the eagle, the king of
birds, and the dung-beetle, the meanest, vilest, most evil-smelling of insects,
which is born and gives birth in dung, and feeds on the same material. The
eagle gathers scarabs to eat and the scarab for its part invades eagles' nests
and by pushing the eggs to the edge tips them out. Aristophanes in the *Lysistrata*: Ὑπερχολῶ γὰρ αἰετὸν τίκτοντα κάνθαρός σε / Μαιεύσομαι 'For I am furiously angry; when you the eagle lay your eggs, I the dung-beetle will pursue
you.'

There is a fable [Aldus 1505 page 24; Aesop 3 Perry] about this: the scarab
was spurned on some occasion by the eagle and set himself to think of some
means of getting his revenge. He sought out where the eagle had sited her
nest, and crawled up to it secretly, for the eagle was quite unaware of such
a tiny creature. Working in the way this insect usually does, he pushed all
the eggs one by one to the edge and out of the nest. The eagle was much an-
noyed by this, and, since she did not know who was the author of her misfortune, moved the nest to a loftier spot. Here too the wicked beetle climbed and
tipped the eggs out by the same trick. However often she moved her home
the eagle could not win, and so she went to Jupiter, her lord, and told him of
her misfortune. The god ordered her to lay her eggs in his lap, for there they
would be safe. And here too, up the skirts and folds of his clothing, the per-
sistent beetle climbed, without being noticed by Jupiter. When finally Jupiter
saw the eggs being moved about but could not see what was doing it, he took
fright at the strange phenomenon, shook them out of his lap and dropped
them to the ground.

In converting this in *1515* to the present substantial satire on abuse of power,
Erasmus gave both eagle and scarab beetle quite new roles. The adage is
an extended allegory based on the Aesopic fable; this, if applied throughout
as Erasmus surely intended, leads to a view of the two contestants that is far
from a simple opposition of absolute power and oppressed innocence. The eagle becomes the portrait of the tyrant (though devious and obsequious when
dealing with a greater power), progressively generalized in later editions and
detached from the potentially dangerous, more particular references of *1515*
(see the introductory note ASD II-6 395–7 and, for example, n48 below). The
beetle, from being the 'meanest, vilest, most evil-smelling of insects,' persis-
tent and malicious, becomes at one moment a champion of the weak, something of a hero, a fighter of tyrants, then the 'leader' (*dux*), small certainly, but
tenacious and resourceful, of an ineradicable resistance to the nominal power,
and finally of 'little men, of the meanest sort but malicious nevertheless.' Although the portrait, like that of the eagle, is painted with a strong colouring
of irony, it is clear that the beetle has all the virtues of an effective general

judgment is more correct: Ὁ κάνθαρος ἀετὸν μαιεύεται[1] 'The dung-beetle is midwife to the eagle.' The meaning is almost the same whether you read μαίεται or μαιεύεται, for the adage is applicable to a weak and insignificant man who plots harm to someone far stronger by means of malicious traps and secret wiles. Aristophanes in the *Lysistrata*: 'I am furiously angry with you; when you the eagle lay your eggs, I shall be the dung-beetle serving as your midwife.'[2] On this subject there is a rather fine Greek fable, by Aesop according to Lucian, when he says in *Icaromenippus* that Aesop related how once upon a time the beetles and the camels went up to heaven together. As far as the story of the beetle and the eagle is concerned it goes like this:

> For a long time there has been, between the race of the eagles and the whole tribe of beetles an old hostility, a long-standing, absolutely deadly feud; in fact what the Greeks call a 'war without truce.'[3] For they hate each other more than

* * * * *

and politician, a dangerous, implacable, and ambitious enemy. Without going into the delicate question of particular contemporary references, we can say that there seems to be no question here of the beetle representing popular or democratic rights; his moment as champion of the hare is a 'point de départ' for his hatred and soon forgotten. He turns out to be, if not morally as reprehensible as the eagle, still malicious and at least as warlike, a portrait of the sort of hidden, ever-present and unrelenting opponent whom the monarch must be forever wary of and forever fighting. That this adage constituted some such warning for the young prince and future emperor Charles is plainly stated in Erasmus' contemporaneous *Institutio principis christiani* (CWE 27 211–12).

The new version was published separately, with the *Sileni Alcibiadis* (*Adagia* III iii 1) and the *Dulce bellum inexpertis* (*Adagia* IV I 1, 399 below), by Froben in May 1517 (Beatus Rhenanus had suggested publishing it with the *Moriae encomium* as early as April 1515 – Ep 318) and this was followed by further separate editions at Leuwen in September 1517, Leipzig 1521, Strasburg 1522, and [Cologne] 1524; it also appeared with Aesop's fables at Antwerp in 1521.

1 In the *Collectanea* and in *1508* Erasmus had accepted μαιεύεται 'to serve as midwife to' as found in Aristophanes (n2 below); it was the Latin translation, *quaerit*, which was at fault. Erasmus however tried to justify his Latin by introducing the Greek word μαίεται, to seek, which hardly gives 'almost the same' meaning.

2 Aristophanes *Lysistrata* 694–5: 'serving as your midwife' is μαιεύσομαι; translated by B.B. Rogers (Loeb) 'Nay, if one sour word ye say, I'll be like the midwife beetle, / Following till the eagle lay.' Erasmus translates *Supra modum irascor tibi . . .*

3 In Greek ἄσπονδος πόλεμος; see *Adagia* III iii 84 A truceless war, and the introductory note (CWE 34 422 84n).

people hated Vatinius;[4] so much in fact that not even Jupiter himself, 'who has the supreme power'[5] and 'at whose nod all Olympus trembles,'[6] has been able to settle the matter between them and put an end to their strife – if the fables tell the truth.[7]

In short, there was no more agreement between them than there is between our palace gods and humble, obscure folk nowadays. But perhaps someone, ignorant[8] of Aesop's fables or unfamiliar with them, will wonder what business a beetle could ever have with an eagle, what kinship, what similarity, what affinity there could be between two such different creatures; for it is between those who have close ties that enmity usually arises, especially between rulers. Besides, whatever could be the cause of such a terrible hatred? And then where did the beetle find courage enough to undertake without second thought a war with the eagle folk? What outrage offended the 'haughty spirit'[9] of the eagle so deeply that he did not treat such a petty enemy with contempt and deem it unworthy of even his hatred? Clearly this is a vast subject, the injury is of long standing, the subsequent history long and tangled too, and the whole matter is beyond human eloquence to explain. But if the Muses, who were not reluctant at one time to dictate to Homer the 'Battle of the Frogs and Mice,'[10] will condescend to leave Helicon for a moment and come to me, I shall try to give a complete account of the matter to the best of my ability. For nothing is too difficult for men to dare if the Muses help. But to provide a clearer light on the subject, before I come to the story itself, I shall describe in as few words as I can the habits, the appearance, the character, and the capabilities of the two protagonists.

First then it occurs to me to wonder what came into the heads of the Romans – sensible people in other respects. Having taken this bird as their symbol, they extol themselves above all other peoples and count themselves

* * * * *

4 Vatinius was a tribune and later consul, attacked by Cicero in one case but defended in another. Vatinius wrote *Ad familiares* 5.9 and 10. Cf *Adagia* II ii 94 Hate worthy of Vatinius, based on a phrase of Catullus 14.3.
5 Homer *Odyssey* 5.4, *Iliad* 2.118 and 9.25
6 Virgil *Aeneid* 9.106 and 10.115
7 Lucian *Icaromenippus* 10; Aesop 3 Perry
8 In Greek ἀνήκοος
9 In Greek θυμὸς ἀγήνωρ; Homer *Iliad* 12.300, referring to a lion
10 In Greek Βατραχομυομαχία 'Batrachomyomachia'; the text is in the Loeb edition of *Hesiod, The Homeric Hymns and Homerica*. Erasmus is echoing the preface of Statius' *Silvae*. See also Plutarch *Moralia* 873F *De Herodoti malignitate*.

closest to the gods, they win so many victories under its auspices and hold so many triumphs, yet far from being grateful to the well-deserving bird, they show an intolerable contempt for it. For this bird, of all birds the most masculine and most vigorous, they emasculate and castrate,[11] turn it into a sort of Tiresias,[12] thereby making themselves less masculine, for in Greek ἀετός is certainly masculine. And this, if I am not mistaken, is much more fitting for one to whom the supreme father and king 'of men and of gods'[13] 'gave dominion over the wandering birds, for Jupiter had found him trustworthy in the matter of flaxen-haired Ganymede.'[14] He alone dares hand to angry Jove his 'triple bolt'[15] while the other gods keep their distance; he is not frightened by the proverb 'Away from Jove and from the thunderbolt.'[16] With good reason, I think, from among so many nations of birds and so many tribes the eagle has been considered the most suitable candidate for the monarchy, not only by the 'brotherhoods'[17] of the birds but by the unanimous vote of the 'senate and people' of the poets. As far as the judgment of the birds is concerned, many were inclined to entrust the supremacy to the peacock; for kingship seemed to be its due because of its beauty, magnificence, exalted character, and quite regal loftiness. And the voting would have gone that way immediately if some birds with long experience, like the rooks and the crows, had not foreseen that, if they put the peacock in charge, things would turn out as we have seen for some years past in certain monarchies, namely that he would be king in name only and by the noise he made, and the eagle would rule just the same even without the popular vote. As for the poets, the wisest of men, I believe they realized that no better image to represent the conduct and life of kings could be conceived. I am speaking of most kings, not all (for in any field there always has been and always will be a scarcity of good people, and different times bring different men).[18]

But let me, if I may, look briefly at the dispute from the point of view of both parties. In the first place, if there is anything to be divined from a name (and there certainly is) the eagle is aptly called ἀετός in Greek, from

* * * * *

11 Because Latin makes *aquila* 'eagle' feminine
12 Ovid 3.323–31
13 Virgil *Aeneid* 1.229
14 Horace *Odes* 4.4.2–4
15 Ovid *Ibis* 469, *Metamorphoses* 2.848
16 *Adagia* I iii 96
17 *Phratrai*; cf *Adagia* III iv 34 (20 above) and III vi 93 (173 above).
18 The parenthesis was added in 1533.

ἀΐσσω, which means roughly 'to rush violently along,' 'to plunge rapidly.'[19] Some birds are quiet by nature and gentle, whilst some are wild but can be tamed and quietened by skill and training. The eagle alone is neither amenable to any training nor can be tamed by any effort. It is simply driven headlong by the force of instinct, and whatever it has conceived an appetite for it demands to be given. Would you like to see a picture of a chick of really aquiline spirit? It has been graphically painted by Horace:

> 'a winged servant of lightning ... Once youthfulness and inborn drive impel him, unaware of hardships, from the nest, and the spring winds, sweeping away the clouds, teach the startled bird their unaccustomed ways, then a swift dive sends him down to attack the sheep-folds, then love of feast and battle makes the writhing snakes his prey.'[20]

This enigmatic simile is better understood by territories that have experienced the many evils that such unbridled violence in young rulers has cost them.[21] It is philosophers who control their appetites and follow the guidance of reason in everything. 'But,' says the satirist, 'there is nothing more open to violence than the ear of a tyrant.'[22] He is always ready with these words: 'This is what I want; this is what I order; let my will be the reason.'[23] Then, while there are six kinds of eagle known,[24] they all have in common a sharply hooked beak and no less sharply hooked claws, so that from the physical characteristics you can see the bird is a carnivore, an enemy of peace and quiet, born for fighting, rapine, and plunder. And as if it were not enough to be carnivores, there are some that are called bone-crushers[25] – and well they may be.

But at this point, dear reader, I hear immediately your unspoken question: what has this picture to do with a king whose proper claim to glory

* * * * *

19 *Etymologicum magnum* 20.54
20 Horace *Odes* 4.4.1 and 5–12
21 This sentence was added in *1517/18*.
22 Juvenal 4.86, quoted from memory; Juvenal says: 'What is more open ...'
23 Juvenal 6.223
24 The following account of eagles and their habits down to 'its fortress' (190 below) is based on Aristotle *Historia animalium* 8(9).32–4 (618b18–620a12) and Pliny *Naturalis historia* 10.6–15, who often follows Aristotle quite closely. The comments on the characteristics of the bird, as opposed to the zoological facts, are Erasmus' own.
25 Pliny *Naturalis historia* 10.11 gives *ossifraga* merely as the name of a variety of eagle.

is to be merciful, to wish harm to no one despite being all-powerful, to be the only bee in the hive without a sting,[26] and to devote himself entirely to the well-being of his people? This is so true that when the wise Niloxenus was asked what was the most helpful of all things he replied, 'A king,'[27] signifying thereby that the proper quality of a true ruler is to harm no one as far as in him lies, to benefit everyone, and to be the best rather than the greatest. However, there is no way in which he can be the greatest other than by being the best, that is by being the most beneficent to all. For my part I admire the model ruler skilfully portrayed by philosophers, and I rather think the princes who administer Plato's state are of such a kind. But in history you will scarcely find one or two whom you would dare to compare with this portrait. Moreover if you consider the rulers of more recent times, I fear you may discover at every point they deserve the terrible reproach that Achilles hurls at Agamemnon in Homer: 'people-devouring king.' (Hesiod uses the expression 'gift-devouring' though he should have said 'all-devouring.')[28] Aristotle distinguished between a king and a tyrant by the very obvious sign that the latter thinks of his own private advantage and the former consults the good of his people.[29] To the early and really great emperors of Rome the title of 'king' seemed excessive and one to be avoided for fear of envy, yet to some it is hardly enough unless it is accompanied by a long train of the most resounding lies: they must be called 'divine' when they are scarcely men; 'invincible' when they never came out of a battle except defeated; 'majestic' when they are petty-minded in everything; 'most serene' when they shake the world with the storms of war and mad political struggles; 'most illustrious' when they are enveloped

* * * * *

26 The tradition that the king (ie queen) bee's lack of a sting, or reluctance to use it, is a symbol of royal clemency derives from Pliny 11.52–3 and Seneca *De clementia* 1.19.3. Erasmus also used the image in the *Institutio principis christiani* (CWE 27 212 and 28 511 n26). Louis XII used a device of a beehive and bees with the motto *Non utitur aculeo rex* – see the picture attributed to Jean Bourdichon in Jean Marot's 'Le Livre du voyage de Gênes' (BN Ms. fr. 5091 folio 15 v) reproduced by André Maurois in *Histoire de la France* (Hachette 1957) page 44.

27 Niloxenus was one of the participants in Plutarch's 'Dinner of the Seven Wise Men' *Moralia* 153A *Septem sapientium convivium*. Erasmus' memory is at fault. The story is told by Niloxenus; it concerns questions put to the king of Ethiopia by Amasis, king of Egypt, and the answer to this question is not 'a king' but 'god.'

28 Homer *Iliad* 1.231: δημοβόρος βασιλεύς 'people-devouring king' (cf Erasmus *Institutio principis christiani* CWE 27 229); Hesiod *Works and Days* 39 and 264: δωροφάγοι 'gift-devouring' and παμφάγοι 'all-devouring'

29 Aristotle *Ethica Nicomachea* 8.10.2 (1160a37–1160b2)

in a black night of ignorance of all that is good; 'catholic' when they have anything in mind but Christ. And if these gods, these famous men, these victors[30] have any leisure left from dicing, drinking, hunting, and whoring, they devote it to truly regal considerations. They have no other thought but how they may organize laws, edicts, wars, treaties, alliances, councils, and courts, ecclesiastical and lay, in such a way that they sweep the whole wealth of the community into their own treasury[31] – which is like collecting it in a leaky barrel[32] – and, like the eagle, cram themselves and their young with the entrails of innocent birds. Come now, if some honest reader of faces will take a careful look at the features and the mien of the eagle, the greedy, evil eyes, the menacing gape, the cruel eyelids, the fierce brow, and most of all the feature that Cyrus the Persian king found so pleasing in a ruler, the hook nose,[33] will he not recognize a clearly royal likeness, splendid and full of majesty? Add to this the very colour, mournful, hideous, ill-omened, a filthy, dark grey. Hence anything dark or approaching black is called *aquilus*.[34] Then there is the harsh voice, the frightening, paralysing, threatening screech that every species of living thing dreads. Now this symbol is immediately recognized by anyone who has endured or indeed has seen the frightening nature of princes' threats, even when uttered in jest, and how all things tremble when this eagle's voice screeches out: 'If they do not give it, I shall come and help myself to your prize, or that of Aias; or I shall walk off with Odysseus'. And what an angry man I shall leave behind me!'[35] Or this, which is no less 'kingly': 'Sit there in silence and be ruled by me, or all the gods in Olympus will not be strong enough to keep me off and save you from my unconquerable hands.'[36] At this screech

* * * * *

30 Cf Erasmus *Institutio principis christiani* (CWE 27 249) and *Adagia* III iii 1 The Sileni of Alcibiades (CWE 34 267–8), III vi 95 'Good-looking' on the doorpost (174 above).

31 Cf *Adagia* I ix 12 To exact tribute from the dead, and Erasmus *Institutio principis christiani* (CWE 27 260).

32 Cf *Adagia* I iv 60 To draw water in a sieve, and I x 33 A great jar that cannot be filled.

33 In Greek γρυπός; Erasmus has misunderstood Plutarch 172E or 821E–F, where the Persians are said to be enamoured of hook-nosed persons because Cyrus had a nose of that shape.

34 See Pompeius Festus page 20 Lindsay. There is no similarly derived word in English that refers to colour.

35 Achilles in *Iliad* 1.137–9; translation by E.V. Rieu (Penguin). Erasmus gives no *Agamemnon* Latin for this or the following quotation.

36 'Kingly' is given in Greek: βασιλική; the rest is said by Zeus to Hera in *Iliad* 1.566–7, translation by E.V. Rieu (Penguin).

of the eagle, I declare, the common folk immediately tremble, the senate huddles together, the nobles fall into line,[37] judges become obsequious, theologians are silent, lawyers assent, laws give way, and established custom yields: nothing can stand against it, not right, not duty, not justice, not humanity. However many eloquent, however many musical birds there are, however various are their voices and their tunes, which may even move stones, more powerful than all these is the harsh and unmusical screech of one single eagle. But there is one species of eagle that Aristotle approved of particularly,[38] perhaps because he wanted Alexander, his own chick, to be like it: no less predatory and greedy than other species, but still a little more modest and quiet, and certainly having a little more compassion, because it rears its own chicks – others do the same as undutiful parents who abandon their young, though even tigers look after their cubs. And for this reason it is called γνήσιος[39] meaning 'true-bred' and 'natural.' Homer[40] saw this species, blind as he was; for he calls it μελάνωτος and θηρευτής, that is, 'black-backed' and 'a hunter,' words that would fit very well such rulers as Nero and Caligula and very many others. But some of these are much more like the true eagle, God knows, γνησιώτεροι 'more aquiline' if I may say so; although close to the gods because of their sceptre and the images of their ancestors,[41] yet sometimes they stoop to flatter even the common

* * * * *

37 The Latin is *observit nobilitas*; the verb *ob-servio* is not attested in classical Latin, nor recorded by Du Cange *Glossarium mediae et infimae latinitatis* (Paris 1937–8). The *Lexicon latinitatis nederlandicae medii aevi* (Leiden 2002) however quotes a *Vocabularius copiosus et singularis . . .* of circa 1480 and gives among other meanings *obedire* 'listen to, obey,' *satisfacere* 'give satisfaction,' *consonare* 'agree.' R.E. Latham, *Revised Medieval Latin Word-List* (London 1975) records one occurrence dated 1537. The *Lexicon mediae et infimae latinitatis polonorum* (Warsaw 1953) records another dated 1278.

38 Aristotle *Historia animalium* 8(9).32 (618b26–31 and 619a27–29); Aristotle does not explicitly state a preference.

39 Aristotle *Historia animalium* 8(9).32 (619a8)

40 Homer *Iliad* 21.252, to which Erasmus refers directly, not to Pliny's citation (10.7)

41 The Romans used images of ancestors, kept on altars in their houses and paraded in funeral processions, as symbols of nobility. The expression *imagines familiae* is to be found in Cicero *De lege agraria* 2.1; other references in Cicero are *Pro T. Annio Milone* 32.86, *In L. Pisonem* 1, *Ad familiares* 9.21.2, *Verrines* 2.1.14.36. See also Polybius *Histories* 6.53, Pliny *Naturalis historia* 35.6. Some account of them had been given in 1508 by Guillaume Budé in his *Annotationes in Pandectas* (*Opera omnia*, 1557, 52D–53B *De origine iuris*).

people and as it were play the sponger if they can expect some worthwhile plunder.

We are told in literature that the eagle is long-lived. When it reaches extreme old age it desires no other drink but blood and by drinking this it prolongs a life that is universally hated; in fact the 'upper beak grows so long'[42] that it cannot eat flesh. This is the source of that very well-known adage 'An eagle's old age,'[43] applied to old men who become addicted to wine, because all other birds of this genus that have hooked talons either do not drink at all or do so very rarely, if we are to believe Aristotle.[44] When they do drink, however, they drink water. Only the eagle thirsts for blood. So by deforming the beak, Nature, who is certainly not always an unkind stepmother,[45] seems to have taken thought for other animals and put some limit to this insatiable greed. For the same reason she has provided that the eagle should not be permitted to lay more than three eggs or to rear more than two chicks. In fact if we are to believe the line of Musaeus that Aristotle quotes as authority: 'It hatches two, lays three, and rears one.'[46] And during the days in which it sits on its eggs – as it does for about thirty days – Nature's providence ensures that 'it has no food' by keeping the claws withdrawn, so that 'it cannot snatch the young of all the other wild creatures.' During that time 'their feathers become white through lack of food,' and therefore they come to hate their own young.[47] (One can only wish for this constraint in the case of the Roman eagles,[48] for it does not happen; they observe neither limit nor measure in pillaging

* * * * *

42 Pliny *Naturalis historia* 10.15
43 *Adagia* I ix 56
44 Aristotle *Historia animalium* 7(8).3 (593b29), 7(8).18 (601b1)
45 Cf *Adagia* I viii 64, which quotes Pliny *Naturalis historia* 7.1. Pliny says he is not sure whether nature shows herself more often as a stepmother or as a mother, considering the way she produces so many poisons and at the same time so many remedies. Cf also Quintilian 12.1.2.
46 Musaeus 2 B 3 Diels-Kranz I.22 in Aristotle *Historia animalium* 6.6 (563a19). Erasmus does not have the Greek but uses the Latin translation of Aristotle by Theodorus Gaza.
47 Erasmus is following and quoting fragments of Pliny *Naturalis historia* 10.13; for the thirty-day hatching time, see 10.165.
48 From 1515 to 1530 this read 'our eagles,' a plainly contemporary reference to imperial troops. The change to 'Roman eagles' in 1533 barely disguises this since the verbs remain in the present tense. According to James D. Tracy, *The Politics of Erasmus*, chapter 2 n110, this is a reference to a subsidy demanded by Maximilian when Charles was emancipated (January 1515).

the common people. Their thirst for spoil increases with age and they never oppress more heavily than when they have hatched a chick. Then indeed the population is struck with one tax after another.) As well as all these characteristics, Nature gave this one bird many enemies, about which we shall say more later.[49] And no one will wonder at this careful provision of Nature if we accept as true what Pliny relates: this extraordinary evidence of insatiable voracity – hardly credible even on the testimony of Democritus,[50] and even though Plutarch, one of the most serious of authors, tells it as established and acknowledged fact[51] – namely, that even the feathers of eagles, if mingled with the plumes of other birds, eat them away and in a short time reduce them to almost nothing – such is the power of their innate greed.[52] For myself I believe the same would happen if the bones of tyrants were mingled with the bones of common people, and that their blood can no more be mixed than that of the *aegithus* and the *florus*.[53]

Now just tell me whether this does not apply quite well to certain rulers. (I am not talking about the ones who are pious and good;[54] and having said this once, I should like the reader to remember it at all times.)[55] One pair of eagles needs a large tract of land to plunder, and they allow no other predator in the area, so they fix the limits of their territories. And among our eagles too, what sovereignty is not thought to be too circumscribed? What zeal to keep enlarging their kingdoms! What sparring with

* * * * *

49 In the paragraph beginning 'It remains for us to describe in a few words what enemies' (191 below)
50 Latin *haud scio an* 'hardly' usually has a positive sense 'probably, possibly.' Here Erasmus is adding his own ironic comment to what Pliny says; Democritus is usually cited as untrustworthy. See *Adagia* I iv 82, II iii 62, IV iv 43. Cf also the colloquy 'Sympathy' (1531) CWE 40 1044 line 7, which has several points of contact with this adage. For the sources of Erasmus' anti-epicureanism see ASD II-6 405:188n.
51 Plutarch *Moralia* 680E *Quaestionum convivialium*
52 Pliny *Naturalis historia* 10.8, 9, 14, 17
53 Cf *Colloquia* 'Sympathy' CWE 40 1042 lines 38–9. For *aegithus* and *anthos* (*florus* in Erasmus and Gaza's translation; the word can mean 'flower' or 'brilliancy') see Aristotle *Historia animalium* 8(9).1 (609b16–20, 610a7), 8(9).15 (616b10). Both names are identified by editors with some hesitation; in one passage in Pliny the *aegithus* (*Naturalis historia* 10.21) is clearly a type of hawk, probably a sparrow-hawk, but later (10.204) probably a titmouse, and the *anthus* (10.116) probably a wagtail. See further D'Arcy W. Thompson *A Glossary of Greek Birds* (Oxford 1936) pages 23 and 51.
54 The phrase 'I am not talking ... good' was added in *1517/18*.
55 The more emphatic disclaimer was added in *1533*.

neighbouring eagles or hawks about the limits of the kingdom, or rather of the area to be plundered! Perhaps the comparison is not quite exact in that this bird, however rapacious, does not plunder its neighbour, probably for fear that the harm it does will sooner or later fall back on its own head, but brings its plunder to the nest from much further away. Tyrants however do not spare even their own friends, or keep their greedy claws off their closest relatives or members of their household; indeed one is more exposed to this danger the closer one is to the prince, as if close to Jupiter and his thunderbolt.[56] This ingrained greed for plunder, inherited from the parents, is much increased by upbringing too. For it is said that the eagle pushes its young out of the nest to hunt when they are barely able to fly, so that straight away and 'from the time their claws are soft,' as they say,[57] they are accustomed to robbery and to living by their own talons. And in the case of many rulers, ye gods, how many incitements are added to this rapacity! In addition to a thoroughly corrupt upbringing, such a swarm of flatterers, so many unprincipled officials, corrupt advisors, stupid friends, and profligate companions who take delight in being able to do the public harm, even without provocation. Add to these pomp, pleasures, luxury, and entertainments, which no plundering can ever suffice to pay for; add silliness and inexperience, the most intractable of all evils if it is combined with wealth; and since even the most promising minds can be corrupted by these factors, what do you think will be the result if they are infused in a greedy and worthless nature like oil poured onto a fire?[58]

But the eagle would not have been equipped βασιλικῶς 'in kingly fashion' if it were armed only with hooked beak and hooked talons to carry off its prey; it had to have in addition eyes sharper than those of Lynceus,[59] able to look unblinking at the brightest sunlight. It is said they use this ability as a test to decide whether their young are genuine.[60] So any prey they intend to attack they can observe from a great distance. However the

* * * * *

56 See n15 above.
57 *Adagia* I vii 52, where the metaphor is described as deriving from puppies and applying to people.
58 For 'And in the case ... fire' cf Erasmus *Institutio principis christiani* CWE 27 209. For 'oil onto a fire' see *Adagia* I ii 9, with a pertinent reference to Jerome *Letters* 22.8.2.
59 *Adagia* II i 54 More clear-sighted than Lynceus
60 Aristotle *Historia animalium* 8(9).34 (620a2); Pliny *Naturalis historia* 10.10, speaking of the sea-eagle, uses the words *adulterinus* 'bastard' and *degener* 'not true to stock.' Curiously, he then goes on to say that sea-eagles have 'no breed of their own, but are born from cross-breeding with other eagles'; cf *Adagia* I ix 18.

king of birds has only two eyes, one beak, a limited number of claws, and one stomach. But our eagles, wonderful to relate,[61] have goodness knows how many eavesdroppers' ears,[62] spies' eyes, officials' claws, governors' beaks, judges' and lawyers' stomachs with utterly unquenchable appetites, so that nothing can ever satisfy or be safe from them, not even things that are kept in the most private chambers or most secret drawers.

Nevertheless, the eagle would perhaps not be so dangerous if its physical weapons and powers were not reinforced by a cunning mind – if, so to speak, the steel, deadly enough in itself, were not tipped with poison. It retracts its claws when it walks in order not to blunt their points and make them less effective in hunting, something which it has in common with lions.[63] And it does not attack at random, but only if it believes itself to be the stronger. Nor does it swoop suddenly down to the ground like other birds as it attacks but descends gradually so that the prey is not startled by a violent movement and frightened off. The eagle will not attack even a hare, its favourite prey, unless it sees that the hare has moved down onto level country. It does not rove about at all times, so that it cannot be caught out through weariness, but flies out hunting from breakfast time to noon, and sits idle for the rest of the time, until men gather again to do their business.[64] Then it does not immediately devour what it has killed on the spot, lest a sudden hostile attack catch it off guard on its prey, but first tests its strength[65] and, once it has recovered, carries off its prize to its nest, which is its fortress – I shall relate shortly the means by which it takes a stag,[66] so much stronger than itself. One proof of its intelligence is particularly memorable: when it has caught a tortoise, it flies high, picks out a suitable place and drops the tortoise on a stone, so that it can eat the flesh from the broken shell. However, in the case of Aeschylus, the eagle that killed the poor man by dropping a tortoise on his shiny pate thinking it was a stone[67] was

* * * * *

61 Erasmus uses the interjection *Papae!* which he explains in *Adagia* III v 51 (98 above).
62 *Corycaeorum aures*. See *Adagia* I ii 44 and Otto 449.
63 Pliny *Naturalis historia* 8.41 talks of 'lions and similar animals'; it is Erasmus who makes this comparison.
64 Aristotle 8(9).32 (619a15–18), and Pliny *Naturalis historia* 10.15 say the eagle hunts in the afternoon and that it is idle in the morning till market time. The muddle is due to Erasmus' use of Gaza's translation.
65 The Latin is *exploratis ... viribus*. Both Aristotle and Pliny speak of testing the weight of the prey; Erasmus has presumably misunderstood the Greek.
66 Below in the next paragraph
67 Pliny *Naturalis historia* 10.7, Valerius Maximus 9.12 ext. 2; cf Aelian *De natura animalium* 7.16.

scarcely 'eagle-eyed,' and for this one very good reason it has attracted the hatred of all the poets; and it still goes on doing it as if by right. In fact the eagle first tricked the tortoise, persuading it that it would learn to fly by itself.[68] Then when the tortoise with this hope allowed itself to be carried up into the sky, the eagle dashed it down on a stone, so that, in the typical way of tyrants, it converted the tortoise's misfortune into its own pleasure. Nevertheless, anyone who considers the multifarious devices, the numerous contrivances, schemes, and juggling tricks that dishonest rulers make use of to despoil the common people – levies, fines, false titles, sham wars, denunciations, marriage duties[69] – will declare the eagle is almost unworthy to be taken as an example of monarchy.

It remains for us to describe in a few words what enemies this noble predator usually has to deal with. For it is true what the proverbs say: the eagle does not hunt flies,[70] or look for worms.[71] It disregards any prey that seems unworthy of its royal claws, unless there are some eagles related to Vespasian[72] who thought 'profit smells good whatever it comes from.'[73] There are some degenerate eagles that live on fish and that have no shame in taking carcasses left by others.[74] But the more noble ones are like tyrants who leave something for the pirates and the robbers, from whom they are no different, as that famous pirate said in the presence of Alexander of Macedon,[75] except in that tyrants ravage and plunder most of the world with their larger ships and greater forces. Eagles leave small fry to hawks and sparrow-hawks[76] while they do battle with the four-footed beasts. This they do, not without danger to themselves, but on the other hand not without hope of victory, as befits an enterprising leader. Among the quadrupeds,

* * * * *

68 In the fable of Aesop, 230 Perry, the tortoise asks the eagle to teach it to fly.
69 Cf *Adagia* I ix 12 To exact tribute from the dead (CWE 32, especially 185–6).
70 *Adagia* III ii 65
71 Cf *Adagia* I ix 71, where Erasmus rejects the meaning given in Zenobius and Diogenianus of Greek θρίψ as a type of bird and mistranslates it 'worm.'
72 Suetonius *Vespasian* 23.3
73 *Adagia* III vii 13 (223 below), from Juvenal 14.204–5
74 The disparaging terms are introduced by Erasmus, who is no doubt thinking allegorically. Pliny *Naturalis historia* 10.8 says of the hawk-eagle *sola aquilarum exanimata aufert*, which H. Rackham (Loeb) translates as 'It is the only eagle that carries away the dead bodies of its prey.' The eagle to which Pliny attributes the habit of catching fish is the osprey.
75 Cf Erasmus *Apophthegmata* IV Alexander Magnus 63, following Augustine *De civitate dei* 4.4; cf Cicero *De republica* 3.24.
76 Here called *Nisi*, from Nisus the legendary king of Megara who was changed into this bird. See Virgil *Georgics* 1.404–9, Ovid *Metamorphoses* 8.146 (*haliaeetus* 'sea eagle') and the pseudo-Virgilian *Ciris*.

as I have said,[77] the eagle hunts particularly the hare; whence one species has been given the additional name 'hare-hunter,'[78] just as you might give a leader the title 'Africanus' or 'Numantinus.'[79] It does not scorn unwarlike enemies, but hunts them as food, so that even if it gains little glory from the victory, it gets much benefit from it. But, as happens at times, it is especially when it is catching a hare that it is most likely to be caught itself, struck by a feathered arrow, and it may well utter the proverb we owe to it: 'We are shot with our own feathers.'[80] It dares to do battle even with the stag, but is likely to be the loser if it does not 'put on a fox's skin';[81] for it makes up with craftiness what it lacks in strength. When it is about to engage in battle it first rolls in dust, then, alighting on the stag's antlers, it shakes the dust collected on its feathers into the stag's eyes and beats on its face with its wings until the stag is blinded and crashes into rocks. But with the snake the eagle has a fiercer, much more uncertain battle, even though it takes place in the air. The snake hunts for eagle's eggs with deadly cunning, whilst the eagle seizes a snake whenever it sees one.[82]

Now there is an irreconcilable feud between the eagle and the fox, and this will be no surprise to anyone who has heard how royally the one treated the other in days gone by. The eagle had formed a close friendship with her neighbour the fox, but when she was sitting on her eggs and had no food, she stole her neighbour's cubs and took them up to her nest. When the fox, on her return, saw the mangled remains of her brood, she did the only thing she could, which was to call on the gods and particularly on Jupiter Philios,[83] avenger of violated friendship. And some god seems to have heard this prayer. A few days later the careless eagle chanced to deposit in her

* * * * *

77 In the paragraph beginning 'Nevertheless the eagle' (190 above)
78 Latin *leporaria*, a word used by Theodorus Gaza to translate Aristotle's λαγω-φόνος (*Historia animalium* 8(9).32.29 [618b28]).
79 Titles of two members of the Scipio family. They replaced in 1533 the titles 'Britannicus' and 'Germanicus,' which belonged respectively to the emperor Claudius and to Nero Claudius Drusus. According to Thomas F. Mayer ('Tournai and Tyranny' in his *Cardinal Pole in European Context* Variorum Collected Studies Series CS 686, Ashgate Variorum 2000, page 274) 'Britannicus' was an allusion to Henry VIII; 'Germanicus' could, of course, have meant Charles V. Did Erasmus choose the replacements because he preferred to evoke for his readers the traditionally liberal policy of the Scipios with respect to the war against the Carthaginians?
80 *Adagia* I vi 52 and Aesop 276 Perry. Cf also *Adagia* IV i 96 He dies twice who dies by his own arms (499 below).
81 Pliny *Naturalis historia* 10.17; *Adagia* III v 81 (114 above)
82 Following Pliny
83 Jupiter, god of friendship; cf n191 below.

nest a live coal, which was stuck to some meat she had snatched from a sacrifice. When the eagle was away the wind fanned the fire and the nest began to burn. The chicks were terrified and threw themselves out, all unfledged as they were. The fox seized them when they fell, took them to her hole and ate them.[84] From that moment no agreement of any sort has been possible between the eagle and the fox, although at great cost to the latter. I rather think the foxes deserve this, for at one time they refused help to the hares who sought an alliance against the eagle.[85] This story is told in the chronicles of the quadrupeds, from which Homer took his 'Battle of the Frogs and Mice.'[86]

Then again there is bitter enmity between the eagle and the vulture, which uses the same methods and competes in greed; although in this respect the eagle is both more cruel and more noble because it eats only what it has killed and does not, out of laziness, settle on carcasses killed by others. It has reason to hate the nuthatch, which tries with marvellous cunning to break the eagle's eggs. And it fights with herons, for this bird, relying on its claws,[87] is not afraid to attack it sometimes, fighting so fiercely that it dies in the struggle. Nor is it surprising that there is little accord between the eagle and swans, truly birds of poetry; what is surprising is that they often get the better of such a warlike creature.[88] The race of poets has not been too popular with kings who have a bad conscience, because they are free and talkative, and because sometimes, like Philoxenus,[89] they prefer to be sent back to the quarries rather than keep silence. For if something pains them, they write it down in their black books,[90] and divulge the secrets of kings to their own successors. Eagles have little liking for cranes too (I think because the latter have a strong preference for democracy,[91] so hated by monarchs). Yet cranes are more intelligent, for when they migrate from

* * * * *

84 Aesop 1 Perry
85 Aesop 256 Perry
86 See n10 above.
87 According to ASD Erasmus has misunderstood Aristotle, who says the heron is at war with the eagle 'which seizes it' (translation by D.M. Balme in the Loeb edition).
88 For the context of this paragraph down to here, cf Aristotle *Historia animalium* 8(9).1 (609b7–610a1).
89 Cf *Adagia* II i 31 To the quarries; Erasmus *Apophthegmata* VI LB IV 313D no 16.
90 According to ASD the expression *chartis illinunt atris* is a contamination of Horace's *quodcunque semel chartis illeverit* 'whatever he has once scribbled in his books' (*Satires* 1.4.36) and *quem versibus oblinat atris* 'whom he may besmear with black verses' (*Epistles* 1.19.30).
91 Pliny *Naturalis historia* 10.58 says that cranes 'agree when to start' and 'choose a leader.'

Cilicia and are about to cross the mountains of Taurus, which are the haunt
of many eagles, they carry large stones in their beaks to muffle their cries
and fly in silence at night, thus deceiving the eagles and passing safely.[92]
But the eagle has a particular hostility toward the wren,[93] as it is called, for
no other reason, as that great old rambler[94] thinks, than that it is also called
king-bird and βουληφόρος 'counsellor,' most commonly among the Latins.
The eagle pursues it with extreme hate as a pretender to power, although
this is not an enemy whose strength the eagle might fear, for the wren is
weak and inclined to flee, but being skilful and intelligent it hides in thick-
ets and holes so that it cannot easily be caught even by a more powerful
enemy. And once, when it accepted a challenge to fly a race with the eagle,
it won more by cunning than by strength.[95] Finally the eagle wages war to
the death with the *cybindus*,[96] so deadly that they are often caught locked together. The *cybindus* is a nocturnal hawk, and no kind of man is more hated
by tyrants than those who do not conform in any way with commonly held
opinion and can see all too clearly in the dark.

   But would I not be very foolish to try and enumerate all the enemies of
a creature that is at war with everyone? Among the other species of living
things there is sometimes war between them and sometimes friendship.
The fox has many enemies, but it has a friend in the raven, who gives it
help when the merlin[97] harasses its cubs. It has a friendly relationship with

* * * * *

92 Plutarch *Moralia* 510A and B *De garrulitate* and 967B *De sollertia animalium*, where
    Plutarch talks of χῆνες 'geese' not γέρανοι 'cranes.' What Erasmus says here is
    not consistent with *Adagia* III vi 68 Cranes that swallow a stone (158 above),
    where he followed Pliny for the explanation.
93 The Latin is *trochilus*; cf *Colloquia* 'Sympathy' CWE 40 1042 lines 15–16. Aris-
    totle *Historia animalium* 8(9).11 (615a18) and Pliny *Naturalis historia* 8.90 both
    appear to use the word for the Egyptian crocodile-bird, or Egyptian plover,
    and for the wren. Aristotle does not use the word βουληφόρος but πρέσβυς
    'old man.' Pliny's reference to the two birds' enmity (*Naturalis historia* 10.203)
    is ambiguous; H. Rackham (Loeb) translates 'the eagle is called the king of
    birds,' though the phrase could be in apposition to *trochilus*.
94 Latin *deambulator*, a humorous reference to Aristotle as peripatetic
95 Plutarch *Moralia* 806E–F *Praecepta gerendae reipublicae*. See Aesop 434 Perry.
96 Pliny *Naturalis historia* 10.24; the correct form of the word is *cybindis* – Erasmus
    declines it incorrectly because he is following the Venice edition of 1496 or
    1507; cf *Colloquia* 'Sympathy' CWE 40 1040 lines 25–6 where he reproduces the
    alternative Greek form *kymindis* given by Aristotle *Historia animalium* 8(9).12
    (615b6).
97 The Latin is *aesalon*; 'merlin' in the translation of Aristotle *Historia animalium*
    8(9).1 (609b32) by D.M. Balme (Loeb). Pliny *Naturalis historia* 10.205 also uses
    the form *aesalon*.

snakes too, because they both like using rabbit-warrens.[98] The crocodile has an enemy in the Nile rat, but a close intimacy with the crocodile-bird, so close that the bird is allowed to get right between the animal's jaws without harm.[99] The eagle alone has no friendship with any animal at all, no kinship, no comradeship, no intercourse, no alliance, no truce. It is everyone's enemy and everyone is its enemy. For he who lives and gets fat by the misfortune of all cannot but be the enemy of all. Therefore, well aware of its guilt, it does not nest on the plain but on broken and lofty rocks, sometimes in trees, but only in the tallest, like one who repeats over and over to himself the tyrant's motto: 'Let them hate, as long as they are afraid.'[100] And so, while storks are so sacred for the Egyptians that it is a capital offence to kill one,[101] while geese were sacred for the Romans, while among the Britons no one will harm a kite,[102] the Jews will not kill pigs, the ancients would not hunt dolphins[103] (it was not permitted to harm one and if anyone did harm one by mistake while hunting, they were punished as if they were boys with a few lashes of the whip). For the eagle there is the same law among all nations as for the wolf and the tyrant, there is a reward for the one who kills the common enemy. Therefore the eagle has no love for, nor is loved by, any animal, any more than bad rulers are loved when they rule their empires for themselves and to the great harm of the state. Perhaps such affections are for private individuals; great satraps[104] are so remote from them that sometimes they do not even love their own children, except for the gain they may bring, and often hold them in suspicion and hatred.

Almost everyone believes that an animal as savage as the lion repaid a man who deserved well of it and saved his life because he had healed its paw.[105] Many believe in the snake that rescued the man who had fed it and came swiftly at the call of his familiar voice.[106] There are some who

* * * * *

98 Aristotle *Historia animalium* 8(9).1 (610a12) says, 'because they both live in holes.'
99 Pliny *Naturalis historia* 8.90; Aristotle *Historia animalium* 8(9).6 (612a20)
100 *Adagia* II ix 62
101 Plutarch *Moralia* 380F *De Iside et Osiride*; Plutarch is speaking of the Thessalians, not the Egyptians.
102 The editors of ASD suggest an allusion to the English predilection for falcons in the time of Henry VIII (*Encyclopaedia Britannica* 'Falconry' in the 1911 or older editions).
103 Plutarch *Moralia* 163A *Septem sapientium convivium*
104 Cf *Adagia* III iii 1 The Sileni of Alcibiades (CWE 34 270–1 and 281). Satraps are strictly of course Persian provincial governors. The term is also used of warmongering rulers in *Adagia* III ix 84 (350 below).
105 Aulus Gellius *Noctes Atticae* 5.14, the story of Androcles and the lion
106 Pliny *Naturalis historia* 8.61; Aelian *Varia historia* 13.46, *De natura animalium* 6.63

believe the story told by Philarchus of the viper that used to come every
day to a certain man's table; when it learned that its host's son had been
killed by one of its own young, it killed its child to avenge the outrage
to hospitality by its own offspring and out of shame never returned to
that house.[107] Then there is a story of a panther, which Demetrius Physicus
thought worth writing down and Pliny took the trouble to recount: because
a man had rescued her cubs from a pit, she obligingly led him out of the
desert and back to a road where people were to be found.[108] Aristophanes
the grammarian, who loved a girl of Stephanopolis, had an elephant as
a rival; Plutarch recorded this as something well known to all and much
talked about.[109] He also speaks of a snake passionately in love with an
Aetolian girl.[110] The dolphins' love for man is generally acknowledged:[111]
one saved the life of Arion,[112] one carried Hesiod to the shore, one saved
the girl from Lesbos and her lover,[113] and one gave a boy rides out of sheer
friendliness.[114] But even those who believe all these things do not believe
that a virgin could be loved by an eagle. You may judge how ill-omened
this creature is and what hatred it has for man by the fact that it was chosen
to be the tormentor on Mount Caucasus of Prometheus,[115] of all the gods
the one who loved man the most. And yet with so many vices there is one
thing we can approve. These most rapacious of creatures are not at all given
to drink[116] or lust.[117] For when the eagle abducted Ganymede,[118] it did so
for Jupiter and not for itself. But you will find many of our 'eagles' who

* * * * *

107 Pliny *Naturalis historia* 10.208. 'Philarchus,' so spelt in the early editions, is
    Phylarchus (*FGrHist* 81 F 28).
108 Pliny *Naturalis historia* 8.59; Demetrius of Apamea (second century BC?), a
    physician of the Alexandrian school of Herophilus, wrote treatises *On Affec-
    tions* and *On Signs*.
109 Plutarch *Moralia* 972D *Terrestriane an aquatilia animalia sint callidiora*; cf Pliny
    Naturalis historia 8.13.
110 Plutarch *Moralia* 972E *Terrestriane an aquatilia animalia sint callidiora*
111 Pliny *Naturalis historia* 9.24–8, Aulus Gellius *Noctes Atticae* 6.8
112 Herodotus 1.23–24, Ovid *Fasti* 2.79–118, Plutarch *Moralia* 161A *Septem sapien-
    tium convivium*, Aulus Gellius *Noctes Atticae* 16.19
113 Plutarch *Moralia* 162D and163A–c *Septem sapientium convivium*
114 Pliny *Letters* 9.33
115 Hesiod *Theogony* 506–616, but the place is given by Lucian *De sacrificiis* 6 and
    Deorum dialogi 5.205.
116 Aristotle *Historia animalium* 7(8).3 and 7(8).18 (593b29and 601b1) of crooked-
    taloned birds in general
117 Aristotle *De generatione animalium* 3.1 (749b10); cf *Adagia* III vii 21 His progeny
    are full of wind (228 below).
118 Cf Xenophon *Symposium* 8.28–30 and Horace (n14 above).

do commit abductions for themselves, and not just one Ganymede, but they abduct girls for themselves, they abduct married women for themselves, so that in this respect they are almost more insufferable than in their pillaging, for which they are already absolutely intolerable.

So, there are innumerable species of birds, and among them some are admirable for their rich and brilliant plumage like the peacocks, others are remarkable for their snowy whiteness like the swans; some, by contrast, are a beautiful shiny black like the ravens, others are of extraordinary physical size like the ostriches, some are famous for legendary miracles like the phoenix, some are praised for their fertility like the doves, or appreciated at the tables of the great like partridges and pheasants; some are entertaining for their talk like parrots, or marvellous for their song like nightingales; some are outstanding for their courage like cockerels, others are born to be men's pets like sparrows. Yet of all of them the eagle alone has seemed to wise men to be a suitable image of the king, not beautiful, not melodious, not good to eat, but a carnivore, a raptor, a predator, a plunderer, a warmonger, solitary, hated by all, a universal bane, capable of the maximum of harm, yet seeking to do even more. On the same basis the lion is adjudged monarch of the quadrupeds, for there is no beast that is fiercer or more noisome.[119] Dogs are useful for many purposes, and in particular for guarding people's property. Oxen till the soil. Horses and elephants go to war. Mules and asses are useful for carrying loads. A monkey can play the scrounger. Even the snake is useful in that it showed the value of fennel for improving the eyesight.[120] The lion has no quality but that of tyrant, enemy, and devourer of all, whose survival depends only on its strength and the fear it inspires – a right royal animal just like the eagle. This seems to have been understood by those who emblazoned on their noble shields lions with jaws agape and claws spread to catch their prey – though it seems Pyrrhus, who liked to be called an eagle, understood this better than Antiochus, who rejoiced in the nickname of the Hawk.[121] But it is no surprise that the lion should rule over the four-footed kinds, since even among the gods invented by the poets it was Jupiter who was considered to be best fitted to exercise rule: undutiful son who castrated and drove out his father,[122] incestuous husband of his

* * * * *

119 Pliny *Naturalis historia* 8.46; cf Aristotle *Historia animalium* 7(8).5 (594b18–28).
120 Plutarch *Moralia* 974B *Terrestriane an aquatilia animalia sint callidiora*; Pliny *Naturalis historia* 8.99
121 Plutarch *Moralia* 975B *Terrestriane an aquatilia animalia sint callidiora*
122 This is a slip on Erasmus' part. In the commonest version of the myth it was Cronus who castrated Ouranos, not Zeus who castrated Cronus. Freud made the same error, though whether it was a 'Freudian' one or not is perhaps

sister, distinguished by so much debauchery, so many adulterous affairs, so many rapes, and despite all this, 'with sable brow and 'flaming bolt'[123] striking terror into everyone. Even if many praise the state system of the bees,[124] in which the king is the only one who may not bear a sting, no one imitates it, any more than they do the state system of Plato.

But I come back to the eagle; for the truly royal qualities I have described and the extraordinary services it has rendered to every kind of animal, the 'senate and people' of the poets have unanimously declared, first, that it should receive the title of 'universal king' and even be called θεῖος, that is 'divine.'[125] Second, they gave it a quite important place among the constellations and decorated it with a few little stars.[126] Finally they gave it the honourable divine task of alone bringing to angry Jupiter the arms with which he makes the whole world tremble. And so that it can do this with impunity, they also gave it the power, alone among living creatures, to be unafraid of the thunderbolt and not to be harmed by it,[127] but to look on a flash of lightning with the same stare that it turns directly on the sun. To these attributes those very wise, ancient Romans added this, that the eagle should have first place among the standards of their legions, that it should be, as it were, the ensign-bearer of all their standards, taking precedence over wolves, the nurses of the Roman nation, over minotaurs and boars, not animals of the greatest rapacity, finally even over horses. For standards decorated with these four creatures followed the eagle in those times. In a short while it would not allow them even to accompany it, but leaving them behind in camp went forth to battle alone.[128] This bird alone, I repeat, they considered worthy to be the ornament on everything belonging to the monarch of the whole world: sceptre, banner, shield, house, clothing, cups, and livery, although, if I am not mistaken, it was on an augury given by vultures, not by eagles, that Roman rule was founded.[129] The college of

* * * * *

a matter for debate (see S. Timpanaro *The Freudian Slip* [London 1985] pages 165–6).
123 In Greek κυανέοις ὀφρύσι καὶ ψολόεντι κεραυνῷ; the 'sable brow' is found in Homer *Iliad* 1.528, the 'flaming bolt' in Homer *Odyssey* 23.330.
124 See n26 above.
125 Aristotle *Historia animalium* 8(9).32 (619b6); Pindar *Olympians* 2.88
126 Manilius 1.343–5; Ovid *Fasti* 5.732
127 Pliny *Naturalis historia* 2.146 and 10.15
128 Pliny *Naturalis historia* 10.16, who refers to the second consulate of Gaius Marius (104 BC). The personification in the last sentence is Erasmus' adaptation, which makes the eagle appear to follow the usual autocratic course of a tyrant.
129 Livy 1.7.1

augurs added this: that if an eagle should perch on anyone's house,[130] or drop a cap on his head, it was a portent that he would rule.[131]

So much for one of these leaders; I come now to the dung beetle. It is an animal – perhaps scarcely even an animal since it lacks some senses – belonging to the lowest order of insects, which the Greeks call by the notorious term *kantharos*[132] and the Romans 'scarab,' nasty to look at, nastier to smell, and nastiest of all in the noise it makes; its wings[133] are covered by a scaly sheath. Indeed it would be more exact to say this whole scarab is nothing but a shell. It is born in excrement, that is in the droppings of animals, and it is in these that it lives, makes its home, delights, and revels. Its chief occupation is to make balls as large as possible, like pastilles, not out of sweet-smelling materials but with dung, especially goat's dung, which smells to the beetle like marjoram.[134] These it rolls backwards with tremendous efforts, thrusting upwards with its back legs, which are extra long, and with its head touching the ground. If, as happens sometimes when they are pushing their burden uphill, the balls slip away from them and run back down the slope, you would think you were watching Sisyphus rolling his stone.[135] They never tire, they never rest, so eager are they to pursue their labour until they have got the ball down into their hole. They themselves were born in these balls, and they bring up their new-born in the same way,[136] and continue to keep them warm in these nests against the winter's cold while they are young. I of course am aware that the dung-beetle is well known to everyone, for it is to be found everywhere, except perhaps where there is no dung. But they are not all of the same species; for there are some whose shell is a sort of shiny greenish black, and several are a repellent filthy black.[137] Some are larger, armed with extra long two-

* * * * *

130 According to Suetonius, an eagle perched on Augustus' tent (*Augustus* 96.1) and on the house of Tiberius (*Tiberius* 14.4).

131 Tarquin was designated by this omen according to Livy 1.34.8; cf Cicero *De legibus* 1.4.

132 *Suda* K 310, where the word is derived from κάνθων 'pack-ass' and ὄνος 'ass'

133 The zoological data are from Pliny *Naturalis historia* 11.97–99. Much of it is repeated in *Adagia* IV viii 94 You would sooner persuade a dung-beetle.

134 Cf *Adagia* I iv 38 A pig has nothing to do with marjoram, where marjoram is described, following Dioscorides and Pliny, as the most highly prized perfume; the dung-beetle is mentioned in CWE 31 348 line 40.

135 Cf *Adagia* II iv 40 To roll a stone.

136 In addition to Pliny (n133 above), cf Plutarch *Moralia* 355A and 381A *De Iside et Osiride*.

137 Cf *Adagia* III ii 39 As black as a beetle.

pronged horns with serrated tips like pincers; with these they can grip and squeeze to bite at will. Some are reddish, and these are very large; they dig in dry ground and make their nests there. There are some that make a terrible loud buzzing noise as they fly and give quite a fright to the unwary.[138] There are others that differ by their shapes. But this they all have in common: they are born in dung, they feed on dung, their life and their delight is in dung.

I imagine there will be some eager supporter of Roman generals who will deplore the lot of the eagle, such a regal bird, destined to fight such a humble and low-born enemy, whom it would be no glory to conquer, by whom it would be utter disgrace to be defeated, and who would gain enormous credit by confronting the eagle even if he is beaten. According to the poets, Ajax was ashamed to have such an unwarlike opponent as Ulysses;[139] was the eagle to be obliged to contend with the beetle? Another person will wonder rather where this basest of insects found such courage, such daring, that it was not afraid of beginning a war with this by far the most bellicose of birds. And where did it find the resources, the strength, the means, the allies to be able to carry on the war for so many years? But in truth, if anyone will open up this Silenus[140] and look more closely at this despised creature, in its own setting as it were, he will see it has so many uncommon gifts that, all things well considered, he will almost prefer to be a scarab rather than an eagle. But let no one cry out or contradict me before he knows the facts.

First of all, even the dung-beetle has an advantage over the eagle in this, that every year it casts off its old age[141] and immediately regains its youth. This in itself is such an advantage that I imagine even certain Roman pontiffs, who may go straight to heaven because they have the keys, would nevertheless prefer, when they reach an unlovable old age, which obliges them to renounce all pleasures, to slough off their old shell[142] like the scarab sooner than accept a sevenfold crown[143] in place of the triple one. Second,

* * * * *

138 Cf *Adagia* III ii 45 Shades of a dung-beetle.
139 Ovid *Metamorphoses* 13.1–20
140 Cf *Adagia* III iii 1 The Sileni of Alcibiades (first paragraph).
141 Cf Aristotle *Historia animalium* 8(9).17 (601a2).
142 In Greek σύφαρ: the 'slough' of a snake or cast shell of a beetle. Cf *Adagia* I i 26 As bare as a snake's sloughed skin, I iii 56 As blind as a sloughed skin and III vii 73 As happy as someone casting off old age (264 below).
143 The expression seems to be Erasmus' invention, meaning a crown of eternal life; cf 1 Cor 9:25, James 1:12, 1 Peter 5:4, Rev 2:10, and Jean Daniélou, *Les Sym-*

what strength of heart it has in such a small body, what heroic mental powers, what energy in attack! Homer's fly[144] is nothing compared to the dung-beetle! This is why, if I am not mistaken, some beetles are called bulls.[145] And since not even lions will rashly attack bulls, it is even less likely that eagles will. It is also endowed with no ordinary intelligence – or are we to think the Greek proverb 'As cunning as Cantharus,'[146] which seems to assign to the beetle a quite unusual and unrivalled wisdom, arose and became universally known for no good reason?

It makes no difference to my argument if someone objects that the beetle is poorly lodged in an ugly house. As far as even physical beauty goes, if we only keep our judgment free of vulgar prejudice, there is no reason to despise the scarab. For if the philosophers are right when they say that the shape they call a sphere is not only the most beautiful but in every way the best, and that the demiurge found this the most pleasing for the shape of the heavens, by far the fairest of all things,[147] why should the scarab not seem beautiful, which comes far closer to this shape than the eagle? If a horse or a dog is beautiful among its kind, why should a beetle not be beautiful among its kind too? Or must we measure the beauty of all other things by our own, so that whatever does not conform to human beauty will always be judged ugly?[148] The colour of the scarab, I think, no one will denigrate for it has the quality of jewels. The fact that it uses the droppings of animals for its own purposes is a matter for praise, not accusation. As if doctors do not do exactly the same, not only smearing their patients with various animal and even human excrement, but putting it in potions for the sick. Alchemists,[149] obviously godlike men, are not ashamed to use dung in the search for their 'fifth essence'; nor farmers, who were at one time the most honoured sort of men, to feed their fields with manure. There are also some peoples who use dung instead of gypsum to plaster

* * * * *

boles chrétiens primitifs (Seuil 1961) 21–31. There is no reference in the Bible to a sevenfold crown, though the number seven is commonly used as a symbol of perfection (see St Cyprian Treatises 11.11 in Ante-Nicene Fathers 5 page 503).
144 Iliad 17.570–4; cf Adagia III viii 95 The depravity of the fly (316 below).
145 Pliny Naturalis historia 30.39
146 Adagia III ii 42 As cunning as Cantharus, in which 'Cantharus' is considered first as a proper name, then as the word for 'beetle,' with reference to Aesop 3 Perry.
147 According to Plato Timaeus 33B
148 Cf Cicero De natura deorum 1.77.
149 Cf Erasmus Colloquia 'Alcumistica' CWE 39 545–56.

their walls. This same material, pounded and dried in the sun, is used to keep fires going instead of wood. The Cypriots fatten their cattle with human dung,[150] and not only fatten them but doctor them even.

But, you say, this stuff, however putrid, smells sweet to the beetle. Well, it would be stupid to expect the beetle to have the nose of a man. As a matter of fact man is peculiar in that he finds the smell of his own excrement offensive; this is not the case with any other creature. So the beetle is not dirtier than us, it is luckier. But it is also true that men are offended not so much by excrement itself as by the current view of it; to the earliest mortals this substance was not so disgusting as it is to us, for they called it by the very auspicious name of *laetamen*,[151] and they had no hesitation in giving the god Saturn the nickname of *Sterculeus*, and this was a compliment if we believe Macrobius.[152] According to Pliny, Stercutus the son of Faunus acquired not only a name from this source, but even an immortal memory in Italy.[153] Further, in Greece the same substance brought fame to two kings: Augeas who devised the task and Hercules who made it famous.[154] Then there is the unforgettable story of the regal old man whom Homer pictured for posterity (as Cicero[155] tells in his *Cato*) fertilizing his fields with his own hands[156] and with the very substance that is the beetle's delight. The stench of urine did not trouble a certain Roman emperor if there was money attached to it.[157] And why should a beetle be frightened away from a thing of so many uses by such a slight inconvenience? – if it is an inconvenience at all. Finally, seeing that the beetle in the midst of dung remains clean and always keeps its shell shining, whilst the eagle stinks even in the air, pray tell me which of the two

* * * * *

150 Pliny *Naturalis historia* 28.266 says that oxen treat themselves by eating human excrement; cf *Adagia* I x 95 A Cyprus ox.
151 Palladius *Opus agriculturae* 1.6.18, Servius on Virgil *Georgics* 1.1; from the same root as the verbs *laeto* and *laetifico* (used in the story of Laertes below), which mean both 'to make happy' and 'to enrich' or 'fertilize'
152 From *stercus* 'dung'; Macrobius *Saturnalia* 1.7.25
153 Pliny *Naturalis historia* 17.50
154 See Apollodorus 2.5.5.
155 Cicero *De senectute* 54
156 Homer *Odyssey* 24.226–31. The old man is Laertes, Odysseus' father. Erasmus' text is much closer to the passage in Pliny just quoted (n153 above): *Iam apud Homerum regius senex agrum ita laetificans suis manibus reperitur* (translation by H. Rackham in the Loeb edition).
157 Vespasian according to Suetonius; cf n72 above.

is the cleaner? Indeed I think the name is derived from this; it is called κάνθαρος, as if it were καθαρός 'clean, pure' (unless one prefers the derivation of *cantharus* from *Centaurus*).[158] For you should not think, because it is of a squalid nature, that the beetle despises luxurious living; it has an extreme fondness for roses and covets them above all else – if we believe Pliny.[159]

These qualities may seem slight and commonplace, but there is one that no one will deny makes the beetle great, a real feather in its cap.[160] In ancient times it was given first place among sacred images and in sacred rites as the most apt symbol of the eminent warrior. Plutarch tells us in his essay 'On Isis and Osiris' among the hieroglyphic images of the Egyptians the picture of the king was an eye placed on a sceptre, signifying watchfulness combined with just government of the state;[161] in those days, I believe, kings were of this nature, very different from eagles.[162] He says that at Thebes there were preserved images without hands representing judges, who must distance themselves as far as possible from all bribery by gifts; among these images there was one without eyes also, which signified the president of the court because he must be entirely without preference, and consider only the case itself without thought of the person.[163] There too, not like 'blue pimpernel among the vegetables' as the proverb says,[164] but among the sacred images, was the scarab, carved on a seal. And what pray did those wisest of theologians intimate to us by this new symbol? Not

* * * * *

158 Derivations, apparently not very serious, invented by Erasmus to oppose to the *Suda* (cf n132 above)

159 Pliny *Naturalis historia* 11.279. But there is a discrepancy here due perhaps to Erasmus' edition of Pliny. The sentence is translated by H. Rackham (Loeb) as 'The creatures we have designated insects can all be killed by sprinkling with oil; vultures are killed by ointment (they are attracted by the scent which repels other birds), and beetles by a rose.'

160 The Latin is *ingenti crista dignum*; in *Adagia* I viii 69 To raise one's crest is described as a sign of eagerness and pugnacity in birds, and the military crest as something 'insolent and stupid' rather than as a sign of legitimate pride. There may be irony or consciousness of a somewhat playful use of materials here. See also Otto 467.

161 Plutarch *Moralia* 354F *De Iside et Osiride*; for the king, Plutarch says specifically Osiris.

162 Cf *Adagia* I iii 1, II i 1, and Erasmus *Institutio principis christiani* CWE 27 241.

163 Plutarch *Moralia* 355A *De Iside et Osiride*: 'the statue of the chief judge had its eyes closed'; translation by F.C. Babbitt (Loeb)

164 *Adagia* I vii 21 and III vi 73 (161 above)

something banal at all, but a great and undefeated general. This too is in Plutarch,[165] in case anyone thinks I have made it up, as some ignorant theologians sometimes contrive allegories.

But some uninformed person will ask, 'What has a beetle to do with a military general?' In fact they have many points in common. In the first place you can see that the beetle is covered with gleaming armour and no part of its body is not carefully protected by scales and plates; Mars does not seem to be better armed when Homer equips him in his fullest panoply. Then there is its aggressive approach with terrifying, unnerving thrum[166] and truly warlike voice. For what is harsher than the blare of trumpets, what is more vulgar[167] than the roll of drums?[168] The sound of trumpets, which delights kings so much nowadays, was intolerable to the Busiritae[169] of old, because it seemed to them like the braying of an ass, and the ass was one of the things that nation considered detestable. Then there is the beetle's patient labour in rolling its burdens along, its unconquerable courage and its disregard for its own life. Add to this that it is claimed no female scarabs are to be found but that all are males.[170] What, I ask, could be more apt for a strong leader? Indeed it is also fitting, as Plutarch also reports, that they use those dainty balls I have described to give birth to, nurture, feed, and bring up their offspring; their birthplace is their food. Do not think this esoteric aptness is easy for me to explain. It could be better explained by military commanders who know what it is 'to be the guest of one's shield,'[171] who are familiar with χαμευνίαι 'beds on the ground,' who have endured hard winters lightly clad during sieges and often harder famines, who have dragged out a grim life by eating not only roots of plants but rotten food, who have spent months at sea. If you consider the squalor of this life, the beetle will seem pure; if you consider its wretchedness, the beetle is to be envied. What I have described, in case anyone should sneer at it, is the lot and the condition of the most brilliant generals. In passing,

* * * * *

165 Plutarch *Moralia* 355A *De Iside et Osiride*: 'The military class had their seals engraved with the form of a beetle.'
166 Latin *panico bombo*; cf *Adagia* III vii 3 A panic attack (215 below).
167 Greek ἀμουσότερον, literally 'more opposed to the Muses'; cf II vi 18 Ἄμουσοι, Strangers to the Muses.
168 Cf Ep 1756 line 95 and the following for Erasmus' aversion to drums.
169 Plutarch *Moralia* 362F *De Iside et Osiride*
170 Plutarch 355A and 381A; Aelian *De natura animalium* 10.15
171 Greek ἐν ἀσπίδι ξενίζεσθαι; cf *Adagia* II vii 75 Like a hero to entertain in my shield, which is from Zenobius 1.64 or Apostolius 18.65.

I like to wonder why our sabre-rattlers[172] prefer to have in their coats of arms, which they think are the foundation of their whole title to nobility, leopards, lions, dogs, dragons, wolves, or some other animal, which either chance has thrown in their way or they have adopted themselves; whereas their proper symbol is the beetle, which is both the most appropriate and is attested and consecrated by that very antiquity that is the sole begetter of nobility.

Finally no one will think the dung-beetle is entirely despicable if they consider that wise men and doctors obtain remedies from the creature for the worst human ills. For example the horns of the stag-beetle, or 'lucanian beetle' as this species is called, are not only carried in purses, but hung around the neck, sometimes set in gold, as a protection against all childhood diseases.[173] Shall not the beetle be granted equal power with the eagle for offering the most effective cures, and ones that would be hard to believe if it were not for the authority of Pliny?[174] I mean 'that formidable type'[175] of scarab that is carved on an emerald, for as the proverb says 'you can't carve a Mercury out of any and every wood';[176] the scarab does not consider every gem worthy of itself, but if carved on the emerald, the brightest of all gems, and hung from the neck as I said (but only with the hair of an ape or at least a swallow's feathers), it affords an immediate remedy against all poisons,[177] and is no whit less effective than the 'moly' that Mercury once gave to Ulysses.[178] It is not only effective against poisons, but also an uncommon asset for anyone seeking an audience somehow or other with a king,[179] so this sort of ring should be worn especially by those who have it in mind to ask the king for some fat benefice or archdeaconry or bishopric, as they are called.[180] Likewise it prevents headaches – not a minor ill, by heaven, especially for drinkers. As far as these quite remarkable curative

* * * * *

172 The Latin is *nostris Pyrgopolynicis*. Pyrgopolynices is the boasting soldier in Plautus' *Miles gloriosus*.
173 Pliny *Naturalis historia* 11.97 and 30.138
174 Pliny *Naturalis historia* 37.124, where Pliny explicitly rejects the following claims made for emeralds carved with scarabs as an insult to humanity
175 Greek ὁ δεινὸς ἐκεῖνος; cf *Adagia* III i 56 A formidable man.
176 *Adagia* II v 47
177 Pliny *Naturalis historia* 37.124
178 Homer *Odyssey* 10.305
179 Pliny *Naturalis historia* 37.124
180 The Latin terms *archidiaconatus* and *episcopatus* are found respectively in Gregory I (the Great) *Epistolae* 2.14 PL 77 549–50 and Tertullian *De baptismo* 17

powers are concerned, wise physicians make no distinction between the eagle and the scarab. So who would scorn this beetle, whose very image carved on a stone has such power? The mention of gems suggests to me that I should add this too: if the eagle takes some pride in a gemstone called 'eagle-stone,'[181] the scarab yields nothing to it in this respect either. For to the scarab the cantharias[182] owes its name, presenting a wonderfully complete picture of the animal, so that you would say it is not a picture but the real living beetle set in the stone. To conclude with something which is perhaps also to the point, this beetle, born in dung, is distinguished by no fewer proverbs than the eagle, king of birds. If some supporter of the eagle's party should say that in this respect the scarab is not to be compared with it because the eagle used to be considered one of the divinities by those loutish fellows, the Thebans,[183] I shall not deny it; but let him remember that this sort of honour is shared by the eagle with crocodiles and long-tailed apes, together with onions and the rumblings of the stomach, inasmuch as all these portents were honoured as divine among the Egyptians.[184] And if the word 'divinity,' meaningless in this assemblage of things divine, is worth anything on this argument,[185] many attributed divinity to the scarab also.[186]

Now we have painted both leaders, such as they are. It remains for us to examine the causes of such a ferocious war. Once upon a time[187] on Mount Etna an eagle was pursuing a hare; its claws were poised and it was so close to grasping its prey that the hare, timid by nature and terrified by the eagle's hot breath, fled for refuge into the nearest beetle's hole. So it is at a critical moment, when things are desperate, we look and hope for shelter

* * * * *

PL 1 1217–20. Erasmus may be thinking however of the literal meaning of the Greek ἐπίσκοπος 'inspector, guardian.'
181 Latin aëtites or aëtitis (which Erasmus is relating, of course to ἀετός – see 210 at n201 below), the hollow nodule of argilaceous oxide of iron having a loose nucleus, found according to fable, in eagles' nests. Pliny Naturalis historia 10.12, 30.130, 36.149 and 37.187
182 A precious stone that has in it the figure of the cantharis, or Spanish fly: Pliny Naturalis historia 37.187
183 Diodorus Siculus 1.87.9
184 See Juvenal 15.1–10 who mentions all these portents except rumblings of the stomach.
185 Latin quo calculo; cf Adagia I v 55 To take back a move (or counter).
186 Pliny Naturalis historia 30.99 states that 'the greater part of Egypt' worships the scarab.
187 Aesop 3 Perry. Erasmus sets the location on Mount Etna, following the scholiast of Aristophanes Peace 73 (Dübner page 173).

wherever we can. However, this scarab was, in Homer's words, 'good and great';[188] for on that mountain the scarab nation was considered to be of a particularly healthy stock, so that the 'Etna beetle'[189] has become proverbial, probably because of its exceptional physical size. So the hare took refuge in this hole and threw itself at the beetle's feet begging and praying that his household gods should protect him against this cruellest of enemies.

Now the beetle was not a little pleased by the very fact that someone existed who, first, was willing to owe his life to him and believed that such a great thing was in his power; and who, second, found his hole, which all men passed by cursing and holding their noses, suitable as a place in which to hide for safety, like a sacred altar or the king's statue. Without delay therefore the scarab flew to meet the eagle and sought to mollify the angry creature with these words: 'The greater your power the more becoming it is that you should spare the harmless. Do not defile my household gods with the death of an innocent animal. In return, may your nest be always safe from such disaster. It is the mark of a noble and kingly spirit to pardon, even the unworthy. One who has committed no crime should have the right to respect for his home, which should be safe and inviolate for everyone, as justice wills, the law allows, and custom approves. If the suppliant has no authority, at least let his zeal speak for him.

> For though you may despise our race and scarabean arms,
> Yet be certain the gods are mindful of good and ill.[190]

If you are not worried that your own hearth may be violated – a fate that will befall you some day – at least respect supreme Jupiter, whom you will offend in three ways with the same deed. This is my guest, so you will offend against the law of hospitality; he is my suppliant and thereby he is also yours, so you will offend against the law of supplication; finally I am a friend supplicating for a friend, so you will offend against the law of friendship.[191] You know how sure is the wrath that Jupiter conceives when

*　*　*　*　*

188 Greek ἠΰς τε μέγας, a common attribute of Homer's heroes; see *Iliad* 2.653, where A.T. Murray (Loeb) translates 'valiant and tall.'
189 *Adagia* II vi 65 ὁ Αἰτναῖος κάνθαρος (of things that are large and filthy)
190 A parody of Virgil *Aeneid* 1.542–3
191 Erasmus gives the Greek words ξένιον . . . ἱκετήσιον . . . φίλιον, three titles of Jupiter, which he could find in Lucian *Timon* 1 and *Piscator* 3; the rare form ἱκετήσιος, instead of the more common ἱκέσιος, is in Homer *Odyssey* 13.213; cf note 83 above.

he is angered, how sharp is his revenge when he is provoked, you who bring him his weapons when he rages. Not everything is allowed to his people, nor is everything condoned for those he loves.'

The beetle was about to say more, but the eagle beat him with her wings and threw him contemptuously to the ground. The hare pleaded in vain; she slew it with the greatest cruelty before the beetle's eyes, tore it to pieces and carried the mangled remains away to her savage nest. Neither prayers nor threats from the beetle had the slightest effect on her. But she would not have scorned the beetle in this fashion if her good sense had been equal to her audacity and strength, nor if it had occurred to her that once upon a time a lion in immediate peril of its life had been saved by a mouse; the king of all the quadrupeds was given at the right moment a gift that was almost beyond the power of the gods by such a weak and despised little beast.[192] Or she might have remembered that the ant was inspired by a kindness received and saved the life of the dove by biting the heel of the bird-catcher.[193] In truth, none is so humble, so lowly, that he cannot on occasion be a beneficent friend or a dangerous enemy even to the most powerful. But at that time none of this occurred to the eagle, who was concerned only to take the present booty and to enjoy it.

This outrage sank deeper into the heart of the generous scarab than anyone would have believed. His lofty and titanic soul was roused by shame that his authority had been worth little in such a just cause, by pity that a harmless and peaceful animal had been so savagely torn to pieces, and by grief that the eagle's savage contempt for him could go unpunished when, as it seemed to him, he deserved no contempt at all. For personal dignity is no slight matter to anyone. Already it occurred to him that the whole race of beetles would be put to shame if the eagle's deed should go at all unpunished. At that moment the beetle, though powerless to take his revenge, showed an altogether regal quality, the one that Calchas spoke of with respect to Agamemnon and other kings: 'Even if the king swallows his anger for the moment, he will nurse his grievance till the day he can settle the account.'[194] And so he pondered all sorts of arts and tricks. It was no common punishment but extermination and 'total destruction'[195] he

* * * * *

192 Aesop 150 Perry
193 Aesop 235 Perry
194 Homer *Iliad* 1.81–3; translation by E.V. Rieu (Penguin). Erasmus gives no Latin at this point.
195 Greek πανολεθρία, the title of *Adagia* I x 27 Root and branch; cf the name *Cantharolethrus* (n214 below).

contemplated. But he considered it too dangerous to risk war directly with such a fierce enemy as the eagle, not only because his forces were inferior, but because Mars is a stupid and frenzied god, as blind as Plutus[196] himself, or Cupid, and usually backs the guiltier cause. For even if their forces were exactly equal, even if those who had right on their side were to win, he saw there was a way to torment the eagle more and to satisfy his hatred with greater vengeance, if she was deprived of descendants and suffered a slow death while still alive and fully aware.

There is no means by which parents can be tormented more than through their children; those who can ignore the cruellest tortures of their own bodies cannot endure the sufferings of their children. He had seen asses plunge through fire to save their colts with marvellous disregard for their own lives, he had seen examples of this courage in many living creatures. He believed the eagle was no stranger to these common feelings. Finally he judged it would be safer for his species if he destroyed the very stock,[197] as they say, of such a tenacious enemy. I think he had heard that well-known proverb 'He's a fool who kills the father and spares the children.'[198] He was also tickled by a certain alluring hope that, if the act succeeded and the eagle were overthrown, he might himself take power. And since grief not only gives strength and courage but wisdom too he looked industriously for the place where his enemy had hidden her hope of posterity. When he had found it he went to Vulcan, who was something of a friend of his because of their similarity in colour. He persuaded the god to forge armour for him, which, without being too heavy for a flying creature, would protect him against an attack of moderate force. Vulcan armed the scarab from the top of his head to his hindmost heels[199] with the armour that he still wears (for before that he was unarmed, like a fly).

The eyrie was far away from there, on a high, sheer crag, hedged around and defended with lots of branches and brushwood. Whether our extraordinary beetle flew there forthwith or crawled there is not clear, but he did reach it. Some say when he was struck by the feathers of the eagle he clung to them in secret and was carried unwittingly by her up into the nest. And so the beetle found a way into a place where not even man, who is more cunning and more ingenious at doing harm than any other creature,

* * * * *

196 Cf *Adagia* III iii 6 and I vii 84.
197 Latin *ab ipsa stirpe*, translating the Greek ἐκ τῶν ῥιζῶν; cf *Adagia* II iv 86 From the eggs to the apples (CWE 33 232), in the last sentence but one.
198 *Adagia* I x 53. Erasmus gives the Greek here but no Latin.
199 Cf *Adagia* I ii 37 From head to heel.

had been able to reach. He lay in ambush, hidden among the brushwood, and grasping his opportunity pushed the eggs out of the nest,[200] one after the other, until not one was left. They were smashed by the fall, and the still unformed chicks were dashed pitifully on the rocks, deprived of life before they had any consciousness at all.

With even this cruel punishment the beetle's wrath was not satisfied. There is a precious stone, one of the best known, called by the Greeks from the name of the eagle *aëtites* 'eagle-stone';[201] it is not unlike an egg, and there is a male and a female form, for in the female you can find a foetus enclosed rather like a chicken. It has a marvellous power to induce delivery at birth,[202] and for this reason it is still placed nowadays on women in labour to speed delivery. So the eagle, who would otherwise never be able to lay eggs and certainly not to hatch them, usually places a couple of these stones in its nest.[203] It was this great treasure that the scarab threw out of the nest, thereby destroying all power of bearing offspring; the stones were shattered into fragments as they struck the pointed rocks. Yet not even this was enough to assuage the beetle's anger; he thought it would be too slight an outrage unless he could enjoy the enemy's grief and lamentations, and so he hid again in the twigs. The eagle returned, perceived the calamity that had just struck her offspring, saw their mangled and torn entrails, and the incalculable loss of the noble stone. She moaned, she cried, she howled, she shrieked, she wailed, she called on the gods, and searched around with those eyes of hers, already sharpened even more by grief, for the enemy with such power. And as she thought, anything and everything came into her mind rather than the despised beetle. Terrible were her threats, terrible her curses on whoever was the author of this outrage. Imagine what delight meanwhile the beetle felt in his heart as he listened to this. What could the wretched eagle do? She had to fly off again to the Fortunate Isles to find another pair of eagle-stones, for it is not to be obtained anywhere else. The nest she removed to another much more isolated and lofty place. Once again she laid eggs, and here again, just the same, the unknown enemy penetrated; everything was destroyed and the whole preceding tragedy played again.[204] Once again the eagle moved to a safer refuge,

* * * * *

200 'Some say . . . out of the nest' is drawn from Aesop 3 Perry.
201 See n181 above.
202 Pliny *Naturalis historia* 30.130 and 36.151 where he speaks rather of preventing abortion and miscarriage
203 Pliny *Naturalis historia* 36.149
204 Cf *Adagia* IV iii 40 A tragic misfortune.

laid more eggs, obtained more eagle-stones. And once again the beetle was there.

There was no limit to flight and no end to pursuit until, exhausted by so many disasters, the bird decided to 'let go the sheet anchor,'[205] to stop trusting in her own powers and flee to the gods for protection. She went to Jupiter and explained the whole drama of her misfortune: how her enemy was powerful and, worst of all, anonymous, so that however much she suffered, she had no means of revenge. She added that this calamity of hers concerned Jove himself, for the imperial office that he had bestowed would cease to exist and he would have to change his armour-bearer, if the enemy continued to do what he had started; there was some value in using known and established servants, even if the novelty of Ganymede's appointment had turned out well.[206] Jupiter was moved by the danger in which his attendant stood, especially as her recent service in the abduction of Ganymede was still in his mind. He commanded the eagle to lay her eggs, if she wished, in his very own bosom. There they would be absolutely safe, if nowhere else. The eagle complied and laid the last hope of her race in the bosom of supreme Jove, entreating him by the blessed eggs that Leda bore him long ago to guard her own faithfully.

What can deep-seated grief of mind not do? I fear the story may seem to some beyond belief. Up to the very stronghold of supreme Jove flew the unconquerable beetle, helped, I rather think, by some divine power. Into his bosom he dropped a ball of dung specially made for the purpose. Jupiter is not used to squalor for he lives in the purest region of the world, separated from earthy contamination by a very wide space. Offended by the filthy smell he tried to shake the dung out of his bosom and carelessly dropped the eagle's eggs, which perished as they fell from that great height even before they hit the ground. Then at last the author of so many deaths became known; and this was the culmination of the beetle's joy, for he had the pleasure of being acknowledged. On the other hand, for the eagle – she learned the whole story from Jupiter himself – there was the very heavy additional grief that the author of her calamity was such a contemptible creature. (It is no small consolation for misfortune if one is beaten by a noble enemy.) Hence the pitiless war broke out anew between them: the eagle harried the beetle race with all her strength wherever she found it,

* * * * *

205 Cf *Adagia* I i 24, meaning to fall back on one's final resource; cf also *Adagia* IV i 1 War is a treat for those who have not tried it n10 (403 below).
206 See Lucian *Deorum dialogi* 8(5). One may note the craven nature of the eagle's argument.

carrying them off, trampling them down, destroying them; the beetle for his part strained every nerve to ruin the eagle. And so it seemed 'there would never be pause or rest,'[207] nor any end to predation, ambush, and slaughter, except by the complete and equal destruction of both races – a Cadmean victory,[208] you might say – such was 'the gladiatorial spirit with which they attacked each other.'[209] The eagle could not be defeated; the beetle did not know the meaning of surrender.

In the end Jupiter thought he should intervene in such a dangerous state of affairs and tried to settle the matter between them privately. The harder he tried the more violent their hatred became, the hotter their anger, the fiercer their battles. He was himself, without a doubt, more inclined to the eagle's side; on the other hand, he was influenced by the fact that a very harmful example was set if anyone were to be allowed to hold the laws of supplication, friendship, and hospitality[210] in contempt. So he did what he usually does at critical moments; he called a council of the gods. After making a few preliminary remarks, he explained the course of the affair. Through his herald Mercury, opinions were asked and given.[211] Their inclinations were divergent. Almost all the lesser gods supported the beetle, and even among the greatest Juno was strongly on his side, being hostile to the eagle's cause out of hatred for Ganymede.[212] Finally they agreed to the decree proclaimed in a clear voice by Mercury and carved in bronze by Vulcan: that the scarab and the eagle should wage eternal war as they wished; that if either suffered harm, he could not complain in law, it must be considered the fortune of war. Whatever each one seized, he would hold by right of conquest. Nevertheless the gods did not desire the extermination of any species. For this reason there was to be a cessation of fighting and a truce was to be observed for the thirty days in which the eagle sits on her eggs. The beetle was forbidden to appear in public during that time so that the eagle should not be burdened with the fatigue of war as well as fasting and the labour of caring for her brood. Because of his partiality Jupiter also declared, despite the protests of not a few: 'It is fair that a small corner of this vast world should be a refuge for my attendant,

* * * * *

207 Latin *nec mora nec requies*: Virgil *Georgics* 3.110, *Aeneid* 5.458, 12.553
208 *Adagia* II viii 34
209 Cf Terence *Phormio* 964 and *Adagia* I iii 76, III viii 72 (308 below).
210 See n191 above.
211 Cf Lucian *Deorum concilium* 1.
212 Lucian *Deorum dialogi* 8(5)

where she may be safe from the scarabs' attacks. I am not creating a prece-
dent. There are places where there are no wolves, where no poisons can
enter, where moles cannot live.[213] I myself will measure out an area of a
certain number of acres in Thrace near Olynthus in which it shall be a capital offence for the beetle to set foot, deliberately or not, willingly or not;
he shall not leave if once he has entered, but shall live in torment there
until he die. The name that is given to this place is Beetlebane,[214] so that,
warned by this name, the beetle may know that it will be the end of him
if he dares to intrude into that place against our decree. The eagle is ban-
ished from Rhodes,[215] lest anyone should think it cruel that the beetle is
shut out of Olynthus.' Thus he spoke and made all Olympus tremble at
his nod.[216] The whole assembly of the gods murmured their assent. The
decree holds good to this day and always will. War to the death continues between scarabs and eagles; during the days when the eagle sits on
her eggs, the descendants of the beetle are nowhere to be seen. The place
that Jupiter designated is carefully avoided; any beetle taken there dies at
once. This is a fact, and if anyone asks, Pliny is witness to it in book 11
chapter 28,[217] as is Plutarch, a weightier author, in his essay 'On Tranquillity of Mind.'[218]

But I know well enough, dear reader, that you have been thinking
for some time, 'What is this fellow thinking of, chattering on to us with so
much nonsense about nothing and making, not exactly an elephant out of
a fly as they say,[219] but a giant out of a beetle? Has he not made enough
work for us to go through all the pages of these thousands of proverbs
without tormenting us as well with these never-ending fables?' But let me
say a word. Everyone has his own opinion, and some will think that my
explanations of these adages are pinched and starved, for they think that
the really grand thing is to expand a volume to an immense size. I wanted
to show these people certainly that I have chosen to be brief in the rest of
the book; otherwise I would not have been short of matter to enrich it if I
had thought more of showing off my eloquence than of giving pleasure to

* * * * *

213 For the moles, cf *Adagia* III vi 16 Water to a frog (131 n6 above).
214 Latin *Cantharolethrus*; see Pliny *Naturalis historia* 11.99.
215 Pliny *Naturalis historia* 10.76
216 See n6 above.
217 Pliny *Naturalis historia* 11.99
218 Plutarch *Moralia* 473E *De tranquillitate animi*
219 *Adagia* I ix 69

the reader. But let us come back to the business of proverbs: the comic poet Aristophanes recalls this tale in his *Peace* in these lines:

> It is said in Aesop's fables
> To be the only creature with wings that ever reached the gods.

> O Father, Father, that's an incredible story,
> That a filthy stinking brute should reach the gods.

> Yet once he did get there, I say, because of the bitter feud
> He had with the eagle, rolling out her eggs
> And seeking revenge upon his enemy.[220]

The fable teaches us that no one should despise an enemy however humble. There are some little men, of the meanest sort but malicious nevertheless, no less black than scarabs, no less evil-smelling, no less mean-spirited, but by their obstinately malicious spirit (since they can do no good to any mortal) they often make trouble for great men. Their blackness is terrifying, their noise is disturbing, their stench is an annoyance; they fly round and round, they cannot be shaken off, they wait in ambush. It is preferable by far sometimes to contend with powerful men than to provoke these beetles whom one may even be ashamed to beat. You cannot shake them off nor fight with them without coming away defiled.[221]

2 Timidus Plutus
Plutus is a coward

Δειλὸς ὁ πλοῦτος, Plutus is a coward. This is how Aristophanes introduces his Plutus,[1] as does Lucian imitating him in his *Timon*,[2] as one who is afraid of everything and trusts no one. Wealth brings a very similar state of mind to the rich, whereas poverty, on the contrary, sleeps sound on either ear.[3] Aristophanes indicates that the fearfulness of the wealthy was a common

* * * * *

220 Aristophanes *Peace* 129–34
221 The lesson drawn in this last paragraph is unchanged from the version of *1508* and shows that the essay was always more than a portrait of tyranny.

2 Zenobius 3.35 = Zenobius (Aldus) column 67, Apostolius 5.89A
1 Aristophanes *Plutus* 203
2 Lucian *Timon* 11–40
3 *Adagia* I viii 19

joke when he says: 'Nay all repeat it, / The most cowardly state of all is wealth.' The scholiast[4] tells us the comic poet was alluding to this line of Euripides: Δειλόν θ' ὁ πλοῦτος καὶ φιλόψυχον κακόν 'Prosperity is a thing that is eager for life, an evil state full of fear.' The reason for this saying is that there are many who set traps for the rich: robbers, would-be heirs, rulers, flatterers, sometimes even a wife and children. This is why Euripides adds φιλόψυχον κακόν 'an evil state clinging to life': because of their wealth they want to live longer than people of meagre fortune, or are often in fear of their lives for the same reason. Juvenal explains it neatly when he says:

> Though you carry but few plain silver vessels
> With you in a night journey, you will be afraid of the sword and cudgel of
>   a freebooter,
> You will tremble at the shadow of a reed shaking in the moonlight;
> But the empty-handed traveller will whistle in the robber's face.[5]

In short, in any business the rich man is more fearful than the poor. He is more careful in making his house secure for fear of thieves. He is afraid of storms because of the crops in his fields, and because of the cargoes that he has at sea. He fears his friends in case he is obliged to give them something when they ask; he fears his enemies who may do him harm. He is more timid in reviling others because he is afraid of being fined. All his words and deeds are more cautious for fear of the false accusations that are brought particularly against the rich because they have the resources that can be taken from them. If war threatens, it is the rich man who is most worried. And finally he is not free of the superstition that some unfriendly god intends him harm.

3 Panicus casus
A panic attack

Πανικόν is what the ancients called a sudden but irrational confusion of mind. For the ancients believed that the god Pan inspired sudden terror and confusion of mind, very like insane ravings, which are so unrestrained

* * * * *

4 The scholiast of Aristophanes *Plutus* 203 (Dübner page 335) citing Euripides *Phoenissae* 597
5 Juvenal 10.19–22; translation by G.G. Ramsey (Loeb)

3 *Collectanea* no 779

that they are not just unreasonable but mindless. In fact it happens not uncommonly, as in an army when both men and horses are thrown into confusion with no apparent sufficient cause.[1] This is something Euripides recalls too in the *Rhesus*: 'Hath Zeus' son Pan with the scourge of quaking / Struck thee'[2] are the words that Hector speaks to the guards who bring the message that a new disturbance has occurred in the camp, and Hector replies that it is a panic impulse. In the *Nemean Odes* Pindar writes that brave men ought not to be blamed if they flee during such a disturbance: 'Faced with divine terrors even the children of the gods flee,'[3] using the expression 'divine terrors' for panic. The same god is said in legend to have been the first to discover the twisted, cone-shaped shell that is called in Greek κόχλος 'tortoise';[4] by blowing through this, he is said to have put the Titans to flight when he was waging war against them.[5] In his book on Phocis Pausanias says: 'But at night a panic fear broke out among them, such groundless terrors as they say are inspired by this god.'[6] The subject is discussed at greater length with quotations from other Greek sources by Angelo Poliziano in his *Miscellanies*, chapter 28. This proverbial expression is used several times by Cicero in his *Letters to Atticus*: 'I believe there will be a most terrible war, unless, to use an expression you are familiar with, there is a "wave of panic."'[7] In another passage: 'In the case of Ventidius I believe there was a panic.'[8] Again: 'They bring a strong rumour that all the corn is being taken to Antony at Rome, this is certainly a panic.'[9] Elsewhere: 'Meanwhile (for you know such words as "panic" and "the uncertainties of

* * * * *

1 Following Poliziano *Miscellanea* 28
2 Euripides *Rhesus* 36–7; translation by A.S. Way (Loeb). Erasmus gives no Latin here.
3 Pindar *Nemeans* 9.27
4 Erasmus translated κόχλος as *testudo* in *1508*, an error, as Poliziano's text would have told him (his source is the scholiast of Aratus 283): the correct equivalent Latin is *concha*, the Triton's trumpet shell. In *Adagia* III iii 38, in a passage from Plutarch added in *1526*, Erasmus translated χελῶναι correctly as 'tortoises,' but failed to correct this.
5 Following Poliziano; see n1 above.
6 Pausanias 10.23.7; added in *1526*
7 Cicero *Ad Atticum* 7.26.3; Erasmus has *Panicus casus*; Cicero has *Parthicus casus*, translated by E.O. Winstedt (Loeb) as 'a Parthian incident,' ie a sudden retreat.
8 Cicero *Ad Atticum* 16.1.4; here Cicero uses *panicon*, and the phrase is translated by E.O. Winstedt (Loeb) as 'I think the report about Ventidius is a false alarm.'
9 Cicero *Ad Atticum* 14.3.1; Erasmus' text has *Romae dum ad Antonium*, which is presumably just an error for the accepted *Romae domum ad Antonium* 'to Antony's house at Rome.' The proverbial expression, here *πανικόν certe*, is again translated by E.O. Winstedt (Loeb) 'Of course it is a false alarm.'

war" are bandied about) at the rumour of my arrival even Cassius, who was besieged in Antioch, took courage, and fear was spread among the Parthians.'[10] Likewise in the letter to Tyro: 'And yet our Atticus, who thought that I had at one time been upset by "panic," still thinks the same and does not see by what philosophical defences I am protected. And by Hercules, because he himself is a coward, θορυβοποιεῖ "he makes an uproar," and is affected by panic.'[11] I think Apuleius too alluded to this in his *Golden Ass*, when he causes Pan to meet Psyche as she is trying to commit suicide.[12]

4 Nihil minus expedit quam agrum optime colere
Nothing pays less well than really good farming

Pliny states in book 18 chapter 6 that among the ancients this was considered as good as a proverb. He says:

> One dictum of the ancients it may seem rash to quote, and perhaps it will be judged almost unbelievable; it is that nothing pays less well than really good farming. Lucius Tatius[1] Rufus was of the humblest birth, but won a consulship by his efficiency as a soldier. Though he was in other respects a man of old-fashioned thriftiness, he spent about one thousand *sicli* (or, as some prefer to read it, *sestertii*),[2] which he had accumulated through the generosity of the emperor Augustus, even to the point of disadvantaging his heir, by buying up land in Picenum and farming it with a view to making a name for himself. Do I think then that this meant ruination and starvation? No indeed, but in my judgment moderation in all things is the most useful criterion. It is essential to be a good farmer, but to be the best is ruinous.[3]

This is what Pliny has to say. Terence referred to this too when he says in the *Phormio*: 'It is our fault that it is profitable for men to be rogues, while we try too hard to be known as honest and generous.'[4] Then there is this line of Horace: 'Avoiding a fault leads to error, if it is done without

* * * * *

10 Cicero *Ad Atticum* 5.20.3; here 'panic' is πανικά. Added in *1533*
11 Cicero *Ad familiares* 16.23.2: 'I had at one time been upset by "panic"' translates *me quondam moveri* πανικοῖς and 'affected by panic' *panicis movetur*.
12 Apuleius *Metamorphoses* 5.25

4 Pliny (see n3 below). Otto 39
1 Pliny has *Tarius*. See ASD II-6 427:879n.
2 The phrase 'or ... *sestertii*' was added in *1526*.
3 Pliny *Naturalis historia* 18.36
4 Terence *Phormio* 766–7

skill.'⁵ And finally there is the Hebrew proverb that warns us not to be too rigorous in justice.⁶

5 Citius quam asparagi coquuntur
As quick as boiled asparagus

Cooked as quick as asparagus. Said of something done with great speed. There are certain proverbial expressions that were particular favourites of Octavius Augustus, and among them this one is recorded by Suetonius, who writes that he used to talk of the speed of some rapid action by saying 'Cooked as quick as asparagus.' He often uses it in his letters too. Asparagus is a prickly type of grass,¹ a useful medicine² and pleasant food as well; before it grows hard, the top is cooked lightly, but only enough to take away the rawness. It is called asparagus because, as Athenaeus says, the finest types do not grow from seed.³ Scholars tell us that there is a similar expression about pickled fish, 'Cooked as quick as pickled fish,' because some sorts of fish that have been preserved in salt or dried in smoke or the open air are also eaten raw or lightly cooked, but I have not found the proverb in Athenaeus whom they give as their source.⁴ It is very close to a proverb that will be given elsewhere: 'Whitebait on the fire.'⁵

6 Amicitiae personam
The mask of friendship

Τὸ προσωπεῖον ἀφελεῖν τῇ φιλίᾳ, To remove the mask of friendship, as we are said to do when we act and talk frankly as we feel among friends, and show

* * * * *

5 Horace *Ars poetica* 31
6 Ecclesiastes 7:16 'Be not righteous overmuch.' Added in *1515*

5 Suetonius *Augustus* 87.1. Otto 195. The suggested English equivalent is due to Robert Graves.
1 Pliny *Naturalis historia* 21.91
2 Pliny *Naturalis historia* 20.108–11; Athenaeus 2.62E–F. Added in *1528*
3 Athenaeus is not talking of etymology, but Erasmus takes οὐ (negative) and σπείρονται (grow from seed) as having the same derivation as ἄσπαρτος, not sown, growing wild; ἀσπάραγος, properly ἀσφάραγος, is of uncertain origin.
4 Athenaeus 3.119E; translated by C.B. Gulick (Loeb) as 'Broiled salt-fish, if it but see the fire ...' 'Scholars ... source' was added in *1533*.
5 *Adagia* II ii 12; 'will be given' is an uncorrected future tense from *1508*, in which II ii 12 appeared later than III vii 5.

6 *Collectanea* no 405. Poliziano *Epistolae* 1.11 (Basle 1553 page 8). The Greek form appears to have been invented by Erasmus.

outwardly what is hidden in our heart. For a face that does not reflect the mind is more truly a mask than a face. Seneca had a very neat remark about Caesar: 'The mask he prefers rather than the face,'[1] meaning how he prefers to appear rather than how he is. Marcus Tullius writes in the fifth book of his *Tusculan Disputations* that Epicurus did no more than wear the mask of philosophy.[2] Martial says: 'You falsely ape youth, Lentinus, with dyed hair, / So suddenly a raven who were but now a swan. / You don't deceive all; Proserpine knows you are hoary: / She shall pluck the mask from off your head.'[3] But the word 'mask' does not always have a pejorative sense. When Marcus Tullius writes in his *On Moral Obligation*: 'For he puts off the mask of a friend when he wears that of a judge,'[4] he does not speak of a false friend or a false judge. The source of the saying is the masks of the theatre.

7 Utere curru, de asinis nihil laborans
Use a cart and you won't have to worry about asses

Ἀπονέμου τῆς σῆς ἁμάξης, τῶν δ' ὄνων οὐδὲν μέλει, Use your own wagons and you won't have to worry about asses. The line is a trochaic tetrameter.[1] The proverb counselled people to look after their own property and to enjoy it, without being concerned or worried for that of others. The figure is derived from the idea that those who have their own wagon at home have no need to hire asses from somewhere else to carry their loads.

8 Libyca fera
An African beast

Λιβυκὸν θηρίον, An African beast. This is recorded by Diogenianus. It used to be said of a cunning man, shrewd, changeable, equivocal, double-natured. Catiline was a monstrous prodigy of this sort according to Cicero.[1] The

* * * * *

1 Seneca *De beneficiis* 2.13.2, referring to Caligula
2 Cicero *Tusculan Disputations* 5.73; this reference and the remainder were added in 1526.
3 Martial *Epigrams* 3.43; cf Otto 1385.
4 Cicero *De officiis* 3.43

7 *Suda* A 3450
1 Not so in the *Suda*; Erasmus added the word σῆς 'your' from the start, but from 1515 to 1526 he called it a trimeter.

8 *Collectanea* no 621. Diogenianus 6.11, from whom Erasmus takes everything except the reference to Cicero; cf Apostolius 10.75.
1 Cicero *In L. Catilinam* especially 2.1–2

origin is the practice they have in Africa of mixing different species and from them producing for the circus strange new monsters, which provincial rulers export to Rome.

9 Semper adfert Libya mali quippiam
Africa always produces something evil

From the same source comes this too: Ἀεὶ φέρει τι Λιβύη κακόν, Africa always produces something evil, because, as I have said, monsters were exported from there to Rome. From this sense it can be turned to apply to the customs and mentality of a race; for if a region is prolific in poisons, the people who inhabit it are malevolent by nature. It will be particularly appropriate for those who break alliances and make changes to agreements.[1]

10 Semper Africa novi aliquid apportat
Africa always produces something novel

Very similar to that is this one from Pliny, which he records in his *History of the World*: 'Africa always produces something novel.'[1] The saying came about because in a very dry region many species of wild animals were obliged to come together at one particular river bank to drink, and there, through various violent interbreedings, different forms of monsters were continually born.[2] Moreover Pliny took this from Aristotle who relates it in book 2 chapter 5 of *On the Generation of Animals*.[3] In Athenaeus book 14 Anaxilas turned it wittily to the subject in hand:

* * * * *

9 *Collectanea* no 526. Diogenianus 1.68 (= Apostolius 1.49, Zenobius [Aldus] column 7)
  1 According to ASD Erasmus is thinking of the bad faith for which Hannibal and Jugurtha were reproached (Livy 21.4.9: *perfidia plus quam punica*; Sallust *Bellum Jugurthinum* 108.3: *fides punica*). In 1508 Erasmus may also have been thinking of Julius II, or Louis XII.

10 Pliny (see n1 below). *Collectanea* no 46. Cf Zenobius 2.51. Otto 35
  1 Pliny *Naturalis historia* 8.42; Erasmus would have found the variant title *Historia mundi* in Ermolao Barbaro's preface to his *Castigationes plinianae* (Rome 1493); see the edition by G. Pozzi I (Padua 1973) 23.
  2 Following Pliny; cf *Adagia* III vii 8 (219 above).
  3 Aristotle *De generatione animalium* 2.7 (746b8) and *Historia animalium* 7(8).28 (606b20). Surprisingly, Erasmus has not taken a Greek version of the proverb from these passages.

Ἡ μουσικὴ δ᾿ ὥσπερ Λιβύη πρὸς τῶν θεῶν
Ἀεί τι καινὸν καθ᾿ ἐνιαυτὸν τίκτει θηρίον

But music, by heaven, just like Africa
Always brings forth each year some new creature.[4]

I know that the last Greek line does not hold good, but this is what is found in the Aldine edition, and I cannot make a satisfactory surmise about how it can be restored, unless perhaps we should read ἐν αὐτῇ for καθ᾿ ἐνιαυτόν, although even so the metre is still incorrect; perhaps θηρίον should be left out and καθ᾿ ἡνιαυτόν should be put in place of καθ᾿ ἐνιαυτόν.[5] It will be suitably applied to men of slippery faith who are forever greedy of change.

11 Afra avis
An African bird

Λιβυκὸν ὄρνεον, An African bird. Applied according to Suidas to exceptionally big things,[1] because birds of immense size are exported from that region. Horace used it of a particularly splendid one:

> No African bird would make for me a meal
> . . .
> More pleasing than olives gathered
> From the most fertile branches of the trees.[2]

In former times Africa provided particularly big fowl, which are also called Numidian fowl.[3] Acron seems to take it to mean the ostrich, a bird that is also said to have a marvellously large body.[4] In my opinion it would

* * * * *

4 Athenaeus 14.623F:; PCG 2 Anaxilas fragment 27; added in 1517/18
5 Added in 1528; the reading accepted nowadays is Ἀεί τι καινὸν κατ᾿ ἐνιαυτὸν θηρίον, the word τίκτει belonging to the next line.

11 Horace (see n2 below). Suda Λ 495
1 Latin praegrandibus; Erasmus appears to have misunderstood the Suda who says ἐκτραπέλων 'extraordinary.'
2 Horace Epodes 2.53 and 55–6
3 Columella De re rustica 8.2.2; Pliny Naturalis historia 10.132
4 Acron Pseudoacronis Scholia in Horatium vetustiora ed O. Keller (Leipzig 1902–4) I 387. Helenius Acron's work (second century AD) is lost. The scholia partly incorporated in later commentaries of Pomponius Porphyrio and Servius may be his but the attribution does not antedate the Renaissance.

not be inappropriate to use it of a man who is remarkable for his strange dress. Plautus somewhere calls his Carthaginian a bird because of his long sleeves hanging down on each side like wings.[5] The proverb is recorded in Aristophanes' *Birds*. The scholiast indicates that it suits barbarians and timid people.[6] Exceptionally big men are mostly rather timid, as in Terence: 'This big fellow is a good-for-nothing.'[7]

12 Boni pastoris est tondere pecus, non deglubere
A good shepherd should shear his sheep, not skin them

This is still commonly used even nowadays, when someone is too demanding, too hard and insistent: 'What? Do you want my skin as well?'[1] – as if to say it would be enough to be satisfied with the wool. As a proverb it was invented or certainly used by Tiberius Caesar, according to Suetonius. When he was advised by friends that he should raise taxes in the provinces, he wrote back: 'A good shepherd should shear his sheep, not skin them.'[2] *Deglubere* means to remove the skin, and the expression is derived from peasants who say *deglubere* for 'to tear open a shell or pod' and 'to strip the peel from a seed.'[3] Because of this Catullus gave it an obscene sense, saying that a man is 'skinned' by a woman;[4] and Fotis in Apuleius says she is accustomed to 'skin men alive.'[5] Those who 'shear' therefore strip in such a way that they leave a portion from which growth can occur; those who 'skin,' leave nothing. For fleece that has been shorn grows again; when the skin is torn off there is nothing that you can subsequently remove. Alexander, king of the Macedonians titled the Great, expressed the same idea with a different metaphor: when someone proposed to him that much more tax could be extracted from the population, he replied thus: 'And I hate the herbalist who pulls out the herb root and all.'[6] And to conclude there is

* * * * *

5 Plautus *Poenulus* 975; from 'In former times' to here was added in 1515.
6 Aristophanes *Birds* 65 and the scholiast (Dübner page 212). Added in 1526
7 Terence *Eunuchus* 785: *Hic nebulo magnus est*, where *magnus* does not in fact refer to the physical size of the subject *hic* but intensifies *nebulo*; J. Sargeaunt (Loeb) translates as 'he's a craven rogue.' Added in 1526

12 Suetonius (see n2 below). Otto 1354
1 Cf Suringar 29.
2 Suetonius *Tiberius* 32.2
3 Cf Varro *De re rustica* 1.48.2.
4 Catullus 58.5
5 The editors of ASD suggest this may be a vague memory of passages such as Apuleius *Metamorphoses* 2.7, 2.17, and 3.18.
6 Apostolius 9.24D from Maximus the Confessor *Loci communes* 13 PG 91 805B–C; the phrase 'root and all' is quoted in *Adagia* II iv 86 From the eggs to the

this: ἀπὸ ῥιζῶν and ἀπορρίζειν,[7] and likewise in Latin *radicitus* 'roots and all,' *stirpium tenus* 'down to the roots,' *a stirpe* 'by the root,' *ab ima stirpe* 'by the deepest root,' and other figures of this sort have something of a proverbial flavour.

13 Lucri bonus est odor ex re qualibet
Profit smells good whatever it comes from

The following was a witty but disgusting *mot* of Vespasian;[1] he put a tax on urine, being greedy to the point of baseness, and was reproved over what he had done by his son for making a profit out of such a malodorous thing. Shortly afterwards he waved the money so collected under his son's nose and asked him, 'Does this stink somehow?' Whence this line of Juvenal: 'Profit smells good whatever it comes from.'[2] Ammianus alluded to this in book 22 when he said: 'And they smell out a profit from every opportunity ...'[3] And then there was that line of Ennius that not only entered into men's speech but right into the way they thought and lived: 'Where you get it from no one cares, but it is important to have it.'[4] And why should we not take seriously what Horace said ironically:[5] 'O citizens, citizens, seek money first, / Virtue after coin.'[6] Cephisodorus[7] in Athenaeus book 3 tells us in the writings of famous poets and wise men there are some blameworthy statements to be found,[8] such as this one of Archilochus: 'Fleece (or despoil) any man.'[9] In Theodorus: 'urging people to seek superiority of possessions,

* * * * *

apples (CWE 33 232 second paragraph) as are several of the following items.
7 The first of these phrases, not found in the literature, is apparently taken by Erasmus as equivalent to ἐκ ῥιζῶν 'from the root' (Plutarch *Pompey* 21.2, Athenaeus 12.523F, and *Adagia* II iv 86). For ἀπορρίζειν, cf ἀπερρίζωσα for 'having rooted out' (of hair) in Alciphron 3 *Letters of Parasites* 30.5 Benner-Fobes.

13 Juvenal (see n2 below). Cf *Adagia* III vii 1 (191 with n73 above). Otto 974 note
 1 Suetonius *Vespasian* 23.3; also quoted in Adagia III vii 1 A dung-beetle hunting an eagle (191 with n72 above)
 2 Juvenal 14.204
 3 Ammianus Marcellinus 22.4.3; added in *1526*. See *Adagia* I vii 10 (CWE 32 310 n4).
 4 The verse, Juvenal 14.207, was ascribed to Ennius in earlier editions of Juvenal. Cf *Adagia* III iii 52 Gain ill-gotten is as bad as loss.
 5 In Greek εἰρωνικῶς
 6 Horace *Epistles* 1.1.53–4; *Adagia* II ix 38 Seek riches first, then virtue; Otto 1910. This and the whole of the remainder were added in *1528*.
 7 Pupil of Isocrates, wrote a history of the Sacred Wars and a treatise against Aristotle; Cephisodorus *FGrHist* 112
 8 Athenaeus 3.122A–B whom Erasmus draws on for all the following cases
 9 Archilochus fragment 39 West

but to praise equality.'[10] In Euripides: 'As for what he may have said, only his tongue has sworn,'[11] which I have discussed elsewhere.[12] In Sophocles:

> I say these things to please you, I do not command,
> But you yourself, do as wise men are accustomed to,
> Praise just deeds, but keep the profit firmly in mind.[13]

The same writer said somewhere else: 'Nothing is bad that brings profit with it.'[14] Homer has Juno plotting against Jupiter, he pictures Mars as an adulterer.[15] All this is in Athenaeus. It is surprising however that people become indignant at poets and actors whenever they speak of such things in the theatre; they should be more indignant at themselves, because they do things in real life that they could not tolerate being shown in the theatre.

14 Lucrum pudori praestat
Profit before shame

Κέρδος αἰσχύνης ἄμεινον, Profit is preferable to shame. Plautus in the *Pseudolus*: 'What causes shame is far easier to bear than what causes annoyance.'[1] He expressed the same idea in another way in the *Trinummus*: 'By Pollux! Shame beats annoyance, and with the same number of letters.'[2] – a sentiment unworthy of a good man, and that is why in the former case it is uttered by a pimp and in the latter by an old man. But the sen-

* * * * *

10 Quoted but not identified by Bergk *Poetae lyrici graeci* (1915) II 375–6. See Diogenes Laertius 2.97–104 ('Aristippus').
11 Euripides *Hippolytus* 612. Erasmus takes his Greek from Athenaeus where the sense seems to be 'saying that only his tongue has sworn.' The accepted reading of this line is: ἡ γλῶσσ' ὀμώμοχ', ἡ δὲ φρὴν ἀνώμοτος, translated by A.S. Way (Loeb) as 'My tongue hath sworn: no oath is on my soul.'
12 *Adagia* II v 41 My tongue did swear it
13 Sophocles fragment 25 Nauck = 28 Pearson and Lloyd-Jones
14 Sophocles *Electra* 61; Lloyd-Jones translates 'No word that brings you gain is bad.'
15 Homer *Iliad* 14.153–160 and *Odyssey* 8.266–70

14 *Collectanea* no 522. Diogenianus 5.42 (= Apostolius 9.68); cf Zenobius 4.67 and Zenobius (Aldus) column 103.
1 Plautus *Pseudolus* 281
2 Plautus *Trinummus* 345. In Latin the words are *pudere* and *pigere*. Paul Nixon (Loeb) translates 'Better feel disgraced than disgusted, despite their being words of equal length.'

timent is aptly brought in to convince the audience even if it is dishonourable. In general it is far better to accept the sacrifice of a thing than
loss of reputation. This is what Terence alluded to in the *Phormio*: 'Aren't
you ashamed of your vanity? – No, as long as it's to my advantage.'[3] Indeed even nowadays there is a common proverb that bids us say farewell
to shame where money is concerned.[4] In his essay 'On Listening to Poets'
Plutarch quotes these lines from an unknown poet: 'Scorn[5] the opinion of
the just and follow the man / Who does whatever offers hope of profit.'[6]
He also records this from Sophocles: 'Profit is pleasant even when gained
by lies.'[7]

15 Baeta tum hyeme tum aestate bona
A baeta is fine in winter and in summer

Βαίτη κὰν θέρει καὶ ἐν χειμῶνι ἀγαθόν, A *baeta* is fine in winter and in summer. Suidas recalls this adage and adds that a *baeta* is a type of leather
garment that seems to be suitable for both seasons, for in winter it keeps
out the winds and in summer the heat. Julius Pollux in book 7 of his *Vocabulary* mentions *baeta* when listing leather clothing; he says it was an extra long tunic, which covered the whole body.[1] So the expression is suitable for something that will be useful for many purposes, such as learning, which is an ornament for both young and old, or philosophy, which
in prosperity keeps us from arrogance, and in adversity protects us from
discouragement.

* * * * *

3 Terence *Phormio* 525–6
4 Suringar 109
5 Erasmus has *spernito* for Greek ἄρνυσο, which means 'earn, seek to win.' ASD
   suggests a confusion with ἀρνεῖσθαι 'to deny, decline.'
6 Plutarch *Moralia* 18D *Quomodo adolescens poetas audire debeat*; adespota 4 Nauck
   = Euripides *Ixion* fragment 426A Snell
7 Sophocles fragment 749 Nauck = 833 Pearson and Lloyd-Jones; found in the
   same work of Plutarch *Moralia* 21A (see n6 above)

15 *Suda* B 212. In *1508* a proverb, Τοῦ Βάυνος χορός 'Baynis' chorus,' taken from
   Suda T 810, appeared between the adages here numbered III vi 15 and 16. In
   it Erasmus suggested the correct reading 'Babys' (the brother of Marsyas) for
   'Baynis'; 'Babys' is found in Zenobius (Aldus) column 159. The content of this
   proverb was added as a paragraph to *Adagia* II vii 34 in *1520* (CWE 34 18 and
   324 n2).
1 Pollux *Onomasticon* 7.70; added in *1515*, as was most of the final sentence, from
   'such as' to the end

16 Anicularum deliramenta
Ravings of silly old women

Γραῶν ὕθλος, Ravings of silly old women. Describes the meaningless trifles
that old women babble about when the defect of age is added to the defect
of their sex and multiplies their disease of talking nonsense. The proverb
occurs in Plato's *Theaetetus*: 'For these are indeed what are usually called
ravings of silly old women.'[1] Likewise Cicero talked in the speech *Concerning His House* about 'old women's superstition.'[2]

17 Ante pedes
Before your feet

Something is said to be 'before your feet' when it is obvious, and present
or about to appear. Terence: 'This is to be wise, to see not only what is
before your feet but to foresee even things that are to come.'[1] Likewise
Pindar in his last ode: 'Whatever is before your feet is always better.'[2]
Lucian in the *Pretended Critic*: 'Because you are ignorant of these things
both commonly known and everywhere in your way.'[3] Philostratus in the
Phoenix: 'But where are you going, with your nose in the air and despising
what is before your feet?'[4] And the expression 'at your feet' means what is
close or imminent; to be ἐμποδών[5] means to be in the way, and ἐκποδών the
opposite. Προκυλίνδεσθαι τῶν ποδῶν is found several times in Plato, meaning
'thrown at one's feet,' what has been revealed, as it were. For example in the
Republic book 4: 'For a long time now, O happy one, it seems to lie before
our feet (φαίνεται πρὸ ποδῶν), and we do not see it; but we were silly, like

* * * * *

16 Zenobius 3.5; cf Diogenianus 3.79; Apostolius 5.63 and *Suda* Γ 432. Otto 12
1 Plato *Theaetetus* 176B; added in 1520
2 Cicero *De domo sua* 105; added in 1533

17 *Collectanea* no 800. Otto 1389
1 Terence *Adelphoe* 386–7; cf *Adagia* III vi 52 (150 above).
2 Pindar *Isthmians* 8.14; added in 1526
3 Lucian *Pseudologista* 2; 'in your way' is ἐν ποσὶν, which Erasmus translates in
this case as *passim obvia*.
4 Philostratus *Heroicus* 1, 2 Lannoy; 283, 7 Kayser ed maior; 128, 1 Kayser ed
minor. The subtitle of this dialogue is 'The Speakers are Ampelourgos and
Phoenix,' but it is not otherwise called the *Phoenix* by any editor; ἐν ποσί
'before your feet' is given in Greek.
5 See the quotation from Plutarch *Moralia* 971C–D in *Adagia* III v 21 n3 (78 above).

people who hold something in their hands, yet search for what they already have.'[6] Using a not dissimilar figure Maro said 'at hand': 'The land is near at hand; I shall not keep you here with a long ode,[7] with digressions and lengthy preludes.'[8]

18 Albo rete aliena captant bona
They use a white net to hunt for other people's goods

A proverb in appearance is this expression of Plautus in the *Persian*: 'I warrant those fellows would never appear, / Who attack other people's property with their white nets.'[1] By 'net' he means the tricks of informers and spongers. 'White' refers to the petitions, actions, and summonses by which a dispute is instituted and conducted. And it would be quite amusing if it were to refer to the praetor's tablet on which laws and rules for disputes were published. For laws, according to Solon even, are like spiders' webs.[2]

19 Ad suum quemque quaestum aequum est esse callidum
Each for his own advantage is rightly hard-headed

This is a proverbial phrase in Plautus' *Truculentus* and in the *Comedy of Asses* too: 'Everyone ought to keep a sharp eye for his own advantage.'[1] If this is used more broadly in a figurative sense, it will be rather more witty. For example one may be after money, another seeks fame, another is greedy for pleasures, another hungry for literature, another may strive after piety. Each one is watchful for what he desires.

* * * * *

6 Cf Plato *Republic* 4.432D πρὸ ποδῶν ... κυλίνδεσθαι and *Theaetetus* 174A and 174C παρὰ πόδας, but προκυλίνδεσθαι with genitive τῶν ποδῶν is not attested in Plato. For the use of προκυλίνδεσθαι see the quotation from Aristotle *Historia animalium* 8(9) in III v 21 n2 (78 above), and from Aristophanes *Birds* in *Adagia* III vi 8 n2 (128 above).

7 Latin *carmine longo*; modern editions have *carmine ficto* 'fabulous ode.'

8 Virgil *Georgics* 2.45–6: *In manibus terrae* ... From 'For example' to the end was added in *1528*.

18 *Collectanea* no 219

1 Plautus *Persa* 73–4; mentioned by Otto 51n, but rejected as corrupt

2 Cf *Adagia* III v 73, where Erasmus refers to Plutarch's *Life of Solon* 5 but quotes in fact from Diogenes Laertius 1.58 (109 with n2 above).

19 *Collectanea* no 60. Plautus (see n1 below). Otto 1500

1 Plautus *Truculentus* 416; in the *Asinaria* 186 it has a rather different form.

20 Vel acum invenisses
You would have found even a needle

In the *The Two Menaechmuses* by the same author there is a proverbial hyperbole for 'searching carefully for something': 'I believe you would have found a needle, if you were looking for a needle.'[1] For a needle is an extremely difficult thing to find, because its fineness makes it easily invisible to the eye of the searcher.

21 Subventanea parit
His progeny are full of wind

Ὑπηνέμια τίκτει, His progeny are full of wind. Said of ideas that are empty and trivial, a figure derived from birds, which, in the false belief that they have had sexual intercourse, conceive eggs that are empty, that is, in which no foetus is formed. Aristophanes in the *Birds*: 'Blackfeathered night bears first a wind-egg.'[1] These births happen mostly among birds that are not good fliers and do not have crooked claws, such as the partridge, and the cock, as Aristotle shows in book 3 of *On the Generation of Animals*; the cause is that they produce greater quantities of excrement. Birds that fly and have crooked claws are not lustful and not prolific, because in them a fertile part of the excrement goes to form feathers and claws.[2] Such foetuses[3] are conceived in some cases from the sound of the voice of the male, as in the case of partridges,[4] in some cases when the birds rub themselves in the dust, and sometimes when the females, because of a shortage of males, cover each

* * * * *

20 *Collectanea* no 204. Otto 13
1 Plautus *Menaechmi* 238–9; quoted from memory

21 Apostolius 17.67. Cf *Suda* Υ 423. The word *subventanea* and several other words in the Latin account of Aristotle below are not attested in classical Latin but taken from Theodorus Gaza's translation.
1 Aristophanes *Birds* 695; translated by B.B. Rogers (Loeb): 'Of Darkness an egg, from the whirlwind conceived, was laid by the sable-plumed Night.' This egg however is not infertile.
2 Aristotle *De generatione animalium* 3.1 (749b1), a passage also cited in *Adagia* III vii 1 A dung-beetle hunting an eagle (196 with n117 above).
3 Latin *huiusmodi foetus*; this hardly makes sense – Erasmus appears to mean 'such unfertilized eggs.'
4 For more on this subject and a modern source used by Erasmus cf *Adagia* III vii 66 Before the cock crows twice (257 below).

other. The authority for this is Pliny.[5] Such eggs the Greeks call ὑπηνέμια 'wind eggs,' or ζεφύρια 'zephyr eggs,' after the west wind.[6] From this useless ideas are said to be ἀνεμίδια 'full of wind.' Plato in the *Theaetetus*: 'But come now let us look at this together and see whether it is a real conception or a wind egg.'[7] And Homer: 'to speak words of wind,' meaning empty utterances like so much wind.[8] Marcus Tullius in the *Letters to Atticus* uses 'airy nothings' of empty rumours that are carried by the wind: 'About the gladiators and the other things you call 'airy nothings,' keep me informed daily.'[9]

22 Phrynondas alter
Another Phrynondas

Φρυνώνδας ἄλλος, Another Phrynondas. Said of a dishonest man. Lucian in the *False Prophet* recalls this name among other wicked celebrities.[1] Phrynondas, though a stranger in Athens, was involved in the Peloponnesian negotiations. He was crafty, maleficent, and mendacious, a masterly contriver of evil deeds, with the result that the name of the man became the term for the thing, and in fact whenever they wanted to characterize someone as particularly evil and wicked they referred to him as 'Phrynondas.' Thus we find Aristophanes in the *Amphiareus*, as Suidas quotes him: 'You abomination, you vilest Phrynondas.'[2] Plato used it too in the *Protagoras*.[3] Such men are recalled too by Aeschines in the speech against Ctesiphon: 'Not Phrynondas, not Eurybatus,[4] nor any other of the old evil-doers was ever such a quack and a liar.'[5]

* * * * *

5 Pliny *Naturalis historia* 10.102, 160, 166
6 Aristotle in the passage cited in n2 above. The whole passage 'These births . . . west wind' was added in 1515.
7 Plato *Theaetetus* 151E: 'wind egg' is ἀνεμίδιον.
8 Homer *Odyssey* 11.464: Κακὸν δ' ἀνεμώλια βάζειν
9 Cicero *Ad Atticum* 13.37.4: 'airy nothings' is ἀνεμοφόρητα; added in 1523

22 Apostolius 18.2. Cf *Suda* Φ 770.
1 Lucian *Alexander* 4
2 PCG 3.2 Aristophanes fragment 26. From 'among other wicked celebrities' to here was added in 1515.
3 Plato *Protagoras* 327D; added in 1520
4 Cf *Adagia* I ii 86 To play Eurybatus, where the passage from Lucian is also quoted.
5 Aeschines 3.137; added in 1526

23 Sus per rosas
A pig among the roses

Ὗς διὰ ῥόδων, A pig among the roses. However in other sources I find Ὗς διὰ ῥοίδων.[1] For me neither version seems right; I believe we should read διὰ ῥοιίδων, from ῥοιᾶ, making a diminutive form of it. And *rhoea* is the Greek word for pomegranate.[2] Eudemus quotes the proverb from the play by Crates entitled *The Neighbours*, where he indicates that it is usually said of rustic, or intransigeant people. They are like pigs that cannot easily be lead past apples.[3]

24 Asinus avis
The ass is a bird

Ὄνος ὄρνις, The ass is a bird. This is in the *Birds* of Aristophanes.[1] It is derived from some augury. A certain man, consulted about a person who was in bad health, saw by chance an ass getting to its feet from a fall and at the same time heard someone else saying, 'See how he got up, even though he is an ass.' Seizing on this as an omen our man immediately takes it to mean that the sick man would recover.[2] So Aristophanes' joke is that an ass is also like a bird in being something of an omen. The origin of this proverb is not the comedy but popular speech used for a humorous purpose by the comic poet.[3] The right moment for it is when we infer something from some silly sign or other.

* * * * *

23 *Suda* Υ 675; Zenobius (Aldus) column 166
  1 Apostolius 17.71 (Ὗς Διαροίδων)
  2 In Latin *malum punicum* 'Carthaginian apple,' or *malum granatum* 'having many seeds.' The correct diminutive form in Greek would be τὸ ῥοίδιον.
  3 PCG 4 Crates fragment 6; on Eudemus, see *Adagia* III v 1 n48 (66 above).

24 Aristophanes (see n1 below); cf *Suda* O 378. From here to III vii 75 the adages are taken from Aristophanes, interrupted at numbers 49–58 by items mainly from Plautus and Stobaeus. From 77–82 the source is Plautus, and from 83–99 the proverbs are attributed to Plutarch from the codex Laurentianus 80.13 (see *Adagia* III v 30n and n1, 83–4 above).
  1 Aristophanes *Birds* 721
  2 Following the scholiast of Aristophanes (Dübner page 226)
  3 'The origin ... comic poet' was added in 1533.

25 **Sisyphi artes**
The wiles of Sisyphus

Σισύφου μηχαναί, The wiles of Sisyphus, a term for resourceful and cunning
advice. Aristophanes in the *Acharnians*: 'Then bring out the clever tricks
of Sisyphus.'[1] Further, the reason why the name of Sisyphus should be
proverbial for cunning is this line of Homer: 'Sisyphus, the craftiest man
in the world.'[2] And again in the *Iliad* book 6: 'Here lived a man called
Sisyphus, as cunning a rogue as ever there was.'[3] From him was descended
Ulysses, whom Homer always portrays as crafty and clever.[4]

26 **Homo Thales**
A man like Thales

Ἄνθρωπος Θαλῆς, A man like Thales. A proverbial irony for a fool who
strives to be thought wise. Aristophanes in the *Birds*: 'Meton is a man
like Thales.'[1] In the *Clouds* by the same author: 'What reason then had we
for regarding this man as a Thales?'[2] – for Thales was one of the seven
wise men. In Plautus too there is 'Hail Thales!' though it designates a
fool.[3]

* * * * *

25 Aristophanes (see n1 below); cf *Adagia* IV i 63n (479 below).
  1 Aristophanes *Acharnians* 391
  2 Not found in this form in Homer, but in the scholion of the Aldine edition of
    Aristophanes (1498), which Erasmus is following here
  3 Homer *Iliad* 6.153, given in Greek, translation by E.V. Rieu (Penguin) (Erasmus
    gives no Latin); added in 1526
  4 Added in *1515*; in post-Homeric stories Sisyphus seduced Anticleia, daughter
    of the other great trickster Autolycus and wife of Laertes: Hyginus *Fabulae*
    201; Euripides *Cyclops* 104–5 and *Iphigenia Aulidensis* 524; Sophocles 417 and
    Ajax 189; *Suda* Σ 490.

26 Aristophanes (see n1 below)
  1 Aristophanes *Birds* 1009; Meton is a character in the play, addressed directly
    here: 'The man's a Thales! Meton!' Meton was a fifth-century Athenian as-
    tronomer, but in Aristophanes he is a comic town-planner. Also mentioned by
    Cicero *Ad Atticum* 12.3.2
  2 Aristophanes *Clouds* 180; B.B. Rogers (Loeb) translates: 'Good heavens! Why
    Thales was a fool to this!'
  3 Plautus *Rudens* 1003; Otto 1775

27 Sardanapalus
A Sardanapalus

Σαρδανάπαλος, A Sardanapalus. His name became a proverb because of the man's extraordinary effeminacy. Aristophanes in the *Birds*: 'Who is this Sardanapalus?'[1] Sardanapalus was the son of Anacyndaraxis and king of Nineveh, a region of Persia,[2] who occupied[3] both Tarsus and Anchialea, two cities of Cilicia, on the same day, but was so effeminate in his vices that he habitually lounged among his eunuchs and girls dressed as a girl himself.[4] Apollodorus, who is quoted by the scholiast of Aristophanes, reports that the epitaph on his tomb, carved in Assyrian letters, said 'Eat, drink, make love, for all else is nothing.'[5] Suidas recounts this version from Callisthenes: 'But you, my guest, eat, drink, play, and give not a fig for any other mortal thing.'[6]

28 Quid tandem non efficiant manus?
What in the end cannot be done with hands?

In the *Birds* Aristophanes says: 'What is there in the end that feet could not do?'[1] The scholiast shows that this is an allusion to the proverb Τί δῆτα χεῖρες οὐκ ἂν ἐργασαίατο; 'What is there finally that cannot be made with hands?' suggesting that there is nothing in the world that cannot be made with

* * * * *

27 Aristophanes (see n1 below)
1 Aristophanes *Birds* 1021
2 Estienne (LB II 890) points out that Nineveh is a city, not a region, and in Assyria, not Persia. He obligingly excuses Erasmus' poor geographical knowledge on the grounds of his lack of resources, and affirms that he would not go to such trouble if he did not sincerely admire the man. In fact Erasmus appears to have mistranslated a Greek phrase which means 'of (i.e. in) Persian land' as being in apposition with Nineveh.
3 Latin *obtinuit*, a mistranslation of the scholion (see n4 below), which says 'founded'
4 For 'Sardanapalus was the son ... women' Erasmus is following the scholiast of Aristophanes (Dübner page 233).
5 Apollodorus *FGrHist* 244 F 303
6 Callisthenes *FGrHist* 124 F 34; *Suda* Σ 122; added in *1526*

28 As he admits, Erasmus accepts the word of the scholiast on Aristophanes *Birds* (Dübner page 236) that this is a proverb, but Aristophanes is parodying a line of tragedy (adespota 46 Nauck) not a proverb.
1 Aristophanes *Birds* 1147: τί δῆτα πόδες ἂν οὐκ ἀπεργασαίατο;

skill and labour. Aristophanes' version might aptly be applied to cowardly infantry for whom any protection and hope of safety lies not in their hands but in their feet.

29 Testa collisa testae
One pot smashed against another

We say 'One pot smashed against another' when two forces come into conflict to the ruin of both. Aristophanes in the *Peace*: 'And reacting in anger one pot damages another.'[1] Disputes between warring kings are just like the dashing of one pot against another: frequently both perish. Certainly neither one escapes without very serious harm. But it seems to me fate disposes things most unfairly: although the misfortunes of war should fall on the heads of those who start the war and whose advantage is in conquest, the greater share of evil falls on those who take up the fight against their will and in detestation of it, and those to whom, even if they fight successfully, not a farthing[2] will be paid in compensation.

30 Animus est in coriis
My mind is on hides

Aristophanes in the *Peace*:

> I was indeed mistaken in this,[1] but you will forgive me;
> For my mind at that moment was entirely on hides.[2]

* * * * *

29 Aristophanes (see n1 below); the whole comment on war was added in *1515*, date of the major expansions of *Adagia* III vii 1 A dung-beetle hunting an eagle (178 above), and IV i 1 War is a treat for those who have not tried it (399 below).
1 Aristophanes *Peace* 613: καὶ πόθος πληγεὶς ὑπ᾽ ὀργῆς ἀντελάκτισεν πίθῳ.
2 In Latin *ne teruncius quidem*, an expression of Cicero *Ad Atticum* 5.20.6: *teruncium sumptus nullum fore* 'not a penny's expense' and 6.2.4; it is used in a different context in *Adagia* I viii 9 He did not spend a farthing.

30 Aristophanes (see n2 below)
1 Estienne remarks (LB II 890) that Erasmus' translation *In his quidem sum lapsus* suggests he had read ἥμαρτον μέν, but that this is metrically impossible. B.B. Rogers (Loeb) translates: 'We erred in that ...'
2 Aristophanes *Peace* 668–9, given in Greek: Ἡμάρτομεν ταῦτ᾽, ἀλλὰ συγγνώμην ἔχε· / Ὁ νοῦς γὰρ ἡμῶν ἦν τότ᾽ ἐν τοῖς σκύτεσι.

However I have recalled this proverb elsewhere.[3] It is very like Terence's expression 'My mind is on dishes.'[4] Then there is what Athenaeus has in book 1 of the *Doctors at Dinner*: 'Let no one speak; we shall never be able to understand, / For the mind itself is too close to the table.'[5] The scholiast reminds us of this proverb: 'He has hides before his eyes,'[6] said of those who expect war, as we have shown elsewhere.[7] A good moment to use it would be when someone is distracted by worry from the matter in hand.

31 Quibus nec ara neque fides
For those who hold to neither altar nor oath

Aristophanes in the *Acharnians*: Οἷσιν οὔτε βωμὸς οὔτε πίστις οὔθ᾽ ὅρκος μένει, For them no altar, no faith, no agreement stands.[1] Used of the utterly treacherous. It was said of the Spartans, who were reproached for their treachery by Euripides: 'Inhabitants of Sparta; counsels of treachery.'[2] Nowadays it fits courtiers not at all badly.[3]

32 Ἄγουσι καὶ φέρουσι
Driving and carrying off

This is very banal certainly but it is a proverbial expression in Greek writers; Ἄγουσι καὶ φέρουσι means figuratively 'they plunder or harass in a hos-

* * * * *

3 *Adagia* II ii 18 My mind is on hides. Added in *1528*; Erasmus seems not to have noticed the duplication of this proverb before then.
4 Terence *Eunuchus* 816; also cited in *Adagia* II ii 18
5 Athenaeus 1.23D; PCG 2 Alexis fragment 279; added in *1520*. The beginning of the quotation is that it is a mistake to lie down before dinner; one cannot sleep or understand a word anybody says. Estienne has a second note correcting Erasmus' mistranslation of the Greek Οὐδ᾽ ἂν λέγῃ τις; the translation should be: 'If someone does speak . . .'
6 Scholiast of Aristophanes *Peace* (Dübner page 191); cf Zenobius 6.2.
7 *Adagia* II ii 19

31 Aristophanes (see n1 below)
1 Aristophanes *Acharnians* 308
2 Euripides *Andromache* 446. Erasmus is following the scholiast of Aristophanes (Dübner page 11).
3 Added in *1515*

32 Aristophanes (see n1 below)

tile manner.' If the expression is applied to a mental state, it will become
much more humorous. Aristophanes does this in the *Clouds*: 'By heavy interest payments and cruellest creditors I am driven and carried off, wretch
that I am, putting up my possessions as security.'[1] Lucian used ἄγει καὶ
φέρει to mean 'He drags you wherever he wants, at his whim.'[2] Cornelius
Tacitus said something very similar in his *Dialogue on Orators*: 'Nowadays
the leading men in the emperor's circle of friends *agunt feruntque cuncta*
"get their own way in everything" and are esteemed by the emperor himself with a sort of reverence.'[3] Homer in book 5 of the *Iliad*: 'For I do not
have anything here / Such as the Greeks could drive away and carry off.'[4]
These are the words of Sarpedon as he exhorts Hector to fight in defence of
his country, for he himself was fighting even though he had nothing that
the Greeks could take away, being from Lycia. Then there is Virgil in book
2 of the *Aeneid*: 'Others rape and rob burning Pergamum,'[5] meaning they
'destroy and plunder it.' In a very similar expression Livy said in book 8 of
his Macedonian War: 'Then at last their endurance was broken as they saw
their possessions carried and driven away.'[6] In Herodotus Croesus says the
same thing to his conqueror Cyrus: 'Now not one of these things is mine,
it is yours they plunder.'[7] The expression seems to be borrowed from military custom, where men and beasts are driven off and burdens are carried
off.

In the *Laws* Plato says: 'Let no one drive or take away anything belonging to anyone else.'[8] Quintus Curtius, in book 4, translated ἄγεσθαι καὶ
φέρεσθαι as *volvi agique*: 'Let them scoff who are persuaded that human affairs are guided and driven arbitrarily and rashly.'[9] In the same book he
used *ferri agique*: 'Still carried away and driven by frenzy, throwing down

* * * * *

1 Aristophanes *Clouds* 240–1: 'I am driven and carried off' is Ἄγομαι, φέρ-
   ομαι.
2 Lucian *Dialogi deorum* 9(6).218
3 Tacitus *Dialogus de oratoribus* 8.3; the emperor in question is Vespasian.
4 Homer *Iliad* 5.483–4
5 Virgil *Aeneid* 2.374; added in *1526*
6 Livy 38.15.10; added in *1533*
7 Herodotus 1.88.3; added in *1533*; Erasmus translates with the single word
   diripiunt 'plunder,' but the Greek contains the two verbs of the proverbial
   expression: φέρουσι τε καὶ ἄγουσι.
8 Plato *Laws* 10.884A; added in *1528*
9 Quintus Curtius *Historia Alexandri* 5.11.10; see *Adagia* I i 11 (CWE 31 60 15n);
   added in *1533*

their arms ...'[10] The words give a clear picture of military disorder and confusion.

33 Salem lingere
To lick salt

"Αλα λείχειν, To lick salt. People are said to lick salt if they live an extremely meagre life. In Persius, for example: 'Varus,[1] if you mean to keep up with Jupiter, you will have to go on being content with scraping the salt cellar with your finger as you have often done before.'[2] When Diogenes was invited by a certain very rich citizen called Craterus to come and enjoy his hospitality and his liberality, he replied that he preferred to lick salt in Athens than to enjoy sumptuous meals in his house.[3] Likewise Plautus in the *Curculio*: 'Today in my house you will have never a lick of salt.'[4]

34 Pedere thus
To fart frankincense

Βδέειν λιβανωτόν, To fart frankincense, has the appearance of a proverb. It will be apt for those who enjoy their own vices or those who are deeply in love. The cause of the former is φιλαυτία 'love of self,' because everyone enjoys his own vices and finds them pleasant, even if they are of the most nauseous sort.[1] The cause of the latter is extravagant love: 'Even Agnes' polyp delights Balbinus,' as Horace writes.[2] And Aristophanes in

* * * * *

10 Quintus Curtius *Historia Alexandri* 4.13.13; added in 1533

33 Diogenes Laertius (see n3 below)
 1 Erasmus' edition gave *Vare*, which may be the vocative case of the proper name, or may mean 'knock-kneed.' The accepted reading nowadays is *Baro* 'simpleton.'
 2 Persius 5.138
 3 Diogenes Laertius 6.57 ('Diogenes the Cynic'); cf Erasmus *Apophthegmata* III Diogenes 144.
 4 Plautus *Curculio* 562; added in 1520; cited by Otto 1571

34 Aristophanes (see n3 below); in Aristophanes the expression is not used proverbially – Erasmus probably associated it with *Adagia* III iv 2 Everyone thinks his own fart smells sweet (4 above).
 1 Cf *Adagia* I ii 15 What is one's own is beautiful, where the passage from Horace (n2 below) is also quoted.
 2 Horace *Satires* 1.3.40

the *Plutus*: 'I am not accustomed to farting frankincense.'³ The expression will also suit flatterers who praise the vilest things instead of the most noble.

35 Pro caeco exoculatus est
Not blind but eyeless

All humorous expressions of this sort have the character of adages; we appear to correct what is said, but with another word that either has the same meaning or has a stronger meaning. As when someone says 'He didn't steal, he purloined' or 'He didn't steal, he plundered.' Aristophanes in the *Plutus*: 'So you did not steal – You robbed?'¹ And in the same play: 'Ἀντὶ γὰρ τυφλοῦ ἐξωμμάτωται 'Not blind, just eyeless.'² The slave is playing on an ambiguous word, which says both that Plutus is endowed with eyes and that he does not make use of them.³

36 Prius lupus ovem ducat uxorem
Sooner a wolf would mate with a sheep

Aristophanes in the *Peace*: Πρίν κεν λύκος οἶν ὑμεναιοῖ, Till the wolf mates with the sheep.¹ Said of those who have an incurable discord between them. Horace used a very similar figure: 'Goats would sooner mate / With the wolves of Apulia.'² Plautus in the *Pseudolus*: 'You would sooner leave wolves among your sheep than these fellows in charge in your house.'³ It will be more humorous if applied to an idea; for example you may say the pursuit of money and the study of literature do not belong together and adapt the proverb to that meaning.

* * * * *

3 Aristophanes *Plutus* 703

35 Aristophanes (see n2 below); lines borrowed from a fragment of Sophocles *Phineas* (fragment 644 Nauck = 710 Pearson and Lloyd-Jones)
1 Aristophanes *Plutus* 372
2 Aristophanes *Plutus* 634–5
3 Erasmus' explanation follows the scholiast of Aristophanes *Plutus* (Dübner pages 359–60).

36 Aristophanes (see n1 below). Otto 981
1 Aristophanes *Peace* 1076
2 Horace *Odes* 1.33.7–8; added in *1526*
3 Plautus *Pseudolus* 140–1; added in *1533*

37 Sphondyla fugiens pessime pedit
When the polecat flees it makes a dreadful smell

The same author in almost exactly the same place: Ὡς ἡ σφονδύλη φεύγουσα
πονηρότατον βδεῖ, When the polecat flees, it usually leaves a bad smell.[1] Said
of people who break ranks and bring shame on themselves. The *sphondyla* is
a kind of insect with an absolutely filthy smell. In book 27 chapter 13 Pliny
recalls a *sphondyla serpens* 'snake beetle,' which does enormous damage to
tree roots,[2] though he does not make it clear what kind it is. There is however
a snake of this sort, slim bodied and blackish in colour, which emits a
very oppressive smell when it dies. Hesychius tells us that among Attic
people *spondyle* was a word for a polecat.[3] In Aristophanes there is the
phrase γαλῆς δριμύτερον 'as pungent as a polecat,' said of acid wind from
the stomach.[4]

38 Nunquam efficies, ut recte ingrediantur cancri
You'll never make crabs walk forwards

Aristophanes in the *Peace*:

* * * * *

37 From *1508* to *1523* Erasmus used what is now the title as the transla-
    tion of the quotation from Aristophanes (see n1 below) correctly render-
    ing σφονδύλη as *sphondyla*, and giving it the Greek meaning of a kind
    of beetle that leaves a strong smell when attacked: 'When the beetle flies
    away it makes a dreadful smell.' In *1526* he changed the translation ren-
    dering σφονδύλη as *feles*, apparently misled by Hesychius (see n3 below)
    who defines σπονδύλη (the Attic form) as ἡ γαλης παρ᾽ Ἀττικοῖς 'What At-
    tic people call a polecat' – meaning perhaps a beetle that stinks like a pole-
    cat. The resulting inconsistency with the information from Pliny remained
    uncorrected. However he did not change the title, which he must have
    now thought of as meaning 'When the polecat flees it makes a dreadful
    smell.'
 1 Aristophanes *Peace* 1077
 2 Pliny *Naturalis historia* 27.143; added in *1517/18*. The source of Erasmus' word
    serpens is a phrase in Pliny *genus id serpentis est*, which is probably a spurious
    interpolation.
 3 Hesychius Σ 1551; added in *1526*
 4 Aristophanes *Plutus* 693

38 Aristophanes (see n1 below); cf *Adagia* III vii 98 Teaching a crab to walk (279
    below). Otto 314

> If you try to make the crab walk forwards you will never succeed,
> And you will never succeed in changing anything that has already
>   been done.[1]

The poet delivers this as a humorous oracle: what has been set by nature you cannot change by any effort. For crabs naturally walk sideways. The second of these lines is pertinent to an adage that was recorded earlier, 'To reopen a closed subject.'[2]

39 Κορυβαντᾶν
To be a Corybant

Aristophanes used κορυβαντᾶν for 'to be in a frenzy' in the *Wasps*: 'Either you are really insane or you are acting like a Corybant.'[1] This term is often used by Lucian, in his *Timon*, in the *Saturnalian Letters*, in *Lexiphanes*, and *Hermotimus*.[2] Its source is the Corybantes, the priests of Cybele who clashed their cymbals as they were seized with a sacred madness, and drove others into a similar madness. Elsewhere the same writer calls this κακοδαιμονᾶν 'being possessed by an evil demon.'[3]

40 Calculo mordere
To bite with a voting token

Ψήφῳ δάκνειν, To bite with a voting token, as people are said to do when they injure or take revenge on a man by means of a vote. Aristophanes in the *Acharnians*: 'They are concerned only with biting with their vote.'[1] For this was the commonest way for the ordinary people to avenge an offence.

* * * * *

1 Aristophanes *Peace* 1083 and 1085: Οὔποτε ποιήσεις τὸν καρκίνον ὀρθὰ βαδίζειν, / Οὐδ᾽ ἐπὶ τῷ πραχθέντι ποιήσεις ὕστερον οὐδέν.
2 *Adagia* I iv 70

39 Aristophanes (see n1 below)
1 Aristophanes *Wasps* 8: κορυβαντιᾷς
2 Lucian *Timon* 26, *Saturnalia* 27, *Lexiphanes* 16, *Hermotimus* 63; added in *1526*
3 Ie Aristophanes; the link was rendered incorrect by the insertion of the reference to Lucian in *1528*; this word is found in Aristophanes' *Plutus* 372.

40 Aristophanes (see n1 below)
1 Aristophanes *Acharnians* 376: ψήφῳ δακεῖν

They expressed their opposition in the assembly when the votes were cast by means of tokens. So they could bite, not with their teeth, which would be unsafe, but with their tokens.[2]

41 Charybdis. Barathrum
A Charybdis. A Barathrum

These are also proverbial hyperboles: a man who is an exceptional glutton, drinker, robber, gourmand is called a Charybdis or a Barathrum. Aristophanes in the *Knights*: 'A tax-gatherer and a ravine[1] and an abyss of plunder.'[2] I think I should add here that Diogenes, according to Laertius, called the stomach the 'Charybdis of one's livelihood.'[3] Horace said of some glutton: 'The maw and whirlwind, the barathrum of the market-place.'[4]

42 Lingua seorsum inciditur
The tongue is cut out separately

Aristophanes in the *Peace*: Ἡ γλῶττα χωρὶς τέμνεται, The tongue is cut out separately.[1] The scholiast tells us this was used as a proverb and derived from Homer, book 3 of the *Odyssey*: 'Well, come now, cut out the tongues';[2] and he quotes Callistratus[3] as author of the phrase. Again in the *Plutus*: 'For

* * * * *

2 'For this ... tokens' was added in *1515*.

41 Aristophanes (see n2 below). See Otto 382 and 400 for other uses of *barathrum* by Horace. The Barathron was a cleft in Athens into which condemned criminals were thrown (Xenophon *Hellenica* 1.7.20).
1 Greek φάραγξ; Erasmus follows the scholiast of Aristophanes (Dübner page 41) in equating φάραγξ with βάραθρον. He would find the latter in the figurative sense in Lucian *Pseudologista* 17, and the Latin *barathrum*, in the sense of stomach, in Plautus *Curculio* 123.
2 Aristophanes *Knights* 248
3 Diogenes Laertius 6.51 ('Diogenes the Cynic')
4 Horace *Epistles* 1.15.31; added in *1526*. Horace has *pernicies* 'ruin,' but Erasmus writes *ingluvies* 'maw,' probably thinking of *Satires* 1.2.8.

42 Aristophanes (see n1 below). Cf also Appendix 3.1.
1 Aristophanes *Peace* 1060
2 Homer *Odyssey* 3.332
3 An Alexandrian grammarian, pupil with Aristarchus of Aristophanes of Byzantium, who wrote commentaries of Homer and Aristophanes the comic poet.

the heralds their tongues were cut out.'[4] Callistratus, according to the scholiast, relates that in ancient sacrifices the tongue was cut out and given to the
heralds. For there are those who say that the tongues of victims are Mercury's
due. But Aristophanes' words contain an ambiguity, not without humour,
because the 'tongues' may be either those of the oxen or of the heralds. The
scholiast[5] tells us there is an allusion to the proverbial saying 'The tongue
for the herald.' We should be using this correctly if we want to signify that
some recompense is due to someone who helped to the best of his ability to
conclude an affair, or that εὐαγγέλιον 'a reward' is to be given to the messenger who brings glad news. Εὐαγγέλιον is what Homer calls the small reward
that was usually given to those who brought good news.[6] In Plutarch, when
Demades, already a weak and broken old man, was mentioned, Antipater
says: 'He is like sacrificial victims, only the stomach and tongue remain'[7]
It seems that the tongue, being a profane organ, is not acceptable in sacred
rites. And Pittacus sends to king Amasis the tongue of a victim as being
both the worst and the best member of the body.[8] Heralds however have ve-
nal tongues, and at sacrifices they admonished the people to 'be favourable
with their tongues.'[9] Thus Plautus in the prologue of the *Carthaginian*:

> Raise your voice, by which you live and worship.
> For unless you shout, famine will come upon you at once.[10]

43 Non capit somnum, nisi hoc aut illud fecerit
He gets no sleep if he hasn't done this or that

There are two proverbial figures that are used to describe an excessive or
uncontrollable desire for something. The first is in Aristophanes *Wasps*:

* * * * *

4 Aristophanes *Plutus* 1110
5 The scholiast of Aristophanes (Dübner page 381)
6 Homer *Odyssey* 14.152
7 Plutarch *Moralia* 183F *Regum et imperatorum apophthegmata*; added in 1526
8 Plutarch *Moralia* fragment 89 Sandbach; cf *Moralia* 506C *De garrulitate*. In
   Moralia 38B and 146F, however, the act is attributed to Bias, not Pittacus.
9 Cicero *De divinatione* 1.102 and 2.83; Horace *Odes* 3.1.2; see also *Adagia* III v 18
   Shut the door, ye profane (76 above).
10 Plautus *Poenulus* 13–14; 'at once' is *statim* in the earlier editions, now replaced
   by *tacitum* 'silently.' From 'Heralds however' to the end was added in 1533.

43 Aristophanes (see n1 below)

Unless he has by chance been the first to sit on the bench
He finds not a grain of sleep all night.[1]

By 'first bench' he means the front row [at the theatre]. *Paspale*[2] is a Greek
word for the most finely ground cornmeal. Juvenal said similarly: 'A dispute
makes some people sleep.'[3] The second figure occurs in the *Eclogues* of Maro:
'For if you had not hurt him in some way, you would have died.'[4] The first is
to be found in the Hebrew paroemiographer: 'For they cannot sleep unless
they have done wrong, and their sleep is taken away unless they have made
someone stumble.'[5]

44 Ventre pleno melior consultatio
You can think better on a full stomach

In book 7 of his 'Table-talk' Plutarch quotes this line of verse: Γαστρὸς ἀπὸ
πλείης βουλὴ καὶ μῆτις ἄμεινων, You will be able to think better when you
have filled your belly.[1] When hunger intrudes, we cannot stop for careful
consideration; consideration requires time and calmness of mind, but hunger
increases bile. This can be turned round to mean that we should do what is
urgent and demanding, and deliberate about what comes later. It will also
apply to those who consult about the most serious matters when they are
drunk, as was the habit of the Persians according to Herodotus book 1.[2]
And Persius: 'See now, over their cups they seek to know, / These sated
sons of Romulus, what divine poetry may have to say.'[3]

* * * * *

1 Aristophanes *Wasps* 90–1: Ἢν μὴ ἐπὶ τοῦ πρώτου καθίζηται ξύλου, / Ὕπνου δ᾽
ὁρᾷ τῆς νυκτὸς οὐδὲ πασπάλην. Erasmus' translation suffers from two errors.
In the Greek, the first line depends on the previous sentence, not on what
follows. Furthermore, as Estienne points out (LB II 893), the Greek πρώτου . . .
ξύλου requires *primo ligno* 'on the first (ie front) bench,' not *ligno . . . primus*,
which makes little sense, though I have translated as it stands. The following
sentence was added from the scholiast (Dübner page 138) in *1528* with no
attempt to reconcile the translation of Aristophanes.
2 The phrase is quoted again in *Adagia* III vii 75 Not even a drop (265 below).
3 Juvenal 3.281–2
4 Virgil *Eclogues* 3.15
5 Proverbs 4:16; added in *1528*

44 Plutarch (see n1 below); the author of the verse is unknown.
1 Plutarch *Moralia* 700E *Quaestiones conviviales*
2 Herodotus 1.133.3; added in *1528*
3 Persius 1.30–1; added in *1528*

45 Tenuis spes
Slender hope

A feeble, uncertain hope is described as 'slender' by the poets, and the figure has been noted as a proverbial one by the commentators, particularly Suidas. Aristophanes in the *Knights*: Λεπτή τις ἐλπίς ἐστ᾽, ἐφ᾽ ἧς ὀχούμεθα 'That hope is a slender one in which we trust.'[1] Euripides talked of a 'cold' hope in the *Iphigenia in Aulis*: 'This is cold hope indeed.'[2] Marcus Tullius in the speech for Roscius the actor: 'It is with a vain, slender hope that you console yourself.'[3] Aristophanes has derived the metaphor from sailors when he says ὀχούμεθα,[4] and it was from them that Marcus Tullius took the expression 'He hopes some breeze will blow from this direction' to mean that some hope is held out; for example, in the sixth indictment against Verres: 'I see what I have done; he sits up, he hopes some breeze may blow his way in this accusation.'[5] This is a figure borrowed from seamen, who, becalmed in a windless sea, predict from some little cloud or from some distant ripple on the water that a wind will come. Plato used a similar figure in book 3 of the *Laws*: 'a poor salvation.'[6] In Athenaeus book 13 there is a quotation from Callimachus: 'Hopes so far troubled that they require help from the enemy.'[7]

46 Anno senior fio
I become a year older

Whenever we want to say something is a great burden to us, we say even in the vernacular[1] that we grow older. Aristophanes in the *Frogs*:

> Take care what you do; for whenever I see

* * * * *

45 Aristophanes (see n1 below). *Suda* Λ 295; cf Apostolius 10.55.
 1 Aristophanes *Knights* 1244
 2 Euripides *Iphigenia Aulidensis* 1014
 3 Cicero *Pro Roscio comoedo* 43; added in *1526*
 4 From ὀχέω 'hold fast,' here 'ride at anchor'; added in *1533*
 5 Cicero *Verrines* 2.1.13.35; added in *1526*
 6 Plato *Laws* 3.699B; added in *1526*
 7 Athenaeus 13.571A; Callimachus fragment 477 Pfeiffer, translated by C.B. Gulick (Loeb): 'Our hopes have not sunk so far in wretchedness that we should summon help from our enemies.' An addition of *1533*

46 Aristophanes (see n2 below)
 1 Suringar 13 page 25

Any of this sort of business,
I come out of it, believe me, a year older immediately.[2]

Weariness and dissatisfaction bring on old age, as Homer declares too:
'Quickly do mortals surrounded by many ills grow old.'[3]

47 Tauricum tueri
To glare like a bull

Βλέπειν ταυρηδόν, To glare like a bull, meaning 'fiercely.' Aristophanes in the
Frogs: 'And so with lowered head he glares up like a bull.'[1] Plato indicates
this was Socrates' habit, to stare with eyes like a bull.[2] And Virgil uses
the word *torva* 'wild' or 'fierce' of a cow: 'The best type of cow is fierce-
looking.'[3]

48 Expedit habere plura cognomina
It's useful to have several names

Aristophanes in the *Plutus*: Ὡς ἀγαθόν ἐστ' ἐπωνυμίας πολλὰς ἔχειν, How
convenient it is if you have several names.[1] This is appropriate for those who
carry on several professions at the same time, so that they can make greater
profits, or who belong to various parties. Like the bat in the fables who is
sometimes a mouse and sometimes a bird.[2] But it is a saying used of Mercury,
who is recorded as having manifold names: he is called *Strophaïos* 'twister,'
either because he brings business round to a good conclusion or because
he is crafty and fickle; *Empolaïos* 'merchant,' because he presides at auctions
and trading; *Hegemonios* because he is a guide, as for Priam in Homer;[3]

* * * * *

2 Aristophanes *Frogs* 16–18: ἐνιαυτῷ πρεσβύτερος ἀπέρχομαι 'I come out of it a
year older.' The speaker, Dionysus, is referring to plays and jokes.
3 Homer *Odyssey* 19.360

47 Aristophanes (see n1 below). *Suda* T 157
 1 Aristophanes *Frogs* 804: ἔβλεψε γοῦν ταυρηδὸν ἐγκύψας κάτω.
 2 Plato *Phaedo* 117B
 3 Virgil *Georgics* 3.51–2; added in 1515; cf *Adagia* III vii 71 (261 with n21 below).

48 Aristophanes (see n1 below)
 1 Aristophanes *Plutus* 1164
 2 Aesop 172 Perry; cf also 566 Perry.
 3 Homer *Iliad* 24.336

Dolios 'deceitful,' because he is the inventor of lying and illusions; *Kerdöos* 'bringer of gain,' because he increases traders' profits; *Enagonios* because he acts as herald in disputes; *Diakonos* 'servant,' because he is the messenger of the gods.[4] Bacchus is also said to have many names. The proverb could also be turned nicely against those who are never without titles and nominations, as they are called, and who are all set, like nets, to catch benefices. Or those who profess several skills, so that they can make their fortune by one means or the other, like the men at royal courts who act as priest, minister, steward, pimp, and buffoon.[5]

49 Λιμοδωριεῖς
Limodorians

Λιμοδωριεῖς, Limodorians. In the collections of proverbs that goes under the name of Plutarch[1] I find the following story: At a time when the Peloponnese[2] was suffering from a failure of the crops, certain people driven by hunger gathered together their goods and emigrated from the region; after wandering hither and thither with no fixed settlement, they were taken by the Tripoliti into their city, and this Tripoli is in Rhodes.[3] They were therefore given the name Limodorians.[4] Hesychius adds, on the authority of Didymus, that the Dorians who lived near Mt Oeta[5] were so called because, given the infertility of the soil, they had to cope often with

* * * * *

4 Most of this list is taken from Aristophanes *Plutus* 1153–61 and the scholiast (Dübner page 384).
5 Another criticism of life at court added in *1515*; cf *Adagia* III iii 1, III vii 1, 29, 74 (178 and 233 above, 264 below).

49 Pseudo-Plutarch (see n1 below)
1 That is, Laurentianus 80.13 (= Pseudo-Plutarch *Alexandrian Proverbs* 1.34, Zenobius [Aldus] column 119, and Zenobius [Athous] 3.61). For a discussion of the proverb see Otto Crusius in *Supplementum* v page 99.
2 According to Estienne (LB II 895 n1), who refers to Thucydides 1.12.3, there were people of Doric race in the Peloponnese, though they did not commonly use the name. However, as Erasmus remarks below, the Dorians of this story came from another area.
3 Presumably a reference to the union of three city-states, Ialysus, Lindus, and Camirus, founded by Dorians on Rhodes. See Strabo *Geographica* 14.2.6, who is quoting Homer *Iliad* 2.656.
4 From λῖμος 'hunger' and Dorian
5 Located in the region defined by Strabo (n8 below); see *Adagia* III vi 74 The Oetaean spirit (161 above).

famine.[6] The name 'Dorians' seems to be derived in Greek from words meaning 'gift' and 'going.'[7] And so those who brought hunger as they moved about were said to be Limodorians (bringing the gift of hunger). Anyway, the Dorians do not live in the Peloponnese, but between the Locrians and the Aetolians, as Strabo says in book 9.[8] The expression will be appropriate for people who are driven by famine to emigrate somewhere, just as the common people in Italy[9] call almost all foreigners Limodorians, as if they were driven by hunger to visit that country. Festus Pompeius tells us that people of little substance and slender fortune were formerly called *canalicolae* 'gutter-snipes,' because they gathered around the *canales* 'gutters' in the forum.[10]

50 **Tribus bolis**
In three throws

Plautus in the *Curculio*: 'If you want it in three throws, I would like a cloak.'[1] He used 'in three throws' to mean 'briefly,' like 'in three words.'[2] I say this because Terence appears to take *bolus* to mean what the Greeks call βλωμός 'a morsel of bread.'[3] And indeed what is swallowed at once is said to be eaten *tribus bolis* 'in three bites.'

* * * * *

6 Hesychius Λ 1047; the passage 'Hesychius . . . Strabo says in book 9' was added in *1526*.
7 Etymology invented by Erasmus
8 Strabo *Geographica* 9.4.10, who refers here to a Dorian Tetrapolis consisting of Erineus, Boeum, Pindus, and Cytinium
9 From *1515* to *1523* Erasmus had *Anglorum vulgus*; after *1528 Italorum vulgus*. The expression he is thinking of must therefore have corresponding forms in the two languages.
10 Pompeius Festus page 40 Lindsay; added in *1533*

50 Plautus (see n1 below). Cf Otto 1869 (*tribus verbis volo*).
1 Plautus *Curculio* 611. Erasmus' text has *velim* 'I would like.' The edition he used – with the commentary by Giambattista Pio, Milan 1500 (see ASD) – has *Si uis tribus bolis uelin* [sic] *clamydem* (folio q ii v). The accepted reading is *vel in*, and the line is translated by P. Nixon (Loeb) as 'three throws if you like, for – oh, well, for a military cloak.'
2 Cf *Adagia* IV iv 84.
3 Terence *Heautontimorumenos* 673. Estienne (LB II 895 n2) points out that the Greek corresponding to Plautus' expression is τρεῖς βολοί, whereas in Terence *bolus* corresponds to βῶλος, a lump of something swallowed. Cf *Adagia* III vi 99 (177 above).

51 **Velut umbra sequi**
Following like a shadow

῞Ωσπερ σκιὰ ἕπεσθαι, To follow like a shadow. This is said of someone who is never absent. For the shadow attends the body, willy-nilly. Plautus in the *Casina*: 'I am resolved / To follow like your shadow, wherever you may go.'[1] Hence individual attendants are called shadows, as are those who, without being asked, accompany others to banquets, as explained elsewhere in the proverb 'Shadows.'[2] Marcus Tullius in the first book of the *Tusculan Disputations*: 'For if there is nothing in fame itself that it should be sought, it nevertheless follows virtue like a shadow.'[3]

52 **Ne nummus quidem plumbeus**
Not a lead penny

A lead penny is a proverbial hyperbole, which stands for the smallest possible amount of money. Plautus in the *Casina*: 'Today this man has not a lead penny to his name.'[1] The same author in the *Trinummus*: 'For the life of me, I would never trust him with a lead penny.'[2] This is very closely related to what he also has in the *Two Captives*: 'Funny people don't rate a farthing with them any more'[3] But this is described elsewhere.[4]

53 **Satietas ferociam parit**
Luxury breeds brutality

In his anthologies Nicolaus Stobaeus quotes this statement as a proverb:

* * * * *

51 Plautus (see n1 below). Otto 1818. Erasmus has made up the Greek version himself.
 1 Plautus *Casina* 91–2
 2 *Adagia* I i 9
 3 Cicero *Tusculan Disputations* 1.109; added in *1526*

52 Plautus (see n1 below). Cf *Adagia* v i 9 A lead penny. Otto 1440n. Cf the modern 'I wouldn't give a brass farthing for ...'
 1 Plautus *Casina* 258
 2 Plautus *Trinummus* 962; added in *1526*
 3 Plautus *Captivi* 477
 4 *Adagia* I viii 9 He did not spend a farthing

53 Stobaeus (see n1 below)

Τίκτει κόρος μὲν ὕβριν, ἀπαιδευσία δὲ μετ᾽ ἐξουσίας ἄνοιαν, Luxury breeds
brutality, inexperience joined with power breeds madness.[1] Wealth saps
intelligence; and if power is joined to inexperience, then the situation can
go as far as madness. It chimes in with that other one, 'He has hay on his
horn.'[2] In the *Olympian Odes* Pindar turns the idea round and says: 'Insolence
is the mother of surfeit.'[3] But he is reproached by the scholiast, who prefers
to approve Homer's verse: 'Luxury breeds arrogance, when a wicked man
acquires wealth.' I do not remember reading this line in Homer, and it does
not seem to be genuinely Homeric; what is certain is that it is extant in the
Maxims of Theognis.[4]

54 Quid caeco cum speculo?
What's a blind man doing with a mirror?

Τί τυφλῷ καὶ κατόπτρῳ; What's a blind man doing with a mirror? This is
very close to 'A jackdaw has no business with a lute.'[1] The verse is quoted
by Stobaeus from Epicharmus: 'To one deprived of eyes what use is there
for a mirror?'[2] What need for books for one who cannot read? To what end
is a kingdom found for a fool, or riches for one who does not know how
to use them?[3]

55 Miseram messem metere
To reap a wretched harvest

To reap a bad harvest is to pay the penalty for one's misdeeds. Not at all
inconsistent with one we have recorded elsewhere, 'As you have sown, so

* * * * *

1 Stobaeus *Eclogae* 3.3.25 Hense III 201 (Aristotle fragment 57 Rose 1886 page
  67 lines 19–21 = 1867 no 89). The editors of ASD suggest that the incorrect
  first name (for 'Johannes') may be explained by the associated reference to
  Nicolaus, a poet of the new comedy, in *Adagia* I iv 1 (CWE 31 319:56–7).
2 *Adagia* I i 81
3 Pindar *Olympians* 13.10 and the scholiast; added in 1526
4 Theognis 153; the verse is not in fact Homeric. Added in 1526.

54 Stobaeus (see n2 below). Cf Eustathius 1587.47 on *Odyssey* 19.104.
1 *Adagia* I iv 37
2 Stobaeus *Eclogae* 4.30.6A Hense V 730. The attribution to Epicharmus is held
  to be an error. The verse is also found in Mantissa 2.100.
3 The two last sentences were added in 1515.

55 Euripides (see n2 below). Cf Otto 1104.

also shall you reap.'[1] Stobaeus quotes these verses from Euripides' *Ion*:

> But at present, you scoundrels, you gather offices
> And prize great wealth, striving to get it from any source
> Indiscriminately by good or bad means; later
> You reap for these deeds a grim and bitter harvest.'[2]

Aeschylus in the *Persians*:

> Flourishing arrogance bore a crop
> Of calamities, whence it reaps a plenteous harvest of tears.[3]

Plato in the *Phaedrus*: 'What sort of harvest do you think he will later reap from the oratory he sowed?'[4] In his *Rhetoric* book 3 Aristotle quotes from Gorgias: 'You have sown foul seeds and reaped a wretched harvest.'[5]

56 Venimus ad summam lineam
We have come to the final line

Euripides in the *Antigone*: Ἐπ᾽ ἄκραν ἥκομεν γραμμὴν κακῶν We have come down to the ultimate mark of evil.[1] And Horace: 'We have come to the ultimate.'[2] The line in the stadium and in games has been described elsewhere more than once.[3]

* * * * *

1 *Adagia* I viii 78
2 Stobaeus *Eclogae* 4.31.56 Hense v 755; Euripides fragment 419 Nauck: the last line reads Ἀμᾶσθε τῶν δε δύστηνην θέρος.
3 Aeschylus *Persians* 821–2; added in *1526*
4 Plato *Phaedrus* 260c–D; this paragraph was added in *1533*.
5 Aristotle *Rhetoric* 3.3.4 (1406b10); Gorgias 82 Diels-Kranz B 16

56 Euripides (see n1 below)
1 Euripides fragment 169 Nauck quoted in Stobaeus *Eclogae* 4.40.8 Hense v 921.
2 Horace *Epistles* 2.1.32, where the phrase is *Venimus ad summum fortunae* 'We have come to the pinnacle of fortune.'
3 *Adagia* I ix 97 Move not the line, and III v 35 To reach the chalk mark (86 above). Two others noted by ASD, I i 25 I will move the counter from the sacred line, which refers to a board game, and I vi 57 To start from scratch, which refers to the starting line in the stadium, hardly seem relevant to this proverb, which is not very distant from the currently popular cliché with yet another reference, the 'bottom line.'

57 Saburratus
Full of ballast

In his *Little Chest* Plautus used a term, original certainly but quite neat: 'ballasted,' for stuffed with food. The metaphor is derived from ships, which
are loaded with sand or clay so that they are not tossed and rolled about in
the waves. I would not have listed this as an adage, if it were not commonly
used even in the vernacular.[1] Plautus' words are as follows:

> I too share what is the vice of a large portion of us women
> Who are in business here. When we are well ballasted,
> We become talkative immediately.[2]

It will be more witty, if the image is taken further: if someone says, for
example, that his ears are ballasted by someone else's endless chatter. Al-
ternatively, someone's mind is ballasted with the precepts of philosophy so
that he is not tossed about by the storms of circumstances.[3]

58 Numero dicis
You talk like 1 2 3

In the *Casina* Plautus used 'Talk like 1 2 3' to mean fluently and concisely.
Festus explains it as 'quickly or rapidly,' quoting many other authors as
well as this passage in Plautus.[1] But in Festus the text is so corrupt that I
would be reluctant to refer to him, if it were not that we learn there that the
ancients not only said 'Talk like 1 2 3,' but 'Learn like 1 2 3,' 'Do like 1 2 3,'
'Rub out like 1 2 3,' 'Believe like 1 2 3,' and 'Arrive like 1 2 3' meaning to
reach a place easily and quickly. Nonius Marcellus thinks *numero* is used
for *multum* 'a great deal,' but the examples he gives show rather that it is
taken to mean 'quickly and easily' or 'immediately' – something which he

*****

57 Plautus (see n2 below)
 1 Suringar 195 page 363
 2 Plautus *Cistellaria* 120–2
 3 The final sentence was added in *1517/18*.

58 Plautus *Casina* 646
 1 Pompeius Festus, page 173 Lindsay, mentions the old Latin poets Naevius (58
   TRF), Accius (503 TRF), Afranius (312 CRF), and Caecilius (2 CRF); see also Varro
   De re rustica 3.16.7.

admits at the end.[2] The same author in the *Amphitryon*: 'It came to my mind like 1 2 3.'[3] It is used by him in several other places.[4]

59 Palpari in tenebris
Groping in the dark

Ψηλαφεῖν ἐν τῷ σκότῳ, To grope with the hand in the dark. This is what people are said to do who try to understand a matter by vague guessing. Aristophanes in the *Peace*: 'Previously we groped with our hands at this business as if in the dark. Now we shall be able to consider everything by the light of the lamp.'[1] The poet has alluded to the trickery by which Hyperbolus, a 'lychnopole' or dealer in lamps, was made ruler.[2] Plato uses the same proverbial saying in the *Phaedo*.[3] And people say this nowadays about uncertain guesses: ψηλαφεῖ.[4]

60 Muscas depellere
Keeping off the flies

Keeping off the flies is still said jokingly nowadays of someone who does an unnecessary and useless job.[1] Aristophanes in the *Wasps*: 'Yes, he has

* * * * *

2 Nonius Marcellus (352M) gives the meanings *ordine* 'in order,' and *cito* 'swiftly,' but nowhere suggests *multum*. 'But in Festus' to here was added in 1533.
3 Plautus *Amphitruo* 180. In Plautus this is a question: *Num numero mi in mentem fuit* 'I was not too quick, was I?' The expression 'same author' is rendered incorrect by an insertion in 1533 (see n2 above).
4 Plautus *Menaechmi* 287, *Mercator* 739, *Poenulus* 1272, *Miles gloriosus* 1400. The phrase is translated by P. Nixon (Loeb) in almost all these cases as 'too soon.'

59 Aristophanes (see n1 below)
1 Aristophanes *Peace* 690–2
2 Following the scholia to Aristophanes *Peace* 681 and 692 (Dübner page 192). Hyperbolus (died 411 BC) was the successor of Cleon, often the butt of comedy, and condemned in severe terms by Thucydides (8.73).
3 Plato *Phaedo* 99B. 'The poet ... *Phaedo*' was added in 1526.
4 For occurrences in German in the sixteenth century see ASD II-6 457:571n; also Suringar 266 page 486 and OED under 'grope.' Ψηλαφεῖ and ψηλαφεῖν are incorrect forms, mistakenly derived by Erasmus from Aristophanes' ἐψηλαφῶμεν.

60 Aristophanes (see n2 below); cf *Adagia* IV vii 25 Fly-flaps.
1 Suringar 126 page 228–9

a vigilant hand, even taking care τὰς μυίας ἀπαμύνει "to drive away the flies."[12]

61 **Tenuiter diducis**
You're combing it out thinly

Λεπτὰ ξαίνεις, You're combing it out thinly. Suidas wrote that this used to be said of people who scrape a living like the poor. The metaphor appears to be derived from women carding wool. (Unless we prefer to read ξέεις, 'scrape'; for in the printed editions[1] we find ξένεις, a word whose meaning is not apparent to me at all.) However, whether you read ξαίνεις or ξέεις, it will refer either way to the carefulness of poor people about very small amounts, which the Greeks call μικρολογία 'pettiness'[2] – so careful that they were said even to 'split cummin.'[3] Moreover, in Latin too poor people are called *tenues*,[4] and Terence said 'rather poorly' of a young man who is in love but has little money.[5] Sometimes *tenuis* is applied to careful precision and fine distinctions, as in Horace's *Satires*: 'For these were subtle matters thoroughly discussed in subtle language.'[6] Likewise in the *Clouds* Aristophanes used λεπτὴ φροντίς 'subtle speculation' and λεπτότατοι λῆροι 'very slender arguments'[7] and λεπτολογεῖν 'to talk subtleties,' when he was mocking the excessively careful and subtle conceits of philosophers.[8] Seneca declared that Chrysippus' intellect was like this, in that he pricked a subject but did not penetrate it.[9]

Moreover, just as appropriate and correct analysis throws much light on language, so this indiscriminate cutting of things into what are more properly bits than organic parts sometimes means that, by seeking to un-

* * * * *

2 Aristophanes *Wasps* 597

61 *Suda* Λ 292
1 For example, Zenobius (Aldus) column 110
2 Cf Plato *Republic* 6.486A; Aristotle *Metaphysics* 2.3.2 (995a10). A closely related meaning is 'hair-splitting' or 'logic-chopping'; cf Plato *Hippias Major* 304B.
3 Cf *Adagia* II i 5 A cummin-splitter; the term is also used by Aristophanes *Wasps* 1353.
4 Cf Cicero *De officiis* 2.70 and *Verrines* 2.2.55.138.
5 Terence *Phormio* 145
6 Horace *Satires* 2.4.9
7 Latin *rationes*, translating λῆροι which means rather 'idle talk' or 'frivolities'
8 Aristophanes *Clouds* 229–230, 359, 320; λεπτολογεῖν is quoted from the same source in *Adagia* I iii 54 To dispute about smoke.
9 Seneca *De beneficiis* 1.4.1

derstand too much, we understand nothing.[10] Hence those who avoid this excessive refinement are said to speak 'roughly and broadly.'[11] Ulpian, in book 15 of the *Pandects*, under the heading 'On Property,' in the section beginning *Quam Tuberonis*: 'One is certainly not obliged of necessity to know each and every detail, but to know it παχυμερέστερον "roughly," and Pomponius inclines to this opinion.'[12] The term seems to be composed from παχύ 'coarse' and μερίς 'division.' In the opposite sense, those who examine every detail however minute are said to talk in quibbles.[13] Instead of παχυμερῶς, Aristotle in book 1 of the *Nicomachean Ethics* said: 'It would be pleasing[14] therefore when discussing such subjects and arguing from them to state the truth παχυλῶς καὶ τύπῳ "roughly and in a summary outline." '[15] He is of the opinion that doubts about exceptions should be left out when dealing with an inexperienced hearer, and that one should speak of things as they commonly are or as they are considered by ordinary people. Again in book 2 of the same work: 'Any statement about moral actions must be made in rough, not precise terms.'[16] In Greek authors we frequently find the expression 'so to speak,'[17] when they feel that they are not expressing the matter exactly as it is, but that they are indicating it with a word or two, alluding to it rather than designating it.[18]

62 Simia fucata
A painted monkey

Πίθηκος ἀνάπλεως ψιμυθίου, A monkey covered with paint. Said of an old woman, ugly but painted and made up with a prostitute's enticements.

* * * * *

10 Cf Terence *Andria* 17.
11 Given in Greek: παχυμερῶς καὶ παχυμερέστερον; cf Strabo *Geographica* 1.4.8–9.
12 Ulpian *Digest* 15.1.7.2; the words *ex necessitate* do not appear in Mommsen's text.
13 In Greek λεπτομερῶς λέγειν; on λεπτομερῶς see Hesychius Λ 687.
14 Latin *gratum*; Estienne (LB II 897) points out that ἀγαπητόν should be translated *sufficiens* 'sufficient.'
15 Aristotle *Ethica Nicomachea* 1.3.4 (1094b20)
16 Aristotle *Ethica Nicomachea* 2.2.3 (1104a1): 'in rough, not precise terms' is τύπῳ καὶ οὐκ ἀκριβῶς
17 In Greek ὡς τύπῳ εἰπεῖν; cf Aristotle *Categories* 10 (11b20), where H.P. Cooke (Loeb) translates 'speaking in outline'; Theophrastus *Historia plantarum* 1.1.6: ὡς τύπῳ λαβεῖν.
18 From 'Moreover' to the end was added in *1533*.

62 Aristophanes (see n2 below)

Ψιμύθιον[1] is what the Greeks call the colouring with which once only prostitutes used to paint their faces and hide the defects of old age and features
– now, God help us, even respectable matrons do so. Aristophanes in the
Women in Parliament:

> Is a monkey painted with different colours?
> Can an old woman return from deepest hell?[2]

It can be adapted to an idea; for example, if someone dresses up an immoral
argument with rhetorical trappings so that it seems honest. Πιθηκίζειν is
'to disguise with pretences and allurements,' whence πιθηκισμός 'aping.'
Aristophanes in the *Knights*: 'O poor me! Would you get round me with
these πιθηκισμοί "monkey tricks"?'[3]

63 Ζοφοροδόρπιδες et similia
A Dusk-diner, and similar expressions

In his 'Table-talk' Plutarch declares that in olden times certain nicknames
were given, by way of a proverbial joke, to those who arrived at a banquet rather late and in leisurely fashion; they were sometimes called κωλυ-
σιδείπνοι 'hinder-dinners,'[1] sometimes ζοφοροδόρπιδες 'dusk-diners,'[2] sometimes τρεχέδειπνοι 'dinner-chasers.'[3] If we may guess at the explanation of
these names, I think those who delayed their arrival were seen to be a hindrance, because others were kept waiting and could not dine; in the second
case, by their slowness they caused the banquet to be prolonged until nightfall. The third nickname seems to be given by way of 'an antiphrasis.'[4] It
is said by someone in Plutarch however that Pittacus was called 'Zophoro-
dorpis' by Alcaeus, not because he arrived late at the banquet but because
he enjoyed sordid, low-class drinking-parties.[5] In ancient times, however,
it was considered unfashionable and uncivil for a guest to arrive late at a

* * * * *

1 Cf *Suda* Ψ 108. The word refers to white lead paint.
2 Aristophanes *Ecclesiazusae* 1072–3: 'painted with different colours' is ψιμυθίου.
3 Aristophanes *Knights* 887; the previous sentence and this were added in 1533.

63 Plutarch (see n2 below)
1 In Athenaeus 2.63D the word means a type of snail.
2 Plutarch *Moralia* 726A–B *Quaestionum convivialium*, more correctly ζοφοδορπίδαι.
   Erasmus uses an incorrect form found in the Aldus Plutarch of 1509, of which
   he must have seen the proofs in 1508.
3 Cf Athenaeus 1.4A and 6.242C.
4 Greek κατ' ἀντίφρασιν
5 Alcaeus fragment 429 Lobel-Page

banquet. Hence Polycharmus, in the defence in which he gave account of his life to the Athenians, included this in his favour: 'In addition to these things, Athenians, I have never arrived late at a meal.' A reason for this view about arriving late for dinner was rather wittily revealed by Battus,[6] a court jester, in the entourage of Augustus Caesar. He used to call those who came late to banquets 'Epithumodipnoi,' 'dinner-devotees' you might say, because, although they were occupied with business, they had a great desire for meals and would not decline any invitations they received. All this is in Plutarch. But Terence in the *Self-Tormentor* indicates that it was impolite to arrive punctually or too early at a banquet, when Chremes says his guests have been in his house for some time and that he is keeping them waiting, no doubt indicating the opposite was usually the case.[7] In Aristophanes' *Women in Parliament* there are several allusions to this: 'I'm coming to the feast.'[8] And in the same play: 'I shall sing some dinner-time song.'[9]

64 **Cui ista arrident, meis ne gaudeat**
Who enjoys such things can have no pleasure in what I do

Aristophanes in the *Clouds*: "Ὅστις οὖν τούτοισι γελᾷ, τοῖς ἐμοῖς μὴ χαιρέτω 'So anyone who finds such things amusing cannot enjoy what I do.' This has the air of a proverb which could be used when we want to indicate that there is a large difference between our thinking and that of others. The Greek line limps, being one syllable short; it will be complete if we read γελάει instead of γελᾷ.[1] Maro has the opposite of this: 'Any one who does not hate Bavius could like your poems, Maevius.'[2] About two poets who were of the same ilk[3] and equally despicable.

* * * * *

6 Augustus' jester was called Gabba; Battus is given by the Aldus Plutarch.
7 Terence *Heautontimorumenos* 171–2
8 Aristophanes *Ecclesiazusae* 1135; added in 1533
9 Aristophanes *Ecclesiazusae* 1153: μελλοδειπνικόν; added in 1533

64 Aristophanes *Clouds* 560
1 Added in 1528; according to the editors of ASD, Erasmus (who simply suggests an uncontracted, instead of a contracted form of the verb γελάω 'to laugh') knew only this isolated line in 1528 and did not realize that it was a Eupolideus, rather than a trochaic tetrameter, and one of a long series of such verses (518–562) at this point in the play.
2 Virgil *Eclogues* 3.90. Bavius and Maevius were mocked by both Virgil and Horace (*Epodes* 10). They are mentioned again in *Adagia* IV v 1 Not even an ox would be lost.
3 Latin *eiusdem farinae*; cf *Adagia* III v 44 (94 above).

65 Βωμολόχος. Βωμολοχεύεσθαι
An altar-scrounger. To lurk around the altar

Βωμολόχοι was a proverbial reproach for knaves and villains. The term seems to have been used in former times of those who were in the habit of lurking about around altars and setting traps to snatch the victims, or who made sacrifices and prayed for a good return from making accusations against others.[1] In the *Icaromenippus* of Lucian, Jupiter hears the prayers of this sort of mortal.[2] Likewise βωμολόχοι is a term for those who, when a sacred rite is being performed, do not pray to the gods but gossip about trivialities[3] – a habit which nowadays is indulged particularly by great personages who think it is perfectly good manners if, during a mass, they busily fill someone's ear with chatter. Aristophanes in the *Clouds* has 'And an altar scrounger.'[4] And in the same play: 'If any one of them should act the altar-scrounger and ring some changes.'[5] There is the suggestion of a proverb in 'ring some changes' too. The same author in the *Knights*: 'Now for some mountebank device, my soul'[6] – meaning that his adversary has conceived some unusual villainy, which he calls βωμολόχος as if it were extraordinarily flattering. The word is derived from βωμός 'altar' and λόχος 'a snare' – for even there, there are those who steal food or seek it by begging. From this sense it is transferred to those who use abject flattery to fill their stomachs, and so base flatteries are called βωμακεύματα and βωμολοχεύματα. Sometimes the term βωμολόχος is used of soothsayers, seers,

* * * * *

65 Aristophanes (see n4 below). *Suda* B 486, 489 and 490
1 Following the scholiast of Aristophanes (see n4 below; Dübner page 120), which according to ASD Erasmus misunderstands in part, though he corrects himself in the final section on the *Knights* added in 1533
2 Lucian *Icaromenippus* 25. The description does not contain the word βωμολόχοι, but some mortals pray to Zeus that they may win their lawsuits. However Lucian goes on to say that Zeus rejects impious prayers.
3 This meaning is not authorized by Greek usage, but is invented by Erasmus for his own obvious purposes. Erasmus refers to similar behaviour of congregations in his *Modus orandi Deum* (CWE 70 217).
4 Aristophanes *Clouds* 910; Erasmus still seems to be speaking of his original meaning, but B.B. Rogers (Loeb) translates 'And a vulgar buffoon.'
5 Aristophanes *Clouds* 970; again Erasmus gives no indication that he understands *bomolochus* to have a different meaning here, but B.B. Rogers (Loeb) translates the line: 'And should anyone dare the tune to impair and with intricate twistings to fill.'
6 Aristophanes *Knights* 1194; translation by B.B. Rogers (Loeb). The passage from the beginning of this sentence to the end was added in 1533.

flute-players and the sort of people who follow the scent of altar smoke. Finally the use of the word spreads to all sorts of people who seek gain by dishonest tricks.[7]

66 Prius quam gallus iterum cecinerit
Before the cock crows twice

Πρὶν ἢ τὸ δεύτερον ἀλεκτρυὼν ἐφθέγγετο, And first let the crested cock crow twice. (This will constitute a line of Greek verse if we read ἀλέκτωρ instead of ἀλεκτρυών.)[1] That is quite early, before daybreak. It is derived from the ancient custom of marking the end of night and the approach of day by the crowing of the cock, since time-keeping sundials had not yet been invented. The cock crows three times to announce the day. Pliny talks about this in book 10 chapter 21: 'And these night watchmen of ours, which Nature created to waken mortals to their work and to put an end to their sleep, know the stars and mark the time of day every three hours with their crowing. They go to sleep with the sun, and recall us to business and labour in the fourth watch, preventing sunrise from stealing up on us unprepared, announcing the approaching day with their call, and the call itself with the flapping of their wings.'[2] All this is in Pliny. The reason why cocks do this is thought by Democritus, quoted by Marcus Tullius, to be that it serves their digestion, their food being propelled at that time from their craw and carried throughout the body.[3] The poets allude to the fable that Lucian recalls in his *Cockerel*.[4] I prefer the reason given by Ambrogio Leoni of Nola,[5] a man whom I do not hesitate in truth to compare, for his researches

* * * * *

7 In 'The word ... tricks' Erasmus is following the *Suda*.

66 Based on Aristophanes (see n9 below) and the gospel of Mark (see n10 below). Cf Otto 753.
1 This parenthesis (ἀλέκτωρ means specifically a cock, ἀλεκτρυών either cock or hen) was added in *1526*. As in *Adagia* III vii 64 (255 with n1 above), the remark is based on observation of the line out of context.
2 Pliny *Naturalis historia* 10.46
3 Democritus 68 Diels-Kranz A 158, quoted in Cicero *De divinatione* 2.57
4 Lucian *Gallus* 3, the story of Ares and Alectryon; cf *Adagia* III iv 31 (19 above).
5 The first known edition of his *Novum opus quaestionum seu problematum* is of Venice 1523; Erasmus was presumably acquainted with the subject matter as early as 1508, the date of this passage, when Leoni was a member of Erasmus' circle of friends in Venice (Ep 868 and *Adagia* I ii 63). Cf also *Adagia* II iii 50 and CEBR 2.322 (Ambrogio Leoni).

on the mysteries of Nature, with any of the ancient philosophers. In his *Quaestiones* this writer gives it as his opinion that the cock's crowing arises from its exceptional lasciviousness. For this bird more than all others is devoted to its hens, and extraordinarily anxious to procreate as much as possible; so much so that one cockerel can rule a large number of hens, can satisfy such a crowd on his own as husband, and will fight with the utmost vigour for his hens and chicks. Moreover there is sufficient support for the idea that the cockerel's crowing is caused by the prospect of intercourse in the fact that before they are mature enough to mate with hens they are silent. Among the other birds likewise there are several that give voice during coitus or when they desire it, such as ducks, sparrows, swallows, and partridges. And indeed the call of the male among birds has such power to stimulate the desire for intercourse that some hens conceive eggs at the mere sound of it. Among these are the partridges.[6] And so the cock, as his food spreads through his entrails and as he wakes up – at a time when bodies are stirred naturally to intercourse – he immediately thinks of his hens and stimulates them with the allurement of his song so that his offspring shall be the more plentiful. The reason for his repeated crowing is that the cock's sleep is intermittent and not at all continuous, especially as they reach mature age, and this, as you will understand also springs from lasciviousness. But to come back to the interpretation of the adage, the ancients set the beginning of the day immediately after the passing of midnight and call the following period *gallicinium* 'cock-crow,' because at that time cocks have a presentiment of daylight long in advance and begin to crow; the third hour was called *conticinium* 'quiet time,' since the cocks were silent and men slept at that time; the fourth hour was called *diluculum* 'break of day,' because daylight begins to appear. The fifth was called *mane* 'morning,' when the day is already bright[7] and the sun risen. So the cock's second call precedes the rising of the sun by a long time. Hence Juvenal:

> But what he does at the second cock-crow
> The nearest shop-keeper will know before daylight.[8]

Very similar is this in Aristophanes' *Women in Parliament*:

> Not in the least.
> Not even if you had been there at the time

* * * * *

6 Cf *Adagia* III vii 21 His progeny are full of wind (228 with n4 above).
7 Cf Macrobius *Saturnalia* 1.3.12.
8 Juvenal 9.107–8

When the cock had crowed a second time.[9]

This expression occurs in the gospels.[10]

67 Ne allii quidem caput
Not even a head of garlic

A proverbial hyperbole Οὐδὲ σκορόδου κεφαλὴν δέδωκεν, He gave not even a head of garlic. Aristophanes in the *Wasps*: 'No one adds even a head of garlic to the stew.'[1] Appropriate for one who is mean and parsimonious in the extreme.

68 Ruminare negocium
To ruminate the business

Ἀναμάσσεσθαι τὸ πρᾶγμα, To ruminate the business, or chew the cud, is said of someone who turns a matter over in his mind, weighing it up again and again. The metaphor originates with animals who bring their food back into their mouths and chew it again, and then transfer it to another stomach. This occurs of course only in those that have two stomachs. Aristophanes in the *Wasps*: 'The case was scarcely known, when they had ruminated.'[1] This is also called ἀναπεμπάζειν.[2] Lucian too uses this adage somewhere.[3]

69 Mordere labrum
To bite one's lip

Ἐσθίειν τὰ χείλη, To chew one's lips. Even nowadays someone is said to do this when he is irritated and angry in his mind.[1] Taken from the action of

* * * * *

9 Aristophanes *Ecclesiazusae* 389–91
10 Mark 14:30; Matt 26:34, Luke 22:34, and John 13:38 omit the word 'twice.'

67 Aristophanes (see n1 below)
1 Aristophanes *Wasps* 679

68 Aristophanes (see n1 below) and the scholiast (Dübner page 153)
1 Aristophanes *Wasps* 783: 'ruminated' is ἀναμασώμενοι.
2 Following the scholiast
3 Lucian uses the word ἀναπεμπάζειν in *Gallus* 5, but not the adage.

69 Aristophanes (see n2 below) and the scholiast (Dübner page 159)
1 Suringar 261 pages 480–1

those who are impatient. Aristophanes in the *Wasps*: 'Chewing his lips with anger.'[2] The same in Homer too, *Odyssey* book 20: 'But they all held their lip with their teeth.'[3]

70 Lesbiari
To behave like a Lesbian

Λεσβιάζειν was a word in ancient times for 'to defile.' Aristophanes in the *Wasps*: 'She who already pollutes her drinking companions.'[1] The infamous vice, which is performed with the mouth, called *fellatio*, I think, or *irrumatio*, is said to have originated with the people of Lesbos, and among them it was first of all something which women had to perform. The scholiast cites as witness to this Theopompus in his *Ulysses*: 'Let me not speak aloud with my own lips of that ancient practice, that the vulgar prate about, which the Lesbians are said to have invented.'[2] He also quotes the *Troilus* of Strattis: 'Do not ever, O son of Jove, come to this point, / Leave this to the Lesbians and let them bid farewell to it.'[3] These appear to be two senarii, but somewhat corrupt.[4] Aristophanes points to the same in the *Women in Parliament*: 'But you seem to me to be the *lambda* of Lesbians.'[5] alluding to the ordinary letter *lambda*, which is the first letter of both 'Lesbians' and the obscene verb λειχάζειν.[6] This, if I am not mistaken, is Greek for what the Latins call 'performing fellatio.' The term remains of course, but I think the practice has been eliminated.[7]

* * * * *

2 Aristophanes *Wasps* 1083
3 Homer *Odyssey* 20.268

70 Aristophanes (see n1 below) and the scholiast (Dübner page 165). In the *Wasps* Aristophanes has λεσβιεῖν; the form λεσβιάζειν is found in the *Frogs* 1308, Lucian *Pseudologista* 28 and Apostolius 10.57A. See also Appendix 4.73 and *Adagia* III v 85 To give a Siphnian wave (117 above).
1 Aristophanes *Wasps* 1346: λεσβιεῖν 'to pollute'
2 PCG 7 Theopompus fragment 36
3 PCG 7 Strattis fragment 42. Strattis, an Athenian comic poet of the late fifth century BC of whom nineteen titles are known, is quoted here from the scholiast of Aristophanes.
4 Added in 1520; they are only slightly corrupt – see the version in PCG.
5 Aristophanes *Ecclesiazusae* 920
6 A form surmised by Erasmus on the basis of λαιχάζουσιν, an incorrect spelling in the scholiast for λαικάζουσιν 'womanize' (corrected in Dübner page 321, but see page 541) by analogy with λείχειν 'to lick.'
7 The two last sentences were added in 1515 and 1517/18 respectively.

71 Pyrrichen oculis prae se ferens
To cast a Pyrrhic look

Πυρρίχην βλέπειν, To have a fierce and warlike expression. This derives from
the *pyrriche*, a dance that is performed by armed youths. Athenaeus testifies
to it in the *Doctors at Dinner* book 14,[1] where he explains that it represents an
image of fighting, the drive and fierceness of those advancing and the haste
of those retreating. And Aelius Spartianus in his *Hadrian* says, 'He often
put on displays of military *pyrriche* dances for the people.'[2] Tranquillus
likewise recalls the *pyrriche* dances: 'The children of the princes of Asia
and Bithynia performed Pyrrhic dances.'[3] Julius Pollux, book 4 chapter 14,
among several kinds of dance records the *emmeleia* of the tragedians, the
cordax of the comedians, the *sicinnis* of the satirical drama, and the *pyrriche*
and the *telesia*, which he calls *enoplioi* 'war dances,' because they were danced
by armed men. He also indicates here that the *xifismos* was so called because
it was performed with swords, and the *podismos* because they made their
bodies spin with wonderfully fast steps. The same author also records other
sorts of dance that represented war, the *komos* and the *tetrakomos*, which he
says was sacred to Hercules. And another, called the *Karike* 'Carian,'[4] which
was also performed with weapons.[5] In book 7 of the *Laws* Plato tells us that
there were two principal types of dance, one warlike and frenzied, which
was called the *pyrriche*, the other was more restrained, which was the *emmeleia*.[6] He describes the *pyrriche* thus: 'You are right to call this the *pyrriche*,
which imitates movements to avoid blows and missiles by the bending of
bodies and every sort of pliancy, by crouching down and leaping up, and
on the other hand the opposite actions to these, which train the body to
movements designed to make it agile, which seek to represent images of
fighting, first with the firing of bows and the hurling of spears, and then
striking all sorts of blows. At the same time the uprightness and strength

* * * * *

71 Aristophanes (see n13 below). Erasmus added considerably to this adage in
   1528, notably the references to Suetonius, Pollux, Plato, and Xenophon. As
   in ASD, the Latin spelling here of *pyrriche* / *pyrrhice* follows the apparently
   arbitrary spelling of *1536*; the Greek word is also transcribed as *pyrriche*.
 1 Athenaeus 14.630D–631A; added in *1517/18*, but the following expansion is
   only very loosely based on Athenaeus.
 2 Aelius Spartianus *Historia Augusti* 1.19.8
 3 Suetonius *Julius* 39.1
 4 Cf *Adagia* I viii 79 Carian music.
 5 Pollux *Onomasticon* 4.99
 6 Plato *Laws* 7.816B

seen in all these representations of healthy bodies and minds, which do a
great deal for the physical fitness of those who take part, is held to be right,
and whatever spoils it wrong.'[7] The scholiast of Homer's *Iliad* book 16 too
recalls three kinds of dances, the *pyrriche*, the *sicinnis* (which is performed at
sacred rites) and the *cordax*,[8] which is not respectable and is suitable for lay
people.[9] The *pyrriche* was Cretan and was performed with weapons. Hence
Homer, when he wants to signify a man who is nimble in warlike actions,
calls him a dancer: ὀρχηστήν περ᾽ ἐόντα.[10] This sort of fighting is neatly described in a passage from Xenophon quoted by Athenaeus, book 1: 'First the
Thracians got up and danced to the tibia and leapt in the air, very lightly
and brandishing their swords. At the climax one struck another, so that he
seemed to everyone to have landed the blow. The man struck pretended
to fall, and everyone immediately cried out. Then the one who appeared
to have struck the blow, having stripped the other of his arms, went off
singing the Sitalcas, and the other Thracians carried off the fallen man as if
he were dead, though he was not harmed at all.'[11] Athenaeus also describes
three other sorts of dance, if anyone would like to know about them. Finally
Homer,[12] in the *Iliad* book 16, calls a Cretan who is a vigorous fighter a
'dancer,' because of the *pyrriche* we have talked about which is familiar
to the Thracians. The scholiast describes the three sorts of dance thus: the
pyrriche is a war-dance, the *sicinnis* was suited to sacred rites, and the *cordax*
was base and profane. Aristophanes in the *Birds*: 'The messenger / Runs up
to us looking like one dancing the *pyrriche*.'[13] Hence the name of the 'pyrrhic'
measure, because it has the rhythm of soldiers rushing into battle, either
from Pyrrhus the son of Achilles (which Pliny in book 7 chapter 56 seems to
accept when he writes: 'The Curetes taught dancing with weapons, Pyrrhus
taught the *pyrriche*, both in Crete'),[14] or, as Athenaeus thinks, from a Spartan

* * * * *

7 Plato *Laws* 7.815A–B
8 Erasmus has *scordacismus* here, a corrupt form, which he took from the scholiast available to him; in the A-Scholia he would have found κορδακισμὸς 'dancing of the *cordax*.' In the *Moria* (CWE 27 94) Silenus is mentioned as 'obscenely
   dancing the *cordax*.'
9 The scholiast of Homer *Iliad* 16.617; Erasmus knew only the *Scholia minora*
   printed in 1517 and 1521.
10 The passage 'The scholiast . . . ἐόντα' was inserted in 1533 into the long addition
   – 'Tranquillus . . . base and profane' – of 1528, creating some repetition, which
   Erasmus failed to eliminate.
11 Xenophon *Anabasis* 6.1.5; Athenaeus 1.15E
12 See nn8 and 10.
13 Aristophanes *Birds* 1168–9; Erasmus prints Ἐλθεῖ for Εἰσθεῖ 'Runs', probably
   through a mistake in the Aldine Aristophanes.
14 Pliny *Naturalis historia* 7.204; added in 1528

called Pyrrhichus[15] (for there are some very warlike Spartans to whom this dance was special and they learned it as children right from the age of five; they called it πυρριχίζειν and the dancers *pyrrichistae*[16]), or it gets its name from its fiery vigour.[17] Julius Pollux, in the passage that I have just quoted,[18] says the *pyrriche* is the same as the *telesia* and that both men[19] were judges of competitions of this sort. Indeed this expression too will look like an adage, if someone who is raging and burning with anger is said to be 'dancing the *pyrriche*.' Using a similar figure Timocles in Athenaeus book 6 says:

> A man who hates speech, never contradicting
> Anything, but speaking war in his ferocious mien.[20]

The poets also say *torva tuens* 'looking daggers,'[21] and the Greeks ὑπόδρα βλέπων 'looking fierce.'[22]

72 Non est oleum in lecytho
There's no oil in the bottle

Ἔλαιον οὐκ ἔνεστιν ἐν τῷ ληκύθῳ, There's not a drop of olive oil in the bottle. Used of course when we want to say that prayers are useless with a pitiless man. It is found in Aristophanes' *Birds*. However, there is a play on the word, because ἔλαιον means 'oil' and ἔλεος 'pity,' and I rather think one is derived from the other.[1]

* * * * *

15 Athenaeus 14.630E quoting Aristoxenos fragment 103 Wehrli; an addition of 1517/18
16 The word is found in Lysias 21.1, Isaeus 5.36, Lucian *Piscator* 36, and the *Etymologicum magnum* 697.24.
17 The suggested derivations from the Greek for fire, πῦρ (pyr), and from Pyrrhus son of Achilles, are both in Hesychius Π 4464.
18 See n5 above.
19 That is Pyrrhichus and Telesias, named by Pollux in the passage just quoted
20 PCG 7 Timocles fragment 12; Athenaeus 6.224A; added in 1528. C.B. Gulick (Loeb) translates οὐδεπώποτε Ἀντίθετον εἰπὼν οὐδέν as 'who has never uttered an antithesis in his life.' The later editions, from 1528 to 1536 and LB, mistakenly have 'Aristophanes' for 'Athenaeus.'
21 For example Virgil *Aeneid* 6.467, of Dido, and *Georgics* 3.51–2 in *Adagia* III vii 47 (244 above)
22 Homer has ὑπόδρα ἰδών, eg at *Iliad* 1.148.

72 Aristophanes *Birds* 1589
 1 Following the scholiast (Dübner page 245), but there seems to be no etymological justification for the association of the two words.

73 Magis gaudet eo qui senectam exuit
As happy as someone casting off old age

Γέγηθε μᾶλλον ἢ τὸ γῆρας ἐκδύς, He is happier than someone who sloughs off old age. Of someone who is extremely happy and exulting in his enjoyment. Aristophanes in the *Peace*:

> Indeed I am happy at having got rid of my shield; I rejoice, I fart,
> I laugh more than someone who has cast off old age,[1]

It is derived from snakes and grasshoppers, which periodically slough off old age and are, as it were, reborn.[2]

74 Hic bonorum virorum est morbus
This is a malady of good men

Αὕτη γε χρηστῶν ἐστιν ἀνδρῶν ἡ νόσος, But this is plainly the malady of an honest man. Suidas quotes this as more or less a proverb, and indeed it is to be found in Aristophanes' *Wasps*.[1] It could be used when something is held to be shameful which ought rather to be considered praiseworthy. It is very close to this from Euripides' *Iphigenia in Aulis*: 'You have upbraided me with an honourable reproach.'[2] Or it can be used ironically of dreadful deeds and serious vices, which although they may be quite terrible, are yet less likely to cause scandal because great and respected men are afflicted with them. Who, for example, would not deplore theft? But adultery is far more detestable, yet princes almost congratulate themselves on it. To be envious, to slander, to seek to accumulate wealth, is far more heinous than to have a girl whom you take into your bed because of her fear of the dark, as St Jerome says.[3] But the priest who does this is called a good-for-nothing

* * * * *

73 Aristophanes (see n1 below)
1 Aristophanes *Peace* 335–6
2 Following the scholiast (Dübner page 181) and Aristotle *Historia animalium* 7(8).17 (600b25 and 601a6). Cf *Adagia* I i 26, I iii 56, III i 85, III vii 1 (200 with n141 above). This was added in *1515*.

74 *Suda* A 4470. Zenobius (Aldus) columns 47–8
1 Aristophanes *Wasps* 80
2 Euripides *Iphigenia Aulidensis* 305
3 Jerome *Letters* 50.5.5

and a cesspit, whilst those who are swollen with ambition, who waste away with avarice, who breathe the poison of envy on everyone, are considered wholesome and holy because, if you please, these are the maladies of good men.[4]

75 Ne guttam quidem
Not even a drop

'Not even a drop' remains even nowadays a very banal hyperbole for 'very little.'[1] Aristophanes in the *Acharnians*: 'But give me one little drop of peace.'[2] The same author in the *Wasps* had an expression of similar form: "Ὕπνου οὐδὲ πασπάλην 'Not even a grain of sleep,'[3] meaning 'Not even the least sleep.' For *paspalē* is the Greek word for the smallest particle of copper or grain, as we have said before.[4] Plautus in the *Pseudolus*: 'Not one drop of sound advice ready, / Let alone a silver coin.'[5] These expressions, of course, are more pleasing if they are used figuratively of abstract things; for example, 'He has not a drop, or a crumb,[6] or a single hair,[7] of good sense.'

76 Βατταρίζειν
To be a Battarist

Βατταρίζειν was a popular word used of those who stuttered and whose

* * * * *

4 From 'Or it can' to here is an addition of *1515*, which pursues the same themes as *Adagia* III ii 1 The Sileni of Alcibiades, III vii 1 A dung-beetle hunting an eagle (178–214 above), III vii 29 One pot smashed against another (233 above), III vii 31 For those who hold to neither altar nor oath (234 above), and III vii 48 It's a good idea to have several names (244–5 above).

75 Aristophanes (see n2 below)
1 See Suringar 132 page 238.
2 Aristophanes *Acharnians* 1033
3 Aristophanes *Wasps* 91; added in *1517/18*. Also used in *Adagia* III vii 43 (241 above).
4 *Adagia* I x 10 Not a splinter. Not even a straw, and for *paspale* III vii 43 (241 above).
5 Plautus *Pseudolus* 397–8; added in *1533*; Otto 773
6 Latin *mica*; cf the quotation from Catullus (86.4) in *Adagia* II iii 51.
7 Latin *pilum*; cf *Adagia* I viii 4 I count it not worth a hair.

76 Zenobius (Aldus) column 53. Cf Erasmus *De pronuntiatione* CWE 26 403–9.

tongue was hesitant and hampered, something the Greeks call τραυλίζειν.
Marcus Tullius in the *Letters to Atticus* book 6: 'I infer from the βατταρίζειν
"stuttering" of my wife's freedman ...'[1] This defect arises from an excess
of humours, according to Hippocrates, and Galen confirms this in his sixth
Commentary.[2] Hence it often occurs in children and in intoxicated people;
although he says there are other causes, pointing out that it happens most
frequently with the letters *t* and *r*, which are pronounced as *tl*, so that
they proclaim their own defect painfully, τραύλωσις 'stuttering.' The question of children and why they stutter more than adults, is examined by
Aristotle in problem 30 of section 11. The philosopher distinguishes there
between 'lisping,' 'defective speech,' and 'stammering.' *Traulosis* 'lisping'
he defines as when someone cannot pronounce a letter, not any letter but
some particular one (this is what Theodorus renders as *blesitas*); 'defective speech' is when some letter or syllable is omitted, as when people say
πιττεύει for πιστεύει (this Theodorus renders as *balbuties*); and 'stammering' when people are unable to link one syllable to another smoothly as
they speak (which Theodorus renders as *linguae hesitantia* 'being tongue-
tied').[3] These defects occur more frequently, as we have said, in children,
old people and the intoxicated, so that Flaccus talks of 'stammering old
age.'[4] The cause, Aristotle thinks, is a physical weakness that cannot be
brought under the control of the mind.[5] Yet Tullius seems to take βατταρίζειν to mean almost 'chatter.' In this way it can be applied to those
who babble trifles, and so βατταρισμός is a word for triviality, a word borrowed from the name Battus, a certain Theban[6] who had a weak voice
and barely articulate speech.[7] The Pythian priestess said to him, 'Battus,
you have come to ask for a voice.' Hesychius recounts this, adding that
some take the word to be an onomatopoeia, like φλοῖσβος 'din' and many

* * * * *

1 Cicero *Ad Atticum* 6.5.1
2 According to the editors of ASD Erasmus' source is exclusively Galen *Commen-
   tarius in Hippocrates aphorismos* 6.32.
3 Aristotle *Problemata* 11.30 (902b16). I have used the English terms used by
   W.S. Hett (Loeb): τραυλότης 'lisping,' ψελλότης 'defective speech,' ἰσχνοφωνία
   'stammering.' Erasmus is also citing the translation of Aristotle by Theodorus
   Gaza. For πιττεύει see *Adagia* I vi 51 and n13 below.
4 Horace *Epistles* 1.20.18; Horace's expression is *balba senectus*.
5 From 'This defect arises' to here all added in *1528*
6 Erasmus has apparently misread Θηραῖος 'Theran' in *Suda* B 180 as Θηβαῖος
   'Theban.' Battus was a Lacedemonian who founded the city of Cyrene in 631
   BC with a colony from Thera.
7 Following *Suda* B 180 and 185

others.[8] They also use the term βαττολογία 'verbosity' from Battus a certain poet who was in the habit of padding out his poems with repetitions. Suidas recalls both of them.[9] But this adds nothing to what Cicero means. It seems to me rather that he said βατταρίζειν for 'to act deceitfully,' because among the Cyrenians the fox is called βάσσαρος, as Herodotus testifies,[10] just as Latin speakers also say *vulpinari* 'to play the fox.'[11] Battarus was the leader of a colony sent to Cyrene.[12] We have talked about *psellismus* elsewhere.[13]

77 Unde excoquat sevum
He could get dripping from it

In the *Two Captives* Plautus used a proverbial hyperbole: 'The old man could get dripping from it,' meaning enormous riches. However the passage seems to be corrupt. The measure of the trochaic line tells us we should read *opimae* 'fertile,' 'rich,' not *optimae* 'best.' This is Plautus' line as it appears in the printed editions:

> *Quid divitiae, suntne optimae? Unde excoquat sevum senex.*

> – How about his property? Pretty fat one, eh?
> – Old Goldfields could get dripping from it.[1]

Sevum, or as others have it *sebum*, is the harder fat of animals, which the Greeks call στέαρ 'stear.'

* * * * *

8 Hesychius B 353; the story is in Herodotus 4.155. Erasmus creates his own Latin word for onomatopoeia, *imitatitia*. 'The Pythian priestess ... many others' was added in *1528*.

9 *Suda* B 183 and 185. For *battologia* cf *Adagia* II i 92 Vain repetition. Spartan brevity.

10 Herodotus 4.192, though Erasmus is quoting the *Etymologicum magnum* on βασσάρα 190.57–191.1. Apart from this phrase added in *1528*, the passage 'They also use ... Cyrene' is an addition of *1515*.

11 Nonius Marcellus 46M citing Varro *Satyrae Menippeae (Mysteria)* 327; cf Apuleius *Metamorphoses* 4.22.

12 Battarus or Battus: Hesychius B 353; Herodotus 4.155; *Suda* B 187

13 *Adagia* I vi 51 The girl who stammers doesn't b-b-believe, and IV iv 28 To act like Sellus

77 Plautus (see n1 below)

1 Plautus *Captivi* 280; Erasmus' correction, usually attributed to Camerarius, is now accepted; the translation is by P. Nixon (Loeb).

78 Iactare iugum
To shake the yoke

'To shake the yoke' is to bear the obligation of service improperly. A figure derived from oxen insufficiently trained to the yoke. Juvenal: 'They have learned under the schooling of life not to fret against the yoke.'[1] Rather like 'You are kicking against the goad.'[2] The misfortune that you bear too impatiently is doubled, but diminished by tranquillity of mind. As Plautus says: 'In an evil pass it helps if you face it with courage.'[3]

79 Ut in velabro olearii
Like oil merchants in the Velabrum

Like oil merchants in the Velabrum. A proverbial comparison for people who have conspired and carry on a business by collusion. Plautus in the *Two Captives*: 'It's the same story. They collude to do all their business, like the oil merchants in the Velabrum.'[1] Varro tells us that the Velabrum was the place in Rome where the oil merchants put up their oil for sale. It is the custom of this class of individuals to collude among themselves about the price and so to sell at a higher price.[2]

80 Imi subsellii
Belonging on the lowest bench

The same author in the same play talks of parasites as 'men belonging on the lowest bench,' because they were admitted to feasts provided they sat in the lowest places. He says: 'Not a bit of use have they nowadays for Spartans,

* * * * *

78 Juvenal (see n1 below), also quoted in *Adagia* III iv 29 (18–19 with n2 above)
1 Juvenal 13.21–22; Erasmus omits *ferre incommoda vitae* 'to endure the ills of life' from the previous line.
2 *Adagia* I iii 46
3 Plautus *Captivi* 202. Used as *Adagia* III iv 68 (42 above)

79 Plautus (see n1 below)
1 Plautus *Captivi* 489
2 Varro mentions the Velabrum in *De lingua latina* 5.43–44, but does not refer to oil-merchants or sales, only to the ferrying of goods.

80 Plautus (see n1 below). Otto 1704n

men of the lowest bench.'[1] And in his *Stichus* the parasite comes on saying, 'I do not demand to be seated on the highest couch. You know that for some time I have been a man of the lowest bench.'[2] Horace too says: 'And a mocker of the lowest couch,' meaning a jester.[3] It will be appropriate for the humble sort of guests whom these wealthy people never invite except to the lowest places. The figure will be wittier if it is extended further, for example to those who are of the lowest rank among nobles at court or the last among scholars, those whom we might call lower class,[4] the bottom class,[5] and those of lowest quality.[6] The last of these expressions seems to derive from merchandise having a label attached that shows the maximum price; the first comes from the ancient Romans' census. For those who belonged to the first class possessed one hundred and twenty thousand asses in bronze, and these alone were known as *classici* – all the rest, for there were several classes, were said to be *infra classem* 'lower class.' The authority for this is Aulus Gellius book 7 chapter 13.[7] However, some versions of the text have *xxv* instead of *xx*, and Titus Livy says 'one hundred thousand asses in bronze.'[8]

81 Manticulari
Rifling wallets

Festus Pompeius shows that the poets used this word *manticulari* for 'to deceive,' or 'to act slyly,' and he quotes Pacuvius as saying: 'Adroitly he moves closer to rifle the wallet.'[1] It is derived from *manticulae*, the 'wallets'

* * * * *

1 Plautus *Captivi* 471; added in 1526. The accepted reading now, here and in the *Stichus* (n2 below), is *unisubsellium*, a bench accommodating one person, as used by parasites who were not allowed to use the *lecti* 'couches.'
2 Plautus *Stichus* 489. Erasmus' text differs in other minor respects from the accepted reading.
3 Horace *Epistles* 1.18.10–11
4 Latin *infra classem*; see Aulus Gellius n7 below.
5 Latin *extremae classis*; Cicero *Academica* 2.73 uses *quintae classis* 'of the fifth class' for 'the lowest class.'
6 Latin *infimae notae*
7 Aulus Gellius *Noctes Atticae* 6(7 in early editions).13. The passage 'The figure will be wittier ... Aulus Gellius' was added in 1515.
8 Livy 1.43.1; this sentence was added in 1528.

81 Pompeius Festus page 118 Lindsay
1 Pacuvius 377 TRF

that thieves run their fingers over in order, of course, to steal from them. As for myself, I am inclined to think the metaphor is derived from the fact that people who wish to dissemble at feasts cover their faces with their napkins[2] as if wiping their mouths. As Horace says in his *Satires*: 'Using a napkin to stifle laughter.'[3] Plautus too in the *Two Captives* uses *mantellum* for a cloak and hiding place by which a piece of trickery could be covered:

> There is no cloak anywhere for my crafty lies.
> No cloak is ready at hand for my flatteries and deceits.[4]

For my part I rather think this figure is what we have in Origen's fifth *Homily on Ezekiel*: 'He says to his neighbour "God forgives us our sins." For even in these sacraments we make a joke, promising each other in turn "God will provide a napkin," '[5] that is, He will cover our infamies by placing a napkin over them. But since I do not have access to the Greek manuscript,[6] it would be better to play the sceptic on this point. Let the scholars who do have access to it examine this passage now I have called their attention to it. Tertullian uses the same expression in his book *Against the Valentinians*: 'But with the drop of a napkin, as they say.'[7]

82 Auro habet suppactum solum
He has gold-plated soles

A proverbial figure used by Plautus in the *Bacchis Sisters*:

* * * * *

2 Latin *mantiles*; Estienne (LB II 904) accepts that *manticulae* may be equated with *mantiles*, but not that the action of wiping the face explains the verb *manticulari*. He refers to some lines of Catullus (12.1–3) from which he deduces that guests at some banquets used napkins to distract attention and hide thefts.
3 Horace *Satires* 2.8.63: 'napkin' is *mappa*
4 Plautus *Captivi* 520–1; Erasmus' second line *Nec sycophantiis, nec fucis ullum mantellum obvium est* bears little resemblance to the accepted text *Neque deprecatio perfidis meis nec male factis fuga est* 'My falsehoods can't beg themselves off, or my transgressions take to their heels,' but, with the exception of *obviam* for *obvium*, is taken from Giambattista Pio's edition (folio n i r).
5 Origen *Homilia in Ezekiel* 5.5 PG 13 708D: *mappam mittet deus* 'God will give the signal.' Cf Suetonius *Nero* 22.2 and see n7 below.
6 Erasmus is using Jerome's Latin translation of Origen.
7 Tertullian *Adversus Valentinianos* 36 CSEL 47 210:14; added in 1526. Cf Otto 1059 who gives the correct meaning: 'At a given signal.' Here and in Origen the *mappa* is the cloth used in the circus to signal the start of a race.

82 *Collectanea* no 228. Plautus (see n1 below). Otto 220

> But isn't this Theotimus a rich man? – How can you ask?
> The soles of his sandals are fastened with gold.[1]

Said of an exceptionally rich person who has such an immense quantity of gold that he wears it on his feet. He used the word *solum* 'sole' for the bottom of the sandals, or at least for the flooring.[2]

83 Ad aras
At the altars

Ἐπὶ βωμούς, At the altars. This is contained in the *Collected Proverbs* that are ascribed to Plutarch in the title, but without explanation.[1] For my part I think it means much the same as if one says 'once the business is actually in hand,' as in the proverb we have quoted elsewhere in which we are forbidden to have discussions at the altar.[2]

84 Samiorum laura
The Laura at Samos

Σαμίων λαύρα, The Laura at Samos. A saying commonly directed against those given to shameful pleasures. The Laura at Samos was a narrow street in which the luxuries of eating houses and cabarets were sold by prostitutes trained for this purpose. This adage too is extant in the commentaries attributed to Plutarch,[1] and Athenaeus[2] repeats it from Clearchus[3] in book

* * * * *

1 Plautus *Bacchides* 331–2
2 Latin *aut certe pro pavimento*; Estienne (LB II 904) asserts this addition of *1515* is entirely at odds with Plautus' meaning and quotes Athenaeus 12.539C and Plutarch *Alexander* 40.1 to illustrate the practice of using gold studs in shoes.

83 Pseudo-Plutarch (see n1 below). Cf Zenobius (Aldus) column 84.
1 Ie the first collection in Laurentianus 80.13 (see *Adagia* III v 30n, 83 above). This proverb is to be found in *Alexandrian Proverbs* 1.70, the first of a series taken from this manuscript. The series is interrupted by the proverbs taken from Homer, which run from *Adagia* III viii 1 to III x 75 (282–383 below); it ends, with some other minor intercalations, at III x 84 (389 below).
2 *Adagia* III iv 28 But the place for deliberation is not before the altar (17 above)

84 Pseudo-Plutarch (see n1 below). Cf Zenobius (Aldus) column 147 and *Adagia* II ix 23 The flowers of Samos.
1 Pseudo-Plutarch *Alexandrian Proverbs* 1.61
2 Athenaeus 12.540F; added in *1517/18*
3 Clearchus fragment 44 Wehrli

12 adding that it was introduced by Polycrates, the tyrant of Samos, and that he planned this corruption of the city on the model of the Elbow at Sardis, which was proverbially called the Sweet Elbow according to Plato.[4]

85 Taenarium malum
A Taenarian bane

Ταινάριον κακόν, A Taenarian bane. If some exceptionally cruel punishment was inflicted on slaves it was called a Taenarian bane, because in former times the Spartans put to death recaptured slaves who had fled to Taenarus. In this case Taenarus is a city of Laconia, whose inhabitants are called Taenaritae, and a headland of that country with a cave that is an entrance to the underworld.[1]

86 Lesbius Prylis
Lesbian Prylis

Ὁ Λέσβιος Πρύλις, Lesbian Prylis. In the Collected Proverbs[1] Plutarch, if the title is not wrong, informs us that this proverbial expression is derived from an allegorical figure. Prylis was the son of Mercury and skilled in divination. However πρύλις means in Greek a foot soldier.[2]

* * * * *

4 Plato Phaedrus 257D. Plato uses the term to mean something like 'sour grapes,' but does not refer to the Elbow at Sardis. Cf Adagia II i 38 Sweet elbow. According to H.N. Fowler (Loeb), the reference there to the 'elbow formed by the Nile' is an addition to the text by some commentator.

85 Pseudo-Plutarch Alexandrian Proverbs 1.54. Cf Suda T 205 and Zenobius (Aldus) column 154.
1 Information from Stephanus Byzantinus (Ταίναρος, page 598 Meineke) and Suda T 206, but the essential point is that a sanctuary near the headland, containing a temple to Poseidon, had a traditional right of sanctuary (Thucydides 1.133) and private slaves were manumitted there. The cave was the one through which Hercules dragged Cerberus up from Hades.

86 Pseudo-Plutarch (see n1 below)
1 Pseudo-Plutarch Alexandrian Proverbs 1.42; see the introductory note to adage 83 above.
2 Prylis was a soothsayer of Lesbos who, inspired by Athene, revealed to Agamemnon that Troy could be taken only by a wooden horse. He is not mentioned in Homer. See Tzetzes Lycophronis Alexandra Scholia lines 219–22,

87 Agas asellum
You can drive the ass

This adage is recorded in an amputated form and it is not completely clear what it means. It is recorded by Cicero in book 2 of *The Making of an Orator* thus: 'In this class are included proverbs like the one used by Scipio, when Asellus boasted that he had visited every province while he was a soldier: "You can drive the ass, etc." '[1] That is all Tully says, and I do not want to repeat what Omniboni proposes here,[2] though he is otherwise a good com-

* * * * *

and Eustathius 601.4 on *Iliad* 5.744 and 893.40 on *Iliad* 12.77, where πρύλις appears as 'foot soldier'; cf *Suda* Π 2984, Hesychius Π 4114, *Etymologicum magnum* 693.31.

87 Cicero (see n1 below). Otto 188 and Otto *Nachträge* page 137. It is difficult to know how Erasmus understood the phrase as it stands, since he thought it was incomplete. Estienne (LB II 905–6) believes the phrase in Cicero is complete and he refers to Martial's epigram 1.79, which has the expression *agis mulas* (line 3), 'do the job of mules' or 'drive mules,' but see also the note by E.W. Sutton (Loeb), according to whom the complete saying is plausibly *Agas asellum; cursum non docebitur* 'Drive the ass; he will not be taught the way,' and the remarks of M.C. Sutphen reproduced in Otto *Nachträge.*

1 Cicero *De oratore* 2.258; E.W. Sutton (Loeb) suggests the innuendo may be that the boasted travels of Ti. Claudius Asellus were solely attributable to compulsory military activity. There is of course a double play on words: *Asellus* is either a name or the word for an ass's colt, and *agas* may mean 'drive' or 'play the part of.' Estienne (LB II 905–6) affirms that *et cetera* does not appear in the manuscript he has seen.

2 Omniboni Leoniceno (*In Marci Tullii Oratorem ad Quintum fratrem commentarium* Vicenza 1476, folio q [7v]) seeks to explain the passage in Cicero by an answer Scipio Africanus is said to have made to one Asellus, a plebeian whom, as censor, he had condemned to the status of *aerarius* 'tax-payer without citizen's rights.' Asellus was released by Scipio's colleague in the censorship of Lucius Mumius (146 BC) at the time of the lustral sacrifice. The following year the plague struck and Asellus complained to Scipio that the sacrifice had been inauspicious; Scipio replied that it was no wonder, because it was performed by Mumius who had released him from the status of *aerarius.* Omniboni seems to be saying that the reply is a harsh joke, which blames Asellus for the plague. Erasmus' impatience is understandable: the story, which really concerns Scipio's objections to Mumius as a colleague in the censorship, contains no proverbial expression such as seems to be implied by Cicero and the explanation it offers is too remote from the context in Cicero. For Mumius Omniboni refers to Valerius Maximus (6.4.2A) but the story of Asellus is not there.

mentator. However it seemed proper to put this adage on the table so that I could at all events offer scholars an occasion for research. Perhaps the reading should be *agaso asellum* 'A stable boy for an ass,' for the ancient Romans elided vowels, like the Greeks, even in writing. Then the meaning would be that each man does the things that are appropriate to him: prodigals get drunk, the glutton eats himself to ruin, the soldier fights, the pimp commits perjury, the lawyer tells lies. This word *agaso* became a proverbial term of contempt,[3] which is more humorous in Greek because of the nature of the language. For the Dorians call an ass not ὄνος like the others but κίλλος, and a stable-boy not ὀνηλάτης but κιλλακτήρ, as Pollux affirms in the *Vocabulary* book 7.[4] Relevant to this perhaps is what Flaccus wrote in his epistle 19 to Lollius: 'In the end / He will become a gladiator, or the hired driver of a greengrocer's nag.[5]

88 Samium comatum
A long-haired Samian

Τὸν ἐν Σάμῳ κομήτην, A long-haired Samian. This was said of someone, considered naïve at first, who conducted himself in an affair more cleverly than expected. It is said that some boxer in Samos was treated as a joke by his opponents because he had long hair, but he won his bouts when matched with them. Hence the expression became proverbial whenever anyone undertakes to compete with people who turn out to be stronger than expected.[1] Not unlike Sulla's warning: 'Beware the ill girt boy.'[2] The adage is included in the *Collected Proverbs* of Plutarch.

* * * * *

3 See the lines quoted from Persius 5.76 in *Adagia* I viii 11 A three-ha'penny fellow.
4 Pollux *Onomasticon* 7.56
5 Horace *Epistles* 1.18(not 19).35–6; translation by H. Rushton Fairclough (Loeb). Added in 1520 and also quoted by Estienne in support of his reading (see headnote and n1 above)

88 Pseudo-Plutarch (see n1 below). Cf Diogenianus 4.58 and Zenobius (Aldus) column 160.
1 Following Pseudo-Plutarch *Alexandrian Proverbs* 2.8
2 Latin *Cavendum a puero male cincto*; Suetonius *Julius* 45.3. Not an exact quotation though the meaning is the same. Suetonius has *ut male praecinctum puerum caverent*, an allusion to Caesar's idiosyncratic habit of wearing a loose girdle over his senator's tunic.

89 Servum haud veho
I maintain no servant

Δοῦλον οὐκ ἄγω, / Εἰ μὴ νεναυμάχηκε τὸν περὶ τῶν κρεῶν, I maintain no servant, / Unless he fought to save his flesh / In the sea battle. That is: 'I accept no servant unless he is proved by a lot of serious tests.' This verse is in
Aristophanes' *Frogs*,[1] and is quoted by me elsewhere.[2] The commentators[3]
point out that there are two readings, 'for his flesh' and 'for the bodies.'[4]
'For his flesh' is taken to mean 'for his life,' 'flesh' being used for the body,
and when slaves fight, since they have no possessions, they are struggling
only for their life. Those who read 'bodies' adduce this story. In the naval
battle that took place at Arginusae the Athenians were the victors; they ordered that the bodies of the dead should not be taken away, and there was
a quarrel over this. In this battle we read that the slaves acted so zealously
that they were given their freedom.[5] The proverb is recorded in the *Collected
Proverbs* of Plutarch.

90 Tertium caput
A third head

Τρίτη κεφαλὴ καὶ τρίτῳ ἐγκεφάλῳ, A third head and For a third brain.[1] Said
of porters who carry their loads not only on their shoulders but on their

* * * * *

89 Pseudo-Plutarch (see n3 below)
1 Aristophanes *Frogs* 190–1
2 *Adagia* II i 80 A hare because of its meat
3 Pseudo-Plutarch *Alexandrian Proverbs* 2.7, and the scholiast of Aristophanes
(Dübner page 280)
4 In Greek, περὶ τῶν κρεῶν 'flesh' and περὶ τῶν νεκρῶν 'bodies,' translated by
Erasmus as *pro carnibus* and *pro cadaveribus*
5 Arginusae was fought by the Athenians against the Spartans in 406 BC. The
subsequent quarrel concerned a failure to pick up the survivors for which
several generals were put to death. Xenophon *Hellenica* 1.6.24; Diodorus Siculus
13.97–100

90 Pseudo-Plutarch (see n1 below) and Zenobius (Aldus) column 162. Cf Mantissa
3.28 and *Suda* T 1016.
1 Pseudo-Plutarch *Alexandrian Proverbs* 1.99; Erasmus would have found both
expressions, one in the nominative and one in the dative, in the *Alexandrian
Proverbs* or in Zenobius (Aldus). The *Suda* offers only the nominative. Estienne
(LB II 906) thought both should be in the dative.

head. Recorded in the same *Collected Proverbs* that I have just mentioned. It could be fittingly adapted to men torn this way and that by diverse affairs.[2]

91 Ut Corinthia videris
You seem like a Corinthian woman

ʽΑ Κορινθία ἔοικας χοιροπωλήσειν, You seem to want to sell yourself like a Corinthian woman. Against a woman behaving wantonly at an unsuitable age.[1] We have spoken elsewhere of the women prostitutes at Corinth.[2] Χοιροπωλῶ is a neologism, which I take to mean 'to sell one's body for money,' since χοῖρος means a woman's sex.[3] This adage too is recorded in the same *Collected Proverbs*.

92 Cyrnia iactura
A Cyrnian disaster

Κυρνία ἄτη, A Cyrnian disaster. Used of great losses and plunderings. The island of Cyrnus is off the coast of Apulia, and its inhabitants are believed to be long-lived because of the honey that they eat commonly (they are neighbours of the island of Sardinia)[1] of which there is a great supply there, according to Stephanus.[2] This island was formerly inaccessible to sailors be-

* * * * *

2 The last sentence was added in *1533*.

91 Pseudo-Plutarch *Alexandrian Proverbs* 1.92. Zenobius (Aldus) column 19. *Suda* X 601 has Ἀκροκορινθία.
1 Latin *intempestivius*, which translates literally παρ᾽ ὥραν in the manuscript
2 *Adagia* I iv 1 It is not given to everyone to land at Corinth
3 The first meaning of χοῖρος is 'pig' and χοιροπώλης 'dealer in swine'; the comic poets frequently make puns on the word, and it is Pseudo-Plutarch or the *Suda* who says it is a Corinthian usage.

92 Pseudo-Plutarch *Alexandrian Proverbs* 1.90. Zenobius (Aldus) column 108
1 Erasmus' uncertain geography, also apparent in *Adagia* III i 74 A land like Cyrnus, where this adage is recalled, may be traced to Stephanus Byzantinus (see n2 below) and Pliny (see n3 below), who both locate the island off Apulia but also mention Corsica. Erasmus had originally omitted 'they are neighbours of the island of Sardinia' here, but introduced it in additions of *1528* without resolving the inconsistencies.
2 Stephanus Byzantinus page 397 Meineke, who says the island is to the east off Iapygia (modern Calabria) but also mentions an island called Corsica in the Ionian Sea.

cause of the robbers and pirates that frequented the waters around it. Hence the popular proverb. In book 4 chapter 12 Pliny[3] speaks of Cyrnus but as distinct from Corsica, though Strabo[4] tells us Cyrnus is the place that the Romans call Corsica, a sparsely populated island because of the roughness of the terrain and inaccessibility of much of the area, but particularly because the people who control the mountains and live by robbery are more savage than the very beasts. If on occasion some of them were captured by Roman commanders and taken to Rome, it was a source of wonder how wild and bestial their behaviour was. For they either killed themselves or, if they lived, they so exhausted their masters with their sullenness and stupidity that, however little the latter had paid for them, they still regretted the purchase. This was Corsica in former times; now it supplies the pleasure-seekers of Rome with the most highly praised wines. So it was because of the barbarity of the robber bands and the wildness of the people that the saying 'A Cyrnian disaster' arose, just like 'A Cilician ending,' which we have noted elsewhere.[5] We mentioned this present adage earlier in 'A land like Cyrnus.'[6]

93 Rapina Cotytiis
Pillage at the Cotytia

Ἁρπαγὰ Κοτυτίοις, Pillage at the Cotytia. The Cotytia was a festival of the Sicilians[1] in which traditionally little cakes and the fruits of trees were bound up with twigs and these bundles were offered up and torn apart. The expression is recorded in the *Collected Proverbs* of Plutarch without explanation. However it is easily seen that it would be said of good things heedlessly squandered and pillaged.

* * * * *

3 Pliny *Naturalis historia* 4.53, where the island is said to be 'off Aetolia' (and therefore also in the Ionian Sea), but in 3.80 is identified with Corsica. The passage from this point to 'elsewhere' is an addition of 1528.
4 Strabo *Geographica* 5.2.7
5 *Adagia* III ii 25
6 See n1 above.

93 Pseudo-Plutarch *Alexandrian Proverbs* 1.78
1 Cotys, or Cotyt(t)o was originally a Thracian goddess associated with orgiastic rites, found later in Corinth and Sicily. Her Corinthian devotees and their rites were the subject of Eupolis' comedy *Baptae*. Erasmus' only source is Pseudo-Plutarch.

94 Quae ex antiqua
What comes from the old city

Τὰ ἐκ παλαιᾶς, What comes from the old city, 'of Tyre' being understood. This amounts to exactly the same as saying the greatest trouble and the worst evil. Tyre, which was called the 'Old' (the words are put together in the form *Palaityros*), was cruelly treated by Alexander when he captured it and joined the island to the mainland by creating a dyke. He inflicted many penalties on it, giving rise to the proverb 'What comes from the old city,' meaning wrongs as numerous as those suffered by ancient Tyre. It is recorded in the Proverbs of Plutarch and in Zenodotus.[1] The story is to be found in Quintus Curtius.[2]

95 Triceps Mercurius
Three-headed Mercury

Τρικέφαλος Ἑρμῆς, Three-headed Mercury. Seems to have been said about people whose nature or intention is uncertain or who are extremely cunning. Mercury was represented thus in ancient times either because of the great power of the spoken word or because this same god is the one who indicates the road to take. So on each head he had an inscription showing where this or that road would lead. According to Philochorus, the first to portray this sort of Mercury was Proclides.[1]

96 Danace
A copper

Δανάκη, A *danakē*. This was the name of the small copper coin that was the fare paid to Charon for transport across the Stygian marsh; Lucian recalls it

* * * * *

94 Pseudo-Plutarch Laurentianus 2.4 Jungblut page 403. See also Appendix IV 79.
 1 Zenobius (Aldus) column 154
 2 Quintus Curtius *Historia Alexandri* 4.2–4. Palaetyros (4.2.4) is described by Curtius as a separate settlement on the mainland, site of a temple of Hercules.

95 Apostolius 17.23. Cf *Suda* T 981.
 1 Philochorus *FGrHist* 328 F 22. The suggestion about the power of the spoken word is only in Apostolius; all the rest is in both Apostolius and the *Suda*.

96 Pseudo-Plutarch Laurentianus 2.5 Jungblut page 403. Zenobius (Aldus) column 66. *Suda* Δ 59

in his *Charon*[1] and Apuleius in the tale of Psyche.[2] It is recorded in the *Collected Proverbs* of Plutarch but the use is not indicated. I think it is used correctly when an old person is told to get his *danakē* ready, signifying that it is time for him to leave this life. Or, if someone has left absolutely nothing, that not a *danakē* remained to him. Juvenal has an expression with this meaning in his third *Satire*, though he calls the coin a *triens*: 'The unhappy man has no hope of a ferry to cross the murky flood, no copper in his mouth to tender.'[3]

97 Ut Bagas constitisti
You stood like Bagas

Βάγας ἕστηκας, You were standing like Bagas. Said of someone dull and speechless. Bagas was like someone struck dumb – dull and insipid. He is mentioned in the *Collected Proverbs* of Plutarch. I think the name should be Bagoas rather than Bagas; Bagoas was a eunuch and this sort is fearful and cowardly.[1]

98 Cancrum ingredi doces
You're teaching a crab to walk

Καρκίνον ὀρθὰ βαδίζειν διδάσκεις, You're teaching a crab to walk forwards. Of someone who teaches the unteachable. It is recorded in the same *Collected Proverbs*. Very similar to, or rather the same as, the one I noted not far back from Aristophanes in the proverb, 'You'll never make crabs walk forwards.'[1] It belongs to the class of ἀδύνατα 'impossibles': 'You are washing an Ethiopian,' etc.[2] For this animal walks only with its body turned side-

* * * * *

1 Lucian *Charon* 11, where the word used is ὀβολός. Erasmus could have seen δανάκη also in Pollux 9.82, Hesychius Δ 219, and *Etymologicum magnum* 247.41.
2 Apuleius *Metamorphoses* 6.18; Apuleius uses *stips*.
3 Juvenal 3.266–7; the *triens* was one third of an *as*.

97 Pseudo-Plutarch Laurentianus 2.15 Jungblut page 404. Cf Zenobius (Aldus) column 50. In Apostolius 4.90 the name is Βησᾶς.
1 Bagoas is the name of the eunuch in Lucian's dialogue *Eunuchus*, which Erasmus had translated in 1514, just before this sentence was added.

98 Pseudo-Plutarch Laurentianus 3.16 Jungblut page 416 = Zenobius (Aldus) column 14
1 *Adagia* III vii 38 (238 above)
2 *Adagia* I iv 50. There is a series of *impossibilia* from I iv 48–61; the class is mentioned in Erasmus' introductory discussion of proverbial metaphors (CWE 31 22), and provided a large number of epigrams of the *Greek Anthology*.

ways and moves thus in all directions. It is thought that it is called καρκίνος from καράκινον 'by moving the head.'³ It is said to give birth through the head.⁴

99 Mare exhauris
You are emptying out the sea

Θάλασσαν ἀντλεῖς, You are emptying out the sea. Said of someone who attempts what cannot be done. For mountains can be penetrated by some means or other, but the sea cannot be emptied.¹

100 Canes timidi vehementius latrant
Nervous dogs bark louder

Curtius declares in book 7 that a proverb commonly used by the Bactrians went something like this: 'A nervous dog barks more violently than he bites.'¹ It is the role of a Thraso to hurl exaggerated threats of calamities but a Chremes is quicker to get something done.² History records too that the Athenians were more adept at speaking eloquently than at acting energetically. Ajax was not a ready speaker nor Ulysses a ready fighter.³ And the Spartans were very sparing of words but outstanding in courage. In Homer the Greeks go into battle silently but breathing fury, whilst the barbarians

* * * * *

3 Ie, deriving the word from κάρα 'head' and κινέω 'move'; *Etymologicum magnum* 491.53
4 Probably an inexact memory of Pliny *Naturalis historia* 9.158 who says *cancri ore [coeunt]* 'Crabs copulate through the mouth,' in turn a misunderstanding of Aristotle *Historia animalium* 5.7 (541b25)

99 Zenobius (Aldus) column 94. Pseudo-Plutarch Laurentianus 3.17 Jungblut page 416. Cf Otto 1062.
1 The last sentence added in *1515*

100 Cf *Collectanea* no 724, though the proverb is not attested in that form in ancient literature. The whole adage dates from *1517/18* and uses a new wording found in Quintus Curtius *History of Alexander* (see n1 below), which Erasmus had edited in the interval and which was published in 1518. Cf Suringar 34. Otto 321
1 Quintus Curtius *History of Alexander* 7.4.13
2 Thraso and Chremes are characters in Terence's *Eunuchus*.
3 Cf Ovid *Metamorphoses* 13.10–11.

rush forward with a frightful noise.[4] And finally women wage war with their tongues better than men. Quintus Curtius adds in the same passage an allegorical figure similar to this: 'The deepest rivers flow with the least sound.'[5]

Some proverbial lines from Homer

Homer was held in such high esteem by the ancients, as Macrobius testifies,[1] that almost every one of his verses was commonly quoted as a proverb. Some of these I have examined at scattered intervals in this work, especially those I have observed to be used in literature. So now I think it will be worthwhile to sort out from the whole corpus of Homer's poetry those verses that look so much like proverbs there can be no doubt that they

* * * * *

4 Homer *Iliad* 3.2–9
5 Quintus Curtius *History of Alexander* 7.4.13; Otto 679; Otto *Nachträge* pages 57 and 271

Some proverbial lines from Homer

The adages based on Homeric verses that constitute *Adagia* centuries III viii and III ix and continue (with only two exceptions) to III x 75 were added to the collection in *1508*. Many of them are untypical in two respects. First, Erasmus has not in many cases made the selected verse or expression from Homer, which he proposes as proverbial, the title of the item – which is his almost invariable practice elsewhere – but has used instead a phrase indicating the person, event or circumstance to which it may be applied (eg III viii 1–10). In other cases he has given a parallel proverbial phrase or precept as his title though still intending the Homeric verse or expression to be his adage (III ix 32–6, III ix 35, and, for a particularly clear case, III ix 67). Second, these verses are not for the most part expressions that are authenticated as proverbs by subsequent usage, but only, in Erasmus' words, 'those verses that look so much like proverbs there can be no doubt that they ... were the ones that antiquity used as proverbial expressions.' In practice he chooses verses that can be used to express judgments of persons and situations commonly encountered, though in some cases he suggests figurative applications particularly distant from the meaning of the phrase in its original context, and in other cases quotes in ways that seem quite opposed to Homer's meanings (III viii 15, 24, 64; III x 21). For his condemnation of 'distortions' of Ovid and Seneca to give Christian interpretations and his own allegorization of Homer and Virgil, see Anthony Grafton 'Renaissance Readers and Ancient Texts: Comments on some Commentaries' *Renaissance Quarterly* 38.4 (1985) 615–49, especially page 637.

1 Macrobius *Saturnalia* 5.16.6

at least of the whole total were the ones that antiquity used as proverbial expressions. Although there is almost no verse by this poet that cannot be turned to some proverbial use, I have preferred to select a few of the many, partly so that no one can say that I have been too assiduous in this rather exotic pursuit, partly because somehow the most pleasing of this kind are those that each person might choose for himself. So I believe it was enough to show in a few cases how they should be adapted. But in these very cases, although I have pointed to the use of the verse that occurred to me as I wrote, there is nothing to prevent other uses of this same verse being admitted. But I would not allow the same licence with other poets, unless it may be thought permissible with Maro, who can very rightly be called the Latin Homer. However Homer has a certain sublime nature which makes this practice appropriate, whatever one may derive from him and however it is done, even if, as often happens in verse made up from borrowings, the words are stretched to give a vastly different sense. Since I am also aware that these would have no charm except to those who could use them in Greek, in order to make them comprehensible for the majority, I have also translated them. But it is time to begin.

1 Non probantis
For a dissenter

'Αλλ' οὐκ 'Ατρείδῃ 'Αγαμέμνονι ἥνδανε θυμῷ, But this was not at all to the liking of Agamemnon, son of Atreus.[1] This is used in a proverbial fashion by Lucian in *The Lapiths*.[2] We shall be using it correctly when we admit that something is the right thing to do but that the opposite is favoured by those whose wishes prevail over justice. Or when someone pursues in tyrannical fashion not what fairness demands but what his whim dictates. Or when one person disagrees with everyone else. Its source is book 1 of Homer's *Iliad*, where this verse is also repeated:

> But the rest of the Greek troops favour the idea
> That the priest should be treated with honour and the magnificent gifts
>   accepted;
> But this was not at all to the liking of Agamemnon

* * * * *

1 Homer *Iliad* (see n1 below)
1 *Iliad* 1.24 and 1.378
2 Lucian *Convivium sive Lapithae* 12

Who dismisses the man rudely and sends him away with harsh words.[3]

2 Refutantis laudem immodicam
For one who rejects excessive praise

Οὔ τοι ἐγὼ θεός εἰμι, τί μ' ἀθανάτοισιν ἐΐσκεις; I am no god; why do you liken me to the immortals?[1] In his essay on 'Progress in Virtue' Plutarch advises us to keep this line of Homer always in mind as a remedy for the poison of flattery, or for the occasions when someone praises us more generously than we deserve.[2] It is used by Lucian in the *Icaromenippus*.[3] The verse comes from book 16 of the *Odyssey* and is part of a speech of Ulysses to his son Telemachus.

3 Caventis clancularias insidias
Of someone wary of hidden treachery

Μή τίς σοι φεύγοντι μεταφρένῳ ἐν δόρυ πήξῃ, Take care that no one spears you in the back as you flee.[1] To be used when we want to recommend action with some caution, so that the rash do not come to harm. Diogenes used it, changing one word, to address a handsome youth who slept without a guard: 'Take care that no one spears you in the back as you sleep.'[2] However, these are the words of Diomedes calling the fleeing Ulysses back to the battle in Homer's *Iliad* book 8. We find the same in the *Iliad* book 22:

> You will never plant your spear in my back as I flee
> But twist it rather in my chest as I face you.[3]

This can be used when someone is not refusing to dispute openly.

* * * * *

3 *Iliad* 1.22–5

2 Homer *Odyssey* (see n1 below)
1 *Odyssey* 16.187
2 Plutarch *Moralia* 81D *Quomodo quis suos in virtute sentiat profectus*
3 Lucian *Icaromenippus* 13

3 Homer *Iliad* (see n1 below)
1 *Iliad* 8.95
2 Diogenes Laertius ('Diogenes the Cynic') 6.53
3 *Iliad* 22.283–4

4 Iubentis aperte loqui
Of one who commends frank speech

If we wish to advise someone to speak out about the reasons for their grief
or hatred and not hide it in their heart, we could quite neatly quote this
from book 1 of the *Iliad*: 'Speak out, do not hide it, so that we may both
know.'[1]

5 Pollicentis se promissa re praestiturum
Of one who promises to stand by what has been promised

When we want to say that confidence in things promised will not be vain,
but that we will guarantee by our actions what we have promised in words,
we could use these lines from the same book:

> Nothing that I say can be revoked or will be invalidated or unfulfilled,
> Whatever I have bowed my head to and promised.[1]

This is Jove speaking to Thetis.

6 In absurde locutum
Against one who has spoken out of place

When someone seems to have said something absurd or when through
inattention some word seems to have slipped out that it would have been
better to restrain, then it will be a moment for the phrase that is to be
found in several places in Homer and, to be precise, in the first book of
the *Odyssey*: 'What word has slipped past the barrier of your teeth?'[1] This

* * * * *

4 Homer *Iliad* (see n1 below)
1 *Iliad* 1.363: Ἐξαύδα, μὴ κεῦθε νόῳ, ἵνα εἴδομεν ἄμφω.

5 Homer *Iliad* (see n1 below)
1 *Iliad* 1.526–7: Οὐ γὰρ ἐμὸν παλινάγρετον οὐδ᾽ ἀπατηλὸν / Οὐδ᾽ ἀτελεύτητόν γ᾽, ὅ τί
κεν κεφαλῇ κατανεύσω.

6 Homer *Odyssey* and *Iliad* (see n1 below)
1 *Odyssey* 1.64: Ποῖόν σε ἔπος φύγεν ἕρκος ὀδόντων; – cf *Odyssey* 5.22, 19.492 and
Iliad 4.350. Erasmus is perhaps also thinking of ἀμείψεται ἕρκος ὀδόντων (*Iliad*
9.409 – see *Adagia* III viii 48 n3 (299 below) – and *Odyssey* 10.328).

verse is praised by Aulus Gellius in book 1 chapter 15 of his *Attic Nights* because it gives noble advice on the need to speak sparingly, 'for Nature surrounded the tongue with the fence of the teeth and the enclosure of the lips' but gave us wide open ears.[2]

7 In spem frustratam
On disappointed hope

If we want to indicate that someone has been disappointed in his hope and that something has turned out otherwise than he expected, it would be quite amusing to apply this from book 2 of the *Iliad*: 'Fool that he was, for Jupiter was devising things quite different from these / For the unwitting man.'[1]

8 Inanis conatus
Vain effort

When we feel that work has been undertaken in vain and that nothing is gained by prolonged labours, it would be rather apt to bring in this from the same book: 'Waging a fruitless battle and a useless war.'[1]

9 Adiurantis se facturum aliquid
Of one who swears to perform some act

When we want to swear on our life that we will perform some act, we may adapt this line from the same book: 'May this head rest no more on Ulysses' shoulders.'[1] Again in book 5 of the *Iliad*: 'Then may some barbarian sword cut off this head of mine.'[2] For this is how ordinary people swear even

* * * * *

2 Aulus Gellius *Noctes Atticae* 1.15.3–4. The phrase concerning ears is added by Erasmus.

7 Homer *Iliad* (see n1 below)
1 *Iliad* 2.38: Νήπιος οὐδὲ τὰ ἤδη, ἅ ῥα Ζεὺς μήδετο ἔργα.

8 Homer *Iliad* (see n1 below)
1 *Iliad* 2.121: Ἄπρηκτον πόλεμον πολεμίζειν ἠδὲ μάχεσθαι

9 Homer *Iliad* (see n1 below)
1 *Iliad* 2.259: Μηκέτ' ἔπειτ' Ὀδυσῆι κάρη ὤμοισι ἐπείη.
2 *Iliad* 5.214: Αὐτίκ' ἔπειτ' ἀπ' ἐμοῖο κάρη τάμοι ἀλλότριος φώς.

nowadays.[3] And among Latin speakers *emoriar* 'may I die' and *dispeream* 'may I perish utterly' are well known.[4]

10 Quae sero contingunt, sed magnifica
Rewards coming late, but generously

Whenever we wish to imply that fame or some reward comes late but is the more brilliant or lasting precisely because it has been rather long delayed, so that delay is compensated by security and permanence, it will not be inappropriate to employ this verse from book 2 of the *Iliad*,[1] which Cicero translates thus: 'Slow and very late, but of everlasting fame and praise.'[2] They are the words of Chalcas[3] as he encouraged the Greeks to endure, for although victory would not come until the tenth year of the war, the glory of it would be undying.

11 Consulendum et consiliis parendum
Consider well and take advice

When we warn someone that he should both give just advice to others and accept it from them in return, or that he should consider a matter thoroughly in his own mind and listen carefully to the opinion of others, it will be a good moment for this, from the same book: 'Come, O king, give good advice yourself and accept good counsel too.'[1]

12 Non interpellandus famelicus
Don't hinder a hungry man

Whenever we want to imply that there is no leisure for chatter if the

* * * * *

3 Suringar 5 page 5
4 See Suringar and Lewis and Short for other examples of *emoriar* and *dispeream*.

10 Homer *Iliad* (see n1 below)
1 *Iliad* 2.325: Ὄψιμον ὀψιτέλεστον, ὅου κλέος οὐκ ἀπολεῖται; Erasmus does not give his own Latin version.
2 Cicero *De divinatione* 2.64: *Tarda et sera nimis, sed fama et laude perenni*
3 Sic for 'Calchas.'

11 Homer *Iliad* (see n1 below)
1 *Iliad* 2.360: Ἀλλά, ἄναξ, αὐτὸς δ᾽ εὖ μήδεο, πείθεό τ᾽ ἄλλῳ.

12 Homer *Iliad* and *Odyssey* (see n2 below)

ravenous, barking stomach,[1] as Horace calls it, has not first been satisfied, or when we want to indicate that someone, as soon as he has obtained what he sought, turns immediately to other things, we might quite aptly utter this formulaic line found in the same book and elsewhere in Homer: 'But after the desire for food and drink was taken away ...,'[2] which Virgil renders thus: 'After hunger was taken away and the urgent desire to eat ...'[3]

13 Ingens rerum multitudo
An enormous number of things

When we want to signify an astonishing multitude of men, of things, of evils for example, a suitable expression will be the following found in the same book and frequently elsewhere:[1]

> As many as are the leaves and flowers in spring,
> As the many swarms of flies in their masses.[2]

14 Quae divinitus contingunt
Things which come by divine providence

If someone wants to say that not everything comes to everybody, no matter who makes the wish, but is given by divine providence, whether it be intelligence, beauty or strength, he could use this expression of Homer from book 3 of the *Iliad*: 'Not every man will gain what he wants.'[1] The words are spoken by Alexander[2] to Hector who had reproached him for

* * * * *

1 Latin *latrantem et iratum ... ventrem*. Horace *Satires* 2.2.18 *latrantem stomachum*; *Satires* 2.8.5 *iratum ventrem*
2 Repeated at *Iliad* 2.432, 1.469 and *Odyssey* 1.150: Αὐτὰρ ἐπεὶ πόσιος καὶ ἐδητύος ἐξ ἔρον ἕντο
3 Virgil *Aeneid* 8.184: *Postquam exempta fames et amor compressus edendi*. The Homeric source is indicated by Macrobius *Saturnalia* 5.8.5.

13 Homer *Iliad* (see n2 below)
1 Only in *Odyssey* 9.51
2 *Iliad* 2.468–9: Ὅσσα τε φύλλα καὶ ἄνθεα γίγνεται ὥρῃ, / Ἠΰ γε μυιάων ἀδινάων ἔθνεα πολλά. In modern editions there is a full stop at the end of the first line; in the early editions there was either a comma or no punctuation at all.

14 Homer *Iliad* (see n1 below)
1 *Iliad* 3.66: Ἑκὼν δ' οὐκ ἄν τις ἕλοιτο.
2 Homer commonly gives Paris the title Alexandros, defender of men; see also Apollodorus 3.12.5.

his hair, his figure, and his unwarlike lyre:

> They will be worth nothing to you, your music and the gifts of
>   Venus,
> Your locks and your beauty, when you join battle in the dust.[3]

To which Paris responds:

> Do not reproach me for the desirable gifts of the Cytherean;
> Not to be despised are the glorious gifts of the gods,
> Which they give of their own accord; nor does every man immediately
>   gain what he wants.[4]

Laertius relates that when Diogenes the Cynic was blamed for accepting gifts from Antipater, he replied with the Homeric verse that I have just quoted: 'Not to be despised, etc.'[5]

15 In senem libidinosum
For a salacious old man

Against those who are no longer capable of action because of age, but still talk at great length – for example if you want to reproach some 'old wether,' as Plautus says, who talks obscenities but is incapable of making love,[1] then you might aptly quote this from the same book: 'Now because of age they are veterans of war, but they are admirable / If it is only a matter of talking.'[2] This is how he describes the son of Tydeus in the fourth book: 'Inferior in battle, but first in talking.'[3]

* * * * *

3 *Iliad* 3.54–55
4 *Iliad* 3.64–66
5 Diogenes Laertius 6.66 ('Diogenes the Cynic'); cf Erasmus *Apophthegmata* III Diogenes 187.

15 Homer *Iliad* (see n2 below)
1 Plautus *Casina* 535; in Plautus *Mercator* Demipho is called *vetulus decrepitus senex* 'little, decrepit old man' in line 314 and *vervex* 'wether' in line 567.
2 *Iliad* 3.150–1: Γήραϊ δὴ πολέμοιο πεπαυμένοι, ἀλλ' ἀγορηταὶ / Ἐσθλοί.
3 *Iliad* 4.400. The words are spoken by Agamemnon, upbraiding Diomedes to provoke him.

16 Fatis imputandum
Put it down to fate

When we want to declare a man free of a fault and attribute it to destiny
or chance, we could use what Priam says to Helen there: 'There is nothing
I blame you for, rather it is the gods themselves I blame.'[1]

17 Diu dissimulatum aperientis
For someone revealing what he has long concealed

For someone who finally speaks out angrily about what he has long concealed, there is an apt expression which is applied in the same passage to
Ulysses: 'But when he does speak with his great voice from deep in his
chest . . .'[1]

18 Pertinax contentio
Stubborn quarrelling

When we want to indicate that it is perverse and unmanly for people of
equal standing to carry on quarrelling because neither one wants to appear
inferior to the other, it will be appropriate to quote from the fourth book
of the *Iliad* what Juno says to Jupiter: 'I too am a god, my birth was from
the same parentage as yours.'[1]

19 Cum uterque concedit alteri
When each yields to the other

On the other hand when quarrelling is laid aside and each yields to the

* * * * *

16 Homer *Iliad*, in the same description of the council of Priam in which the
previous adage occurs (see n1 below).
1 *Iliad* 3.164: Οὔτι μοι αἰτίη ἐσσί, θεοί νύ μοι αἴτιοί εἰσιν.

17 Homer *Iliad* (see n1 below)
1 *Iliad* 3.221: Ἀλλ' ὅτε δή ῥ' ὄπα τε μεγάλην ἐκ στήθεος ἵει

18 Homer *Iliad* (see n1 below)
1 *Iliad* 4.58: Καὶ γὰρ ἐγὼ θεός εἰμι, γένος δέ μοι ἔνθεν ὅθεν σοί.

19 Homer *Iliad* (see n1 below)

other, it will be a suitable moment for what follows immediately in the same passage: 'Nay rather let us both yield in this to the other, / You to me, and I thereon to you.'[1]

20 Adamantis tenere
Of one who loves tenderly

To someone who loves another tenderly or loves so much that he will not suffer his loved one to be affected by the least trouble from anyone, you might quite appropriately apply this from the same book: 'Just as a mother / Carefully brushes away a fly from her child as he lies asleep,' a description of Athena treating Menelaus' wound.[1]

21 Contemnentis dicterium
For one who is not troubled by mockery

When we want to indicate that we are only slightly affected by a joke or an insult and do not take it too deeply to heart, the following passage also from book 4 of the *Iliad* will be appropriate:

> The flying arrow did not penetrate to my vitals,
> But my belt stopped it in my skin, and the plated armour
> With applied bronze which the smith attached to it.[1]

22 Malorum oblivio
Forgetting wrongs

Someone who wants to turn aside an unfavourable omen or wants the

* * * * *

1 *Iliad* 4.62–3: Ἀλλ᾽ ἤτοι γὰρ ταῦθ᾽ ὑποείξομεν ἀλλήλοισιν, / Σοὶ μὲν ἐγώ, σὺ δέ μοι.

20 Homer *Iliad* (see n1 below)
1 *Iliad* 4.130–1: Ὡς ὅτε μήτηρ / Παιδὸς, ἐέργει μυῖαν, ὅθ᾽ ἡδέϊ λέξεται ὕπνῳ; Erasmus' *curante vulnus* 'treating ... wound' is not strictly correct: Athena is diverting Pandarus' arrow.

21 Homer *Iliad* (see n1 below); Erasmus speaks of this in Ep 1342:782 as an 'old Homeric tag.' A more succinct equivalent might be 'Names will never hurt me.'
1 *Iliad* 4.185–7: Οὐκ ἐν καιρίῳ ὀξὺ πάγη βέλος, ἀλλὰ πάροιθεν / Εἰρύσατο ζωστήρ τε παναίολος, ἡ δ᾽ ὑπένερθεν / Ζῶμά τε καὶ μίτρη, τὴν χαλκῆες κάμον ἄνδρες.

22 Homer *Iliad* (see n1 below)

memory of wrongs to be obliterated could aptly use this from the same book:

> And may the gods blow all these things away and bring them to naught.[1]

23 Ex minimis initiis maxima
Greatest things from smallest beginnings

To signify that the greatest animosities are sometimes born of the slightest wrongs, just as the worst fire is born from the smallest spark, the lines from the same book about Eris, goddess of discord, will be wonderfully apt: 'At first she rises only a little, but then her head / Reaches to heaven while her feet still mark the earth.'[1] In the *Aeneid* book 4 Virgil turned this expression to apply to Rumour: 'Small at first through fear, soon she rises to the heavens; / She walks on the ground and her head reaches to the clouds.'[2]

24 Diversarum partium
Conflicting loyalties

If you want to imply that someone is a Metius[1] or conspires with both sides or is a lying witness or a treacherous leader,[2] you could quite neatly use this from book 5 of the *Iliad*:

> But of Tydeus' son you could scarcely tell
> Whether he belonged to the Trojan or to the Achaean army.[3]

* * * * *

1 *Iliad* 4.363: Τὰ δὲ πάντα θεοὶ μεταμώλια θεῖεν.

23 Homer *Iliad* (see n1 below)
1 *Iliad* 4.442–3: "Η τ᾽ ὀλίγη μὲν πρῶτα κορύσσεται, αὐτὰρ ἔπειτα / Οὐρανῷ ἐστήριξε κάρη καὶ ἐπὶ χθονὶ βαίνει.
2 Virgil *Aeneid* 4.176–7. Erasmus may have found the reference to Virgil in Macrobius *Saturnalia* 5.13.31, though the latter thought Virgil's use inappropriate.

24 Homer *Iliad* (see n3 below)
1 Sic. The reference is to Mettius Fufetius, the treacherous dictator of Alba Longa. Livy 1.23.4–1.28.10
2 Homer's line does not imply treachery at all, but describes the speed with which Diomedes dashes about the battlefield.
3 *Iliad* 5.85–6: Τυτείδην δ᾽ οὐκ ἂν γνοίης, ποτέροισι μετείη, / Ἡὲ μετὰ Τρώεσσιν ὁμιλέοι ἢ μετ᾽ Ἀχαιοῖς. ASD notes that the mistaken spelling Τυτείδην is repeated in the Latin Tytiden.

25 Alieno ferox praesidio
Fierce with someone else's help

If someone is being aggressive and acting wickedly and you want to imply that he is doing this relying not on his own strength but with the support and protection of someone more powerful who is secretly supplying him with confidence and resources (as our people suspect the Duke of Geldern has troubled us these many years with the hidden support of the French),[1] you could adapt this from the same book: 'Such things this man could never dare without inspiration, / But some god stands beside him, his shoulders hidden in the dark.'[2]

26 Fortuna prorsus adversa
Absolutely hostile fortune

When something is undertaken with thorough deliberation but still turns out badly you might aptly quote this from the same book: 'Some god is angry.'[1] And this in book 6: 'When he too came to be hated by every one of the gods.'[2]

27 Arripe negocii curam
Seize control of the affair

When we advise someone to take some business firmly in hand and to approach the affair with zeal, we shall use this verse from the same passage, where Aeneas exhorts his charioteer: 'Nay, come now, grasp the whip in your hand / And the glittering reins.'[1]

* * * * *

25 Homer *Iliad* (see n2 below)
 1 The Duke of Geldern is Karl von Egmont. This remark was added in *1517/18*. See Allen Ep 549:23 (10 March 1517), Epp 584:35, 3119:31; Erasmus *Institutio principis christiani* CWE 27 256 and CEBR 1.422 (Karel van Egmond).
 2 *Iliad* 5.185–6: Οὐχ ὅ γ᾽ ἄνευθε θεοῦ τάδε μαίνεται, ἀλλά τις ἄγχι / Ἕστηκ᾽ ἀθανάτων νεφέλῃ εἰλυμένος ὤμους.

26 Homer *Iliad* (see n1 below)
 1 *Iliad* 5.191: Θεός νύ τίς ἐστι κοτήεις.
 2 *Iliad* 6.200: Ἀλλ᾽ ὅτε δὴ κἀκεῖνος ἀπήχθετο πᾶσι θεοῖσι

27 Homer *Iliad* (see n1 below)
 1 *Iliad* 5.226–7: Ἀλλ᾽ ἄγε νῦν μάστιγα καὶ ἡνία σιγαλόεντα / Δέξαι.

28 Reiicientis autorem formidinis
Rejecting talk of fear

To someone who causes terror and inspires groundless fear one could recite this line from the same book where Diomedes addresses Sthenelus: 'Talk not to me of fear.'[1]

29 Omni conatu invadere
Attack with every effort

If we want to affirm that someone is putting all his efforts into attacking someone else, this line from the same book will be appropriate: 'Forward leapt Aeneas with shield and spear.'[1]

30 Summa vi defendere
Strongest defence

On the other hand if someone wants to protect another with all his strength, then what follows in the same passage will be fitting: 'On all sides he covered him with his spear and round shield.'[1]

31 Aequa concertatio
Contest between equals

When we want to say that two parties are equally matched to debate or to fight we may apply these verses from the same book: 'Ready to do immediate battle with each other, / They raise their hands and sharp-pointed spears.'[1]

* * * * *

28 Homer *Iliad* (see n1 below)
1 *Iliad* 5.252: Μή τι φόβονδ' ἀγόρευε.

29 Homer *Iliad* (see n1 below)
1 *Iliad* 5.297: Αἰνείας δ' ἐπόρουσε σὺν ἀσπίδι δουρί τε μακρῷ.

30 Homer *Iliad* (see n1 below)
1 *Iliad* 5.300: Πρόσθε δέ οἱ δόρυ τ' ἔσχε καὶ ἀσπίδα πάντοσε ἴσην.

31 Homer *Iliad* (see n1 below)
1 *Iliad* 5.568–9: Τὼ μὲν δὴ χεῖράς τε καὶ ἔγχεα ὀξυόεντα / 'Αντίον ἀλλήλων ἐχέτην μεμαῶτε μάχεσθαι.

32 **Incitare currentem**
Cheering on a willing runner

If one wants to talk of encouraging someone to do what he is inclined to
do of his own accord, one could use this from the same book, though it is
found elsewhere too[1] in the same author: 'The whip strikes the horses, but
they were willingly flying.'[2] This originates with charioteers.

33 **Ad utrumvis paratus**
Ready for good or bad

A man who is prepared for good or bad fortune, who is able to play as
well as to be serious, or who knows how to deal with both good men and
bad, might be symbolized by this verse, which is in book 7 of the *Iliad*: 'I
have learned to wield my buckler on both right and left.'[1]

34 **Nullus delectus**
No discrimination

In book 2 of his *Politics* Aristotle quotes this line as well known: 'Equal
honour to the coward and the brave.'[1] This could be used when we want to
say no distinction is made between the scholar and the imposter, between
the deserving and the culpable, between the honourable and the dishonourable. They are the words of Achilles, angry that he is not given his due
by Agamemnon though he was by far the bravest of all. A mistake was
made here by the translator Leonardo Aretino,[2] a man both learned and
eloquent but still a man, for he translates Homer's line thus: 'The coward

* * * * *

32 Homer *Iliad* (see n2 below); cf *Adagia* I ii 46 and 47.
1 *Iliad* 11.519
2 *Iliad* 5.768: Μάστιξεν δ᾽ ἵππους, τὼ δ᾽ οὐκ ἄκοντε πετέσθην; 1533, 1536, and LB
  have ἵππους instead of δ᾽ ἵππους. To be consistent with Erasmus' purpose, it
  seems Latin *ast*, Greek δέ, must be given some adversative force, ie 'but'; if
  this is so he is distorting the meaning here. E.V. Rieu (Penguin) translates:
  '[Hera] Flicked her horses with the whip, and the willing pair flew off . . .'

33 Homer *Iliad* (see n1 below)
1 *Iliad* 7.238: Οἶδ᾽ ἐπὶ δεξιά, οἶδ᾽ ἐπ᾽ ἀριστερὰ νωμῆσαι βῶν.

34 Aristotle quoting Homer *Iliad* (see n1 below)
1 Aristotle *Politics* 2.4.7 (1267a3) quoting *Iliad* 9.319: Ἐν δ᾽ ἰῇ τιμῇ ἠμὲν κακὸς ἠδὲ
  καὶ ἐσθλός.
2 Leonardo Bruni (1374–1444) whose translation of the *Politics* was made in 1420
  and first printed at Strasbourg in 1475

strives for honour as much as the brave man'; he must have been misled by the man who lectured to him[3] on these books. Nor did he notice that ἰῇ appears in place of μιᾷ.[4]

35 Muneribus res agitur
Gifts get the business done

If someone wants to say that there is no place for things done properly and for fair arguments, but that everything is achieved by bribery and flattery, he might adapt this line from book 9 of the *Iliad*: 'With lavish gifts and smooth words.'[1] A verse in which gifts are given first place quite deliberately.

36 Frustratus conatus
A vain attempt

Someone who is disappointed in his hope and fails to obtain what he was soliciting could be quite suitably described by this from book 8 of the *Iliad*: 'The heart willed the arrow to transfix him, / But the hand failed and he missed.'[1] Or this: 'But once again he deceived.'[2]

37 Alieno auxilio potentes
Strong with someone else's help

People who rely on others' resources to commit some unusual crime, or do

* * * * *

3 Probably Manuel Chrysoloras, who taught in Florence from 1397 to 1400, and whose grammar, *Erotemata*, was printed in 1471 and used by Erasmus. See L.D. Reynolds and N.G. Wilson *Scribes and Scholars* (Clarendon Press 1974) 131.
4 Usual feminine form of the word for 'one'; ἰῇ is a form found in Homer. The implication is presumably that Bruni did not realize the line was from Homer.

35 Homer *Iliad* (see n1 below)
1 *Iliad* 9.113: Δώροισίν τ' ἀγανοῖσιν ἔπεσσί τε μειλιχίοισι. Again Erasmus diverts the phrase to a sense quite foreign to Homer's; Nestor is persuading Agamemnon to think of conciliating Achilles.

36 Homer *Iliad* (see n1 below)
1 *Iliad* 8.301–2: Βαλέειν ὁ δὲ ἵετο θυμός, / Καὶ τοῦ μέν ῥ' ἀφάμαρτο.
2 *Iliad* 8.311: Ἀλλ' ὅ γε καὶ τόθ' ἅμαρτε, which is preceded by exactly the same phrase as in 8.301. Estienne (LB II 913) points out that Erasmus' Latin *fefellit* 'deceived' is incorrect, and that the passive form, meaning 'missed' or 'failed,' would be better, though he is not wholly satisfied with this either.

37 Homer *Iliad* (see n2 below)

something under the cloak of someone else's name, might be aptly labelled
with what is said in the same book about Teucer the brother of Telamonian
Ajax; for he hides behind his brother's shield and fires some arrows at the
Trojans: 'He stood covered by the seven-layered[1] shield of Ajax.'[2]

38 Cavendum a potentiore
Beware of a more powerful man

Someone who wants to say he has no wish to deal with a much more
powerful person who could do him great harm could justly adapt this from
the same book: 'With Jove I have no desire at all to start a fight.'[1]

39 Subitum remedium periculi
Swift relief from danger

When we want to say that an affair had reached the point of crisis and it
was all over if salvation had not suddenly appeared, as if sent directly by
some god, then this from the same book, which occurs frequently elsewhere
too,[1] will be appropriate: 'If the father of both gods and men had not been
quick to see.'[2]

40 Perplexus animique consternati
Entangled and fearful at heart

For someone who is frightened by a dangerous business and cannot find a
way to extricate himself, this from the same book will be appropriate:

* * * * *

1 Erasmus has filled up his Latin verse with a translation of ἑπταβόειον 'of
   sevenfold bull's hide,' which does not appear in the Greek he quotes but
   which occurs in the previous book (*Iliad* 7.220).
2 *Iliad* 8.267: Στῆ δ' ἄρ' ὑπ' Αἴαντος σάκεϊ Τελαμωνιάδαο.

38 Homer *Iliad* (see n1 below)
1 *Iliad* 8.210: Οὐ γὰρ ἐγώ γ' ἐθέλοιμι Διὶ Κρονίωνι μάχεσθαι.

39 Homer *Iliad* (see n2 below)
1 The expression is used of various figures other than Jove: *Iliad* 5.312 and 680,
   8.91, 20.291.
2 *Iliad* 8.132: Εἰ μὴ ἄρ' ὀξὺ νόησε πατὴρ ἀνδρῶν τε θεῶν τε·

40 Homer *Iliad* (see n1 below)

From Nestor's hands the shining reins slipped.'[1]

41 Litem incipere
To start a dispute

For one who when challenged proceeds to shout insults, the following from
book 10 of the *Iliad* will fit: 'A spear he seized, stout and sharp-tipped.'[1]
This is the opposite of 'He threw away his spear,' which I have included
elsewhere from Cicero.[2]

42 In formidolosum
For a man dismayed

For a man who is extremely afraid and dismayed at heart these lines from
the same book will suit:

> Nor is my mind firm, but is tossed to and fro; my heart
> Leaps out of my breast and the limbs of my body tremble.[1]

They are spoken by Agamemnon fearful for his people.

43 Blandius alloqui
Speaking with gentler words

A person who persuades someone with gentle and respectful words, using his family names, such as 'Quintus' or 'Publius,'[1] so that he can gain
some favour with him, will rightly be described with the words used by
Agamemnon in the same book when he orders Menelaus to coax the Greek

* * * * *

1 *Iliad* 8.137: Νέστορα δ' ἐκ χειρῶν φύγον ἡνία σιγαλόεντα.

41 Homer *Iliad* (see n1 below)
1 *Iliad* 10.135: Εἵλετο δ' ἄλκιμον ἔγχος, ἀκαχμένον ὀξέϊ χαλκῷ.
2 *Adagia* I ix 81

42 Homer *Âlliad* (see n1 below)
1 *Iliad* 10.93–5: Οὐδέ μοι ἦτορ / Ἔμπεδον, ἀλλ' ἀλαλύκτημαι, κραδίη δέ μοι ἔξω /
Στηθέων ἐκθρῴσκει, τρομέει δ' ὑποφαίδιμα γυῖα.

43 Homer *Iliad* (see n2 below)
1 Cf Horace *Satires* 2.5.32.

troops: 'Calling each man by his father's and his family's name.'[2]

44 Inexorabilis
Unbending

For one who will not listen to prayers, who is stern and must be left to his own way of thinking, or one whose service we have no regard for, we may suitably borrow what Diomedes said of Achilles in book 9 of the *Iliad*, when the latter rejected the envoys and the gifts of Agamemnon: 'Let us rather leave him to his own devices, / Whether he wishes to come or remain here.'[1]

45 Ausculta et perpende
Pay heed and consider

Whenever we want to indicate that we are about to say something that is relevant and will be proved true, it will be suitable to quote this, which occurs in the same book, though quite often elsewhere in this poet:[1] 'Nay, one other thing I shall say; and you must take it to heart.'[2]

46 Non statim decernendum
Not to be resolved at once

If you are going to indicate that there should be a pause before a decision is made, and that a matter should be postponed to a later day, a suitable phrase from the same book would be Achilles' reply to Phoenix, who was sent by Agamemnon with a delegation to regain his good will: 'When the dawn comes up tomorrow, / We shall take counsel.'[1] This seems to be the source of the well-known Greek proverb 'Night is the mother of counsel,' which I have quoted in another place.[2]

* * * * *

2 *Iliad* 10.68: Πατρόθεν ἐκ γενεῆς ὀνομάζων ἄνδρα ἕκαστον

44 Homer *Iliad* (see n1 below); cf *Adagia* III x 72 (382 below).
1 *Iliad* 9.701–2: Ἀλλ' ἤτοι κεῖνον μὲν ἐάσομεν, ἤ κεν ἴῃσιν / Ἦ κε μένῃ.

45 Homer *Iliad* (see n2 below)
1 *Iliad* 1.297, 4.39, 5.259, etc.
2 *Iliad* 9.611: Ἄλλο δέ τοι ἐρέω, σὺ δ' ἐνὶ φρεσὶ βάλλεο σῇσι.

46 Homer *Iliad* (see n1 below)
1 *Iliad* 9.618–19: Ἅμ' ἠοῖ φαινομένηφι / Φρασσόμεθα.
2 *Adagia* II ii 43 Ἐν νυκτὶ βουλή

47 Nemo cogendus amicus
No one may be forced to be a friend

When you want to signify that a person should not be ordered to agree to treat against his will, or that a duty should not be imposed on one who will neither recognize it nor accept it of his own free will, this remark of Achilles about Phoenix in the same book would be suitable: 'If he wishes. I will not force this man to go anywhere against his will.'[1]

48 Omnibus antevertenda vitae cura
Life comes before all else

If one wants to say everything must be counted of lesser importance when we are considering life itself, one can adapt this from the same book:

> For me, no wealth is worth the same as life, not even the same
> As the wealth of Ilium,[1] which men say this rich city
> Possessed of old in time of peace.[2]

And the reason is given immediately, for a life can neither be recalled nor restored once breath has left the lips: 'But that a man's spirit should come back ... neither pillage avails nor winning.'[3]

49 Evenit malo male
Wrong to the wrong-doer

When things turn out for some villain as everyone prayed and wished, it

* * * * *

47 Homer *Iliad* (see n1 below)
 1 *Iliad* 9.429: ῏Ην ἐθέλῃσιν· ἀνάγκῃ δ᾽ οὔ τί μιν ἄξω.

48 Homer *Iliad* (see n2 below)
 1 Sic: Erasmus has *Nullum equidem precium cum vita confero, nec cum / Iliacis opibus* but the Greek seems to require *neque Iliacas opes* 'not even the wealth of Ilium.'
 2 *Iliad* 9.401–3: Οὐ γὰρ ἐμοὶ ψυχῆς ἀντάξιον οὐδ᾽ ὅσα φασὶν / Ἴλιον ἐκτῆσθαι, εὖ ναιόμενον πτολίεθρον, / Τὸ πρὶν ἐπ᾽ εἰρήνης.
 3 *Iliad* 9.408–9; translation by A.T. Murray revised by William F. Wyatt (Loeb); Erasmus does not translate here. (The Greek in LB omits the vital phrase at the end of the second line: ἐπεὶ ἄρ᾽ κεν ἀμείψεται ἕρκος ὀδόντων 'when once it has passed the barrier of his teeth.')

49 Homer *Iliad* (see n1 below)

will be the moment to quote this from the same book: 'The curses were fulfilled by the gods.'[1] These are the words of Phoenix recounting how all the ills befell him that his father had earlier prayed for.

50 Nec dignus, qui me intueatur
Not worthy to look me in the eye

If you want to express contempt for someone who you think is cowardly and altogether inferior to yourself, then it would be quite humorous to adapt this remark of Achilles about Agamemnon from the same book: 'He would not dare, / Despite his shameless mien[1] to look me in the face.'[2] The same expression is still common nowadays.[3] It is a sign of consciousness of guilt if you do not dare to look directly in the face of the one you have offended. This is why Menelaus, in the *Iphigenia in Aulis*, especially orders Agamemnon to look at him, so that he can gather the best proof of what he had done.[4]

51 Cavendum ab eo, qui semel imposuit
Beware of the man who has cheated once

If you want to say you have no wish to deal with someone who has once cheated you, you might use this from the same book:

> I will undertake nothing with this man, nor is it in any way right that I should;
> For now he has cheated once and deceived me with lies,
> He will not make a fool of me again with words.
> Let it suffice that he has done this once, and let him henceforth be silent,
> And go to hell.[1]

* * * * *

1 *Iliad* 9.456: Θεοὶ δ᾽ ἐτέλειον ἐπαράς.

50 Homer *Iliad* (see n2 below)
1 Latin *Quamvis perfricta sit fronte*; cf *Adagia* I viii 47 *Faciem perfricare. Frontis perfrictae* To wipe off your blushes. To put a bold front on it.
2 *Iliad* 9.372–3: Οὐδ᾽ ἂν ἔμοιγε / Τετλαίη κύνεός περ ἐὼν εἰς ὦπα ἰδέσθαι.
3 Suringar 129 page 234
4 Euripides *Iphigenia Aulidensis* 320

51 Homer *Iliad* (see n1 below)
1 *Iliad* 9.374–7: Οὐδέ τί οἱ βουλὰς συμφράσσομαι οὐδὲ μὲν ἔργον· / Ἐκ γὰρ δή μ᾽ ἀπάτησε καὶ ἤλιτεν οὐδ᾽ ἂν ἔτ᾽ αὖτις / Ἐξαπάφοιτ᾽ ἐπέεσσιν, ἅλις δέ οἱ, ἀλλὰ ἔκηλος / Ἐρρέτω.

52 Amicorum est admonere mutuum
It is the duty of friends to admonish each other

There seems to be a proverbial phrase in this line of book 11 of the *Iliad*: 'Effective are the words of a friend who advises.'[1] This phrase might be used when we want to say that it is the duty of one friend to admonish another quite freely if he has somehow gone astray.

53 Unus multorum instar
One who is equal to many

The praise of physicians in the same book could be adapted to any out-standing virtue. The verse goes like this: 'One physician is worth many other men.'[1] This is wittily turned against Eryximachus by Alcibiades who says he cannot resist his orders because a physician is the equal of many men.[2] It will be funnier if it is used figuratively of ideas, as Plato does in book 4 of the *Republic*: 'Providing they have preserved the one big thing,'[3] as they say. He indicates that this ἓν μέγα 'one big thing' is a proverbial expression. See the adage 'The fox knows many things, etc.'[4] The same lesson is taught by the very remarkable parables in the gospels of the precious pearl and the treasure in the field.[5] A good mind therefore is 'worth all other things,' and learning and reputation are 'worth many other things.'[6]

54 Contemnentis inimicum
Of a man who despises his enemy

Anyone who wants to say he is not alarmed by the insults of some despised

* * * * *

52 Homer *Iliad* (see n1 below)
   1 *Iliad* 11.793: Ἀγαθὴ δὲ παραίφασίς ἐστιν ἑταίρου.

53 Homer *Iliad* (see n1 below)
   1 *Iliad* 11.514: Ἰητρὸς γὰρ ἀνὴρ πολλῶν ἀντάξιος ἄλλων; it is referred to in *Adagia* I viii 13 Not worth a one.
   2 Plato *Symposium* 214B
   3 Plato *Republic* 4.423E: Ἐὰν τὸ λεγόμενον ἓν μέγα φυλάττωσι
   4 *Adagia* I v 18 The fox knows many things, but the hedgehog one big thing
   5 Matt 13:44–46. Erasmus uses the singular *parabola* but these are of course two separate parables.
   6 The quoted phrases are given in Greek and echo the Homeric verse (see n1 above).

54 Homer *Iliad* (see n1 below)

person might neatly turn to his use what Diomedes says in the same book:
'I care no more than if a woman or some child / Had aimed a dart at me,
for your arrows are those of a coward and fly to no effect.'[1]

55 In voti compotem
On one whose wish is fulfilled

When someone has achieved what he hoped for and desired, for example
if someone sends a gift to a prince in the hope of a church benefice and
obtains that benefice by favour of the prince, then this from the same book
will be appropriate: 'He hit him, not for nothing was the sharp arrow fired
by his hand.'[1]

56 Lupus in fabula
The wolf in the fable

When by chance in the middle of a conversation someone appears who was
the subject of discussion, this from book 10 of the *Iliad* will be appropriate: 'Suddenly there they were themselves before the word was out of his
mouth.'[1]

57 Corrigentis quod dictum est ab alio
For one who corrects what someone else has said

When we want to indicate politely that someone has not expressed his
real opinion or when what is proposed would be improper, we can adapt
this line from book 12 of the *Iliad*, which Plutarch also used in this way
somewhere:[1] 'You know how to devise better words than these.'[2]

* * * * *

1 *Iliad* 11.389–90: Οὐκ ἀλέγω, ὡς εἴ με γυνὴ βάλοι ἢ πάϊς ἄφρων. / Κωφὸν γὰρ βέλος
   ἀνδρὸς ἀνάλκιδος οὐτιδανοῖο.

55 Homer *Iliad* (see n1 below)
   1 *Iliad* 11.376: Καὶ βάλεν, οὐδ᾽ ἄρα μιν ἅλιον βέλος ἔκφυγε χειρός.

56 Homer *Iliad* (see n1 below); the Latin proverb appears in the *Collectanea* no
   517 and *Adagia* IV v 50 The wolf in the fable. It was used by Terence *Adelphoe*
   537 and quoted by Servius on Virgil's *Aeneid* 3.477. Cf also *Adagia* I vii 86 The
   wolves have seen him first, and IV iv 91 Mercury has now arrived. Otto 988
   1 *Iliad* 10.540: Οὔπω πᾶν εἴρητο ἔπος, ὅτ᾽ ἄρ᾽ ἤλυθον αὐτοί.

57 Homer *Iliad* (see n2 below)
   1 Plutarch *Moralia* 20E *Quomodo adolescens poetas audire debeat*
   2 *Iliad* 12.232: Οἶσθα καὶ ἄλλον μῦθον ἀμείνονα τοῦδε νοῆσαι.

58 Aliter cum aliis agendum
Different people should be treated differently

If someone wants to say that some people should be treated more gently, others more harshly, each according to his intelligence or fortune and rank, he may bring in this from the same book: 'One man with gentle words, another with harsher words / They chided.'[1]

59 Ut nunc sunt homines
That's how men are now

If you want to say that the morals of your time are continually declining from the standards of your elders, for example if you say this or that monarch should be praised, considering how monarchs are nowadays, you can apply this from the same book: 'Such as mortals are now.'[1] This hemistich is found in several places in Homer; in this book it is used of Ajax and Hector who easily pick up huge stones from the ground; in book 5 of the *Iliad* it is used to describe Tydeus likewise picking up a stone.[2]

60 Non suscipiendum negocium temere
A deal not to be undertaken rashly

Against some exceptionally powerful person with whom you should not compete or fight unless you have some strong protection, this from the same book will be suitable:

> None facing him could have stood against him,
> Except the gods.[1]

This describes Hector, armed with two spears, leaping into battle after he had thrown the great stone.

* * * * *

58 Homer *Iliad* (see n1 below)
 1 *Iliad* 12.267–8: Ἄλλον μελιχίοις, ἄλλον στερεοῖς ἐπέεσσι / Νείκεον.

59 Homer *Iliad* (see n1 below)
 1 *Iliad* 12.383 and 12.449: Οἷοι νῦν βροτοί εἰσιν. Erasmus allows his title to stand as the translation of this phrase.
 2 *Iliad* 5.304

60 Homer *Iliad* (see n1 below)
 1 *Iliad* 12.465–6: Οὐκ ἄν τίς μιν ἐρυκάκοι ἀντιβολήσας / Νόσφι θεῶν.

61 Vehementer cupientis
For someone with a powerful longing

When the heart itself prompts us strongly to do something, this from book 13 of the *Iliad* will be suitable:

My heart, welling up of itself in my breast,
Is ever more eager to fight and come to close grips;
My feet below and my hands above both hasten me forward.[1]

62 Elucet egregia virtus
Exceptional virtue shines out

Exceptional virtue, even when it is concealed, always stands out among other people; it is visible in the cast of the face and shines, so to speak, on the brow. True nobility too shows in the human face just as virtue does. This notion is expressed by the following verse of Homer from the same book: 'The might of the gods is unmistakable.'[1]

62A Mutua defensatio
Mutual defence

Agreement by many people among themselves and mutual defence can be indicated quite humorously with these lines from the same book:

Spears were packed against spears,
Shield against serried shield, buckler supported buckler,
Helmets interlocked with helmets, man with man.[1]

* * * * *

61 Homer *Iliad* (see n1 below)
1 *Iliad* 13.73–5: Κὰδ δ' ἐμοὶ αὐτῷ θυμὸς ἐνὶ στήθεσσι φίλοισι / Μᾶλλον ἐφορμᾶται πολεμίζειν ἠδὲ μάχεσθαι, / Μαιμώωσι δ' ἔνερθε πόδες, καὶ χεῖρες ὕπερθεν.

62 Homer *Iliad* (see n1 below)
1 *Iliad* 13.72: Ἀρίγνωτοι δὲ θεοί περ.

62A Homer *Iliad* (see n1 below); cf *Adagia* III viii 71 (308 below) with a similar title. In 1536 the number 62 appears twice (in earlier editions a similar error occurs); LB accommodates the extra adage by having the number 74 twice. We have followed the numbering used by ASD.
1 *Iliad* 13.130–1: Φράξαντες δόρυ δουρί, σάκος σάκεϊ προθελύμνῳ, / Ἀσπίδ' ἄρ' ἀσπὶς ἔρειδε, κόρυς κόρυν, ἀνέρα δ' ἀνήρ. For Latin *virum vir* 'man with man' cf Virgil *Aeneid* 10.361. The verses of Homer and Virgil are mentioned together by Macrobius *Saturnalia* 6.3.5.

Likewise Juvenal talking about effeminate people:

> But they are defended
> By their number and phalanxes of joined shields.[2]

63 Concordia fulciuntur opes etiam exiguae
With unanimity even slender resources are strengthened

In the same passage there is a proverbial phrase which goes like this: 'When they join together even the most unskilled are a force.'[1] This can be used appropriately when we want to say that we should not disregard the alliance or the rivalry of the multitude, even if they are otherwise weak and, as individuals, easily despised. For, in Ovid's words, just as 'Things that taken singly are of no benefit, in large numbers do help,'[2] – so things that do not hurt singly, in large numbers do harm.

64 Extra periculum ferox
Brave when there is no danger

Against a cowardly person and one who is brave only when danger is far away, like a secret critic who has not dared to take issue face to face, this line from the same passage will be suitable: 'Knowing how to fight, but at a distance and when the enemy is far away.'[1] This recalls what Demosthenes says in his speech *On the Crown*: 'They welcomed us in such a friendly manner that, although their infantry and cavalry were there,[2] they gave the

* * * * *

2 Juvenal 2.46; Juvenal's remark in fact is about men in general.

63 Homer *Iliad* (see n1 below)
1 *Iliad* 13.237: Συμφερτὴ δ᾽ ἀρετὴ πέλει ἀνδρῶν καὶ μάλα λυγρῶν.
2 Ovid *Remedia amoris* 420. All editions of the *Adagia* mistakenly give the following phrase as part of the quotation.

64 Homer *Iliad* (see n1 below)
1 *Iliad* 13.263: Ἀνδρῶν δυσμενέων ἑκὰς ἱστάμενος πολεμίζειν; Erasmus has misread the Greek ἱστάμενος 'standing' as ἐπιστάμενος 'knowing how to.' He has also reversed Homer's meaning by omitting the part of the sentence in the previous line that contains a negative; E.V. Rieu (Penguin) translates: 'I do not believe in fighting the enemy at a distance.'
2 Latin *adessent*; Erasmus omits the word ἔξω, which C.A. and J.H. Vince (Loeb) translate as 'outside the walls.' The omission is strange since ἑκὰς in the Homeric line, translated *eminus* 'at a distance,' seems to be one reason at least for his recall. ASD suggests Erasmus evidently sees the parallel in the unwarlike behaviour.

army access to their homes, to their city, to their children and their wives
and to everything that was most precious to them.'³ 'Out of range,' we
have recorded before; the opposite is 'Within range.'⁴ Marcus Tullius, in
the fourth speech against Verres: 'I should not have come myself the short
voyage from Vibo within range of your arrows and those of the revolted
slaves and pirates.'⁵ 'Within range,' as the Greeks say.⁶

65 Quisquis is fuerit
No matter who it might be

We can show that we mean any man at all without any exception with this
line, which is in the same book: 'Providing he is mortal and eats the gifts of
Ceres.'¹ For example, if someone says that human laws are different from
place to place but that the law of nature is the same for everyone 'providing
he is mortal . . .'

66 Iuventa viribus pollet
Youth abounds in physical strength

Youth is a time that brings the greatest development of physical strength.
This is suitably expressed by this line about Aeneas from the same book:
'And he is in the flower of youth, in which strength is at its greatest.'¹

67 Ancipitis consilii
In two minds

A person who is perplexed, in two minds, and hesitating, could be suitably

* * * * *

3 Demosthenes 18.215; added in *1528*
4 *Adagia* I iii 93 *Extra telorum iactum*, Out of range, which also mentions Ἐντὸς
   βελῶν *Intra tela*, Within range; added in *1533*
5 Cicero *Verrines* 2.2.40.99; added in *1533*
6 In Greek Ἐντὸς βελῶν; see n4 above.

65 Homer *Iliad* (see n1 below)
1 *Iliad* 13.322: Ὃς θνητός τ᾽ εἴη καὶ ἔδοι Δημήτερος ἀκτήν

66 Homer *Iliad* (see n1 below)
1 *Iliad* 13.484: Καὶ δ᾽ ἔχει ἥβης ἄνθος, ὅτε κράτος ἐστὶ μέγιστον.

67 Homer *Iliad* (see n1 below); cf *Adagia* III viii 89 *Ancipitis animi* 'In two minds'
   (314 below).

described with this from book 5 of the *Iliad*: 'Halfway between earth and starry Olympus.'[1] These are the words of the poet describing the horses of Juno flying swiftly between heaven and earth.

68 Praedives
Very wealthy

We can signify a very wealthy person with these lines, which are in books 6, 10, and 11 of the *Iliad*:

> Many treasures are hidden in my wealthy father's house,
> Bronze and gold and much wrought iron.[1]

The same idea is suitably expressed in these words from book 10 of the *Iliad*: 'Rich in gold and rich in bronze.'[2]

69 Aegre quidem, sed facimus tamen
With difficulty, but still we do it

When we do something with difficulty and with much inconvenience, but do it nevertheless because we are forced to by necessity, then this line from book 6 of the *Iliad* will be apt: 'Though we are much distressed, yet so fate forces us.'[1]

70 Quod alibi diminutum exaequatur alibi
What is lacking in one way is made up for in another

For someone who is thought to be lacking in some virtue but whose deficiency is compensated by some other gift – for example if we want to give

* * * * *

1 *Iliad* 5.769: Μεσσηγὺς γαίης καὶ οὐρανοῦ ἀστερόεντος

68 Homer *Iliad* (see n1 below)
1 *Iliad* 6.47–48, 10.379 (second line only), 11.132–3 (in the house of Antimachus): Πολλὰ δ᾽ ἐν ἀφνειοῦ πατρὸς κειμήλια κεῖται, / Χαλκός τε χρυσός τε πολύκμητός τε σίδηρος.
2 *Iliad* 10.315: Πολύχρυσος πολύχαλκος

69 Homer *Iliad* (see n1 below)
1 *Iliad* 6.85: Καὶ μάλα τειρόμενοί περ, ἀναγκαίη γὰρ ἐπείγει.

70 Homer *Iliad* (see n2 below)

the idea that someone is not very eloquent but has admirable judgment, or if someone is uneducated but well endowed, then this line from the same passage in book 10 of the *Iliad* that we have just quoted[1] will be appropriate: 'A man who was ugly in appearance, but swift of foot.'[2]

71 Mutua defensio tutissima
Mutual protection is the surest

If someone wants to say that the least vulnerable people are those who agree to protect each other and, on the other hand, those who are divided by internal factions are exposed to all sorts of harm, then these lines from book 17 of the *Iliad* will be appropriate: 'Far fewer died, for in battle they always strove / To support each other and to ward off harm.'[1]

72 Qui cum contemptu vitae invadunt
Those who attack with no regard for their life

For those who, as Terence says, attack someone 'in the spirit of a gladiator'[1] so that they either kill or are killed, this phrase from book 12 of the Â*lliad* will be suitable: 'Like wild boars.'[2] Hunters say that these animals when challenged charge straight at the challenger without avoiding the spear.[3]

73 Aliis prospiciens, non sibi
Foresight for others, not for oneself

If we want to amuse ourselves with a joke at the expense of someone who claimed to know the art of divination and predicted the misfortunes of others but failed to foresee his own, we can quite aptly use this from the

* * * * *

1 At the end of *Adagia* III viii 68 (307 above)
2 *Iliad* 10.316: Ὃς δή τοι εἶδος μὲν ἔην κακός, ἀλλὰ ποδώκης·

71 Homer *Iliad* (see n1 below); cf *Adagia* III viii 62A (304 above) with a similar title.
1 *Iliad* 17.364–5: Παυρότεροι δὲ πολὺ φθίνυθον, μέμνηντο γὰρ αἰεὶ / Ἀλλήλοις ἀν' ὅμιλον ἀλεξέμεναι πόνον αἰπύν.

72 Homer *Iliad* (see n2 below)
1 Terence *Phormio* 964. Used as *Adagia* I iii 76 With a gladiator's spirit; cf also III vii 1 (212 with n209 above).
2 *Iliad* 12.146: Ἀγροτέροισι σύεσσι ἐοικότες
3 Cf Xenophon *Cynegeticus* 10.16.

73 Homer *Iliad* (see n2 below)

'Boeotia' of Homer:[1] 'But for all his auguries he did not ward off his black fate.'[2] The line was imitated by Maro: 'But auguries were not enough to ward off his doom.'[3] This is said of Eunomus,[4] leader of the Mysians, a skilled augur, who was nevertheless killed by Achilles.

74 Dedecus publicum
Public shame

You could signify something altogether dishonourable and destructive quite wittily with these lines, in which Hector upbraids Paris in book 3 of the *Iliad*:

> Enormous harm to your city, your people, and your father,
> A joy to your enemy, but to yourself shame and grief.[1]

75 Ne depugnes in alieno negocio
Don't contend in other people's business

When we wish to indicate that we do not want to be embroiled in someone else's dispute which has nothing to do with us, but that we will allow those whose business it is to fight it out between themselves at their own risk, then there will be a place for this line from the same book: 'They alone should do battle for Helen and all her wealth.'[1] Said of Menelaus and Paris when they were about to meet in single combat.

76 Prudentia coniuncta cum viribus
Wisdom joined with strength

For someone who knows both how to tell others what has to be done, and

* * * * *

1 The name 'Boeotia' appears with the words 'Catalogue of ships' in the Aldine edition of *Iliad* 2, above line 494.
2 *Iliad* 2.859: Ἀλλ' οὐκ οἰωνοῖσιν ἐρύσσατο κῆρα μέλαιναν.
3 Virgil *Aeneid* 9.328. The connection is noted by Macrobius *Saturnalia* 5.9.10.
4 Sic, for 'Ennomus' (*Iliad* 2.858).

74 Homer *Iliad* (see n1 below)
1 *Iliad* 3.50–1: Πατρί τε σῷ μέγα πῆμα πόληί τε παντί τε δήμῳ, / Δυσμενέσιν μὲν χάρμα, κατηφείην δὲ σοὶ αὐτῷ

75 Homer *Iliad* (see n1 below)
1 *Iliad* 3.91: Οἴους ἀμφ' Ἑλένῃ καὶ κτήμασι πᾶσι μάχεσθαι

76 Homer *Iliad* (see n1 below)

to carry out himself, when necessary, the orders he gives to others, the following from the same book will be apt: 'Equally a good leader and powerful in battle.'[1] For there are some who know how to play the commander
but not how to be a soldier.

77 Pauciloquus, sed eruditus
Sparing of words, but knowledgeable

For someone whose words are few but worth hearing, there is a suitable
line from the same book that describes Menelaus, who is laconic,[1] but who
speaks pleasantly and clearly: 'Not at length, but very clearly, seeing he was
a man of few words.'[2]

78 Duobus malis resistere difficillimum
Against two evils it is very difficult to stand firm

'Now war and sickness alike subdue the Greeks'[1] – for a time when we
want to say that the same individual is oppressed by two or several ills.
The line is in book 1 of Homer's *Iliad*.

79 A fronte simul et occipitio
With both the front and the back of the head

When we want to describe a wonderful understanding of everything or
exceptional wisdom, which consists not only of knowledge of things present
but remembrance of things past and foresight for things to come, we can
aptly use this from the same book: 'He knows the past and present, and

* * * * *

1 *Iliad* 3.179: Ἀμφότερον βασιλεύς τ᾽ ἀγαθὸς κρατερός τ᾽ αἰχμητής

77 Homer *Iliad* (see n2 below). *Pauciloquus*, also used in the translation of the
verse, is a neologism created by Erasmus, probably on the model of Plautus'
multiloquus (*Pseudolus* 794).
1 Latin *breviloquo Laconum more*; cf *Adagia* II i 92 and II x 49, both titled
Laconismus.
2 *Iliad* 3.214: Παῦρα μέν, ἀλλὰ μάλα λιγέως, ἐπεὶ οὐ πολύμυθος

78 Homer *Iliad* (see n1 below); Erasmus seems to have reverted here, and in
the next three items, to his usual format, giving an expression of proverbial
appearance as his title; the Homeric phrase is then suggested as a parallel.
1 *Iliad* 1.61: Εἰ δὴ ὁμοῦ πόλεμός τε δαμᾷ καὶ λοιμὸς Ἀχαιούς.

79 Homer *Iliad* (see n1 below). Erasmus relates the Homeric line to the common
tradition of the three forms of knowledge composing the virtue of prudence:

what will be later.'[1] Virgil translated the line like this: 'What is, what was, what the future may soon bring ...'[2]

80 Nocuit et nocebit
It has done harm and will do so again

Whenever the cause of past ills has been proven and we want to warn that there may be worse to come unless someone comes to his senses, we can make timely use of this line of Homer from the same book:

> For these acts Apollo has sent many ills and will send more.[1]

For example, if a physician, given the proven danger of the sickness, advises his recovering patient to abstain from too much love-making, otherwise the illness will recur in worse measure.

81 Ingens discrimen
An enormous difference

Whenever we want to say there is a very big difference between men, or that things differ in great measure from one another, or there is a large gap between widely divided people, we can neatly adapt the following from the same book:

> Much stands between, both shadowy mountains
> And straits full of the frightful crash of breaking seas.[1]

* * * * *

remembrance, knowledge of things present, and foresight (cf Cicero *De inventione* 2.160). These arise in the three faculties of memory, reason, and imagination located in the back, middle, and front of the head respectively (cf Bartolomaeus Anglicus *De proprietatibus rerum* 3.22). The meaning here is quite different from that of *Adagia* I ii 19 Forehead before occiput. Cf *Adagia* III i 53 Forward and backward, and the dictum of Timotheus in III x 75 A good commander and a hard soldier too (383 below).
1 *Iliad* 1.70: Ὃς ἤδη τά τ' ἐόντα τά τ' ἐσσόμενα, πρό τ' ἐόντα.
2 Virgil *Georgics* 4.393; Servius commenting on this line points out the Homeric parallel.

80 Homer *Iliad* (see n1 below)
1 *Iliad* 1.96: Τοὔνεκ' ἄρ' ἄλγε' ἔδωκε ἑκηβόλος, ἠδ' ἔτι δώσει.

81 Homer *Iliad* (see n1 below); cf *Adagia* III ix 70 (344 below) with the same title.
1 *Iliad* 1.156–7: Ἐπεὶ ἦ μάλα πολλὰ μεταξὺ / Οὐρεά τε σκιόεντα θάλασσά τε ἠχήεσσα.

82 Adhortantis ad gloriam
For someone giving encouragement to seek fame

When we want to encourage people to procure everlasting fame with extraordinary deeds, it will be appropriate to adduce this verse, which Marcus Tullius used in several places:[1] 'Strive so that posterity too may praise
you.'[2] The verse exists in other places in Homer including the *Odyssey*
book 1. For this is how Athena, in the shape of Mentor, exhorts Telemachus
to valour with the example of other famous men: 'Come, you too, for I
see you are tall and handsome, / Strive so that posterity too may praise
you.'[3]

83 Qui paratus ad resistendum
Someone ready to resist

Someone who wants to indicate that he will certainly not decline to fight,
but has abundant resources to protect his possessions, can use this from
book 13 of the *Iliad*: 'I have slender spears and round shields, / Helmets
and far-flashing breast-plates.'[1]

84 In discrimine apparet qui vir
A crisis reveals who is a man

For a dangerous and difficult situation, and such as calls for a man both
prudent and decisive, this verse will be suitable, spoken by Idomeneus,
leader of the Cretans: 'There the situation itself tells us who is the coward
and who the man of valour.'[1] What follows in the next verse is suitable for

* * * * *

82 Homer *Odyssey* (see n2 below)
  1 Cicero *Ad familiares* 13.15.1; this seems to be the only place where Cicero refers
    to the line.
  2 *Odyssey* 3.199–200: Ἄλκιμος ἔσσ', ἵνα τίς σε καὶ ὀψιγόνων εὖ εἴπῃ (Nestor to
    Telemachus)
  3 *Odyssey* 1.301-2 where Athena has assumed the appearance of Mentes (see line
    180), not Mentor. She adopts the latter disguise in 2.401 and 24.548.

83 Homer *Iliad* (see n1 below)
  1 *Iliad* 13.264–5: Τῷ μοι δούρατά ἐστι καὶ ἀσπίδες ὀμφαλόεσσαι / Καὶ κόρυθες καὶ
    θώρηκες λαμπρὸν γανόωντες.

84 Homer *Iliad* (see n1 below)
  1 *Iliad* 13.278: Ἔνθ' ὅ τε δειλὸς ἀνὴρ ὅς τ' ἄλκιμος ἐξεφαάνθη.

the same purpose: 'A coward changes colour back and forth.'[2] This has been mentioned by me elsewhere.[3]

85 Non cedendum malis
Never yield to misfortunes

Whenever you want to warn someone that he should not give in to enemies or the assaults of hostile fortune, or be like those who run away, you could quite neatly turn this to the purpose from the same book:

> May the javelin not strike[1] behind on your neck or back,
> May the enemy's arrow strike your stomach or your breast. [2]

86 Ipse sibi perniciem accersivit
He brought calamity on himself

For a man who obstinately brings disaster on himself as if he is condemned to it by fate, this line from the same book will be suitable: 'An evil Fate was drawing him on to this fatal end.'[1]

87 Ultra vires nihil aggrediendum
Do not engage in what is beyond your powers

If you want to say that you should not begin an undertaking that you do not have the power to complete, then this from the same book could be adapted quite appropriately: 'No one should seek a battle beyond his

*　*　*　*　*

2 *Iliad* 13.279: Τοῦ μὲν γάρ τε κακοῦ τρέπεται χρὼς ἄλλυδις ἄλλῃ. Erasmus gives no translation here.
3 *Adagia* I ii 89 The coward changes colour, where Erasmus quotes lines 279–84 from *Iliad* 13. In *1508* and *1515* these had appeared here with their translation, but were replaced by the two lines given above in *1517/18*.

85 Homer *Iliad* (see n2 below)
1 Erasmus translates the Greek potential optative, equivalent here to a conditional 'would not strike,' with a Latin optative.
2 *Iliad* 13.289–90: Οὐκ ἂν ἐν αὐχέν᾽ ὄπισθε πέσοι βέλος οὐδ᾽ ἐνὶ νώτῳ, / Ἀλλά κεν ἢ στέρνων ἢ νηδύος ἀντιάσειε.

86 Homer *Iliad* (see n1 below)
1 *Iliad* 13.602: Τὸν δ᾽ ἄγε μοῖρα κακὴ θανάτοιο τέλοσδε.

87 Homer *Iliad* (see n1 below)

strength, / However eager he may be.'[1] These are the words of Paris speaking to Hector.

88 Ocyor accipitre
As swift as a hawk

It is possible to signify wonderful speed with a proverbial hyperbole which is to be found in the same book: 'As swift as a hawk.'[1] The phrase will be more stylish if it is used to refer to fame, or intelligence, or a message, or anything like that.

89 Ancipitis animi
In two minds

A mind divided in two and undecided could be described with the lines in book 14 of the *Iliad*:

> So the old man turned it over in his mind and pondered,
> Inclining one way and the other.[1]

This was imitated by Maro: 'And his mind is divided, going rapidly now this way now that.'[2] In the *Iliad* again, book 16: 'My mind inclined this way and that as I pondered.'[3]

90 Correctio dicti
Mending what we say

A remark that is improper and such as should be withheld by respectable people, or any absurd remark, we can denote with this couplet from the *Iliad* book 14:

* * * * *

1 *Iliad* 13.787: Πὰρ δύναμιν δ᾽ οὐκ ἔστι καὶ ἐσσύμενον πολεμίζειν.

88 Homer *Iliad* (see n1 below)
1 *Iliad* 13.819: Θάσσονες ἰρήκων

89 Homer *Iliad* (see n1 below); cf *Adagia* III viii 67 (306 above).
1 *Iliad* 14.20–21: Ὡς ὁ γέρων ὥρμαινε δαϊζόμενος κατὰ θυμὸν / Διχθάδια.
2 Virgil *Aeneid* 4.285 and 8.20. The editors of ASD remark that Erasmus seems to be the first to note the parallel.
3 *Iliad* 16.435: Διχθὰ δέ μοι κραδίη μέμονε φρεσὶν ὁρμαίνοντι.

90 Homer *Iliad* (see n1 below)

Speech such as may never be uttered by any man
Who has the least idea of how to speak prudent and sensible words.[1]

91 In clamosos
Against people who shout

We can describe loud shouting during lawsuits or disputes with this couplet of Homer's about Neptune in the same passage:

Shouting loud as the war cry of nine
Or ten thousand men as they join battle.[1]

The same couplet is found also in book 5 of the *Iliad* where it refers to Mars.[2]

92 Pro mea virili
To the utmost of my ability

When we want to promise that we shall give something our attention to the utmost of our ability, this remark of Venus to Juno from the same book will be appropriate: 'If I can fulfil it and if it is something that can be fulfilled.'[1] The same verse is to be found in book 5 of the *Odyssey* and book 18 of the *Iliad*.[2] Plutarch uses it as if it were a proverb in his essay 'On Distinguishing a Flatterer from a Friend': 'For it was rightly said by our ancestors that a friend makes a promise like this: "If I can fulfil it and if it is something that can be fulfilled," but a flatterer does it like this: "Tell me whatever you have in your heart."'[3]

* * * * *

1 *Iliad* 14.91–2: Μῦθον, ὃν οὔ κεν ἀνήρ γε διὰ στόμα πάμπαν ἄγοιτο, / Ὅς τις ἐπίσταιτο ᾗσι φρεσὶν ἄρτια βάζειν

91 Homer *Iliad* (see n1 below)
1 *Iliad* 14.148–9: Ὅσσον τ' ἐννεάχιλοι ἐπίαχον ἢ δεκάχιλοι / Ἀνέρες ἐν πολέμῳ, ἔριδα ξυνάγοντες Ἄρηος.
2 *Iliad* 5.860–1, where Mars' cry is provoked by a wound from the spear of Diomedes guided by Athena

92 Homer *Iliad* (see n1 below)
1 *Iliad* 14.196: Εἰ δύναμαι τελέσαι γε καὶ εἰ τετελεσμένον ἔσται
2 *Odyssey* 5.90 and *Iliad* 18.427
3 Plutarch *Moralia* 62E *Quomodo adulator ab amico internoscatur*: Εἶ γὰρ εἴρηται τοῖς πρὸ ἡμῶν, φίλου μὲν ἐκείνην εἶναι τὴν ἐπαγγελίαν· Εἰ δύναμαι τελέσαι γε καὶ εἰ τετελεσμένον ἔσται, κόλακος δὲ ταύτην, Αὔδα ὅ τι φρονέεις.

93 Pro dignitate cuiusque
To each according to his status

When roles are assigned to each person according to his suitability and status, for example if difficult business is entrusted to someone wise and experienced and less important things to someone young and inexperienced, then this also from book 14 of the *Iliad* will be suitable: 'The best warrior was now the best equipped, and passed on / His inferior gear to the inferior man.'[1]

94 Omnia ex sententia cedunt
Everything is happening as planned

For the extremely fortunate, for whom everything undertaken whether rightly or wrongly turns out happily, this couplet from the *Iliad* book 17 will be suitable:

> All their darts strike home, whether they are fired
> By coward or brave man, for Jupiter himself
> Guides them.[1]

95 Improbitas muscae
The depravity of the fly

For the reprobate who immediately returns to crime even if he is driven off in disgrace, this from the same book will be appropriate:

> And in his heart she set the daring of the fly
> That however often it is driven off a man's skin,
> Still returns to attack and bite.[1]

* * * * *

93 Homer *Iliad* (see n1 below)
1 *Iliad* 14.382: Ἐσθλὰ μὲν ἐσθλὸς ἔδυνε, χέρεια δὲ χείρονι δόσκεν.

94 Homer *Iliad* (see n1 below)
1 *Iliad* 17.631–2: Τῶν μὲν γὰρ πάντων βέλε᾽ ἅπτεται, ὅς τις ἀφείη, / Ἢ κακὸς ἢ ἀγαθός, Ζεὺς δ᾽ ἔμπης πάντ᾽ ἰθύνει.

95 Homer *Iliad* (see n1 below)
1 *Iliad* 17.570–2: Καί οἱ μυίης θάρσος ἐνὶ στήθεσσιν ἐνῆκεν, / Ἢ τε καὶ ἐργομένη μάλα περ χροὸς ἀνδρομένοιο / Ἰσχανάᾳ δακέειν.

96 Deo fortunaeque committo
I trust to God and fortune

For someone who has decided to put an affair to the test and commit the outcome of it to fortune, the following from the same book will suit: 'I too will cast; all these things shall be Jupiter's concern.'[1]

97 Consilium in melius commutandum
Change your plan for a better one

Whenever we want to enjoin someone to change their intention because it is repugnant or stupid, or when we want to condemn something as done ill-advisedly, then this from the same book will be useful: 'What god has given you such unprofitable counsel / And driven good sense out of your heart?'[1]

98 Modis omnibus incitat
By every means he urges

When someone uses every means to persuade someone else, prayers, flattery, censure, threats, you can make use of this from the same book, spoken of Automedon and the horses of Achilles: 'Again and again he commanded them with lashes of his whip, / Again and again he coaxed them with soft words, again and again he threatened.'[1]

99 Eidem inhiantes testamento
Mouths agape for the same will

It will be harsh perhaps, but quite clever nevertheless, if the verse in the

* * * * *

96 Homer *Iliad* (see n1 below)
1 *Iliad* 17.515: Ἥσω γὰρ καὶ ἐγώ, τὰ δέ κεν Διὶ πάντα μελήσει.

97 Homer *Iliad* (see n1 below)
1 *Iliad* 17.469–70: Τίς τοί νυ θεῶν νηκερδέα βουλὴν / Ἐν στήθεσσιν ἔθηκε καὶ ἐξέλετο φρένας ἐσθλάς;

98 Homer *Iliad* (see n1 below)
1 *Iliad* 17.430–1: Πολλὰ μὲν ἄρ μάστιγι θοῇ ἐπεμαίετο θείνων, / Πολλὰ δὲ μειλιχίοισι προσηύδα, πολλὰ δ' ἀρειῇ.

99 Homer *Iliad* (see n1 below)

same book about the Greeks and Trojans fighting over the body of Patroclus is adapted to describe inheritance hunters vying over the same old man as if he were a corpse: 'Even so in the scant space they haul the corpse / This way and that.'[1]

100 Praematura mors
Early death

For one who has met an early death while his parents survive, we can adapt from the same book what is said of the Pelasgian Hippothous son of Lethus whom Telamonian Ajax killed because he seized the body of Patroclus by the foot and tried to drag it off to Troy: 'But neither did he repay his parents For his upbringing, his life was too short.'[1]

1 Alia dantur, alia negantur
Some things are given, some are denied

Whenever one of a natural pair of gifts has been granted and the other has been denied – for example if someone is of handsome appearance and has no intelligence to boast of – or when only one of two requests is fulfilled, there will be a place for this line from book 16 of the *Iliad*: 'To him one thing the divine father granted, the other he denied.'[1] This line was used by Pliny in one of his letters.[2] The words refer to Achilles; in the prayers he made for Patroclus, who was about to go into battle in Achilles' own armour, he asked for two things: one that Patroclus should fight gloriously, the second that after the battle he should return safe himself and with the armour. Jupiter granted one of these requests, namely that he should fight bravely. But the arms of Achilles he did not bring back nor did he return safely. The verse was used wittily by Stratonicus the lyre-player,[3] who quoted the Homeric line when he heard someone singing to the lyre: 'To him one thing

* * * * *

1 *Iliad* 17.394–5: "Ὡς οἵ γ᾽ ἔνθα καὶ ἔνθα νέκυν ὀλίγῃ ἐνὶ χώρῃ, / Εἵλκεον ἀμφότεροι.

100 Homer *Iliad* (see n1 below)
1 *Iliad* 17.301–2: Οὐδὲ τοκεῦσι / Θρέπτα φίλοις ἀπέδωκε, μινυνθάδιος δέ οἱ αἰών.

1 Homer *Iliad* (see n1 below)
1 *Iliad* 16.250: Τῷ δ᾽ ἕτερον μὲν ἔδωκε πατήρ, ἕτερον δ᾽ ἀνένευσεν.
2 Pliny *Letters* 1.7.1
3 A famous citharist, 410[?]–360 BC; cf Erasmus *Apophthegmata* VI Stratonicus 11.

the divine father granted, the other he denied.' And when somebody else asked him why he said this he replied, 'Because he gave him a talent for playing the lyre badly, but denied him a talent for singing well.' This is all in Athenaeus book 8.[4]

2 Victoria non incruenta
Not a bloodless victory

In general not only the corruption of judges but also the greed of advocates causes both parties in a lawsuit to suffer damage, so much so that it is not uncommon for the one who has won the case to regret it. For such people a suitable quote is this from book 17 of the *Iliad*: 'And these too did not fight without bloodshed.'[1]

3 Filius degenerans
A son going to the bad

For a son who falls short of the upbringing given by his father, or one who does not long enjoy his father's inheritance but is driven out of his ancestral possessions, we can aptly transpose this from the same book:

But the son did not grow old in his father's armour.[1]

4 Eventus praeter expectationem
An unexpected outcome

Whenever something turns out very differently from what was intended or seemed likely to happen, then this from the same book will be fitting: 'But

* * * * *

4 Athenaeus 8.350D; Erasmus gives Stratonicus' quotation from Homer only in Greek.

2 Homer *Iliad* (see n1 below)
1 *Iliad* 17.363: Οὐδ᾽ οἱ γὰρ ἀναιμωτί γ᾽ ἐμάχοντο.

3 Homer *Iliad* (see n1 below)
1 *Iliad* 17.197: Ἀλλ᾽ οὐχ υἱὸς ἐν ἔντεσι πατρὸς ἐγήρα.

4 Homer *Iliad* (see n1 below); cf *Adagia* III i 19 All does not come to pass that you have set your heart on.

the will of great Jove prevails at every moment.'[1] Pindar in the last *Pythian Ode*: 'For what is in the fates cannot be avoided; but there will be times when to someone cast down in despair one thing will be granted beyond all expectation, but another will not.'[2] And again in book 16 of the *Iliad*: 'But greater than that of men at all times is the will of Jove.'[3]

5 Reprehensio cogitationis
Censuring what we think

When we reproach ourselves for our intentions or for dishonourable or unhelpful thoughts, it would be a good place for this from book 17 of the *Iliad*: 'But why does my mind put this into my heart?'[1] The same is to be found in other passages.[2]

6 Praebere viros
Prove yourselves men

We can encourage people to act or suffer bravely with this line, also from book 17 of the *Iliad*, though it is also found repeatedly in other places:[1] 'Come then, be men, show vigour and strength.'[2]

7 Re opitulandum, non verbis
Help is in the deed, not in words

When action is required, words are no help; for example, if someone needs financial support, what use is it to fill his ears with advice? On the other

* * * * *

1 *Iliad* 17.176: Ἀλλ' αἰεί τε Διὸς κρείσσων νόος αἰγιόχοιο.
2 Pindar *Pythians* 12.30–2
3 *Iliad* 16.688

5 Homer *Iliad* (see n1 below)
1 *Iliad* 17.97: Ἀλλὰ τίη μοι ταῦτα φίλος διελέξατο θυμός;
2 *Iliad* 11.407, 21.562, 22.122 and 385

6 Homer *Iliad* (see n2 below)
1 *Iliad* 6.112, 8.174, 11.287, 15.487 and 734, 16.270
2 *Iliad* 17.185: Ἀνέρες ἔστε, φίλοι, μνήσασθε δὲ θούριδος ἀλκῆς.

7 Homer *Iliad* (see n1 below)

hand in deliberations and decisions it is a matter of arguments, not action. This Homeric line from book 16 of the *Iliad* is suitable for this:

The council is the place for words, in battle what matters is fortitude.[1]

8 Corrupta iudicia
Corrupt judgments

The case of those who give corrupt judgments or who cast their votes not with the good of the state in mind but their private advantage, or who stifle law by tyranny, is met by this couplet from the same book:

Men who by violence in public meetings
Pervert the common laws and seek to drive out justice,
Having no respect for the voice[1] of the gods.[2]

9 Apta provincia
A suitable function

For a person who takes up a function suited to his abilities and refrains from affairs to which he is not equal – for example if someone accepts a bishopric and declines the papacy – this couplet from the same book will be suitable: 'He seizes any huge spears that fit his grasp, / Only the spear of Achilles he does not take.'[1] This refers to Patroclus who put on Achilles' armour but refrained from taking the spear because it was too heavy for any of the Greeks to wield except Achilles alone. Homer pictured the bow of Ulysses in the same way in the *Odyssey*.[2]

* * * * *

1 *Iliad* 16.630: Ἐν γὰρ χερσὶ τέλος πολέμου, ἐπέων δ' ἐνὶ βουλῇ.

8 Homer *Iliad* (see n2 below)
1 Latin *vocem*; Erasmus has confused ὄπις, accusative ὄπιν 'vengeance,' with ὄψ, accusative ὄπα 'voice.'
2 *Iliad* 16.387–8: Οἳ βίῃ ἐν ἀγορῇ σκολιὰς κρίνωσι θέμιστας, / Ἐκ δὲ δίκην ἐλάσωσι, θεῶν ὄπιν οὐκ ἀλέγοντες.

9 Homer *Iliad* (see n1 below); for *provincia* see *Adagia* II iv 41.
1 *Iliad* 16.139–40: Εἵλετο δ' ἄλκιμα δοῦρα, τά οἱ παλάμηφιν ἀρήρει, / Ἔγχος δ' οὐχ ἕλετ' οἶον ἀμύμονος Αἰακίδαο.
2 *Odyssey* 21.91–4 and 124–8

10 **Pudor et metus**
Shame and fear

When we refrain from something because it seems improper to do it and
also dangerous, there will be a place for this from book 15 of the *Iliad*: 'For
shame and fear forbid it.'[1] Homer is speaking of a compact battle formation
which was prevented from breaking up partly by shame and partly by fear.
He shows that shame is a great spur[2] to acting bravely in the same book
when he says: 'Of those who feel shame more are saved than fall.'[3]

11 **Qui obticescit**
One who falls silent

For someone who is stunned by fear or struck dumb with wonder and falls
silent, or who can find no answer, a good phrase would be this from book
17 of the *Iliad*: 'He was stunned and struck dumb.'[1]

12 **Mors omnibus communis**
Death is the common lot

Anyone who wants to say that death must come to all equally and that no
force can ward off the necessity of fate can quote this from the *Iliad* book 18:
'Not even Hercules was strong enough to avoid pitiless death.'[1]

13 **Alius aliis in rebus praestantior**
People excel in different ways

If we want to say that different people have different talents, we can borrow
what is said in the same book of Polydamas and Hector: 'This man is far

* * * * *

10 Homer *Iliad* (see n1 below)
 1 *Iliad* 15.657–8: Ἴσχε γὰρ αἰδὼς / Καὶ δέος.
 2 Latin *addere calcar*; cf *Adagia* I ii 47 To spur on the running horse.
 3 *Iliad* 15.563

11 Homer *Iliad* (see n1 below)
 1 *Iliad* 17.695: Δὴν δέ μιν ἀμφασίη ἐπέων λάβε.

12 Homer *Iliad* (see n1 below)
 1 *Iliad* 18.117: Οὐδὲ γὰρ οὐδὲ βίη Ἡρακλῆος φύγε κῆρα.

13 Homer *Iliad* (see n1 below)

better with words and that one with a spear.'[1] The same view is expressed
at greater length in book 13 of the *Iliad* by Polydamas when he speaks to
Hector:

> Hector, you are not good at gaining hearts with words.'[2]
> But just because the gods have granted you to be a great fighter,
> Do you think your ideas should be given precedence over others' in council?
> But you cannot take on alone all responsibilities at the same time,
> For the god has given to one to excel in fighting,
> Another earns praise for dancing, another for playing the lyre and singing
>> sweet songs,
> And in another's mind great Jupiter has planted
> A brilliant intelligence.[3]

14 In periculoso negocio non est dormitandum
In a dangerous affair you cannot afford to doze

When we want to warn that you must not be negligent in the middle of a
difficult business, a fitting phrase could be this found in Homer's *Iliad* book
16: 'There is little breathing space in battle.'[1] This could be applied to legal
battles or to some other such unpleasant, difficult business.

15 Mens laeva
Wrong-headed

The minds of men are often perverse; they pursue the worst instead of
the best, and reject the best in favour of the worst. The idea is suitably
expressed by this from book 18 of the *Iliad*:

*****

1 *Iliad* 18.252: Ἀλλ᾽ ὁ μὲν ἄρ μύθοισιν, ὁ δ᾽ ἔγχεϊ πολλὸν ἐνίκα.
2 In 1526 Erasmus had *Haud dictis Hector didicisti moriger esse* 'Hector, you have
not learned to be amenable to persuasion,' which corresponds better with the
Greek, usually translated as something like 'you are hard to persuade.' In
1528 however he changed this to *Hector, non potis es deflectere pectora dictis*,
explaining in the Corrigenda of the 1528 edition: '[Polydamas] acknowledges
Hector's valour in war, but denies his eloquence in council.'
3 *Iliad* 13.726–33; added in 1526

14 Homer *Iliad* (see n1 below)
1 *Iliad* 16.43 and 11.801: Ὀλίγη δ᾽ ἀνάπνευσις πολέμοιο.

15 Homer *Iliad* (see n1 below). *Mens laeva* is borrowed from Virgil *Aeneid* 2.54.

Everyone praised the advice of Hector, which was bad,
And no one that of Polydamas, though his alone was good.[1]

16 Verbis pugnas, non re
You are fighting with words, not facts

It is easy to exchange insults, but difficult to convince by the facts. This
idea can be suitably expressed by the following from book 20 of the *Iliad*
spoken by Aeneas when he is about to encounter Achilles: 'Seeing I too
know well / How to attack with insults and to utter taunts.'[1] Shortly after
this he repeats the same idea at greater length:

It is easy for both of us to hurl plenty of insults;
A hundred-oared ship could not carry the weight of them.
For the tongue of man is glib; it has many and varied sorts
Of speech at its command, a wide pasturage[2] of words
On every side and many alternatives, but the sort of words
You utter will be the sort you hear in answer.[3]

17 Ne quid moveare verborum strepitu
Don't be put off by loud words

If you want to warn someone not to be dissuaded from trying to achieve
something by violent words and threats, you can adapt this from the same
book where Apollo speaks to Aeneas: 'Nay, with unwavering sword go
forward rather to meet him, / And never let him put you off with violent
words and threats.'[1]

* * * * *

1 *Iliad* 18.312–13: Ἕκτορι μὲν γὰρ ἐπήνησαν κακὰ μητιόωντι, / Πουλυδάμαντι δ' ἄρ'
οὔτις, ὃς ἐσθλὴν φράζετο βουλήν.

16 Homer *Iliad* (see n1 below)
1 *Iliad* 20.201–2: Ἐπεὶ σάφα ὃιδα καὶ αὐτὸς / Ἠμὲν κερτομίας ἠδ' αἴσυλα μυθήσασθαι.
2 Erasmus translates the Greek ἐπέων δὲ πολὺς νομός as *pascua dictis*. Estienne (LB
II 924) points out that it has the sense of πλῆθος 'great number' and suggests
copia dictorum. The phrase is usually translated as 'a wide range of words.'
3 *Iliad* 20.246–50; cf *Adagia* I i 27 He who says what he would will hear what he
would not.

17 Homer *Iliad* (see n1 below)
1 *Iliad* 20.108–9: Ἀλλ' ἰθὺς φέρε χαλκὸν ἀτειρέα, μηδέ σε πάμπαν / Λευγαλέοις
ἐπέεσσιν ἀποτρεπέτω καὶ ἀρειῇ.

18 **Cibo opus duraturis in labore**
Those who face a long task need food

Those who are about to go into battle should not go in the least hungry lest
they are deprived of their strength. This could be applied to literary studies,
to the practice of piety and many other things. Homer's verses from book
19 of the *Iliad* fit here:

> For what man can keep going from sunrise to sunset
> Enduring the struggle of continuous battle without food?
> However eager he may be to fight, his limbs gradually
> Become heavy, a burning thirst and hunger attack him
> And his knees give way as he struggles against the enemy.
> On the contrary, one who has had his fill of wine and food
> Will be able to fight the enemy all day long.
> His spirits remain ever fierce, his limbs do not tire
> Until, victorious, he drives all before him.[1]

19 **Omnibus armis praesidiisque destitutus**
Without arms or protection

We can signify a man without weapons and deprived of any protection with
this line, which is in the *Iliad* book 21: 'Stripped of everything, shield and
helmet and spear.'[1]

20 **Frustra habet qui non utitur**
Possessions are worthless if not used

If you want to reproach someone for not using the intelligence, wealth or

* * * * *

18 Homer *Iliad* (see n1 below)
  1 *Iliad* 19.162–70: Οὐ γὰρ ἀνὴρ πρόπαν ἦμαρ ἐς ἠέλιον καταδύντα / Ἄκμηνος σίτοιο
  δυνήσεται ἄντα μάχεσθαι· / Εἴ περ γὰρ θυμῷ γε μενοινάᾳ πολεμίζειν, / Ἀλλά τε
  λάθρῃ γυῖα βαρύνεται, ἠδὲ κιχάνει / Δίψα τε καὶ λιμός, βλάβεται δέ τε γούνατ᾽
  ἰόντι. / Ὃς δέ κ᾽ ἀνὴρ οἴνοιο κορεσσάμενος καὶ ἐδωδῆς / Ἀνδράσι δυσμενέεσσι παν-
  ημέριος πολεμίζει, / Θαρσαλέον νύ οἱ ἦτορ ἐνὶ φρεσίν, οὐδέ τι γυῖα / Πρὶν κάμνει,
  πρὶν πάντας ἐρωῆσαι πολέμοιο.

19 Homer *Iliad* (see n1 below)
  1 *Iliad* 21.50: Γυμνὸς ἄτερ κόρυθός τε καὶ ἀσπίδος οὐδ᾽ ἔχεν ἔγχος.

20 Homer *Iliad* (see n1 below)

learning that he has, this line from the same book 21 of the *Iliad* will do:
'Why do you carry your bow about unused?'[1]

21 In fugitivum
For a runaway

When someone is incited by unbridled greed to want something, especially
something ignoble, or more still if someone runs away like a coward, it will
be apt if you say, 'He is being dragged off by the *cynamyia*.'[1] In the same
book Juno describes Mars as he runs away from the battle like this: 'Plague-
bearing Mars is being led off by the *cynamyia*.'[2] The *cynamyia* is the dog-fly.

22 Cum diis non pugnandum
You may not fight with the gods

If you want to warn that we should not fight with a spirit, with the immortal
gods, or with great princes that even the Hebrew scriptures call gods,[1] you
can use this from the same book: 'But men are lower than the gods.'[2] I have
spoken about 'Fighting against the gods,' elsewhere.[3] Pindar expressed this
idea in the second Pythian ode thus: 'And it is right not to strive with God.'[4]

23 Autor omnium et fons
Author and source of everything

When we want to point to the first originator of everything, from whom

* * * * *

1 *Iliad* 21.474: Τί νυ τόξον ἔχεις ἀνεμώλιον αὔτως;

21 Homer *Iliad* (see n1 below)
1 *Iliad* 21.421: Τοῦτον ἡ κυνάμυια ἄγει.
2 Mars is escaping from an encounter with Athena; Juno uses 'dog-fly' as an
epithet for Venus who is helping him.

22 Homer *Iliad* (see n2 below)
1 Exodus 21:6 ; 22:8, 9 (AV 'judges,' RSV 'God'); 22:28 (AV 'gods,' RSV 'God'); Ps
82:1 and 6; John 10:34
2 *Iliad* 21.264: Θεοὶ δέ τε φέρτεροι ἀνδρῶν; the Greek means literally 'The gods are
mightier than men.'
3 *Adagia* II v 44 Θεομαχεῖν, where Erasmus mentions this dictum from Homer
and the line from Pindar
4 Pindar *Pythians* 2.88

23 Homer *Iliad* (see n2 below)

everything, from the greatest to the smallest, proceeds as from the head (for example, if someone says pride is the father of all evils, faith is the source of all virtues, Homer is the father of all poetry) it will be quite fitting to adapt from the same book this couplet referring to Ocean:[1]

> From whom alone flow all seas and all rivers,
> All springs and deep lakes stream forth.[2]

24 Prorsus ignotus
Utterly unknown

If we wish to make it apparent that a person is emphatically unknown to us, we can jokingly turn against him this line, which occurs in the same book[1] and often elsewhere in Homer, such as the *Odyssey* books 1 and 14: 'Tell me, who are you, where do you come from, where are your country and your parents?'[2] This is close to the adage 'I know not whether you are dark or fair.'[3] It could also be applied to a circumstance, for example, let us say that someone entirely ignorant of philosophy has come across a book on the subject: 'Tell me, who are you, where do you come from, where are your country and your parents?'[4]

25 Quoad vixero
For as long as I live

Something that we want to declare we will always hold to in life can be signalled with Homer's verse in book 22 of the *Iliad*: 'While I move / Among the living, while I am supported by these knees.'[1] Maro imitated this: 'While I am mindful of myself, while my spirit rules these limbs.'[2]

* * * * *

1 Cf Quintilian 10.1.46 and Erasmus *De conscribendis epistolis* CWE 25 87.
2 *Iliad* 21.196–7: Ἐξ οὗ περ πάντες ποταμοὶ καὶ πᾶσα θάλασσα / Καὶ πᾶσαι κρῆναι καὶ φρείατα μακρὰ νάουσιν.

24 Homer *Iliad* (see n1 below)
1 *Iliad* 21.150
2 *Odyssey* 1.170 and 14.187: Τίς πόθεν εἰς ἀνδρῶν, πόθι τοι πόλις ἠδὲ τοκῆες;
3 *Adagia* I vi 99
4 Erasmus repeats the Greek without translating it again.

25 Homer *Iliad* (see n1 below)
1 *Iliad* 22.387–8: Ὄφρ' ἂν ἔγωγε / Ζωοῖσιν μετέω καί μοι φίλα γούνατ' ὀρώρα
2 Virgil *Aeneid* 4.336, a parallel first noticed by Erasmus, according to ASD

26 Gloriosum et apud posteros
A deed glorious to posterity too

When we want to signify a deed whose glory will be celebrated by posterity too, this from the same book will be fitting:

Nay rather he achieved[1] a great deed
Such that posterity itself would hear of.[2]

27 Vindicta tarda, sed gravis
Vengeance falling late, but heavily

When someone who has committed many crimes over a long period with impunity is at last brought to his downfall, and pays once and for all for his earlier misdeeds, this from the same book will be fitting: 'Now you shall pay once and for all for all your accumulated misdeeds.'[1] These are the words of Achilles to Hector.

28 Anceps eventus rei
Two possible outcomes

When we point out that a situation has two possible outcomes and that it is uncertain which way victory inclines, this line from the same book will be appropriate: 'Then the father balanced the two pans of his golden scales.'[1] The same line occurs in book 8 of the *Iliad*.[2]

* * * * *

26 Homer *Iliad* (see n2 below)
1 Erasmus' verb *peregit* completes the sense of the Greek phrase he translates but disregards the context. The phrase is part of Hector's wish: 'Let me not die ... ingloriously, but in the working of some great deed ...'
2 *Iliad* 22.305: Ἀλλὰ μέγα ῥέξας τι καὶ ἐσσομένοισι πυθέσθαι.

27 Homer *Iliad* (see n1 below)
1 *Iliad* 22.271: Νῦν δ' ἀθρόα πάντ' ἀποτίσεις. 'All your accumulated misdeeds' is *cuncta ... adglomerata*; this is the meaning of Erasmus' Latin as suggested by his context ('earlier misdeeds'), but in the Greek that he omits Achilles speaks of 'all my sorrows for my comrades.'

28 Homer *Iliad* (see n1 below)
1 *Iliad* 22.209: Καὶ τότε δὴ χρύσεια πατὴρ ἐτίταινε τάλαντα.
2 *Iliad* 8.69

29 Magna de re disceptatur
A great matter being debated

When we want to say that there is great dispute and that what is to be gained is neither insignificant nor absurd,[1] these lines from the same book will be appropriate: 'For it was not for a sacrificial animal / Or a heifer[2] that they strove.'[3] This is said of Achilles and Hector in mortal combat. It is used by Lucian in his *Eunuch* where he makes fun of philosophers quarrelling disgracefully before the judges about their fees.[4] The whole verse goes like this:

> For it was not for a sacrificial animal
> Or a heifer that they strove, such as are the prizes for a race;
> They were running for Hector's life.

Virgil renders this in book 12 of the *Aeneid*: 'For it is not petty or sporting prizes they seek; / They are fighting for the life and blood of Turnus.'[5]

30 Omissis nugis rem experiamur
Trifling aside, let's put it to the test

If you want to stop trading insults and demand that it should actually be put to the test to decide which one shall win or lose, then this from the same book will not be inopportune:

> But it would be better to come to grips, so that it may be clear
> As soon as possible[1] to whom Jupiter wants the fame
> And the glory to go.[2]

* * * * *

29 Homer *Iliad* (see n3 below)
1 Latin *nec levia aut ludicra peti praemia*, suggested by the lines from Virgil quoted at the end
2 Erasmus translates the Greek βοείη 'ox-hide' or 'shield of ox-hide' with *bucula*.
3 *Iliad* 22.159–60: Ἐπεὶ οὐχ ἱερήιον οὐδὲ βοείην / Ἀρνύσθην
4 Lucian *Eunuchus* 3
5 Virgil *Aeneid* 12.764–5; added in 1526

30 Homer *Iliad* (see n2 below)
1 In the Aldine edition the full stop at the end of line 129, after ὅττι τάχιστα, is missing. Erasmus therefore links this phrase with what follows.
2 *Iliad* 22.129–30: Βέλτερον αὖτ᾽ ἔριδι ξυνελαυνέμεν, ὅττι τάχιστα / Εἴδομεν, ὁπποτέρῳ κεν Ὀλύμπιος εὖχος ὀρέξῃ.

31 Metus infamiae
Fear of disgrace

When we want to say that people's opinion of us and their murmurings influence us so that we do not waver in our purpose, this from the same book and book 6 of the *Iliad*, which is used often by Marcus Tullius in his *Letters to Atticus*, will be suitable: 'I stand in awe of the men and women of Troy and feel shame before them.'[1] These are the words of Hector unwilling for shame to withdraw into the city lest anyone should reproach him and blame him for the deaths of the Trojans.

32 Aliam aetatem alia decent
Different ages different conduct

If we want to say that someone is older now and that something that was fitting for the young does not befit the old, we can use this, which is from the same book though it is repeated elsewhere:[1]

But when the head is grey and grey the chin ...[2]

33 Quod aliis vitio vertas, ipse ne feceris
Don't do yourself what you criticize in others

What you would condemn in others you should not do yourself. This line from the *Iliad* book 23 will be suitable here:

What is more, if anyone else were about to commit
Such an act, you would condemn it and brand it a vice.[1]

* * * * *

31 Homer *Iliad* (see n1 below)
  1 *Iliad* 22.105 and 6.442: Αἰδέομαι Τρῶας καὶ Τρῳάδας ἑλκεσιπέπλους, quoted by Cicero *Ad Atticum* 7.12.3, 8.16.2, 13.13.2, 13.24; Cicero uses only Αἰδέομαι Τρῶας.

32 Homer *Iliad* (see n2 below)
  1 *Iliad* 24.516 (in part)
  2 *Iliad* 22.74: Ἀλλ' ὅτε δὴ πολιόν τε κάρη πολιόν τε γένειον

33 Homer *Iliad* (see n1 below)
  1 *Iliad* 23.494: Καὶ δ' ἄλλῳ νεμεσᾶτον, ὅτις τοιαῦτά γε ῥέζοι.

34 Aut ipse fuisti aut tui simillimus
It was either you or someone very like you

If we want to say jokingly that a person was present who nevertheless denies that he was – for example, if you accuse someone of drinking with habitual drunkards and he denies that it was he and says it was someone else – it would be quite amusing to adapt this from the same book, where Homer spoke of the shade of Patroclus: 'It was in all things like him – voice, handsome eyes, / Stature – and wore similar dress.'[1]

35 Audiens non audit
He has ears and hears not

There are some people who pretend not to know what they do not like; for example, they deny that they have received a letter reminding them of a duty they would prefer to avoid rather than fulfil. For such people this phrase from the *Iliad* book 23 will be suitable: 'Pretending not to have heard.' This is said of Antilochus who, although he heard Menelaus calling him back from the race, drove all the faster as if he had not heard:

> But Antilochus raced all the faster,
> Plying the whip as if he had not heard.[1]

36 Ex habitu bonum virum prae se fert
Appearance tells you if a man is good

If you want to say that a man's probity can be seen from his face, you can quote this line from book 1 of the *Odyssey*: 'From his face alone he seemed to be no scoundrel.'[1] Marcus Tullius, in the eighth book of the *Verrine Orations*:

* * * * *

34 Homer *Iliad* (see n1 below)
1 *Iliad* 23.66–7: Πάντ᾽ αὐτῷ μέγεθός τε καὶ ὄμματα κάλ᾽ εἰκυῖα, / Καὶ φωνήν, καὶ τοῖα περὶ χροῒ εἵματα ἔστο.

35 Homer *Iliad* (see n1 below). Erasmus' title is an echo of Matt 13:13: *Audientes non audiunt*, though it is the phrase from Homer which he suggests may be used proverbially.
1 *Iliad* 23.429–30: Ὡς οὐκ ἀΐοντι ἐοικώς

36 Homer *Odyssey* (see n1 below)
1 *Odyssey* 1.411: Οὐ μὲν γάρ τι κακῷ εἰς ὦπα ἐῴκει; Erasmus has *improbus*

'This was the Apronius who, as he himself proclaims not only by the way he lives but in his person and face, was a monstrous chasm or abyss of every sort of vice and immorality.'[2]

37 Absit clamor in colloquio aut lusu
Against brawling in conversation or in games

If we want to recommend at a banquet or in a conversation that we should refrain from shouting, this from the same book will be fitting:

> Now let us dine merrily, and let there be no brawling.[1]

38 Grata novitas
Novelty finds favour

When you want to say that it is the newest things that please the common people most, it would be quite opportune to quote this from the same book:

> For the song that is most praised by far by the majority of men
> And most pleasing is the one that has come most recently to their ears.[1]

There is an ode on this by Pindar, number 9 of the *Olympian Odes*: 'Praise wine that is old, but praise also the flowers of songs that are new,'[2] meaning that songs celebrating recent achievements are more welcome than those that deal with ancient deeds. Novelty renders many things agreeable, especially to the inexperienced. On the other hand, in literature it is age that wins favour, and novelty attracts envy. This is why Flaccus says in his *Epistles*: 'I find it offensive that anything is blamed, not because it is thought / To

* * * * *

'scoundrel,' but κακός in the Greek certainly refers to rank, and corresponds more to 'menial.'
2 Cicero *Verrines* 2.3.9.23. According to the old numbering that Erasmus uses elsewhere, this was the fifth book; it is the eighth in Cratander's edition of 1528, used by Erasmus for the additions of *1533*. See *Adagia* III iv n7 (11 above).

37 Homer *Odyssey* (see n1 below)
1 *Odyssey* 1.369–70: Νῦν μὲν δαινύμενοι τερπώμεθα, μηδὲ βοητὺς / Ἔστω.

38 Homer *Odyssey* (see n1 below)
1 *Odyssey* 1.351–2: Τὴν γὰρ ἀοιδὴν μᾶλλον ἐπικλείουσ᾽ ἄνθρωποι, / Ἥ τις ἀκουόν-τεσσι νεωτάτη ἀμφιπέληται.
2 Pindar *Olympians* 9.48; added in *1533*

be a crude or dull composition, but because it is new.'[3] But in almost every other field the partiality for novelty makes people forget the attraction of older things. This is why David, bishop of Utrecht – a learned and wise man,[4] son of Philip duke of Burgundy, the great grandfather of the one who died recently[5] – when counselled by certain people to allow a bishop elect to be appointed alongside him, because of his advancing age, said that he was persuaded by the example of St Antony not to do this.[6] For the latter was disregarded as soon as the later saint Roche took over his functions.[7] Human nature manifests a similar boredom with what is familiar, and we marvel at the exotic even if we have better things at home. This happens most particularly with physicians: we become tired of our own, even if they are learned, and we revere a monster originating in some remote foreign place.[8] Likewise pharmacists buy up at a great price herbs that have been brought from great distances, even though better ones are to be found in a neighbouring garden. This was neatly illustrated by Alexis in Athenaeus book 3: 'We love a stranger and despise our kin.'[9]

39 Mulier pudica ne sola sit usquam
A modest woman should not be alone anywhere

When we want to warn that it is not suitable for a modest woman to be

* * * * *

3 Horace *Epistles* 2.1.76–7
4 David of Burgundy, illegitimate son of Philip the Good, ordained Erasmus on 25 April 1492. Allen Ep 603, note to line 11; CEBR 1.226–7. Philip of Burgundy, bishop of Utrecht, did eventually become his co-adjutor.
5 Philip the Handsome, Philip I of Castille, son of the emperor Maximilian and Maria of Burgundy, father of Charles V, died 1506; see Erasmus' *Panegyricus ad Philippum*, CWE 27; CEBR 1.229–30.
6 Antony of Padua died in 1231, and was beatified in 1232.
7 St Roche of Montpellier, died 1327, object of a popular cult as protector against the plague, though he was never officially canonized
8 An addition of *1528*; according to ASD possibly a reference to Paracelsus, though from the tone of Erasmus' letter, Ep 1808, and the fact that Paracelsus was born in Einsiedeln near Zurich, this seems unlikely. See CEBR 3.29–30 and W.A. Murray, 'Erasmus and Paracelsus' *Bibliothèque d'Humanisme et Renaissance* XX (1958) 560–4. Paracelsus arrived in Basle in 1526, and acted as physician to Johann Froben and Erasmus himself; he was appointed *Stadtphysicus* and professor, but refused to lecture on Hippocrates, Galen, and Avicenna. He fled in 1528, having no powerful protector.
9 Athenaeus 3.123F; Alexis PCG 2 fragment 145. 'Human nature' to the end is also an addition of *1528*.

39 Homer *Odyssey* (see n2 below)

talking to men alone and without witnesses, we could make use of this line about Penelope, which occurs often in Homer:[1] 'Not alone, but with two waiting-women in attendance.'[2]

40 Fatale vitae tempus exactum
His allotted span fulfilled

For the very old, whose time seems to be completed, this line from the same book will fit: 'Fools, for they devoured the oxen sacred to you, / Highest Apollo.'[1] For I think by the oxen of the sun the poet means the allotted span of years.[2]

41 Non luctu, sed remedio opus in malis
Misfortunes need healing not mourning

In misfortunes we should not indulge in lamentation but seek help. This can be illustrated by this line in the *Iliad* book 24, although it is repeated in other places:[1] 'For wretched weeping and lamentation do no good at all.'[2]

42 Adhuc aliquis deus respicit nos
Thus far some god has cared for us

When we wish to say, in particularly calamitous circumstances, that we have not entirely lost courage but that there is some hope, then there will be a place for this, which is spoken by Priam in the same book: 'Some friendly divinity hitherto has held out his hand to me.'[1]

* * * * *

1 It recurs only at *Odyssey* 18.207.
2 *Odyssey* 1.331: Οὐκ οἴη, ἄμα τῇ γε καὶ ἀμφίπολοι δύ᾽ ἕποντο.

40 Homer *Odyssey* (see n1 below)
  1 *Odyssey* 1.8–9: Νήπιοι, οἳ κατὰ βοῦς Ὑπερίονος Ἡελίοιο / Ἤσθιον.
  2 Following Eustathius 1717.33 on *Odyssey* 12.130 (= Aristotle fragment 175 Rose)

41 Homer *Iliad* (see n2 below)
  1 *Odyssey* 10.202 and 568, though with a different conclusion to the phrase
  2 *Iliad* 24.524: Οὐ γάρ τις πρῆξις πέλεται κρυεροῖο γόοιο.

42 Homer *Iliad* (see n1 below)
  1 *Iliad* 24.374: Ἀλλ᾽ ἔτι τις καὶ ἐμοῖο θεῶν ὑπερέσχεθε χεῖρα.

43 Mors optima rapit, deterrima relinquit
Death snatches away the best and leaves the worst

The best things are snatched away by death, the worst are left. Accordingly we see some good-for-nothing people live as long as Tithonus,[1] and very few who are endowed with unusual intelligence reach the threshold of old age. This idea is well expressed by the following from the same book:

> These have been slain by Mars, yet evil things are left,
> Shameful things are left, liars, mountebanks,
> Leaders of the dance, robbers of lambs
> And kids.[2]

This passage of Maro is famous: 'Life's fairest days are ever the first to flee / For hapless mortals; on creep diseases.'[3] Theocritus too sings the same theme in the *Epitaph of Bion*:

> So the Nymphs have ordained; the wretched frog sings his song for ever;
> But I am not envious of him for he does not make good music.[4]

44 Domi manendum
Better stay at home

A warning that it is fruitless to be absent a long while from home and to leave one's property. This idea is aptly expressed by this from the *Odyssey* book 3: 'You too, my friend, beware of staying long away from home, / Leaving wealth and men under your roof.'[1] Hesiod says the same: 'It is better

* * * * *

43 Homer *Iliad* (see n2 below)
 1 Partner of Eos, goddess of the day, who won immortality for him from Jupiter but forgot to ask also for perpetual youth
 2 *Iliad* 24.260–2: Τοὺς μὲν ἀπώλεσ᾽ Ἄρης, τὰ δ᾽ ἐλέγχεα πάντα λέλειπται, / Ψεῦσταί τ᾽ ὀρχησταί τε χοροιτυπίῃσιν ἄριστοι, / Ἀρνῶν ἠδ᾽ ἐρίφων ἐπιδήμιοι ἁρπακτῆρες.
 3 Virgil *Georgics* 3.66–7, translation by H. Rushton Fairclough (Loeb); added in 1526
 4 Ie Moschus *Lament for Bion* 3.106–7; added in 1526

44 Homer *Odyssey* (see n1 below); cf *Adagia* III i 13 He who is well off should stay at home, and IV ii 66 A poor man on dry land (535 below).
 1 *Odyssey* 3.313–14: Καὶ σύ, φίλος, μὴ δηθὰ δόμων ἄπο τῆλ᾽ ἀλάλησο, / Κτήματά τε προλιπὼν ἄνδρας δ᾽ ἐν σοῖσι δόμοισι.

to be at home, for ruin lies abroad.'² And this verse of Euripides is recorded:

> Blest is he who remains in prosperity at home,
> For a cargo that is kept on land
> Can be sent to sea again.³

45 A sacris abstinendae manus
Do not lay hands on sacred things

It is a popular belief that misfortune threatens the man who has laid hands on objects that are sacred or dedicated to a god, or who has fought against pious men or those who exercise sacred offices, such as the Roman pontiff, bishops, abbots, even if they were not of pious habits. Something very like this was said long ago by Homer in book 17 of the *Iliad*:

> When someone seeks to contend against both a god and a man
> Whom the god favours, disaster threatens him very shortly.¹

46 Turpis iactantia
Boasting is ignoble

It is not the act of a noble soul to boast about what one has achieved either by courage or by good fortune. On this subject there is a remark of Menelaus in the same book: 'It does not look well to boast proudly of oneself.'¹

47 Prior occupat
He who acts first wins

When someone seizes an advantage by being quicker than someone else,

* * * * *

2 Hesiod *Works and Days* 365
3 Euripides fragment 793 Nauck, found in Stobaeus *Eclogae* 4.17.18 Hense IV 404

45 Homer *Iliad* (see n1 below)
1 *Iliad* 17.98–9: Ὁππότ᾽ ἀνὴρ ἐθέλει πρὸς δαίμονα φωτὶ μάχεσθαι, / Ὅν τε θεὸς τιμᾷ, τάχα οἱ μέγα πῆμα κυλίσθη.

46 Homer *Iliad* (see n1 below)
1 *Iliad* 17.19: Οὐ μὲν καλὸν ὑπέρβιον εὐχετάασθαι.

47 Homer *Iliad* (see n1 below)

this line from book 22 of the *Iliad* will be pertinent:

> Lest someone, by throwing a spear, should snatch the glory and the
>   honour,
> And he himself come too late in second place.[1]

This is said of Achilles, who signals to the rest of the Achaeans that no one should cast a spear at Hector, so that he should have all the glory to himself.

48 Sacra celerius absolvenda
Perform sacred rites promptly

It is desirable to give more thought rather than more time to church services so that they are not cheapened by being too long, contrary to the habit of certain priests who spend too much time on the rites and prayers called 'hours.' The point could be illustrated by this from book 3 of the *Odyssey*: 'Nor is it right / To sit too long at the feast of the gods, / But we should rise promptly.'[1]

49 Ne dii quidem a morte liberant
Not even the gods free us from death

No one is so dear to the gods that he may evade death by their favour. This idea can be supported by the testimony of Homer from the same book:

> But death, the common lot of all,
> The gods cannot ward off from a man they love
> When the dreadful day of bitter destiny is finally upon him.[1]

* * * * *

1 *Iliad* 22.207: Μή τις κῦδος ἄροιτο βαλών, ὁ δὲ δεύτερος ἔλθοι.

48 Homer *Odyssey* (see n1 below)
1 *Odyssey* 3.335–6: Οὐδὲ ἔοικε / Δηθὰ θεῶν ἐν δαιτὶ θαασσέμεν, ἀλλὰ νέεσθαι.

49 Homer *Odyssey* (see n1 below)
1 *Odyssey* 3.236–8: Ἀλλ᾿ ἦ τοι θάνατον μὲν ὁμοίϊον οὐδὲ θεοί περ / Καὶ φίλῳ ἀνδρὶ δύνανται ἀλαλκέμεν, ὁππότε κεν δὴ / Μοῖρ᾿ ὀλοὴ καθέλῃσι τανηλεγέος θανάτοιο.

50 Deus undecunque iuvat, si modo propitius
God's help is everywhere, if only he is so inclined

God is everywhere present if he so chooses, nor does it matter where in the world you may live if he protects you. The idea can be expressed by adapting this from the same book:

If they will, from far away too the gods can keep one safe.[1]

51 De lautitiis
On sumptuous displays

For sumptuous foods this line from book 3 of the *Odyssey* will be suitable: 'Delicacies such as purple-clad kings eat.'[1] It will be more pleasing if it is used metaphorically of speech that is excessively ornate, as if it were worthy of the ears of the gods.[2]

52 Concordia
Harmony

For complete harmony and agreement on all points, this couplet from the same book will be apt:

Our assembly and our council never heard us
Battle in words, but saw us always of the same mind,
Having the same ideas and coming to the same conclusions.[1]

This is Nestor speaking about himself and Ulysses.

* * * * *

50 Homer *Odyssey* (see n1 below)
1 *Odyssey* 3.231: Ῥεῖα θεός κ᾽ ἐθέλων καὶ τηλόθεν ἄνδρα σαῶσαι.

51 Homer *Odyssey* (see n2 below)
1 *Odyssey* 3.480: Ὄψα τε, οἷα ἔδουσι διοτρεφέες βασιλῆες. The Greek διοτρεφής means 'cherished by Jove'; Erasmus' word is *purpurei* 'purple-clad.'
2 The last sentence was added in 1515.

52 Homer *Odyssey* (see n1 below)
1 *Odyssey* 3.127–8: Οὐδέποτ᾽ εἰν ἀγορῇ, δίχ᾽ ἐβάζομεν οὔτ᾽ ἐνὶ βουλῇ, / Ἀλλ᾽ ἕνα θυμὸν ἔχοντε νόῳ καὶ ἐπίφρονι βουλῇ.

53 Fatum immutabile
Destiny cannot be changed

Divine decrees cannot be changed, human laws vary over time, as do customs and ambitions. This idea is suitably expressed by this from the same
book: 'For the mind of the star-dwelling[1] gods is not changed.'[2]

54 Sine ope divina nihil valemus
Without divine help we avail nothing

All human effort and undertakings are lame unless God breathes favourably
on them. The idea may be expressed in this Homeric phrase from the same
book:

> Every mortal has need of divine help.[1]

55 Industriam adiuvat deus
God helps those who work hard

When we enter on an undertaking, we can foresee some things by use of
human reason; other elements are provided by the disposition of chance and
the situation itself. The idea is found in several places[1] in Homer including
the book I have just quoted: 'Part of this you will work out for yourself
with your native wit, / Part some god will provide for you.'[2]

* * * * *

53 Homer *Odyssey* (see n2 below); cf *Adagia* III ix 86 Destiny is unavoidable (351
below), which uses *Odyssey* 5.103–4, and III x 7 Fate is inevitable (360 below),
based on *Odyssey* 7.196–8.
1 Erasmus' word *astricola* has no classical authority. It may be modelled on
agricola and mean 'star-herding, or, as J.N. Grant has suggested, 'inhabiting
the stars,' which would be closer to the Greek 'everlasting.'
2 *Odyssey* 3.147: Οὐ γάρ τ᾽ αἶψα θεῶν τρέπεται νόος αἰὲν ἐόντων.

54 Homer *Odyssey* (see n1 below)
1 *Odyssey* 3.48: Πάντες δὲ θεῶν χατέουσ᾽ ἄνθρωποι.

55 Homer *Odyssey* (see n2 below)
1 ASD suggests in addition only the rather remote description of Achilles by
Diomedes in *Iliad* 9.702–3.
2 *Odyssey* 3.26–7: Τηλέμαχ᾽, ἄλλα μὲν αὐτὸς ἐνὶ φρεσὶ σῇσι νοήσεις, / Ἄλλα δὲ καὶ
δαίμον ὑποθήσεται.

56 Faustus exitus
A lucky outcome

When we want to express the idea that something we have begun is going to turn out well and has some divine favour, this line from book 2 of the *Odyssey* will suit: 'Have faith, nurse, this plan is not without a god's inspiration.'[1]

57 Aetate prudentiores reddimur
Age makes us wiser

If we want to say that now we are older we no longer approve the things we enjoyed before in our youthful ignorance, but have grown wiser with experience, then this passage from the same book will fit:

> I was till now a boy, but now I have come of age;
> I have gained knowledge by converse with others
> And my own mind has grown.[1]

– the words of Telemachus to the suitors.

58 Ociosus esto
Relax!

If we want to recommend to someone to stop worrying, to go and just look after their dainty skin,[1] and leave others to take care of affairs, we can adapt this from the same book:

> Take care;
> You will torture yourself with thoughts of what to say or do;

* * * * *

56 Homer *Odyssey* (see n1 below)
1 *Odyssey* 2.372: Θάρσει, μαῖ᾽, ἐπεὶ οὔ τι ἄνευ θεοῦ ἥδε γε βουλή.

57 Homer *Odyssey* (see n1 below)
1 *Odyssey* 2.313–15: Ἐγὼ δ᾽ ἔτι νήπιος ἦα. / Νῦν δ᾽ ὅτε δὴ μέγας εἰμί, καὶ ἄλλων μῦθον ἀκούων / Πυνθάνομαι, καὶ δή μοι ἀέξεται ἔνδοθι θυμός.

58 Homer *Odyssey* (see n2 below)
1 Latin *curare cuticulam*; cf *Adagia* II iv 75 To cultivate one's dainty skin. Otto 494

Come rather, eat and drink in peace as you did before.[2]

59 Haud perficiet
He will never finish

If you want to say that some business begun by someone else cannot in any way be completed, you could say it in Homer's words:

> But this journey he will never accomplish.[1]

60 Cedendum multitudini
Yield to numbers

If you want to persuade someone that one person cannot fight against many, and that one should always give in to a multitude, you can bring in this from the same book: 'He will at once bring on himself a harsh fate, / If he seeks to fight against a great number.'[1] The same suitors just before: 'It is a hard thing to fight alone over a banquet / With men that outnumber you.'[2]

61 Vanae coniecturae
Empty guesses

Against those who are in the habit of giving predictions about the outcome of an undertaking, there is this from the same book:

> But a great multitude of birds whirl around in the air,
> And not every one is apt for predicting destiny.[1]

* * * * *

2 *Odyssey* 2.303–5: Μήτε τοι ἄλλο / Ἐν στήθεσσι κακὸν μελέτω ἔργον τε ἔπος τε, / Ἀλλὰ μάλ᾽ ἐσθιέμεν καὶ πινέμεν ὡς τὸ πάρος περ.

59 Homer *Odyssey* (see n1 below)
1 *Odyssey* 2.256: Τελέει δ᾽ ὁδὸν οὔποτε ταύτην.

60 Homer *Odyssey* (see n1 below)
1 *Odyssey* 2.250–1: Ἀλλά κεν αὐτοῦ ἀεικέα πότμον ἐπίσποι, / Εἰ πλεόνεσσι μάχοιτο.
2 *Odyssey* 2.244–5

61 Homer *Odyssey* (see n1 below)
1 *Odyssey* 2.181–2: Ὄρνιθες δέ τε πολλοὶ ὑπ᾽ αὐγὰς ἠελίοιο / Φοιτῶσ᾽, οὐδέ τε πάντες ἐναίσιμοι.

62 **Certum prospicio**
I foresee it for certain

If we want to say we are not making a rash prediction about the good or
bad outcome of anything, but that we have adduced sound arguments and
made observations in several trials, we can adapt this from the same book:

> For I am not unskilled in prophecy, but
> Particularly well experienced.[1]

63 **Deus ulciscetur**
God will punish

When we want to say that at the moment we do not have the power to deter
someone, but hope the gods will punish eventually, it is a moment to use
this from the same book:

> But for my part I shall beg the immortal gods
> That Jupiter himself may eventually provide requital.[1]

64 **In tempore cavenda poena mali**
Beware in good time of the penalty for wrongdoing

Whenever we want to warn someone that he will encounter misfortune long
before he might crush us, or that he should desist from sin before divine
vengeance falls on him, we will find this from the same book useful:

> But long before that let us seek to set a limit
> And an end.[1]

These are the words of the seer threatening the suitors with the return of
Ulysses.

* * * * *

62 Homer *Odyssey* (see n1 below)
1 *Odyssey* 2.170: Οὐ γὰρ ἀπείρητος μαντεύσομαι, ἀλλὰ εὖ εἰδώς.

63 Homer *Odyssey* (see n1 below)
1 *Odyssey* 2.143–4: Ἐγὼ δὲ θεοὺς ἐπιβώσομαι αἰὲν ἐόντας, / Αἴ κέ ποθι Ζεὺς δῷσι παλίντιτα ἔργα γενέσθαι.

64 Homer *Odyssey* (see n1 below)
1 *Odyssey* 2.167–8: Ἀλλὰ πολὺ πρὶν / Φραζώμεσθ᾽ ὥς κεν καταπαύσομεν.

65 Domesticum malum
Private misfortune

To signify a private or family misfortune which does not concern other people, we might aptly use this from the same book: 'Moreover a misfortune that befalls in my house, / Concerns me alone.'[1] Marcus Tullius in the fifth speech against Verres, calls a crime that is committed in the home and that does not become common knowledge a 'domestic or household crime.'[2]

66 Senum prudentia
Wisdom of the aged

For an old man who is experienced in the handling of most situations and who remembers many of the deeds of past years a suitable quotation would be this from the same book:

> Who is wise in many and ancient ways.[1]

67 Premenda occasio
Seize the opportunity

If you want to say that every means should be used to press forward and an opportunity once offered should not be allowed to slip through our hands, a suitable phrase will be this from book 4 of the *Odyssey*: 'Hold your captive fast and tie him all the tighter.'[1] This could also be used when we want to say that our natural impulses must be all the more constrained by the guidance

* * * * *

65 Homer *Odyssey* (see n1 below)
1 *Odyssey* 2.45: Ἀλλ' ἐμὸν αὐτοῦ χρεῖος, ὅ μοι κακὸν ἔμπεσεν οἴκῳ.
2 Cicero *Verrines* 2.3.61.141, although this is the speech that Erasmus called the eighth above (see *Adagia* III ix 36 n2, 332 above); added in *1533*

66 Homer *Odyssey* (see n1 below); cf *Adagia* III x 74 (382 below) for another quotation with the same title.
1 *Odyssey* 2.188: Παλαιά τε πολλά τε εἰδώς

67 Homer *Odyssey* (see n1 below). The title is a phrase quoted in *Adagia* I vii 70 Consider the due time (CWE 32 109 and 323 n8). The last sentence suggests a quite different idea of restraint, and is clearly a second independent interpretation of the quotation, not a second application of the injunction in the title, which confirms that Erasmus' proverbial expression, his adage, is the Homeric phrase, not the precept with which he has headed it. The whole item is of *1508*.
1 *Odyssey* 4.419: Ὑμεῖς δ' ἀστεμφέως ἐχέμεν μᾶλλόν τε πιέζειν.

of reason the more they boil up and entice us towards wrong-doing.

68 Omnibus nervis
With every nerve

When we want to indicate that we should put out all our strength in some undertaking, straining every nerve, the following from the same passage will be appropriate: 'Then make use of your strength and courage.'[1] Pindar uses a similar figure in the tenth Olympian ode: 'Who in the end has attained the desired crown with hands and feet and chariots?'[2] This passage should have been added to the adage 'With hands and feet,' but those pages were already out of my hands.[3] Marcus Tullius in the fifth speech *Against Verres*: 'Listen carefully, members of the jury, for I have to insist with all my strength.'[4]

69 Cum principe non pugnandum
Do not dispute with a ruler

If we want to say that it is hard for a private person to overcome a ruler or very difficult to defeat nature, we could use this from the same book: 'It is hard for a mortal man to defeat a god.'[1]

70 Ingens discrimen
An enormous difference

An enormous gap – for example if one believes there is a great difference between the pursuit of money and wisdom – could be indicated by this couplet from the same book:

* * * * *

68 Homer *Odyssey* (see n1 below). The title is also that of *Adagia* I iv 16. Otto *Nachträge* page 255
1 *Odyssey* 4.415: Καὶ τότ᾽ ἔπειθ᾽ ὑμῖν μελέτω κάρτος τε βίη τε.
2 Pindar *Olympians* 10.60–1. This and everything that follows were added in 1533.
3 *Adagia* I iv 15
4 Cicero *Verrines* 2.3.56.130. Again this is the speech that Erasmus called the eighth in *Adagia* III ix 36 n2 (see 332 above).

69 Homer *Odyssey* (see n1 below)
1 *Odyssey* 4.397: Ἀργαλέος γάρ τ᾽ ἐστὶ θεὸς βροτῷ ἀνδρὶ δαμῆναι.

70 Homer *Odyssey* (see n1 below); *Adagia* III viii 81 (311 above) has the same title.

It was as far as a well-steered ship may cover
In a day's run when driven by a following wind.[1]

71 Aperte simpliciterque loqui
Speaking literally and simply

We can indicate that we are going to speak simply, literally, and directly
with this verse, which is in the same book: 'I shall not mislead and cheat
you with contrived deceits.'[1]

72 Rerum omnium vicissitudo
All things do change

The shifts of fortune are ever changing, and to each man comes now happiness, now sadness. To this idea we can apply, from the same book: 'Now
to this one, now to that, / Jupiter sends now joy, now grief.'[1]

73 Festivus sermo
Lively conversation

When someone at a banquet starts some amusing and witty conversation that dispels any gloom, then there is a place for this passage from
the same book where Homer pictures Helen putting in the banqueters'
cups a drug that induces forgetfulness of everything they had done
before:

* * * * *

1 *Odyssey* 4.356–7: Τόσσον ἄνευθ', ὅσσον τε πανημερίη γλαφυρὴ νηῦς / Ἤνυσεν, ᾗ
λιγὺς οὖρος ἐπιπνείησεν ὄπισθεν.

71 Homer *Odyssey* (see n1 below)
1 *Odyssey* 4.347–8: Οὐκ ἂν ἔγωγε / Ἄλλα παρὲξ εἴποιμι παρακλιδὸν οὐδ' ἀπα-
τήσω.

72 Homer *Odyssey* (see n1 below); this adage has virtually the same title, based
on a phrase from Terence's *Eunuchus* 276 (Otto 1292), as *Adagia* I vii 63; cf also
I vii 64 Variety's the spice of life.
1 *Odyssey* 4.236–7: Ἀτὰρ θεὸς ἄλλοτ' ἐπ' ἄλλῳ / Ζεὺς ἀγαθόν τε κακόν τε δι-
δοῖ.

73 Homer *Odyssey* (see n1 below); Erasmus makes use of the adage at the beginning of the *Praise of Folly*, CWE 27.

Straightway into the wine they drank she put a drug,
Forgetfulness of all grief, all anger, all wrongs.[1]

This is recalled by Pliny in book 25. He talks of 'that noble drug that brings indulgence and forgetfulness of grief, and is to be administered especially by Helen to all mortals.'[2] Dioscorides, in book 4, mentions the herb ἄλυπον, which when taken below is good for black bile.[3] This is where the name comes from, it seems, for it means 'having no pain,'[4] just like νηπενθής 'soothing' and ἄδιψον 'without thirst,'[5] because they dispel grief and thirst.

74 Qui nocere potest et idem prodesse
One who can both harm and benefit

For inexperienced physicians, who often give a poison instead of a cure, a suitable adage from the same book is this, which Lucian used in his *False Prophet*[1] and which is to be found in several places in Homer: 'Mixed drugs, many health-giving, but many harmful.'[2] The same would suit a man proficient in good and bad skills who can either give pleasure if he wishes or do harm.

75 Asseverantius dicere
Speaking out firmly

When we are about to speak rather boldly and firmly, because it seems to us necessary, we can quote from the same book this line which Helen applies to Telemachus: 'Shall I lie or speak the truth? But my heart / Bids

* * * * *

1 *Odyssey* 4.220–1: Αὐτίκ' ἄρ' εἰς οἶνον βάλε φάρμακον, ἔνθεν ἔπινον, / Νηπενθές τ' ἄχολόν τε, κακῶν ἐπίληθον ἁπάντων.
2 Pliny *Naturalis historia* 25.12; added in 1526
3 Dioscorides *De materia medica* 4.178; added in 1526
4 Latin *dolore carens*, translating ἄλυπος
5 Dioscorides *De materia medica* 3.5. Erasmus might have included here ἄχολον from the *Odyssey* passage above, which I have rendered as 'forgetfulness of ... anger.' Black bile is *atra bilis* or *melancholia*.

74 Homer *Odyssey* (see n2 below)
1 Lucian *Alexander* 5
2 *Odyssey* 4.230: Φάρμακα, πολλὰ μὲν ἐσθλὰ μεμιγμένα, πολλὰ δὲ λυγρά; not found elsewhere

75 Homer *Odyssey* (see n1 below)

me to speak.'[1] The same line is to be found in book 10 of the *Iliad*.[2]

76 Arripienda quae offeruntur
Seize what is offered

A standard verse, repeated in many places, is this: 'Each laid ready hands on anything useful[1] which was set before him.'[2] This could be taken to apply to guardians who find something belonging to their wards, take it, share it among themselves, and claim it as their own. Or to similar types of people who attack and carry off the property of others.

77 Principum favor necessarius
Support from influential people is essential

When someone tries, against the wishes of influential people, to disentangle himself from some difficult situation or dispute, from which he cannot escape without their help and support, there will be a place for these words from the same book. They refer to Ajax, son of Oïleus: 'He boasted he would escape from the deep waves / Of the great gulf in spite of the will of the gods.'[1]

78 Negocium non aptum
An unsuitable undertaking

If someone refuses an office or a responsibility which is not suitable for him

* * * * *

1 *Odyssey* 4.140: Ψεύσομαι ἢ ἔτυμον ἐρέω, κέλεται δέ με θυμός.
2 *Iliad* 10.534

76 Homer *Odyssey* (see n2 below)
 1 The Greek ὄνειαρ means first 'anything helpful, advantageous,' and second 'refreshment, food.' The line is usually translated simply with something like 'they helped themselves to the good things spread before them,' as the context requires. Erasmus' rendering, *si quid foret utile*, seems to be designed to drag the sense towards the pejorative applications he envisages.
 2 *Odyssey* 4.67 and 218: Οἱ δ' ἐπ' ὀνείαθ' ἑτοῖμα προκείμενα χεῖρας ἴαλλον. Also *Odyssey* 1.149, 5.200, 8.71; *Iliad* 9.91 and 221, 24.627

77 Homer *Odyssey* (see n1 below)
 1 *Odyssey* 4.504: Φῆ ῥ' ἀέκητι θεῶν φυγέειν μέγα λαῖτμα θαλάσσης.

78 Homer *Odyssey* (see n1 below)

or says that he does not wish to appoint to some responsibility anyone who does not seem fit to carry it out, he could use this from the same book: 'But horses I shall not take to Ithaca.'[1] These are the words of Telemachus when he refuses the horses offered as a gift by Menelaus because the island of Ithaca is not suitable for feeding horses, being stony and ill-suited to pasturage.

79 Obtestatio veterum meritorum
Invoking past deserts

When we want to make an entreaty by recalling our past services, it will be apt to quote this from the same book (it is also found elsewhere in this poet's work): 'If I have burned[1] fat limbs of ox or sheep for you, / Remember them now.'[2] These are the words of Penelope begging the goddess to remember the sacrifices and the savour on which she had often fed and to come now to her aid in return.

80 Conviva non conviva
Invited but not to take part

To someone who sits down at a feast, but only to be a spectator of what is offered – for this is how some mean nobles treat their guests[1] – one could apply what is said in the same book about Penelope: 'Fasting, he[2] sat tasting neither food / Nor drink.'[3]

* * * * *

1 *Odyssey* 4.601: Ἵππους δ᾽ εἰς Ἰθάκην οὐκ ἄξομαι.

79 Homer *Odyssey* (see n2 below)
1 Latin *incendi*, though Penelope says 'If ever Odysseus burned ...' From *1508* to *1517/18* the Greek also had a first person verb, ἔκηα, but after *1520* the third person ἔκηε appeared; this was probably not intended by Erasmus since he did not change his Latin, and the slightly adapted version serves his stated purpose better.
2 *Odyssey* 4.764–5: Ἦ βοὸς ἦ ὄϊος κατὰ πίονα μηρί᾽ ἔκηα, / Τῶν νῦν μοι μνῆσαι. *Iliad* 15.373 is similar.

80 Homer *Odyssey* (see n3 below)
1 Borrowed from Lucian *De mercede conductis* 26.
2 The Greek adjectives have a common masculine and feminine ending; Erasmus translates with the masculine *Incoenatus et impastus ...*, clearly thinking of his own subject rather than of Penelope.
3 *Odyssey* 4.788: Κεῖτ᾽ ἄρ᾽ ἄσιτος, ἄπαστος ἐδητύος ἠδὲ ποτῆτος.

81 Undecunque lucrum captant
No matter where from, it's profit they're after

For lawyers, informers, bad doctors, who hunt everywhere for someone to 'fall into the net,'[1] someone they can plunder, a suitable quotation is this, which is in the same book:

> All the time, on every accessible coast of the island, they hunted about
> For fish to hook, for grim hunger pinched their stomachs.[2]

82 Ingratitudo vulgi
Public ingratitude

If someone wants to declare that he is troubled by ingratitude because he feels that no regard is given to the services of high officials, he might quite aptly use this from book 5 of the *Odyssey* (the same lines are to be found in other places):

> Henceforth let no sceptre-bearing king be gentle and kind
> Nor mild nor firm in justice, but let him be
> Always harsh and always work unrighteousness.[1]

83 Munerum corruptela
Bribery with gifts

For someone who approaches a business with money and gifts, you might quite humorously adapt from the same book what is said of Mercury as he takes up his caduceus: 'He seized the staff with which he lulls to sleep the

* * * * *

81 Homer *Odyssey* (see n2 below)
  1 Cf Ovid *Ars amatoria* 2.2.
  2 *Odyssey* 4.368–9: Αἰεὶ γὰρ περὶ νῆσον ἀλώμενοι ἰχθυάασκον / Γναμπτοῖς ἀγκί-
    στροισι, ἔτειρε δὲ γαστέρα λιμός.

82 Homer *Odyssey* (see n1 below)
  1 *Odyssey* 5.8–10: Μή τις ἔτι πρόφρων ἀγανὸς καὶ ἤπιος ἔστω / Σκηπτοῦχος βασιλεύς,
    μηδὲ φρεσὶν αἴσιμα εἰδώς, / Ἀλλ᾽ αἰεὶ χαλεπός τ᾽ εἴη καὶ αἴσυλα ῥέζοι; also *Odyssey*
    2.230–2

83 Homer *Odyssey* (see n1 below)

eyes / Of whom he will, and awakens others too.'[1] What is said of Mercury's staff is admirably appropriate for the gifts with which, for example, judges who were dozing before are woken up, and on the other hand the hostile ones are placated so that during the case they go to sleep, as it were, and close their eyes. Aristophanes, in the *Women in Parliament* says the gods too are won over by gifts and that is why they stand with a hand out palm up:

> For when we pray to them to send us good things,
> They stand holding out a hand palm up,
> As if they will give nothing, but rather will accept.[2]

The scholiast informs us that in olden times the statues of the gods were almost always carved with hands held out 'supine,'[3] and by 'supine' he means 'cupped,' 'positioned so as to receive.'

84 Principes inter se noti
Rulers know each other

If we want to say that rulers or scholars communicate among themselves even if they live in different and widely separated countries, we could use this from the same book:

> The immortal gods are not unknown to each other,
> Though they dwell far apart in different abodes.[1]

This could also be turned to apply to those worldly princes[2] who, even if they are visibly at war and clashing in universal turmoil, still conspire secretly among themselves, and this they do for the sole purpose that each may impoverish his own people and, diminishing public authority, reinforce their own tyranny.

* * * * *

1 *Odyssey* 5.47–8: Εἵλετο δὲ ῥάβδον, τῇ τ᾿ ἀνδρῶν ὄμματα θέλγει, / ῾Ων ἐθέλει, τοὺς δ᾿ αὖτε καὶ ὑπώοντας ἐγείρει.
2 Aristophanes *Ecclesiazusae* 781–3; added in 1533
3 Scholiast of Aristophanes (Dübner page 320)

84 Homer *Odyssey* (see n1 below)
1 *Odyssey* 5.79–80: Οὐ γάρ τ᾿ ἀγνῶτες θεοὶ ἀλλήλοισι πέλονται / ᾿Αθάνατοι, οὐδ᾿ εἴ τις ἀπόπροθι δώματα ναίει.
2 Latin *satrapae*; cf *Adagia* III iii 1 The Sileni of Alcibiades (CWE 34 28 and 270–1) and III vii 1 A dung-beetle hunting an eagle (195 with n104 above). This paragraph was added in 1515.

85 **Periculum ne temere subeas**
Do not take a rash risk

No one undertakes a long voyage for pleasure but when impelled by some
serious need, and no one enters heedlessly on a long and serious piece of
work. This idea is suitably expressed by this from the same book: 'Who
would rush of his own accord over such an expanse of sea?'[1]

86 **Fatum inevitabile**
Destiny is unavoidable

What is decreed by fate no one can avoid. The idea can be suitably expressed
by this from the same book: 'But it is not lawful for any one of the gods /
To evade or subvert by any means the will of Jupiter.'[1]

87 **Fatis adactus**
Driven by fate

For someone who falls into some way of life, not of his own will but as if
circumstances and the fates drove him, this line from the same book will
be suitable: 'But this man was driven hither, born by the winds and the
waves.'[1]

88 **Male coniugati**
Unhappily married

For a man who is bound in marriage to a woman whose deep love he cannot return, though she is loved for the pleasure a wife gives, the following

* * * * *

85 Homer *Odyssey* (see n1 below)
 1 *Odyssey* 5.100: Τίς δ' ἂν ἑκὼν τοσσόνδε διαδράμοι ἁλμυρὸν ὕδωρ;

86 Homer *Odyssey* (see n1 below); cf *Adagia* III ix 53 Destiny cannot be changed
 (339 above), based on *Odyssey* 4.147, and III x 7 Unavoidable fate (360 below),
 which uses *Odyssey* 7.196–8.
 1 *Odyssey* 5.103–4: Ἀλλὰ μάλ' οὔπως ἐστὶ Διὸς νόον αἰγιόχοιο / Οὔτε παρεξελθεῖν
 ἄλλον θεὸν οὐδ' ἁλιῶσαι.

87 Homer *Odyssey* (see n1 below)
 1 *Odyssey* 5.134: Τὸν δ' ἄρα δεῦρ' ἄνεμός τε φέρων καὶ κῦμα πέλασσε.

88 Homer *Odyssey* (see n1 below)

lines from the same book can be quite humorously applied:

> But unwilling and perforce he lay beside her at night,
> Unwilling beside the willing nymph in the dark cave.
> All through the day however he sat on the rocks and the shore,
> Torturing his soul with tears, cares and groans.[1]

89 Si deus voluerit
God willing

Said of some future matter whose outcome depends on the favour of a god;
for even among ordinary people they say for good luck 'God willing,' and
the apostle James teaches us to use the expression.[1] In joking conversation
among scholars, it can be expressed in a Homeric verse: 'If it is the will of
the gods whom Olympus holds.'[2]

90 Suadeo, quod ipse facturus essem
I am advising what I myself would do

When we give someone else advice which we would not be unwilling to
follow ourselves in a similar case, Calypso's words from the same book
will be fitting: 'I have in mind and will give you advice that I would not
hesitate / To follow myself, if a similar circumstance befell me.'[1]

91 Malorum assuetudo
Familiarity with misfortune

Someone who has become familiar with misfortunes and born a great number bears more easily any other ill that occurs. This idea is suitably expressed

* * * * *

1 *Odyssey* 5.154–7: Ἀλλ᾽ ἦ τοι νύκτας μὲν ἰαύεσκεν μὲν ἀνάγκῃ / Ἐν σπέσσι γλα-
φυροῖσι παρ᾽ οὐκ ἐθέλων ἐθελούσῃ, / Ἤματα δ᾽ ἐν πέτρῃσι καὶ ἠϊόνεσσι καθίζων /
Δάκρυσί τε στοναχῇ τε καὶ ἄλγεσι θυμὸν ἐρέχθων.

89 Homer *Odyssey* (see n2 below)
1 James 4:15
2 *Odyssey* 5.169: Αἴ κε θεοί γ᾽ ἐθέλωσι, τοὶ οὐρανὸν εὐρὺν ἔχουσιν

90 Homer *Odyssey* (see n1 below)
1 *Odyssey* 5.188–9: Ἀλλὰ τὰ μὲν νοέω καὶ φράσσομαι, ὅσσ᾽ ἂν ἐμοί περ / Αὐτῇ μη-
δοίμην, ὅτε με χρειὼ τόσον ἵκοι.

91 Homer *Odyssey* (see n1 below)

in the same book by what Ulysses says: 'I have already born many ills and
many labours / Amidst the waves and in wars; let this too be added to those.'[1]

92 Fortuna reddit insolentes
Good luck makes people arrogant

Someone whom fortune has looked on favourably and who then puts on
airs and behaves rather too confidently will be aptly described with this
from the same book: 'Gladly he spread his sails to the favourable winds.'[1]

93 Moderator negocii
An arbitrator

The line that follows immediately after this will be appropriate for one who
arbitrates in some affair with wisdom and authority: 'He steered the craft
with the oar skilfully and wisely.'[1]

94 Tacite stomachari
Silent vexation

For someone who is angry within himself a suitable phrase is this from
the same book: 'His heart becomes more and more inflamed with anger.'[1]
It refers to Neptune who is angry that Ulysses was having a prosperous
voyage.

95 Qui conturbat omnia
He causes havoc everywhere

For one who creates enormous, widespread commotion, we can aptly

* * * * *

1 *Odyssey* 5.223–4: Ἤδη γὰρ μάλα πόλλ᾽ ἔπαθον καὶ πολλὰ μόγησα / Κύμασι καὶ
πολέμῳ, μετὰ καὶ τόδε τοῖσι γενέσθω.

92 Homer *Odyssey* (see n1 below)
1 *Odyssey* 5.269: Γηθόσυνος δ᾽ οὔρῳ πέτασ᾽ ἱστία δῖος Ὀδυσσεύς.

93 Homer *Odyssey* (see n1 below)
1 *Odyssey* 5.270: Αὐτὰρ ὁ πηδαλίῳ ἰθύνετο τεχνηέντως.

94 Homer *Odyssey* (see n1 below)
1 *Odyssey* 5.284: Ὁ δ᾽ ἐχώσατο κηρόθι μᾶλλον.

95 Homer *Odyssey* (see n1 below)

borrow this from the same book: 'Every sort of storm of every sort of wind / He roused.'[1]

96 Non abiicit animum
Not losing heart

Concerning someone who does not give up hope or resolution even in the most wretched circumstances – as Latinus did, in Virgil, when he 'resigned the reins of government'[1] – but who thinks of how to recover by any means whatever, we might aptly say what is said in this passage about Ulysses:

> But not even in this distress did he forget
> His raft.[2]

97 Malis mala succedunt
One misfortune after another

For someone who is wearied by multiple misfortunes, first sickness, then robberies, then other ills and more again, this from the same book will be apt:

> Sometimes the south wind would fling it to the north to carry along,
> Now again the east wind passed it to the west to toss about.[1]

In one of his epigrams Ausonius used the elegant expression *catenatos labores* 'chains of toils,'[2] because every affair is linked to another. The opposite of this is what Pindar says in the eighth Olympian ode where he wishes that Jupiter 'will heap blessings on blessings for him.'[3]

* * * * *

1 *Odyssey* 5.292–3: Πάσας δ' ὀρόθυνεν ἀέλλας / Παντοίων ἀνέμων.

96 Homer *Odyssey* (see n2 below)
1 Virgil *Aeneid* 7.600
2 *Odyssey* 5.324: Ἀλλ' οὐδ' ὡς σχεδίης ἐπελήθετο τειρόμενός περ.

97 Homer *Odyssey* (see n1 below)
1 *Odyssey* 5.331–2: Ἄλλοτε μέν τε νότος βορέῃ προβάλεσκε φέρεσθαι, / Ἄλλοτε δ' αὖτ' εὖρος ζεφύρῳ εἴξασκε διώκειν.
2 Ausonius *Eclogae* 7.2.14 Peiper (Loeb). Ausonius borrowed the phrase from Martial *Epigrams* 1.15.7; cf *Adagia* II x 27 A throng of misfortunes CWE 34 363 n3; added in *1533*.
3 Pindar *Olympians* 8.84–5; added in *1533*

98 Hospitis habenda cura
A stranger must be cared for

If you want to say we should have respect for strangers, you could use this passage from the same book: 'For even the immortal gods treat with respect the man / Who is driven ashore after many wanderings, / As I am now.'[1]

99 Divitiae non semper optimis contingunt
Wealth is not always the lot of the best

If you want to say that it is not always the most prudent people who become wealthy, but that it is a matter of chance, now one now the other, you can quote this from book 6 of the *Odyssey*:

> Jupiter himself measures out wealth to mortals
> To each as he sees fit, to good or to bad.[1]

The words are spoken by Nausicaa to Ulysses when he approaches her as a beggar; and she does not despise him for being poor, because fortune is to be blamed for that not the man, providing he is not imprudent.

100 Munus exiguum, sed opportunum
A small gift, but a timely one

When we describe a gift as costing very little but still most welcome to the receiver at that time – for example if you offer bread to one in danger of starving to death – we may quote this from the same book: 'A small gift, but a welcome one.'[1] The same line is to be found in book 14.[2]

* * * * *

98 Homer *Odyssey* (see n1 below)
1 *Odyssey* 5.447–8: Αἰδοῖος μέν τ᾽ ἐστὶ καὶ ἀθανάτοισι θεοῖσι, / Ἀνδρῶν ὅς τις ἵκηται ἀλώμενος ὥσπερ ἐγὼ νῦν.

99 Homer *Odyssey* (see n1 below)
1 *Odyssey* 6.188–9: Ζεὺς αὐτὸς νέμει ὄλβον Ὀλύμπιος ἀνθρώποισι, / Ἐσθλοῖς ἠδὲ κακοῖσιν, ὅπως ἐθέλησιν ἑκάστῳ.

100 Homer *Odyssey* (see n1 below)
1 *Odyssey* 6.208: Δόσις δ᾽ ὀλίγη τε φίλη τε
2 *Odyssey* 14.58

1 Quo transgressus etc.
Where have I transgressed, etc?

Among the philosophers you will hardly find one who educated young people more conscientiously than Pythagoras. This caused him to mingle with his teaching much superstition, because untrained youth, like the uneducated masses, cannot be ruled by precepts in clear and unadorned philosophical language. To these superstitions certainly belonged the prohibition on eating meat, the praise of vegetables, and the five-year 'silence,'[1] and finally certain of the precepts, almost of an oracular nature, which had to be learned by heart before they could be understood. Our modern monks, who are monks in name only, seem to have imitated some of this man's teachings, and those who control their bellies and their tongues are the ones who sin least. However, because it is not in man's nature to be on his guard against wavering all the time, the next best thing is that each should constantly demand of himself an account of his actions and, if he has erred in any way, he should correct himself; if he has performed according to his duty, he should persevere therein and make even better progress. One of Pythagoras' salutary teachings, in the form of a symbolic figure, is preserved in a line of verse (its author is unknown for I cannot find it in Homer) which Plutarch seems to have taken delight in,[2] for no one among the pagan philosophers is more saintly than this man. The verse goes like this: Πῆ παρέβην; τί δ᾽ ἔρεξα; τί μοι δέον οὐκ ἐτελέσθη; 'Where have I slipped?[3] What have I done? Or what duty have I omitted?'[4] For every failure in human living consists of one of three things. We do otherwise than we should,

* * * * *

1 This adage was added in 1526, when some related changes were made to *Adagia* I i 2 (see CWE 31 32); it replaced 'Glaucus has eaten grass and lives in the sea,' now IV i 63. The title suggests both the pseudo-Virgilian *De viro bono* (see n5 below) and the first element of the line from the pseudo-Pythagorean *Golden Verses* (see n4 below).

1 Greek: ἐχεμυθία. For the five-year silence see Diogenes Laertius 8.10 ('Pythagoras'). An epigram on the subject, *Anthologia Palatina* 10.46, was among those translated by Thomas More (no 127 in the Yale edition of his *Complete Works*). Cf *Adagia* IV iii 72 Less talkative than Pythagoreans, and Otto 1496.

2 Plutarch *Moralia* 168B *De superstitione*; cf 515F *De curiositate*.

3 At this point Erasmus translates παρέβην as *lapsus* rather than the *transgressus* he uses in the title or the *praetergressus* he would have found in the *De viro bono* (see below).

4 Pseudo-Pythagoras *Carmen aureum* in D. Young ed *Theognis* (Leipzig 1971) 5.42; Diehl pages 82–90. The attribution to Pythagoras is due to Diogenes Laertius 8.22 and is repeated by the *Suda* Π 3123.

that is, more or less than is required; to this error corresponds the question 'Where have I transgressed?' Or we do what we should not have done, to which corresponds the phrase 'What have I done?' Or we fail to do what we should have done, and to this corresponds the last phrase 'What duty have I not done?' If someone admonishes his son or his wife more leniently than is necessary when they sin or rebukes them too harshly, on reflection he will rightly ask, 'Where have I transgressed?' One who teaches a son un-worthy things will ask, 'What have I done?' One who neglects a son's sins when it would be opportune to admonish him will ask, 'What duty have I not done?' Pythagoras was in the habit of admonishing young people to recite this verse in their minds whenever they returned home. If they had been wanting perchance in any way or if they had picked up some vice from their contact with men, this meditation made them anxious to correct it and to be wary of it in the future. This idea was developed at greater length and more fully by the person who wrote the poem 'On the Good Man,' which is to be found in the appendices of the works of Virgil:

> Before he allows his eyes to close in gentle sleep,
> He will have thought over all his deeds the whole day through:
> Where have I transgressed? what have I done at the right time? what have
>   I not done?
> Why was this deed not fitting? or that one not sensible?[5]

These ideas have been taught by men who did not know Christ. What then should Christians do? If only priests and monks would say to themselves when they returned to their beds from generous and splendid feasts: 'Where have I slipped? What have I done? Or what duty have I not done?'[6] God in heaven, how many things would occur to us to be ashamed of and to repent?

2 Suo quisque studio gaudet
Everyone rejoices in his own pursuit

Anyone who wants to say that different people are engrossed in different pursuits and each person lives by his own means will quote this from the

* * * * *

5 *De institutione viri boni* 14–17 = Ausonius *Eclogae* 4.14–17
6 Erasmus repeats this in Greek without translating

2 Homer *Odyssey* (see n2 below)

same book:[1] 'For the Phaeacians have no regard for arrows or quivers, / But for oars and a ship well-made with even planks.'[2] This is rather like 'Smiths their hammers ply.'[3] And Pindar in the tenth Pythian ode: 'The minds of different men are stimulated by love of different things.'[4]

3 Demittere sese ad aliorum mediocritatem
Coming down to the level of others

When someone limits his effort deliberately to conform to other people's lower level, for example if a teacher provides his listeners not with everything he can teach but with as much as they can take in, then there will be a place for this verse from the same book about Nausicaa who controls the pace of her mules with the reins so that her followers and Ulysses could keep up with her on foot:

> She drives so that Ulysses can accompany her on foot
> And the whole crowd of her followers, using the whip
> With moderation and sure skill.[1]

4 Mihi curae erit hoc negocium
This business will be my concern

When we want to declare to someone that we will take care of a matter so that he himself can be free of worry and hand over the whole task to us, these words from book 7 of the *Odyssey* will be suitable: 'But proceed quietly, I will lead the way here.'[1]

* * * * *

1 In the earliest editions this adage immediately followed *Adagia* III ix 100 (355 above) in which there was a reference to *Odyssey* 6.208.
2 *Odyssey* 6.270–1: Οὐ γὰρ Φαιήκεσσι μέλει ἰὸς ἠδὲ φαρέτρη, / ᾿Αλλ᾿ ἱστοὶ καὶ ἐρετμὰ νεῶν καὶ νῆες εἶσαι.
3 Horace *Epistles* 2.1.116, quoted in *Adagia* I vi 15 To learn the potter's art on a big jar
4 Pindar *Pythians* 10.60; added in *1526*

3 Homer *Odyssey* (see n1 below)
1 *Odyssey* 6.319–20: Ἡ δὲ μάλ᾿ ἡνιόχευεν, ὅπως ἅμ᾿ ἑποίατο πεζοὶ / ᾿Αμφίπολοί τ᾿ ᾿Οδυσεύς τε, νόῳ δ᾿ ἐπέβαλλεν ἱμάσθλην.

4 Homer *Odyssey* (see n1 below)
1 *Odyssey* 7.30: ᾿Αλλ᾿ ἴθι σιγῇ τοῖον, ἐγὼ δ᾿ ὁδὸν ἡγεμονεύσω.

5 Animus praesens
A firm mind

Firmness of mind is valuable at all times, because timidity seems to be
caused either by a bad conscience or by petty-mindedness. This idea is
supported by this verse of Homer from the same book: 'A brave and bold
man is better in all things, / Even if he is a stranger and comes from
distant shores.'[1] This is how Pallas encourages Ulysses not to be afraid as
he goes into Alcinous' house. It coincides with an adage recorded elsewhere:
'Fortune favours the brave.'[2] Livy in book 8 of *From the Foundation of the
City*:

> But the outcome showed that fortune favours the brave.[3]

6 Locupletum reditus
The profits of the wealthy

For the wealthy, for whom one profit follows another, we can adapt this,
which is said in the same book about the orchards of Alcinous:

> And there is no fresh summer each year,[1]
> But the west wind blowing with perpetual breath produces
> These fruits and drops them ripe from the trees;
> Pears follow full-grown upon pears, apples upon apples,
> Figs upon figs mature, and grapes upon grapes.[2]

* * * * *

5 Homer *Odyssey* (see n1 below)
1 *Odyssey* 7.51–2: Θαρσαλέος γὰρ ἀνὴρ ἐν πᾶσιν ἀμείνων / Ἔργοισι τελέθει, εἰ καί
ποθεν ἄλλοθεν ἔλθοι.
2 *Adagia* I ii 45; added in *1528*
3 Livy 8.29.5; added in *1528*

6 Homer *Odyssey* (see n2 below)
1 As Estienne points out (LB II 936), Erasmus has misunderstood this phrase because in the Aldine edition it is separated by a colon from the beginning of
the sentence which precedes. In addition he has made a non-existent nominative θερεύς from the genitive θέρευς. A.T. Murray (Loeb) translates: '[Of these
the fruit perishes not nor fails in winter or in] summer, but lasts throughout
the year; and ever does the west wind ...'
2 *Odyssey* 7.118–121: Οὐδὲ θερεὺς ἐπετήσιος, ἀλλὰ μάλ' αἰεὶ / Ζεφυρίη πνείουσα τὰ
μὲν φύει, ἄλλα δὲ πέσσει, / Ὄχνη ἐπ' ὄχνῃ γηράσκει, μῆλον δ' ἐπὶ μήλῳ, / Αὐτὰρ
ἐπὶ σταφυλῇ σταφυλή, σῦκον δ' ἐπὶ σύκῳ.

7 Inevitabile fatum
Unavoidable fate

What is decreed for man by the fates will happen. On this idea we have
Homer's lines in the same book:

> Thereafter he will suffer
> Whatever fate and the grim spinners have spun for him
> At his birth when he emerged from his mother's womb.[1]

But this passage about the fates should be used only in a humorous way;
for example if someone sends his son to some rather remote place for his
education and says he would not care what he does there, but leaves it to
the gods and fortune.

8 Aliud cura
Worry about something else

When you want to say that there is no reason why someone should doubt
or continue to be worried by some concern that has been removed,[1] this
from the same book will fit: 'Alcinous, worry about something else.'[2] Then
there is Terence: 'I have already thought of one; worry about something
else.'[3]

9 Molestus interpellator venter
The belly is a troublesome heckler

The stomach is a shameless intruder which never allows anyone to forget
it. It could be used figuratively of extreme poverty, which always forces

* * * * *

7 Homer *Odyssey* (see n1 below); cf *Adagia* III ix 53 Destiny cannot be changed
(339 above), which is based on *Odyssey* 3.147, and III ix 86 Destiny is unavoidable (351 above), which uses *Odyssey* 5.103–4.
1 *Odyssey* 7.196–8: Ἐνθάδ' ἔπειτα / Πείσεται, ὅσσα οἱ αἶσα κατακλῶθές τε βαρεῖαι /
Γεινομένῳ νήσαντο λίνῳ, ὅτε μιν τέκε μήτηρ.

8 Homer *Odyssey* (see n2 below)
1 Cf *Adagia* IV v 66 To cast a pebble.
2 *Odyssey* 7.208: Ἀλκίνο', ἄλλο τί τοι μελέτω φρεσίν.
3 Terence *Phormio* 235

9 Homer *Odyssey* (see n1 below)

mortals to do and suffer all sorts of things. This is what Ulysses says in the same book:

> There is no other thing more shameless than a troublesome stomach,
> Which bids a man take thought for it even against his will,
> However distressed you may be at heart, whatever affliction torments
> your breast.[1]

10 Vulgus suspicax
Ordinary people are suspicious

Common people are suspicious and often take things in a bad sense. Homer in the same book: 'For we men are mostly quick to suspect the worst.'[1]

11 Nemo cogendus officii causa
Do not force anyone by kindness

No guest should be kept against his inclination and will. No one should be forced to accept anyone's hospitality if he does not wish it. This idea can be illustrated by this from the same book: 'If you choose to remain, no one shall keep you against your will.'[1] The words are addressed to Ulysses by Alcinous king of the Phaeacians.

12 Malum bono pensatum
Misfortune compensated with good

Whenever Nature bestows some extraordinary gift but counterbalances it with some flaw, or when a person spoils his kindness with some malice,

* * * * *

1 *Odyssey* 7.216–18: Οὐ γάρ τι στυγερῇ ἐπὶ γαστέρι κύντερον ἄλλο / Ἔπλετο, ἥ τ᾽ ἐκέλευσεν ἕο μνήσασθαι ἀνάγκῃ / Καὶ μάλα τειρόμενον καὶ ἐνὶ φρεσὶ πένθος ἔχοντα.

10 Homer *Odyssey* (see n1 below)
 1 *Odyssey* 7.307: Δύσζηλοι γάρ τ᾽ εἰμὲν ἐπὶ χθονὶ φῦλ᾽ ἀνθρώπων.

11 Homer *Odyssey* (see n1 below)
 1 *Odyssey* 7.315: Εἴ κ᾽ ἐθέλων τε μένοις, ἀέκοντα δέ σ᾽ οὔ τις ἐρύξει. The Aldine edition has a stop at the end of line 314. A.T. Murray (Loeb) translates: 'a house and possessions would I give thee, if thou shouldst choose to remain, but against thy will shall no one keep thee ...'

12 Homer *Odyssey* (see n1 below)

then there will be a place for these words from book 8 of the *Odyssey* spoken about Demodocus the minstrel:

> This man the Muse loved above all others and gave him
> Both good and evil. For she deprived him of his sight,
> But gave him the gift of softening hearts with sweet song.[1]

13 Omni certaminis genere
In any sort of contention

When we imply that we have engaged in every sort of contention, for example if someone says that there has been bitter argument on every point of doctrine, then this from the same book will be appropriate: 'In boxing and in racing, in leaping and in wrestling.'[1] Likewise, when someone declares that he refuses no competition, but is prepared for any sort of mental test, the following from the same book will do:

> Come here, for I am greatly angered;
> Let anyone who wishes try me out in boxing or in wrestling,
> Or racing if he will, I care not.[2]

14 Longe vicit
First by far

If we feel someone is so pre-eminent that there is no danger anyone will take the palm from him, then this from the same book will suit: 'But set your mind at rest, as far as this competition is concerned, / No one of the Phaeacians will throw as well or further.'[1]

* * * * *

1 *Odyssey* 8.63–4: Τὸν περὶ Μοῦσ' ἐφίλησε, δίδου δ' ἀγαθόν τε κακόν τε / Ὀφθαλμῶν γὰρ ἄμερσε, δίδου δ' ἡδεῖαν ἀοιδήν.

13 Homer *Odyssey* (see n1 below)
1 *Odyssey* 8.103: Πύξ τε παλαισμοσύνη τε καὶ ἄλμασιν ἠδὲ πόδεσσιν
2 *Odyssey* 8.205–6: Δεῦρ' ἄγε πειρηθήτω, ἐπεί μ' ἐχολώσατε λίην, / Ἢ πὺξ ἠὲ πάλη ἢ καὶ ποσίν, οὔ τι μεγαίρω.

14 Homer *Odyssey* (see n1 below)
1 *Odyssey* 8.197–8: Σὺ δὲ θάρσει, τόνδε γ' ἄεθλον / Οὔ τις Φαιήκων τῶνδ' εἴξεται οὐδ' ὑπερήσει.

15 Antiquis debetur veneratio
The ancients should be treated with reverence

We should not compete with the greatest and the invincible, or with the ancients, for these seem to be placed beyond the hazards of mortals; to them we should yield willingly. For example, if someone says he does not wish to vie in eloquence with Cicero, but does not want to refuse ordinary rivals, he can use what Ulysses says in the same passage:

> With the men of olden times I will not compete,
> With Hercules' excellence[1] or with Eurytus of Oechalia.'[2]

16 Flagitiorum turpis exitus
Crime has an ugly outcome

When an affair that has been wrongly undertaken turns out badly, the following verse from the same book will suit: 'Wicked deeds never turn out well.'[1] This is said of the adultery of Mars when it was discovered.[2]

17 Fidus amicus
A faithful friend

A faithful friend is to be valued no less than a brother. Homer says in the same book: 'Someone whom chance makes a pleasant and good friend / Is to be valued no less than a brother.'[1]

* * * * *

15 Homer *Odyssey* (see n2 below)
1 Latin *Herculea virtute*; it is with the marksmanship of Hercules and Eurytus as bowmen that Ulysses refuses to compete.
2 *Odyssey* 8.223–4: Ἀνδράσι δὲ προτέροισιν ἐριζέμεν οὐκ ἐθελήσω / Οὔθ' Ἡρακλῆϊ οὔτ' Εὐρύτῳ Οἰχαλιῆϊ.

16 Homer *Odyssey* (see n1 below)
1 *Odyssey* 8.329: Οὐκ ἀρετᾷ κακὰ ἔργα.
2 'This ... discovered' is omitted in LB.

17 Homer *Odyssey* (see n1 below); the punctuation in the Aldine edition has led Erasmus to separate these two lines from the preceding and following lines.
1 *Odyssey* 8.584–5: Ἦ τίς που καὶ ἑταῖρος ἀνὴρ κεχαρισμένα εἰδώς, / Ἐσθλός, ἐπεὶ οὐ μέν τι κασιγνήτοιο χερείων.

18 Patria sua cuique iucundissima
To every man his own country is most agreeable

Every man finds his own country most agreeable, whatever land he happens to be in. Homer in book 9 of the *Odyssey*: 'For nothing is sweeter to any man than his fatherland / And his own parents.'[1]

19 Fuga tutior
Flight is safer

Someone who wants to say that it is safer to overcome a violent desire by fleeing from it than by fighting it could adapt what is said about Charybdis in book 12 of the *Odyssey*: 'There is no remedy; the best thing is to flee far from her.'[1]

20 Alia committenda, alia caelanda
Some things must be trusted to others, some concealed

One should not without good reason divulge no matter what to no matter whom, and not all secrets should be spread around the household; some should be trusted to friends or wives, others hidden. The idea is suitably expressed by this from book 11 of the *Odyssey*: 'One thing may be said, another, on the other hand, should be withheld.'[1]

21 Foemina nihil pestilentius
Nothing is more noxious than a woman

Nothing is more noxious than a woman. The opinion is expressed by Homer[1] in the same book: 'Nothing is more shameless and worse than

* * * * *

18 Homer *Odyssey* (see n1 below)
  1 *Odyssey* 9.34–5: Ὡς οὐδὲν γλύκιον ἧς πατρίδος οὐδὲ τοκήων / Γίγνεται.

19 Homer *Odyssey* (see n1 below)
  1 *Odyssey* 12.120: Οὐδέ τις ἔστ᾽ ἀλκή, φυγέειν κάρτιστον ἀπ᾽ αὐτῆς.

20 Homer *Odyssey* (see n1 below)
  1 *Odyssey* 11.443: Ἀλλὰ τὸ μὲν φάσθαι, τὸ δέ γ᾽ αὖ κεκρυμμένον εἶναι.

21 Homer *Odyssey* (see n2 below)
  1 Erasmus, who names the speaker often enough elsewhere, seems deliberately to give a quite misleading impression here: these are the words of the shade

a woman.'[2] In the ancient poets the female sex is often spoken of badly. And in our own times they constantly strive to ensure that the poets should not seem to have been liars.

22 Effoeta senecta
The weakness of old age

The words in book 11 of the *Odyssey* about the dead can be applied to a man who has lived too long and lost his strength, or to someone who is frightened: 'For sinews no longer hold flesh and bone together.'[1]

23 Aegre, sed tamen contigit
It was difficult, but he achieved it

For those who achieve what they want, even if with difficulty, this line from the same book will be appropriate: 'You will reach home, though you will have suffered many ills.'[1] These words are spoken to Ulysses by Tiresias.

24 Cum amico non certandum aemulatione
Do not compete in rivalry with a friend

We should not seek to compete with a friend and one who deserves well of us in case our friendship is overshadowed by the rivalry that accompanies this sort of contention. Homer implies this in book 8 of the *Odyssey* when Ulysses excludes Laodamas as a competitor because he was his host: 'For who would quarrel with a benevolent host?'[1] It will also be appropriate when we want to say that it is the duty of the guest to give way to those

* * * * *

of Agamemnon concerning Clytemnestra and are completed by '... who puts into her heart such deeds' (translation by A.T. Murray in the Loeb edition). See the introductory note to *Adagia* III iv 77 When the lamp is removed there's no difference between women (49 above).
2 *Odyssey* 11.427: Ὡς οὐκ αἰνότερον καὶ κύντερον ἄλλο γυναικός.

22 Homer *Odyssey* (see n1 below)
1 *Odyssey* 11.219: Οὐ γὰρ ἔτι σάρκας τε καὶ ὀστέα ἶνες ἔχουσιν.

23 Homer *Odyssey* (see n1 below)
1 *Odyssey* 11.104: Ἀλλ' ἔτι μέν γε καὶ ὡς κακά περ πάσχοντες ἵκοισθε.

24 Homer *Odyssey* (see n1 below)
1 *Odyssey* 8.208: Τίς ἂν φιλέοντι μάχοιτο;

with whom he lodges, even if he could win. For in the same passage there is immediately added this thought:

> For he is indeed a foolish man and worthless,
> Who would challenge to the outcome of a contest the one
> From whose hospitality he benefits and whose house he enjoys.[2]

25 Reiicientis culpam
For one who won't accept blame

Against the man who throws the cause of his misfortune on someone else, as people commonly do, one can aptly turn this line from book 11 of the *Odyssey*. It is spoken by the shade of Elpenor who had died because he was drunk in Circe's house: 'An evil fate of the gods was my undoing and too much wine.'[1] There's another place too where Agamemnon similarly throws the blame for a dispute on Ate.[2]

26 Voluptas foeda
Abominable pleasures

For shameful pleasures, or for a prostitute who is skilled in all the arts that cause the ruin of young people, the following words from book 10 of the *Odyssey* will suit. They are said of Circe: 'She will change us all to swine or wolves or fierce lions.'[1]

27 Aspera vita, sed salubris
A hard life, but a healthy one

For a way of life that is rather hard but suitable for the proper teach-

* * * * *

2 *Odyssey* 8.209–10

25 Homer *Odyssey* (see n1 below)
1 *Odyssey* 11.61: Ἆσέ με δαίμονος αἶσα κακὴ καὶ ἀθέσφατος οἶνος.
2 *Iliad* 19.86–92

26 Homer *Odyssey* (see n1 below)
1 *Odyssey* 10.432–3: Ἢ κεν ἅπαντας / Ἢ σῦς ἠὲ λύκους ποιήσεται ἠὲ λέοντας.

27 Homer *Odyssey* (see n1 below)

ing of morality, an apt verse would be the following about Ithaca from the *Odyssey* book 9: 'A rugged island, but a good nurse for young men.'[1]

28 Consiliis simul et facto valens
Effective both in advice and in action

For a man who is as distinguished in counsel as in action a suitable verse will be this one from book 14 of the *Odyssey*: 'Such a man was this, whether in battle or in counsel.'[1]

29 Non possum non dicere
I cannot help speaking

When someone says he cannot keep silent about what he thinks, he can adapt this humorously from the same book: 'For my part I shall say something rather bold, / For foolish wine impels me.'[1] In the same passage Ulysses declares eloquently what wine can do, for he goes on:

> Wine excites a man however serious and modest to sing,
> And drives him to easy laughter and dancing,
> And sometimes he opens up his heart and babbles out
> What it would have been better to keep silent.[2]

30 Perplexus
Trapped

Anyone who wants to say that he finds himself in the greatest danger and that no help is at hand, can use this from the same book: 'No other land

* * * * *

1 *Odyssey* 9.27: Τραχεῖ᾿, ἀλλ᾿ ἀγαθὴ κουροτρόφος

28 Homer *Odyssey* (see n1 below)
1 *Odyssey* 14.491: Οἷος ἐκεῖνος ἔην βουλευέμεν ἠδὲ μάχεσθαι

29 Homer *Odyssey* (see n1 below)
1 *Odyssey* 14.463–4: Εὐξάμενός τι ἔπος ἐρέω, οἶνος γὰρ ἀνώγει / Ἥλιος.
2 *Odyssey* 14.464–6

30 Homer *Odyssey* (see n1 below)

appeared, / But everywhere around us only sky and sea.'[1] The same expression is found in book 12.[2]

31 Abhorrentis ac detestantis
For one who loathes and detests

When we want to say that we are violently repelled by some vice, we can use this from the same book: 'This man is hateful to me as the threshold of the dark gods.'[1] The same verse is found in book 9 of the *Iliad* spoken by Achilles.[2] Here it is spoken by Ulysses.

32 Sui dissimilis
A different face

For someone who presents a different face a suitable expression would be this, from book 13 of the *Odyssey*, which Ulysses says of Athena: 'Now you put on one face and now another.'[1] The same expression will be marvellously suitable for the wisdom that is concealed with different wrappings in the ancient writers and is presented in ever changing images, especially in holy scripture, which consists almost entirely of allegories.[2]

33 Nihil ad rem
Nothing to do with the subject

For someone who has said something out of place and irrelevant to the subject under discussion, a suitable expression will be this from the same

* * * * *

1 *Odyssey* 14.301–2: Οὐδέ τις ἄλλη / Φαίνετο γαιάων, ἀλλ' οὐρανὸς ἠδὲ θάλασσα; cf Virgil *Aeneid* 3.193 *coelum undique et undique pontus*.
2 *Odyssey* 12.403–4

31 Homer *Odyssey* (see n1 below)
1 *Odyssey* 14.156: Ἐχθρὸς γάρ μοι κεῖνος ὁμοῦ Ἀΐδαο πύλῃσι.
2 *Iliad* 9.312

32 Homer *Odyssey* (see n1 below)
1 *Odyssey* 13.313: Σὲ γὰρ αὐτὴν πάντα ἐΐσκεις.
2 For Erasmus' ideas on allegory in holy scripture see for example the *Enchiridion militis christiani* CWE 66 30–8.

33 Homer *Odyssey* (see n1 below)

book, although the same is to be found in other places:

> Stranger, you are foolish, or a foreigner recently come
> From distant shores.[1]

34 Quod adest, boni consule
Accept things as they are in good part

If someone wants to warn that we ought to accept in good part what fortune allows us he will use this from book 14 of the *Odyssey*:

> Stranger, take this food and enjoy such bounty as there is,
> For fate will give one thing and refuse another
> According to its whim, for it can do all things.[1]

With these words the swineherd Eumaeus invites Ulysses to accept in good part his humble rustic food such as it is. They can be used metaphorically of any aspect of human life whenever we want to recommend that we should live happily and quietly in the position fate has given us. In book 10 of Athenaeus is recorded this verse: 'Whatever is at hand, weave your life with that.'[2] In his speech *On the Peace* Isocrates says it is very difficult for some men 'to be content with what is present' and that this is why they prefer war to peace.[3]

35 Officium ne collocaris in invitum
Do not place an obligation on someone who does not want it

It would be in the nature of an insult if a person placed an obligation on

* * * * *

1 *Odyssey* 13.237: Νήπιός εἰς, ὦ ξεῖν', ἢ τηλόθεν εἰλήλουθας; also found at *Odyssey* 9.273

34 Homer *Odyssey* (see n1 below); cf *Adagia* II ix 33 Take your present fortune in good part, and IV ii 43 What is given ... (525 below).
1 *Odyssey* 14.443–5: Ἔσθιε, δαιμόνιε ξείνων, καὶ τέρπεο τοῖσδε, / Οἷα πάρεστι· θεὸς δὲ τὸ μὲν δώσει, τὸ δ' ἐάσει, / Ὅττι κεν ᾧ θυμῷ ἐθέλει· δύναται γὰρ ἅπαντα.
2 Athenaeus 10.458B; PCG 8 adespota 121.4, 231 Kock; 'They can be used' to here was added in *1528*.
3 Isocrates 8.6–8; added in *1533*

35 Homer *Odyssey* (see n1 below)

someone who does not want it. This idea is expressed by Homer in book 15 of the *Odyssey*:

Both commit a wrong: the man who drives out a guest
Who is unwilling to go, and the man who detains one who wishes to leave.
As long as he wishes to stay, a guest should be treated kindly;
And when he seeks to leave, he should be allowed to go.[1]

36 Bona spes ostensa
Appearance of hope

When a sure hope of achieving what we set out to do appears from somewhere, a suitable adage will be the following from the same book: 'Even as he speaks a bird of good omen flies by on the right.'[1]

37 Arrogantia non ferenda
Intolerable arrogance

For those who show unbearable arrogance, we can adapt quite neatly from the same book the words of Eumaeus about the suitors: 'Their wantonness and violence reaches heaven.'[1] The same expression is used in book 17 by Ulysses speaking to Eumaeus.[2]

38 Domus optima
Home is best

The most unhappy condition is to be a vagrant without fixed abode, as the

* * * * *

1 *Odyssey* 15.72–4: Ἴσόν τοι κακόν ἐσθ᾽, ὅς τ᾽ οὐκ ἐθέλοντα νέεσθαι / Ξεῖνον ἐποτρύνῃ καὶ ὃς ἐσσύμενον κατερύκῃ. / Χρὴ ξεῖνον παρεόντα φιλεῖν, ἐθέλοντα δὲ πέμπειν.

36 Homer *Odyssey* (see n1 below)
1 *Odyssey* 15.160: Ὣς ἄρα οἱ εἰπόντι ἐπέπτατο δεξιὸς ὄρνις.

37 Homer *Odyssey* (see n1 below)
1 *Odyssey* 15.329: Τῶν ὕβρις τε βίη τε σιδήρεον οὐρανὸν ἥκει.
2 *Odyssey* 17.565

38 Homer *Odyssey* (see n2 below). According to the editors of ASD the title is to be understood as in *Adagia* III iii 38 *Domus amica, domus optima,* A loved home is the best home.

ἀνέστιοι 'homeless'[1] always are, and those who live in foreign countries. Support for this is given in the same book: 'Nothing is more wretched than wandering with no fixed abode.'[2] This could be used metaphorically of those who are pushed this way and that by every sort of idea or who change their friends or their way of life repeatedly.[3]

39 Non omnibus contingit
It is not given to everyone

Not everyone has the opportunity to confer with kings; not everyone is given the power to penetrate the mysteries of holy scripture. This meaning may be given quite elegantly by the following line from book 16 of the *Odyssey*: 'Not to everyone is the will of the gods made manifest.'[1]

40 Auctoritas divinitus
Prestige divinely given

It is the will of god that the same man should be highly revered at one moment and despised at another. The following from the same book is suitable for this:

> It is easy for the gods, whom broad Olympus houses,
> To make a man despised or to grant him honour.[1]

41 Tollenda mali occasio
Remove the opportunity for evil

If you want to persuade people to remove the opportunity for evil, it would

* * * * *

1 Cf *Adagia* III iv 62 n1 (38 above).
2 *Odyssey* 15.343: Πλαγκτοσύνης δ᾽ οὐκ ἔστι κακώτερον ἄλλο βροτοῖσιν.
3 The last sentence was added in *1528*.

39 Homer *Odyssey* (see n1 below)
1 *Odyssey* 16.161: Οὐ γάρ πω πάντεσσι θεοὶ φαίνονται ἐναργεῖς.

40 Homer *Odyssey* (see n1 below)
1 *Odyssey* 16.211–12: Ῥηίδιον δὲ θεοῖσι, τοὶ οὐρανὸν εὐρὺν ἔχουσιν, / Ἠμὲν κυδῆναι θνητὸν βροτὸν ἠδὲ κακῶσαι.

41 Homer *Odyssey* (see n1 below)

not be out of place to quote this from the same book: 'For the iron draws men to it of itself.'[1] Thus wealth tempts one to luxury and familiarity with girls stirs one to lust.[2]

42 Ubi cognitum est quod erat occultum
When what was hidden becomes known

When a matter that was concealed with great care is somehow detected, a suitable adage will be this from the same book:

> Either some god pointed this out to them
> Or they saw it themselves.[1]

43 Abstinenda vis a regibus
Never do violence to kings

If you want to say that for good reason one should not lay hands on kings, on rulers, or on men dedicated to god, you can bring in this from the same book:

> It is a fearful thing and full of danger
> To have killed one of royal stock.[1]

44 Domesticum dissidium
Discord in the home

For the abominable quarrelling that takes place in the home and the discord and intrigues of those who live together, a suitable expression is this from the same book: 'It is an impious thing to plot evil one against the other.'[1]

* * * * *

1 *Odyssey* 16.294: Αὐτὸς γὰρ ἐφέλκεται ἄνδρα σίδηρος.
2 The last sentence was added in 1515.

42 Homer *Odyssey* (see n1 below)
1 *Odyssey* 16.356: Ἤ τίς σφιν τόδ' ἔειπε θεῶν, ἢ εἴσιδον αὐτοί.

43 Homer *Odyssey* (see n1 below)
1 *Odyssey* 16.401–2: Δεινὸν δὲ γένος βασιλήϊόν ἐστιν / Κτείνειν.

44 Homer *Odyssey* (see n1 below)
1 *Odyssey* 16.423: Οὐχ ὁσίη κακὰ ῥάπτειν ἀλλήλοισιν.

45 Qui eget, in turba versetur
The needy man should keep with the crowd

The story is still commonly told nowadays of the blind beggar who ordered
his servant to lead him to where there were most people, adding the opinion
well known in popular humour that profit is to be made where there are
lots of people.[1] Homer has it in book 17 of the *Odyssey*: 'A beggar does
better to beg for his meal in a crowded town / Than in the country.'[2]

46 Officium humilius
An unworthy office

When someone refuses an office as too humble and not worthy of him, he
could apply this line which is also from book 17 of the *Odyssey*: 'For my
age does not require that I should stay at the farmstead.'[1] This is Ulysses
speaking to the swineherd.

47 Vitandae potentum offensae
Avoid the rancours of the powerful

If you want to say that the rancours of the rich and of rulers are to be
dreaded because, however slightly they are injured, they take serious offence and, as Plautus says, 'their wrath is a load of lead,'[1] then you may
apply this line from the same book:

The rancours and threats of kings are to be feared.[2]

* * * * *

45 Homer *Odyssey* (see n2 below); the story of the blind beggar is also in the
Convivium religiosum, Colloquies CWE 39 175; cf also Suringar 188 and Apostolius
15.8A.
1 Suringar 188 page 346
2 *Odyssey* 17.18–19: Πτωχῷ βέλτιόν ἐστι κατὰ πτόλιν ἠὲ κατ᾽ ἀγροὺς / Δαῖτα
πτωχεύειν.

46 Homer *Odyssey* (see n1 below)
1 *Odyssey* 17.20: Οὐ γὰρ ἐπὶ σταθμοῖσι μένειν ἔτι τηλίκος εἰμί. The following line
makes Odysseus' reason clearer: 'at a master's beck and call.'

47 Homer *Odyssey* (see n2 below)
1 Plautus *Poenulus* 813; translation by P. Nixon (Loeb). Cf *Collectanea* 209 *Plumbea
ira*. Otto 1440 note
2 *Odyssey* 17.189: Χαλεπαὶ δέ τ᾽ ἀνάκτων εἰσὶν ὁμοκλαί.

48 Princeps indiligens
The negligent ruler

A careless tutor corrupts the child, a bad teacher spoils the student, and a wicked king corrupts the nation. The idea is effectively expressed by this line from the same book: 'The bad shepherd ruins the sheep.'[1] These words are spoken by the swineherd Eumaeus to the goatherd.

49 Assuevit malis
He has grown used to ills

For one who has become accustomed to putting up with injuries, a suitable adage will be this from the same book:

Not at all unused to blows and peltings.[1]

50 De alieno liberalis
Generous with others' goods

We give easily of other people's goods, but it is not the same with our own. This idea was expressed by Antinous in the same book:

For there is no hindrance or regret
In giving away another's possessions.[1]

Seneca in book 2 of his *Letters* number 16: 'You need not wonder at my genius; so far, I have been lavish with other men's possessions.'[2] And when Aeschinus in *The Brothers* says, 'Do it; I have promised them,' Mitio replies, 'Promised, did you? Be generous with what is your own, my boy.'[3]

* * * * *

48 Homer *Odyssey* (see n1 below)
1 *Odyssey* 17.246: Αὐτὰρ μῆλα κακοὶ φθείρουσι νομῆες.

49 Homer *Odyssey* (see n1 below)
1 *Odyssey* 17.283: Οὐ γάρ τι πληγέων ἀδαήμων οὐδὲ βολάων

50 Homer *Odyssey* (see n1 below). Otto 63
1 *Odyssey* 17.451–2: Ἐπεὶ οὔ τις ἐπίσχεσις οὐδ᾽ ἐλεητὺς / Ἀλλοτρίων χαρίσασθαι.
2 Seneca *Letters* 16.7; cf *De clementia* 1.20.3; added in *1528*
3 Terence *Adelphoe* 940; added in *1528*

51 Pauper, sed ingeniosus
Poor but talented

For a man who is poorly dressed but nevertheless of outstanding physical appearance,[1] a suitable adage will be this from book 18 of the *Odyssey*: 'Such shoulders[2] the old man shows beneath his humble rags.'[3] This is said of Ulysses when he is about to wrestle with Irus. In his 'Gallic Hercules' Lucian applies it to an old man who is outstandingly clever and eloquent.[4]

52 Iactantiae comes invidia
Envy is the companion of boasting

If someone wants to warn against boasting excessively of good fortune or natural gifts lest at any time Nemesis overhears and takes them away, it would be a good time to use this from the same book: 'Let him keep in silence whatever gifts he may have of the gods.'[1]

53 Verbo tenus amicus
A friend in words alone

For one whose words make a pretence of good will but who plots something very different a suitable phrase will be this from the same book: 'She

* * * * *

51 Homer *Odyssey* (see n3 below); an adage that might be grouped with The Sileni of Alcibiades (*Adagia* III iii 1)
  1 Latin *egregio ... corpore*. At this point Erasmus usually suggests a figurative interpretation of the Homeric expression, often in an amplification of the title. Here however he seems to be applying it again on the literal level of physical appearance, which seems pointless. The title is normal, offering a figurative meaning suggested by Lucian (see n4 below).
  2 The Greek ἐπιγουνίς means 'thigh'; Erasmus' word is *armus*, normally the shoulder of a man.
  3 *Odyssey* 18.74: Οἵην ἐκ ῥακέων ὁ γέρων ἐπιγουνίδα φαίνει.
  4 Lucian *Heracles* 8

52 Homer *Odyssey* (see n1 below)
  1 *Odyssey* 18.142: Ἀλλ' ὅ γε σιγῇ δῶρα θεῶν ἔχοι, ὅττι διδοῖεν.

53 Homer *Odyssey* (see n1 below). For the sentiment cf *Collectanea* no 443 and Aulus Gellius *Noctes Atticae* 17.19.1, both referred to in ASD.

beguiled his mind / With gentle words but her thoughts were on other things.'[1]

54 Nihil recusandum, quod donatur
Never refuse a gift

If on occasion you want to say that we should never refuse a gift, whatever is offered, or that we should seize the chance of some advantage whenever it occurs, a suitable adage would be this from the same book: 'It is never a good idea to refuse a gift.'[1]

55 Adminicula vitae
The comforts of life

All those things that are important to comfortable living can be quite neatly symbolized by this line from book 19 of the *Odyssey*: 'Things by which they live well and are reputed wealthy.'[1]

56 Qui per se sufficit
A self-sufficient man

For the man who would say he does not need the help of others and is quite fit to complete a task by himself a suitable adage will be this from book 20 of the *Odyssey*:

> I have eyes, ears, and two feet,
> And intelligence in my breast that is neither simple nor foolish.[1]

* * * * *

1 *Odyssey* 18.282–3: Θέλγε δὲ θυμὸν / Μειλιχίοις ἐπέεσσι, νόος δέ οἱ ἄλλα μενοίνα.

54 Homer *Odyssey* (see n1 below)
1 *Odyssey* 18.287: Οὐ γὰρ καλὸν ἀνήνασθαι δόσιν ἐστίν.

55 Homer *Odyssey* (see n1 below)
1 *Odyssey* 19.79: Οἷσίν τ᾽ εὖ ζώουσι καὶ ἀφνειοὶ καλέονται

56 Homer *Odyssey* (see n1 below)
1 *Odyssey*: 20.365–6: Εἰσί μοι ὀφθαλμοί τε καὶ οὔατα καὶ πόδες ἄμφω, / Καὶ νόος ἐν στήθεσσι τετυγμένος οὐδὲν ἀεικής.

57 Novit mala et bona
He knows the bad and the good

For one who through age and experience of affairs is able to discern between things to be avoided and things to be desired a suitable adage will be this from the same book:

> For a long time now I have known and understood all things,
> Both what is good and what is evil.[1]

Even nowadays no expression is more common than this.[2]

58 Neque enim ignari sumus
For we are no strangers

When someone takes heart and bears present discomforts by remembering past ills he can with some humour use this from the same book: 'Stand firm, my soul; in the past you have borne worse.'[1] Virgil imitated and developed this with:

> You have had worse to bear than this. Now, as before,
> Providence will bring your suffering to an end
>
> ...
>
> Hold hard, therefore. Preserve yourselves for better days.[2]

Likewise Horace in the *Odes*: 'You who have stayed by me through worse disasters, heroes ...'[3]

* * * * *

57 Homer *Odyssey* (see n1 below)
1 *Odyssey* 20.309–10: Δὴ γὰρ νοέω καὶ οἶδα ἕκαστα / Ἐσθλά τε καὶ τὰ χέρεια.
2 Suringar 152 page 278

58 Homer *Odyssey* (see n1 below); the title is borrowed from Virgil *Aeneid* 1.198: *Neque enim ignari sumus ante malorum*, and Erasmus follows Ovid closely for his translation (*Tristia* 5.11.7).
1 *Odyssey* 20.18: Τέτλαθι δή, κραδίη, καὶ κύντερον ἄλλο ποτ᾿ ἔτλης.
2 Virgil *Aeneid* 1.199 and 207; translation by W.F. Jackson Knight (Penguin). Macrobius *Saturnalia* 5.11.5–6 links this passage to Homer *Odyssey* 12.208–213, but it is Erasmus who seems to have noticed the parallel he quotes.
3 Horace *Odes* 1.7.30; translation by James Michie (Penguin)

59 Danda venia lapso
A slip should be pardoned

If you want to say that we should pardon a mistake that has occurred through neglect, and that a man cannot be expected to give careful attention at every moment, you can use this from book 19 of the *Odyssey*: 'For it is in no way possible for a mortal to remain / Forever awake.'[1]

60 Non quidvis contingit quod optaris
Not everything you wish for happens

If you want to say that not everything happens as you may have hoped or imagined you can apply this from the same book:

> Some dreams, of course, are trifling and vain,
> Nor does everything you see turn out to be real.[1]

And in this passage he introduces the very beautiful image of the two gates for dreams which Virgil describes in book 6.[2]

61 Gaudium dolori iunctum
Joy is linked to pain

When something happens at which we rejoice and grieve equally – for example, when someone's wealthy parents depart this life, on the one hand he is tormented by their death, on the other he rejoices at gaining his inheritance and becoming free – a suitable adage will be this from the same book:

> Joy and grief together came upon her heart.[1]

* * * * *

59 Homer *Odyssey* (see n1 below)
1 *Odyssey* 19.591: Ἀλλ' οὐ γάρ πως ἔστιν ἄυπνους ἔμμεναι αἰὲν / Ἀνθρώπους.

60 Homer *Odyssey* (see n1 below)
1 *Odyssey* 19.560–1: Ἤ τοι μὲν ὄνειροι ἀμήχανοι ἀκριτόμυθοι / Γίγνοντ', οὐδέ τε πάντα τελείεται ἀνθρώποισι.
2 Virgil *Aeneid* 6.893–6, a parallel noted by Servius

61 Homer *Odyssey* (see n1 below); the words refer to the old nurse Eurycleia as she recognizes Odysseus, though the Latin could refer to either gender.
1 *Odyssey* 19.471: Τὴν δ' ἅμα χάρμα καὶ ἄλγος ἔλε φρένα.

62 Mala senium accelerant
Misfortunes hasten age

If you want to say we should not measure age by years, because when men
are tormented by frequent labours and troubles they become old before
their time, you can use this from the same book: 'For quickly do men grow
old with cares and misfortunes.'[1]

63 Vita mortalium brevis
The life of mortals is short

If you want to warn that we should do our best to leave with our descendants a worthy memory that will live for ever, for this life is bound by
narrow limits, you can apply this from the same book: 'But mortals' lives
are confined to brief spans.'[1]

64 Verisimiliter mentiens
Lies that sound like truth

For one who tells a falsehood just as if it were the truth a suitable expression
would be this from the same book: 'He made the many falsehoods of his
tale seem like truth.'[1] This is said about Ulysses. Plato also remarked that
Homer represented Ulysses as a liar, and Achilles on the other hand as
truthful.[2]

65 Sibi malum repperit
He invented his own misfortune

For the man who is harmed by his own discovery, a suitable expression will

*****

62 Homer *Odyssey* (see n1 below)
  1 *Odyssey* 19.360: Αἶψα γὰρ ἐν κακότητι βροτοὶ καταγηράσκουσι.

63 Homer *Odyssey* (see n1 below)
  1 *Odyssey* 19.328: Ἄνθρωποι δὲ μινυνθάδιοι τελέθουσι.

64 Homer *Odyssey* (see n1 below)
  1 *Odyssey* 19.203: Ἴσκε ψεύδεα πολλὰ λέγων ἐτύμοισιν ὅμοια.
  2 Plato *Lesser Hippias* 365B

65 Homer *Odyssey* (see n1 below)

be this from book 21 of the *Odyssey*: 'But it was his own harm he caused first, being overcome with wine.'[1] This is said of Eurytion, who was the first to discover the use of wine and was killed by the Lapiths.[2]

66 Qui continet arcanum
The man who keeps a secret

For a man who conceals a secret that has been entrusted to him and does not blurt it out to anyone a suitable saying will be this in book 21 of the *Odyssey*:

> For him[1] the words lacked wings.[2]

That is, they flew no further.

67 Rem novam aggredior
It is a new thing I begin

If at some time you want to indicate that you are about to undertake something difficult and new, something not attempted by anyone else, you can apply this from book 22 of the *Odyssey*: 'Now I shall attempt another target, to see if I can hit it, one that no one else has hit so far.'[1] These are the words of Ulysses as he prepares to kill the suitors.

* * * * *

1 *Odyssey* 21.304: Οἵ τ' αὐτῷ πρώτῳ κακὸν εὕρετο οἰνοβαρείων.
2 The editors of ASD suggest that Erasmus takes this as the implication of the quoted verse. But Erasmus' Latin verse is not inconsistent with, for example, E.V. Rieu's translation (Penguin): 'He was the first to suffer and he brought his troubles on himself by getting drunk.' It seems likely that the comment means Eurytion was the first Centaur to learn the effect of wine, thus starting the battle of the Centaurs and the Lapiths. The story begins at *Odyssey* 21.295.

66 Homer *Odyssey* (see n2 below)
1 The Latin *huic* is of common gender, and is translated 'him' because Erasmus has started with *In eum qui* 'For a man who,' but the Greek τῇ is feminine and the person referred to in Homer is again Eurycleia; cf *Adagia* III x 61 (378 above).
2 *Odyssey* 21.386: Τῇ δ' ἄπτερος ἔπλετο μῦθος.

67 Homer *Odyssey* (see n1 below)
1 *Odyssey* 22.6–7: Νῦν αὖτε σκοπὸν ἄλλον, ὃν οὔπω τις βάλεν ἀνήρ, / Εἴσομαι, αἴ κε τύχοιμι.

68 Benefactorum memoria
The memory of good deeds

When a person receives a benefit because someone has remembered past good deeds, a suitable adage will be this from the same book: 'It is far better to do one's duty than to commit evil.'[1]

69 Mortuis non conviciandum
Do not insult the dead

A beaten man should not be scoffed at nor should insults be heaped further on a dead man, even if he was justifiably killed. Homer approves of this in the same book: 'It is an inauspicious thing to boast over slain men'[1] – the words of Ulysses about the dead suitors.

70 Focus luculentus in aedibus
A glowing hearth at home

The best ornament of a house is a glowing hearth; this is why those who move into a new house or come to an inn bid first of all that a fire be lit. The idea seems to come from book 22 of Homer, who makes Ulysses say, 'Now first of all let a fire be made for me in the hall.'[1] And this famous line: 'For the home is brighter when the fire is lit.'[2] This verse seems to have greatly delighted Plutarch, so often does he use it and adapt it to various meanings. In the essay 'On Virtue and Vice' he applies it to wealth, power, and fame, which become the more pleasing if the soul is free of troubles; again in the book entitled 'The Lover' he applies it to the heart of the suitor, which glows far more brightly if it is fired by the warmth of love.[3]

* * * * *

68 Homer *Odyssey* (see n1 below)
1 *Odyssey* 22.374: Ὡς κακοεργίης εὐεργεσίη μέγ᾽ ἀμείνων.

69 Homer *Odyssey* (see n1 below)
1 *Odyssey* 22.412: Οὐχ ὁσίη κταμένοισιν ἐπ᾽ ἀνδράσιν εὐχετάασθαι.

70 Homer *Odyssey* (see n1 below)
1 *Odyssey* 22.491: Πῦρ νῦν μοι πρώτιστον ἐνὶ μεγάροισι γενέσθω.
2 Attributed to Homer in *Certamen Homeri et Hesiodi* 324: Αἰθομένου δὲ πυρὸς γεραρώτερος οἶκος ἰδέσθαι in the Loeb edition of *Hesiod, The Homeric Hymns and Homerica* 592. This and what follows were added in 1515.
3 Plutarch *Moralia* 100D *De virtute et vitio* and 762D *Amatorius*

71 Qui iure perierunt
Those who deserved to die

For those who deserve to die a suitable line will be this from the same book: 'These men were destined to be killed, destroyed by their own misdeeds.'[1] The words refer to the suitors.

72 Inexorabilis
Unbending

For one who is hard and pitiless a fitting adage is this line from book 23 of the *Odyssey*: 'But your heart is ever harder than any stone.'[1] So Telemachus to his mother.

73 Recipere animum
Regaining courage

When someone is confused by a sudden event and then recovers himself, a suitable adage will be this line from book 24 of the *Odyssey*:

As he caught his breath and his spirit returned into his breast.[1]

74 Senum prudentia
Wisdom of the aged

Speaking of people who may be old certainly, but who, because of their experience of affairs, are nevertheless quite fit to carry on some occupation, we might aptly say this from the same book: 'Hoary age indeed, but not unfit for war.'[1]

* * * * *

71 Homer *Odyssey* (see n1 below)
1 *Odyssey* 22.413: Τούσδε δὲ μοῖρ᾽ ἐδάμασσε θεῶν καὶ σχέτλια ἔργα.

72 Homer *Odyssey* (see n1 below); cf *Adagia* III viii 44 (298 above) for the same title.
1 *Odyssey* 23.103: Σοὶ δ᾽ αἰεὶ κραδίη στερεωτέρη ἐστὶ λίθοιο.

73 Homer *Odyssey* (see n1 below)
1 *Odyssey* 24.349: Αὐτὰρ ἐπεί ῥ᾽ ἄμπνυτο καὶ ἐς φρένα θυμὸς ἀγέρθη

74 Homer *Odyssey* (see n1 below); cf *Adagia* III ix 66 (343 above) for the same title.
1 *Odyssey* 24.499: Καὶ πολιοί περ ἐόντες ἀναγκαῖοι πολεμισταί

75 Imperator bonus et idem robustus miles
A good commander and a hard soldier too

There is a story by Plutarch in the essay on the 'Fortune of Alexander'
(if indeed this book is by him): 'When the question was raised at dinner,
which of the verses of Homer was most praiseworthy, and different people
expressed their preference for different verses, Alexander awarded the palm
to this line which is in book 3 of the *Iliad*:

> A good leader and an outstandingly strong soldier too.[1]

For with this line he both sang the praise of Agamemnon and prophesied
the courage of Alexander.'[2] However, in my opinion physical strength does
not count for much in a prince, but deliberation and wisdom count for
a great deal. For this reason, when orators sang the praises of a certain
Chares, a young man of notable physical strength, and gave their opinion
that the Athenians should seek to have this sort of leader in war, Timotheus said vehemently, 'Not at all. I would have that sort of man carry mat-
tresses and blankets for the army, but as commander I would have a man
who has eyes for "what is both before and behind,"[3] and who is not hindered in his determination of what is for the best by any disturbance of his
reasoning.'[4]

76 Capram coelestem orientem conspexerunt
They have seen the heavenly she-goat rising

Αἶγα τὴν οὐρανίαν ἐπιτέλλουσαν ἐθεάσαντο, They have gazed at the heavenly she-goat rising. This used to be said of those for whom everything

* * * * *

75 Homer *Iliad* (see n1 below), added in *1515* to the adages from Homer
1 *Iliad* 3.179: Ἀμφότερον, βασιλεύς τ᾽ ἀγαθὸς κρατερός τ᾽ αἰχμητής
2 Plutarch *Moralia* 331C *De Alexandri magni fortuna aut virtute*
3 *Iliad* 1.343; cf *Adagia* III viii 79 With both the front and the back of the head
(310 above), and III i 53 Forward and backward.
4 Plutarch *Moralia* 788D–E *An seni respublica gerenda sit*. A shorter version is found
in *Moralia* 187C *Regum et imperatorum apophthegmata*, which Erasmus uses in
his *Apophthegmata* v Alcibiades 25 (LB IV 249B).

76 Pseudo-Plutarch (see n2 below); cf Zenobius (Aldus) column 10, and Zenobius
1.26. From here to *Adagia* III x 84, except 82, and with the addition of 96 and 97,
Erasmus continues the series from Pseudo-Plutarch (see III v 30n, 83 above),
which he had begun at the end of century III vii.

prospered as well as they wished, because in antiquity according to popular opinion it was accepted that those who had observed the she-goat – the one that had been Jupiter's nurse and was therefore placed among the constellations – would be the possessors of whatever they prayed for. This story is explained at greater length in the adage 'Amaltheia's horn.'[1] This one, however, is to be found in the *Collected Proverbs* of Plutarch.[2] It is also in the essay 'On Listening to Poetry': 'How happy is the owner of many fields[3] who keeps οὐράνιον αἶγα "a heavenly goat" to bring him wealth.'[4] However, in Athenaeus book 9, Antiphanes I think mentions the heavenly goat among animals suitable for the table: 'Wild goat, αἶξ οὐρανία "heavenly she-goat," castrated ram.'[5]

77 Capra ad festum
A she-goat to the festival

Αἶξ εἰς τὴν ἑορτήν, A she-goat to the festival. Used to be said when someone came into an affair opportunely, or when someone exposed himself openly to his own destruction.[1] This was because, at festivals, particularly those of Bacchus, they sacrificed a she-goat. It is recorded in the same collection.[2]

78 Mox sciemus melius vate
Soon we shall know better than the prophet

Τάχ᾽ εἰσόμεσθα μάντεων ὑπέρτερον, Soon we shall know the matter better than the prophet himself. This expression was used by people who did not foretell a thing by guessing but tried to understand it by testing it. For there is no better proof than a test. It is recorded in the same *Collected Proverbs* of

* * * * *

1 *Adagia* I vi 2 Ἀμαλθείας κέρας A horn of plenty
2 Pseudo-Plutarch Laurentianus 3.27 Jungblut page 417
3 Latin *multorum agrorum possessor* translating the word 'Polyagros' in the Greek, which is in fact a proper name
4 Plutarch *Moralia* 27C *Quomodo adolescens poetas audire debeat*; added in 1526
5 Athenaeus 9.402E; PCG 2 Antiphanes fragment 131.3–4; added in 1528

77 Pseudo-Plutarch (see n2 below); cf Zenobius (Aldus) column 10.
1 'or when ... destruction' was added in 1515.
2 Pseudo-Plutarch Laurentianus 3.28 Jungblut page 417

78 Pseudo-Plutarch (see n1 below)

Plutarch,[1] but it originates in Sophocles' *Antigone*.[2] However, in the second book of the *Punic War* Livy says: 'The outcome is the teacher of fools.'[3]

79 Tinctura Cyzicena
Cyzicene dye

Βάμμα Κυζικηνόν, Cyzicene dye, was an expression among the Athenians for an ineradicable disgrace.[1] It was said of those who did something shameful from fear, for the Cyzicenes had a reputation for both cowardice and effeminacy. It is listed in the same *Collected Proverbs*.[2] Hesychius recalls it too, adding that the Cyzicenes were known for their effeminacy, being Ionians.[3] The scholiast of Aristophanes says roughly the same.[4] Stephanus Byzantinus adds that they were overwhelmed by the repeated plundering of the Tyrrhenians.[5] The expression is found in Aristophanes' *Peace*: 'But if ever it is necessary to fight and wear the scarlet, he himself is immediately "stained with Cyzicene dye."'[6] Distinctive dyes are usually known by the names of places, for not all dyes found everywhere colour well. Thus people speak of 'Syracusan dye' and 'Sardinian dye.'[7] This was used proverbially of men's conduct, for the appraisal and the rumour that follow men's lives act like a dye. Whence people are said to be 'marked with coal' when they are condemned.[8]

* * * * *

1 Pseudo-Plutarch Laurentianus 3.60 Jungblut page 419
2 Sophocles *Antigone* 631; added in *1520*
3 Livy 22.39.10; the speaker is Fabius Maximus. Added in *1528*. Cf Otto 613 and *Adagia* I i 31 Trouble experienced makes a fool wise.

79 Pseudo-Plutarch (see n2 below). The text of *1508* runs from Ἡάμμα ... *Collected Proverbs*'; the remainder is of *1533*, except the quotation from Aristophanes, which was added in *1526*.
1 Following *Suda* B 89
2 Pseudo-Plutarch Laurentianus 3.76 Jungblut page 420; cf Zenobius (Aldus) column 52.
3 Hesychius B 186
4 Scholiast of Aristophanes *Peace* 1176 (Dübner page 205)
5 Stephanus Byzantinus Κύζικος, page 391 Meineke. According to the editors of ASD the text is defective and was misunderstood by Erasmus. His Latin may mean 'they were hard to deal with (or 'embittered') because of the repeated plunderings of the Tyrrhenians,' but the translation given seems more likely in the context.
6 Aristophanes *Peace* 1175–6: βέβαπται βάμμα Κυζικηνικόν; added in *1528*
7 Following Hesychius; see n3 above.
8 Cf *Adagia* I v 54 To mark with chalk, with coal.

Well known too is this line of Ennius quoted in Aulus Gellius: 'Affairs dyed with evil or others good to speak of.'[9] The scholiast of Aristophanes tells us the Spartans used to wear red tunics so that they should not be seen to be wounded by the enemy because the colour would be the same.[10] Cowards and weak people on the other hand turn pale.[11] Let me add something that is in book 4 of Herodotus: 'When the king of the Ethiopians looked at a purple cloak sent to him by the Persian king, he asked how it had been dyed. When he learned it was done by the Fish-eaters[12] he said it was not only the men who were cunning, but that even their clothes were deceitful.'[13]

80 Servabis bovem
You will keep watch on the ox

Βουκολήσεις, You will be a cowherd. This was in the nature of a riddle which meant exile. Those who were ostracized went into exile in Argiva[1] where there was a bronze ox of great size. This is recorded in the *Collected Proverbs* of Plutarch.[2] Hesychius states that it appeared in the *Phasma* of Menander.[3]

81 Embarus sum
I am Embarus

Ἔμβαρός εἰμι, I am Embarus. This was said formerly of a mad or delirious person. The adage is explained by reference to a story that goes like this. In

* * * * *

9 Ennius *Annales* 274 Skutsch, in Aulus Gellius *Noctes Atticae* 12.4.4. Erasmus follows the wording of the Venice 1509 edition: *Quae tincta malis aut quae bona dicto.*
10 Scholiast of Aristophanes *Peace* 1173 (Dübner page 205)
11 Cf *Adagia* I ii 89 The coward changes colour.
12 *Ichthyophagi*, a name given to various little known peoples, here most probably a tribe living on the Arabian Gulf (Strabo *Geographica* 16.4.4) or one on the Persian Gulf (Strabo 15.2.1–2 and Pliny *Naturalis historia* 6.149).
13 Herodotus 3.22.1 (not book 4)

80 Pseudo-Plutarch (see n2 below)
1 Probably a guess by Erasmus for Ἄργινα, the equally unknown name used in the *Collected Proverbs*
2 Pseudo-Plutarch Laurentianus 3.79 Jungblut page 420
3 The last sentence is an addition of 1526 which belongs not here but at the end of the next adage (see III x 81 n3 below).

81 Pseudo-Plutarch (see nn1 and 2 below)

olden times Piraeus was an island, something that the name itself indicates because περᾶν is 'to send across.' When Munychus became the ruler, he built a temple to Diana, to whom the title 'Munychian' was added. Later, when a bear, which is sacred to Diana, was discovered there and was killed by some Athenians, a famine occurred. People resorted to the oracle and sought a remedy for the evil. The god answered that there would be an end to the evil only if someone sacrificed his daughter to the deity. And Embarus alone was found who was mad enough to promise that he would sacrifice his daughter on condition that the priestly office should be granted to his descendants. So his daughter was dressed in the customary way and sacrificed.[1] This too is mentioned in the *Collected Proverbs* of Plutarch.[2] Hesychius states that it appeared in the *Phasma* of Menander.[3]

82 Colophonium suffragium
The Colophonian vote

Κολοφωνία ψῆφος, The Colophonian vote. This is used in a letter of Plato to Dionysius.[1] The adage differs in words rather than in meaning from the one we noted in the second chiliad, 'He added the colophon.'[2] The source of the adage is explained in this way. At a time when the Colophonians were in uproar with internal rebellions, some of them happened to move

* * * * *

1 Zenobius (Aldus) column 79 and Apostolius 7.10. According to ASD the end of Erasmus' version of the story is deficient and consequently garbled. In *Suda* E 937, which Erasmus apparently overlooked, Embaros sacrifices a goat in place of his daughter. Cf Eustathius 331.26–30, Pausanias Atticista fragment ε 35 Erbse, and Zenobius (Athous) 1.8 where Embaros, in contrast to Erasmus' version, appears as a clever man.
2 Pseudo-Plutarch Laurentianus 4.5 Jungblut page 406
3 Hesychius E 2291, merely naming Embaros; *Phasma* fragment 2 Körte-Thierfelder; in the Loeb edition of Menander by W.G. Arnott 3.390 line 80. This sentence was intended as an addition here in 1526 but printed at the end of the preceding adage – see n3 to III x 80 above.

82 *Collectanea* nos 680 and 608; according to the editors of ASD no 680 was based on Ficino's translation of Plato (see n1 below) and the Greek is a back-translation of *Colophonium suffragium*.
1 Plato *Letters* 3.318B. The expression is translated by R.G. Bury (Loeb) as 'the coping-stone.'
2 *Adagia* II iii 45 Τήν Κολοφῶνα ἐπέθηκεν; see R.B. Mynors' introductory note and n1 (CWE 33 392) for the confusion between the masculine noun 'colophon' and the feminine place name 'Colophon.'

residence and migrated to Smyrna. Later, when the Smyrnaeans were at war and were repeatedly defeated, they finally accepted the help of the Colophonians whom they had welcomed into the city and who had proved themselves superior. Thus the belief was established that, just as the Smyrnaeans had not been able to win in war without the support of the Colophonians, so they would not win elections if they did not also have their vote. Hence when the Ionian[3] rule extended over twelve cities, of which one was Smyrna, and when the votes of the Smyrnaeans were equally divided in public meetings, the party that won was the one that had the support of the Colophonians who had helped them conquer in the war.[4] Relevant to this too are some things related by a Greek writer called Iabenus.[5] The twelve cities of Ionia were accustomed to meet together, and this was called the Pan-Ionian council. If it happened that no decision could be made because the votes on each side were equal, the Colophonians were summoned and victory was accorded to whichever party they supported. So the adage will fit when we want to indicate that someone's judgment or vote is of great moment in some matter. I have already mentioned this adage.[6]

83 Mihi ista curae futura sunt etc.
These things will be my care, etc.

Ἐμοὶ μελήσει ταῦτα καὶ λευκαῖς κόραις, These things I and the white maidens will take care of. This is an oracular trimeter which has been taken into popular speech. When Brennus[1] attacked Delphi with his Gallic forces, the

* * * * *

3 From 1508 to 1526 'Ionian' was 'Colophonian' following the *Suda* (Milan 1499); it was corrected in 1528 in accordance with the 1526 addition that follows.
4 From 'The source' to here follows Zenobius (Aldus) column 160 and *Suda* K 766 or Apostolius 16.92; the proverb is also in Diogenianus 8.36.
5 Under this name Erasmus quotes the fourteenth-century Georgius Lacapenus whose 'Grammar' was unpublished at that time, but who reproduces an article (T 765) of the *Suda*. The three sentences 'Relevant ... supported' and the final sentence, an unnecessary repetition (see n2 above), are additions of 1526.
6 See n2 above.

83 Pseudo-Plutarch (see n2 below); cf Zenobius (Aldus) column 80 and Appendix 2.55.
1 The name is introduced from Cicero (see n3 below) in 1526; before that Erasmus had said only 'The barbarians attacked ...' This is not the Brennus who sacked Rome circa 390 BC but a Galatian chieftain who invaded Macedonia and Greece in 279. He was defeated and wounded at Delphi and committed suicide during the retreat through Thessaly.

Delphians asked the oracle what they should do. The answer was in the form of the verse I have just quoted. Shortly afterwards Apollo was seen with the two maidens Pallas and Diana, for there are temples to them as well at Delphi. It can be properly used whenever we want to signify that there is no danger, that an affair will be looked after by those whose concern it is. It is included in the *Collected Proverbs* of Plutarch.[2] Cicero translates the Greek verse in book 1 of *On Divination* as follows: 'It is I and the white maidens who shall provide for this.'[3]

84 Festum multas habens
A festival has many

Ἑορτὴ πολλὰς ἔχουσα, A festival has many, 'troubles' or 'pre-occupations' being understood. Said of people who make up great packages to carry when they are about to travel somewhere. It will be more humorous if it is applied to certain people who do nothing, however trivial, without great effort, long delay, and extraordinary preparation, such that they often exhaust both themselves and everyone else with their preparations before they start anything. It derives from people going to festivals, who were in the habit of taking a great many goods with them: jars, clothes, sacred objects, bread, and lots of other things of that sort, in case anything necessary for the ceremony should be lacking. It is extant in the same *Collected Proverbs*.[1]

85 Nihil aliae civitates ad Crotonem
Other cities are nothing beside Croton

Μάταια τἆλλα παρὰ Κρότωνα τἄστεα, Compared with Croton the rest are wretched little towns. The scholiast of Theocritus recalls this proverb. It can be applied to a thing or a man so outstanding that others seem nothing when placed alongside. The origin is perhaps the excellence of Crotonian boxers, one of whom was the Milo we have mentioned elsewhere, namely in the proverb 'Healthier than Croton.'[1]

* * * * *

2 Pseudo-Plutarch Laurentianus 4.20 Jungblut page 407
3 Cicero *De divinatione* 1.81; added in 1526

84 Pseudo-Plutarch (see n1 below); cf Zenobius (Aldus) column 84.
1 Pseudo-Plutarch Laurentianus 4.24 Jungblut page 407

85 Scholiast of Theocritus 4.33; cf Mantissa 2.2.
1 *Adagia* II iv 43

86 Canis panes somnians
A dog dreaming of bread

There are certain people who seem to be the target of a proverbial figure
in the *Fishermen* of Theocritus: 'Every dog dreams of ἄρτος "bread" in his
sleep, but I of fish.'[1] The meaning is that everybody dreams about the things
he desires eagerly and to which he is most committed. Aristotle attributes
dreams not only to men but to all the other animals,[2] although this is most
apparent in dogs because, as they sleep, we often hear them dreaming
of hunting, as can be quite easily deduced from the nature of the barks
they utter while asleep. Therefore, it would seem to me to fit better if
instead of ἄρτος 'bread' we read ἀγρός or ἄγρα 'field' or 'hunt.' But I am
merely suggesting this should be considered by scholars who can decide on
the matter when they have found a more correct manuscript. This has not
happened to me so far. Dreams are used to prophesy future events by many
people even in our own time, although Aristotle does not approve of it.[3]

87 Canis
You keep on singing

Ἄιδεις ἔχων, You keep on singing. I find this means 'You are being frivolous,
talking nonsense, talking vainly.' It is an Attic expression,[1] like παίζεις ἔχων
'you keep on playing, or joking.'[2] So those who are singing are not doing
anything serious, but just seeking to charm our ears with a passing pleasure.

88 Aethiops non albescit
The African cannot become white

Αἰθίοψ οὐ λευκαίνεται, The African cannot become shining white. Usually
said about those who will never change their nature. For an inborn trait
cannot easily be changed. There is a fable of Aesop about a man who bought

* * * * *

86 Theocritus (see n1 below)
  1 Theocritus 21.44–5: Καὶ γὰρ ἐν ὕπνοις / Πᾶσα κύων ἄρτως μαντεύεται, ἰχθύα κῆγών.
  2 Aristotle *Historia animalium* 4.10 (536b27)
  3 Aristotle *De divinatione* 1 (462b20)

87 Zenobius (Aldus) column 5 (Ἄδεις) = Apostolius 1.32. Hesychius A 1766
  1 Cf the scholiast of Aristophanes *Clouds* 509: Ἀττικῶς (Dübner page 105).
  2 Lucian *Icaromenippus* 24, Theocritus 14.8

88 Zenobius (Aldus) column 14 = Apostolius 1.68; cf *Adagia* I iv 50 You are washing an Ethiopian.

an African and thinking that the colour of his skin was not natural but had come about because of the neglect of a former master, scrubbed his face for so long that he even made him ill, whilst the colour was no better than it had been before.[1] There is also an epigram attributed to Lucian: 'You wash the African in vain; why not give up the task? / You will never manage to turn black night into day.'[2]

89 Annas clibanum
Annas and the oven

Ἄννας κρίβανον, Annas and the oven. We should understand 'Annas invented the oven.' It does not escape me that I have dealt with this expression elsewhere,[1] but since it crops up so often in collections of proverbs in a different form, I am glad to advise that the written form is threefold. In another place, in several places in fact, I find the reading Ἄνθρωπος κρίβανον 'The man and the oven.'[2] Personally, I think this reading is corrupt. Nor is it difficult to see the source of the corruption for those who know Greek script.[3] In another place I find Ἄννος,[4] so that it seems to have been a man in question. In some I am surprised to find the spelling Ἄννας, as if it were a woman's name or at least a foreign word. *Clibanus* 'oven,' however, I understand not in the common sense – what would be extraordinary or new about that? – but as the earthenware pot that is put in common ovens with the bread inside, and in which bread or even fish or meat is cooked gradually by a slow heat.[5]

90 Archilochum teris
Wearing out Archilochus

Ἀρχίλοχον πατεῖς, You are wearing out or treading Archilochus, was used

* * * * *

1 Aesop 393 Perry
2 Lucian *Epigrams* 19 Jacobitz; *Anthologia Palatina* 11.428. Erasmus added the epigram in 1533.

89 Pseudo-Plutarch Laurentianus 2.26 Jungblut page 405
1 *Adagia* I x 75; see also the end of *Adagia* II i 91.
2 Zenobius (Aldus) column 34; *Suda* A 2570 and 4052
3 Erasmus is suggesting that ἄννος (see the next sentence) has been misread as the common abbreviation for ἄνθρωπος.
4 Scholiast of Aristophanes *Acharnians* 86 (Dübner page 5) and the *Suda* (see n2 above)
5 Cf *Adagia* III i 9.

90 *Suda* A 4112; cf Diogenianus 2.95 and Zenobius (Aldus) column 46.

to describe a scandal-monger. Πατεῖν 'to tread' was used either because the scandal-monger seemed to be eager to trot out the verses of this poet or because he followed in his footsteps.[1] Archilochus is described by Horace too: 'It was rage that armed Archilochus with his own iambus.'[2] Personally I think this adage is the same as the one I have noted elsewhere, Ἀρχιλόχου πατρίς 'Archilochus' native land,'[3] the word πατεῖς being corrupted to πατρίς.

91 Culicem colant
Straining at a gnat

There are many expressions in the gospels taken from popular speech. And this was not unworthy of Christ, but rather highly suitable because, just as by assuming a body he wished to be one of us, so he used expressions as familiar as possible in order to raise our humble understanding by every means to his divinity. But it did not seem proper to me to include a large number of these expressions,[1] partly because to people excessively devoted to poetry anything that smacks of sacred scriptures seems unattractive; partly because I believe they are clear enough to anyone; but mostly because I am afraid that some pious individual might consider that I insult holy scripture if I intermingle them in this work where there are not only pagan expressions, but even some not very decent ones. The few I have referred to in spite of this and as discreetly as I could are by no means all. But of all the adages in the gospels I could not leave out this one. It was applied by our lord Jesus Christ to certain superstitious and absurdly punctilious people who do not know or disregard what constitutes real Christian piety, but are delighted or alarmed in turn by trifles, are unconcerned with the most important things, are full of Judaizing superstitions and devoid of true charity.[2] It is against these people, in Matthew 23, that Christ, the teacher of real piety, turns the adage thus: Τὸν κώνωπα διυλίζουσι τὴν

* * * * *

1 ASD remarks that Erasmus' explanation is supported by that of Adagia II vi 27 You have not even thumbed your Aesop, which uses the same verb in Greek.
2 Horace Ars poetica 79; added in 1526
3 Adagia II ii 58; see also II ii 57 for Archilochus; cf Apostolius 4.2.

91 Matt 23:24
1 Polydore Vergil attempted to fill this gap in 1519 with a new edition of his Adagiorum libellus, first published in 1498, containing a second book of 503 'sacred' adages.
2 For 'certain superstitious people ... true charity,' cf especially Moria CWE 27 130–2.

κάμηλον καταπίνοντες [Blind guides who] 'strain at a gnat and swallow a camel.' This is not far from the adage we have recorded elsewhere: Ἀν-δριάντα γαργαλίζειν 'To try to drink a statue.'[3]

92 Non inest illi dentale
It has no tree

Γύης οὐκ ἔνεστιν αὐτῷ, It has no tree. This used to be said of anything that was of no use for some particular purpose. The source of the figure is the plough, of which the γύης 'plough-tree' is a part. Some think this is what Latin speakers called the *dentale*.[1] Apparently if this particular part is missing, nothing can be done with the plough. Hesiod spoke of 'a plough-tree of holm-oak'[2] in this sense, but Homer used it to mean *iugerum*, talking of a field as 'fifty *guai*,'[3] that is measuring one hundred *iugera*.[4]

93 Gigantum arrogantia
The pride of the giants

Γιγάντων ἀπόνοια, The folly of the giants. This used to be said when, relying on his own strength, someone rashly and inconsiderately undertook things that should not have been attempted. The origin is the well-known story of the giants. The adage tells us that anything undertaken unreasonably and by force against the gods, against piety, against the law, against justice will turn out to be ill-fated. Horace in his *Odes*:

* * * * *

3 *Adagia* III iv 56 You are trying to drink a statue (35 above), where Erasmus gives the verb in the second person singular; here it is in the infinitive

92 *Suda* Γ 474; cf Apostolius 5.70A and Zenobius (Aldus) column 65.
1 For *dentale* see Pliny *Naturalis historia* 18.171, Virgil *Georgics* 1.172, and Isidore *Etymologiae* 20.14.2. The plough-tree is the curved piece of wood to which the blade or 'share' is attached.
2 Hesiod *Works and Days* 436: πρίνου δὲ γύης; added in 1515
3 Homer *Iliad* 9.579: πεντηκοντόγυον
4 Erasmus appears to be inconsistent in saying Homer uses γύης to mean *iugerum* and then translating πεντηκοντόγυον 'fifty *guai*,' as if one *gues* equals two *iugera*. The *iugerum* measured 240 by 120 feet.

93 Zenobius (Aldus) column 60 = Apostolius 5.44. The story of the Titans' folly and Jupiter's revenge is told in the preceding verses of Horace's ode (see n1 below).

Force without reason topples to its own ruin,
Force moderated is raised by the gods to even greater heights.[1]

In book 23 of the *Iliad* Homer declares in some very elegant lines that in every sort of affair reason and deliberation are of much greater weight than physical strength:

By cunning much more than by strength
You can cut down heavy timber;
By cunning too the helmsman steers the ship
Buffeted by wind and waves on the dark sea,
By cunning one charioteer beats another and comes first.[2]

In book 2 of the *Rhetoric* Aristotle quotes this trochaic verse, without naming the author:

It is not proper that one who is mortal should be concerned with
immortal things,
But rather one who is mortal should think of mortal things.[3]

94 Per ignem incedis
You are stepping into fire

Ἐν πυρὶ βέβηκας, You are stepping into fire, that is 'You are involved in a risky affair.' It is found in Aristophanes' *Lysistrata*: 'I would even be willing to step into the fire, if it were necessary.' [1] Horace in his *Odes*:

You are concerned with a work
That is full of hazards and you step on fire

* * * * *

1 Horace *Odes* 3.4.65–7
2 Homer *Iliad* 23.315–18
3 Aristotle *Rhetoric* 2.21.6 (1394b25): Θνατὰ χρὴ τὸν θνατόν, οὐκ ἀθάνατα τὸν θνατὸν φρονεῖν; fragment 263 Kaibel, adespota 79 Nauck, attributed by earlier authorities to Epicharmus. Added in *1528*. Erasmus' translation is in two lines.

94 *Suda* E 1429; cf Diogenianus 4.52, Apostolius 7.43 and Zenobius (Aldus) column 83; cf *Adagia* IV vi 32 You are not walking on fire.
1 Aristophanes *Lysistrata* 133–4; added in *1526*

Lying beneath deceptive ash.[2]

This is said to fit a person who seeks to finish a task rapidly. Someone who steps on fire suffers less harm if he goes quickly on the tips of his toes.[3] This is similar to what a rhetorician in Seneca said: 'I am stepping on thorns.'[4]

95 Fortis in alium fortiorem incidit
One strong man meets another who is stronger

Ἐσθλὸς ἐὼν ἄλλου κρείττονος ἀντέτυχεν, One strong man met another stronger and better. This expression is used when someone relies too much on his own strength and then finds someone who beats him. The origin is believed to be Hyllus the son of Hercules and Euchemus of Aegea. This is what Zenodotus says.[1] Suidas records these words without mentioning the author's name: 'It sometimes happens as the proverb says[2] that some matter of its own accord may resist the efforts of good men; on the other hand it happens sometimes [as the proverb says], "For one strong man, another comes along stronger and better."'[3] The idea is visibly taken from the *Iliad* book 22, when Hector encounters Achilles:

One who was previously brave fled, pursued by one yet braver.'[4]

* * * * *

2 Horace *Odes* 2.1.6–8. The second phrase 'you step ... ash' is cited by Otto 847.
3 This sentence was added in 1533.
4 Seneca the Elder *Controversiae* 1 praef. 22. The rhetorician (*declamator*, the word used by Seneca) is Marullus. Erasmus' *suspensis pedibus* in the previous sentence, translated as 'on the tips of his toes,' is also from the same passage.

95 Zenobius (see n1 below) and *Suda* E 2239
1 Zenobius (Aldus) column 86. For Hyllus' death at the hands of Echemus, king of Tegea in Arcadia, see Pausanias 8.5.1 and 8.40.1, and Diodorus Siculus 4.58.1–4.
2 The phrase 'as the proverb says' is misplaced, and should follow 'sometimes' two lines lower.
3 *Suda* E 314; at the beginning of E 2239 however, the *Suda* names Polybius (15.16, on Hannibal), not quoted by Zenobius. The proverb is a verse, adespota 8 Bergk.
4 Homer *Iliad* 22.158; added in 1526. Erasmus has translated the Greek πρόσθε with *prius* 'previously,' giving a temporal sense instead of a locative one, and attached it to the word *acer* 'brave.' The Greek should be translated 'In front fled one who was brave, pursued by one yet braver.'

96 Gloria futuri
Glory is for the future

Τὸ δέ τοι κλέος ἐσσομένοιο, Glory is for the future. This is a half line of heroic verse.[1] It is cited in the same *Collected Proverbs* of Plutarch.[2] It warns us that for the most part we achieve fame and reputation for our good deeds in the eyes of those who come after us. Moreover, as Ovid rightly says: 'It is the living envy feeds on; after death it is silent.'[3]

97 Insania non omnibus eadem
Not everyone is mad in the same way

Μανία γ᾽ οὐ πᾶσιν ὁμοία, Not everyone has the same insanity. A half-line of heroic verse, like the previous one, which is extant in the same *Collections*. The meaning is that there is no mortal who is not in some way foolish, although each one suffers from a different sickness, one from avarice, another from lust, one from ambition, another from envy. This is what Damasippus the Stoic proves amply in Horace's *Satires*.[1] This ruinous characteristic of men is a game played with wonderful variety by Nature.[2] Among those whose mind has gone there are some who think they have bull's horns, others a very long nose, some think they are earthenware pots, some believe they are dead, some think they are princes, others that they are learned

* * * * *

96 Pseudo-Plutarch (see n2 below); cf Zenobius (Aldus) column 158 and Appendix 4.95.
  1 Added in 1533. The editors of ASD suggest *Iliad* 3.287, 3.460, and 17.232 as possible Homeric parallels.
  2 Pseudo-Plutarch Laurentianus 4.60 Jungblut page 410 (= Zenobius [Athous] 1.77). The word 'same' refers to *Adagia* III x 84 (389 above)
  3 Ovid *Amores* 1.15.39; also quoted in *Adagia* II vii 11 You deserve no praise even at a feast

97 Pseudo-Plutarch Laurentianus 4.67 Jungblut page 410; cf Diogenianus 6.47, Apostolius 11.8, Zenobius (Aldus) column 116. Apart from the passing reference to the vices in the second sentence, Erasmus' thoughts on madness run on quite different lines here to those of the *Moria* where another kind of madness, the state of ecstatic rapture, akin to the Platonic fury of the lover, is described as the highest form of happiness (CWE 27 152).
  1 Horace *Satires* 2.3.31–2
  2 This sentence and the remainder of the adage were added in *1528*. For the idea that Nature enjoys variety for its own sake, cf Pliny *Naturalis historia* 9.102, 11.123, 21.1.

philosophers. I know a man who thinks he is by far the most villainous among the living or the dead; I know a man who believes no one is better in any way than he; I know a man who thinks he is Jesus Christ and another who believes he is God. There was a man of Argos who applauded in an empty theatre fancying he was listening to wonderful tragic actors.[3] In book 12 Athenaeus talks of a certain Athenian who was convinced that he owned all the ships calling at Piraeus; he counted them, sent them forth, or brought them back, welcoming all those visiting the port with as much joy as if he were master of all they carried. But if there was any loss, he made no further enquiry about whether survivors had arrived. He enjoyed himself leading a very pleasant life all the time until his brother Crito came from Sicily and took him to a doctor whose care freed him from his madness. When he had recovered, however, he would say that he had never lived more happily.[4]

98 Hydrus in dolio
A snake in the jar

Ὕδρος ἐν τῷ πίθῳ, A snake in the jar. This is a proverb, I freely confess, which I have so far not located in any ancient author, neither Greek nor Latin; it is perhaps borrowed from the vernacular, for I do not like to believe that a good writer, with no small reputation in letters, has lied knowingly, because it is reported by Antonio Sabellico in one of his *Familiar Letters*. And he adds a story that was the source of the proverb, which goes like this:

> A certain peasant noticed that some wine stored in a cask was diminishing in quantity and, wondering what the cause was, began looking for the crack by which the liquid was leaking away. Finding nothing of this sort, he next suspected his neighbours of breaking the seal on the cask in his absence and drinking the wine. So he sealed the cask carefully when he was about to go out to work. But when he came back he found the seals unbroken and the wine

* * * * *

3 Horace *Epistles* 2.2.128–40, where the story has a somewhat similar ending to the following one from Athenaeus. Cf *Moria* CWE 27 111.
4 Athenaeus 12.554E–F citing Heraclides Ponticus fragment 56 Wehrli

98 Marcantonio Sabellico (see n1 below) lived from 1436 to 1506; Erasmus' relation of his story is a paraphrase not a quotation and the Greek form of the proverb is Erasmus' own.

still diminished. Then indeed he bewailed the luck of farmers, for whom ruin
waited not only in their vines but in their casks. Finally, when the cask was
empty they found at the bottom a snake, which was drinking the wine.[1]

The story became a popular joke. Pliny tells us in book 10 chapter 72 that
although snakes generally drink little, they are particularly attracted to wine
if they have a chance.[2] Juvenal in his sixth satire says of a bibulous woman:
'Like a long snake she falls into a deep barrel and drinks and vomits.'[3] The
adage in itself is by no means inelegant or contemptible. And if you are not
put off by its modern source you can use it when someone is struck by a
disaster that is unexpected because the cause or the author is not obvious,[4]
or when the author of a longstanding ill is at last perceived. The snake, for
which the Greek word is *hydros*, is called *natrix* in Latin because it lives in
water.[5] From the swelling made by its bite there flows a plentiful humour
which is watery and fetid – this according to Dioscorides book 6.[6] Pliny in
book 6 chapter 23 reports that between certain islands off Persia sea snakes
twenty cubits long terrified a fleet.[7]

99 E Massilia venisti
You're from Massilia

Ἐκ Μασσαλίας ἥκεις, You're from Massilia. Suidas affirms this used to
be said of those who dressed themselves up in an unmanly way, because the Massilians were given to luxury and adorned themselves like
women, besmearing their hair with unguents and tying it up. Related to
this is what Athenaeus records in book 12 of the *Doctors at Dinner*: 'You
should sail to Massilia,'[1] which I have mentioned elsewhere in the adage

* * * * *

1 Marcantonio Coccio Sabellico *Epistolarum familiarum libri duodecim* in *Opera
  omnia* Basle 1560 tome IV column 377B.
2 Pliny *Naturalis historia* 10.198
3 Juvenal 6.431–2; added in *1526*
4 Following Sabellico
5 Erasmus associates *natrix*, incorrectly it seems, though following a very old
  popular etymology, with *natator* 'swimmer,' or the verbs *nare* and *natare* 'to
  swim.'
6 Pseudo-Dioscorides Περὶ ἰοβόλων (*On Venomous Animals*) 14, *Medici Graeci* 26
  page 72
7 Pliny *Naturalis historia* 6.99; from 'The snake, to which' to the end was added
  in *1528*.

99 *Suda* E 499 and Zenobius (Aldus) column 77
1 Athenaeus 12.523C: Πλεύσειας εἰς Μασσαλίαν (given in Greek); this expression
  is also in Pseudo-Plutarch *Alexandrian Proverbs* 1.60.

'You should take ship for Massilia,' and I have explained what I think of this.[2]

100 Tibicines mente capti
The delirium of flute-players

In book 8 of the *Doctors at Dinner* Athenaeus writes that there was a proverb among the ancients to the effect that flute-players had no intelligence: 'It is an ancient saying that "The gods never endowed flute-players with sense, / For when they blow sense is blown away too."'[1] I have made several remarks about this sort of person in the adage 'You live the life of a flute-player.'[2]

1 Dulce bellum inexpertis
War is a treat for those who have not tried it

This is one of the finest of proverbs and is widely used in literature: Γλυ-κὺς ἀπείρῳ πόλεμος, War is a treat for one who has not tried it. In book 3

* * * * *

   2 *Adagia* II iii 98 *Naviges Massiliam,* where Erasmus raises doubts as to the identity of the city and the meaning of the phrase

100 Athenaeus (see n1 below); this whole adage was added in *1517/18.*
   1 Athenaeus 8.337E–F
   2 *Adagia* II iii 34

   1 Diogenianus 3.94 or Zenobius (Aldus) column 62 (= Apostolius 5.51; *Suda* Γ 317). Tilley W 58 Wars are sweet to them that know them not. Cf Otto 1481.
   With the exception of the three lines of *1508* and a few later passages, which are noted as they occur, this long essay dates from *1515.* Most of its arguments were adumbrated in a letter to Antoon van Bergen, abbot of St Bertin, dated from London on 14 March 1514 (Ep 288), but a reference to a lost work entitled *Antipolemus,* composed during Erasmus' stay in Rome (see n161 below), shows that he had given systematic thought to the subject in that period. Several passages of the argument are repeated in the slightly later *Institutio principis christiani* (CWE 27). Unlike 'A dung-beetle hunting an eagle' (*Adagia* III vii 1, 178 above) this adage has no continuing metaphor or allegory, but is a literal condemnation of war, particularly as an instrument of diplomacy or religious conversion. It constitutes a reasoned statement of Christian pacifism, which portrays war as utterly opposed to the nature of man, as an evolutionary decline from innocence to barbarism, and as a madness that defies common sense, economics, and religion. On the latter subject Erasmus notably blames a development of scholarship that has led to the notion of heresy and the persecutions which have resulted. He concludes with a condemnation of the wars against the Turks (in the course of which he makes his one very limited concession to the advocates of war when he allows that he would approve a

chapter 14 of his *Art of War* Vegetius puts it this way: 'Do not put too much trust in a novice who is eager for battle, for it is to the inexperienced that fighting is attractive.'[1] From Pindar we have: 'War is sweet for those who have not tried it, but anyone who knows what it is is horrified beyond measure if he meets it in his heart.'[2] You can have no idea of the dangers and evils of some aspects of human affairs until you have tried them.

> It is pleasant, for those who have never tried, to seek the favour of a
>   powerful friend,
> But the experienced dread it.[3]

It seems fine and glorious to move among nobles at court and to busy oneself with the affairs of kings, but old men who know all about the business from experience willingly deny themselves this pleasure. It seems delightful to be in love with girls, but only to those who have not yet tasted the bitter in the sweet.[4] The adage could be applied in the same way to any affair carrying great risk and attended by suffering such as no one would face unless he were young and inexperienced. In his *Rhetoric* Aristotle suggests that youth is bolder and age is diffident because the former are given confidence by their inexperience and the latter are made diffident and hesitant by their long acquaintance with suffering.[5] If there is any human

* * * * *

defensive expedition in case of unprovoked attack), and an appeal to leaders to pursue the Christian ideal of peace as their highest aim. For a summary bibliography of Erasmus' pacifism see the introductory note by R. Hoven, the editor of ASD II-7.

Separate editions of this adage appeared in Basle 1517 and 1519, Louvain 1517, Zwolle 1520, Leipzig 1521[?], Paris 1530 and London 1533.

1 Vegetius *De re militari* 3.12; added in *1526*; cited in Otto 1481
2 Pindar fragment 110 Snell, cited by Stobaeus *Eclogae* 4.9.3 Hense IV 321–2; added in *1533*. As ASD points out (II-7 13:6–8n), Erasmus' Greek (ἐμπείρων δέ τις ταρβεῖ προσιόντα νιν καρδία περισσῶς) is taken from a partial edition of Stobaeus published by Froben in 1532. A note by Estienne (LB II 951) points out that the dative καρδίᾳ (sic) should stand with ταρβεῖ, and that Erasmus should have translated 'is horrified in his heart.'
3 Horace *Epistles* 1.18.86–7; the last two words, *expertus metuit*, are cited by Otto 617.
4 Erasmus makes a play on the words *amor* 'love' and *amarum* 'bitter'; cf Virgil *Eclogues* 3.109–10.
5 A slightly confused memory of Aristotle *Rhetoric* 2.12.6–9 (1389a) and 2.13.7 (1389b). Aristotle actually connects courage and cowardice directly with passion and the lack of it.

activity that should be approached with caution, or rather that should be avoided by all possible means, resisted and shunned, that activity is war, for there is nothing more wicked, more disastrous, more widely destructive, more persistently ingrained, more hateful, more unworthy in every respect of a man, not to say a Christian.

Yet it is remarkable how widely these days, how rashly, for what trivial reasons war is begun, how cruelly and barbarously it is waged, not only by pagans, but even by Christians, not only by laymen, but even by priests and bishops, not only by the young and inexperienced, but even by older people who have known it already so many times, not only by common folk and the naturally fickle mob, but most especially by princes whose duty is to restrain with prudence and reason the rash impulses of the foolish mob. And there are plenty of lawyers and theologians who add fuel to the fire of these outrages and, as the saying goes, 'sprinkle them with cold water.'[6] Because of this war is now such an accepted thing that people are astonished to find anyone who does not like it, and such a respectable thing that it is wicked and, I might almost say, 'heretical' to disapprove of this, which of all things is the most abominable and the most wretched. How much more reasonable it would be to marvel at what evil genius, what plague, what excess, what madness[7] first put into the mind of man something so beastly that this gentle animal, which Nature created to be peaceful and well disposed to its fellow creatures, the only one she intended for the preservation of all the others, should plunge with such savage insanity, such mad clamour, into mutual slaughter. This will cause even more wonder to anyone who has rejected popularly accepted opinions and turned his thoughts to discerning the real meaning and nature of things, looking with a truly philosophical eye on the one hand at the image of man and on the other at the picture of war.

First then, if we consider just the condition and appearance of the human body, is it not apparent at once that Nature, or rather God, created this animal not for war but for friendship, not for destruction but for preservation, not for aggression but to be helpful? For he gave every other living thing its own weapons. He armed the charging bull with horns, the raging lion with claws; he fitted the boar with slashing tusks; he protected elephants not only with their hide and their size but with their trunk as well. The crocodile is armour-clad at every point with plate-like scales, dolphins

* * * * *

6 Plautus *Cistellaria* 35: *frigidam ... suffundunt*, which does not quite mean 'To pour cold water'; see *Adagia* I x 51n (CWE 32 379–80).
7 For 'what evil ... madness,' cf Virgil's description of the Fury Allecto in *Aeneid* 7.324–492 (see nn14 and 15 below).

are equipped with flippers as weapons; porcupines have the defence of quills, the ray has a sting; the cock is equipped with spurs. Some Nature fortified with a shell, others with a hide, others with a scaly covering. There are some whose safety she provided for by giving them speed, like the doves; again there are others to whom she gave poison as a weapon. To these features she added hideous, savage appearance, fierce eyes, and harsh voices, and implanted inborn enmities. Man alone she produced naked, weak, delicate, unarmed, with very soft flesh and a smooth skin. No part of his body seems to be intended for fighting and violence, not to mention the fact that other animals are capable of protecting themselves almost as soon as they are born; only man is born in such a state that he must be long dependent entirely on the help of others. He cannot speak, he cannot walk, he cannot feed himself, he only wails for help, so that we may conclude that this creature alone was born entirely for friendship, which is formed and cemented most effectively by mutual assistance.[8] It follows that Nature wanted man to owe the gift of living not so much to himself as to the good will of others, so that he should learn that his end was thankfulness and friendship. Then she gave him an appearance that was not hideous and terrifying, as with the others, but mild and gentle, bearing the signs of love and goodness. She gave him friendly eyes, revealing the soul; she gave him arms that embrace; she gave him the kiss, an experience in which souls touch and unite. Man alone she endowed with laughter, the sign of merriment; man alone she endowed with tears, the symbol of mercy and pity. To him she also gave a voice that was not threatening and fierce as with the beasts, but friendly and caressing.

Not content with these gifts Nature gave to man alone the use of speech and reason, the thing that is able above all else to create and nourish good will, so that nothing should be managed among men by force. She implanted a dislike of solitude and a love of companionship. She sowed deep in his heart the seed of goodwill. She arranged that what is most salutary should also be the most pleasant. For what is more agreeable than a friend, and at the same time what equally necessary? So, even if it were possible to lead a comfortable life without the society of others, still nothing would seem pleasant without a companion – unless one were to put off human nature altogether and sink to the level of a wild animal. Further she added the pursuit of learning and the desire for knowledge, the most effective means of drawing the mind of man away from all savagery, just

* * * * *

8 Cf Pliny *Naturalis historia* 7.1–5.

as it has special power in forming friendships. For neither close family nor blood relationships bind souls together with stronger or firmer chains of friendship than does a shared interest in worthwhile studies.

In addition to these she distributed among mankind a wonderful variety of gifts both intellectual and physical, so that everyone could find in someone else something to love and respect for its excellence, or to pursue and prize for its usefulness and necessity. Finally she implanted in man a tiny spark of the divine mind so that, even with no prospect of reward, he would take pleasure in deserving well of everyone. For this above all is the property and nature of God that by his benefits he has regard for all. Otherwise, what is that exquisite pleasure that we feel in our souls when we learn that we have been the means of someone's salvation? And this is why one man is dear to another,[9] that he is bound by some great benefit bestowed. Therefore God placed man in this world as an image in some sense of himself, so that he should, like a sort of earthly divinity, take thought for the salvation of all. Even the brute beasts feel this, for we see not only the gentle ones, but leopards and lions and fiercer animals than these, fly for help to man when in great danger. He is the final refuge for all creatures, he is the most hallowed sanctuary for all, he is without exception their sheet anchor.[10]

We have sketched some sort of portrait of man. Now let us compare with this on the other hand, if you will, a picture of war.[11] Imagine now that you see the barbarous cohorts that inspire terror by their very faces and the sound of their voices. On both sides iron-clad battle lines, the fearful clash and glitter of arms, the hateful roar of a great multitude, the threatening looks, harsh bugles, the terrifying blare of trumpets, the thunder of bombardons, no less frightening than real thunder but more harmful, the mad uproar, the furious clash of battle, the monstrous butchery, the merciless fate of the slain and those who kill, the slaughtered lying in heaps, the

* * * * *

9 Cf *Adagia* I i 69 Man is a god to man. This whole sentence was added in 1526.
10 Cf *Adagia* I i 24 To let go the sheet anchor. The largest anchor on a ship, the sheet anchor, was called in Latin the *sacra ancora*. In his religious writings Erasmus usually makes it an image of sacred scripture. See the *Ratio verae theologiae* (LB v 89D), Ep 858 (CWE 6 77:175) to Paul Volz, and M. O'Rourke Boyle, *Erasmus on Language and Method in Theology* (University of Toronto Press 1977) 59–61.
11 Margaret Mann Phillips (*The Adages of Erasmus* [Cambridge 1964] 313 n1) draws attention to the parallel passage in Ep 273 to Andreas Ammonius dated 1 September 1513 (CWE 2 253). Another model for Erasmus' general development of his theme may be Hippolytus' speech (483–564) in Seneca's tragedy of that name.

fields running with gore, the rivers dyed with human blood. Sometimes brother falls on brother, kinsman on kinsman, friend on friend, as the general madness rages, and plunges his sword into the vitals of one who never harmed him even by a word. In short a tragedy like this contains such a mass of evils that the heart of man is loath even to remember it.

I refrain from recounting other evils, common and trivial by comparison, such as crops trampled far and wide, farms burnt out, villages set on fire, cattle driven away, virgins raped, old men dragged off in captivity, churches sacked, and robbery, pillaging, violence and confusion everywhere. And I say nothing of the consequences of even the most successful and just war: peasants plundered, land-owners oppressed; so many old men left desolate, more tormented by the slaughter of their children than if the enemy had killed them and taken away the knowledge of their grief;[12] so many old women left destitute, condemned to a crueller death than by the sword; so many wives left widows, children left orphans, homes filled with mourning, rich folk reduced to poverty. As for the harm it does to the way people behave, what use is it to speak of that when everyone knows that general moral standards are ruined once and for all by war? It is the cause of contempt for duty, disregard for law, readiness to dare any sort of crime. It is the source of the huge teeming flood we have of mercenaries, robbers, despoilers of churches and assassins. Worst of all, this deadly pestilence cannot be contained within its original limits, but, having begun in one quarter, it infects not only neighbouring regions like a contagious disease but even, through the effects of trade, of family or political alliances, drags remote ones into the general uproar and turmoil. In fact war is born from war, a real war from a counterfeit one, a huge war grows from a tiny one, and it is not unusual to see the same thing happen in these cases as the fables tell us about the Lernaean monster.[13]

It was for these reasons, I believe, that the ancient poets, who penetrated with the greatest discernment into the significance and nature of things and also pictured them in the most suggestive images, have related that war was sent into the world from the infernal regions by means of the Furies and that not just any Fury was suitable to carry through this work – it was the most deadly one of all that was chosen:

* * * * *

12 'than if the enemy ... grief' was added in 1526.
13 The multi-headed hydra, which grew two or three heads to replace one cut off (Hesiod *Theogony* 313–15, Servius on *Aeneid* 6.287), finally killed by Hercules; cf *Adagia* I iii 27 A Lerna of troubles (to which might be added references in Pausanias 2.37.1 and 4) and n52 below.

she who has a thousand names,
A thousand ways of causing harm.[14]

Armed with countless serpents she blows her hellish horn.[15] Pan fills everything with mindless tumult.[16] Bellona cracks her furious whip.[17] Godless Rage, breaking all his knotted chains, flies out with gory mouth,[18] hideous to see. This has not escaped grammarians either, some of whom would have it that war is called *bellum* by antiphrasis because it has nothing good or *bellum* 'beautiful' about it;[19] war is 'beautiful' in the same way that the Furies are the Eumenides 'the Kindly Ones.'[20] Other grammarians prefer to think it is derived from *bellua* 'beast' because it is an act of brute beasts not of men to come together to destroy each other.[21] But to me it seems worse than savage, worse than brutish, to resort to armed conflict. In the first place, most animals live in harmony and good order with their own kind, moving in herds and ensuring mutual protection. Not even all wild animals are fighters by nature (there are harmless ones as well, like deer and hares), it is only the most savage like lions, wolves, and tigers. But even these do not make war on each other as we do.[22] Dog does not eat dog-flesh,[23] lions do not inflict their ferocity on each other,[24] snake lives in peace with snake, between venomous creatures there is an understanding. But for man no wild beast is more dangerous than man.[25] And then, when they do fight, animals fight with their own weapons; we men equip ourselves to destroy men with unnatural instruments devised by the art of devils.

* * * * *

14 Virgil *Aeneid* 7.337–8, where Allecto is named as the Fury or Erinys
15 In Erasmus' Latin 'hellish' is *tartareus*; Virgil uses it of Allecto's sisters in the preceding passage and speaks of her 'countless black serpents'; her horn is mentioned in *Aeneid* 7.513.
16 Cf *Adagia* III vii 3 A panic attack (215 above).
17 A Roman goddess of war (cf *Aeneid* 8.703) but it is Allecto who cracks her whip in *Aeneid* 7.451.
18 Cf *Aeneid* 1.294–6.
19 Servius on *Aeneid* 1.22 (*bellum a nulla re bella*); Donatus *Ars grammatica* 3.6 in H. Keil ed *Grammatici latini* (Leipzig 1855–80) IV 402
20 See Sophocles *Oedipus Coloneus* 42–3, Servius on *Aeneid* 6.250, Suda K 215.
21 Cf Pompeius Festus page 30 Lindsay.
22 Cf Ep 288 (CWE 2 280:27–33), *De copia* II (CWE 24 601:2–4), *Querela pacis* (CWE 27 306–7).
23 Varro *De lingua latina* 7.31. Otto 323. Not listed in its own right in the *Adagia* though alluded to in II i 86 Keep wolf-cubs
24 Pliny *Naturalis historia* 7.5
25 Cf *Adagia* I i 70 Man is a wolf to man.

And animals do not become fierce for trivial reasons, but when hunger drives them mad, or when they feel they are being hunted, or when they fear for their young. But, God in heaven, we humans, what tragedies of wars we stir up, and for what frivolous causes! For the emptiest of territorial claims, out of childish anger, because some woman we intended to marry has been denied us,[26] for reasons even more ridiculous than these. And then among animals combat is always one to one, and very brief, and however bloody the fight may be, one or the other breaks away when wounded. When did anyone hear of a hundred thousand animals falling dead together after tearing each other to pieces, as men do everywhere? Remember too that just as some animals have a natural hostility for others of a different species, so conversely with some they have a real and permanent friendship. But between man and man, any man and any other, warfare is perpetual, and no treaty is capable of holding between any mortals – so true is it that anything that has departed from its own nature degenerates into a species worse than if Nature herself had implanted the vice. Do you want to know what a savage, foul thing war is, how unworthy of man? Have you ever seen a lion forced to fight a bear? What grimaces, what roaring, what growling, what ferocity, what tearing of flesh! It strikes horror in anyone who sees it even from a safe distance. But how much more loathsome, how much more savage, is the sight of a man fighting a man armed with so many weapons and so many missiles. I ask you, who would believe these were human beings if familiarity with the evil had not taken away our sense of wonder? Their eyes burn, their faces are pale, their step betokens madness, the voice grates, the shouting is mindless, the man is entirely turned to iron; their weapons clang, their cannons spout flashes of lightning. It would be more humane if man devoured man for food and drank his blood; some indeed have even gone this far, doing out of hatred what custom or necessity would have rendered more excusable.[27] But now the same thing is done in a crueller way, with poisoned darts and hellish machines. There is no trace of man in it anywhere.

Do you think Nature herself would recognize here what she created? And if anyone were to point it out to her, would she not be right to curse her deed as wicked, saying: 'What new sight is this I see? What hell has

* * * * *

26 Cf *Querela pacis* (CWE 27 305). The editor, Betty Radice, suggests (nn103 and 104) that the first part may be a reference to the French claim on Milan and Naples and the last an allusion to Anne of Brittany, betrothed to Maximilian but married to Charles VIII in 1491.
27 'what ... excusable' was added in *1526*.

produced this monstrosity for us? There are some who call me a harsh stepmother[28] because in the whole grand total of things I made a few poisonous
creatures – although even these were meant to yield benefit to man – because I made a few animals that were not gentle – although no beast is
so savage that it cannot be tamed by skill and kindness. The art of man
can make lions tame, serpents gentle, and bears obedient. Who then is this,
worse than a stepmother, who has given us this new beast, a plague to all
the world? There was one creature I brought forth made entirely for kindly
actions – peaceful, friendly, helpful. What has happened to make him degenerate into a beast like this? I recognize nothing in him of the man I created. What evil genius has degraded my work?[29] What sorceress has con-
jured away his human mind and called up an animal's in its place? What
Circe has changed his native shape? I would order the unhappy creature
to look at himself in a mirror; but what can the eyes see when the mind
is gone? But look at yourself, you raging warmonger, if you can somehow
come to your senses. Where did you get that threatening crest on your head,
that glittering helmet, those iron horns, those winged elbow-pieces, those
scales, those brazen teeth, that plate-armour, those deadly arrows, that more
than savage voice, that more than bestial face, that thunder and lightening
more terrifying and more deadly than Jupiter's own bolt? I made you a
creature in some sense divine; what came into your head to change yourself into a brute so monstrous that no beast will be a brute in future if compared to man?' I think Nature, the great builder of all things, would say all
this and much more.

This then is how man is constituted, as we have shown, and this is
what war is like, as we experience it all too often. So it seems a matter for
considerable wonder what god, what sickness or what chance first put it into
the heart of man to plunge a deadly sword into human vitals. It must have
been by many stages that he descended to such an extraordinary madness.
Indeed, 'No one ever fell all at once to the worst depths of shame ...' as
the satirist says,[30] and the greatest evils have always crept into the lives
of men in the shadow and semblance of good. Long ago therefore when
the first primitive men lived in the forests, naked, without fortifications or
homes, they were sometimes attacked by savage beasts. It was with these
that man first went to war, and a man was considered brave and a leader

* * * * *

28 In Latin *noverca*; cf Pliny *Naturalis historia* 7.1, Quintilian 12.1.2, and *Adagia* I
    viii 64 One day's a stepmother and one's a mother.
29 Cf *Adagia* I i 72 An evil genius.
30 Juvenal 2.83

if he had driven off attacking beasts from his fellow humans. Moreover it seemed entirely just that slayers should be slain and butchers should be butchered, especially when they suffered no harm from us and attacked our kind without provocation. Since such deeds won high praise – this was the reason Hercules was deified – spirited young people began to hunt wild animals everywhere and to show off the skins as trophies. Then, not content with having killed, they protected themselves with the skins against the cold of winter. Such were the first murders and the first spoils.

After this they went further and dared to do a thing that Pythagoras deemed thoroughly wicked[31] and that might seem unnatural to us if custom did not tell us otherwise. Custom has such force everywhere that among certain peoples it was considered a matter of duty to beat up an aged parent, throw him into a pit and so deprive of life the one who had given it;[32] it was thought pious to eat the flesh of one's intimate friends; it was held to be a fine thing that a virgin should become a common prostitute in the temple of Venus; and there were many other things more absurd than these that would be shocking to anyone if they were so much as mentioned here, so true is it that nothing is too villainous, or too cruel to gain approval if custom recommends it. So, what was the crime they dared to commit? It was that they did not shrink from taking the carcasses of slain animals for food, to tear dead flesh with their teeth, to drink the blood and suck the gore, to 'stuff their entrails with other entrails' as Ovid says.[33] That crime, however monstrous it might seem to gentler minds, was nevertheless sanctioned by usage and convenience. It has even become a pleasure to see, among the luxuries of the table, the semblance of a corpse. Meats are covered under crusts like buried corpses, they are embalmed with scents, an inscription is placed on them: 'Here lies a boar,' 'This is the grave of a bear' – What carrion pleasures![34] And they went further: from dangerous beasts they moved to harmless animals. There was a general onslaught on sheep, 'a creature without trickery or guile'[35] There was an onslaught on the hare, whose only crime was to be edible. Nor did they refrain from eating the

* * * * *

31 Diogenes Laertius 8.13 ('Pythagoras'), Plutarch *Moralia* 993A *De esu carnium*, and Ovid *Metamorphoses* 15.60–142. ASD also suggests parallels in the passage with Herodotus 3.38, 1.216, 3.99, and 1.199.
32 Cf in *Adagia* III v 1 A Sardonic laugh (59 above), the account of the Sardinians.
33 Ovid *Metamorphoses* 15.88
34 'It has even become … pleasures' was added in *1526*.
35 Ovid *Metamorphoses* 15.120, although Ovid is speaking of the ox. Erasmus' reference to an ox in the next sentence is probably an echo of the same passage.

domestic ox who had supported the ungrateful family for so long with his hard labour; no species of bird or fish was spared, and this tyranny of the stomach reached the point that no animal was ever safe from the cruelty of man. But custom also induced them to believe that this was not cruelty to any species providing it was not men they slaughtered.

Vice however is like the sea: we may have the choice of shutting it out, but to let it in and then contain it, no one has that power; once admitted, neither is controlled by our will but is driven by its own momentum. After they had had some practice in killing with these beginnings, anger convinced them that man should assault man with clubs or stones, or their fists. For up till then it was with such weapons that they fought, I imagine, and by killing beasts they would have learned that a man too can be slaughtered with very little trouble. But this kind of barbarity remained for a long time a matter of fighting between individuals. When one was defeated, the war was over; sometimes both fell, but then both were unworthy to live.[36] Moreover there was some appearance of right in having killed an enemy, and it began to be a matter for praise if one killed some violent or pernicious man, such as Cacus and Busiris[37] were said to be, and freed the world of such monsters. We see such titles to praise among the achievements of Hercules. The next step was that numbers of people banded together according to kinship, neighbourhood, or close connection, and what is now called brigandage was then called war. Up till then it was a matter of stones and stakes with fire-hardened points; a stream in the way or a crag or some such obstacle would put an end to the fighting. Meanwhile, as savagery increased with habit, as anger rose and ambition became more and more inflamed, ingenuity provided weapons to match their violence. Men invented any sort of arms they could to defend themselves and missiles to destroy the enemy. Now they began to make war everywhere, now in greater numbers, now with weapons. But this obvious madness had its own code of honour: they called it *bellum* 'beautiful' or 'war,'[38] and sought to make it a virtue if a man defended children, wife, herds, or places of retreat from enemy attacks at the risk of his own life. And so malice[39] grew

* * * * *

36 'When ... live' was added in 1526.
37 Cacus was a brigand (Virgil *Aeneid* 8.194, Livy 1.7.5, Ovid *Fasti* 1.550) and Busiris an Egyptian king (Cicero *De republica* 3.15, Virgil *Georgics* 3.5), both killed by Hercules.
38 See the passage at 405 with nn19 and 21 above.
39 *Malitia* [sic] from 1515 to 1520. In 1523 it was mistakenly printed as *militia*, but corrected to *malitia* in the copy of this edition with manuscript corrections by

gradually side by side with civilization; city began to declare war on city, region on region, kingdom on kingdom, although there still remained at this time, in something that was excessively cruel in itself, traces of the humanity of the earliest times. Priests were sent to demand satisfaction,[40] they called the gods to witness, they skirmished with words before they came to blows. The battle was fought with ordinary weapons, and courage, not trickery. It was a crime to strike the enemy if the signal for battle had not been given; it was forbidden to go on fighting when the general had ordered the retreat to be sounded. In short, it was a contest in bravery and honour rather than a desire to kill.

And as yet there was no resort to arms except against foreigners, who because of this were called *hostes* 'enemies,' a word like *hospites* 'strangers.'[41] From these beginnings empires were born – and no nation ever achieved empire without great shedding of human blood. Since then there has been constant warfare back and forth, as one man drives another out of the seat of empire and seizes it for himself. Subsequently, as power had fallen into the hands of the most criminal sorts of mortals, armed attacks were made on anybody at will, and it was not the evildoers but the wealthy who began to be most exposed to the dangers of war, and the aim of fighting was no longer glory but filthy lucre or something even more base than that. I have no doubt that Pythagoras, wisest of men, foresaw this when he sought by his philosophical teaching to deter the inexperienced multitude from slaughtering flocks.[42] He could see that someone who, without any provocation or injury, was accustomed to shedding the blood of harmless animals, would not hesitate to kill a man when angry or roused by insults. What is war anyway but murder and brigandage committed by many, all the more criminal because it is more widespread? But these ideas are laughed at as

* * * * *

Erasmus that R. Hoven, editor of ASD, calls π. However the incorrect *militia* continued to appear in all subsequent editions, including LB.

40 Latin *repetebantur res per fecialem*; for the office of the *fetialis* see Varro *De lingua latina* 5.86, Livy 1.24.4–6 and 1.32.5–6, Cicero *De legibus* 2.21 and *De officiis* 1.36, Sallust *Historiarum fragmenta* 3.61.17; cf *Adagia* II ix 61 Hands off the holy man.
41 Cf Servius on *Aeneid* 4.424.
42 There is no specific instruction to this effect among the Symbols of Pythagoras (see *Adagia* I i 2), in the Pseudo-Pythagorean *Carmen aureum*, in Diogenes Laertius, who reports a number of precepts, in Plutarch (see n31 above), nor in Iamblichus *Protrepticus* 21, which has the fullest listing of them (ed H. Pistelli [Stuttgart 1967] 106–8). Erasmus seems to be suggesting it as a general tendency of Pythagorean teaching for the uninitiated, possibly inspired by Ovid *Metamorphoses* 15.72–126.

the ravings of schoolmen by the boorish lords of our own time, who have nothing human beyond the appearance of men but think themselves gods.[43]

And yet from these beginnings we find the madness has reached such a point that life consists of nothing else. We are continually at war, nation clashes with nation, kingdom with kingdom, city with city, prince with prince, people with people and, as even the heathen admit is wicked, relative with relative, kinsman with kinsman, brother with brother, son with father; finally, worse in my opinion than all these, Christian with fellow man, and worst of all, I must add reluctantly, Christian with Christian. And men are so blind in their thinking that no one is surprised at this, no one denounces it. There are some who applaud it, make a glorious parade of it, call it 'holy' when it is worse than hellish, and inflame rulers already crazed with fury, pouring oil on the fire, as they say.[44] One uses the sanctity of the pulpit to promise pardon for all sins committed by those who fight under his prince's flag. Another declaims, 'Invincible prince, if you only continue your present support of religion, God will fight on your side.' A third promises certain victory, and distorts the words of the prophets to a wicked purpose with his interpretations of 'You will not be afraid of the terror by night nor of the arrow that flies by day, nor of the demon of midday,' and 'A thousand will fall at your side, and ten thousand on your right,' and 'You will walk upon the asp and the basilisk, and tread underfoot the lion and the dragon.'[45] In short, the whole of this mystical psalm was perverted to apply to profane things, to fit the case of this or that ruler. There were plenty of such prophets on both sides, and plenty of people to applaud such prophets. We have heard bellicose sermons of this sort from monks, theologians, and bishops.[46] So the decrepit make war,[47] priests make war, monks make war, and we involve Christ in something so diabolical! Two armies advance on each other and both carry the standard of the cross, which in itself could teach them how appropriate it is to conquer Christians. From that heavenly banner, which represents the complete and ineffable union of all Christians, they rush to mutual slaughter; and of this wicked deed

* * * * *

43 'who have ... gods' was added in 1517/18.
44 *Adagia* I ii 9 To pour oil on the fire
45 The phrases 'You will not be afraid ... dragon' are from Psalm 91:5–7 and 13. LB has *a sagitta volante in te* 'of the arrow that flies towards you,' but 1536 has the biblical *in die* 'by day.'
46 From 'inflame rulers' to here added in 1526
47 Latin *decrepiti*; probably an allusion to Julius II, who was over sixty years old when he began his reign in 1503. Cf *Moria* (CWE 27 139).

we make Christ the witness and the author. Where is the kingdom of the devil if it is not in war? Why do we drag Christ into this when he would be more at home in any brothel than in a war? Paul the Apostle considers it unworthy that any dispute should arise among Christians that needs a judge to settle the case.[48] What if he could see us making war the whole world over, for such trivial reasons, more savagely than any pagans fought, more cruelly than any barbarians? What if he could see that this is done with the authority, encouragement, and help of representatives of the pope – the peacemaker, the unifier of all things – of those who greet the people with the sign of peace? I am not deaf to what has long been shouted at me by the Carians[49] who reap their profit from public misfortune.[50] 'We did not want war! We were forced into it by the crimes of other people! We are taking our rights! Whatever evil war brings, the responsibility should lie with those who gave cause for it.' But let them keep quiet for a moment; I will refute their special pleadings and remove this cosmetic we use to hide our disease.

Just as I have contrasted man and war, that is, the most peaceable of animals with what is by far the most barbarous activity, so that the horror of it should be clearer, let me now contrast war and peace, the most wretched and wicked of conditions with the happiest and best; it will then be clear what madness it is to resort to war with so much clamour, so much effort, so much expense, so much danger, and so many disasters, when concord could be bought at much less cost. In the first place, what is there in the whole world better and sweeter than friendship? Absolutely nothing. But what is peace if not friendship among many people? Conversely, war is likewise nothing but hatred between large numbers. It is the characteristic of good things that the more widespread they are the more advantage they bring. Therefore since friendship between one person and another is such a pleasant and salutary thing, how great the happiness will be if kingdom is united with kingdom and nation with nation in bonds of friendship. Conversely it is in the nature of evils that the wider they spread the more they deserve their appellation. Therefore if it is deplorable, if it is criminal for a man to attack another with the sword, how much more destructive it is, how much more criminal for the same deed to be done by so many thousands of men? In concord, small things grow; in discord, even great

* * * * *

48 Cf 1 Cor 6:1.
49 Mercenaries; cf *Adagia* I vi 14 Risk it on a Carian.
50 'who reap ... misfortune' was added in *1517/18*.

things decline.[51] Peace is the mother and the nurse of all that is good. War immediately and once and for all buries, extinguishes and destroys all that is joyous and beautiful, and pours out a veritable Lerna of evils into the lives of men.[52] In times of peace it is just as if a fresh spring sun has begun to shine on human affairs; fields are cultivated, gardens turn green, flocks graze contentedly, farms are established and towns rise, fallen buildings are restored, others ornamented and enlarged, wealth increases, pleasures are nurtured, law is in repute, statecraft flourishes, religion is fervent, justice reigns, goodwill prevails, artisans practise their crafts with skill, the earnings of the poor are greater and the opulence of the rich more splendid. The study of the most noble subjects thrives, youth is educated, old age enjoys a peaceful leisure, girls are happily married, 'Young mothers are praised for children who resemble their fathers.'[53] Good men prosper, bad men are less bad.[54] But as soon as the raging storm of war irrupts, ye gods, what a monstrous sea of troubles[55] rushes in, flooding and overwhelming everything. Flocks are driven off, crops trampled, farmers slaughtered, farms burned, flourishing cities built over so many centuries are overturned by a single onslaught, so much easier is it to do harm than good! Citizens' wealth falls into the hands of damnable brigands and assassins; homes grieve with fear, mourning, and complaints; everything is filled with lamentations. The skills of craftsmen grow cold, the poor must starve or resort to wicked means. The rich either mourn their plundered wealth or tremble for what they have left, much to be pitied in either case. If girls marry, they do so with sadness and foreboding. Deserted wives remain childless in their homes, the laws are silent,[56] goodwill is mocked, there is no place for justice, religion is a subject of scorn, there is no distinction at all between sacred and profane. Youth is corrupted with every sort of vice, the old weep and curse the length of their days. Study and learning are without honour. In short, we find more evils in war than any man's words can express, still less any words of mine.

* * * * *

51 Sallust *Bellum Jugurthinum* 10.6; Seneca *Letters* 94.46; Otto 418. Cf *Adagia* III viii 63 With unanimity even slender resources are strengthened (305 above).
52 The lake at Lerna (n13 above) was notoriously a sewer and rubbish tip. Erasmus uses the image of the mess some men make of their life in the *Moria* (CWE 27 114).
53 Horace *Odes* 4.5.23
54 This sentence was added in *1517/18*.
55 *Adagia* I iii 28 Sea of troubles
56 Cf Cicero *Pro T. Annio Milone* 4.11.

Perhaps it could be borne if wars only made us miserable and not malevolent and wicked too, if peace only made us happier and not better too. But it is a wicked man who resorts to war.[57] There are already, alas! too many evils that never cease to worry hard-pressed mortals whether they will or no, wearing them down and consuming them. About two thousand years ago there were some three hundred names of illnesses noted by physicians,[58] not including sub-types – the new diseases that develop every day – and old age itself, the malady with no cure.[59] We read of whole cities in one place destroyed by an earthquake, set on fire by lightning in another, solid areas of ground in yet another swallowed up by a gaping hole, towns undermined by excavations and collapsing, not to mention the vast number of people carried off by events so common as to be ignored: flooding of seas and rivers, avalanches and collapsing buildings, poisonings, falls, attacks by wild animals, eating, drinking, sleeping. One person chokes on a hair while drinking milk, another on a grape-seed, a third on a fish-bone stuck in his throat. Some have died of sudden joy – though to die of great sorrow is less extraordinary. Then there are the fatal epidemics that rage quite commonly everywhere. There is no part of the world where human life, in any case so brief in itself, is not in danger. It is prey to so many woes that Homer was right to declare man the most wretched of living creatures.[60] But these woes cannot easily be avoided and do not happen by our own fault, so they make us wretched but not guilty. What is it that makes creatures exposed to such a multitude of calamities go looking for further trouble as if they had none already? And looking not for just any trouble but the most terrible of all: so destructive that it alone beats all the others, so fertile that it alone contains all the others, so deadly that it makes people as wicked[61] as it makes them tormented, utterly wretched yet not to be pitied, except those who want war the least and suffer from it the most.[62] Add to all this that the advantages of peace spread very widely and most people have a share in them. In war, if anything turns out happily – though heaven knows whether anything in war could be called happy! – it affects only a few, and unworthy ones at that. The salvation of one is the ruin of another;

* * * * *

57 This sentence was added in 1526.
58 Pliny *Naturalis historia* 26.9
59 Latin *immedicabilem* in 1526, *inevitabilem* in 1515–23; cf Terence *Phormio* 575, Seneca *Letters* 108.28 (*insanabilis*), and *Adagia* II vi 37 Old age is sickness itself.
60 Homer *Iliad* 17.446–7
61 LB omits *impios*.
62 'except ... most' was added in 1523.

one man's wealth is the spoils taken from another; this man's triumph is that man's grief, with the result that the unhappiness is bitter, but the happiness is monstrous and bloody. Most often both sides weep over 'a Cadmean victory,' as it is called.[63] I wonder whether any war has ever ended so successfully that a sensible victor did not regret having undertaken it. So, since peace is of all states both the best and most joyful, and since war, conversely, is the most wretched and most unjust, how can we believe that people are in their right mind when they can ensure peace with little trouble yet prefer to resort to war, even at the cost of the greatest difficulties?

What an unpleasant thing it is in the first place, that first rumour of war. And then what resentment the ruler must face as he strips his subjects bare with frequent taxes, how much trouble in raising and keeping extra troops, in bringing in foreign troops and mercenaries. What trouble and expense too fitting out ships, building and repairing fortresses and camps, furnishing tents, constructing and moving machines, weapons, missiles, baggage, transport, provisions. What labours must be put into raising walls, digging trenches and underground passages, in setting watches, posting sentries, holding manoeuvres. I am still saying nothing of alarms and dangers – for what is not to be feared in war? Who could possibly tell how many hardships these idiots of soldiers put up with in their camps? And they deserve worse just for being willing to put up with them:[64] food at which a Cyprian ox would turn up its nose,[65] sleeping quarters that would be scorned by a dung-beetle,[66] few hours of sleep and those not of their own choosing, a tent that lets in the wind from every direction, or no tent at all. They have to endure an open-air life, sleep on the ground, stand in their arms, bear hunger, cold, heat, dust, rain. They have to obey their commanders, they have to bear floggings with rods; for no slave's bondage is more humiliating than soldiers' service. Add to this that when the fatal signal is given you have to go and face up to death, either to kill mercilessly or to fall miserably. We undergo all these woes in order to get to the most wretched part of all.[67] We afflict ourselves first with these countless woes, just in order to inflict them on others.

* * * * *

63 *Adagia* II viii 34
64 'And they' to here added in *1517/18*.
65 *Adagia* I x 95
66 'sleeping quarters' to here added in *1526*; cf *Adagia* III vii 1 A dung beetle hunting an eagle (199 above with n136).
67 Latin *res omnium miserrima*, ie war – the same phrase as was used at the end of the previous paragraph

If we will only do the arithmetic[68] and weigh up in honest terms the cost of war and the cost of peace, we shall soon discover that the latter can be bought for a tenth part of the worry, effort, distress, risk, expense, and bloodshed that war involves. You lead forth into danger a huge host of men to demolish some town; but with the labour of these men, and with no danger at all, you could have built another town, and a far finer one! But you want to harm the enemy. That alone is inhumane, but just think: Could you harm them without first harming your own men? And it seems the act of a madman to accept such certain trouble when it is uncertain which way the dice of war will fall.

But admitting that the heathen might have been brought to this state of madness by stupidity, anger, ambition, greed, or barbarity, or, as I more readily suppose, by the Furies sent from Hell, where did we get the idea that Christian should draw a bloody sword on Christian? It is called parricide if one brother kills another, but Christian is united with Christian more closely than any blood brother, unless the bonds of nature are tighter than those of Christ. What an absurdity that there should be almost continuous warfare between those whom the church holds under one roof, who boast of being members of the same body with the same head, who is Christ.[69] They have one father in heaven, they are given life by the same spirit, initiated into the same mysteries, redeemed by the same blood, reborn in the same baptism, nourished by the same sacraments; they serve the same commander, eat the same bread, share the same cup; they have a common enemy in the devil and finally are called every one to the same inheritance.[70] Where else are there so many symbols of perfect concord? So many lessons of peace? One commandment Christ called his own – the commandment of love.[71] What is more opposed to love than war? He greets his own with the blessed sign of peace.[72] To his disciples he gives nothing but peace and leaves nothing but peace.[73] In those holy prayers of his, he prays to the Father particularly that, as he was one with God,[74] so his own (that is, Christians) should be one with him. As you can hear, this is something more than peace, or friendship or concord. The prefiguration of Christ was Solomon, whose name means

* * * * *

68 Latin *rem ad calculum vocare*; cf in *Adagia* I v 55 (CWE 31 432:12): *ad calculos revocare* 'reduces ... to a question of figures.'
69 Cf Romans 12:5 and n86 below.
70 Cf Romans 8:17.
71 John 13:34 and 15:12
72 Cf Luke 24:36; John 20:19, 21, 26.
73 John 14:27. LB omits the phrase *nihil donat, praeter pacem* here, but all the early editions have the complete biblical quotation.
74 John 17:21

'Peacemaker' in Hebrew;[75] he was chosen by God to build the temple. David, who was greatly beloved[76] for his other virtues, was nevertheless kept away from the building of the temple because he was a man of blood.[77] But he made war at God's command usually against the wicked and that in an age which had not yet learned from Him, who came to complete the law of Moses, that we should love even our enemies.[78] When Christ was born, it was not of war or triumphs that the angels sang, but of peace.[79] Even before he was born, the mystic prophet sang of him: 'And his place was made in peace.'[80]

Search the whole of his teaching; nowhere will you find anything that does not breathe peace, that does not ring of friendship, that does not savour of love. And since he knew that peace cannot exist except when we sincerely despise the things for which this world is prepared to fight, he commanded us to learn from him to be meek.[81] 'Blessed' was his word for those who thought nothing of riches and of their daughter Pride, for he called them the 'poor in spirit'; 'blessed' were those who reject the pleasures of this world – he called them those that mourn; those who allow themselves to be turned out of their property knowing that this world is nothing but an exile and that the real homeland and the real treasure of the devout are in heaven. 'Blessed' are those who do good to everyone, and yet men revile and persecute them with impunity.[82] He forbad anyone to resist evil.[83] To keep the matter short, just as the whole of his doctrine teaches tolerance and love, so his whole life is a lesson in gentleness. This was how he reigned, how he fought, how he conquered, how he triumphed. The apostles, who drank the spirit of Christ in its purest form and were gloriously drunk with that wine,[84] have no other teaching.

What is the sound that rings everywhere in Paul's letters but peace, gentleness and charity? What does John talk of, repeatedly, but love? What

* * * * *

75 1 Chron 22:9
76 Latin *egregie charum*; LB has *clarum*, an error that crept in from *1528* on.
77 2 Sam 7:12–17, 1 Kings 8:16–19, 1 Chron 17:3–15, 22:8, 28:2–3
78 From 'David' to here was added in *1523*; Matt 5:17 and 44, Luke 6:27
79 Luke 2:14
80 Ps 76:2; an interpretation rather than a quotation from the psalm, which actually says 'in Salem ... in Zion.' This psalm is one of the Songs of Asaph. Asaph was a seer (2 Chron 29:30) and one of the three musicians whom David put in charge of music in the temple (1 Chron 6:31); twelve psalms (Ps 50 and 73–83), all of a prophetic character, are assigned to him.
81 Matt 11:29
82 Matt 5:3–12
83 Matt 5:39
84 A reference to Acts 2:13–17; cf *Moria* (CWE 27 149).

else does Peter say? What else do all truly Christian writers say? Where does all this noise of wars come from among the sons of peace? Is it nothing but a fable when Christ calls himself the vine and his followers the branches?[85] Who ever saw a branch fighting with a branch? Is it meaningless, the figure that Paul used more than once: that the Church is nothing if not one body composed of different members, joined to one head, who is Christ?[86] Who ever saw the eye fighting with the hand, or the stomach with the foot? In this universe there is a harmony of all the very different elements. In the body of a living creature, there is peace between one member and another, and the gift that each part has, it has not for itself alone but for all in common. If anything happens to one part, the whole body comes to its aid. Is the bond of nature in a perishable body more powerful that the spiritual bond uniting the mystical and immortal body? Is it in vain that we pray as Christ taught us: 'Thy will be done on earth, as it is in heaven'?[87] In the heavenly city there is complete concord, and Christ wanted his church to be no less than a heavenly people on earth living, as far as possible, in the image of that city, hastening towards him and depending on it.

Let me ask you to picture now some strange visitor, from the cities on the moon where Empedocles lives or from one of those innumerable worlds that Democritus imagined,[88] who had come to this world of ours seeking to learn what goes on here. Suppose that he has learned a lot about different things and has heard that there is one animal that is a wonderful combination of a body, which it has in common with the beasts, and a soul which is an image of the divine mind. This creature is so noble that although it lives here in exile it rules over all other animals because, owing to its heavenly origin, it always strives towards heavenly and immortal things. He has heard that God cared for it so much that, seeing that it could not achieve what it strove for either by its own natural strength or by philosophical reasoning, he sent his only son here to bring a new kind of teaching. Suppose then that, having learned everything about the life and teachings of Christ, he wishes to observe from some lofty observatory[89]

* * * * *

85 John 15:5
86 Rom 12:5, Eph 4:16 and 5:23
87 Matt 6:10
88 Diogenes Laertius 8.62, 66, 68 ('Empedocles') records stories that Empedocles made claims to immortality. The editor of ASD suggests this passage may reflect an idea that Diogenes Laertius attributes to Heraclides (8.72). For Democritus' unlimited worlds see Diogenes Laertius 9.44 ('Democritus').
89 Latin *specula*; cf *Adagia* IV iii 95 As if from a watch-tower.

what he had heard about. When he observes all the other animals behaving properly, each following the laws of nature according to its own kind and seeking nothing except what Nature prescribes, and one animal trafficking, bargaining, quarrelling, and warring, will he not surmise that the 'man' he has heard about is any animal but man himself? Finally when man is pointed out to him and he tries to discern the whereabouts of the Christian flock that follows the teaching of its heavenly master and offers an image of the angelic city, will he not judge that the Christians live anywhere but in those countries in which he has seen such opulence, luxury, licence, pomp, tyranny, ambition, deceit, envy, anger, dissension, brawls, fights, wars, and tumults; in short a Lerna[90] of all those things that Christ condemns, worse than any to be found among the Turks or Saracens?

Where did it creep in from then, this plague that has infected the people of Christ? Doubtless this evil, like most others, found acceptance gradually with the heedless. For every bad thing either slips by degrees into the life of men or insinuates itself under the pretext of something good. The first thing to creep in in this case was erudition, apparently ideal for confuting heretics, armed as they were with the writings of philosophers, poets and orators. At the very beginning such things were not studied by Christians, but people who had to do with them before they knew Christ turned what they had acquired to pious uses. Eloquence too, at first disguised rather than spurned, was later openly approved. Then, on the pretext of overthrowing heresy, an ostentatious love of controversy crept in, which was a major scourge to the church. Finally things went so far that the whole of Aristotle was accepted into the heart of theology, and accepted to the extent that his authority was almost more sacred than that of Christ. For if anything Christ said is not easily seen as fitted to the way we live, we are permitted to interpret it differently, but anyone who dares to oppose in the slightest degree the oracles of Aristotle is immediately hissed off the stage. From the latter we have learned that human happiness is not complete without bodily comforts and worldly goods. From him we have learned that a state in which all property is held in common cannot flourish. We try to fuse together all his decrees and the teachings of Christ, which is like mixing fire and water.[91] We have also accepted some things from Roman law because of their obvious fairness, and in order to reconcile the two better we have twisted gospel teaching as far as we could to fit them.

* * * * *

90 See nn13 and 52 above.
91 *Adagia* IV iii 94 Mixing fire and water

But Roman law allows us to meet force with force[92] and each person to pursue his own rights; it sanctions bargaining, it allows usury, providing it is moderate, and describes war as praiseworthy, providing it is just. 'Just,' however, is defined as what has been ordered by the ruler, even if he is a minor or a fool.[93] In fact the whole teaching of Christ is so contaminated by the writings of pagan dialecticians, sophists, mathematicians, orators, poets, philosophers, and lawyers that the greater part of a lifetime must be spent before you are free to investigate the sacred scriptures; and when you do get to them you are inevitably so corrupted with all these worldly ideas that the precepts of Christ either seem utterly repugnant or they are distorted to fit the teachings of the pagans. And we are so far from condemning this state of affairs that it is regarded as a sin for anyone to speak about Christian scriptures if he has not first crammed himself 'up to both ears,' as they say,[94] with nonsense out of Aristotle, or rather out of the sophists. As if the teachings of Christ were not truly something that could be entirely shared by all, or had any kind of common ground with the wisdom of the philosophers.

The next stage was that we were accorded much honour, but spontaneously offered;[95] then we began to demand it as our due. That seemed not unfair. Then we were given money, but to be distributed as alms to the poor; then it was given even for our own use. Why not? For we have learned that this is the order of charity, that each must be his own neighbour.[96] There was no lack of excuses for this fault: it is one's duty to consider the needs of one's children, it is fair that one should prepare in advance for old age. Finally 'Why should I refuse riches,' they say, 'if they are gained honestly?' By these stages it has gradually reached the point where the richest is considered the best, and never was wealth held in greater honour among pagans than it is nowadays[97] among Christians. What is there anywhere, either sacred or profane, that is not controlled by wealth? It seemed some power

* * * * *

92 Latin *vim vi repellere*; cf Ulpian in the *Digest* 4.2.12.1.
93 For Erasmus' understanding of the word in this context, as opposed to the legal definition, see 425 below in the paragraph beginning 'Moreover, if Christ approved ...': 'just,' however, means any war declared in any way against anybody by any prince. This sentence was also added in 1526.
94 *Adagia* II iii 27 Up to both ears
95 'but spontaneously offered' was added in 1523.
96 Latin *sibi quisque sit proximus*; cf *sibi quisque amicus est* in *Adagia* I iii 91 Everybody wants things to go better for himself than for others, or Charity begins at home.
97 Latin *apud ethnicos, quam hodie sit*, added in 1515–36, omitted in LB

should go with these honours; and there was no lack of people willing to cede it. This also became an accepted thing, but somewhat reluctantly and sparingly. Then they were satisfied with the title alone and willingly left the business to others. In the end, bit by bit, it has reached the point where a bishop does not think he is a bishop unless he has some worldly power; and an abbot who can never do what tyrants do is scarcely a proper abbot. Finally, brazen-faced,[98] we have thrown away all shame and broken down all the barriers of modesty. Whatever sort of avarice existed among the heathen – whatever ambition, luxury, pomp, tyranny – we imitate, equal and outdo.

I say nothing of less important things, but was there ever war among the heathen as continuous and as cruel as among Christians? What storms have we not seen these past few years, what waves of war, what broken treaties, what bloodshed! What nation has not clashed swords with what other? And then we abominate the Turk; as if there could be any spectacle more agreeable to the Turks than what we ourselves provide for them daily with our massacres of each other. Madness seized Xerxes[99] when he led that huge multitude to invade Greece; does he seem sane to you, writing threatening letters to Mount Athos commanding it to move aside, ordering the Hellespont to be whipped because it did not favour him when he wanted to sail across? Rage overcame Alexander the Great; who denies it? That demigod wished for more worlds to conquer,[100] such was the fever for glory that obsessed his immature mind. And yet these men, whom Seneca does not hesitate to call raving bandits,[101] made war more humanely than we do, made war in better faith, without such machines, without such techniques and not for such frivolous causes as we Christians.[102] If you read the histories of the pagans you will find many leaders who resorted to extraordinary tactics to avoid war, who preferred to fetter the enemy by obligations rather

* * * * *

98 Latin *perfricta facie*; cf *Adagia* I viii 47 *Faciem perfricare. Frontis perfrictae*, To wipe off your blushes. To put a bold front on it, and III viii 50 Not worthy to look me in the eye (300 above).

99 Herodotus 7.20 and 35, Plutarch *Moralia* 455D *De cohibenda ira*; cf *Adagia* I iii 1 One ought to be born a king or a fool, CWE 31 229:60–2.

100 Quintus Curtius *Life of Alexander* 9.6.20; Valerius Maximus 8.14 ext 2; Plutarch *Moralia* 466D *De tranquillitate animi*; Juvenal 10.168 (who refers to Alexander as *Pellaeo iuveni* – Alexander was born at Pella 356 BC)

101 On Xerxes, see Seneca *De beneficiis* 6.31.1 and *De ira* 3.16.4; on Alexander, *De beneficiis* 1.13.3, *De ira* 2.23.3 and 3 17.1.

102 The passage from here to 'our own cause is!' at the beginning of the next paragraph but one (423 below) was added in 1526; see ASD II-7 31:556–91n.

than to defeat them by force of arms.[103] Some even considered it better to give up their power than to go to war. But as for us pseudo-Christians, there is nothing we do not snatch at as a pretext for war. Before pagan warriors resorted to arms, they would meet to talk. Among the Romans, when everything else had been tried, a *fetialis* was sent forward with the *paterpatratus*;[104] certain ceremonies were performed; undoubtedly, they were trying to find means of delay, so that the war fever could be cooled. And when all this was completed it was not permitted to engage the enemy until the signal was given, and this was given in such a way that the ordinary soldier would not know when it was to be given. And even when it was given, anyone who was not bound by the military oath was not allowed to challenge or strike the enemy, even if he were living in the camp. Thus Cato the Elder wrote to his son, who was idling in camp, to tell him either to come back to Rome or, if he preferred to remain with the army, to seek the commander's permission to engage in fighting with the enemy.[105] Just as the signal for battle gave the power to fight only to those who were bound by the oath, so the signal by which the retreat was sounded took away from everyone the right to kill. This is why Cyrus praised a certain soldier who had his sword raised to kill his enemy and, hearing the retreat sounded, forthwith let his opponent go.[106] These practices had the effect that no one thought he had the right to kill a man unless necessity forced him to.

Nowadays if, by chance in a wood, a man meets one of the people with whom he is at war – not carrying arms but money, not seeking to fight but running away somewhere to avoid fighting – if he kills him, and having killed him strips him, and having stripped him buries him, this is held to be valour among Christians. 'Soldiers' are those who rush into a fight of their own accord in the hope of some small loot, and fight on either side like gladiators, brothers against brothers, and subjects of the same ruler. Such men come home from battles like these and tell the story of their exploits like soldiers; yet they are not punished as robbers and traitors to their country and deserters of their prince's cause. We loath an executioner because he is hired by the legal authority and puts to death the guilty and the condemned; but men who abandon their parents, wives and children and rush off to war of their own accord, not hired but asking to be hired for

* * * * *

103 There is a play on words here with *devincire* 'fetter' and *devincere* 'defeat.'
104 See n40 above; the *paterpatratus* was the chief of the priests called *fetiales*.
105 Plutarch *Moralia* 273E–F *Quaestiones Romanae*
106 Plutarch in the same passage (n105 above); the source is Xenophon, *Cyropaedia* 4.1.3–4; the soldier was called Chrysantas.

some wicked butchery, are almost more welcome when they go home than if they had never been away. They think they have won some sort of nobility from their villainies. The man who has stolen a garment is infamous; the man who has robbed so many innocent people while he was on his way to join his army, while he was serving as a soldier and when he was coming back is considered a respectable citizen. And the soldier who has conducted himself with the most brutality is thought worthy to play the commander in the next war. So, if you consider the rules of military service in olden times, you will see that military service among Christians is not military service at all but brigandage.

If you compare Christian monarchs with pagan ones, how weak our own cause is![107] They had no ambition but glory;[108] they took pleasure in increasing the prosperity of the provinces they had subjugated in war; where rustic peoples were without education or law and living like wild beasts, they brought refinement and the arts of civilization; they populated uncultivated regions by building towns; they fortified unsafe places, and made men's lives easier by building bridges, wharves, embankments, and a thousand other such amenities, so that it turned out beneficial to be conquered. How many stories are told of things wisely said or soberly done by them, even in the midst of war! But the things done in wars between Christians are too disgusting and too cruel to be mentioned here. The fact is that we copy only the worst practices of the pagans, or rather we outdo them.

But it would be worthwhile to hear how we justify this great madness of ours. 'If it were always a sin to make war,' we are told, 'God would not have commanded the Jews to fight against their enemies.' I hear you, but you should take into account the fact that the Jews hardly ever[109] went to war among themselves, only against foreigners and unbelievers. We Christians fight with Christians. Their reason for fighting was a difference of religion, different gods; we are drawn into it by childish anger, by hunger for money or thirst for glory, often by sordid wages. They fought by divine command, but it is passion that makes us draw the sword. However, if the example of the Jews is so attractive, why do we not by the same token practise circumcision? Why do we not make animal sacrifices? Why do we not abstain from pig's flesh? Why do we not each marry several wives? Since

* * * * *

107 End of the long addition of *1526* (see n102 above)
108 Cf *Querela pacis* (CWE 27 305).
109 Latin *vix unquam* in *1523*; *nunquam* 'never' in *1515, 1517/18*, and *1520*; see ASD II-7 33:603–4n.

we condemn these practices, why is their example in war alone acceptable? Why in a word do we here follow 'the letter that kills'?[110] War was allowed for the Jews, but like divorce, doubtless 'because of the hardness of their hearts.'[111] But after Christ ordered the sword to be put away,[112] it is not proper[113] for Christians to fight, except in the noblest of all battles against the most shameful enemies of the church, against love of money, against anger, against ambition, against the fear of death. These are our Philistines, our Nabuchodonosors, our Moabites, and our Ammonites,[114] with whom we must make no truce, with whom we must be unceasingly at war until the enemy is completely eliminated and peace is installed in their place. Unless we subdue these, there can be no real peace for anyone either with himself or with anyone else. This is the only war that can produce true peace. Anyone who has conquered in this war can have no wish to engage in war with any other mortal. I am not influenced by the fact that some interpret the 'two swords'[115] as the two powers, ecclesiastical and civil – which are both claimed for the successors of Peter[116] – for Christ allowed Peter to err on this very point,[117] so that after he was ordered to put up his sword, no one

* * * * *

110 2 Cor 3:6
111 Matt 19:8, Mark 10:4–5
112 Matt 26:52 and John 18:11
113 Latin *non decet* in *1520–33*; *nefas est* 'it is a sin' in *1515* and *1517/18*. This sentence and the following may be compared with a passage in *Adagia* III iii 1 The Sileni of Alcibiades (CWE 34 475:9–12).
114 Traditional enemies of the Jews, here allegorical figures of love of money, anger, ambition, and fear of death. For a similar allegorization of seven tribes as the seven deadly sins see the *Enchiridion militis christiani* (CWE 66 30).
115 Luke 22:38. First elaborated by Popes Innocent III and IV on the basis of the teachings of St Bernard and as a product of their struggles with the German emperors, the doctrine of the 'two swords' was promulgated by Boniface VIII during his disputes with Philippe IV of France, in the bull *Unam sanctam* (18 November 1302). The doctrine declares that there are two swords in the power of the Church, the spiritual and the temporal. The first is in the hand of the priest; the second is in the hand of kings and knights, but is to be used only with the permission of the priest. The most extreme expressions of the theory are to be found in Giles of Rome (*De ecclesiastica potestate*, 1301) and Augustine of Ancona (*Summa de ecclesiastica potestate*, 1326), but the best known defence of the doctrine was probably that found in the *Summa copiosa* (1253) of the canonist Henry of Segusio (Hostiensis), which was a handbook for canonists down to the seventeenth century.
116 'which ... Peter' was added in *1526*.
117 That is, Christ allowed Peter to carry a sword at this moment (Matt 26:51–2, John 18:11) for the express purpose of being able to order him to put it up. Cf *Julius exclusus* (CWE 27 174–5).

should be left in any doubt that war, which seemed permissible before, was now forbidden. 'But Peter fought,' we are told. He fought, but still as a Jew who had not yet received the truly Christian spirit. And he fought, not for his rights or his property as we do, nor for his own life, but for the life of his master. And lastly, the man who fought was the one who a little later made the denial. If the example of his fighting attracts you, then so should his denial. And though he erred out of honest affection, he was still reproved.

Moreover, if Christ approved[118] this sort of defence – a quite absurd interpretation adopted by certain people – why is it that his whole life and teaching proclaim nothing but tolerance? Why does he send his disciples to meet tyrants armed only with their staff and their pouch? If the sword that Christ ordered them to buy after selling everything else stands for temperate defence against persecutors – as some interpret it, not only ignorantly but wickedly[119] – why did the martyrs never use it?[120] This is where those Rabbinical distinctions are brought forward: 'It is lawful for a paid soldier to fight, just as it is lawful for a butcher to exercise his skill in preparing meat. For the latter has learned to cut up animals, and the former men; even citizens may fight, but in a just war' ('just,' however, means any war declared in any way against anybody by any prince). 'Priests and monks are not allowed to brandish a sword, but they are allowed to be present and take command. It is a sin to make war in a spirit of vengeance, but not out of concern for justice.' But who does not think his own cause is just? 'Christ sent out his disciples without means of defence, but while he was still with them they had no need of defence. When the time came for him to depart, he told them to take a pouch and a sword, the pouch against lack of food, the sword against their enemies. Anyway the words "Take no thought for the morrow," "Do good to them that hate you,"[121] and others of that sort were valid up to the time of his departure. Similar teachings of Paul or Peter are advice, not instructions.'

It is with brilliant teachings of this kind that we feed the greed of princes and offer them the means of self-flattery. As if there were a danger

* * * * *

118 Latin *probabat* in *1515–36*; LB has the present tense *probat*.
119 Luke 22:36. The only meaning for the sword of which Erasmus seems to approve here is that given in the letter to the Ephesians (see n154 below), 'the gospel word.' In the *Moria*, he refers to the 'sword of the spirit' and attacks the fourteenth-century theologian Nicholas of Lyra, alluded to indirectly through a mention of the adage 'An ass to the lyre' (*Adagia* I iv 35), for interpreting the sword as something that could serve for physical defence (CWE 27 145–6).
120 From here to the end of the paragraph there is another lengthy addition of 1526.
121 Matt 6:34, Matt 5:44, Luke 6:27

that the world would have a rest from war one day, we defend war with the words of Christ; and as if we were afraid that men in their greed would get tired of piling up riches, we make Christ our authority for it, twisting his words to the point that it seems he commanded, not tolerated, the practices he had previously forbidden. Before the gospel came, the world had its laws; it punished, made war, gathered stores of wealth and food. Our Lord came not merely to tell us what was allowed – how far we might fall below perfection – but what goal we must strive for with all our might. Anyone who tries earnestly to dissuade men from war is suspected of heresy; and those who water down the strength of gospel teaching with falsehoods like these and offer princes opportunities to flatter their own desires, they are orthodox and 'doctors of divinity.' A doctor who is truly Christian never approves of war; perhaps he admits it is permissible sometimes, but with reluctance and sorrow.

But this is dictated, we are told, by the law of nature, it has legal sanction, it is accepted by custom that we should meet force with force, that each of us should defend our own life, and our money too since it is 'our very life,' as Hesiod says.[122] I admit that. But the grace of the gospel[123] is more effective than all these, and prescribes that we should not curse those who curse us, that we should repay evil with good, that if someone takes away part of our possessions, we should give the whole, that we should pray even for those who try to kill us.[124] 'These sayings are addressed to the apostles,' we are told; but they apply still more to the whole people of Christ, and to the body, as we have said, which must be whole and complete, even if one member excels another in endowments. It may be that the teaching of Christ is not addressed to those who do not hope for their reward in Christ; fighting for money, lands and power is for those who scoff at Christ's words, 'Blessed are the poor in spirit'[125] – that is, the rich are those who desire nothing of wealth or honour[126] in this world. Those for whom the greatest happiness is in riches fight to save their own lives, but they are people who do not understand that this is death rather than life, and that for the faithful immortality is prepared.

The objection is raised that some Roman pontiffs have both instigated and abetted wars, that there are pronouncements of the church fathers in

* * * * *

122 Hesiod *Works and Days* 686
123 Latin *Evangelica*; the word was added in 1523.
124 Matt 5:42 and 44, Luke 6:27–35
125 Matt 5:3
126 'or honour' was added in 1526.

which war is apparently mentioned with approval. There are indeed some like this, but they are from the later period, when the vigour of the Christian spirit was waning; and they are very few, whereas there are countless examples, among writers of proven sanctity, which argue against war. Why do those few come to mind rather than the rest? Why do we turn our eyes from Christ towards men and prefer to follow uncertain examples rather than the unquestioned authority? In the first place the popes were men. Second, it is possible that they were badly advised, or not attentive, or lacking in prudence or piety.[127] However, even in these cases, you will find there was no approval of the sort of war we are constantly waging. I could prove this with the clearest documentation if I did not want to avoid any longer delay in such a digression. St Bernard praised warriors, but in terms that condemn all our forms of soldiering.[128] But why am I influenced by a work of Bernard, or an argument of Thomas,[129] rather than by the teaching of Christ, who forbids us absolutely to resist evil,[130] certainly in the way that the common man resists?

'But,' it is said, 'it is legitimate to sentence one criminal to punishment; therefore it is legitimate to take revenge on a state by war.' The answer that can be given to this is too long to be set out here. I shall say only that there is this difference: that in the courts a convicted criminal is punished in accordance with the laws, in war each side treats the other as guilty. In the first case, only the one who did wrong suffers and the example is visible for everyone. In the second case the greatest part of the suffering falls on those who least deserve to suffer, namely on farmers, old people, wives, orphans and young girls.[131] Moreover, if there is any advantage to be gained from this most evil of all activities, it goes entirely to a small number of utterly criminal bandits, to the mercenary soldiery, to the brazen profiteers, perhaps to the few leaders who connived to stir up the war for this very purpose and who are never better off than when the state is on the rocks. In the courts, an individual is not spared in order to ensure the safety of all; in war, in order to take revenge on a few, or even on one person perhaps, we inflict cruel suffering on so many thousands of people who in no sense deserve it. It is better for the fault of a few to go unpunished

* * * * *

127 'badly advised ... piety' is from 1526; in 1515–23 the text read *aut stulti fuerint aut mali* 'they were either stupid or bad.'
128 Bernard *Sermo* II *Ad milites* 3 PL 182 924–5
129 Thomas Aquinas *Summa theologica* II–II q 40
130 Matt 5:39
131 Cf *Adagia* III vii 29 One pot smashed against another (233 above).

than to demand some vague punishment of one individual or another and in the process draw ourselves and our loved ones, as well as our 'innocent enemies' – as we call them – into certain danger. Better leave the wound alone if you cannot treat it without serious harm to the whole body. If anyone cries out that it is unjust not to punish a sinner, my answer is that it is much more unjust to call down utter disaster on so many thousands of innocents who have not deserved it.

But these days almost every war we see is caused by some 'title' or other and by the ambitious[132] alliances of princes who, in order to assert their dominion over some small town, seriously imperil their whole realm.[133] Then this same thing that they have laid claim to with so much blood they sell or give away. Someone will say, 'Would you have princes fail to assert their rights?' I know it is not for someone like me to argue boldly about the business of princes, and even if it were safe to do so, it would take longer than I have time for here. I will say this only: if some claim or other seems to constitute a cause for war, then human affairs are in such a confused state, and there have been so many changes, that there can be no one who does not have a claim. What nation has not at some time both been driven out of its homeland and driven others out? How many migrations have there been from one place to another? How many times has there been a transfer of power this way and that, either by chance or by treaty? The Paduans should try to recover the site of Troy because Antenor was once a Trojan.[134] The Romans should try to recover Africa and Spain because these were once provinces of Rome. In addition, what we call 'rule' is administration; rights over men, free by nature, are not the same as rights over cattle. This same 'right' that you have was given by the consent of the people, and the same people who gave it, if I am not mistaken, have the power to take it away. Moreover, look what petty affairs are in question: it is not a matter of whether this or that state is to be subject to a good prince or slave to a tyrant, but whether it is reckoned to be Ferdinand's or Sigismund's, whether it pays tax to Philip or to Louis.[135] This is the all-

* * * * *

132 'ambitious' was added in 1526.
133 Latin *totum imperium adducunt in extremum discrimen*; in 1515-23 we find *periclitantur imperium* 'risk their realm.'
134 Virgil *Aeneid* 1.242-9. Erasmus' sarcasm may show that some inhabitants of the city still believed the early Paduan humanist Lovato Lovati (1241–1309), who discovered a skeleton which he optimistically identified as that of Antenor (L.D. Reynolds and N.G. Wilson *Scribes and Scholars* 111).
135 Ferdinand, Sigismund, Philip, and Louis were all familiar names of rulers in recent Spanish, Polish, imperial, and French history, but used probably as a

important right for which the whole world is to be entangled in war and slaughter.

But let us admit that this 'right' is worth something, that there is no difference between a privately owned field and a state, no difference between the cattle bought with your money and men who are not only free but Christians. Still it is prudent to give some thought to whether this right is worth so much that you should pursue it at the cost of such huge detriment to your people. If you cannot show that you have the mind of a prince, at least act like a man of business. This man takes no account of expense if he has seen clearly that it cannot be avoided except at the cost of heavier loss, and he considers it a gain if he has the good fortune to cut off a business with very small loss. At all events, in the case of a danger to the state you might follow the example from private life about which[136] there is a popular, rather amusing story. There was a disagreement between two kinsmen about the division of property and since neither would yield to the other it looked as if the affair would go to court and the quarrel would be settled by the decision of the judges. Counsel were being consulted, the action was prepared, it was in the hands of the lawyers. The judges were addressed, the case opened, and the pleading began – that is, war was declared. At this moment one of them came to his senses just in time, invited his opponent to visit him privately, and spoke to him in these words: 'To start with, it is indecent for those whom Nature has joined to be separated by money. In the second place the outcome of legal action is almost as uncertain as war. We have the power to start this but we cannot put an end to it. This whole case is about a hundred gold pieces. We shall spend twice that amount if we go to law on clerks, on investigators, on barristers, on solicitors, on judges, and on judges' friends. We shall have to be polite to them, flatter them, and give them presents; and I say nothing of the worry of canvassing and the effort of running here and there. Even if I win on all possible points, it is still more trouble than gain. Why don't we think more of ourselves, rather than of these robbers, and share between us the money that would be wasted on them? You give up half of yours, and I will give up the same of mine. In this way we shall enrich our friendship, which would otherwise be destroyed, and we shall avoid a great deal of trouble. And if you refuse to give up anything, I cede the whole case to you. I prefer to see this money go to a friend, not to those insatiable robbers.

* * * * *

collective symbol of the major powers rather than as individual targets for criticism.
136 'in the case ... about which' was added in 1526.

I shall have made an ample profit if I preserve my reputation, keep a friend, and avoid such a host of troubles.' His opponent was moved both by the truth of this and by his kinsman's good humour. The matter was settled between themselves, to the rage of those gaping crows, the lawyers and the judges, whom they had tricked.[137]

In a matter of much greater danger, you should try to imitate the good sense of these men. Do not consider only what you may hope to gain, but the sacrifice of so many amenities, the dangers, the disasters you will also incur in order to gain it. If you weigh, as in a balance, advantages and disadvantages and find that an unjust peace is preferable by far to a just war, why should you prefer a throw of the dice with Mars? Who but a madman would fish with a golden hook?[138] If you see that the cost is far greater than the profit, even if everything falls out well for you, is it not better to give way a little on your rights than to buy a small advantage for such countless ills? I would rather anyone had the title if my claim must be justified by the sacrifice of so much Christian blood. One man, whoever he may be, has held possession for many years, has become accustomed to the reins of government, is acknowledged by his subjects and carries out the office of ruler; then up will come another who has discovered some old claim from the chronicles or from some worn inscriptions, and turns a settled state of affairs upside down.[139] In these times especially, when we see that nothing in human affairs keeps its place for long, but is the plaything of chance and ebbs and flows like the tide,[140] what is the use of asserting one's claim with so much noise to something that will soon, by some quirk of chance, pass to someone else?

Finally, if Christians cannot bring themselves to despise such trivialities as these, what need is there to fly immediately to arms? There are so many earnest and learned bishops in the world, so many venerable abbots, so many nobles of great age with the wisdom of long experience, so many councils, so many assemblies set up, not without reason, by our ancestors.[141] Why are the childish disputes of such princes not settled by means of their

* * * * *

137 Cf *Adagia* I vii 15 He's tricked the gaping crow.
138 *Adagia* II ii 60
139 Cf *Adagia* I iii 85 Up and down, especially the references to Plato and Aristides (CWE 31 303).
140 All editions, including LB, have a full stop here, but I have preferred to follow ASD, which has a comma, and to join the clause to the next sentence.
141 'set up ... ancestors' was added in 1526.

arbitration? 'But the argument of those who make the pretext of defending the Church is more "honourable"' – as if indeed the people were not really the Church, or as if the whole dignity of the Church were in the wealth of the clergy, or as if the Church had originated, grown, and become established by means of wars and slaughter instead of by the blood of the martyrs, by their tolerance, and by their scorn for life.

To me it does not even seem such a commendable matter that we repeatedly prepare war against the Turks. The Christian religion is indeed in a bad way if its safety depends on this sort of defence. Nor is it reasonable to expect good Christians to be born from such beginnings: what is obtained with the sword is also lost by the sword.[142] Would you bring the Turks to Christ? Let us not display our wealth, our armies, our strength. Let them see in us not just the name 'Christians' but the sure marks of Christians: an innocent life, the desire to do good even to our enemies, an unshakeable tolerance of all injuries, a scorn for money, a disregard for glory, a life held cheap; and let them hear the heavenly teaching that accords with this sort of life. The best way to subdue the Turk is with these weapons. All too often nowadays we are wicked people fighting other wicked people. I will put it another way – and would that it were too daring rather than too true! – if you take away the name and sign of the cross, we are Turks fighting with Turks. If it is by armies that religion has been established, if it has been strengthened by the sword, and increased by wars, then let us defend it by the same means. But if everything has been achieved by different means to these, why do we adopt pagan ways as if we distrusted Christ's protection? 'Why should I not cut the throats[143] of those who cut ours?' they say. Do you feel inferior if someone is more of a criminal than you are? Why do you not rob the robber, or revile the man who reviles you, or hate the man who hates you?[144] Do you think it is a Christian act to kill even the wicked – as we judge them to be,[145] but who are still men whom Christ died to save – and so make a welcome sacrifice to the devil? You would give double pleasure to the enemy, because a man has been killed and because it was a Christian who did the killing. Most people,

* * * * *

142 Matt 26:52
143 All early editions have the singular *iugulem*; LB has *iugulemus*, which fits the other plurals in the sentence.
144 Allusions to Luke 6:27–8
145 From here to 'providing there is no contention' at the end of the next four paragraphs (435 below), the text is almost entirely an addition of 1523.

wishing to seem truly Christian, try to do as much harm as possible to the Turks; and what they cannot do they call down in the form of curses, although one might perceive this, on this very evidence, as unchristian. In the same way some who wish to appear strictly orthodox heap fearful curses on those they call heretics when they themselves are perhaps more deserving of the name. If someone wants to appear orthodox, let him do his best to bring back the erring to a right mind by gentle reasoning. We spit on the Turks and think we are by this action fine Christians, when perhaps we are more detestable to God than the Turks themselves. If the first messengers of the gospel had had the same attitude towards us as we have towards the Turks, where should we be now who are Christian because of their forbearance? Help the Turks! Make the ungodly godly, if you can; if you cannot, then pray and I will recognize your Christian spirit.

There are so many orders of monks in the world who live by begging and who want to be thought of as pillars of the church; but out of all these thousands how many are there who hold life cheap when it comes to spreading the religion of Christ? 'But there is no hope of that,' they say. On the contrary there would be the greatest hope if they followed the ways of their founders, Dominic and Francis; they were men who, I think, held the life of this world in supreme contempt,[146] to say nothing meanwhile of apostolic morals. There would be no lack of miracles among us; indeed the glory of Christ would require it. At present those who pride themselves on being the vicars and successors of Peter, the prince of the church, and the other apostles, generally put their whole trust in human defences. They are in truth strict proponents of the true religion; they live in wealthy cities given over to luxury, where they are corrupted themselves more quickly than they can reform others and where there is an ample supply of pastors to teach the people and priests to sing God's praises. They dwell in Princes' courts – and this is not the place to tell what they do there. If only it were nothing worse than 'a dog in a bath.'[147] They sniff around for wills, they hunt for money, they are subject to the tyranny of princes; and in order not to appear idle they censure passages in books as erroneous, suspect, scandalous, irreverent, heretical, or schismatic.

The fact is they prefer to rule to the detriment of the Christian people than to extend the kingdom of Christ at any risk to themselves. But those whom we call Turks are in large part half-Christian and perhaps nearer to

* * * * *

146 Latin *summum mundi huius contemptum*; LB omits *mundi*.
147 Cf *Adagia* I iv 39 What has a dog to do with a bath? Sentence added in *1526*

true Christianity than most of our own folk. How many are there among us who do not believe in the resurrection of the body and do not believe either that the soul survives the body?[148] And meanwhile it is through them that an attack is directed against petty heretics who question whether the Roman pontiff has jurisdiction over souls tormented by the fires of purgatory.[149] Let us first cast out the beam from our own eye, then we can cast out the mote from our brother's eye.[150] The purpose of gospel faith is conduct worthy of Christ. Why do we insist on things that have no effect on morality and neglect others that are like pillars of faith and will cause the whole structure to collapse at once if they are removed? Finally, who will believe us when we bear the cross as our device and the name of the gospel, if our whole life speaks at every moment of nothing but the world? Add to this that Christ, in whom there was no imperfection, nevertheless does not quench the smoking flax nor break the bruised reed, as the prophecy said,[151] but cherishes and tolerates the imperfect until it could become better. We are preparing to quench the whole of Asia and Africa with the sword, though most of the population there is either Christian or half-Christian. Why do we not rather acknowledge the first and cherish the second, reforming them mercifully?

But if we are seeking to expand the Empire, or if we crave their wealth, why to such a worldly enterprise do we put the name of Christ? What of the fact that, at the same time, we attack them with purely human means and bring into obvious peril the whole of that very thing which remains to us in the world? What a small corner of the world is left to us! What

* * * * *

148 A reflection of Aristotelian (Paduan?) tendencies, which, as it appears from the next sentence, Erasmus attributes to some Dominicans. The grounds for the doctrinal accusation may well be that the minister general of the order, Thomas de Vio, Cardinal Cajetan, had held in his commentary on Aristotle's *De anima* (1509) that the immortality of the soul cannot be proved on philosophical grounds, and had voted against the Lateran decree of 1513 on this question (see *The Cambridge History of Renaissance Philosophy* [1988] 500 and 504). Cf also Erasmus' portrayal of the Dominicans in the colloquy 'The Apotheosis of ... Johann Reuchlin' (CWE 39 248:32–38). For a summary account of Erasmus' relations with the Dominicans see Allen Ep 1006 n4. This is part of the long insertion of 1523, which begins with the reference to orders of monks and Dominic and Francis (cf n145 above).

149 The allusion is to Lutheran objections to the traffic in indulgences; the Dominicans in particular were commissioned to oppose these objections; see A. Renaudet *Etudes érasmiennes* (Paris 1939) 167 and 153 n2.

150 Matt 7:3

151 Matt 12:20, Isaiah 42:3

a multitude of barbarians, and what a few we are to challenge them! But someone will say, 'If God be for us, who can be against us?'[152] And he will have the right to say this if he relies on the protection of God alone. But what does Jesus Christ our commander say to those who rely on other forms of protection? 'He who strikes with the sword shall perish by the sword.'[153] If we wish to conquer for Christ, let us gird on the sword of the gospel word; let us take the helmet of salvation and the shield of faith,[154] and the rest of the truly apostolic armour. This is how it will come about that when we are conquered we shall make our greatest conquest.[155] But suppose that we are successful in war, who ever saw people being made true Christians by the sword, by slaughter, fire, and pillage? It is a lesser evil to be openly Turk or Jew than to be a Christian hypocrite.[156] 'But their assault on us must be driven off.' Why then do we invite them to assault us by our quarrels with each other? Certainly, if we are in agreement, they will not be able to attack us easily, and they are more likely to be converted to the faith by our good offices if they are spared than if they are killed. I would rather have a genuine Turk than a fake Christian. It is our business to sow the seed of the gospel; Christ will give the increase.[157] The harvest is plentiful, if the labourers are not lacking.[158] And yet for the sake of making a few Turks into bad and false Christians, how many good Christians will we make bad, and how many bad ones worse? For what else can be the result of such a turmoil of wars? I am reluctant to voice here the suspicion – which has all too often turned out to be true, alas! – that the rumour of war with the Turks has been put forward as an excuse for robbing the Christian population, so that it is broken with every sort of oppression and therefore is more servile to the tyranny of both sorts of princes.[159]

I say these things, not because I would entirely condemn an expedition against the Turks if they attack us of their own accord, but in order to ensure that we prosecute the war, which we claim to wage in the name of Christ, in a Christian spirit and with Christ's own protection. Let them feel that they are being invited to be saved, not attacked for booty. Let us show them

* * * * *

152 Rom 8:31
153 Matt 26:52
154 Eph 6:17 and 16
155 An allusion to Rom 8:36–7?
156 This sentence was added in 1526.
157 Cf 1 Cor 3:6–7.
158 Matt 9:37, Luke 10:2
159 That is, secular and ecclesiastical

conduct worthy of the gospel. If we do not have the language to converse with them, our manner of life itself will have considerable eloquence. Let us offer them a simple and truly apostolic profession of faith, not loaded with superfluous transient riders. Let us demand of them most of all those things that are plainly taught us by the sacred books and writings of the apostles. Agreement will be easier to reach on a few points and harmony will be more easily established if each is free to make his own sense of most questions, providing there is no contention.[160]

But I shall have rather more to say about all these matters when I publish my book, which I have entitled *Antipolemus*,[161] and which I wrote some time ago during my stay in Rome, addressing it to Pope Julius II during deliberations about whether to make war against the Venetians – something to be deplored rather than refuted. If you examine the matter more closely you will find that almost all wars between Christians have arisen either from stupidity or from malice. A few youths, with no experience, have been inflamed by the bad examples of their forbears and by the records of the histories that fools have spread about fools. Then they have been encouraged by the calls of flatterers, goaded by lawyers and theologians, with the consent or connivance of bishops, perhaps even at their demand, and, rashly, rather than wickedly, they go to war; and to the enormous suffering of the

* * * * *

160 End of the long addition of 1523, which begins at 'as we judge them to be' (n145 above)
161 In the *Catalogus lucubrationum*, published in CWE 9 as Ep 1341A to Johann von Botzheim (1523), there is a brief account of this tract (CWE 9 351:1452–60), though not under this title. It was lost, apparently at some time after this passage was written in 1515, and has since disappeared. In 1523 Erasmus states that it was composed to please Raffaele Riario, cardinal of San Giorgio, who had asked for it in Julius' name, since the subject was under discussion at the time in the sacred college (Erasmus is referring to preparations for the League of Cambrai in early 1509). He then wrote a second speech, putting the opposite case, which won the day, though he had put more effort into the first and written it more from the heart. The arguments against war (in summary, that it is improper for the church, improper for a Christian, involves unacceptable risks and unacceptable consequences) were used as an example in the *De copia* (CWE 24 598–600). Erasmus apparently regretted losing the tract and in 1523 writes that he had begun to jot down again from memory some of the heads of the argument. See also the note by M.M. Phillips in 'Erasmus and the Art of Writing' in *Scrinium Erasmianum* ed. J. Coppens (Leiden 1969) I 347. The work with this title that appeared in London in 1794 (*BLC* [to 1975] 102 15) is a partial translation into English of *Dulce bellum inexpertis*.

whole world they learn that war is something to be avoided at all costs. Some are driven to war by a secret hatred, others by ambition, others again by their ferocity of mind. For it is true that even our *Iliad* contains 'nothing but the feverish doings of stupid kings and peoples.'[162]

There are some whose only reason for inciting war is to use it as a means to exercise their tyranny over their subjects more easily. For in times of peace the authority of the assembly, the dignity of the magistrates, the force of the laws stand in the way to some extent of the ruler being allowed to do what he likes. But once war is declared then the whole business of state is subject to the will of a few. Those whom the prince regards with favour are promoted; those with whom he is angry are cast down. They demand as much money as they like. Why say more? It is only then that they feel they are really kings. Meanwhile the generals act in collusion to pick the bones of the unhappy population. With people of this mentality, do you think they would be slow to seize any opportunity offered of making war?

Then we cloak our disease with respectable names. I crave the riches of the Turks and hide this with the defence of religion; I do what my hatred dictates and use the rights of the Church as an excuse. I am the slave of ambition, I gratify my anger, carried away by my wild, undisciplined character, and I give as an excuse some treaty broken, some friendship violated, some omission in regard to the laws of betrothal, or something else of the kind. It is astonishing how they can fail to achieve the very thing they are striving for, and while they are stupidly dodging this or that misfortune, they fall into another, or even much deeper into the original one. For really, if they are led by desire for glory, it is much more splendid to preserve than to destroy, much finer to construct a city than to demolish it. Then, even supposing the war has the best possible outcome, it is a very small share of the glory that can be given to the prince, whereas a large part is due to the people whose money paid for the whole thing, a greater part usually to foreign soldiers and mercenaries, some to the generals, and the greatest part to luck, which is always the greatest factor, in war as in all other business. If it is high-mindedness that incites you to war, think, I beg you, how mistaken you are to act on that basis. You are not willing to yield to one person, a neighbouring ruler for instance, perhaps a kinsman, perhaps one who has deserved well of you in the past, yet how much more humiliating it is for you to make yourself a suppliant, begging for help

* * * * *

162 Horace *Epistles* 1.2.8

from barbarians – and what is even more unworthy, from men besmirched with every sort of crime, if indeed brutes of this sort can be called men[163] – persuading, flattering, and wheedling blackguards, murderers, and robbers, for these are the people through whom war is most commonly waged. You try to look rather fierce to your equal, and you have to force yourself to be servile to the lowest dregs of humanity. You get ready to drive some close neighbour out of his territory, and you have to let a rabble of the dirtiest scoundrels into your own. You don't trust your kinsman, yet you trust yourself to an armed mob? How much safer peace would have made you!

If you are lured by the idea of gain, make some calculations. War may seem attractive as long as you have not realized that you are incurring immeasurable expenditure for a return that is not only much smaller but uncertain too. But you are thinking of the interests of the state? There is no other way[164] by which states go more quickly and completely to ruin than by war. Before you start, the harm you have already done to your country is greater than the good you would do if you were victorious. You exhaust the wealth of your citizens, you defile their homes with mourning and fill the whole country with robbers, thieves and rapists. For these are the waste that war produces. And whereas before you could have enjoyed control of the whole of France, you are now excluded by your own act from many parts of it.[165] If you really love your people, why do you not think of questions like these? 'Why should I expose this flower of youth to all these evils? Why am I going to deprive so many wives of their husbands, so many children of their parents? Why should some title or other, some uncertain right, be claimed at the price of my people's blood?' When war was undertaken on the pretext of defending the church, we have seen the clergy so crushed by

* * * * *

163 'and what ... men' was added in *1517/18*.
164 LB has *vitia* 'vices,' a misprint for *via* 'way.'
165 Part of a passage added in *1517/18*, this sentence may, as Margaret Mann Phillips suggested (*The Adages of Erasmus* [Cambridge 1964] 351 n1), be addressed to Francis I or refer to Louis XII. Given the date, it is possible at least that it is aimed rather at the French monarchy as an institution and that Erasmus had in mind the French defeat at Guinegatte on 16 August 1513 (Battle of the Spurs). As a result of this battle Henry VIII took Tournai from Louis XII and did not sell it back to Francis I until 1518. Erasmus' admonition may also betray some satisfaction on his part for he had a personal interest there: Mountjoy was made lieutenant of Tournai (Ep 301n) and secured a canonry for him from Wolsey (Epp 360, 371, 388, 390, 410n), which he eventually failed to take up (Ep 806). He also wrote an epigram mocking the behaviour of the French soldiers at the battle (CWE 85 no 58).

frequent tithes that no enemy could have treated them with greater enmity. So because we use some silly means to avoid one pitfall, we throw ourselves of our own accord into another. Because we cannot suffer some slight insult, we subject ourselves to the greatest humiliations. Because we are ashamed to seem compliant to a prince, we become the suppliants of the basest of men. Because we rashly demand freedom, we entangle ourselves in the heaviest servitude. Because we chase after a little gain, we inflict immense losses on ourselves and on our people. A prudent man would weigh all this up in his mind; for a Christian, if he is truly Christian, a thing so hellish, so alien to both the life and teachings of Christ, is something to be avoided, averted and excluded by all possible means.

If, because of general perversity, there is no way of avoiding it, when you have left nothing untried and no stone unturned in your search for peace, then the best expedient will be to ensure that, being an evil thing, it is the exclusive responsibility of evil people, and is settled with a minimum of bloodshed. For if we strive to be in fact what is said of us, that is, admiring or desiring nothing of this world, seeking only to take flight from it with as little burden as possible, striving with all our might towards heavenly things, placing our whole happiness in Christ alone, believing that whatever is truly good, truly glorious, truly joyful is founded only on him, holding firmly that the faithful cannot be harmed, pondering how empty and fleeting are the playthings of mortal existence, reflecting deeply what a difficult thing it is for man somehow to become like God and by a sort of untiring meditation be so purged here of the contagion of this world that, once this bodily cloak is laid aside, he can pass directly into the company of the angels – in short, if we show we have those three qualities without which no one deserves the name of Christian – innocence, so that we may be free of all vice, charity, so that we may do good as far as we can, and patience, so that we may bear with the wicked and, if possible, overcome evil with good – what war over trifles, I ask you, could possibly exist between us? If Christ is merely a story, why do we not frankly spurn it? Why do we glory in his name? If he is really 'the way, the truth and the life'[166] why is there such a difference between this model and our whole way of thinking? If we acknowledge Christ as our authority, and if he is love, if he taught nothing, handed down nothing but love and peace, well, let us declare him, not by wearing his name and badge, but in our deeds and lives.

* * * * *

166 John 14:6

Let us embrace the cause of peace, so that Christ in return may acknowledge his own. It is to this end that popes, princes, and states must take counsel together. There has been enough shedding of Christian blood now. We have provided enough amusements for the enemies of the name of Christ. If the populace is in something of an uproar, as it usually is, it must be restrained by the rulers, who should be to the state what the eye is to the body, or reason to the mind. Or again, if the rulers make trouble, then it is up to popes to settle the disturbance with their wisdom and authority. Or rather may we become sated in the end of everlasting wars and be touched by the desire for peace. Calamity itself draws us to it; the world, exhausted by wrongs, begs for it;[167] Christ beckons us to it; and to it we are exhorted by Pope Leo, tenth of this name, representative on earth of Jesus Christ, the true peacemaking Solomon,[168] a lamb when it comes to doing harm, but a roaring lion against all that is opposed to piety,[169] whose every wish, every counsel, and every effort are directed to uniting those joined by a common faith in a common bond of harmony. He is endeavouring to make the Church flourish, not by wealth or power, but by its own proper gifts. A magnificent task indeed, and one worthy of such a hero, descendant of the illustrious Medici whose civic wisdom brought the famous city of Florence its great flowering with a long period of peace, whose house was the fortress of all good learning. Leo himself was endowed with a serene and gentle character and was introduced, from earliest childhood, as they say,[170] to the humanities and the gentler Muses; he was educated among the most learned men, as if in the very lap of the Muses, and brought to the office of pontiff a life and reputation quite unsullied, unstained by the slightest suspicion of slander even in that freest of all cities, Rome. Leo did not thrust himself forward for this office but, when he least expected it, his name was called as by a divine voice to bring help to a world grown weary with a prolonged turmoil of war. Let Julius have the glory of making war; let him keep his victories; let him keep his splendid triumphs. Whether such things are fitting for a Christian pontiff is not for such as myself to

* * * * *

167 'the world ... for it' was added in 1526.
168 The name is used as a title whose meaning has already been given (417 with n75 above).
169 'a lamb ... piety' was added in 1526; according to the editor of ASD this addition first appears as manuscript in Erasmus' own hand in the copy of the Froben edition of 1523, which he designates as π. It is in any case a curious addition, given that Leo had died in 1521, and was perhaps intended as a criticism of Clement VII.
170 Latin *a teneris ... unguiculis*; *Adagia* I vii 52 Since the time their nails were soft

declare. I shall say only this: that man's glory, such as it was, was accompanied by the ruin and misery of a very great number of people. The return of peace to the world will produce far more true glory for our Leo than all those wars valiantly undertaken or successfully waged all over the world could produce for Julius. But this digression will seem to be an undue delay for those who prefer to hear about proverbs rather than about peace and war.

2 Argivos vides
You are seeing Argives

'Αργείους ὁρᾷς, You are seeing Argives, that is, 'You look with stupefied and dazed eyes.' I think the source is Orestes driven mad by the Furies.[1] Hesychius sheds some light on this when he informs us that those who were distinguished and of some authority among the Helots were customarily called 'Argives,'[2] for the Helots are inhabitants of the Peloponnese and the principal city of the Peloponnese is Argos. It was a sign of ambition among them therefore that they preferred to be called Argives rather than Helots. I am not forgetting that among the Spartans the slaves were called Helots because the Spartans conquered them and made them their slaves. And perhaps of these the ones trusted more by their masters preferred to be called Argives rather than Helots. You can find a similar feeling even nowadays in certain people who were born in some quite obscure village but take a surname from some famous city. Aristophanes in his *Plutus* used the expression 'to look mad,'[3] in the same sense.[4] It is referred to as proverbial by Suidas.

* * * * *

2 In *1508* this consisted of the first two sentences and the last only. Zenobius (Aldus) column 43 = *Suda* A 3770. Cf Appendix 3.35.
1 Cf Aeschylus *Choephori* (possibly 1061) and *Eumenides* for the story of Orestes, and Virgil *Aeneid* 3.331 for *Oreste, Furiis agitato*, but since Orestes is himself an Argive (*Eumenides* 757) Erasmus' association of him with this adage is problematical.
2 Hesychius A 7022 and E 944
3 Cf *Adagia* III iv 13 Having a Gorgon's eyes (10 above), and IV ii 7 Born of the Furies (506 below).
4 Aristophanes *Plutus* 424: μανικὸν βλέπειν, added in *1515*. The expression 'in the same sense' is detached from its reference by all the material inserted in *1533*, which runs from 'Hesychius' to 'famous city'; it refers in fact to 'with stupefied and dazed eyes.'

3 Argivi fures
Argive thieves

Ἀργεῖοι φῶρες, Argive thieves. Said of those who are openly dishonest. In ancient times the Argives suffered from a bad reputation for their inclination to steal. This is recorded in Suidas;[1] but there seems to be an allusion to the word itself, for *argos* in Greek means 'lazy' and 'unoccupied.' Such people in fact are in the habit of living by theft.[2] The Romans, using a word humorously derived as it seems, commonly call thieves *Laverniones*, because they are under the protection of the goddess Laverna,[3] in whose dark and secret grove they are accustomed to bury their booty and the gains of their thieving. The authority for this is Festus Pompeius.[4]

4 Mars Rex
Mars is king

Ἄρης τύραννος, Mars is king. Suidas explains this as applying to a ruler who controls the state by force, not by law. Zenodotus believes the origin may have been Timotheus, ruler[1] of the Athenians who achieved many successes against the Persians and Asian forces, and whose leadership brought

* * * * *

3 The *Suda* or Zenobius (Aldus) (see n1 below); cf *Adagia* III iv 11 Argive accusation (9 above). Also found in Macarius 2.28
1 *Suda* A 3771 = Zenobius (Aldus) column 43. PCG 3.2 Aristophanes fragment 60.
2 The comment 'but there seems ... theft,' added in 1533, seems to be Erasmus' own.
3 Plautus *Aulularia* 445, Horace *Epistles* 1.16.60
4 Pompeius Festus pages 104–5 Lindsay. From 'The Romans' to the end was added in 1515.

4 *Suda* A 3853 or Zenobius (Aldus) column 44. The adage dates from 1508, but the text 'Zenodotus ... force' was revised in 1526. The earlier version read: 'There are those who say this began among the Persians whom Timotheus commanded. Because he safeguarded the Athenian state with enduring prosperity in all its affair, he was called "King Mars," and this became proverbial.' Timotheus took service with Artaxerxes II for a time in 372 BC, but see n2 below.
1 Erasmus' Latin is *imperator*. Timotheus was, of course, never 'ruler' of Athens, but Erasmus may be thinking of the Athenian office of *strategos* 'general'; see n2 below.

prosperity to Attica.[2] The expression 'Mars is king' comes from this. Hesychius merely records the proverb.[3] Suidas tells us that the Greeks sometimes called iron itself 'Ares,'[4] so this could be the meaning of the use of the proverb 'Iron is king' whenever something is done by force.

5 Attagen
Woodcock

Ἀτταγᾶς, Woodcock.[1] Suidas tells us that branded slaves were called by this nickname as a sort of proverbial joke, because the woodcock has feathers distinguished by diverse patches of colour. In the *Birds* Aristophanes says:

> If anyone among you is going to be a deserter and branded with marks,
> Among us he will certainly be called a variegated woodcock.[2]

For this reason, in the same play, he calls this bird 'motley feathered.'[3] In the same way the Greeks call 'peacocks' people who adorn themselves brilliantly and wear multi-coloured clothes.[4] However I shall have several things to say about the woodcock in the proverb 'The woodcock's new moon.'[5]

* * * * *

2 Zenobius (Athous) 2.47 (Crusius *Analecta* 151) and Zenobius (Aldus) column 44 (= Laurentianus 5 29, Jungblut page 412). The editor of ASD points out that Zenobius says in fact that the proverb is taken from the *Persians* of Timotheus; see Plutarch *Agesilaus* 14.2. The ruler in question appears to be Agesilaus, and Timotheus, the dithyrambic poet, the author of the saying (Timotheus fragment 10 Bergk = 15 Wilamowitz).
3 Hesychius A 7176
4 *Suda* A 3852. Both Greek σίδηρος and Latin *ferrum* can mean 'iron' and 'sword'; cf *Odyssey* 16.294 in *Adagia* III x 41 Remove the opportunity for evil (371 above).

5 *Suda* A 4307
1 Also translated as 'francolin' and 'heathcock' (Horace *Epodes* 2.54, Pliny *Naturalis historia* 10.133, Martial *Epigrams* 2.37.3). See D'Arcy W. Thompson *A Glossary of Greek Birds* (Oxford 1936) 59–61.
2 Aristophanes *Birds* 760–1
3 Aristophanes *Birds* 249
4 Eg Aristophanes *Acharnians* 63, *Birds* 102 and 268
5 *Adagia* IV iii 73 A francolin's new moon. 'In the same way' to the end was added in 1533.

6 Tenedius homo
A man of Tenedos

Τενέδιος ἄνθρωπος, A man of Tenedos. In the *Collected Proverbs* Plutarch[1]
says this was used of a man of severe and formidable appearance. The
source, as is generally the case for other proverbs, is variously reported.
Suidas says there was a certain king of Tenedos, called Tenes, who made
a law and brought in the custom that behind the judge there should stand
someone holding an axe clearly ready to strike immediately anyone who
said anything untruthful during a trial[2] – meaning, I believe, a deliberate
lie or false testimony. This sort of interpretation fits clearly with what I
have recalled in the adage 'An axe from Tenedos.'[3]

Others tell the story in the following way, which is, however, not incompatible with this. Cygnus, the son of Neptune and father of Hemithea
and Tenes, introduced to his children a stepmother. Subsequently however
Tenes was accused by the stepmother before his father of having impor-
tuned her to commit adultery. The father, believing this to be true, shut
the young man up in a chest with his sister Hemithea, because she wanted
to be with her brother in his fate, and threw them both into the sea. The
box was thrown up on Leucophrys, whose name was later changed to Tenedos, after Tenes the son of Cygnus, of course. In the course of time, Tenedos obtained power on the island and, as we have just said, introduced the
warning custom whereby there should be a person in the courts who held
a quivering axe over the head of an accuser. For if anyone were convicted
of making false accusation he would be immediately cut down as he stood.
Since this was seen as a fearful spectacle, it became proverbial to call 'a
man of Tenedos' anyone who was of threatening and fierce appearance.

In his book on *Phocis* Pausanias tells a somewhat different story, as
I have recounted elsewhere in the proverb 'An axe from Tenedos.'[4] In the
second book of his *Letters to his brother Quintus* Cicero says: 'So the freedom
of the Tenedians was cut off by the Tenedian axe, when, apart from myself,

* * * * *

6 Pseudo-Plutarch (see n1 below). Cf Zenobius 6.9 and Zenobius (Aldus) column
  157. Otto 1759
1 Pseudo-Plutarch Laurentianus 4.40, Jungblut page 408
2 *Suda* T 309
3 *Adagia* I ix 29, where the Latin title is *Tenedia bipennis* not *Tenedia securis* as here,
  and where he relates the slightly different version of Pausanias (see below)
4 Pausanias 10.14.1–4. See *Adagia* I ix 29. The story is used again in *Adagia* IV
  ix 67 Lay the axe (added in 1533). From 'Pausanias' to the end was added in
  1526.

Bibulus, Calidus, and Favonius, no one would defend them.'[5] He means that freedom had been strictly and entirely denied.

7 Tenedius patronus
A Tenedian defender

Τενέδιος συνήγορος, a Tenedian advocate. This has come from the same source[1] and was usually said of a lawyer who dispatches a case with economy and cuts through the tangle of a dispute swiftly. The origin is the Tenedian axe, which I spoke of in the previous adage. Suidas states that among the Tenedians two axes were hung on display.[2] According to the same author Aristotle says, in addition to the points I have noted, that in Asserina,[3] which is some place in Tenedos, there is a stream where they use the shells of crabs as boats. They cut these open in such a way that they look like an axe. Stephanus recalls the proverb in his *Catalogue* of places where he adds that the expression was used of a lawyer who was stern and austere, for in Tenedos it was not safe to babble on in any way you liked in the courts.[4]

8 Ἐγκεῶτις ἡμέρα
Which day in Ceos?

Ἐγκεῶτις ἡμέρα. In his *Collected Proverbs* Plutarch (if the title is correct) reports that this used to be said of those who propose or offer a feast, and that it comes from the fact that among the Ceans it was the custom for any-

* * * * *

5 Cicero *Ad Quintum fratrem* 2.11.2

7 Apostolius 16.26 = Zenobius (Aldus) column 157 (ξυνήγορος)
1 The *Suda* or Apostolius, not pseudo-Plutarch
2 *Suda* T 311
3 The form of the name and the following information are attributed to Aristotle only in the *Suda* and Apostolius. They are not in the Aristotelian fragments recorded by Rose (1886 no 593 = 1867 no 551). By *1515* Erasmus had found *Asterium* (Ἀστέριον) and the account of the crabs with the mark of an axe in Plutarch *Moralia* 399F *De Pythiae oraculis* (see *Adagia* I ix 29 An axe from Tenedos). The editor of ASD reports that a correction is made at this point in π, but this is not carried through in subsequent editions.
4 Stephanus Byzantinus pages 615–16 Meineke. The last sentence was added in *1517/18*.

8 Pseudo-Plutarch (see n1 below)

one who went into the magistracy to offer a banquet to the people.[1] When several people became magistrates they shared out days among themselves, and so, when they met each other they asked τίς ἡμέρα; 'Which day is it?'[2] The expression became a popular joke. It seems however that the word ἐγκεῶτις was a deliberate, absurd contraction of the words ἐν Κείῳ τις 'In Ceos which?' – 'day' being understood.

9 Versatilis Artemon
An Artemon, going the rounds

Ὁ περιφόρητος Ἀρτέμων, An Artemon, 'rotating.' This is found in the same *Collected Proverbs*.[1] It is stated there that it was customarily said about those whose good looks are the object of much competition, that this Artemon was a certain young man who was greatly loved by women for his outstanding beauty. I suspect that he was said to be 'rotating,' either because his name was bandied about on everyone's lips or because he walked around to show himself off.[2] Others prefer to believe that Artemon was a maker of machines in the time of Pericles, who was outstanding in his craft, and, being lame, carried his machines around everywhere.[3] In book 12 of his *Doctors at Dinner* Athenaeus refers to this proverb and quotes the authority of Chameleon of Pontus[4] who states that Artemon was given the nickname

* * * * *

1 Pseudo-Plutarch Laurentianus 4.43, Jungblut page 408 (Ἐγκεῶ τις), but it appears to have been Erasmus who read the whole expression as one word. For the doubt expressed in the parenthesis see *Adagia* III v 30n (83 above) and III vii 83 n1 (271 above).
2 Zenobius (Aldus) column 81, Hesychius E 3167, and Athenaeus 3.117B (PCG 4 Crates fragment 32) all have in fact Ἐν Κέῳ τίς.

9 Pseudo-Plutarch (see n1 below)
1 Pseudo-Plutarch Laurentianus 4.50, Jungblut page 409. See also Zenobius (Athous) 1.64 and Appendix 4.32.
2 Estienne (LB II 972 n2) asks, 'Where is περιφόρητος to be found with either of these meanings?'
3 Plutarch *Pericles* 27.3–4. The Latin *suas machinas circumferebat* is found in all editions of the *Adagia*. But Estienne (LB II 972 n3) suggests the more likely reading: 'But who would deny that περιφόρητος has a passive, not an active meaning?' That is, Artemon 'was carried around' in, or by, *suis machinis* 'his machines.'
4 Chameleon of Pontus fragment 36 Wehrli. In *1508–23 citat hoc proverbium ex Clearcho, testatur dictum fuisse quod . . .*; in *1526 de Chamaeleone Pontico* was added, and 'Clearchus,' the result of a confused reading of Athenaeus, was dropped in *1528*.

'rotating' because he had himself carried around in a litter for the pleasure
of it, or because, having at first been poor, he subsequently began to lead
a life of ease and luxury. Athenaeus quotes the following about the same
person from Anacreon:

> He wore at his side the thin ox-hide covering
> Of a poor shield and associated with dealers in loaves
> And prostitutes, making a fraudulent living; often,
> To survive, he had to submit his neck to the spear, or else
> To the wheel, often his hair and beard were plucked.[5]

From these words it seems the adage refers to a man who is inconstant
and changeable in his habits, such as Alcibiades was reputed to be. He, as
Satyrus tells us, when he was among the Ionians was more luxurious than
the Ionians; when among the Thebans he was more Boeotian in physical
exercise than any Boeotian; among the Thessalians he was more devoted
to horsemanship than they; among the Spartans more temperate and hardy
than the Spartans; in Thrace more of a wine-bibber than the Thracians.[6]
He could even earn praise in becoming these things. But περίτριμμα is an
abusive term for someone who is a shuffler in every sort of matter. This is
shown by Pollux in book 6.[7] Plutarch tells us Artemon was a certain lame
man who was carried around in a litter and who was somewhat fearful
and inclined to remain most of the time at home with two slaves holding
a bronze shield over his head in case something fell on it from above.
Whenever he did have to go out, he was carried in a litter, but close to
the ground for fear of falling. Plutarch relates something like this in his

* * * * *

5 Athenaeus 12.533E–534A; Anacreon PMG fragment 388; Erasmus' quotation
  of the Greek, and consequently his translation, is faulty. Athenaeus does
  not distinguish Artemon, the rival of Anacreon, from the engineer contemporary of Pericles of the same name, nor does Erasmus (see above *de eodem* 'about the same person'), though Pericles lived some eighty years later
  than Anacreon. C.B. Gulick in the Loeb edition of Athenaeus translates this
  phrase, 'rotating Artemon,' which Anacreon uses of his rival, as 'litter-borne.'
  See also J.M. Edmonds ed *Lyra graeca* (Loeb) II fragment 96, Diehl fragment
  16.
6 Satyrus was a peripatetic writer of the third century BC known largely from
  citations by Athenaeus and Diogenes Laertius; this passage is part of a quotation by Athenaeus 12.534B, *FHG* III 160. Cf Plutarch *Alcibiades* 23.4–5.
7 Pollux *Onomasticon* 6.183 and 5.144. The word is found in Aristophanes *Clouds*
  447 with the meaning of a legal charlatan.

life of Pericles.[8] The word seems therefore to be used of soft-living and fearful people. Indeed Pliny too, in book 34 chapter 8, recalls an Artemon among the works of Polycletus called περιφόρητος.[9] There is also a play here on the word *artemo*,[10] a tackle-block on a ship by which the sails can be turned and cargo lifted out of ships – sailors still use the yard-arms for both purposes nowadays. *Artemon* in Greek is, properly speaking, a device for raising loads which Latin speakers, if I am not mistaken, call a *troclea*.[11] It is constructed so that it can be rotated easily.

10 Placiadae
   Placiadae

Πλακιάδαι καὶ στέλαιον,[1] Placiadae and a hoe handle. In the same collection[2] Plutarch declares this used to be said of those taken in adultery and dragged off, as they deserved, with insults. There is a village in the territory of Attica whose inhabitants are called Placiadae.[3] It was their custom to inflict punishment and disgrace on those taken in adultery by pushing radishes up the anus;[4] the radishes in their country are said to be of extraordinary size, and if radishes were not available they used the handle of a hoe. I am aware that I have spoken of this elsewhere, but incorrectly,[5] and I thought it was necessary to set it down here afresh.

* * * * *

8 Plutarch (see n3 above) attributes the story of Artemon's fearfulness to Heracleides Ponticus, not Chameleon Ponticus. The passage shows clear signs of being one of those Erasmus failed to correct.
9 Pliny *Naturalis historia* 34.56
10 Cf Vitruvius 10.2.9.
11 Cf Vitruvius 9.9.3.

10 Pseudo-Plutarch Laurentianus 4.57, Jungblut page 410. Or Zenobius (Athous) 1.73 (see n2 below and Crusius *Analecta* 64 and Zenobius (Aldus) column 142.
 1 The word στέλαιον seems to be a misspelling of στελεόν or στειλειόν 'haft or handle of an axe.' In the third sentence Erasmus defines his Latin *stelaeum* as the handle of a hoe (*ligo*).
 2 Latin *iisdem commentariis*; that is, the proverbs attributed to Plutarch (see III v 30n, 83 above), which were the source of IV i 9
 3 *Suda* Π 1683 (see also n5 below)
 4 Latin *raphanus* from the Greek ῥαφανίς; there is also a Greek verb ῥαφανιδόω 'to punish as an adulterer' (Aristophanes *Clouds* 1083, Lucian *Peregrinus* 9).
 5 *Adagia* II x 53, where Erasmus uses the form Laciadae, following *Suda* Ω 62. Both refer to citizens of the deme of Lacia in Attica, mentioned by Plutarch in the *Pericles* and the *Cimon*.

11 Iustitiae oculus
A paragon of justice

Δίκης ὀφθαλμός, An eye of justice, is an expression used of an upright and
uncorrupted judge, or of a judgment itself. The adage is recalled by Suidas.
It seems to derive from the description by Chrysippus in Aulus Gellius
book 14 chapter 4 in which he attributes to Justice penetrating, direct, and
unmoving eyes.[1] It is important that one who is to judge rightly should not
allow his gaze to be diverted this way or that from what is honest. This
proverbial verse is famous: 'There is an eye of justice which perceives all.'[2]

12 Iustitia iustior
More just than justice

Δίκης δικαιότερος, More just than justice. This is a proverbial hyperbole for
the rigorously upright and uncorrupted. The ancients made Justice a goddess, and there is an elegant description of her image by Chrysippus, as I
have just said,[1] in Aulus Gellius.[2]

13 Quantum ex Bacchanalibus
As old as the Bacchanalia

῍Οσον ἐκ Διονυσίων, As old as the Dionysia or Bacchanalia. Suidas records
this as a proverb, but somewhat confusedly as usual. In ancient times the

* * * * *

11 *Suda* Δ 1096 = Zenobius (Aldus) column 70. Cf also *Suda* E 3228 and Apostolius
6.8. Otto 886
1 Aulus Gellius *Noctes Atticae* 14.4.4. Chrysippus Περὶ τοῦ καλοῦ fragment 1 von
Arnim (*Stoicorum veterum fragmenta* 3.197–8)
2 Menander *Sententiae* 225 Jäkel = Philemon fragment 246 line 5 Kock = adespota
421 Nauck. PCG 5 Diphilus (Spuria) fragment 136 line 5; also quoted, without
an author's name, by Plutarch in *Moralia* 1124F *An recte dictum sit latenter esse
vivendum*

12 *Collectanea* no 323. Diogenianus 4.22, Apostolius 6.13
1 'as I have just said' was added in *1533*.
2 See n1 to the preceeding adage. From 'The ancients' to the end was added in
1515.

13 *Suda* Δ 1168 deriving from Aristophanes *Thesmophoriazusae* 746–7. Cf Zenobius
(Aldus) column 83. The title from *1508–23 Ex eo prope tantum* 'Almost as far
from that,' became *Quantum ex Bacchanalibus* in *1526*. The whole expression in
Suda ἐξ αὐτοῦ σχεδὸν τοσοῦτον, ὅσον ἐκ Διονυσίων seems to mean 'As far from
that as from the Bacchanalia' or possibly 'That is as old as the Bacchanalia.'

Athenians used to calculate the years and the number attached to them from the Dionysia, as they did from the Olympiads. The festival of the Dionysia was repeated every third year.[1] This is why Virgil calls them *trieterica*.[2] The complete phrase used by Suidas is as follows: 'Almost as far from that as from the Bacchanalia.' He adds that it is said about things that are very desirable and fervently awaited.[3] This is supported by what he relates from some unknown author: 'O the Bacchanalia, they are fragrant with ambrosia and nectar.'[4]

14 Mercator est
He's a shopkeeper

Ἔμπορός ἐστι σκηπτόμενος, He pretends to be a shopkeeper. Can be said of someone who is fearful and makes up false reasons to avoid being put in danger. Suidas quotes it from Aristophanes; in both the *Plutus* and the *Women in Parliament* by this author someone is introduced who says something like this: that he pretends to be a shopkeeper whenever he is ordered to go to war, because business men were not obliged to turn out. It was useful to release them so that they could look after provisioning. In the *Plutus* the passage is as follows:

> Are you a tiller of the field?
> – Do you think I am so mad?
> Are you a business man?
> – I pretend I am when it's necessary.[1]

The other passage is: 'I behave as if I were a business man.'[2] This is not entirely different from the gospel parable about those who are invited to a wedding and excuse themselves for various reasons.[3]

* * * * *

1 Since the Romans counted inclusively, this means in fact every second year.
2 Virgil *Aeneid* 4.302–3 *trieterica Baccho orgia* translated as 'biennial revels.' See R.G. Austin's commentary page 97.
3 Estienne (LB II 973) points out that the *Suda* says the Dionysia themselves were fervently awaited; his words are not a paraphrase of the proverb.
4 Aristophanes *Acharnians* 195–6. Erasmus quotes from the *Suda*. From 'The complete phrase' to the end was added in 1526.

14 *Suda* E 1047 (= Zenobius [Aldus] column 79) citing Aristophanes (see n1 below)

1 Aristophanes *Plutus* 904
2 Aristophanes *Ecclesiazusae* 1027; from 'In the *Plutus*' to here was added in 1526.
3 Matt 22:1–11

15 Donum quodcunque dat aliquis proba
For any gift that is given be grateful

Δῶρον δ᾿ ὅτι δῷ τις ἐπαίνει, For any gift be grateful. The adage tells us that a
gift, a service or advice offered by a friend is to be appreciated. The source
is indicated by Strabo the Geographer in book 6. When the Greeks were
commanded by the oracle to establish the city of Croton[1] a certain Myscellus
was sent to inspect the future site of the city. When he saw Sybaris already
built and thought the site was the most suitable, he returned to the oracle
and consulted the god as to whether it was permitted to found Sybaris
instead of Croton. The god answers thus: Μύσκελλε βραχύνωτε, πάρες σέθεν
ἄλλο ματεύων, / Κλάσματα θηρεύεις, ὀρθὸν δ᾿ ὅτι δῷ τις ἐπαίνει. These lines
are rendered by the translator[2] thus:

> Expel it from your breast, short-backed Myscellus;
> When you seek other answers, see! you strive in vain for what is unjust.
> But take whatever is rightly given with appreciation.[3]

This is also extant in the *Collected Proverbs*, but in a very corrupt state; however, from the ruins of words, if I may use the expression, the following reading might be put together: Μύσκελλε βραχύνωτε, παρὲκ θεὸν ἄλλα
ματεύων. / Οὔδαλα θηρεύεις, δῶρον δ᾿ ὅτι δῷ τις ἐπαίνει.

> When you ask the god for something different, hump-backed Myscellus,
> You may get something worthless; be happy with the gift that is given.[4]

He was called Myscellus, it seems, because of his thin legs, which were like
those of a mouse, and Brachynotus because of his bent back.[5] I have said

* * * * *

15 In *1508* Chiliad IV began at this point. Zenobius 3.42, Zenobius (Aldus) column
   73, Apostolius 6.42A. *Suda* Δ 1474
 1 In the 'toe' of Italy; a colony was established there around 710 BC. Ovid *Metamorphoses* 15.15–59
 2 Guarino of Verona, Venice 1498 folio LII r
 3 Strabo *Geographica* 6.1.12; there is a fuller account of the oracle in Diodorus
   Siculus 8.17.
 4 Zenobius 3.42, Zenobius (Athous) 3.83 and Zenobius (Aldus) column 73. Erasmus does not appear to be referring on this occasion to Pseudo-Plutarch; cf
   Adagia III v 30n, 83 above.
 5 Sentence added in *1517/18*; in the earlier editions Erasmus had suggested an
   emendation of the Greek verse. The attempt to explain the name as μῦς 'mouse'

elsewhere that Croton was a very healthy place, and Sybaris was insalubri-ous.[6] Suidas relates other things concerning oracles given to Myscellus, but not relevant to the explanation of this proverb.[7]

16 Ithorus
Ithorus

Ἴθορος. Suidas affirms this expression was proverbial for someone who stimulated and encouraged others. I think it is taken from the usage of sailors, who are exhorted to work hard when they are rowing by the voice of the captain, or from horse racing.[1] In decade 7 question 5 of his 'Table-talk' Plutarch writes that the chant for encouraging horses was called the ἱππόθορος.[2] He relates very similar things in the 'Precepts on Marriage.'[3] In Greek θορεῖν means 'to leap in with a rush.'[4] So too in Homer Ares is called θούριος 'impetuous' from his swift assault.[5] It seems the Greek word is made up from ἴθι 'exceedingly'[6] and ὀρεῖν 'to exhort.'[7]

17 Ne allia comedas et fabas
Eat neither garlic nor beans

Ἵνα μὴ φάγῃ σκόροδα, μηδὲ κυάμους, Eat neither garlic nor beans. This seems to have been said by way of a proverbial riddle, meaning 'Do not go either to war or to court.' Garlic used to be carried into battle as part of the soldiers' provisions. (If only it were in such abundant supply, that those

* * * * *

and σκέλος 'leg' or 'paw' is Erasmus' own, but the derivation of Brachynotus is correct.
6 *Adagia* II iv 43 and I ii 94
7 *Suda* M 1473 and M 1474

16 *Suda* I 241
1 'or from horse racing' was added in 1517/18.
2 Plutarch *Moralia* 704F *Symposiaca problemata*
3 Plutarch *Moralia* 138B *Coniugalia praecepta*; added in 1526
4 θορεῖν is the infinitive of θρώσκω; this is correct, but the etymology suggested in the last sentence is quite inconsistent with it.
5 Homer *Iliad* 5.30, 35, 355, 454, 507, 830, 903; 15.127, 142; 24.498 (θούρος)
6 Latin *valde*; ἴθι is the imperative of εἰμί meaning 'Come on!' J.N. Grant suggests Erasmus may be thinking of the Homeric ἶφι 'strongly,' 'with force.'
7 Presumably from ὄρνυμι or the root ὄρω, Latin *hortor*

17 *Suda* I 364; cf Aristophanes *Lysistrata* 687–9.

who delight in wars, the foulest of men, should have nothing but garlic to eat – or whatever is worse!)¹ In the courts people commonly ate beans to stop themselves going to sleep. This is what Suidas says in fact, though I think it is rather a reference to the bean-shaped pebbles that were used as votes in ancient times.²

18 Mortuus per somnum vacabis curis
If you dream that you die, you will be free of your cares

Θανὼν καθ᾽ ὕπνους φροντίδων ἔσῃ δίχα, If you dream that you die, you will be free of your cares. This is a line of verse commonly recited by the Greeks, and arising from superstitious observation of dreams. They believed that someone who dreamed he died would be freed from his cares and troubles, because death seems to mark an end to griefs, and clearly does so for those who depart from this life for a better one. Relevant to this same idea perhaps is the line I have recorded elsewhere: 'Your business will fail if you dream of the dead.'¹

19 Animus heptaboëus
A heart of seven ox-hides

Θυμὸς ἑπταβόειος, A heart of seven ox-hides; another version is 'a seven-hide rage.' Said of someone who is big and strong, and invincible. The epithet originates with the shield of Ajax, which Homer calls ἑπταβόειος because it was covered with the hides of seven oxen and therefore impenetrable.¹ Ovid too has: 'Ajax, Lord of the seven-fold shield.'² The adage

* * * * *

1 Erasmus' own comments added in 1515 and 1517/18
2 Cf *Adagia* i i 2:170–4 following Plutarch, who says that the Pythagorean 'Abstain from beans' means that one should keep out of politics because beans were used for voting on the removal of magistrates (*Moralia* 12E–F *De liberis educandis*). Cf *Adagia* iv vi 37 A bean-gnawer.

18 *Suda* Θ 43, Apostolius 8.83G
1 *Adagia* iii vi 40 Seeing the dead (144 above). See Astrampsychus *Oneirocriticon* ed Joseph Scaliger in *Oracula metrica ... a Ioanne Opsopoeo collecta* (Paris 1607) 94. Erasmus gives the line only in Greek.

19 *Suda* Θ 574
1 Homer *Iliad* 7.220, 222, 245, 266; 11.545
2 Ovid *Amores* 1.7.7, *Metamorphoses* 13.2; added in 1515

comes from the *Frogs* of Aristophanes:

> But belching javelins and spears, white plumes on their heads,
> With helmets and greaves, and hearts of seven ox-hides.[3]

20 Semper Ilio mala
Troy is ill-fated ever

Ἀεὶ Ἰλίῳ κακά, Troy is ill-fated ever. Said of those who are exceedingly wretched and distressed. The fall of Troy offered the poets many subjects of tragedies, and this is how the proverb arose. It is mentioned by Eustathius in his commentary on the fourth book of the *Iliad*. And when Stratonicus was asked why he did not wish to live with the Trojans he replied, 'Troy is ill-fated ever.' The authority for this is Athenaeus in book 8 of the *Doctors at Dinner* (though this passage is not entirely without error).[1]

21 Libera Corcyra, caca ubi libet
Corcyra is free, shit where you will

Ἐλευθέρα Κόρκυρα, χέζ᾽ ὅπου θέλεις, Corcyra is free, shit where you will. Said when we want to indicate that one is free to do anything. It is cited by Eustathius in his commentary on Dionysius, but it would be more apt when we want to signify that there is no punishment for the wicked.[1] Here, I think, we can appropriately relate what Plutarch says. Certain Chians, sojourning with the Spartans, not only vomited after a banquet but emptied their bowels on the ephors' couches. At first there was a careful inquiry about who had committed such a villainy, for they would certainly be punished if they were citizens. But when it was found that it had been done

* * * * *

3 Aristophanes *Frogs* 1016–17; added in *1526*

20 Eustathius 444.23 on *Iliad* 4.48. Cf Diogenianus 5.26, Apostolius 9.3 and *Adagia* I iii 26 An Iliad of troubles.
1 Athenaeus 8.351A; Stratonicus was a famous citharist whose witticisms are quoted extensively in this section of Athenaeus; cf *Adagia* IV i 56 (475 below). From 'And when Stratonicus' to the end was added in *1518*.

21 Eustathius *Commentary on Dionysius Periegetes* line 494, ed G. Bernhardy (Leipzig 1828) 194 line 11. Corcyra is modern Corfu.
1 'but it would be ... wicked' was added in *1515* and everything that follows in *1533*.

by the Chians, the Spartans went about saying, 'Chians have permission to behave outrageously.'²

22 Decernetur equa Thessalica
The prize will be the Thessalian mare

Ἐπικρινεῖται ἵππος Θεσσαλική, The prize will be the Thessalian mare. This expression was used for winning the first prize, because in ancient times Thessalian mares had the best reputation. This is clearly indicated by the oracle given to the Aeginetans.¹ Eustathius quotes it with reference to the second book of the *Iliad*. Suidas, following I know not which author, says: 'Cavalry in Thessaly and Thrace, archers and lighter-armed infantry in India, Crete and Caria.'² This adage is closely related to one discussed elsewhere: 'A tunic Pellene-style.'³ It will be wittier if used ironically.

23 Canis vivens e magdalia
A dog living on breadcrumb

Κύων ζῶν ἀπὸ μαγδαλιᾶς, A dog living on breadcrumb. Eustathius, commenting on the *Iliad* book 4, shows that this expression was used of parasites and those who lived on food provided by others. He says *magdalia* has something like the meaning of 'scurf' or 'scrapings from the hands.' But among

* * * * *

2 Plutarch *Moralia* 232F–233A *Laconum apophthegmata*; cf *Adagia* IV ii 38 A Chian (523 below), where the story was added in *1526*.

22 Eustathius 340.11 on *Iliad* 2.763. The Latin could mean 'It will be decided by a Thessalian mare' but Erasmus is quoting Eustathius, ἐπικρίνεται ἵππος Θετταλική, where 'Thessalian horse' is nominative and the verb is passive, as if that were the actual proverb. This is not certain, and the original proverb may have been something like 'Choose a Thessalian mare'; cf *Adagia* IV ii 70 Acarnanian horses (538 below).

1 Thessalian mares are mentioned in the answer given by the oracle of Delphi, not to the Aeginetans of the island of Aegina but to the Aegians, inhabitants of Aegium in Achaia. *Suda* Υ 108. Cf *Anthologia Palatina* 14.73 line 2.

2 *Suda* I 538. The author quoted is Julian the Apostate *Orationes* 7.205D.

3 *Adagia* III iii 17

23 Eustathius 462.35–6 on *Iliad* 4.190. In *1508* this consisted only of the reference to Eustathius. Most of the rest, including the discussion of the Plutarchan passage, was added in *1526*, but 'He also relates ... crossroads' was added in *1528*, and 'This is what Aristophanes ... to refute' in *1533*.

other authors I find the phrase is written as one word, as in Hesychius. He says: '*Apomagdalia* is the *adeps* "soft crumb" on which they wiped their hands at banquets; they threw this to the dogs when they left the table.'[1] Then we have Julius Pollux in book 6 chapter 14 of his *Vocabulary*: 'But the ancients made use of the *apomagdaliai*, which is what they called the soft, fatty part of bread; they wiped up their food with it and then threw it to the dogs. Hence the Spartans call *apomagdalia κυνάς* "dog food."'[2] In the *Knights* of Aristophanes, the *halantopola* 'sausage-seller' declares that he will surpass Cleon in shameless and wicked tricks, or else his diet of *apomagdaliai* has been to no avail. Cleon answers him:

> *Apomagdaliai*, like a dog? You villain; if you live on dog's food,
> How can you defend yourself against this dog-faced monkey?[3]

Apomagdaliai are mentioned in Plutarch too in the *Lycurgus*, though I doubt if the translator[4] has followed the meaning of the passage. The Greek words are as follows: [see n6]. I would translate the Greek more or less thus:

> A person who wanted to take part in a banquet was tested, so it is said, in the following manner. Each of the guests took a piece of breadcrumb in his hand and placed it in silence, like a voting pebble, into a κάδδος "bowl" which a servant was carrying on his head. Those who approved did simply that, others passed condemnation by squeezing it hard in their hand. Such a flattened piece of bread was the equivalent of a perforated pebble. If even one such vote was found, they did not allow the applicant to join, for they wanted everyone to have pleasure in eating together. But the person who was rejected[5]

* * * * *

1 Hesychius Ἀπομαγδαλία A 6477. *Suda* A 3432
2 Pollux *Onomasticon* 6.93
3 The sausage-seller's words (there should be no initial 'h' in *alantopola*) come from Aristophanes *Knights* 413–14, translated by B.B. Rogers (Loeb): 'I think in shamelessness I'll win; else vainly in the slums / Have I to such a bulk been reared on finger cleaning crumbs?' Cleon's reply is *Knights* 415–16.
4 Named below as Lapus, that is Lapo Birago da Castiglionchio; his 'Life of Lycurgus and Numa' was first published in a collective translation of the *Lives* of Plutarch in Rome in 1470. See the *Dizionario biografico degli italiani*. His mistakes are also exposed in *Adagia* II viii 11 and 21. Erasmus' text differs in several respects from the accepted one.
5 Somewhat misleadingly Erasmus here translates ἀποδοκιμασθέντα as *probatus* having translated δοκιμάζων as *probans* 'approved,' in the third sentence of the quotation. As the editor of ASD suggests (II-7 59:294n), the Latin should probably be *reprobatus*.

in this way was said to be *caddissatus* "caddied" for *cadus* was the word for the bowl into which they put the pieces of bread.'[6]

Lapus however translates thus:

Anyone who wanted to be a participant in a banquet was tested as follows: first each person took a piece of breadcrumb in his hand and put it like a voting pebble, without saying anything, into a bowl which a servant carried on his head; those who *reprobaret* 'disapproved' did simply that, but those who *approbaret* 'approved' squeezed it hard with their hand. If any piece of bread were flattened it had the same meaning as a perforated pebble. If they found just one piece which was not flattened they did not admit the applicant, because they wanted everyone to enjoy themselves together. But the person who was thus *reprobatus* 'rejected' was said to be 'caddied,' for *caddiscus* [sic] was the word for the bowl into which the pieces of bread were put.[7]

If you compare this with what Plutarch wrote, you will see that the Greek text that Lapus followed was different from that which the Aldine press gave us recently.[8] Be that as it may, Athenaeus also recalls some points in book 9 about pieces of bread which were offered before meals for wiping hands.[9] He also relates in book 4 that among the Arcadians, if I am not mistaken, it was the custom to make a sacrifice after the meal, without actually washing their hands but simply wiping them with some broth and a piece of bread, and whatever they wiped their hands with each one took away with him. This they did to ward off the night-time terrors that tend to haunt crossroads. This is what Athenaeus says.[10] I think this is obviously also a useful remedy for the dogs that assault travellers at crossroads. This is what Aristophanes was remembering, I think, in the *Knights* when he charges Cleon with the fact that while other outstanding people are driven

* * * * *

6 Plutarch *Lycurgus* 12.5–6: Δοκιμάζεσθαι δὲ τὸν βουλόμενον τοῦ συσσιτίου μετασχεῖν οὕτω φασί. Λαβὼν τῶν συσσίτων ἕκαστος ἀπομαγδαλίαν εἰς τὴν χεῖρα, τοῦ διακόνου φέροντος ἀγγεῖον ἐπὶ τῆς κεφαλῆς, ἔβαλλε σιωπῇ καθάπερ ψῆφον, ὁ μὲν δοκιμάζων ἁπλῶς, ὁ δὲ κρίνων σφόδρα τῇ χειρὶ πιέσας. Ἡ γὰρ πεπιεσμένη τῆς τετρημμένης ἔχει δύναμιν. Κἂν μίαν εὕρωσι τοιαύτην, οὐ προσδέχονται τὸν προσιόντα, βουλόμενοι πάντας ἡδομένους ἀλλήλοις συνιέναι. Τὸν δὲ οὕτως ἀποδοκιμασθέντα κεκαδδεῖσθαι λέγουσι· κάδδος γὰρ καλεῖται τὸ ἀγγεῖον εἰς ὃ τὰς ἀπομαγδαλίας ἐμβάλλουσι.

7 See n5 above and ASD II-7 59:302–4n.

8 Venice 1519

9 Athenaeus 9.409D

10 Athenaeus 4.149C

into exile he wipes his hands with the most delicate barley cakes: 'And he is in exile while you wipe your hands on cakes of Ἀχιλλείων "finest barley."' The scholiast adds that this sort of barley is called *Achilleum*, as if it were more noble.[11] It is not surprising then that an argument is called an 'Achillean argument' by theologians if it is effective and difficult to refute.[12]

24 Ficus post piscem
Figs after fish

Σῦκον μετ' ἰχθύν, ὄσπρεον μετὰ κρέα, After fish figs, after meat vegetables. This one is recalled by Athenaeus in the third book of the *Doctors at Dinner*.[1] It will be applicable when we want to say that different things suit different people. Just as it is common for people to like to have cheese after eating meat, and after fish nuts.

25 Ficus avibus gratae
Birds like figs

Σῦκα φίλ᾽ ὀρνίθεσσι φυτεύειν οὐκ ἐθέλουσιν, Birds like figs, but they will not plant them. This heroic hexameter is quoted by Athenaeus immediately after in the same passage as I have just mentioned.[1] It seems to be applicable to lovers of pleasure or those who avoid honest work, though they want the advantages of it.[2]

26 Ingredi Iunonium
Marching in the Junonium

Βαδίζειν Ἡραῖον ἐμπεπλεγμένον, Marching in the sacred procession of Juno. This too is found in Athenaeus, book 12 of the *Doctors at Dinner*. It seems

* * * * *

11 Aristophanes *Knights* 819 and the scholiast (Dübner page 64)
12 Cf *Adagia* I vii 41 (last sentence) and ASD II-7 59:316n.

24 Apostolius 15.70B. Suringar 78
1 Athenaeus 3.80E

25 Apostolius 15.70A
1 Athenaeus 3.80E
2 'though ... advantages of it' was added in *1515*.

26 Athenaeus 12.525E. Otto 878

to have been uttered on the occasion of some splendid, slow procession, which Horace too mentions in his *Satires*: 'As if he were carrying the sacred objects of Juno . . .'[1]

27 Volentem bovem ducito
Lead a willing ox

Τὸν θέλοντα βοῦν ἔλαυνε, Drive a willing ox. Make use of the efforts of those who work willingly. It is madness to 'lead unwilling hounds to hunt' as Plautus says.[1] The adage is recorded by the scholiast of Theocritus. I have mentioned it in the adage 'Milk the one that's handy.' [2]

28 Habet
He's got it!

He's got it! is a proverbial expression uttered when someone achieves what he was longing for or what he deserves: 'He's got what he wants; like lips like lettuce.'[1] It is thought to be derived from fowlers, fishermen or hunters who, when they come home, are greeted with Ἔχεις τι; 'Have you caught anything?' This is quoted from Aristophanes *Clouds*.[2] In his *Agamemnon* Seneca the tragedian says: 'He has it. The deed is done.'[3] In the *Andria* Terence has 'Immediately I say to myself. Indeed he's caught. He's had it.'[4] Donatus shows this is said 'properly of gladiators when others notice they are wounded before they feel it themselves.'[5] The adage seems to have originated with this cry.[6]

* * * * *

1 Horace *Satires* 1.3.10–11. Horace is describing the inconsistency of the musician Tigellius: 'Often he would run as if fleeing from a foe; very often he would stalk as slowly as some bearer of Juno's holy offerings.'

27 Scholiast of Theocritus 11.75. Cf Mantissa 3.14.
 1 Plautus *Stichus* 139; *Adagia* I vii 65
 2 *Adagia* III ii 91 Milk the one that's handy; why pursue him that runs away?

28 Aristophanes (see n2 below)
 1 *Adagia* I x 71
 2 Aristophanes *Clouds* 733; Erasmus adds the name of the author to the information found in Zenobius (Aldus) column 90 or *Suda* E 4002.
 3 Seneca *Agamemnon* 901; added in 1526
 4 Terence *Andria* 82–3, cited by Otto 777; added in 1526
 5 Donatus *Commentum Terentii* ed P. Wessner I 67; added in 1526
 6 The last sentence was added in 1533.

29 Hercules hospitatur
Being a host to Hercules

Ἡρακλῆς ξενίζεται, Being a host to Hercules. Often said when someone seemed to be outstaying his welcome at a feast, because those who received Hercules into their house and to a feast had to wait a long time before he was sated. It was not safe to disturb him while he was still hungry, nor was the glutton easily satisfied; we even read that he ate whole oxen at one meal. This is why he was called ἀδδηφάγος 'the glutton' by the Greeks who consecrated to him the seagull calling it the βουφάγος 'the ox-eater.'[1] We also read that he competed with a certain Lepreus to see which of them could finish an ox more quickly. These and many other stories about his greed are recounted in book 10 by Athenaeus,[2] who adds that a certain athlete of Thasos, named Theagenes, and Milo of Croton finished an ox in one day.[3] May our enemies have such guests![4]

30 Etiam in deorum coetu
Even in the assembly of the gods

Κἀν θεῶν ἀγορᾷ, Even in the assembly, or meeting of the gods. Some take this to refer to persons who are particularly good and just, others to the utterly scurrilous. It is said in addition that there is a place in Eleusis, near the Anactorum,[1] called the Forum of the Gods, which people would not go into without speaking words of good omen. Hence they would say of someone who was outrageously scurrilous, 'This man would speak evil even in the assembly of the gods.'

* * * * *

29 Apostolius 8.63. Suidas H 477 = Zenobius (Aldus) column 93. Aristophanes
  Lysistrata 928
  1 Gulick (Loeb) translates Athenaeus (see n2 below) here as 'which is called the
    scavenger.' For βουφάγος as an epithet for Hercules see Lucian *Amores* 4.
  2 Athenaeus 10.411A–412B
  3 From 'This is why' to here added in *1517/18*
  4 This sentence was added in *1533*. Cf Ovid *Heroides* 16.219 quoted in *Adagia* II iii
    11, III ii 1, III ii 78. Here Erasmus has *convivae* 'guests'; Ovid has *convivia* 'feasts.'

30 Pseudo-Plutarch Laurentianus 4.63 Jungblut page 410 or Zenobius (Aldus) column 102. Cf Zenobius 4.30, Zenobius (Athous) 1.82, Diogenianus 5.21, Apostolius 8.89. *Suda* K 1163
  1 The Greek ἀνάκτορον is a common noun meaning 'palace' or 'temple,' which
    Erasmus appears to have mistaken for the name of the temple at Eleusis.

31 **Calliphanes**
Calliphanes

Καλλιφάνης, Calliphanes. It was this poet's ridiculous way of canvassing favour that gave rise to a proverbial joke. It is said that it was his custom to put together in writing the beginnings of various odes and speeches, up to three or four lines, and to declaim them and show them off in order to seem knowledgeable and learned to people who did not know of the deception. Athenaeus[1] recalls him in book 1 of the *Doctors at Dinner* and says his nickname was Parabrycontis, son of Parabrycon.[2]

Such literary impostors are not unknown in our own times; their method is to learn by heart a few notable passages, not widely published, from some of the best authors of different disciplines. Armed with these they are not afraid to speak in assemblies and attack anyone however learned. And they carry this off, with their ready recitation of these passages, so well that they seem to the inexperienced to be veritable Solons. But these Solons, if it is the third or the fourth time you have encountered them – Heavens above! – there is no one less capable of speech, no one more uneducated than they once their little hoards have been exhausted.

I can hardly avoid laughing as I write this remembering a certain Calliphanes I knew once when I was staying in the family of that most distinguished man Hendrik van Bergen, bishop of Cambrai.[3] But I will spare his name because he was a fellow-guest. This man put together and bound a great many volumes, but with empty pages except that at the front there were certain rather grand titles to be seen, such as 'Odes,' 'Orations,' 'Epistles.' Before each title there was written his full three-part name, so that anyone who happened to read the titles would think this was a learned man producing multiple great works of literature.

32 **Cauda blandiri**
Wagging the tail

Κέρκῳ σαίνειν, Wagging the tail, is said of those who fawn on a person in

* * * * *

31 *Suda* K 243. Cf Zenobius (Aldus) column 102.
1 Athenaeus 1.4C
2 From παρά 'beside' and βρύκω 'gobble'; Gulick (Loeb) translates 'Son of Voracious.'
3 Erasmus was secretary to the bishop from 1492 to 1495. See CEBR 1.132–3 and CWE 1 100.

32 Aristophanes (see n1 below)

the hope of some gratification. Aristophanes in the *Knights*:

> The one who wags his tail as he watches the meal, my friend,
> While you are looking elsewhere, he is the one who eats your food.[1]

He often expresses the same idea with αἰκάλλειν 'fawn,' which is said of dogs fawning with their ears, their tails, and their whole body. In the *Knights* we have: 'These oracles fawn upon me.'[2] Θωπεύειν 'to wheedle' was also derived from the name of an animal, if we believe the Greek etymologist.[3] *Thos* is Greek for a type of wolf, and some wolves fawn in the manner of dogs. *Thoes* is used by Pliny in book 8 chapter 24 for one kind of wolf, but one that is friendly to man.[4] Whether θωπεύειν comes from this, I am doubtful.[5]

33 Crater litium
A basinful of disputes

Κρατὴρ κακῶν, A basinful of evils. Said of something extremely troublesome or of a man who causes disputes. Aristophanes in the *Acharnians* has: 'A basinful of evils, a trafficker in disputes,'[1] meaning a slanderer and an informer.

34 Lampon iurat per anserem
Lampon swears by a gander

Λάμπων ὄμνυσι τὴν χῆνα, Lampon swears by a gander. This expression was used when someone tried to cheat by swearing an oath. Lampon was some

* * * * *

1 Aristophanes *Knights* 1031–2: Ὃς κέκρῳ σαίνων 'The one who wags his tail'
2 Aristophanes *Knights* 211; the same verb is used at *Knights* 48 and *Thesmophoriazusae* 869.
3 *Etymologicum magnum* 459.44
4 Pliny *Naturalis historia* 8.123
5 'He often expresses' to the end was added in *1533*.

33 Aristophanes (see n1 below); cf *Adagia* IV ii 57 Basin and all (531 below). In *1508* there appeared the Greek title Κρατὴρ δικῶν, probably taken from *Suda* K 2338 (= Zenobius [Aldus] column 107), where it is said to be a proverb.
1 Aristophanes *Acharnians* 937; Erasmus' word *sector* 'trafficker' means a purchaser of public goods, a profiteer; the Greek τριπτήρ means the vat into which oil pressed from olives runs, hence the informer who 'squeezes oil' from disputes.

34 *Suda* Λ 93 = Zenobius (Aldus) column 110

sort of priest, a prophet, and a speaker of oracles. He was in the habit of swearing by a gander, as if it were an oracular bird, or because this was formerly so ordained by Rhadamanthus, that there be no swearing by one of the gods, but by a dog, or a gander, something which Socrates does commonly in Plato. It is said that it was on Lampon's proposal that the Athenians sent a colony to Sybaris. The adage is recalled by Aristophanes in the *Birds*: 'Lampon even now swears by a gander when someone deceives him in some matter.'[1]

35 Palpo percutere
Piercing with a caress

'Piercing with a caress' is said of anyone who cajoles, or inspires vain hope with words. Plautus in the *Merchant*:

> – 'I will make a free man of you in a few months.
> – You pierce me with a caress.
> – Would I ever dare to tell you an untruth?'[1]

The same author elsewhere: 'You cannot force me with your caresses.'[2] The image is borrowed from grooms who pacify horses by patting with the hand. Virgil in the third book of the *Georgics*:

> Then more and more to delight in his trainer's
> Caressing praise and to love the sound of patting his neck.[3]

And Horace in his *Satires*:

> Stroke the steed clumsily and back he kicks, at every point on his guard.[4]

* * * * *

1 Aristophanes *Birds* 521; added in 1526. Erasmus' translation is *ubi quis fallit in aliquo* 'when someone deceives him in some matter'; in 1526 he had: *fallit aliquem* 'lets someone down.' Modern editions of Aristophanes give better sense: 'whenever he's going to cheat you.'

35 Plautus (see n1 below). Otto 1327
1 Plautus *Mercator* 152–4; cf *Amphitruo* 526.
2 Plautus *Pseudolus* 945. This line also makes *Adagia* III vi 27 To smother with caresses (139 above).
3 Virgil *Georgics* 3.185–6; translation by H. Rushton Fairclough (Loeb)
4 Horace *Satires* 2.1.20; translation by H. Rushton Fairclough (Loeb)

36 Eximere e manu manubrium
To strike the handle out of his hand

Plautus was using a proverbial figure when he said, 'To strike the handle out of his hand,' meaning to wrest the ability to do something from the person about to do it. The passage is in the *Pot of Gold*:

> I took the cudgel and slew the cock, a red-handed thief.
> By heaven! I think the cooks had promised that cock a reward
> To show them where it is. I struck the handle out of their hand.[1]

The figure is derived from one who has already raised the sword to strike and has the handle struck suddenly out of his hands.

37 Alybantis hospitis munera
Gifts of an Alybantian host

Τὰ δῶρα τοῦ ἐξ Ἀλύβαντος ξένου ἤ τὰ τοῦ Ἀλυβαντίου ἑταίρου ξένια, Gifts of an Alybantian host, or Hospitality of an Alybantian friend. Eustathius the commentator of Homer thinks this can be properly used as a proverb whenever anyone boasts falsely that he has bestowed great gifts, or if kindness is shown only in words and not in deeds. In the last book of Homer's *Odyssey* Ulysses, in disguise, talks to his father Laertes; he pretends he is from Alybas, is the son of the very wealthy Aphidas, and that he had earlier given hospitality to Ulysses and sent him away loaded with generous gifts. He says, 'I am from Alybas, where I have a grand house; / I am the son of King Aphidas, son of Polypemon. / My own name is Eperitus.'[1] And shortly before this:

> I took this man into my home and made him welcome,
> Showering him with all the luxuries
> That overflowed[2] in our house, adding to them

* * * * *

36 Plautus (see n1 below). Otto 1033
  1 Plautus *Aulularia* 469–71; in *1508* Erasmus gave the title as *in Euclione*, correcting this in *1517/18*. Euclio is the character speaking.

37 Eustathius 1961.60 on *Odyssey* 24.304–6
  1 Homer *Odyssey* 24.304–6
  2 All editions have *ex(s)uperant*; I follow ASD in reading *exuberant*.

Guest gifts fit for such a friend.
Seven talents of wrought gold I gave him,
A solid silver, engraved wine-bowl,
Twelve cloaks of single weave,
As many long mantles I added and as many tunics,
And besides all this four servant girls handsome and skilled
In arts and hand crafts whom I allowed him to choose for himself.[3]

38 Fungus
A mushroom

In the *Bacchis Sisters* Plautus uses 'mushroom' to mean someone who is
stupid and too readily trusting. This is perhaps because the mushroom
itself is a rather tasteless thing, or because it is soft and fragile, or because
it bursts suddenly.[1] Plautus' words are as follows: 'Could I have been such
a mushroom as to trust him?'[2] The same author in the same play:

Of all the fools, dullards, idiots, mushrooms, half-wits,
Babblers, ninnies anywhere, who are, were, or will be,
I alone am far ahead for stupidity.[3]

39 Eurycles
Eurycles

Εὐρυκλῆς, Eurycles, was a popular nickname for someone who foresaw anything concerning himself and his own troubles. There was a certain seer of
this name also called Etastrimythos because, if I am not mistaken, he fore-
told true things from the stars, the name being derived from ἐτάζειν 'to
examine.'[1] He is mentioned by Suidas too, although in his case the nick-

* * * * *

3 *Odyssey* 24.271–9

38 Plautus (see n2 below). Otto 736. Cf *Adagia* IV x 98 A rotten mushroom.
1 Latin *vel quod subito prorumpat*. Is Erasmus including puff-balls among mushrooms, suggesting insubstantiality or the sudden deflation of betrayed trust?
2 Plautus *Bacchides* 283
3 Plautus *Bacchides* 1087–8

39 Pseudo-Plutarch (see n3 below)
1 Etastrimythos is an aberrant form, found in Zenobius (Aldus) column 89,
  which leads Erasmus to attempt a fanciful etymology ἐτάζ + ἀστηρ; the correct
  form is as given by the *Suda* (and used by Rabelais).

name is written Engastrimythos, 'prophet' or 'ventriloquist.'[2] It is listed in the *Collected Proverbs* ascribed to Plutarch.[3] It is also used by Plato in the *Sophist*. Having criticized those who betray their own foolishness with their tangled and absurd arguments, he goes on: 'There is no need of others to refute them; they have an enemy at home,[4] as the saying goes, to contradict them, and they always go marching about carrying with them some spirit muttering within like the absurd Eurycles.'[5]

40 **Si quis iuxta civitatem clypeus**
Some shield for the town!

Εἴ τις περὶ πόλιν αἰγίς, Some shield around the city! This was shouted by way of a joke at people who roved about the city here and there in a dissolute manner. It is listed in the *Collected Proverbs* of Plutarch, but is not explained.[1]

41 **Rupta ancora**
His hook has broken

Κράδης ῥαγείσης, His hook has broken. This used to be said about people who had put themselves forward hastily as intending to do some great deed and then, to everyone's disappointment, behaved in a disgraceful and unseemly manner when it came to the deed. The figure is taken from tragic actors; when a god was to be brought on, they used to be raised quickly by certain machinery and appeared high up on the stage building as if suspended in the air, hanging by a rope tied in their belt. Sometimes the hook to

* * * * *

2 *Suda* E 3721. Cf Apostolius 8.14 and Zenobius (Aldus). The ventriloquist Eurycles is also mentioned at Aristophanes *Wasps* 1019; 'because ... ventriloquist' was added in *1515*
3 Pseudo-Plutarch *Alexandrian Proverbs* 2.22
4 Latin *domi*, Greek οἴκοθεν – both have the meaning 'in one's own nature'; cf Terence *Adelphoe* 413, *Domi habuit unde disceret* (Otto 573).
5 Plato *Sophist* 252C; added in *1533* and used already in *1520* in *Adagia* IV v 33 They have an enemy within

40 Pseudo-Plutarch *Alexandrian Proverbs* 2.21. Cf Zenobius (Aldus) column 77.
1 'but is not explained' was added in *1515*.

41 Zenobius (Athous) 3.156. Pseudo-Plutarch *Alexandrian Proverbs* 2.16 = Zenobius (Aldus) column 107. The Greek expression is listed by PCG 8 as adespota 945.

which these people were tied happened to break and they fell, much to the amusement of the spectators and to their own hurt and loss of dignity. *Crada*[1] here does not mean a branch of a fig-tree as it does elsewhere, but the bronze hook by which the actors were secured to the machinery. Julius Pollux in book 4 chapter 19 tells us, Ἡράδη was the word used in comedy for what was called μηχανή in tragedy. It was like a "fig-tree," since in Attic Greek a fig tree is κράδη,'[2] but the branches of any tree are sometimes called *cradae*.[3]

42 Suam quisque homo rem meminit
Each man thinks of his own business

This is Plautus in the *Merchant*: 'Each man thinks of his own business.' It is a proverbial phrase expressing men's usual habit of nodding through another man's business, but each is wide awake and attentive to his own. Hence the good advice of Ennius quoted in Aulus Gellius:

> Let this saying be always ready to your mind:
> Don't expect your friends to do what you can do for yourself.[1]

The same idea is the subject of a very fine fable by Aesop about the crested lark who knew she was not in danger as long as the harvest was left to other people.[2] Plautus alludes to the adage in the *Carthaginian*:

> Is this how you try to see whether we can remember our own affairs?[3]

Terence alludes to it too in the *Phormio*: 'But if he had left an estate of ten talents, etc.'[4] Whatever is dear to us we remember easily, and negligence is generally the mother of forgetfulness.

* * * * *

1 In the title Erasmus has used *ancora*, but the transliteration *crada* in the translation of the Greek.
2 Pollux *Onomasticon* 4.128–9; added in 1526. Cf Hesychius K 3913.
3 From 'but the branches' to the end was added in 1533.

42 Plautus *Mercator* 1011. Otto 1089
1 Ennius *Satirae* 57–8 Vahlen, cited by Aulus Gellius *Noctes Atticae* 2.29.20
2 Aesop 325 Perry (Babrius 88); cited from Aulus Gellius 2.29.2–16. See *Adagia* I iv 41:11n CWE 31 351.
3 Plautus *Poenulus* 557; added in 1526
4 Terence *Phormio* 393; added in 1533

43 In utrumvis dormire oculum
To sleep on either eye

Plautus in the *Pseudolus*: 'As to that, you may sleep on either eye.'[1] It has the same meaning as the one we noted earlier: 'To sleep sound on either ear.'[2] The comic playwright aimed at humour through his novelty of expression. This is why the dialogue goes on at that point: 'Either eye! Don't you mean "ear"?' And the inventive Pseudolus answers: 'But that's too common.'[3] At the same time the passage draws attention to the fact that men often try to invent new sayings of this sort.

44 Corinthiis non indignatur Ilium
Troy is not angry with the Corinthians

Κορινθίοις δ' οὐ μέμφεται τὸ Ἴλιον, Troy places no blame on the Corinthians. With this verse we can covertly reproach the cowardice of someone who has acted in such a way that the enemy has nothing for which it may seriously blame him. It is a verse of Simonides, which, according to Aristotle in book 1 of the *Rhetoric*, the Corinthians were vexed about, believing it to be something composed as an insult to them because in the Trojan War they had not made any great effort to assist. It could be adapted to use when somebody has written in such a gauche way against good letters that his want of eloquence speaks for them rather than against them, 'On the Corinthians etc.'[1] In his life of Dion Plutarch interprets the adage somewhat differently: 'Just as Simonides says, O Sosius Senecio, "Troy is not angry with the Corinthians"[2] for having come to the war with the Greek forces,

* * * * *

43 *Collectanea* no 232. Otto 211
1 Plautus *Pseudolus* 123–4
2 *Adagia* i viii 19
3 Erasmus' text says *pervulgatum est nimis*; the accepted version is *hoc pervolga-tumst minus*, which P. Nixon (Loeb) translates: 'My version is less platitudinous.' But see ASD ii-7 69:532–3n.

44 Aristotle *Rhetoric* 1.6.24 (1363a16) quoting (from memory) Simonides PMG 67 = 50 Bergk and 571 Campbell (*Greek Lyric* [Loeb] 3.456–8). Plutarch (see n2 below) has a different version, and the scholiast of Aristotle (*Commentaria in Aristotelem graeca* xxi part 2 294) a third from the scholiast of Pindar on *Olympians* 13.78. Cf Edmonds *Lyra graeca* ii number 59.
1 'It could be ... etc' was added in *1517/18*.
2 In Greek: τοῖς Κορινθίοις οὐ μηνίειν τὸ Ἴλιον

because the Trojans also had resolute allies in the companions of Glaucus[3] who were themselves descendants of the Corinthians.'[4] From these words of Plutarch we may understand the proverb as meaning that we should feel less hurt if we are harmed by those who were formerly our benefactors, and should forgive the present offence for the sake of earlier services.

45 Maras
Maras

Μάρας, Maras. This name is said to have been that of a certain man of the Syrian city of Beroea,[1] very rich but nonetheless humane and kind to everyone, citizens and strangers. Hence it became popularly accepted to apply the term to men who seemed to be born for the benefit of the many. There is a rather long story about this man in the Greek *Collected Proverbs*,[2] but I think it is sufficient for me just to have mentioned it in order not to waste time, for 'Maras' does not appear to be a genuine or authentic proverb. If anyone really wants to learn about the story, the work is available, published by Aldus when my *Adagia* had already been finished.[3]

46 A Nannaco
Since Nannacus

Ἀπὸ Ναννάκου, Since Nannacus – when we mean that something goes back to the most remote antiquity. Nannacus, so the story says, was a king before Deucalion who foresaw the flood to come. I have mentioned him elsewhere.[1]

*****

3 Glaucus was second in command after Sarpedon of the Lycian contingent at Troy (*Iliad* 2.876) and great grandson of Glaucus of Corinth (*Iliad* 6.154–5), son of Sisyphus.
4 Plutarch *Dion* 1.1; from 'In his life of Dion' to the end is an addition of *1520*.

45 Zenobius (Aldus) column 116. *Suda* M 181
1 Pliny *Naturalis historia* 5.89, Strabo *Geographica* 16.2.7
2 Ie Zenobius (Aldus), published in 1505. See *Adagia* III v 30n and III vii 83 n1 (83 and 271 above).
3 This sentence was added in *1533*, by which time Erasmus' memory may have been slightly confused since, although his *Collectanea* had indeed appeared before 1505, this proverb was not included until the *Chiliades* of *1508*.

46 *Suda* N 24 = Zenobius (Aldus) column 124. Cf also Zenobius 6.10, Zenobius (Aldus) column 41, and *Suda* A 3448.
1 *Adagia* II viii 19 Cannacus' things

He is also recalled, under the word Ἰκόνιον, by Stephanus who reports that
he was the source of another proverb: 'To weep in the time of Cannacus,'
even though there we read 'Annacus' for 'Cannacus.'² Latin speakers use a
similar figure when they say, 'Going back to the time of the Aborigines'³
and 'Just as if you were talking to Evander's mother.'⁴ This is not very
different from 'As old as Codrus'⁵ and 'You are talking of things older than
the diphthera.'⁶

47 Asinus ad tibiam
An ass to the flute

Ὄνος πρὸς αὐλόν, An ass to the flute. This is to be used for someone who
does not notice or understand or approve clever remarks. There are certain
animals in whom there seems to be some sensitivity to music, such as horses,
birds, and serpents. The ass is unmoved by any song. This adage is closely
related to 'An ass to the lyre.'¹

48 Oresti pallium texere
To weave a mantle for Orestes

Ὀρέστῃ χλαῖναν ὑφαίνειν, To weave a cloak for Orestes. Said of one who
made a gift for someone who would waste it. For Orestes in his madness
would tear his clothes to pieces. It is a hemistich of heroic verse taken
from the *Birds* by Aristophanes: 'And then to weave a cloak for Orestes so
that he may not feel cold and strip people of their clothes.'¹ The scholion

* * * * *

2 Stephanus Byzantinus, Ἰκόνιον pages 329–30 Meineke (Ἀννακός); added in
   1520. According to ASD the form 'Nannacus' is correct; 'Annacus' is found
   only in Stephanus Byzantinus, and 'Cannacus' is an error of Erasmus himself.
3 Aulus Gellius *Noctes Atticae* 5.21.7
4 Aulus Gellius 1.10.2; cf *Adagia* IV iv 29 As if you are talking with Evander's
   mother (Otto 612 and Otto *Nachträge* page 25).
5 *Adagia* IV iii 21
6 *Adagia* I v 24

47 *Suda* O 385 = Zenobius (Aldus) column 130. Cf PCG 5 Eupolis fragment 279.
 1 *Adagia* I iv 35, where Erasmus says we are to understand 'An ass listening to
   the lyre'

48 Aristophanes (see n1 below)
 1 Aristophanes *Birds* 712 and 1490–3. The source was identified in 1526, after
   Erasmus had written in 1508 *hemistichium e poeta quopiam*, and in 1515–23

says that Orestes was a λωποδύτης 'a stealer of other people's clothes,' who, pretending insanity, used to approach men in the dark and rob them of their apparel.[2] Hence it will be quite aptly applied when we are warned to give something to a man threatening to steal so that he does not take it by force. The adage did not originate with Aristophanes but is adapted by him, for by this circumlocution he means the winter.

49 Pandeletias sententias
Pandeletian maxims

Πανδελετίους γνώμας, A Pandeletian maxim, is how Cratinus in his *Low-class Men* describes a peevish and annoying saying that people cite.[1] It derives from some informer[2] or other called Pandeletus, of the sort who, in order to make money, 'thrust great law-suits upon you,' as Terence's Phormio says;[3] and they get votes by similar methods.

50 Sibylla vivacior
More long-lived than the Sibyl

The longevity of the Sibyl gave rise to this proverb. Propertius in book 2

* * * * *

hemistichium heroici carminis e poeta quopiam. Erasmus forgot to eliminate his speculation about the metre, which is actually part of an anapaestic tetrameter catalectic, when he discovered that the verse was from Aristophanes (see ASD II-7 71:582–3n).
2 Dübner pages 226 and 242: the word λωποδύτης is used in the second of these; the first has an explanation corresponding to the last part of Erasmus' sentence. Aristophanes himself uses the word in the same play, line 497 (and *Frogs* 772). This whole paragraph was added in 1533. N. Dunbar has a full discussion of the problems of this line and translates, 'And (we reveal the right time for you) to weave a cloak for Orestes, so that he may not feel cold and strip off people's clothes.'

49 *Suda* Π 171 = Zenobius (Aldus) column 140. Cf Aristophanes *Clouds* 924.
1 PCG 4 Cratinus fragment 260. Erasmus' Latin for the title of the play Χείρωνες is *Deteriores*.
2 Latin *sycophanta*; see *Adagia* II iii 81 A sycophant.
3 Terence *Phormio* 439

50 Macarius (CPG 2) 261. ASD suggests the title was inspired by Ovid *Metamorphoses* 14.104.

of his *Elegies*: 'But a Sibyl's whole lifetime shall never alter my love.'[1] He used 'a Sibyl's lifetime' to mean 'a very long time.' The Sibyl is called the 'long-lived priestess' by Virgil in book 6 of the *Aeneid*.[2] Servius, explaining this passage, adds that Apollo fell in love with the Sibyl and gave her the choice of asking for anything she wanted. She demanded to live as many years as there were grains of sand in a heap she had scooped up. Apollo replied that this could be done if she left the island of Erythrea[3] and never looked on it again. And so she came to Cumae where she lost her bodily strength and retained life in her voice alone. When her fellow citizens learned this, whether out of envy or pity, they sent her a letter signed in the ancient manner with chalk. But she, seeing the soil of her native land,[4] was finally freed in death. This is how Phoebus deceived his priestess.[5]

51 E flamma cibum petere
Snatching a dinner out of the fire

In the *Eunuchus* Terence says of a parasite that he is the sort who would even 'snatch a dinner out of the fire,'[1] that is, that he would suffer or do anything for the sake of food. Catullus explains the adage in his *Epigrams*:

> Rufa from Bologna, wife of Menenius,
> Deceives[2] Rufulus. You have seen her often
> In the cemeteries snatching food out of the very pyre,

* * * * *

1 Propertius 2.24.33; cited by Otto 1639. Translation by H.E. Butler (Loeb)
2 Virgil *Aeneid* 6.321. The whole passage from the beginning of this sentence to 'freed in death' (second last sentence) was added in *1515* and the final sentence in *1517/18*.
3 An error of Servius: no island of this name is recorded. The home of this Sibyl was Erythrea in Ionia. Varro (*Res divinae* in Lactantius *Institutiones* 1.6.8–12) lists ten Sibyls including the Erythrean.
4 The adjective *erythreus* means red; the chalk was presumably also red.
5 Servius on the passage cited (see n2 above); cf Ovid *Metamorphoses* 14.132–153.

51 *Collectanea* no 535. Terence (see n1 below). Otto 669.
1 Terence *Eunuchus* 491; translated by J. Sargeaunt (Loeb): 'steal cakes from a corpse.' Also quoted in *Adagia* II iii 55 Through sword and fire we needs must break our way
2 Latin *fallit*; Catullus has *fellat* 'sucks.'

Even though she was cudgelled by a half-shaved corpse-burner
As she chased a loaf that fell out of the fire.[3]

52 Reddidit Harpocratem
He turned him into Harpocrates

In his *Epigrams* Catullus said by way of a proverb: 'He turned him into
Harpocrates,' meaning 'He imposed silence.' The poem goes like this:

> Gellius had heard that his uncle was in the habit of reproving loudly
> Anyone who enjoyed love's pleasures or talked about them.
> Determined that this should not happen to himself, he scorned his own
>   uncle's wife[1]
> And turned his uncle into a figure of Harpocrates.
> He did whatever he liked, for now even if he made his uncle himself
> Perform fellatio,[2] Uncle would not utter a word.[3]

Harpocrates was pictured in ancient times as a god who, by a finger raised
to his lips, enjoined silence,[4] rather like the Roman goddess Angerona.[5]

* * * * *

3 Catullus 59

52 *Collectanea* no 172. Catullus (see n3 below). Otto 791. Tilley H 177 To be a
Harpocrates
1 Latin *patrui perdespuit ipsam / uxorem*; the accepted text is now *patrui perdepsuit
ipsam / uxorem* 'worked over his own uncle's wife.' Peter Whigham (Penguin)
translates 'promptly assaulting his aunt.'
2 Latin *irrumet*; cf *Adagia* III vii 70 (260 above).
3 Catullus 74.4
4 Cf *Collectanea* no 172 *Digito compesce labellum* (from Juvenal 1.160) and Tilley
F 239 Lay thy finger on thy lips. See Plutarch *Moralia* 378c *De Iside et Osiride*;
Ovid *Metamorphoses* 9.691; Poliziano *Miscellanea* 83. The sentence was added
in *1515*. In fact this interpretation of Harpocrates as a symbol of silence is a
complete misunderstanding of the gesture of certain forms of the Egyptian
Horus where it signifies childhood. See 'Horus' in the *Oxford Classical Dictionary*.
5 Represented with a sealed bandage over her mouth; see Pliny *Naturalis historia*
3.65, Macrobius *Saturnalia* 1.10.7. Harpocrates and Angerona are mentioned
together as gods of silence, and therefore of secrecy, in *Adagia* I v 74 (CWE 31
450:56–8). In Ep 47 Erasmus talks of dedicating his work to Harpocrates rather
than Apollo.

53 Qui probus Atheniensis
An Athenian who is honest

Plato mentions this proverb[1] in book 1 of the *Laws*: 'And the popular saying that "those of the Athenians who are good are exceptionally good" seems to be very true.'[2] Plato feels that, in a republic which is badly governed and corrupt, those who are good are instinctively so and to an extraordinary degree. For they are not to be thought of as feigning honesty, certainly not when they are living among dishonest people with whom they would actually find favour if they conducted themselves in the same dishonest way; nor can they be corrupted by the degenerate morals of others and contact with vice. The same can be said of the Roman state in which it is a proof of exceptional integrity to be uncorrupted.[3] By a similar argument Terence's Simo infers the good morals of his son.[4] The adage can be adapted to life at court or the sort of pursuit that offers temptations to ruin.[5]

54 Digna Cedro
Worthy of cedar

Things are said to be 'worthy of cedar' when they deserve to be remembered in perpetuity and are considered to be such as should be bequeathed to posterity. Horace in the *Art of Poetry*

> We hope for poems to be fashioned,
> Worthy to be smeared with cedar oil.[1]

And Persius: 'who has uttered words worthy of cedar oil.'[2] The origin is

* * * * *

53 Plato (see n2 below); cf Ep 1177.
1 From *1508–15* Erasmus had a phrase here qualifying his translation on the grounds of his lack of a Greek manuscript, but was able to omit this in *1517/18*.
2 Plato *Laws* 1.642c: ὅσοι Ἀθηναίων εἰσὶν ἀγαθοὶ διαφερόντως εἰσὶ τοιοῦτοι
3 Is Erasmus thinking of modern Rome or ancient Rome, or deliberately leaving the ambiguity?
4 Terence *Andria* 93–5
5 'The same can be said' to here was added in *1528*.

54 Persius (see n2 below). Cf Epp 47 and 996.
1 Horace *Ars poetica* 331–2; translation by H. Rushton Fairclough (Loeb)
2 Persius 1.42; translation by G.G. Ramsey (Loeb)

the nature of the tree; anything smeared with its sap does not rot. Pliny tells us in book 13 chapter 13 that it was by this means that the books of Numa,[3] although made of paper, lasted five hundred and thirty-five years buried in the ground.[4] The same author in book 16 mentions cedar as being among the materials that last for ever.[5] Dioscorides affirms the sap of this tree is mainly valued for its thickness, clarity, and rather strong smell; it does not run down but forms into solid drops. It has a power which can act in opposite ways: it corrupts living bodies, and preserves dead ones. This is why it is said that some call the tree Νεκροῦ ζωή 'The life of a carcass.'[6] Relevant to this is 'poems that will have nothing to fear from mackerel or from spice.'[7] And in Martial:

> Lest, hurried off to a sooty kitchen,
> You wrap tunny fry in your sodden papyrus . . .[8]

And Horace: 'Or you'll take refuge in Utica, or be despatched in a greasy parcel to Ilerda.'[9]

55 Telemachi olla
A Telemachus pot

Τελεμάχου χύτρα, A Telemachus pot. This adage is recalled by Athenaeus in book 9 where he says that Telemachus was a certain Acharnian who lived for the most part on beans, from which we may suppose that the expression was used of miserly people.

* * * * *

3 Livy 40.29.4–8; Plutarch *Numa* 22.2. Numa Pompilius, second king of Rome, was according to legend the founder of its religious customs. The dates of his reign are traditionally 715–673 BC and Pliny is counting from 181 when the books are said to have been found.
4 Pliny *Naturalis historia* 13.85
5 Pliny *Naturalis historia* 16.213
6 Dioscorides 1.77.1; added in *1528*
7 Persius 1.43; translation by G.G. Ramsey (Loeb); in *1508* this followed on immediately from the other quotation from Persius.
8 Martial *Epigrams* 3.2.3–4; translation by Walter C.A. Ker (Loeb)
9 Horace *Epistles* 1.20.13. Erasmus reads *unctus* 'greasy' not *vinctus* 'bound' as in ASD; cf *Adagia* II viii 96. Added in *1533*

55 Athenaeus 9.407D–408A

56 Alia res sceptrum, alia plectrum
A sceptre is one thing, a plectrum is another

I would not personally assert with complete confidence that it is a proverb, this answer Stratonicus the lyre-player gave to king Ptolemy, who was disputing with him hotly about the art of singing, but still as a turn of speech and figure it is so similar to a proverb that one fig is scarcely more like another.[1] Ἕτερόν ἐστιν, ὦ βασιλεῦ, σκῆπτρον, ἕτερον δὲ πλῆκτρον. 'A sceptre is one thing, o king, a plectrum is another.'[2] The phrase can be used whenever some wealthy and powerful person, relying on what fortune has given him, argues as if on equal terms with a scholar, though it is one thing to be rich or fortunate and something very different to be educated.

57 Quae dolent, ea molestum est contingere
It is unkind to touch on things that give pain

Amphis in the *Ampelurgus*, quoted by Stobaeus:

> On places where a man is not entirely happy
> It is most unkind to lay a hand.[1]

Each one of us is unwilling to hear about our own misfortunes especially those that have gained some notoriety, such as a disgrace in the family or a deformity. Accordingly it is a politeness not to rub anyone's wound or to touch a sore spot.

* * * * *

56 Athenaeus (see n2 below); cf *Adagia* IV i 20 (453 above). The story of Stratonicus was also added in *1528* to II ii 82. This adage was introduced in *1517/18*; in place of it, *1508* and *1515* have *Cucumerem rodens*, which became IV v 16 Gnaw at the gourd, wife, and weave the cloak.
1 *Adagia* II viii 7 As like as two figs
2 Athenaeus 8.350C

57 Stobaeus (see n1 below). ASD suggests that the title is a paraphrase of Erasmus' Latin translation, *minime suave est admovere ad haec manum*, of the Greek phrase πλησιάζειν τόπῳ, which as Estienne (LB II 982) remarks does not mean to 'lay a hand on a place,' but 'to reach a place,' that is, to move the foot, not the hand. Cf Phaedrus (*Babrius and Phaedrus* [Loeb]) 1.18.1 *Nemo libenter recolit qui laesit locum* 'No one likes to revisit the place that has brought him injury.'
1 PCG 2 Amphis fragment 4 cited by Stobaeus *Eclogae* 4.40.6 Hense v 921: Ἐν οἷς ἂν ἀτυχήσῃ ἀνθρώποις τόποις, / Ἥκιστα τούτοις πλησιάζων ἥδεται

58 Aurum igni probatum
Gold tested in the fire

'Ο χρυσὸς τῷ πυρὶ δοκιμασθείς, Gold tested in the fire, is an expression used of someone whose loyalty has been tested and confirmed by adversity. Marcus Tullius uses this figure in book 9 of his *Letters to Friends*.[1] Pindar too in the fourth *Nemean*: 'Gold which has been through the fire shows all its brilliance.'[2] Again in the tenth *Pythian Ode*: 'But gold shines when rigorously tested, and so does a true mind.'[3] Theognis:

> In all things you will find me like pure gold,
> Gently blushing when rubbed with the touchstone.[4]

And the same author elsewhere:

> When it comes to the touchstone and is compared in the test to lead,
> Then it will be completely clear that it is pure gold.[5]

This comparison is used also by St Peter the Apostle in his first letter: 'Much more precious than gold which perishes (or "ruinous gold") although it is through fire that it is tested.'[6] It is nothing short of a wonderful miracle

* * * * *

58 Erasmus probably formed the Greek from the New Testament: χρυσίου ... διὰ πυρὸς δὲ δοκιμαζομένου (see n6 below), but there is also a fragment of Menander (691 Kock): Χρυσὸς μὲν οἶδεν δοκιμάζεσθαι πυρί. ASD suggests for the Latin Seneca *De providentia* 5.10: *Ignis aurum probat* ... 'Fire provides a test for gold.' Otto 843. Tilley G 284 Gold is tried in the fire

1 Cicero *Ad familiares* 9.16.2; the full quotation is in *Adagia* II viii 81.
2 Pindar *Nemeans* 4.82–3
3 Pindar *Pythians* 10.67–8; added in *1526*
4 Theognis 1.449–50
5 Theognis 1.1105–6
6 1 Peter 1:7: πολὺ τιμιώτερον χρυσίου τοῦ ἀπολλυμένου, διὰ πυρὸς δὲ δοκιμαζομένου; added in *1515*. The verb ἀπόλλυμι is translated as middle voice in AV 'which perisheth' and RSV 'which though perishable,' but Erasmus, inserting *sive auro pestifero* in a bracket after *quod perditur*, suggests reading it as active 'which destroys' or 'is ruinous,' which is incorrect, but of course more consistent with his context. He offers the same alternatives, again without indicating a preference, in his New Testament, in the note on *Multo preciosior sit auro*: '*Sit* is redundant [it is omitted in modern editions]; moreover the Greek has πολὺ τιμιώτερον χρυσίου τοῦ ἀπολλυμένου, διὰ πυρὸς δὲ δοκιμαζομένου, that is, "much more precious than gold which is lost, or perishes, though it is assayed by

that gold is not only not dulled by fire but becomes brighter and brighter. Likewise the man who is genuinely good, when he is exposed to the storms of misfortune, does not lose his strength of mind but brings it to light. In book 33 Pliny writes that gold was esteemed above all metals particularly because it was the only thing in no way damaged by fire, surviving safely by its very nature even in conflagrations.[7] Indeed, as a matter of fact, it improves in quality the more often it is fired. It is a proof of the purity of gold if it glows red like fire, and this is called *obrizum* 'assayed gold.'[8]

59 Lunam detrahere
To pull down the moon

Τὴν σελήνην κατασπᾷ, He pulls down the moon. Customarily said of someone whose prospects seemed utterly desperate. The scholiast of Apollonius, on book 4, asserts that the saying originated with Aglaonice daughter of Hegemon, who because of her skill in astrology knew in advance of an eclipse of the moon and boasted that she was going to bring the moon down from heaven to earth. This excessively arrogant declaration was heard by Nemesis who soon took her revenge.[1] And this was how the proverb arose.

60 Leonis vestigia quaeris
It's only the tracks of the lion you look for

Τοῦ λέοντος ἴχνη ζητεῖς, It's the tracks of the lion you look for. A sarcasm against someone who speaks bravely and acts timidly. From some fable of Aesop in which the story is told of a certain hunter who asked a shepherd he met whether he had seen a lion anywhere and to point him out. The

* * * * *

fire," or "lost and ruinous gold."' Cf *Paraphrasis in primam epistolam Petri* (ASD VII-6 190): *aurum – res alioqui et perdita et peritura.*
7 Pliny *Naturalis historia* 33.59; added in *1515*
8 The word *obrizum* is a latinization of the Greek ὄβρυζον. Pliny uses *obrussa* for the process of assaying in the same passage.

59 Scholiast of Apollonius (see n1 below). This proverb is referred to in *Adagia* III ii 2.
1 Scholiast on Apollonius Rhodius 4.59. The practice is also referred to in Apollonius Rhodius 3.533 and in Plutarch *Moralia* 145C and 417A, where Erasmus would find the story of Aglaonice, daughter of Hegetor.

60 Aesop (see n1 below)

shepherd replied, 'I can soon show you the tracks of a lion for they are not far from from here.' Whereupon the hunter said, 'It's only the tracks that I'm interested in; I do not need any more than that.'[1] This adage matches one recorded elsewhere: 'Confronted with the bear you go looking for his tracks.'[2]

61 Non una vehit navis
More than a single ship can carry

Οὐ μία ναῦς ἄγει, More than a single ship can carry. This shows all the character of a proverb, one that it will be appropriate to use whenever we mean a greater number of men than a single ship can hold. One might say, for example, 'The ignorant are more than a single ship can carry.' It is to be found in Theognis: 'Even after searching among them all you will not find / More men than a single ship can carry.'[1]

62 Horna messis
This year's harvest

In the *Haunted House* Plautus uses 'this year's harvest' as a proverbial figure to mean a very large profit, equivalent to 'as much gain as there was to be made this year from the fields.' The comic poet says: 'Heavens! I haven't enjoyed a cold bath more for a long time, / Nor one in which, believe me Scapha, there was better refreshment for me.'[1] These words are spoken by a girl character. Then the procuress says, hoping to take advantage as much as possible of the other's beauty, 'May the outcome be like this year's harvest

* * * * *

1 Aesop 326 Perry (Babrius 92)
2 *Adagia* I x 34

61 Theognis (see n1 below)
1 Theognis 1.83–4

62 Plautus (see n1 below); Erasmus' text of Plautus (Milan 1500) leads him to see a proverbial expression where there is only a piece of mystification by the procuress.
1 Plautus *Mostellaria* 157–60; in early editions Erasmus followed the text of Milan 1500, edited by Giambattista Pio: *Nec cum me melius mea scapha reres aedificatam.* From 1526 this was corrected to: *Nec unde me melius Scapha reres aedificatum,* though it is difficult to see what he could have made even of this. Estienne corrects (LB II 983): *rear esse defaecatam.* The Loeb edition has *deficatam* 'I never had a better scouring.'

for everyone.'[2] The girl who is rather naïve does not understand what this means and says, 'What has this harvest to do with my bath?' The figure is very close to the same author's phrase in the *Curculio*: 'This grape harvest is not enough for this one old woman,'[3] meaning that she is such a drinker that all the wine from that year's harvest is not enough to satisfy her thirst.

63 Glaucus comesa herba habitat in mari
Glaucus has eaten grass and lives in the sea

Γλαῦκος φαγὼν πόαν οἰκεῖ ἐν θαλάσσῃ, Glaucus has eaten grass and lives in the sea. This appears to be said by way of a joke about people who, though dead, are still alive according to popular opinion. This belief occupied the minds of our nation for many years, to the point of madness, in the case of Prince Charles, Duke of Burgundy.[1] When he died in battle there were many who did not hesitate to assert, at great risk to their own interests, that he was still alive. Concerning Glaucus the Greeks tell a story which goes like this:[2]

> Glaucus was a certain fisherman of Anthedon who was by far the best swim-
> mer of all. To inspire greater wonder this man conceived the following de-
> ception: he swam out of the harbour with the Anthedonians watching him

* * * * *

2 Latin *Eventus omnibus velut horna messis fuat*; the accepted reading is: *Eventus rebus omnibus, velut horno messis magna fuit*, which P. Nixon (Loeb) translates: 'Everything has its outcome, just as this year brought a big harvest.'
3 Plautus *Curculio* 110a

63 Zenobius (Aldus) column 61 = Apostolius 5.49. In *1508* this adage was number III 979 and in *1515* number III 994; from *1517/18* to *1523* it was III x 1; it appeared here in *1526*. In its place in earlier editions was an adage entitled *Sisyphi commentum*, which had material in common with III vii 25 The wiles of Sisyphus (231 above), also found in these editions. Translated the text read: A Sisyphian trick. Said of a secret and cunning rather than honest inten-tion. Very like 'An invention worthy of Ulysses' [*Adagia* II viii 79]. Aristo-phanes in the *Acharnians* [391]: 'Then bring out the clever tricks of Sisy-phus.' Ajax in Ovid accuses Ulysses of embodying the cunning of Sisy-phus, from whom he was descended, and whom 'he much resembled by his thefts and deceit' [*Metamorphoses* 13.31].
1 Charles le Téméraire, the Bold or the Rash, killed at the siege of Nancy on 5th January 1477
2 Zenobius (Aldus) or perhaps Palaephatus *De incredibilibus* 28; this work was also published by Aldus in 1505, in the same collective publication as his Ae-sop, the proverbs of Tarrhaeus and Didymus, and the *Hieroglyphs* of Horapollo; it was translated into Latin by Filippo Fasanini in 1515.

until he was out of sight. At that point he turned back to land, hid in a remote spot and stayed there for many days. Then, when he judged it was
right, he swam back into the harbour watched by those who were standing
on the shore. To friends and enquirers who wondered where on earth he
had stayed all that time he pretended that he had lived for a while on the
waves.

He raised further wonder with another deception. During the winter
months, when other fishermen could catch no fish at all, he asked the citizens
what sort of fish they would like to be provided, and whatever they ordered
he brought, for he had already prepared a supply of them for this purpose
and kept them enclosed in another place. Finally it came about that this de-
ceiver was eaten by a sea monster, and that was the end of his comedy. But
since he did not return as was his custom, a popular legend spread about
that Glaucus had tasted grass, become immortal, and lived in the sea.[3] The
scholiast of the poet Apollonius[4] tells very similar stories about Glaucus,
that he was a fisherman who on one occasion was worn out by the weight
of fish he had caught and threw them away when he was half-way home.
But then a wonderful thing happened: one of the fish which was already
dying ate some grass and revived. This was seen by Glaucus who ate the
same grass and became immortal. Finally, wearied of life, he threw himself
into the sea. According to some he was turned into a marine god, according
to others into a fish, something on which there are many details in book 7
of Athenaeus,[5] who also quotes from the *Man with a Cataract* of Alexis.[6] If
you want to learn all the other stories about Glaucus in minor Greek authors you can read the seventh book of Athenaeus who chatters on enough
to put you off and make you sick about Glaucus the fish and Glaucus the
demon; for my part I have no desire to repeat all these trifles here.[7] It was
almost against my better judgment that I included this fanciful story here;
for if I may say plainly what I feel, I suspect this Greek writer, whoever
he was, made up the proverb as a pretext for recalling this story. However
I preferred to amuse myself with this effort rather than offer some half-

* * * * *

3 To this point Erasmus has been following Apostolius.
4 Scholiast of Apollonius Rhodius 1.1310
5 Athenaeus 7.296A–297C
6 Athenaeus 3.117C–118A, 6.224F and 7.301A–B. It is not clear why Erasmus includes this remark, unless he thinks the title significant: *Apeglaukomenos*. Alexis
   was a poet of the middle and new comedy living circa 375–275 BC. PCG 2 Alexis
   fragments 15–18. See W.G. Arnott *Alexis: The Fragments. A Commentary* (Cambridge 1996) 85–104.
7 From 'According to some' to here added in *1517/18*

educated individuals an excuse to say that I had ignorantly omitted what was to be found even in the published commentaries on Greek authors.[8]

64 Pergraecari
To live like a Greek

Since 'To play the Chalcidian,' 'To behave like a Lesbian,' 'To play Cretan,'[1] and several other expressions of this sort are proverbs in Greek, why should the Romans not take as an adage the word that Plautus uses in the *Haunted House*, that is *pergraecari*, meaning 'to lead a pleasant life'? Plautus' own words show clearly enough what *pergraecari* means:

> Get fuddled day and night, live like Greeks,
> Buy girls and set 'em free, feed parasites,
> Go in for fancy catering![2]

That's what Plautus says. Marcus Tullius, in the third speech against Verres, says: 'They had a conversation and an invitation was given to drinks in the Greek manner.'[3] The Greeks are spoken of badly everywhere in the Latin poets, and likewise in Cicero, not only as given to pleasures and softened by luxuries, but also as untrustworthy. This was either because to the somewhat uncivilized Romans of early times, holding to that ancient severity of theirs, the refinement of the Greeks seemed to be extravagance, or because rivalry in their purposes and mutual hatred caused them to write such outrageous things about the Greeks, or because there were in fact not a few Greeks in Italy such as Juvenal describes,[4] something which is not denied by Lucian too in his book *On Payment to Servants*,[5] so that men judged the whole nation on the basis of Greeks such as these.

* * * * *

8 Zenobius (Aldus) or Palaephatus; see n2 above.

64 *Collectanea* no 650. Plautus (see n2 below)
1 *Adagia* III ii 40 *Chalcidissare*, III vii 70 (260 above), I ii 29 *Cretiza cum Cretensi* – all adduced as proverbs referring to ethnic or geographical origins
2 Plautus *Mostellaria* 22–4; translation by Paul Nixon (Loeb). Cf Plautus *Truculentus* 87b.
3 Cicero *Verrines* 2.1.26.66 (see III iv 14 n7, 11 above); added in 1533. L.H.G. Greenwood (Loeb) notes this probably means 'to take wine with' their host, a special courtesy.
4 Juvenal 3.58–125
5 Lucian *De mercede conductis* 40; Erasmus' version of the title is *De mercede servientibus*.

65 Conos artoxya
Bangles and baubles

Κόνος ἀρτοξύη, Bangles and baubles. Said of things that are alike and inter-
changeable.[1] Some scholars believe a *conos* is a baker's instrument, not unlike an *artoxya*, which seems to mean a baker's knife. But from what follows
shortly after in Suidas it appears that *conoi* were small gifts given to children, suitable to their age, like bracelets.[2] So does it not fit the case of those
who reward someone's effort with some mean and petty gift?

66 Ne ligula quidem dignus
Not worth a tiddler

Κορδύλης οὐκ ἄξιος, Not worth a tiddler.[1] Said of a useless, worthless man,
it survives in common parlance among Latin speakers[2] even nowadays.
However I am of the opinion that it was the cheapness of tunny fry that
gave rise to the proverb. *Cordylae* are young tunny, but even smaller, as
Pliny tells us in book 32 chapter 11.[3] The cheapness of tunny fry is also
evident from Martial in book 11:

*****

65 *Suda* K 2045 = Zenobius (Aldus) column 106
  1 Following the *Suda*
  2 *Suda* K 2047. The meaning Erasmus would give to *artoxya* however remains to
    be surmised from the last sentence, which was added in *1515*.

66 *Suda* K 2073, Zenobius (Aldus) column 106, Zenobius Athous 3.109 (= Appendix 3.49). Suringar 135
  1 Latin *ligula*; (σ)κορδύλη (Aristotle *Historia animalium* 6.17 [571a16]), and *cordyla*
    (Pliny; see n3) both mean 'the fry of the tunny fish,' but for *ligula* in this
    context the *Oxford Latin Dictionary* gives only 'tentacle' of a cuttle-fish etc. The
    editor of ASD suggests that in *1508*, when the adage consisted only of the
    first two sentences, Erasmus may have used *ligula* in the sense of the Greek
    δεσμός 'fastening, latch,' the word used in Zenobius and *Suda*. In this case,
    he maintains the word *ligula* would no longer be appropriate for the new
    meaning Erasmus would have derived from Pliny in *1517/18*. However, the
    Oxford Latin Dictionary also cites Plautus' use of *ligula* in *Poenulus* 1309 as a
    term of abuse with uncertain sense, which may explain Erasmus' retention of
    it as a synonym for *cordyla*.
  2 Latin *apud Latinos*; possibly contemporary Italians. *Latini* were originally con-
    quered peoples of Italy who were allowed to keep some of their own laws and
    did not receive the full rights of Roman citizenship; see the *Oxford Classical
    Dictionary* ('Citizenship, Roman' and 'Latini').
  3 Pliny *Naturalis historia* 32.146 (*cordyla*) and 9.47

First there will be given you lettuce useful for relaxing
The bowels, and shoots cut from their parent leeks;
Then tunny salted and bigger than a small lizard fish,
And one which eggs will garnish in leaves of rue.

Shortly afterwards the poet mentions luxuries, so that he can deceive his companion:

I will deceive you to make you come; fish, mussels, sow's paps,
And fat birds of the poultry-yard and the marsh.[4]

67 Iuxta navem
Ship-shape

Κατὰ ναῦν, Ship-shape, is said of things that are arranged in good order, and that fit in or fit together, because the fittings of ships are always put in their proper place. For myself I am inclined to doubt whether the phrase that follows is proverbial: 'Rigging to suit the ship.'[1] Not all sails suit every ship.

68 Iuxta cubitum profecit
He has progressed by the cubit

Κατὰ πῆχυν ἐπεδίδου, He has progressed by the cubit. Said of someone who has risen to a better status, either progressing by regular steps, or advancing by great strides. For *cubitus* means both 'measure' in the sense of nothing excessive[1] and 'a rather large measure,' in the sense of a fairly big increment. We commonly measure very small things either by finger's breadths or by hand's breadths.

* * * * *

4 Martial *Epigrams* 11.52.5–8 and 13–14; translation by Walter C.A. Ker (Loeb). The two references to Martial were added in Â*1526*.

67 *Suda* K 667 = Zenobius (Aldus) column 103
1 Greek given by Erasmus as κατὰ ναῦν ἄρμενα, in the *Suda* κατὰ ναῦν τὰ ἄρμενα

68 *Suda* K 710 = Zenobius (Aldus) column 103
1 Latin *nihil transiliendum*; cf the Pythagorean precept 'Exceed not the balance,' commonly rendered as *Stateram ne transilias* (see for example the edition by Filippo Beroaldo, Bologna 1503, folio A [vi] r), though translated by Erasmus as *Stateram ne transgrediaris* (*Adagia* I i 2, CWE 31 33).

69 De tuo capite aguntur comitia
Your status is at stake in this meeting

There is a proverbial figure used by Plautus in his *Pot of Gold*, I am going to
a meeting where my status[1] is at stake. The discussion was about whether
or not he should marry the girl he was in love with. The origin is the
Roman meetings in which new magistrates were created by the votes of the
citizens. So when a decision is made about anything on which someone's
happiness may depend then the words 'The meeting is about his status'
will be appropriately uttered.

70 Usque ad ravim
Till I'm hoarse

Much as the Greeks say, Ἄχρι κόρου, 'To the point of satiety,'[1] so Plautus
somewhat more wittily says, 'To the point of hoarseness' meaning 'excessively,' or more often, 'too noisily,' so that the voice even of the person who
shouts so much becomes hoarse. The phrase is in the *Pot of Gold* as follows:
'Have you been pushing me off on this miserly old man? / If we ask anything of him, we may ask until we're hoarse / Before anything is given.'[2]

71 Cereri sacrificant
They sacrifice to Ceres

Again just as the Greeks say Ἑστίᾳ θύουσιν, 'They sacrifice to the Lar,'[1] so
Plautus shows more or less that Latin speakers used 'They sacrifice to Ceres'

* * * * *

69 Plautus *Aulularia* 700
  1 In Rome, particularly, *caput* could mean a person's political and social rights
    or citizenship. P. Nixon (Loeb) translates 'Now for the session that decides
    my fate.'

70 Plautus (see n2 below). Otto 1509. The editor of ASD draws attention to the
    discrepancy between the meaning Erasmus gives in defining the expression
    – taken by the editor as the meaning of the adage's title – and the sense in
    Plautus; it seems preferable to translate the title in conformity with Plautus.
  1 *Adagia* II viii 73 To the point of saturation. Zenobius 1.44. Apostolius 4.67.
    Zenobius (Aldus) column 50
  2 Plautus *Aulularia* 335–7. The accepted text has the verbs in the first person
    singular. Again Erasmus follows the edition of Giambattista Pio (k ii v); see
    Adagia IV i 62 n1 (478 above).

71 *Suda* Θ 3214. Cf Zenobius 4.44, Diogenianus 2.40 and 4.68, Apostolius 7.100
  1 *Adagia* I ix 43. Zenobius (Aldus) column 87

at any time at a feast when there is a shortage of wine. In her rites it was forbidden to introduce wine, as it was in the sacrifices of certain goddesses among the Greeks, as I have shown in the adage 'Nephalian wood.'[2] The passage is in the *Pot of Gold*, in these words roughly: 'Are these people going to celebrate a marriage to Ceres, dear Strobilus? / – Why? – Because I notice that no alcohol has been brought.'[3]

72 Inutilior blace
As useless as a catfish

Βλακὸς ἀχρηστότερος, As useless, or as bad, as a *blax*.[1] Said of a good-for-nothing, and someone of no virtue at all. The expression derives from a fish that is so bad, tasteless, and evil-smelling that it is rejected even by dogs. However this fish is rather like the catfish[2] if we are to believe the ramblings of the *Greek Etymologies*.[3] But I have never heard that dogs were eager for fish. And if the catfish is what is popularly called 'sturgeon,'[4] this is considered to be among the best of fish. The etymologist also says there is a place near Cumae, a marsh I suppose and infertile, called Blacia, which he suspects was the source of the proverb. Hesychius too calls the fish *blacia* instead of *blax*.[5] He says in addition that in Alexandria there is a tax, called the βλακεννόμος, paid by astrologers because *blaces*, that is, fools, go constantly to them asking for oracles from the stars.[6] It is certain that

* * * * *

2 *Adagia* II ix 95, though Erasmus might rather be thinking of II ix 96 A Nephalian sacrifice.
3 Plautus *Aulularia* 354–5

72 Apostolius 4.99 = Zenobius (Aldus) column 54. Cf *Suda* B 315 (βλάκα). This first appeared in *1508*, but from 'if we are to believe' to the end, together with 'tasteless, and evil-smelling,' everything is an addition of *1533*.
1 Latinization of Greek βλάξ 'stupid, stolid'; Erasmus later calls the fish *silurus*.
2 Added in *1515* following the *Etymologicum magnum* (see n3 below) or Zenobius (Aldus), who is also a source for the allegation that the *blax* is rejected by dogs. It is also said to be a type of fish by Erotian and Hesychius.
3 *Etymologicum magnum* 198.57–199.12
4 Erasmus' Latin is *sturio*, a variant of *sturgio*. See Du Cange, *Glossarium mediae et infimae latinitatis* (Paris 1937–8), who observes that Paulo Giovio believed the *silurus* mentioned by Ausonius (*Mosella* 135) was the sturgeon. This passage was added in *1533*, but Giovio's speculation is likely to have come too late to be the occasion for Erasmus' remark.
5 Hesychius βλακείας B 673
6 Not in Hesychius; Erasmus returns here to his quotation of the *Etymologicum magnum*, or Zenobius Aldus column 54, who attributes the information about the astrologers of Alexandria to Aristotle.

silly, lazy, effeminate, and dull people are called *blaces*, hence βλακεύειν 'to be effeminate or lazy,' and βλακικῶς 'stupidly, dully.' It seems that it was from this word that Latin speakers took the words *flaccus*, *flaccidus*, and *flaccescere*. But that's enough about catfish.[7]

73 Ἀλιτήριος
A mugger

Ἀλιτήριος was popularly used of someone who seized the property of others by force. It arose from an incident as follows. At the time of the Aetolian wars the Athenians were the victims of such a shortage of grain that poor people, driven by hunger, stole the prisoners' flour[1] by force, and from that incident the term began to be used of any person who was a criminal. In his essay 'On Curiosity' Plutarch gives a different origin for the word, namely that when Athens was suffering extreme starvation and those who had been ordered to do so were not supplying the public with grain but were grinding it secretly in their houses at night, some curious passers-by noticed the noise of the millstones and betrayed them; it was these passers-by who were called *aliterioi*[2] like the sycophants.[3] However he mentions a different explanation to this in the *Problems*, deriving *aliterium* from the verb 'to flee' (in Greek ἀλέω means both 'to grind' and 'to escape')[4] and writes that this term was used to denote a man who was so wicked that anyone who managed to avoid him was considered fortunate.[5] In the *Knights* Aristophanes calls *aliterii* those who violated the temple of Pallas: 'I declare

* * * * *

7 Ἀλλὰ περὶ βλακὸς ἅλις; Erasmus does not translate the Greek.

73 *Suda* A 1258 = Zenobius (Aldus) column 22. Apostolius 2.19. The word is normally an adjective derived from a verb ἀλιταίνω meaning 'to sin,' or 'to offend against.' In a note W.C. Helmbold (Loeb) gives the meaning of the noun as 'transgressor, outlaw.'
1 See ASD II-7 83:874n. Erasmus' Latin *captivorum farinam* is a mistranslation of the Greek and should read 'stole ground flour.'
2 Plutarch has just said that the *aliterios* first acquired the name from being a busybody.
3 Plutarch *Moralia* 523A–B *De curiositate*; 'sycophants' means 'fig-watchers.' See *Adagia* II iii 81, where Erasmus refers to the same passage of Plutarch. From 'In his essay' to here was added in *1515*.
4 Erasmus appears to be confusing ἀλέω 'to grind' and ἀλέομαι 'to flee,' but see the introductory note above.
5 Plutarch *Moralia* 297A *Quaestiones graecae* – Erasmus' title is *Problemata*; added in *1528*

you are one of the *aliterii* who invaded the citadel of the goddess.'[6] The scholiast, among the many things he records, also recalls this: a certain Cylon, wishing to become sole ruler, occupied the citadel and was caught in the act of robbing the temple of Minerva. He himself escaped at an opportune moment but his friends who fled together to the altar of the goddess were dragged away by the Athenians and killed. From this incident the term was applied to those who had violated the supplicants, for those who had violated the temple of the goddess and killed the supplicants later suffered capital punishment.[7] Finally Ceres is called 'Aliteria' and Jupiter 'Aliterius' because when public starvation threatened they guarded the millers so that the flour would not be stolen.[8] Further, we are told that *aliterii* is a term applied to those who are disappointed in their hopes and do not achieve what they sought. There is an ambiguity in the fact that ἀλέω means two things: 'to grind' and 'to wander off.'[9] Hence too ἀλίτης 'a vagabond.' Moreover as *aliterios* means a sacrilegious and wicked person, so ἀλιτραίνειν means 'to commit sacrilege.'

74 Piscis nequam est nisi recens
A fish is no good unless it is fresh

'A fish is no good unless it is fresh' is a very common and popular saying that has survived to this day. It is said especially however of a guest or ordinary friend who is not unwelcome when he first arrives but spoils before the third day. Plautus: 'For a procuress a lover is just like a fish – he's no good if he's not fresh.'[1] In Alexis, quoted by Athenaeus, someone makes a joke that since some rather virtuous people would not eat things that had a soul,[2] he had never brought anything of this kind, that is, the fish

* * * * *

6 Aristophanes *Knights* 445–6, quoted by the *Suda*; this sentence to the end of the adage was added in *1533*.
7 Scholiast on Aristophanes *Knights* Dübner page 50
8 *Etymologicum magnum* 65.40 Ἀλιτήριοι
9 Latin *aberro*; not quite the same as *fugio* 'to flee,' which he had given above (see n4) in *1528*

74 *Collectanea* no 59. Otto 1429. Suringar 171
1 Plautus *Asinaria* 178
2 Latin *ab iis quibus esset anima*. W.G. Arnott (see *Adagia* IV i 63 n6, 480 above) remarks that 'The speaker clearly alludes to Pythagorist vegetarianism, which was much ridiculed by comic poets and others in the second half of the fourth century' (121).

he purchased were dead.[3] But nowadays vendors, by shaking their hands, pretend that fish dead for two days are still alive.

75 Nihil homini amico est opportuno amicius
Nothing is more friendly for a man than a timely friend

A service that is offered in good time is most welcome. On the other hand, untimely attention is usually troublesome. Plautus: 'Nothing is more friendly for a man than a timely friend.' To put it the opposite way, 'Untimely kindness is no different from hostility.'[1]

76 Asinum in rupes protrudere
To push an ass over a cliff

There is an air of a proverb in something Horace writes in his *Letters*: 'A man who pushed his stubborn ass over a cliff.'[1] This will be suitable for certain people of naturally perverse mentality who have no judgment themselves and yet are unwilling to submit to prudent advisers. Such people have to be pushed even further than they wish, so that they learn through punishment and acknowledge their own stupidity. The source was some peasant or other who was leading his ass over snow-covered mountains; the ass would not obey the reins, and he pushed it over a cliff. And rightly so: 'For who would care to save an ass against his will?'[2]

77 Videre mihi labda
I think you are a lambda

Δοκεῖς δέ μοι καὶ λάβδα κατὰ τοὺς Λεσβίους, I think you are a Lesbian lambda. This signifies a woman who performs fellatio, through a riddle based on the

* * * * *

3 PCG 2 Alexis fragment 27, quoted by Athenaeus 9.386c as from his *Atthis*. From 'In Alexis' to the end was added in *1518*.

75 *Collectanea* no 79. Plautus *Epidicus* 425. Cf Tilley F 692 A friend in need is a friend indeed.
  1 *Adagia* I vii 69 Goodwill untimely differs not from hate. There Erasmus uses *simultas* 'hate'; here *inimicitia* 'hostility.' The sentence was added in *1515*.

76 *Collectanea* no 159. Horace (see n1 below)
  1 Horace *Epistles* 1.20.15
  2 The next line in Horace; translation by H. Rushton Fairclough (Loeb)

77 Aristophanes (see n2 below)

first letter, which 'Lesbians' and the vice attributed to them have in common, as I have mentioned elsewhere.[1] The source is Aristophanes' *Women in Parliament*.[2]

78 Postica sanna
A face behind your back

Persius makes a proverbial expression, 'A face behind your back,' for concealed mockery, from the action of those who laugh at someone behind his back: 'Meet the face being made behind your back.' And the same author:

> O Janus, whom no stork ever pecked from behind,[1]
> Behind whom no agile hand ever mimicked white donkey-ears,
> At whom no tongue ever protruded as much as a thirsty Apulian dog's.[2]

For these are the sort of gestures by which some folk express mockery from behind people's backs.

79 Corvus serpentem
Crow and serpent

Κόραξ τὸν ὄφιν, Crow and serpent. When somebody is killed by his own discovery. It originates in some fable of Aesop. A hungry crow noticed a snake sleeping in the sun and seized it but died from its bite.[1] This is very close to one I have noted elsewhere: 'Crow and scorpion.'[2] We can turn this against the man who suffers because of his greed, like Diogenes the Cynic, who died after eating raw octopus.[3]

* * * * *

1 *Adagia* III vii 70 To behave like a Lesbian (260 above); cf also *Adagia* II x 43 Fit for Lesbians.
2 Aristophanes *Ecclesiazusae* 920, first named in 1526

78 *Collectanea* nos 238–9. Persius (see n2 below)
1 The image is of hands imitating the movement of a stork's bill, equivalent to 'making a pair of horns.' Janus, having two faces, could not be mocked from behind. This line is also used in *Adagia* III iii 41 and IV ii 93 (497 below).
2 Persius 1.62 and 58–60

79 Aesop (see n1 below)
1 Aesop 128 Perry; among the fables of Aesop, in the same publication as that of 1505 containing the proverbs of Zenobius (Aldus) page 43
2 *Adagia* I i 58 The crow (caught) the scorpion
3 Diogenes Laertius 6.76 ('Diogenes the Cynic'), but Erasmus is translating Athenaeus 8.341E.

80 Caenei hasta
Caeneus' spear

Τὸ Καινέως δόρυ, Caeneus' spear. Caeneus was the son of Elatus, king of the Lapiths. He was formerly a beautiful girl, but was changed from a girl to a man with the consent of Neptune whom she had allowed to lie with her.[1] As a man it was granted to him that 'he could not be harmed by any wound or perish by the sword,' as Ovid relates in book 12 of the *Metamorphoses*.[2] There is a story that he fought with Apollo and also that it was his habit to command those who approached him to swear by his spear, whence the proverb, as the scholiast of Apollonius on the first book of the *Argonautica* indicates.[3] This passage is cited with reference to the first book of the *Iliad* by Eustathius,[4] who adds that Caeneus, having become the most notable man of his times, planted his javelin in the middle of the market-place and called on the gods to count him in their number. Angered by this arrogance, Jupiter took revenge on him, and when he was fighting in a battle with the Lapiths, invulnerable as he was, the god found a way to destroy the man: the Lapiths, throwing oak-trees and pines at him, pounded him into the ground.[5]

81 Pepones
Water-melons

Πέπονες, Water-melons, a proverbial insult applied to weak, effeminate men, scarcely masculine. Homer in the *Iliad* book 2: 'You water-melons, miserable objects of scorn, Achaean women, not men at all.'[1] Eustathius, commenting on the seventh book of this work, indicates that the figure is taken from

* * * * *

80 Scholiast of Apollonius (see n3 below); not in CPG or the *Suda*. Cf *Adagia* III iv 25 Invulnerable like Caeneus (16 above).
1 Added in *1533*
2 Ovid *Metamorphoses* 12.206–7; the whole story runs from 189–209.
3 Scholiast on Apollonius *Argonautica* 1.57–64
4 Eustathius 101.10–19 on *Iliad* 1.264, but R. Hoven observes (ASD VII-1 87:952n and 954n) that Erasmus, in these additions of *1533*, must in fact have used the scholion of Didymus published by Aldus in 1521.
5 Erasmus appears to become confused here; he has begun by saying Caeneus was a son of the king of the Lapiths and in III iv 25 he has Caeneus fighting alongside the Lapiths against the Centaurs. In Eustathius and Ovid *Metamorphoses* 12.462–535 it is the Centaurs who kill Caeneus.

81 Homer *Iliad* (see nn1 and 2 below)
1 Homer *Iliad* 2.235

the fruit, which, at the moment it ripens, is sweet certainly but soft and inedible.[2] However the same word is on occasion used not to insult but to address someone in a rather gentle, affectionate manner, as in book 6 of the *Iliad*: ᾽Ὦ πέπον, ὦ Μενέλαε 'Soft-hearted Menelaus'[3]

82 Ῥυποκόνδυλος
Dirty knuckles

It is a proverbial insult among the Greeks to call *sordidi* 'dirty' and miserly people 'dirty-knuckles,' the epithet deriving from people who have *sordes* 'dirt' in their nails and who will not even spend the small coin needed to have a barber clean their nails. For ῥύπος means properly the dirt that gathers in the tips of the nails of the hands and toes, and κόνδυλος the joints of the fingers and toes. Julius Pollux in book 6 chapter 4 calls these same people τρυγοβίοι 'living on dregs,' as it were.[1] Some give the adage as follows: ῞Αχθομαι αὐτοῦ τῷ ῥύπῳ 'His dirtiness offends me.'[2] Latin-speakers use *sordes* to mean excessive miserliness – that is, the vice that is the opposite of ostentation – and a man addicted to that vice is called *sordidus*.

83 Iuvenari
Behaving like an adolescent

Iuvenari is used by Horace[1] in both a novel and proverbial way in his *Art of Poetry*. The Greeks likewise use νεάζειν, νεανίζειν, and νεανιεύειν[2] in the same way to mean 'acting in a rather boastful, thoughtless, impetuous way,' or any other way that seems to be peculiar to that age-group. The less literal the application the wittier it will be; for example if someone says that flowery

* * * * *

2 Eustathius 211.9–19, not on the seventh book of the *Iliad* but the second
3 *Iliad* 6.55; Eustathius 624.18. 'Soft-hearted' is a translation of *pepon* 'melon' (more correctly *pepo*) in the Latin version.

82 *Suda* A 4702 = Zenobius (Aldus) column 50, Apostolius 4.64
1 Pollux *Onomasticon* 6.27 (τρυσίβιος; τρυγοβίος in some old editions)
2 The *Suda* cites Aristophanes (PCG 3.2 Aristophanes fragment 931); the editor's note adds fragment 718 Kock (ie PCG 3.2 Aristophanes fragment 736) and Plato comicus 124 Kock (ie PCG 7 Plato fragment 132). Cf Apostolius 4.64.

83 Horace (see n1 below); cf *Adagia* I ii 28 lines 9–10.
1 Horace *Ars poetica* 246. Horace speaks of 'fauns ... playing at times the young bloods with their mawkish verses' (translation by H. Rushton Fairclough, Loeb edition).
2 All editions have νεανεύειν, an error which ASD corrects.

and luxuriant speech is 'adolescent.' The same form is shown by γυναικίζειν, meaning 'to look like a woman in manner and dress.' Because of ignorance and lack of control over their emotions young people are more unstable, which is why the Greeks also say νεανικῶς 'impetuously' for something that is done with more energy than judgment. Basil in one of his letters says: 'And here certainly those who have not yet completed their inner development and have not reached the fullness of maturity, the proverb says they go round in circles and vacillate.'[3] You will also find ἀκμάζειν used to mean 'doing youthful things.' This is the way Hyperides used it in his speech *Against Mantitheus* and Lysias against the flute-player Nicarchus.[4] Laberius, quoted by Nonius, uses *adolescenturire, incipio adolescenturire,* and *nescio quid nugarum facere* 'doing some nonsense or other' with the same meaning.[5]

84 Laudant ut pueri pavonem
Like children admiring a peacock

There is the appearance of a proverb in what Juvenal writes about misers who confine themselves to praising songs and give nothing to the singers:

> When he gives praise[1] the miser
> Has learned to give nothing but admiration, to give the eloquent nothing
>   but praise,
> Like children admiring Juno's bird.[2]

And the same author elsewhere: 'Goodness is praised and grows cold.'[3] The figure is so well known that it is not necessary to explain it. Ovid says somewhere about the peacock:

    * * * * *

3 Basil *Epistolae* 223 1 PG 32 821B
4 Hyperides fragment 122 Blass-Jensen and Lysias fragment 97 Thalheim, both quoted from Harpocration A 61
5 Laberius 137 CRF cited by Nonius Marcellus 74M

84 Juvenal (see n2 below); Erasmus seems to hint that he has formed the title from the text of Juvenal; cf Ovid (n4 below).
1 Erasmus has *Didicit laudator avarus*, where Juvenal has *Didicit iam dives avarus*; translated by G.G. Ramsay (Loeb) as 'Your rich miser has now learnt.'
2 Juvenal 7.30–2
3 Juvenal 1.74

If they are admired, Juno's bird shows its feathers;
But if you look in silence it hides its wealth.[4]

85 Λευκηπατίας
Liver-pale

Λευκηπατίας, Liver-pale was once a term for a timid person. Clearchus, in his *Lives*, quoted by Zenodotus, says that a certain sickness occurred in some people's liver which made them timid and this was how a humorous epithet came to be used proverbially.[1] The word seems to be made up from λευκός 'pale' and ἧπαρ 'liver,' because for the most part people whose liver is affected go pale, something which also appears in animals. And pallor is typical of the timid too.

86 Emori risu
To die laughing

Two proverbial hyperboles are 'To die laughing' and 'To fall down laughing'[1] meaning to laugh heartily. Homer in the *Odyssey* book 18:

Then the brilliant crowd of suitors,
Γέλῳ ἔκθανον 'Nearly dying with laughter,' threw up their hands
To the stars above.[2]

Terence uses this too in the *Eunuchus*: 'They all died laughing.'[3]

* * * * *

4 Ovid *Ars amatoria* 1.627–8; cited by Otto 1362. Cf also Ovid *Metamorphoses* 13.802 *Laudato pavone superbior.*

85 Pseudo-Plutarch *Alexandrian Proverbs* 1.64 and *Suda* Λ 346A. Cf also Zenobius 4.87, Zenobius (Aldus) column 111 (Λευτηπαχίας [sic]) and Zenobius (Athous) 3.95.
1 Clearchus fragment 40 Wehrli; the reference is found only in Zenobius and Zenobius (Aldus).

86 Terence (see n3 below). Otto 1544
1 Latin *diffluere risu,* an expression found in Apuleius *Metamorphoses* 3.7
2 Homer *Odyssey* 18.99–100
3 Terence *Eunuchus* 432. Erasmus quotes from memory: *omnes risu emoriri* for *risu omnes qui aderant emoriri.* The reference was added in 1515 and the [mis]quotation in 1517/18.

87 Hipparchi murus
A wall of Hipparchus

Ἱππάρχου τειχίον, A wall of Hipparchus. This was said of anything that cost a great deal. It arose from the fact that Hipparchus the son of Pisistratus surrounded the Academy with a wall, and on this account exacted a great deal of money from the Athenians. The source is Suidas.

88 Hodie nullus, cras maximus
Today a nobody, tomorrow the greatest

Ὁ νῦν μὲν οὐδείς, αὔριον δ' ὑπέρμεγας, He who is a nobody today will be perhaps the greatest tomorrow. Said of the man to whom, suddenly and beyond all hope, some very high honour comes. And those who are raised from the lowest status to high office are commonly said to have emerged from nothing. The line is in Aristophanes' *Knights*.[1]

89 Samiorum mala metuis
You fear the punishments of the Samians

Τὰ Σαμίων ὑποπτεύεις, You fear the punishments of the Samians. Commonly said of those who feared betrayal. The story is that, whenever the Athenians captured Samians, they dealt with them violently and mercilessly, that they killed some and others they pierced with a *sama*, which is an instrument of torture. For their part, if they captured any Athenians, the Samians made them suffer in the same way. This is where the adage 'Men of letters from Samos' arose;[1] for, as Suidas tells us, it used to be said of people who feared incurable injuries, and the same author says that *samê* was the word for a particular type of Samian injury because the Athenians branded their Samian captives with infamous signs

* * * * *

87 *Suda* T 733. Cf Zenobius (Athous) 2.13 (see Crusius *Analecta* 136), Zenobius (Aldus) column 159, and Apostolius 17.8.

88 Aristophanes *Knights* 158. *Suda* Ω 126 = Zenobius (Aldus) column 171. Suringar 87
1 'And those ... from nothing' was added in *1515*, the last sentence in *1526*.

89 *Suda* T 142. Zenobius (Aldus) column 156. Apostolius 16.14. Laurentianus 5.64, Jungblut page 415
1 *Adagia* IV vi 14 Lettered Samians

and the Samians soon did the same to the Athenians.[2] Duris, a Samian writer, says many exaggerated things, in the tragic mode, about the cruelty of Pericles and the Athenians towards the Samians, things that Plutarch believes were largely made up to stir up hatred of Pericles and the Athenians.[3] A similar figure is found in the adage 'The misfortunes of the Magnesians.'[4]

90 **Pygmaeorum acrothinia Colosso adaptare**
Using the spoils of the pygmies for the Colossus

Ἀκροθίνια τῶν Πυγμαίων Κολοσσῷ ἐφαρμόζειν, People were said to 'use the spoils of the pygmies for the Colossus' if they undertook some work that was vain and silly or if they fitted the very small with the very large; for example if someone greeted some frivolous and petty deed with the highest and most fulsome praise. Philostratus in the *Nicetes*: 'But he could not understand that he was fitting very good but πυγμαῖα "small" parts on to the Colossus.'[1] However when Suidas quotes this passage he says πυγμαίων not πυγμαῖα.[2] Eustathius recalls this adage in his commentary on the *Odyssey* book 21.[3] *Colossi* is the word for statues of enormous, wonderful size.[4] The word is thought to be used by the Greeks because the height of these statues was further than a man could see.[5] The tallest pygmies are not more than two and a quarter feet tall,[6] so their name is thought to have come from πυγμαῖος, meaning 'about a forearm's length.'[7] They are a people inhabiting the most distant parts of Egypt, occupied in agriculture,

* * * * *

2 *Suda* Σ 75
3 Plutarch *Pericles* 28.1; 'This is where ... Athenians' added in *1526*
4 *Adagia* II x 17; added in *1528*

90 Apostolius 15.12. Otto 1495. The proverb is quoted in *Adagia* III i 1 The labours of Hercules.
1 Philostratus *Vitae sophistarum* 1.19.512
2 *Suda* A 1002; that is, the *Suda* uses the genitive plural meaning 'of the Pygmies,' not the neuter accusative adjective, meaning 'of about a forearm's length.' See the information drawn from Augustine (n7 below).
3 Eustathius 1862.35 on *Odyssey* 19.205 (not 21)
4 Cf *Adagia* III ii 5 The size of a Colossus. The sentence was added in *1515*.
5 The *Etymologicum magnum* 525.16 states that κολοσσοί is derived from the verb κολούειν, which it says means 'to diminish (the eyes),' 'as if the eyes are not capable of seeing them.' The sentence was added in *1533*.
6 Aulus Gellius *Noctes Atticae* 9.4.11, added in *1515*
7 Cf Augustine *City of God* 16.8.1 PL 41 485.

who wage a constant war with the cranes.[8] The cause of the war is that the cranes carry off seed and create famine in that region; this is what the scholiast says, in his commentary on the third book of the *Iliad*.[9] Their women bear children in their fifth year and become infertile in the eighth.[10] The Pygmies are recalled by Juvenal in Satire 13.[11] And there is much joking about them in Greek epigrams.[12] I may add that *acrothinia* is the Greek word for the first offerings, because these are usually taken from the top of the heap; *acron* means 'top,' and *thines* 'heaps of grain.'[13]

91 Dii tibi dent tuam mentem
May the gods give you the mind you deserve

May the gods give you the mind you deserve. This is suitable for a mad person and one who deserves his state of mind. For what greater misfortune could we pray for wicked men?[1] Martial says: 'May the gods grant to you, Philoenis, a mind that suits you.'[2] And Horace: 'What can you do with him

* * * * *

8 Homer *Iliad* 3.3–6 and Pliny *Naturalis historia* 7.26–7
9 Eustathius 372.3–24 on *Iliad* 3.6
10 Cf Augustine in the passage immediately following that cited in n7 above. But Erasmus is mistaken in taking this to apply to the pygmies; Augustine is following Pliny 7.30, who speaks of the Calingi of India.
11 Juvenal 13.168, also a reference to the war with the cranes
12 In the *Anthologia Palatina* there are only two references, at 11.265 and 11.369.
13 Estienne (LB II 989 n1) relates this to the original meaning: 'In this case ἀκροθίνια seems to mean arms, such as shields, breast-plates, helmets, etc; if these are taken from small men, they cannot be made to fit the statue of a colossus.'

91 *Collectanea* no 252. Martial (see n2 below)
1 Estienne (LB II 989–90 nn2 and 3) thinks Erasmus' interpretation is illogical: 'On the contrary we do not pray for anything unfortunate for the man to whom we say *Dii tibi dent tuam mentem*. And the expression in which we wish for someone to be given better sense is the same as this, not contrary to it, as Erasmus thinks, who ... understands this expression as if we were to say to a madman "May the gods give you an appropriate mind and such as you deserve," that is, "May the gods give you your own insane mind." For the one who would be mad is the one who calls somebody insane and then wishes him out of his senses. For who is insane if not the person who is out of his senses? Why then wish him to be what it is admitted that he is? I say therefore "May the gods give you your senses" is to be understood as "May the gods restore for you the senses which you had formerly."'
2 Martial *Epigrams* 7.67.16; translation by Walter C.A. Ker (Loeb)

but bid him be miserable, / Since that is his whim.'[3] On the other hand Demea in Terence says, 'Get yourself a better mind.'[4]

92 Cura esse quod audis
Take care to be what you are said to be

This expression of Horace comes into the category of proverbs: 'Take care to be what you are said to be.' It fits the wealthy who were happy precisely insofar as they tried to be what they heard from their flatterers. Horace's verse is as follows:

> You are living a true life if you take care to be what you are said to be.
> All we in Rome have long boasted that you are happy,
> But I fear you may give more credit to others than to yourself.[1]

93 Cautus enim metuit, etc.
The cautious wolf goes in fear, and so on

People who refrain from committing misdeeds not on principle but through fear of punishment will be suitably described by these proverbial phrases all using a similar metaphor: 'For the cautious wolf goes in fear of the pit, and the hawk / Of the suspected nets, the pike of the hidden hook.'[1] For different traps are set for different animals. Wolves are caught in a pit covered with leaves, and this is why in Plautus a slave threatens he will dig a pit for the pimp whose name is Lycus.[2] This one about a stick is similar: 'To change tune for fear of the stick.'[3]

* * * * *

3 Horace *Satires* 1.1.63–4
4 Terence *Adelphoe* 432

92 *Collectanea* no 436. Horace (see n1 below). Tilley s 214 Be what thou wouldst seem to be
1 Horace *Epistles* 1.16.17–19. Cicero attributes the sentiment to Socrates; cf *Adagia* II i 67 n2 (CWE 33 358). It is used again in *Adagia* v i 31 and cited by Otto 65.

93 *Collectanea* no 437. Otto 985
1 Horace *Epistles* 1.16.50–1
2 Plautus *Poenulus* 187. Lycus is so named from λύκος 'a wolf.' From 'For different traps' to here was added in 1533.
3 Horace *Epistles* 2.1.154

94 Si corvus possit tacitus pasci
If the crow can eat quietly

If, as Fabius says, a short fable is a type of proverb,[1] why should we not include among proverbs this one composed by Horace?

> But if the crow could eat quietly he would get
> More of the feast and much less quarrelling and envy.[2]

Some believe this is borrowed from the fable, which is told by Apuleius in the book *On the God of Socrates*, about the crow that found a prize, which a fox snatched away when he artfully persuaded her to start singing.[3] It applies to people who, finding something good, boast about it constantly and show it off, and in this way bring it about that others either prevent them from deriving any advantages from it or defraud them of what they have found.

95 Clavam extorquere Herculi
To snatch Hercules' club

A man who tries to take for himself what someone stronger has already taken possession of can be said not without humour to 'want to snatch Hercules' club.' This has been well known as a proverb among scholars[1] for a long time. It arose from an aphorism of Maro[2] who, when certain emulators of Zoilus[3] found fault with him because he had used many verses of Homer as his own, replied that this was in itself a splendid achievement to seize the thunderbolt of Jupiter or to snatch Hercules' club from his hand. Macrobius in book 5 of the *Saturnalia* says of Maro that he used Homeric verses in such a way that he made them his own: 'Three things were thought

* * * * *

94 *Collectanea* no 440. Quintilian (see n1 below)
1 Quintilian 5.11.21; cited by Otto 262
2 Horace *Epistles* 1.17.50–1
3 Apuleius *Florida* [*De deo Socratis*. Prologus] 4, who quotes Aesop's 'The fox and the crow' 124 Perry

95 *Collectanea* no 739. Macrobius (see n4 below). Otto 804
1 Isidore *Etymologiae* 10.44, Suetonius (or Donatus) *Vita Vergilii* 46
2 Macrobius (see n4 below) does not explicitly attribute the aphorism to Virgil.
3 Zoilus of Amphipolis was a cynic philosopher of the fourth century BC, notorious for the bitterness of his attacks on Isocrates, Plato, and especially Homer.

to be equally impossible: to steal a thunderbolt from Jupiter, a club from Hercules, or a verse from Homer, and even if it were possible it would not be proper for anyone but Jupiter to throw the thunderbolt, anyone but Hercules to wield the oaken club, or anyone to sing what Homer sang, yet Virgil, by translating suitably into his own work what the earlier poet had said, made people believe it was his own.'[4]

96 Bis interimitur qui suis armis perit
He dies twice who dies by his own arms

This is a proverbial line from a mime; it is of uncertain authorship,[1] though falsely attributed to Seneca: 'He dies twice who dies by his own arms.' Greater hurt is caused by the troubles we bring on ourselves. It appears to come from an Aesopic fable and was put into iambic verse by a certain Gabrias thus:

> Once upon a time an eagle, struck in the breast, looked at his wound,
> And weeping many tears for the pain could not go on flying.
> But when he saw the feathered arrow he exclaimed 'Woe is me,
> Feathered as I am, it is by my feathers I am brought to grievous ruin.'[2]

I have mentioned the Greek adage that is derived from this passage elsewhere.[3]

* * * * *

4 Macrobius *Saturnalia* 5.3.16. From 'Macrobius' to the end was added in *1528*.

96 Publilius Syrus line 78 in the Loeb edition of *Minor Latin Poets*. Otto *Nachträge* pages 140–1
1 The phrase must be a vestige of *1508* since Erasmus published an edition of Publilius in 1514; see *Adagia* III v 32 n1 (85 above).
2 Babrius 185 Crusius, corresponding to the prose fable 276 Perry. 'Gabrias' is a Byzantine corruption of 'Babrius,' the author of versified fables of Aesop who wrote not later than the second century AD (see *Adagia* III ii 98n CWE 34 405). Erasmus would have found the name in the Aldine Aesop of 1505 where this fable is on folio d iv r; his text however corresponds to that of Apostolius 4.98A. There is also a Latin version in Aldus, folio D iv v, but Erasmus has made his own translation. The Latin translations in Aldus were added on separate quires in a corrected second issue; they are found after the hieroglyphs of Horapollo and just before the proverbs of Didymus. Cf *Adagia* IV ii 40.
3 *Adagia* I vi 52 We are shot with our own feathers. Also quoted in III vii 1, 192 above with n80.

97 Mulierem ornat silentium
Silence becomes a woman

Sophocles in his *Ajax the Whipbearer*: Γυναιξὶ κόσμον ἡ σιγὴ φέρει 'Silence is always a seemly ornament for women.' This is a proverbial expression which Servius quotes from Sophocles in his commentary on book 1 of the *Aeneid*.[1] Woman is by nature a talkative animal and is respected for nothing as much as for her silence, especially in the company of men when the talk is of serious matters. The source is Homer who says several times: 'Speech shall be for men.'[2] And St Paul does not give women the right to speak even in church, but says they should question their husbands at home.[3]

98 Imitabor nepam
I shall imitate the crab

'Imitating the crab' is said of someone who goes backwards. This will be more like a proverb if it is applied figuratively to one who sinks to worse and worse 'Mandraboulus' fashion.'[1] For Nepa, as Festus Pompeius tells us, is what Africans call the constellation Cancer[2] (or, as some think, Scorpio, which also goes backwards).[3] Nonius Marcellus says this word means simply 'scorpion' and quotes Cicero *De finibus* book 5: 'We may see snakes crawl, ducklings swim, blackbirds fly, oxen using their horns, scorpions

* * * * *

97 Sophocles *Ajax* 293, quoted by Apostolius 5.78A and attributed to Sophocles. Tilley s 447 Silence is the best ornament of a woman
  1 Added in *1526*. ASD II-7 95:125n quotes a reference to *Aeneid* 1.561 which is found in the first edition of Servius (Rome c 1470), placed in brackets in that of Göttingen 1826, but omitted in the modern editions, Teubner 1886 and Harvard 1946.
  2 Homer *Odyssey* 1.358
  3 1 Cor 14:34–5

98 Plautus (see n7 below). Erasmus believes, following Festus' first suggestion, that *Nepa* is the name of the constellation Cancer, not Scorpio, and that Cicero would not have used *nepa* instead of the common *scorpio*. Estienne however remarks (LB II 991 n2) that in translating Aratus Cicero regularly renders the Greek σκορπίος as *nepa*.
  1 *Adagia* I ii 58
  2 Estienne (LB II 991 n1): 'For *Afrorum sydus, appellatur cancer*, read *Afrorum lingua sidus, quod cancer appellatur* "In the African language the star that is called Cancer."'
  3 Pompeius Festus pages 162–3 Lindsay.

their stings, each follows its own nature in living.'[4] He also quotes Manilius: 'Erigone[5] raised among the stars, / The *nepa* "scorpion" by its sting,
and the lion by his skin.'[6] This is what Nonius says. But if *nepa* is no more
than 'scorpion' it is surprising that Cicero should prefer to use the word
nepa. However it is a characteristic of the scorpion also to go backwards
if it attacks something, and the crab attacks by striking [with its claws].
Plautus in the *Casina*: 'I shall retreat to the wall. I shall imitate the *nepa*
'crab.'[7]

99 Quod alius condivit coquus, aliter condiam
What one cook has seasoned I shall season in another way

When someone changes and disturbs everything, a suitable adage will be
this phrase of Plautus from the same play, which is undoubtedly proverbial
in its form:

> I shall go in, and what one cook has seasoned
> I shall in my turn season in another way,
> Whatever is for lunch, will not be for lunch,
> And he will have got what was not prepared.

100 Odi puerulos, praecoci sapientia
I hate striplings who are precociously wise

In the second book of his *Apologia* Apuleius quotes this line from some unknown poet, as if it were very commonly used: 'I hate striplings who are
precociously wise.'[1] A common belief has taken root that children who become wise too early will either not be long-lived or will be mad as soon

* * * * *

4 Cicero *De finibus* 5.42, quoted by Nonius Marcellus 145M. Everything from
  'Nonius Marcellus' to the end, except the quotation from Plautus, given by
  Festus, is an addition of *1526*.
5 Daughter of Icarius, became the constellation Virgo
6 Marcus Manilius, stoic author of the *Astronomica*, 2.31–2 (not cited by Nonius)
7 Plautus *Casina* 443; cited by Otto 314

99 Plautus *Casina* 511–4

100 Apuleius (see n1 below). Quoted in *Moria* (CWE 27 92). Suringar 157 and 498
  1 Apuleius *Apologia* 85 = incert. 95 CRF. Already quoted in *Adagia* III iii 10 Before
    you've grown your beard you teach old men

as they reach adulthood. Pliny relates in book 7 that Cato the Censor proclaimed as if from an oracle 'To be old while still a youth is a sign of early death.'[2] And in Seneca book 2 of the *Controversies*, Controversy 1, Cestius used to prophesy of the intelligence of Alfius Flavius 'that great intelligence, mature at that age,[3] was not long-lived.'[4] A boy like that Sophocles[5] calls ἀνδράπαις [sic] 'A grown-up child'; the verse is quoted by the scholiast on Pindar's second Pythian ode: 'A grown-up child that I his master have myself ruined.'[6] Ἀνδράπαις is his word for one who is a child in age but endowed with mature wisdom. The adage may be used for a pupil who takes pleasure immediately in the elementary things. In book 2 of his *Rhetoric* Aristotle quotes this aphorism from an unknown poet:

> Good sense tells us one should never,
> By teaching boys too much, turn them early into philosophers.[7]

1 Δούρειος ἵππος
A wooden horse

Δούρειος ἵππος, A wooden horse. This expression was used of secret conspiracies, or when a large number of people suddenly appeared who were not visible before. It originated with the horse in Homer in which the leaders of the Greeks hid and from which they suddenly leaped out to capture Troy. This horse Homer described as *durateus* 'wooden,' as in the *Odyssey* book 8, because it was constructed of timbers:

* * * * *

2 Pliny *Naturalis historia* 7.171; added in *1526*

3 Latin *tam mature magnum ingenium*. The accepted text has *tam immature magnum ingenium*. Michael Winterbottom (Loeb) translates 'a talent that was so great so early in life.'

4 Seneca the Elder *Controversiae* 1.1.22 (not book 2); added in *1533*. Otto 1917. Erasmus appears to be quoting from memory. Seneca says *Semper de illius ingenio Cestius et praedicavit et timuit*, which Winterbottom translates 'Cestius was always remarking on his genius – and fearing for it.'

5 Sophocles fragment 562 Nauck, cited by the scholiast of Pindar *Pythians* 2.65. The word itself (ἀνδρόπαις) is in *Suda* A 2187 (anon) and Hesychius A 4768 who refers to Sophocles.

6 Scholiast on Pindar *Pythians* 2.121 (Τὸν ἀνδρόπαιδα δεσπώτης ἀπώλεσα)

7 Aristotle *Rhetoric* 2.21.2 (1394a29) citing Euripides *Medea* 294–5

1 *Suda* Δ 1428–9. Otto 610. Erasmus probably took the form δούρεος (from *1517/18* δούρειος) from Aristophanes, translating it with *dureus*. Below, where he quotes Homer, he uses *durateus*.

For it was the city's destiny to perish at the entry
Of the lofty wooden horse that enclosed all
The leaders of Greeks who would bring grief and death to the Trojans.[1]

In his life of Themistocles Plutarch relates that Themistocles once asked for a horse as a gift from the horse-breeder Philides. When the latter refused he threatened he would soon turn Philides' own house into a wooden horse, meaning that he would bring to light accusations against Philides and his household.[2] It would be an ingenious use to call some learned person's school a 'wooden horse' because over a short period a number of the best men were produced by it.

Men of reputation[3] who have come all at once from some establishment are often said by scholars to have come from that house 'as if from the Trojan horse.'[4] Marcus Tullius in the second *Philippic* used it to mean a company engaged in an extraordinary enterprise: 'I am not unwilling to be included with the leaders in being part of this plan, in a Trojan horse as it were.'[5] In the *Birds* Aristophanes shifts the meaning of the adage towards the idea of strength and size: 'Drawn by horses as bulky as ὁ δούρειος "the wooden one."'[6] The scholiast tells us this is an allusion to the bronze horse of wonderful size which stood on the Acropolis, and was consecrated by

* * * * *

1 Homer *Odyssey* 8.511–13; cf also *Odyssey* 8.492–3: 'lofty wooden horse' is δου-ράτεον μέγαν ἵππον.
2 Plutarch *Themistocles* 5.2; reference added in *1526*. Erasmus paraphrases rather loosely the explanatory phrase 'meaning that . . . household.' Bernadotte Perrin (Loeb) translates 'Darkly intimating that he would stir up accusations against him in his own family, and lawsuits between the man and those of his own household.'
3 The text from here to the end was added in *1533*; this explains perhaps the slight repetitiousness of this and the previous sentence, which dates from *1508*.
4 The classical source of this expression is Cicero *De oratore* 2.94. In 1512 Thomas More had used the figure in a letter to John Colet to describe alumni of St Paul's School, defending it against its critics (*Correspondence of Sir Thomas More* ed Elizabeth Frances Rogers [Princeton 1947] 15, no 8). Erasmus used it in a letter to Leo X dated 21 May 1515 (Ep 335:22), but see also ASD II-7 101:20–37n and 20–1n.
5 Cicero *Philippics* 2.32. The editor of ASD notes (II-7 101:21–3n) that Erasmus' text corresponds both to the *editio princeps* and to that of I.A. Brassicanus *Proverbionim symmicta* 67 (Vienna 1529).
6 Aristophanes *Birds* 1128. Erasmus gives no Latin here. Cf also Euripides *Troades* 14 and Plato *Theaetetus* 184D.

Charidemus to Pallas, as the inscription itself declared.[7] This horse, however, was in its form a copy of the Trojan horse. In the sixth speech against Gaius Verres, Marcus Tullius uses 'Trojan horse' to mean a terrible disaster: 'Picture to yourselves the hurrying to and fro in the town, the cries of grief, and the wailing of the women, too; anyone looking on would have thought that the Trojan horse had been admitted and that the city was in its enemies' hands.'[8] The gates through which the wooden horse was brought in are called by Homer in book 3 of the *Iliad* Σκαίαι 'Scaean' or 'ill-omened,' because it was foolish of the Trojans to bring the horse into the city.[9] Cicero also says in the speech in defence of Murena that the Trojan horse is within when he feels that there is a danger to the state from civil discord: 'The Trojan horse is within, within the city, I say. It will never overwhelm you in your sleep while I am consul.'[10] The same author in the speech in defence of Caelio: 'Was it ... a Trojan horse, which received and protected so many invincible warriors waging war for a woman?'[11]

2 Cum adsit via, semitam quaeris
When the road is before you, you look for a track

Ὁδοῦ παρούσης τὴν ἀτραπὸν ζητέεις, When the road is before you, you look for a track. This is cited by Eustathius in his commentary on *Odyssey* book 13.[1] Ἀτραπός is a 'track,' which is different from the vehicular road called a 'royal' road. The adage will be applicable to shufflers who, to evade an immediate affair, look for diversions.

* * * * *

7 Scholiast to Aristophanes *Birds* Dübner page 235
8 Cicero *Verrines* 2.4.23.52; translation by L.H.G. Greenwood (Loeb)
9 Homer *Iliad* 3.145, 149 and 263. Erasmus' Latin for 'ill-omened' is *sinister*, literally 'left-hand.' Troy's Scaean Gate was its western portal; a Greek augur faced north and therefore had the west, the direction from which an ill-omened portent appeared, on his left (Greek σκαιός, Latin *scaevus*). Likewise Erasmus' Latin for 'foolish' is *laeva mente* where *laevus* is also a word for 'left, left-handed.' Homer's context at this point has nothing to do with the Trojan horse.
10 Cicero *Pro L. Murena* 78; translation by Louis E. Lord (Loeb)
11 Cicero *Pro M. Caelio* 67; translation by R. Gardner (Loeb)

2 Apostolius 12.34. *Suda* O 48 citing PCG 3.2 Aristophanes fragment 47. It is surprising that Erasmus does not justify his application by citing Plautus' *De via in semitam degredere* (*Casina* 675), meaning 'to answer evasively,' which he had quoted, also in *1508*, in *Adagia* III v 16 (75 above). Otto 1888
1 Eustathius 1738.54 on *Odyssey* 13.195

3 E culmo spicam coniicere
To guess from the stalk what the grain was like

Eustathius explains this line from book 14 of the *Odyssey* which we have quoted in another place:[1] 'Yet I think you can tell, if you do but look at the stubble.'[2] He shows that Ulysses was alluding to the proverb which, in full, goes like this: Ἐκ καλάμης δῆλός ἐστιν ὁ τεθερισμένος στάχυς 'From the stalk you can envisage the grain that was harvested.'[3] Even in an old man there are signs of what he was like as a youth.[4] Aristotle mentions this passage in his book on *Rhetoric* and says 'the stalk' is a metaphor for 'old age.'[5]

4 Βυσσοδομεύειν
To lay deep foundations

Βυσσοδομεύειν. This occurs frequently in Homer[1] and has the appearance of a proverb. It means to plan something deep in one's heart and to set an ambush secretly in one's mind. It is a figure drawn from the foundation of buildings that are laid very deep. In the *Odyssey* book 17: 'Who spoke fair, but pondered evil in their minds.'[2] And the same author elsewhere: 'Turning over deceit deep in his mind.'[3]

* * * * *

3 Eustathius (see n2 below). This is a repetition of *Adagia* I x 41 To judge by the stubble, seemingly included only to show that Erasmus had found the reference in Eustathius.
1 *Adagia* I x 41 To judge by the stubble. This is also mentioned in I iii 72 Even the autumn of beauty is beautiful.
2 Eustathius 1758.41 on *Odyssey* 14.214–15: Ἀλλ' ἔμπης καλάμην γέ σ' ὀίομαι εἰσορόωντα / γιγνώσκειν. Erasmus gives no Latin translation here, and seems to have invented the title of the adage himself.
3 Eustathius (see n2 above)
4 Added in *1517/18*. Cf Erasmus' remark about Thomas More in the famous portrait in Ep 999:55–6, which is dated 23 July 1519 (CWE 7 17 lines 55–6): 'How good-looking he was as a young man, one can guess even now by what remains.'
5 Aristotle *Rhetoric* 3.10.2 (1410b14) referring to *Odyssey* 14.213; added in *1533*

4 Homer (see n1 below)
1 Homer *Odyssey* 4.676, 8.273, 9.316, 17.66, 465, 491, 20.184; always in a bad sense (LSJ)
2 Homer *Odyssey* 17.66: Ἐσθλ' ἀγορεύοντες, κακὰ δὲ φρεσὶ βυσσοδόμευον – already used in *Adagia* III i 12 Double men
3 Not Homer, but Hesiod *Shield of Heracles* 30: Δόλον φρεσί βυσσοδομεύων; added in *1533*

5 **Accersitum malum**
Evil brought on oneself

Ἐπίσπαστον κακόν, Evil brought on oneself. Said of something of which you yourself have been the cause. Homer in the *Odyssey* book 18: 'Assuredly dissolute Irus will soon experience the harm that he seeks / Of his own accord.'[1]

6 **Eurymnus**
Eurymnus

Εὔρυμνος, Eurymnus,[1] was formerly a proverbial name for someone who tried to use false accusations to create strife among good friends. This man plotted to sow discord between Castor and Pollux laying blame with each against the other, and when he was subsequently caught was heavily punished by both. This is the common lot of those who seek by wicked means to divide people joined by some unbreakable natural link, such as husband and wife, parent and child, or brothers. For what happens is that, when the victims return to harmony, they both seek punishment from the author for past animosity. This happened at Athens to Hyperbolus who tried to create enmity between Nicias and Alcibiades.[2]

7 **A Furiis oriundus**
Born of the Furies

Ἐρινύων ἀπορρώξ, Born of the Furies. This used to be an expression for

* * * * *

5 Homer (see n1 below). Cf the last sentence added in *1515* to *Adagia* IV ii 62 Evils come of their own accord.
1 Homer *Odyssey* 18.73: Ἦ τάχα Ἶρος Ἄϊρος ἐπίσπαστον κακὸν ἕξει. Erasmus, with *perditus Irus*, makes no attempt to reproduce the play on words in Ἶρος Ἄϊρος; A.T. Murray has 'Irus un-Irused.'

6 Pseudo-Plutarch *Alexandrian Proverbs* 1.74 = Zenobius (Aldus) column 89. Schneidewin (CPG 1.332) cites as source Libanius *Epistolae* 389 Wolf line 12 (= 386 Foerster page 378 line 15).
1 In Libanius he is Εὔρυμος and in Hesychius E 7153 Εὐρυμᾶς.
2 Sentence added in *1533*; Plutarch *Aristides* 7.3–4, *Nicias* 11.3–7, *Alcibiades* 13.4–5. Hyperbolus is also mentioned in *Adagia* IV iii 61 Surpassing Hyperbolus.

7 *Suda* E 2995 = Zenobius (Aldus) column 85, from Aristophanes *Lysistrata* 811

someone of foul and hideous appearance, who 'looked mad,' as Aristophanes says.[1] Anything harmful and destructive is also said to have 'come from the Furies,' as Ajax says in the tragedy: 'Was this sword-point not forged by a Fury from hell?'[2]

8 Similes videntur captivis ex Pylo
They look like captives from Pylos

Ἐοίκασι / Τοῖς ἐκ Πύλου ληφθεῖσι τοῖς Λακωνικοῖς, They look to me like the Spartan captives from Pylos. This is in the *Clouds* of Aristophanes.[1] It was said of people of pitiable appearance, pale, dirty, and thin. Pylos was a city in Laconia, besieged and defeated by Cleon.[2] Those who escaped death he took away to Athens, weak, exhausted, pale, disfigured, as must have happened both because of the length of the siege, especially on a deserted island which could offer a poor supply of the necessary provisions, and because after the fall of the city they were kept for many days in chains. This is all in Zenodotus. Of Pylos I have talked elsewhere in the proverb 'Pylos there is before Pylos.'[3]

9 Γύργαθον φυσᾷς
You're blowing away the stocks

Γύργαθον φυσᾷς, You're blowing away the stocks, a phrase tossed at someone who is mad and shouts vainly. The *gyrgathos* was the couch to which the par-

* * * * *

1 Aristophanes *Plutus* 424, added in 1515 to *Adagia* IV i 2 (440 above) and in 1533 to III iv 13 (10 above)
2 Sophocles *Ajax* 1034: Ἄρα οὐκ Ἐρινύς τοῦτ' ἐχάλκευε ξίφος;

8 Zenobius (Aldus) column 84 (= Appendix 2.74)
1 Aristophanes *Clouds* 185–6. In 1526 the title of the play replaced the expression *ni memoria fallor* 'if my memory does not fail me,' which had stood there from 1508 to 1523.
2 This is Pylos in Messenia identified with Nestor's home by Pausanias (4.36.1–2), though Erasmus was in some doubt because Strabo (*Geographica* 8.3.7) prefers the Pylos in Triphyllia. It was captured by the Athenians in 425 BC together with a contingent of Spartans on the neighbouring island of Sphacteria (Thucydides 4.6–41). The event was the background to Aristophanes' attack on Cleon in his *Knights*.
3 *Adagia* II viii 45; from 'This is all' to here was added in 1526.

9 *Suda* Γ 508, Apostolius 5.70, Zenobius (Aldus) column 66

alytic, the mad, and anyone said to be possessed are chained and on which they thrash about;[1] they shout numerous threats but all in vain. It will be suitable therefore to describe a terrible but ineffectual rage. Hesychius mentions that a *gyrgathos* is also the container in which a baker placed cooked loaves.[2] The Greek word appears to be derived from the word for 'to turn.'[3]

10 **Decora teipsum**
You should adore yourself

Γέραιρε σαυτόν, You should worship yourself. A proverbial joke against someone who behaves too grandiosely. Γεραίρειν is 'to reverence' and 'to honour.'

11 **Byzeni libertas**
The freedom of Byzenus

Βυζήνου παρρησία, The freedom of Byzenus. Said when someone speaks too boldly and too freely. Derived from Byzenus, apparently a son of Neptune,[1] who was in the habit of taking extraordinary liberties in his speech. Stephanus mentions a Byzya, a city in Scythia, whence came the Byzyeni.[2] It was a characteristic of this people to speak without fear.

* * * * *

1 Erasmus' word is *lectus* 'couch' following the *Suda*. Estienne (LB II 993) finds Erasmus' interpretation and explanation awkward and points to an obvious alternative: 'For what does γύργαθος mean? Is it not a "net"? What does φυσᾶν mean if not "to blow"? What does the *Suda* say? "γύργαθον φυσᾷς, a proverb used of those who labour in vain." Who labours more vainly than the man who blows at a net, or who "hunts the winds with a net"? – as another proverb has it [*Adagia* I iv 63]. So let's have no more of this couch for paralytics and the possessed.' LSJ however gives in addition to this 'cage for insane patients,' Paulus Aeginetus 3.14. For the proverb see also Aristaenetus 2.20 (ed R. Hercher *Epistolographi graeci* page 170, who translates *rete inflas* 'you are blowing a net').
2 Hesychius Γ 1019
3 Latin *volvendo*; Erasmus appears to be thinking of γυρόω 'to make round,' 'to bend,' but the etymology is false.

10 *Suda* Γ 193 = Zenobius (Aldus) column 60 (Appendix 1.69 = Mantissa 1.39)

11 Zenobius 2.63 = Zenobius (Aldus) column 58 = Diogenianus 1.99. See also Crusius in CPG 3 Supplementum IIIa 24 no 51.
1 It was Byzas the legendary founder of Byzantium who was said to be a son of Neptune. The name Byzenus is found only in the paroemiographers.
2 Stephanus Byzantinus page 190 Meineke; added with the final sentence in 1533. Ptolemy *Geographia* 5.4.10 places the Byzeni in Galatia in Asia Minor.

12 Ἀχρειόγελως
   A trifler

Ἀχρειόγελως, a proverbial neologism for a 'trifler' and anyone who takes
pleasure in absurdities; ἀχρειόγελως means exactly the same as 'laughing for
no reason,' an aberration that is a sign of foolishness or madness.[1]

13 Protinus apparet quae plantae frugiferae futurae
   Fruitful plants show it straightaway

Ἀυτίκα καὶ φυτὰ δῆλα ἃ μέλλει κάρπιμ᾽ ἔσεσθαι, Straightaway it is apparent
which plant will give fruit. Even in children their future character is clear.
Future progress can be foreseen immediately in the pupil.[1]

14 Periit sus
   The pig has perished

Ἀπόλωλεν ὗς καὶ τάλαντον καὶ γάμος, My pig has gone, and my money, and
my marriage. This used to be said when someone was cheated and lost a
costly investment. Derives from someone who had prepared everything for
his marriage but did not achieve it. Very close to 'I have wasted both oil
and toil.'[1]

15 Ἀμφιθαλὴς ἔρως
   Love blossoming on both sides

Ἀμφιθαλὴς ἔρως, Love blossoming on both sides. This used to be said whenever two persons were complete in each other and loved each other equally.

* * * * *

12 *Suda* A 4714 = Zenobius (Aldus) column 50 = Apostolius 4.65
 1 The word appears in PCG 4 Cratinus 360.1.

13 *Suda* A 4479 = Zenobius (Aldus) column 48
 1 This sentence was added in *1517/18*.

14 Apostolius 3.66 (γνάθος [sic, for γάμος], but Erasmus has taken the correct reading from the commentary) = Zenobius (Aldus) column 42. Gregory Cyprius
   1.80 has the same proverb.
 1 *Adagia* I iv 62; added in *1517/18*

15 Apostolius 2.58 = Zenobius (Aldus) column 31, *Suda* A 1729. For ἀμφιθαλής cf
   also *Adagia* III iv 28 n2, 18 above.

For we say we are 'divided' whenever a friend is taken away, as if he were
a part of us. The expression is to be found in Aristophanes' *Birds* at the end
of the play.[1] And this is the sort of love that Phaedria wishes for in the
Eunuchus: 'If only you loved me / As much as I love you.'[2] Matching this
is the line in Pindar's *Pythian Odes*: 'Loving him who loves, and joyfully
offering my hand to him who offers his.'[3]

16 Ex amphitheto bibisti
You have drunk from the *amphithetos*

Ἀμφιθέτῳ ἔπινες, You have drunk from the *amphithetos*. Used to be said as a
criticism of someone who drank too much undiluted wine. An *amphithetos*
was a sort of cup so fashioned that it would stand whichever way you put
it down, having no clearly defined bottom. It is more likely, as Hesychius
adds among various facts, that an *amphithetos* was a cup that was picked up
and put down with both hands because of its size,[1] what Dutch sailors call
a *busa*.[2]

17 Pronomi barba
Pronomus' beard

Προνόμου πώγων, Pronomus' beard was an expression for a very long beard.
Aristophanes in the *Women in Parliament*:

> So up till now it was not known that Argyrrhius was [a woman]
> Wearing Pronomus' beard.[1]

* * * * *

1 Aristophanes *Birds* 1737. This and everything down to the end were added in
  1526.
2 Terence *Eunuchus* 91–2
3 Pindar *Pythians* 10.66: Φιλέων φιλέοντ', ἄγων ἄγοντα προφρόνως

16 Apostolius 2.57 = Zenobius (Aldus) column 31
1 Hesychius A 4021. *Suda* A 1731. ASD supplies the word *ambabus* 'with both
  [hands],' omitted in all the early editions from 1508 to 1536, but inserted in
  1540, followed by LB; cf Hesychius ἀμφοτέραις ταῖς χερσίν 'with both hands.'
2 See Du Cange *Glossarium mediae et infimae latinitatis* (Paris 1937–8) and Suringar
  71 *Butta*. From 'It is more likely' to here was added in 1533.

17 *Suda* Π 2527. Cf *Adagia* I ii 95 Bearded, therefore wise.
1 Aristophanes *Ecclesiazusae* 102–3

Pronomus was some flute-player with a very long beard, not a very suitable appurtenance for his profession, but proverbs do sometimes mention
the effeminacy of flute-players.[2] Argyrrhius was a general, effeminate and
homosexual, with no manly qualities but a beard. In the same play there
is criticism of the beard of a certain orator Epicrates who, for this reason,
was given the nickname σακεσφόρος 'beard-bearer' by way of a popular
joke;[3] this is shown by the verse that the scholiast of Aristophanes quotes
from Plato the writer of comedies: 'The king with the beard, O Epicrates
the shield-bearer.'[4] He calls a beard a shield because of their similar shape,
and elsewhere we find: 'And loath upon your chins to wear that monstrous
equipage of hair.'[5] Of the same person Aristophanes says: 'My beard is
much more fine than even Epicrates'.'[6] So it will be appropriate for certain
men who are effeminate in other respects but who by the severity of their
countenance and garments give the appearance of a continent life. There are
frequent jokes in Lucian about philosophers' beards.[7] Likewise in Horace:
'And bade me grow a wise man's beard.'[8] Martial too makes fun of such a
person.[9]

18 Omnibus vestigiis inquirere
To investigate every trace

Πᾶσιν ἴχνεσι ζητεῖν, To investigate every trace, is said of someone who traces
an affair with the greatest of care and thoroughness. The metaphor is bor-

* * * * *

2 Eg *Adagia* II iii 34 You live the life of a flute-player
3 Aristophanes *Ecclesiazusae* 71
4 Scholiast of Aristophanes *Ecclesiazusae* 71 (Dübner page 316) citing PCG 7 Plato
   comicus fragment 130; 'shield-bearer' is *scutifer* in Erasmus' translation. ASD
   points out that Erasmus is deliberately playing on the two meanings of the
   Greek σάκος, 'shield' and 'beard,' and that *scutifer* does not distinguish the two
   meanings of σακ(κ)εσφόρος, 'shield-bearer' and 'shaggy bearded.'
5 Aristophanes *Ecclesiazusae* 502: "Απασα καὶ μίσει σάκον πρὸς ταῖν γνάθοιν ἔχουσα.
   Erasmus gives no Latin in this case.
6 See n3 above; this translation and the previous one are by B.B. Rogers (Loeb).
7 Lucian *Demonax* 13, *De mercede conductis* 40, *Eunuchus* 9, *Dialogi mortuorum* 20
   (10) 9
8 Horace *Satires* 2.3.35; translation by H. Rushton Fairclough (Loeb)
9 Martial *Epigrams* 9.47.4 (cf *Adagia* I ii 95), 11.39.3 (cf *Adagia* II vii 9); added in
   1515

18 *Collectanea* no 763. In 1508 this consisted only of the first two sentences; the
   rest was added in 1533. The Greek was probably invented by Erasmus.

rowed from hunters. Marcus Tullius in the fourth speech against Verres: 'You are sure you can escape even from these nets?[1] – for we are following you, not by means of doubtful conjecture, but by your own traces which you left, and recently too, in the public records.'[2] Again in the same speech: 'So that every mortal can see not just the traces of this greed, but its very lairs.'[3] Again in the sixth speech: 'I believe the real prosecutors were those who pursued the thefts of such men by no more than their scent or some faintly traced footprints to guide them. For what are we doing in the case of Verres, who we know has been wallowing in the mire by the traces of his whole body?'[4] In the speech defending Cluentius: 'What? Is the trail of Albius' money to be sniffed out by us, or can we not, following your lead, come straight to his very lair?'[5] And shortly afterwards: 'No trace is to be found of any money of Cluentius given to a magistrate.'[6] In the speech against Piso: 'But do you think I have made insufficient investigation of the disgraces of your rule and the ruins of the province? These I have tracked in fact not by scenting the trail of your comings and goings, but by all the wallowings of your body and your lairs.'[7]

19 Apros immittere fontibus
To allow boars in springs

Someone who brings on or wishes for himself what will cause him harm will be aptly described by this phrase of Virgil: 'I have let in boars to my crystal springs.'[1] And it is obvious this is said with a proverbial sense. Boars do not just drink from a pool with their feet in the water but even wallow in it.[2]

* * * * *

1 All editions have *retibus*; the accepted text has *rebus*, translated by L.H.G. Greenwood (Loeb) as 'our pursuit.'
2 Cicero *Verrines* 2.2.42.105
3 Cicero *Verrines* 2.2.77.190
4 Cicero *Verrines* 2.4.24.53
5 Cicero *Pro A. Cluentio* 82
6 Cicero *Pro A. Cluentio* 102
7 Cicero *In L. Pisonem* 83

19 *Collectanea* nos 812 and 811. Cf *Adagia* III vi 72, of which this is a partial repetition.
1 Virgil *Eclogues* 2.59. Cf in *Adagia* III vi 72 (160 above) the whole sentence: 'Madman, I have let in the south wind to my flowers, and boars to my crystal springs!'
2 Added in *1533*

20 E canis podice
Out of a dog's bottom

Ἐκ κυνὸς πρωκτοῦ, Out of a dog's anus. It seems Lucian used this to mean worrying, tight situations because the organ is rather firmly contracted in this animal so that they excrete with some difficulty. He ends his story the *Ass* with these words: 'Then I sacrificed to my tutelary gods and offered gifts, now that after so long and with such difficulty I reached home in safety, certainly not "out of a dog's bottom" as the popular saying has it, but rather "out of an ass's curiosity."'[1] It was popularly said of Zeno too, as Laertius[2] tells us, that he had written the whole of *On the Republic* on a dog's bottom, either because the work was too difficult to understand or too silly. But I have mentioned this proverb elsewhere.[3]

21 E cantu dignoscitur avis
The bird can be told by its song

This too is reported by certain people, even if I have not yet found it in authors where I would expect it: 'The bird can be told by its song,' which in any case is not unworthy of being classed as a proverb. The meaning matches that of 'As the man is, so is his talk.'[1] A popular saying very similar to this is 'The bird is known from its feathers,'[2] the way of life and the mind of a man are seen from his appearance.

* * * * *

20 Probably a repetition, with slight variation, of *Adagia* II ii 36 To look into a dog's anus – where the expression is explained by reference to Aristophanes *Ecclesiazusae* 255 and the scholiast (Dübner page 317) and *Acharnians* 863 – in order to add the references to Lucian and Diogenes Laertius. Cf *Suda* Π 2950.
1 Lucian *Asinus* 56
2 Diogenes Laertius 7.4 ('Zeno'). The Greek ἐπὶ τῆς τοῦ κυνὸς οὐρᾶς is literally 'on the dog's tail,' but Erasmus, who seems to have missed the possible allusion to Diogenes the Cynic (κύων 'dog'), has *in canis postico*. The *Republic* of Zeno of Citium, whose stoicism was a development of cynicism through Crates (see *Adagia* IV ii 31, 519 n2 below) has not survived.
3 *Adagia* II ii 36

21 Walther 6845. Suringar 64. According to Erasmus' own words, a popular proverb not found in the ancient authors
1 *Adagia* I vi 50
2 Cf Tilley B 269 Every bird is known by his feather.

22 Canis saeviens in lapidem
A dog getting angry with the stone

Κύων εἰς τὸν λίθον ἀγανακτοῦσα, A dog taking offence at the stone. This fits those who attribute the cause of their misfortune not to its source but to something else; for example when someone attributes the vice of anger to youthfulness, not to the stupidity from which it really arises. In book 5 of the *Republic* Plato condemns those who plunder the bodies of the slain and declares they do exactly what dogs do when they get angry with the stone and ignore the person who threw it.[1] And there is Pacuvius in his *Judgment of Arms* quoted in Nonius: 'For when a dog has been struck by a stone he tends to seek not the person who threw it but the stone itself with which he was struck.'[2]

23 Profundum sulcum
A deep furrow

Βαθεῖαν αὔλακα, A deep furrow. This too is recorded in the *Collected Proverbs*.[1] The comment there is that it was said of people who weigh up a matter with profound thoughts that they keep deep within their hearts. It is taken from the tragedy of Aeschylus called *Seven against Thebes*. In this the following verses are spoken about Amphiaraos: 'Gathering the harvest from the deep furrowing of his mind, / Whence well-founded counsels grow.'[2] This is quoted in several places by Plutarch in his *Moralia*[3] and by Plato in the second book of the *Republic*.[4] And there are allusions to the proverb in several places in Marcus Tullius; in a letter to Atticus, book 4: 'Lest the βαθύτης

* * * * *

22 Mentioned in *Collectanea* no 332. Erasmus' Greek is probably his own translation of the Latin. Pliny *Naturalis historia* 29.102 describes it merely as a proverbial expression for quarrelsomeness. Otto 322. Tilley D 542 Silly dogs are more angry with the stone than with the hand that flung it
1 Plato *Republic* 5.469E, quoted in *Adagia* I x 34
2 Pacuvius 38–9 TRF, cited by Nonius Marcellus 124M

23 Apostolius 4.69 = Zenobius (Aldus) column 50. Cf *Suda* B 27.
1 Erasmus' Latin in this case is *Adagionum collectanea*, which might refer either to Apostolius or Zenobius (Aldus), but not, of course, to the *Suda*.
2 Aeschylus *Seven against Thebes* 593–4: Βαθεῖαν αὔλακα διὰ φρενῶν καρπούμενος, / Ἐξ ἧς τὰ κεδνὰ βλαστάνει βουλεύματα
3 Plutarch *Moralia* 32D–E *Quomodo adolescens poetas audire debeat*, 88B *De capienda ex inimicis utilitate*, 186B *Regum et imperatorum apophthegmata*
4 Plato *Republic* 2.362A

"careful thought," which was obvious in my action, should be less clear in my writing.'[5] And in book 5: 'You will wonder at my βαθύτητα "careful thought" when we come home safe, so much attention do I give to this virtue.' Again in the first letter of book 6: 'For there is nothing that I have enjoyed more than the immense pleasure in knowing that you approve my βαθύτητα "careful thought" in the case of Appius and my generosity in that of Brutus.'[6] It seems to me it will also fit well those who judge themselves, not by the opinion of others, but by their consciousness of things done rightly or otherwise.

24 Herniosus usque ad gulam
Circumcised up to the neck

Ψωλὸς μέχρι τοῦ μιρρίνου, Circumcised[1] right up to the neck. This is suitable for someone who is severely injured. There is a verse in Aristophanes' *Knights*: 'You must be circumcised up to the neck.'[2] The scholiast of Aristophanes indicates that the expression was also in Diphilus.[3]

25 Benignior pellace vulpe
As kind as a cunning fox

Ὦ πλεῖον ἵλαος αἱμύλης ἀλώπεκος, He is as kindly as a cunning fox. Said of one who pretends to be kind for his own advantage. Plato mentions

* * * * *

5 Cicero *Ad Atticum* 4.6.3, 5.10.3, 6.1.1–2. E.O. Winstedt (Loeb) translates βαθύτης in all these cases as 'self-restraint' or 'reserve.' Cicero's word βαθύτης retains of course the idea of depth. In the last example, Erasmus' text differs from the received one in joining two sentences together: *Nam nulla re sum delectatus magis quam* [sic for *magis. Quod*] *meam* βαθύτητα *in Appio tibi, liberalitatem in Bruto probari vehementer gaudeo.*
6 From 'by Plato' to here added in 1526

24 Zenobius (Aldus) column 171 quoting Aristophanes (see n2 below); cf *Suda* Ψ 130 (with the correct μυρρίνου) and Appendix 5.41.
1 Erasmus' word *herniosus* has no meaning other than 'ruptured.' Ψωλὸς means 'with the foreskin drawn back, circumcised.' Cf Aristophanes *Birds* 507.
2 Aristophanes *Knights* 964
3 Scholiast on Aristophanes *Knights* 964 Dübner pages 67 and 414. The reference to Diphilus (PCG 5 Diphilus fragment 38), a new comedy poet of the second half of the fourth century, is among material added by Aldus from the *Suda*. The sentence was added in 1526.

25 Zenobius (Aldus) column 172. Cf *Suda* Ω 144. Only the quotation and the following sentence are from 1508; the rest was added in 1533.

the fox of Archilochus in his *Republic* book 2:

> And so, as men endowed with wisdom declare, since appearance masters even
> truth itself and is the key to happiness, I must bow to it wholeheartedly; each
> man must surround himself with a sort of forecourt and shadow-outline of
> virtue, but such that behind his back he may lead the fox of the all-wise
> Archilochus.[1]

He says these things at that point to Glaucus, praising injustice so that
he can provoke Socrates to commend justice.[2] Archilochus' fox is also remembered by St Basil in several places including the book addressed to
his grandsons,[3] and by Philostratus in his *Pictures*.[4] There are many fables
about the fox's cunning, but which of these is by Archilochus is not at all
clear.

26 Non ut prior laedam, sed ut iniuriam retaliem
I shall not be the first to strike, but I shall repay an insult

This senarius is quoted by some as from Menander's *Olynthia*[1] and by others
as from the *Thersites* of Chaeremon: 'I would not willingly be the first to
provoke violence, / But I shall repay violence already done with violence.'[2]
It matches this one from Terence: 'Let him reflect that this is an answer [in
self-defence], not something said [as an attack].'[3]

* * * * *

1 Plato *Republic* 2.365C, citing Archilochus fragment 185 West (= 89 Bergk, 81
  Diehl); but see ASD II-7 111:240n for the part of the quotation omitted by
  Erasmus.
2 The speaker is Adeimantus arguing that injustice is intrinsically superior to
  justice.
3 Basil *De legendis libris gentilium* 8 PG 31 585D–588A, *Sermo* 1 PG 32 1129A
4 The fox referred to in Philostratus *Imagines* 1.3 is Aesop's, not Archilochus'.
  ASD points out that Erasmus found his references to Basil and Philostratus in
  Brassicanus (no. 28).

26 Zenobius 6.51 (= Zenobius [Athous] 3.49 and Zenobius [Aldus] column 172)
1 PCG 6.2 Menander fragment 259 (see also 298 Körte-Thierfelder note)
2 Greek: Ὡς οὐχ ὑπάρχων, ἀλλὰ τιμωρούμενος; *Suda* Ω 237 = Chaeremon fragment
  3 Nauck and Aristarchus fragment 4 Nauck (cf Athenaeus 13.612F)
3 Terence *Eunuchus* 5–6; Erasmus' quotation, which is from the playwright's
  apologetic prologue, is rather cryptic – the line is completed by 'for it was he
  who gave the first provocation.'

27 Non navigamus ad Hippolaïtas
We are not sailing to the Hippolaïtas

Οὐχ ἱππολέκτας περισσὰς πλῶμες. This is how I myself have found it written in published versions, but from these words I do not see what meaning can be extracted. I shall say therefore what seems to me to be closest to the truth, not because I should like others to yield immediately to my powers of divination, but to provide scholars with some chance of conjecturing the true reading. Try reading 'We are not sailing to the abundant Hippolaitas'[1] – as if it were a warning to use what you have more sparingly, and that you are not on a voyage to this place where an abundance of such things is to be had so that you can easily make good what you have rashly spent. In the Greek collections I find only this note: 'About those who possess little.'[2] Hippola was a very ancient Laconian city, not far from the sea, which because of the convenience of its port probably flourished formerly as a trading centre. Pausanias mentions it in his *Laconia* in these words: 'And by the sea there is a temple of Venus with a standing statue in stone. If you go thirty stadia from here, you find the high gates of Taenarum and the ruins of the city of Hippola, and among these a sanctuary of Minerva Hippolaïtis.'[3] Stephanus mentions this city too.[4] And so as not to omit any conjecture, consider too, dear reader, whether instead of 'Hippolaitas' we should read 'Hippobotas.' This is a tribe in Chalcidia mentioned by Plutarch in his life of Pericles and ranked among the greatest in earlier times for their wealth and fame.[5] Their name was given them for the fertility of their lands, 'nursery of horses,' as you might say.[6] The natives of this region were driven out, a colony was introduced, and it was

* * * * *

27 Zenobius (Aldus) column 139 = Pseudo-Plutarch *Alexandrian Proverbs* 1.81
1 Greek: Οὐχ Ἱππολαίτας περισσοὺς πλῶμες.
2 Greek: Ἐπὶ τῶν βραχέα κεκτημένων, in both of the sources given above
3 Pausanias 3.25.9; 'high gates' is *ostia summa* – Erasmus has misunderstood θυρίδες ἄκρα, which H.A. Ormerod (Loeb) translates 'Thyrides, a headland of Taenarum.'
4 Stephanus Byzantinus page 336 Meineke, referring to Pausanias
5 Plutarch *Pericles* 23.2; from 'And so as not' to here was added in *1520*, a second attempt to emend the text; neither is satisfactory, according to the editor of ASD.
6 This sentence was added in *1533*. Erasmus' Latin is *equorum altricem* 'nurse of horses,' but Plutarch's βώτας (or βούτης) means 'herdsman.' Bernadotte Perrin (Loeb) translates 'Knights.'

occupied by the Athenians. This affair is recorded by Herodotus too in the 'Terpsichore.'[7]

28 Epiphyllides
Small grapes

This senarius too, from the comedy of Aristophanes called the *Frogs*, is counted among proverbs: 'These things are small grapes and pure bombast.'[1] It is said to be fitting for smooth talkers and those who make a better show of words than of distinguished deeds. *Epiphyllides* is the Greek word for the smaller grapes forming part of the bunch with the larger ones. Callistratus writes that all very small bunches are called *epiphyllidae* because they are hidden under the leaves.[2] The term comes from the fact that they lie close under the leaves. And indeed this is proof of the fruitfulness of the plant. Theocritus reminds us in the *Aita* that it is used of pustules formed on the nose which are evidence of a liar.[3] This will be dealt with in its proper place.[4]

29 Ἀπ᾽ ἀκροφυσίων
Straight from the bellows

Ἀπ᾽ ἀκροφυσίων, Straight from the bellows, was a proverbial expression for anything that had been produced recently in a workshop, as if straight from the bellows and bronze furnace, for this is where the metaphor is taken from. Aristophanes says: 'Using splendid turns of phrase and jokes, all κινναβεύματα "originals" and straight from the bellows.'[1] *Cinnabeuma*, I may add, is the word for an archetype, an image that painters and sculp-

* * * * *

7 Herodotus 5.77.2; from 'The natives' to here was added in *1526*. For 'Terpsichore' cf *Adagia* III iv 60 n3 (38 above).

28 *Suda* E 2758. Cf Zenobius (Aldus) column 85 and Apostolius 7.66.
1 Aristophanes *Frogs* 92
2 From the *Suda* or Zenobius (Aldus); 'under the leaves' from *epi* 'under' and *phylla* 'leaves'
3 Theocritus 12.24; in fact, the scholiast of Theocritus, commenting on the word ψεύδεα 'lies'
4 *Adagia* IV vi 6 Lie-pimples; from 'Theocritus reminds us' to the end added in *1526*

29 Zenobius (Aldus) column 38 = Apostolius 3.37 = *Suda* A 2874
1 PCG Aristophanes 3.2 fragment 719

tors reproduce in order to create and represent emblematic signs. Hence anything recently created is said to come ἀπὸ τῶν κινναβευμάτων 'from the archetypes.'

30 Super te haec omnia, Leparge
The whole load on your back, Lepargus

Ἀνά σοι τάδε πάντα, Λέπαργε, The whole load on your back, Lepargus. A heroic hemistich, which was said of someone who is not allowed to take breath even after finishing his work. The figure is derived from oxen who, having already endured the labour of ploughing, have still to perform the labour of carrying home the plough and other tools. These are usually loaded on to whichever of the two is the stronger. The bull is called Lepargus[1] because of the whiteness of its coat. These could well be the words of the ass to the ox as he collapsed under his load; the ox was asked to take part of the load but refused, and when the ass died shortly after, the ox was obliged to carry the whole load together with the hide of the ass.[2]

31 Laqueus auxiliari videtur
The snare seems to be a help

Ἀμύνει, ὡς ἔοικεν, ἡ πάγη, The snare, it seems, did some good. This was said customarily whenever some misfortune turned out to someone's advantage. For example, if some Turk, captured in the war, worked among Christians and were converted by this opportunity to the rites of our religion. Or if a rich man, reduced to poverty, were changed by this opportunity from a dissolute character to a sober one, and from an unbeliever to a believer.[1] This is what the philosopher, Zeno if I am not mistaken, was saying when he remarked that he had made a good voyage only after he had been shipwrecked.[2]

* * * * *

30 Zenobius (Aldus) column 32. *Suda* A 2090 and Λ 283
1 Λέπαργος means 'with white skin.'
2 Cf Babrius fable 7 The Horse and the Ass, Aesop 357 Perry. As ASD notes, Erasmus seems to be mixing Plutarch *Moralia* 137D, the fable of the ox and camel, and Aesop. From 'These could well' to the end was added in *1533*.

31 Zenobius (Aldus) column 30 = Apostolius 2.74
1 From 'Or if a rich man' to here was added in *1517/18*.
2 Diogenes Laertius ('Zeno') 7.4–5. It was through suffering shipwreck that Zeno encountered his teacher Crates; see *Adagia* II ix 78 and IV ii 20 n2 (513 above).

32 Ἀμυστὶ πίνειν
To drink at one draught

Ἀμυστὶ πίνειν, To drink at one draught, is said of people who gulp a drink, greedily, without taking a breath as they drink, but tipping it into their bellies as if into a barrel. The word ἀμυστί means the same as 'without swallowing.' It could be used figuratively of people who take what is said too eagerly, without discrimination; or of those who cram their minds with excessive reading when they would do better to mingle reading and thinking together.[1] Such drinking is called ἄμυστις by the Greeks because during the drinking the lips are not closed.[2]

33 Amphidromiam agis
You are celebrating the Amphidromia

Ἀμφιδρομίαν ἄγεις, You are celebrating the Amphidromia. This adage could be adapted to various uses: for example to those who show off their children and carry them around, or those who seek gifts and go around soliciting. It is derived from the ancient custom whereby the women who were present at a birth and who helped at the delivery cleansed their hands five days later and ran around the hearth carrying the child. On the same day little gifts, most often cuttlefish and octopuses, were sent by relatives. On the tenth day after the birth the child was given its name. This sort of small gift is recalled by Terence in the first scene of his *Phormio*.[1] And Plautus in the *Truculentus*, where the prostitute Phronesium orders Dinarchus, who wants to go to bed with her when she was going to sacrifice 'on behalf of her adopted[2] baby,' to do instead what was usually done on the fifth day.[3]

* * * * *

32 Zenobius (Aldus) column 30 = Apostolius 2.62. Cf *Suda* A 1687.
  1 From 'It could be' to here was added in 1515.
  2 Ἄμυστις is formed from a privative and μύω 'to close [the lips or eyes]'; the sentence was added in 1533.

33 Zenobius (Aldus) column 30. Cf Apostolius 2.56 and *Suda* A 1722.
  1 Terence *Phormio* 46–7
  2 The Latin word *accititio* (sic) makes no sense. ASD corrects to *ascititio* which appears in the early editions (see n3 below); it is also used in *Adagia* III iv 100 (58 above).
  3 Plautus *Truculentus* 423–4. Erasmus is paraphrasing the text of Plautus as it appeared in early editions such as Milan 1500. Phronesium says in fact that

However Hesychius writes that the Amphidromia was usually celebrated on the seventh day.[4] In the *Theaetetus* Plato calls the ritual τὰ ἀμφιδρόμια, in the neuter gender,[5] and Ephippus does the same in Athenaeus' *Doctors at Dinner* book 9.[6]

34 Canens vitae palmum
Singing brief life away

Ἄιδων τὴν σπιθαμὴν τοῦ βίου πρὸς ἄνηθον, Singing brief life away with nothing but dill on the table.[1] Said of a frugal man who gets through life on scant, slender resources and yet thinks he lives magnificently. This is visibly the habit of certain people who put nothing that can be eaten on the table, but, so that the meal should not seem to be a complete fast, tell a variety of stories or sing songs to persuade their guests to forget food.

35 Qui non litigat caelebs est
If he has no disputes, he's a bachelor

St Jerome cites this phrase as being a proverbial saying: 'If he has no disputes, he's a bachelor.' The adage tells us that every marriage is full of strife and that the only way to live peacefully is in celibacy. Juvenal:

> There is endless strife and quarrels one after the other
> In the bed where a wife lies; there is no sleep to be had there.[1]

* * * * *

she wishes to offer sacrifice herself (see ASD II-7 115:335–7n). The text from 'And Plautus' to the end was added in 1526.
4 Hesychius Δ 2416 (see also A 3995)
5 Plato *Theaetetus* 160E
6 Athenaeus 9.370D citing PCG 5 Ephippus fragment 3 line 4

34 Zenobius (Aldus) 1505 column 7 = *Suda* A 518. Cf *Adagia* II ii 69 Brief span of life.
1 Latin *ad anethum*. Both Greek πρὸς (LSJ C III 6) and Latin *ad* can mean 'to the accompaniment of'; *ad anethum* appears to be a humorous figure for 'nothing on the table.'

35 Jerome *Adversus Jovinianum* 1.28 PL 23 261B
1 Juvenal 6.268–9

There is support for this aphorism in several proverbial verses: 'A woman in the home means a bad time for the man.' And this: 'A woman's jealousy sets light to any house.' And this: 'There is nothing worse than a woman, even a good one.'[2] But Hesiod, more moderately and so more truthfully I think:

> A better fate never befell any man than a good woman;
> Contrariwise nothing is ever worse than a bad one.[3]

36 Praestat uni malo obnoxium esse quam duobus
It is better to be exposed to one evil than two

In the *Women in Parliament* Aristophanes uses the following proverbial senarius: Ἐνὶ γὰρ ξυνέχθεσθαι κρεῖττον ἢ δυοῖν κακοῖν 'It is better to be entangled in one evil than two.' Whenever it is impossible to avoid one or the other of two evils we should strive to ward off one and meet face-to-face the one that brings the least disadvantage.

37 Utrumque
Both

The scholiast of Apollonius quotes this line from Callimachus: 'It is both: a goad for the oxen and a measure for the land.'[1] This may be used of anything that can be adapted to a different use, as I have shown earlier in the case of the Delphic sword.[2] Callimachus means the stick that the Greeks call an ἄκαινα and the Romans, if I am not mistaken, a *decempeda*. This is said to be an invention of the Thessalians, and is ten feet long. It is the same as shepherds used to use as a crook.

* * * * *

2 Menander *Sententiae* 823, 278 (= adespota 311 Nauck) and 609 Jäkel. ASD points out that the three verses are found together in the collection of the *Sententiae* published, without Menander's name, by Aldus in 1495, following the works of Theocritus and Theognis.
3 Hesiod *Works and Days* 702–3

36 Aristophanes *Ecclesiazusae* 1096

37 Scholiast of Apollonius (see n1 below). The proverb appears to be the line from Callimachus and *Utrumque* an abbreviated form for it.
1 Scholiast of Apollonius 3.1323; Callimachus fragment 24 Trypanis, Pfeiffer line 7 from *Aetia* I
2 *Adagia* II iii 69

38 Chius
A Chian

Χîος ἀποπατῶν, A Chian shitting. The scholiast of Aristophanes' *Peace* shows that this was a proverbial rebuke uttered against those who polluted the city and made it dirty. Any such occasion was used to invent slurs against the Chians. Whence it will be fittingly adapted to those who seize an opportunity to slander someone. Like the wolf in Aesop[1] who accuses the lamb of muddying the water he was drinking. Aristophanes in the play I have just quoted: 'The city of the Chians will incur a fine because of your bowels.'[2] The adage was probably derived from an incident that Plutarch relates in his 'Sayings of Spartans.' Some Chians, travelling in Laconia, vomited after a meal in the Assembly of the Ephors, the highest dignitaries among the Spartans, and emptied their bowels on the seats where the Ephors were accustomed to sit. At first a strict inquiry was made as to who had perpetrated this offence with the intention of dealing severely with any citizen who was responsible. When they discovered that the Chians had done it, they had an edict proclaimed which said, 'Permission is given to the Chians to behave like drunks.'[3]

39 Furari littoris harenas
Stealing the sands of the sea-shore

Someone is said 'to steal the sands of the sea-shore' if he takes what no one wants or guards. Ovid in the *Amores*: 'Who would make love with the wife of a fool / Could steal the sands from a deserted shore.'[1] A good match for this will be the one from Aristotle I noted elsewhere: 'The water-jar on the door-step.'[2] It will be better if the adage is used with a negative implication: 'Who would steal the sands of the sea-shore?'

* * * * *

38 Scholiast of Aristophanes *Peace* 171–2 (Dübner page 176)
 1 Aesop 98 Perry
 2 A Latin translation of the Greek, *Civitas Chiorum ob tuum culum debebit*, was added in 1515–23, but disappeared in 1526.
 3 Plutarch *Moralia* 232F–233A *Apophthegmata Laconica*; the whole story was added in 1526. A slightly different translation of it was also added to *Adagia* IV i 21 Corcyra is free, shit where you will (453 above) in 1533.

39 Ovid (see n1 below). Otto 788
 1 Ovid *Amores* 2.19.45–6; translation by Grant Showerman (Loeb)
 2 *Adagia* II i 65; Aristotle *Rhetoric* 1.6.22 (1363a5): Ἐν θύραις τὴν ὑδρίαν

40 **Colubrum in sinu fovere**
Nourishing a serpent in one's bosom

Ὄφιν ἐν τῷ κόλπῳ θάλπειν, Nourishing a serpent in one's bosom is said of someone who embraces an ungrateful person with affection and zealous attention when he is likely to seize some opportunity to do harm. It comes from a fable which is told under the name of Aesop and which a certain Gabrias put into iambic verse thus:

> A certain farmer was nursing in his lap a viper
> Which was stiff with cold, but the viper felt the warmth
> And bit its nurse, who soon died of the wound.
> This is how the ungrateful treat those who deserve well of them.[1]

There is another fable too about a hen that was incubating a snake's eggs; she was warned by a swallow not to hatch it lest it brought her own destruction.[2]

41 **Praeter Sibyllam leget nemo**
Illegible to anyone but the Sibyl

St Jerome makes fun of the style of Jovinian as confused and obscure and notes that it is aptly described by an expression used about writing in Plautus: 'No one but the Sibyl could read this.' The passage is in Plautus' *Pseudolus* where someone laughs at the handwriting of a woman friend, little marks badly formed, typical of women's writing:

> – These characters are after children, the way
>   They climb on top of each other.
> – The Sibyl may be able to read this, but I don't believe
>   Anyone else can make it out.

* * * * *

40 Pseudo-Babrius (see n1 below). Otto 1903 and Otto *Nachträge* pages 66, 120, 227. Tilley V 68 To nourish a viper in one's bosom
   1 Babrius 147 Crusius; see *Adagia* IV i 96 n2 (499 above). Erasmus could have found this in the Aldine Aesop of 1505 (d 6 r, page 57). A Latin version appears on folio D 5 v, but Erasmus has made his own translation. The fable corresponds to the prose Aesop 176 Perry, where the man is identified as ὁδοιπόρος 'a wayfarer.'
   2 Aesop 192 Perry; added in *1515*

41 Jerome *Adversus Jovinianum* 1 1 PL 23 221B. Otto 1640

– Lord save us! Have hens got any hands?
For it surely was a hen wrote this.[1]

42 Nihil profuerit bulbus
An onion would be no good at all

In the second book of the *Doctors at Dinner* Athenaeus records this senarius
as a proverb: 'Any one who is impotent would not be helped at all by
an onion.' Martial too: 'You can do nothing but satisfy your hunger with
onions.'[1] The onion arouses lust. But we may be allowed to use the adage
for a more seemly purpose to mean that study is of no benefit if intelligence
is lacking.[2]

43 Quae dantur
What is given ...

Marcus Tullius in book 6 of his *Letters to Atticus*: 'When he lost them he left
without an explanation, saying, "I give in. 'Twere shame to tarry long,"[1]
and casting in my teeth the old proverb Τὰ μὲν διδόμενα "Take the goods
the gods provide you."'[2] He uses the same phrase in another place too.[3]
It is not entirely clear what it means[4] unless we may conjecture that τὰ
μὲν διδόμενα 'What is given ...' is a line by some poet, for it is an iambic

* * * * *

1 Plautus *Pseudolus* 23–6, 29–30; translation by P. Nixon (Loeb)

42 Athenaeus 2.64B, adespota 484 Kock
 1 Martial *Epigrams* 13.34.2, already used in *Adagia* III iv 44 He's looking for
   onions (27 above)
 2 Last sentence added *1515*

43 Cicero (see n2 below). Cf *Adagia* III x 34 Accept things as they are in good
   part, IV i 15 Whatever gift anyone gives, be grateful (369 and 450 above), and
   v i 40 What you're given. Otto *Nachträge* page 34
 1 *Iliad* 2.298 Αἰσχρόν τοι δηρόν τε μένειν, cited by Cicero in Greek (see n2 below);
   it forms *Adagia* II viii 87 It is a disgrace to stay too long and return empty-
   handed. I have followed the translation of E.O. Winstedt (Loeb).
 2 Cicero *Ad Atticum* 6.5.2. The passage is largely in Greek, for which Erasmus
   gives no translation.
 3 *Ad Atticum* 15.17.1
 4 Estienne (LB II 999) thinks it is quite clear that it means 'Beggars cannot be
   choosers' and refers to his *Castigationes in Ciceronem* (1557 page 72, where he
   numbers the letter 19, not 17); cf Tilley B 247 Beggars should be no choosers.

hemistich. It counsels us to accept gratefully what fortune gives us and to bear patiently what cannot be changed. In the *Gorgias* Plato seems to point to this proverb: 'But now I am deceived by a lie, and it is necessary, it seems, to take my present fortune in good part, as the old saying runs, and τοῦτο δέχεσθαι τὸ διδόμενον "to accept whatever you give me."'[5] Δῶρον δ᾽ ὅτι δῷ τις ἐπαίνει 'For any gift be grateful' is dealt with elsewhere.[6] The same idea is contained in 'As best we can, since as we would we may not.'[7]

44 Sidera addere coelo
Adding stars to the heavens

Adding stars to the heavens is a proverbial figure meaning to add to what already exists in great abundance. Proof enough of this would be the way Ovid wove it together with two other proverbs in the second book of his love poems:

> Why do you add leaves to the trees, stars to a full sky?
> Why add pond-water to the deep seas?[1]

45 Pamphili furtum
Pamphilus pilfering

Παμφίλου νοσφισμός, Pamphilus' thievery. This Pamphilus is censured and abused in the Old Comedy because he robbed the treasury. The expression will be suitable for embezzlers who steal money from the public.[1]

*****

5 Plato *Gorgias* 499C referred to in *Adagia* II v 1 and quoted in II ix 33. From 'In the *Gorgias*' to the end was added in *1528*.
6 *Adagia* IV i 15 (450 above)
7 *Adagia* I viii 43

44 Ovid (see n1 below). Otto 1643
1 Ovid *Amores* 2.10.13–14; the last line is quoted in *Adagia* III ii 68 Water out of a ditch into the sea.

45 Apostolius 14.4. This is the first of a sequence taken from this source, which runs through to *Adagia* IV iii 64, and with which Erasmus originally finished his *1508* edition. From *1508–20* the title read *Pamphili vindicatio* 'Pamphilus taking revenge,' which is plainly inconsistent with what the text says.
1 Last sentence added in *1533*

46 Pegaso velocior
As fast as Pegasus

Πηγάσου ταχύτερος, As fast as Pegasus. A proverbial exaggeration describing people who can run very fast. From the well known story of the winged horse. Thus we find in Pindar *Olympic Odes* number 9:

Faster than a noble horse or a winged ship.[1]

47 Crepitu probabis
You will prove it by the sound

Πλαταγῇ δοκιμάσεις, You will prove it by the 'pop.'[1] Said of those who try by absurd means to find out others' intentions towards them. The origin is a common game for girls who strike the palm of one hand against a poppy leaf[2] held between the thumb and middle finger of the other; if it makes a pop it is a proof of love, if not, it is a sign that love is absent.[3] Suidas tells us this is done with the leaf of a poppy or anemone which is called πλαταγώνιον, from πλατάσσειν 'to crack.'[4] Ammianus alluded to the adage in book 14: 'For when it is expressed truthfully and from the heart love shows itself by a slight sound.'[5] So it will be a good moment for the proverb when a man's intention is clearly recognizable in his way of speaking plainly. Elsewhere I find πλατάγη for the instrument by which we produce the sound, and πλαταγεῖν for 'to make a snapping sound.'

* * * * *

46 Apostolius 14.28
   1 Pindar *Olympians* 9.23–4: Καὶ ἀγάνορος ἵππου / θᾶσσον καὶ ναὸς ὑποπτέρου; added in *1533*

47 Apostolius 14.36
   1 In this translation Erasmus latinizes the Greek word *plataga*, presumably in order to maintain the play with πλαταγώνιον 'poppy leaf.' According to LSJ the Greek word refers to the petal of a poppy.
   2 Latin *papaveris folium* 'poppy leaf.' A.S.F. Gow *Theocritus* 2.70–1 has a detailed discussion of this in his commentary on *Idylls* 3.29f.
   3 In *1526* the words *Suspicor ex Apostolio sumptum* 'Taken from Apostolius I suspect' stood here – they were replaced in *1528* by the text down to 'Elsewhere I find.'
   4 *Suda* Π 1698.
   5 ASD points to Ammianus Marcellinus 24.3.8 (not book 14): *armorum crepitu leni* 'by a slight clashing of shields,' which in early editions read *amor ex levi crepitu*.

48 Multa docet fames
Hunger teaches many things

Πολλῶν ὁ λιμὸς γίγνεται διδάσκαλος, Hunger is the teacher of many arts. Ovid says: 'Misfortunes often stir the wits.'[1] And Persius: 'That dispenser of genius, the belly, who has a rare skill in getting at words that are not his own.'[2]

49 Multorum festorum Iovis glandes comedit
He has eaten acorns at many feasts of Jupiter

Πολλῶν πανηγύρεων Διὸς βαλάνων ἔφαγεν, He has eaten acorns at many feasts of Jupiter. Said of a man who is old and wise through long and varied experience; it means exactly the same as 'He has lived many Olympiads.' The oak is sacred to Jupiter, whence the expression 'Jove's oak nuts.'[1] People in my country still say nowadays,[2] 'He has eaten many Easter eggs' as a humorous way of referring to an old man.

50 Prodico doctior
As learned as Prodicus

Προδίκου σοφώτερος, As learned as Prodicus. It is asserted that this Prodicus showed the most acute judgment in settling lawsuits and making decisions between disputing friends. Aristophanes in his *Centaur*, as quoted by Suidas: 'For my part, if anyone should commit an injustice, / I want Prodicus to consider the matter.'[1] However there is an underlying allusion to the

* * * * *

48 Menander *Sententiae* 630 (the accepted text has ὁ καιρός 'Time' not 'Hunger'). Apostolius 14.40A. All three quotations are found together in *Adagia* I v 22 Poverty has drawn wisdom as her lot.
  1 Ovid *Ars amatoria* 2.43, cited by Otto 1358 as a parallel to Plautus' *[Paupertas] artis omnis perdocet* '[Poverty] teaches all the arts' (*Stichus* 178).
  2 Persius Prologue 10–11, translation by G.G. Ramsey (Loeb); cited by Otto 640 as a parallel to Seneca's *[Istos quos] nova artificia docuit fames* '[Those whom] hunger has taught new tricks' (*Letters* 15.7) with the Greek from Macarius 7.24

49 Apostolius 14.66
  1 Latin *Nuces iuglandes*, the latter word being a contraction of *Iovis glandes*. This and the final sentence were added in 1533.
  2 Suringar 124 page 225

50 Apostolius 14.76. Prodicus was a native of Ceos, a teacher mainly of rhetoric.
  1 *Suda* Π 2366, citing PCG 3.2 Aristophanes fragment 278

common noun; *prodicus*[2] means much the same as *praeiudicator*, an investigating magistrate who gives an opinion on a case before it is sent before the judges.[3] There was also a sophist of this name whom Plato mentions in several places.[4]

51 Mendico ne parentes quidem amici sunt
For a beggar not even parents are friends

Πτωχοῦ φίλοι οὐδ᾿ οἱ γεννήτορες, For a beggar not even parents are friends. Wealth attracts friends, poverty has no friends, not even those bound by Nature. We give so much importance in our lives to things that should have the least influence if we measured them by their usefulness and not by our greed.[1]

52 Malus ianitor
A bad gatekeeper

Πυλωρὸς κακός, A bad gatekeeper; that is, a negligent leader or custodian. Derived from something a certain Thericyon said when he saw that Philip's troops had occupied the narrows of the Isthmus: 'The Peloponnese has bad gatekeepers in you, men of Corinth.'[1] The Greeks call narrow places *pylae* 'gates.' The story is told by Plutarch in the 'Sayings of Spartans.'[2]

53 Audi Chelidonem
Listen to Chelidon

Πύθου Χελιδόνος, Listen to Chelidon, that is, 'Take care of your affairs in good time.' Some believe this originated with a certain diviner by the name

* * * * *

2 Erasmus appears to be referring to the Greek πρόδικος 'an advocate.'
3 From 'and making decisions' to here added in 1515.
4 Plato *Apology* 19E, *Phaedrus* 267B, *Laches* 197D, *Protagoras* 315E, etc

51 Apostolius 15.7
1 The last sentence was added in 1517/18.

52 Apostolius 15.13
1 In Greek: Κακοὺς πυλωροὺς ὑμᾶς, ὦ Κορίνθιοι, ἡ Πελοπόννησος ἔχει
2 Plutarch *Moralia* 221F *Apophthegmata Laconica*

53 Apostolius 15.14. *Suda* Π 3136

of Chelidon. It is said it was his practice to observe portents and to infer the outcome of events from them. The source of this belief is said to be Mnaseas Patrensis in his *Circumnavigation*.[1] Many prefer to think this is a reference to the swallow, because it is a bird with a screeching and mournful song, or because it announces the arrival of spring.[2]

54 Ominabitur aliquis te conspecto
Anyone who sees you will read it as an omen

Σὲ δ' οἰωνίσαιτ' ἄν τις ἰδών, Anyone who saw you could take it as an omen. This was said at the expense of deformed or ugly people. The ancients used to derive an omen from the first person they encountered. To meet a handsome person was considered a fortunate omen; to meet an ugly or dark person was the opposite. One Roman emperor, Hadrian I think, being very superstitious in every way, saw it as an omen of death when he encountered a certain Moorish jester. The latter, when ordered to go away, made this rather ominous statement: 'You have conquered everything, you have achieved everything; now be a god.'[1] For deceased emperors were included, following certain solemn rites, in the number of the gods.

Juvenal says: 'And whom you would not want to meet at midnight.'[2]

55 Non admodum misces
You are not exactly shaking everything

Οὐ μάλα κυκᾷς, You are not exactly shaking everything. That is, 'You cannot

* * * * *

1 Mnaseas of Patara in Lycia. Erasmus appears to follow Hesychius Π 4311 here, identifying the work in Greek ('Ἐν τῷ περίπλῳ); *FHG* III 149–158 and IV 659. See Pauly-Wissowa XV 2250.
2 'Swallow' is χελιδών in Greek. Cf *Adagia* IV iii 22 A swallow will win by miles.

54 Apostolius 15.42
1 Severus, not Hadrian. See Aelius Spartianus *Severus* 22.4–5 in *Scriptores historiae Augustae*. Erasmus corrected himself in the *Apophthegmata* VI 7 (LB IV 312E).
2 Juvenal 5.54; the quotation evidently refers to the adage, not to the story of Severus.

55 Apostolius 13.38. *Alexandrian Proverbs* 2.4. Diogenianus 8.4. Zenobius (Aldus) column 137

do much either to benefit or to harm.' Pericles was said to have shaken the whole of Greece with his eloquence, because he changed everything to suit his own idea.[1] And in Marcus Tullius people are said to 'shake everything' when they upset the state with their excessive power.[2]

56 Asini cauda
An ass's tail

῎Ονου οὐρὰ τηλίαν οὐ ποιεῖ, An ass's tail does not make a sieve. To be used when someone is said to be unfit for this or that purpose. Sieves used to be made from horse-hair, not from the coarse hair of an ass's tail. I suspect Apostolius took this from the low language of our own age.[1]

57 Ipso cratere
Basin and all

Αὐτῷ κρητῆρι γίνῃ[1] κακά, Let evils fall on him, basin and all. This was often said of those who were the victims of the traps they set for others. 'Basin' is used to mean the source of evils; whence 'A basinful of evils' which is dealt with elsewhere.[2]

* * * * *

1 Aristophanes *Acharnians* 530–1; 'because he changed ... idea' was added in 1515.
2 Cicero *Pro Sexto Roscio Amerino* 91; added in 1533

56 Apostolius 12.90
  In 1508 there was an additional adage before this one (between those now numbered IV ii 55 and IV ii 56) entitled *Quid opus Sapragorae dote?* 'What need has Sapragoras of a dowry?' Its source was Apostolius 16.68, based on Plutarch *Moralia* 525D *De cupiditate divitiarum*. It read as follows:
    Τίς ἀνάγκη Σαπραγόρᾳ προίξ, What need has Sapragoras of a dowry? This used to be said of those who seek things that are quite unnecessary. Sapragoras was a very rich man who preferred his wife to be well behaved rather than well endowed; for her condition required no dowry, but he sought in his wife a well-formed mind.
  1 The last comment was added in 1517/18.

57 Apostolius 4.47. Diogenianus 3.22
  1 Latin: *contingant*; Erasmus takes γίνῃ as if were some form of the optative of γίγνομαι 'happen' – it is probably corrupt.
  2 *Adagia* IV i 33 (461 above); the last sentence was added in 1515.

58 Gutta vini
A drop of wine

Σταλαγμὸς οἴνου μυρίοις χοεῦσιν ὕδατος οὐ μίγνυται, A drop of wine is not mixed too often[1] with water. Used when a little of what is good is mixed with too much evil. For wine is diluted and fades right away if you spoil a small amount with excessive water.

59 Bos porrecto ultra Taygeton capite
An ox putting its head over Taygetus

Ταῦρος ὑπερκύψας τὸ Ταΰγετον ἀπὸ τοῦ Εὐρώτα ἔπιεν, A bull putting its head over Taygetus to drink from the Eurotas. A phrase for anything utterly absurd. Very like 'What if the sky should fall?'[1] The source is a saying of Geradas the Spartan. When he was asked by a guest what the penalty for adulterers was among the Spartans, he denied that there were any adulterers among Spartans. When his guest insisted, saying, 'What penalty would he pay if there were any?' he said, 'He would pay for a bull big enough to stretch its neck out over Mount Taygetus and drink from the Eurotas.' The guest laughed and asked, 'Where would you get such a huge bull?' The Spartan replied, 'Where would you find an adulterer among the Spartans?' The story is told by Plutarch in his life of Lycurgus.[2]

60 Ad cribrum dicta
Pronouncements according to the sieve

Τἀπὶ κοσκίνῳ, Pronouncements according to the sieve. Anything they would

* * * * *

58 Apostolius 15.62
  1 Erasmus has *saepius*. Estienne (LB II 1001) remarks, 'The Greek words mean "A drop of wine is not mixed with endless measures of water" or "with ten thousand measures," μυρίοις being from the nominative μυρίοι, not μυρίοι.' LSJ specifies that according to grammarians μυρίος (paroxytone) is the *indefinite*, μύριος (proparoxytone) the *definite number*.

59 Apostolius 15.90
  1 *Adagia* I v 64
  2 Plutarch *Lycurgus* 15.17 (Geradas); cf *Moralia* 228c *Apophthegmata laconica* (Geradatas). Added in *1526*

60 Apostolius 15.95. Zenobius (Athous) 2.39. *Suda* T 103 and T 22 (Τὰ ἐπὶ κοσκίνου)

want to seem true and certain would be described thus. Very like 'Straight from the tripod.'[1] It is derived from a type of divination that was performed by raising and shaking a sieve, as I have shown elsewhere,[2] drawing on Aristotle[3] and Lucian.

61 Iovis tergus
Jove's hide

Διὸς κῴδιον, Jove's hide.[1] An expression for something paltry in itself but kept for some purpose or other. In early times the skin of a sacrificial victim was kept to be carried in the Eleusinian processions or was laid beneath the feet of those who were under constraint to expiate some impiety.

62 Mala ultro adsunt
Evils come of their own accord

An aphorism like this is found in the *Collected Proverbs*:[1] 'Good fortune rarely comes to those who seek it, bad fortune befalls even those who do not seek it.'[2] And low-class people commonly say, not without some truth, 'Evils come of their own accord, uncalled for.'[3] And yet time and again it is by our own fault that we bring on ourselves war, disputes, and illnesses, as if there were not evils enough of themselves.[4]

* * * * *

1 *Adagia* I vii 90 Τὰ ἐκ τρίποδος
2 *Adagia* I x 8 To divine by a sieve; see Lucian *Alexander* 9.
3 The reference to Aristotle was added in *1528*, but the passage has not been identified.

61 Apostolius 6.10. *Suda* Δ 1210
1 Here and in the title *tergus* replacing the original *vellus* 'fleece' of *1508* and *1515*

62 Apostolius 6.14
1 In this case apparently *Collected Proverbs* means Apostolius; cf *Adagia* IV i 15 n4 (450 above). See also Stobaeus 4.34.58 Hense v 842, where it is attributed to Democritus.
2 Given in Greek: Διζημένοισι τἀγαθὰ μόλις παραγίνεται, τὰ δὲ κακὰ καὶ μὴ διζημένοισι
3 Added in *1517/18*. Suringar 110
4 Sentence added, along with so many other pacifist remarks and most of *Adagia* IV i 1 *Dulce bellum inexpertis* (399–440 above), in *1515*; cf *Adagia* IV ii 5 (506 above).

63 A vicinis exemplum habent
They have the example of their neighbours

Ἐκ τῶν γειτόνων ἔχουσι τὸ παράδειγμα, They follow their neighbours' example. Said of people who do something because they have been induced by the example of others. One man infects a neighbour with his illness; we are made worse by dealings with wicked people.[1] This is certainly what Terence was alluding to in the *Andria*: 'What is so surprising about that, if he follows your example?'[2]

64 My sortitus es
You have drawn M

Ἔλαχες τὸ M, Letter M has fallen to your lot. A riddle meaning stupid people, because in Greek the word μωροί 'fools' has this letter as initial. When the letter M came up for Dionysius[1] as lots were being drawn, someone said jokingly: Μωρολογεῖς, Διονύσιε 'You say foolish things, Dionysius.' But he turned it another way and said Μονομαχήσω μὲν οὖν 'No rather, I shall fight in single combat.' This is how the story is told in the Greek *Collected Proverbs*,[2] but there is an error as is apparent from Plutarch who relates that Dionysius replied μοναρχήσωμεν οὖν, which the translators, misled by the mistake in the text, render as 'We shall be monarchs.'[3] The reading should be μοναρχήσω μενοῦν 'No rather, I shall be monarch,' μενοῦν being one word and adversative rather than inferential, because he corrects someone else's interpretation and adds 'No rather, I shall be monarch.' Who indeed would say, 'We shall be monarchs'? Anyway μοναρχήσωμεν does not mean 'We shall be monarchs' but 'Let us be monarchs.' Finally, if you read

* * * * *

63 Apostolius 6.97. Cf Aristides 1.138.
1 Sentence added in *1515*
2 Terence *Andria* 651; added in *1520*

64 Apostolius 7.7. Everything from 'This is how' to the end was added in *1528*.
1 Ruler of Gela and Syracuse 478–67 BC
2 Here Erasmus' source seems to be Arsenius' version of Apostolius. In Apostolius the proverb is said to apply ἐπὶ τῶν εὐτυχησάντων 'to those who are fortunate,' which is omitted in Arsenius. For Arsenius Apostolius and his father Michael Apostolius, whom Erasmus cited from a manuscript up to 1519, see CEBR 1.68–9 and Ep 1232A.
3 Plutarch *Moralia* 175D *Regum et imperatorum apophthegmata*; the translators are Filelfo and Raphael Regio. For the details see ASD II-7 127:592–3n.

οὖν as indicating a deduction, not a correction, what else is Dionysius saying than that he would be monarch precisely because he is foolish? [4]

65 In Pythii templo cacare
To shit in the temple of Delphi

Ἐν Πυθίου χέσαι, To shit in the temple of Delphi. This was said of someone who committed some abominable and perilous act, for the tyrant Pisistratus, having built the temple, inscribed a notice that no one should empty his bowels in the precinct, and imprisoned a foreigner who was caught in the act.

66 In terra pauperem
A poor man on dry land

Ἐν γῇ πένεσθαι μᾶλλον ἢ πλουτοῦντα πλεῖν, Better to be needy on dry land than a rich man ploughing the waves. It is preferable to possess little in security than a great deal in danger. No one was content with wealth that depended on ship's ropes, much less wealth that can be snatched away by the winds.[1] The proverb teaches us that a secure fortune, even a modest one, is to be preferred to uncertain ones even if they are greater.[2]

67 Inter pueros senex
An old man among boys

Ἐν παισὶ μὲν γέρων, ἐν τοῖς δὲ γέρουσι παῖς, A boy among old men, but the same person is an old man among boys. This will be applicable to someone half-grown, too old to look like a boy, too young to look like a man. The

* * * * *

4 Modern editions print μοναρχήσω μὲν οὖν 'Indeed, I shall be monarch,' agreeing that 'μεν' is a particle not a verb ending, but taking μὲν οὖν as two words; ASD II-7 127:593n agrees with Erasmus on both points.

65 Apostolius 7.17. Cf *Suda* E 1428.

66 Apostolius 7.27. *Suda* E 1150. Diogenianus 4.83. Cf *Adagia* III ix 44 Better stay at home (335 above).
1 Sentence added in *1515*; cf *Adagia* IV iv 6 Do not put all your wealth on one ship.
2 Sentence added in *1528*

67 Apostolius 7.29. *Suda* E 3046

expression was used by rivals against Hermogenes the rhetorician.[1] We may use it for someone who is educated to the point where he can appear quite learned among the uneducated but among scholars is an ignoramus.[2]

68 In sola Sparta expedit senescere
Only in Sparta does it pay to grow old

'Εν Σπάρτη μόνη λυσιτελεῖ γηράσκειν, Sparta is the only place where it pays to grow old. This was said because among the Spartans the greatest respect was accorded to old people in ancient times. It could be used figuratively of any people who place a high price on virtue.[1] Plutarch records this in his 'Sayings of Spartans'[2] but as by an unknown author. It was a remark made by some visitor on seeing how much respect young people accorded to their elders. In his *Cato the Elder* Marcus Tullius attributes a similar remark to Lysander: 'Lysander the Spartan is said to have been in the habit of remarking that the worthiest home of old age was in Sparta. Nowhere is such tribute paid to age, nowhere is age more honoured.'[3] There is a

* * * * *

1 For Hermogenes see Philostratus *Vitae sophistarum* 2.7.577–8. Estienne (LB II 1002) remarks: 'Antiochus the Sophist had nothing of the sort in mind when he made this joke against Hermogenes. His real meaning could have been gathered easily by Erasmus from the account Philostratus gives of him. He relates that Hermogenes, when only fifteen years old, had a very high reputation among sophists, such that he inspired the emperor Marcus with a desire to hear him; but when he reached maturity, he lost the rhetorical power that he used to have. This provided his rivals with an occasion to laugh, for they said his words were truly, as Homer had it, winged, since Hermogenes had moulted them like feathers. To these remarks he adds: "And once Antiochus the sophist, jesting at his expense, said, 'Lo, here is that fellow Hermogenes, who among boys was an old man, but among the old is a boy.'" Having read this I think everyone will agree with me that the meaning of this sally to anyone who affirms it is this: "Someone who was endowed in boyhood with the mind and judgment of an old man (or worthy of an old man) has the mind in old age of a complete child." Philostratus adds that Hermogenes reached extreme old age.' Estienne, it seems, would relate this adage to IV i 100 I hate striplings who are precociously wise (501 above).
2 Sentence added in *1517/18*

68 Apostolius 7.30
1 Sentence added in *1515*
2 Plutarch *Moralia* 235F *Apophthegmata Laconica*
3 Cicero *De senectute* 63. This and the preceding reference to Plutarch were added in *1526*. Erasmus' source for the following story, added with the ref-

well-known story of an old man who went into the theatre and to whom
no one among the Athenians would give a place; only the Spartan ambas-
sadors showed respect for his white hair, honoured him by standing up,
and gave him the most prestigious seat in their midst. When the Athenians
in the crowd applauded what had been done for him, one of the Spartans
remarked that Athenian people knew very well what was right but they
took no heed of it. The story is told by many authors, including Valerius
Maximus book 4 chapter 5, to name one.[4]

69 Ne maior thylaco accessio
Beware the load is not bigger than the bag

In his *Praise of Demosthenes* Lucian says: 'But perhaps you are afraid of
being the butt of the proverbial joke about an ill-judged sense of propor-
tion, namely, "Beware that your little extra bundle isn't bigger than the
bag."'[1] The *thylakos* was a leather saddle-bag or satchel made for carrying
loads.[2] I am aware that in published versions we find τοὐπίγραμμα 'label'
not τοὐπίσαγμα 'extra bundle.' However, unless you make some change in
the text no sense can be derived from it. Ἐπίσαγμα is from σάττω 'load' and
means 'extras to the load.'[3] The figure is derived from muleteers, who in
addition to the proper load put on a number of small containers. So we shall
be right to use this proverb when a digression is longer than the matter itself. Basil expresses the same idea in other words in his book on the Holy
Spirit: 'In this way moreover the accessory would be much bigger than the
main part.'[4]

* * * * *

erence to Valerius Maximus in 1533, is most likely this same passage by
Cicero.
4 Valerius Maximus 4.5 ext 2

69 Pseudo-Lucian (see n1 below). Not in Apostolius
1 Pseudo-Lucian *Demosthenis encomium* 10: Μή σοὶ μεῖζον προσκέοιτο τοὐπίσαγμα
τῷ θυλάκῳ (on τοὐπίσαγμα see n3 below)
2 Sentence added in 1526
3 Modern texts prefer τοὐπίγραμμα and translate 'too large a name tag.' Estienne
(LB II 1003) would keep τοὐπίγραμμα, as in pseudo-Lucian, for τοὐπίσαγμα and
goes on: 'I think it can be translated thus: "Don't attach a label to the bag
bigger than is proper." ... However I freely confess this explanation of mine
does not satisfy me; but such as it is it preserves the whole of the reading that
we have ...'
4 Basil *De spiritu sancto* 14C PG 32 128B: ῍Η οὕτω γε ἂν τὸ ἐπεισόδιον πολλαπλάσιον
εἴη τοῦ κεφαλαίου; added in 1533

70 Acarnici equi
Acarnanian horses

Ἀκαρνικοὶ ἵπποι, Acarnanian horses, was a term for the largest horses.[1] Very like the expression that Aristotle also mentions "Ἵππος Θεσσαλική 'A Thessalian mare.'[2] In his *Georgics* Virgil awards the highest praise to the horses of Epirus:

Epirus [gives us] the Olympian victories of her mares.[3]

The Acarnanians are neighbours of the Epirotes, as are the Thessalians.[4] We can use it suitably for anything outstanding or highly prized.[5]

71 Contribulis factus serva ordinem
When you become a member of the tribe, keep your place

Γεννητὸς γεγονὼς τήρει τὴν τάξιν, When you become a member of the tribe, keep your place; that is, after you are admitted to some body, perform your duty as the others do. The origin is the tribes of Athens. The population of Athens was divided into twelve tribes, following the number of months, and each tribe into thirty *gene*, according to the number of days.[1] Hence γεννητοί, as they were called, were not people joined by close blood relationship, but those enrolled in the same division of a tribe.

* * * * *

70 Apostolius 2.90
1 Apostolius gives the adage as Ἀχαρνικοὶ ἵπποι 'Acharnian horses,' an alternative to Ἀχαρνικοὶ ὄνοι 'Acharnian asses,' which is found in Diogenianus and Macarius. Erasmus misquotes the adage and thinks it refers to Acarnania (see n4 below), and not to Acharnae, a deme in Attica. He follows Apostolius, however, in saying that the adage refers to the largest horses.
2 The expression 'Cavalry in Thessaly and Thrace' was a well-known proverb (cf W.C. Wright ed, Julian the Apostate *Orationes* 7.205D) which Erasmus referred to in *Adagia* IV i 22 The prize will be the Thessalian mare (454); but, as the editor of ASD points out, he did not mention Aristotle there.
3 Virgil *Georgics* 1.59
4 Acarnania, on the northern side of the Gulf of Corinth, was part of Epirus. From 'In his *Georgics*' to here was added in 1526.
5 Last sentence added in 1515

71 Apostolius 5.30
1 Apostolius, whom Erasmus follows throughout here, may echo Heracleides' epitome of the first part of the Aristotle's *Athenian Constitution* fragment 5.

72 Glaucus alter
Another Glaucus

Γλαῦκος ἄλλος ἱππόβρωτος, Another Glaucus, devoured by horses. This will fit a man who exhausts his resources in keeping horses. The origin is a legend, like the one that is told of Actaeon.[1]

73 Gorgonem Perseus aggreditur
Perseus approaches the Gorgon

Γοργόνα Περσεὺς ἐχειρώσατο, Perseus has attacked the Gorgon.[1] Said when someone undertakes some extraordinary deed. The legend is very well known.[2] This is a proverb I would not have included if I had not found it in the Greek *Collected Proverbs*.[3]

74 Vincula Tyrrhena
Tyrrhenian bonds

Δεσμοὶ Τυρρηνοί, Tyrrhenian bonds, was an expression for irksome affairs that overwhelmed a person. Derived from the heavy, fatiguing fetters with which the Tyrrhenians[1] chained their captives.

* * * * *

72 Apostolius 5.47.
1 Glaucus of Potniae was eaten by his horses at the funeral games for Pelias, king of Iolcus; he is identified by Asclepiades of Tragilus (*FGrHist* 12 F 1) and Pausanias (6.20.19) with Glaucus son of Sisyphus of Corinth. Actaeon, of course, was killed by his own hounds (Ovid *Metamorphoses* 3.138ff); the last sentence was added in *1515*. Erasmus' interpretation however seems to come from Palaephatus *De incredibilibus* 26 (see *Adagia* IV i 63 especially n2, 479 above).

73 Apostolius 5.58. Zenobius (Aldus) column 62–4
1 Estienne (LB II 1004 n1) remarks that the Greek verb means rather 'has defeated, subdued.'
2 It is recounted at length in Zenobius (Aldus), but is also found in Palaephatus *De incredibilibus* 32, Apollodorus 2.4.1–5, and Ovid *Metamorphoses* 4.604–803.
3 Again Erasmus' source is Apostolius not Pseudo-Plutarch *Alexandrian Proverbs*. The last sentence was added in *1517/18*.

74 Apostolius 5.97. *Suda* Δ 273. Cf Hesychius Δ 701.
1 Ie Etruscans

75 **Diu delibera**
Take a long time to think

Δηρὸν βουλεύειν, Take a long time to think. A deal is not to be undertaken
hastily. The complete line of verse is recorded thus:

Reflect at length so that you may prevail by far.[1]

You should take time to think slowly, but when you have decided then you
should do what is necessary in good time.[2] Those who do otherwise usually
find what happens is, as Plato says, that they begin in a hurry and finish
too late.[3]

76 **Epimenideum corium**
Epimenides' skin

Ἐπιμενίδειον δέρμα, The hide of Epimenides. Used of something stored and
preserved as a miraculous object. In some manuscripts I encountered the
spelling 'Epimelidium,'[1] but this is a corruption if I am not mistaken. It was

* * * * *

75 Apostolius 6.1
 1 In Greek: Δηρὸν βουλεύειν, ἵν᾽ ἔχῃ καὶ πολλὸν ἄμεινον; Apostolius and Eustathius (127.19) on *Iliad* 1.417
 2 Cf the quotations from Sallust and Aristotle in *Adagia* II i 1 Make haste slowly,
   where Erasmus also has a discussion of the Latin word *mature* translated here
   as 'in good time' (CWE 33 5 and 341 nn54 and 55). Cf also II iii 70 Think before
   you start.
 3 Plato *Republic* 7.528D and several other passages collected in *Adagia* III v 60
   (101–2 above). From 'You should take time' to here was added in *1515*.

76 Apostolius 7.73. *Suda* E 2471. See also *Adagia* I ix 64 You sleep longer than Epimenides (with a quotation from Pliny *Naturalis historia* 7.175). For Epimenides
   as an image of the scholastic theologian see Ep 64:25–76.
   In *1508* this adage occurred where II viii 51 appears in the later editions and,
   because Erasmus wished to correct an error, at this point also, where the following notice was inserted after 'a miraculous object': 'It does not escape me
   that I have placed this proverb elsewhere, but since, after the book was completed, I noticed from some better corrected texts that the published version
   was corrupt, it seemed advisable to warn the reader.' This was deleted in
   1517/18 and the earlier occurrence of the adage at II viii 51 was replaced with
   a new text (see CWE 34 339 51n and n2 below).
 1 Apostolius 17.14 and some manuscripts of Diogenianus 8.28

noted there that this man's skin was concealed and preserved in Sparta as a sacred object.[2] However Eudemus[3] informs us that the source is Epimenides the Cretan, who is recorded as having slept continuously for forty-seven years, or if we believe Laertius, fifty-seven,[4] and to have lived on for many years after that. Hence it is likely that his remains were preserved as the memorial of a miracle.

77 Volaticum iusiurandum
A fleeting oath

Ταχυβάμονες ὅρκοι, Fleeting oaths. This is what they used to call an empty oath that faded and flew away as soon as it was uttered, like those of lovers. This meaning is the one favoured by Suidas,[1] but Aristarchus, quoted by Eudemus,[2] understands it by antiphrasis, as meaning that an oath should be made with deliberation and not uttered rashly, for if you do swear an oath it should not immediately evaporate.

78 Superatus es a gallo quopiam
You have been beaten by some gamecock

Ἡττήθης τινὸς ἀλεκτρυόνος, You have been beaten by some gamecock. A proverbial joke against slaves who walk behind their masters, supplicating and humble, like cocks who have been beaten in a fight. When defeated this bird is silent, but when it wins it crows, as Cicero tells us in *On Divination*.[1] It is also said that a cock defeated in a fight will follow behind the victor of

* * * * *

2 From 'In some manuscripts' to here was added in *1517/18*; see ASD II-7 131: 684–6n.
3 See *Adagia* III v 1 n48 (66 above). Erasmus quotes Eudemus in relation to adages IV ii 76–9, but they are also in Apostolius.
4 Diogenes Laertius 1.109–15 ('Epimenides'). See also Valerius Maximus 8.13 ext 5, Plato *Laws* 1.642D, Plutarch *Moralia* 784D *Septem sapientium convivium*. The phrase 'or, if we believe Laertius, fifty-seven' was added in *1526*.

77 Apostolius 16.21
1 *Suda* T 201, who also refers to Aristarchus; added in *1528*
2 On Eudemus, see *Adagia* III v 1 n48 (66 above).

78 Apostolius 8.70. *Suda* H 620
1 Cicero *De divinatione* 1.74 and 2.26.56; added in *1526*

its own accord. The source is Aristophanes, if my memory does not deceive me.[2] It is recorded by Eudemus.[3]

79 Βατακάρας
Droopy head

Βατακάρας is an expression used of dull people who lack energy. Eudemus mentions it,[1] adding that it should be read as one word κατὰ συστολήν 'joined together.' What the words may mean is still not very clear unless he has understood that it is a reproach for dullness of mind. For a lively mind makes us keep our head up; to have the head bowed is usually a sign of a rather dull, slow mind. And this is the source of the Greek word,[2] for in the Tarentine dialect Βατάς, as Hesychius tells us, means 'inclined forward' and κάρα means 'head.'[3] From this comes βάτταραι used by the Thracians for Bacchantes inspired by the spirit of Bacchus, who are also called Bassarides,[4] as the Etymologist shows.[5] On a lower level the term is used of a prostitute who submits to all and sundry. In Athenaeus book 4 καρηβαροῦντες is a word for people whose heads are fuddled with intoxication.[6] It will be suitable for a drunk or sleepy person, which is how St Basil used it in one of his letters.[7]

* * * * *

2 Aristophanes *Birds* 70–1; this sentence and the previous one added in *1533*.
3 On Eudemus, see *Adagia* III v 1 n48 (66 above).

79 Apostolius 4.75. *Suda* B 175 (Βατὰ Κάρας). Zenobius (Aldus) column 52 (Βάτα κάρα)
1 On Eudemus, see *Adagia* III v 1 n48 (66 above). Erasmus seems to be following Apostolius, who reads ἀδυνάτων 'of weak people' and κατὰ συστολήν 'joined together, in one word,' where the *Suda* has δυνατῶν 'of powerful people' and κατὰ διαστολήν 'in two words.' The latter does not refer to Eudemus at this point.
2 From 'What the words may mean' to here added in *1517/18*
3 Hesychius B 328 and K 756
4 Cf Persius 1.101; Bassareus (Horace *Odes* 1.18.11) was one of the names of Bacchus.
5 *Etymologicum magnum* 191.3
6 Athenaeus 4.130B
7 Erasmus is referring to the expression βαθεῖ κάροι in Basil *Epistolae* 2 (PG 32 233A). Βατακάρας is a conjecture that he had made in a letter of 1528 (Ep 1997) and follows in this addition of *1533*, but he had apparently already withdrawn it in the edition of Basil published under his name in *1532*. See ASD II-7 133:714n.

80 Ex aequo partire
Sharing equally

Ἐξ ἴσου δίδου πᾶσιν, Give equally to all.[1] A figure borrowed from those who share a banquet or an inheritance. It will be suitable for a judge or prince who must administer justice fairly.

81 Ἐπαύλια δῶρα
Wedding gifts

Ἐπαύλια δῶρα was an expression meaning splendid gifts. The Greeks used it for the gifts that the father of the bride brought in a sort of procession to the bride and groom the day after the marriage. In front walked a boy in a white toga[1] carrying a burning torch. After him came one carrying a basket of flowers, and after him a long line of bearers of gold, basins, cleaning instruments, litters, combs, couches, caskets, sandals, cylinders, perfume vases,[2] and sometimes the dowry itself. It is also said[3] that the day itself following the wedding was the ἐπαυλία, because that was when the bride was led to the marriage bed. The adage could be adapted to those who flaunt their good deeds. I believe these gifts are what the lawyers call παράφερνα 'goods that a bride brings over and above her dowry.'[4]

82 In pedes retrocedit
He's going back on his tracks

Ἐπὶ πόδα ἀναχωρεῖ, He's backing down,[1] is an expression for someone who

* * * * *

80 Apostolius 7.51
 1 From Plutarch *Moralia* 208c *Apophthegmata Laconica*

81 Apostolius 7.65. *Suda* E 1990. Eustathius on *Iliad* 24.29 (1337.44). Pausanias Atticista ε 49 Erbse
 1 Latin *toga*; the Greek in Apostolius and the *Suda* is χλανίς, an upper garment of fine wool.
 2 Latin *reliquamque suppellectilem* 'and all the other household furniture' of 1508 to 1526 was replaced in 1528 by 'cleaning instruments ... perfume vases.'
 3 In *Suda* E 1990. The text from here to the end was added in 1528.
 4 Cf Justinian *Digest* 23.3.9.3.

82 Apostolius 7.68
 1 Erasmus uses the plural *pedes* in the title, and the singular, as in the Greek,

gives way through fear to a stronger person and withdraws to safety; it seems to be derived from wrestlers or gladiators. It is the same as the Latin *referre pedem* 'to retreat.'[2] It will be applicable too to people changing their mind.

83 In armis accissat
Looking coy in his armour

Ἐπὶ τοῖς ὅπλοις ἀκκίζεται, Looking coy in his armour. Directed against a man who is pleased with himself and as it were admires his own figure dressed in armour. Suitable for someone who is foolishly self-satisfied. Recorded with others by the Etymologist.[1] Acco, the woman who paid herself silly compliments in her mirror, is described elsewhere in the adage 'To feign indifference.'[2]

84 In Lipsydrio pugnas
You fight in Lypsidrium

Ἐπὶ Λειψυδρίῳ μάχη, You fight in Lypsidrium. Lypsidrium was a place not far from Mt Parnes, which tyrants fleeing from the city had surrounded with a rampart; the Alcmaeonid family was the first to establish itself there, but when they were besieged and defeated by the forces of Pisistratus, a satirical song began to be sung about them, which went like this:

> Alas, alas Lypsidrium! betrayer of friends.
> What men you have ruined, illustrious and brave fighters,
> For they showed what ancestors they were descended from.[1]

* * * * *

here *In pedem retrocedit*. Plautus (*Bacchides* 374) and Terence (*Phormio* 190) have *in pedes se coniicere*.
2 Eg Cicero *Philippics* 12.8

83 Apostolius 7.67
 1 *Etymologicum magnum* 49.3; added in *1533*
 2 *Adagia* II ii 99

84 Apostolius 7.70. Cf *Suda* E 2440, Hesychius Λ 567, *Etymologicum magnum* 361.31, PMG fragment 907 (*Carmina convivialia* 24). The earliest source is Aristotle *Athenian Constitution* 19.3, but see also Athenaeus 15.695E.
 1 Erasmus is following Apostolius, but it was in the last years of Hippias' rule (after 514 BC) that the Alcmaeonids fortified but failed to defend Leipsidrion (Herodotus 5.62).

The proverb was directed against turbulent, belligerent men. The name of the place is due to its lack of water.[2]

85 Desertum obtueri
Staring at a desert

Ἔρημον ἐμβλέπειν, Staring at a desert, was an expression describing someone who was looking with a fixed, thunder-struck gaze. It is a metaphor borrowed from people who gaze silently at a boundless sea or an empty place. A lot of people have trouble with their eyes in that, when they look at things that are a little too far away, they cannot see clearly. We could say sometimes to these people in a crowd that, because they do not focus their eyes on anyone in particular, they seem to be looking at a desert.[1] This is Aristophanes, quoted from his *Polyidus*.[2]

86 Esto promus
Do your job as steward

Ἔστω ταμίας, τἄλλα δ' εἰ βούλει κύων, Do your job as intendant;[1] in everything else you're free to be a dog. The sources say this is a jibe against someone to whom good fortune comes when he does not deserve it, and especially against eunuchs. Suidas tells us that in Athens [the *tamies*] was

* * * * *

2 Greek λείπω 'be wanting,' ὕδωρ 'water'; last two sentences added in *1533*

85 Apostolius 7.92. *Suda* E 2965
1 From 'A lot of people' to here added in *1533*
2 PCG 3.2 Aristophanes fragment 473 from the *Suda* and Apostolius; added in *1533*

86 Apostolius 8.2. In *1508* this consisted only of the first two sentences; everything else, that is, everything taken from the *Suda* (T 58 and 59), was added in *1528*.
1 Erasmus uses *promus* in the title, but *condus* 'intendant, bursar' (cf Plautus *Pseudolus* 608) in his translation of the Greek. Estienne (LB II 1005) rejects Erasmus' somewhat clumsy attempt to relate the saying to eunuchs, and dismisses the *Suda*'s explanations entirely. He believes the saying has nothing to do with stewards, and would replace ταμίας with τομίας 'eunuch,' though without any other evidence than that the verse requires the long ι of the latter, not the short ι of the former. Further, he would translate Ἔστω as a third person imperative 'Let him be' not as a second person imperative or subjunctive (*sis*), taking the adage to mean 'Providing he's a eunuch, he can be as inept as he likes.' The editor of ASD II-7 135:761n, rejects Estienne's suggestion on the grounds that ταμίας is what is found in Apostolius.

a magistrate appointed to the Decemvirate who guarded the monies that were designated sacred and public, and deposited in the temple of Pallas, along with the statue of Pallas itself and the rest of the temple ornaments.[2] There were also *tamiae triremium* 'intendants of triremes,' who accompanied trireme captains as custodians. Though it was essential that uncorrupted men of complete trustworthiness should be appointed to the office, this magistracy was sometimes entrusted to thieves, as if it did not matter what sort of person you were to undertake the responsibility as long as it was assigned. As an irony the expression may be addressed to someone who enters on an office without worrying about what education or what morals the office requires, as if you were to say, 'Be a bishop by your office, and be a dog in your morals if you like.' Kings usually entrust their treasures and their wives to eunuchs.

87 Ephemeri vita
To live as long as Ephemerus

Ἐφημέρου ζωή, To live as long as Ephemerus. An expression used of those who die or perish very suddenly. Derived from creatures called 'ephemerids' because they do not live longer than a day.[1] In book 5 of his *Natural history* Aristotle has the following statement about ephemerids: 'In the summer the Hypanis, a river flowing into the Cimmerian Bosphorus,[2] carries little pods rather bigger than grapes from which four-footed winged creatures emerge. This species of creature lives and flies about until the evening, but as soon as the sun starts to go down it wastes away, becomes weak, and dies as the sun sets; its life lasts no longer than one day, and this is why it is called an "ephemerid."'[3] Pliny has similar things to say in

* * * * *

2 The ταμίης τοῦ ἱροῦ translated by LSJ as 'comptroller of the sacred treasure in the citadel of Athens.' See also Aristotle *Athenian Constitution* 47.1.

87 Apostolius 8.19
1 Greek ἐπὶ ἡμέρα 'for a day'
2 The modern Kerch Strait leading into the Sea of Azov. The river therefore appears to be the Kuban, which flows into this strait from the Caucasus, not the Bug (see the Loeb translations of Pliny and Cicero), which enters the Black Sea to the west of the Crimea. According to Van der Heyden and Scullard, *Atlas of the Classical World* (London and Edinburgh 1963) map 27, both of these rivers were called Hypanis. See also C. Muller *Geographi Graeci minores* ([1855]; reprinted by Georg Olms, 1965) map v.
3 Aristotle *Historia animalium* 5.19 (552b18); added in 1515

book 11 chapter 36, except that he calls the creature *hemerobius*.[4] Aristotle is quoted by Cicero in his *Tusculan Disputations* book 1, where he adds that the Hypanis flows into the Black Sea from the European side.[5]

88 Canis mendico auxilians
A dog helping a beggar

Κύων τῷ πτωχῷ βοηθῶν, A dog helping a beggar. Used when we are faced by an enemy and the one whose help we were relying on supports the other side. For dogs are the enemies of beggars, being ὁμότεχνοι 'practitioners of the same craft,' except when they are bribed with a bit of bread.[1]

89 Iupiter aquilam delegit
Jupiter chose the eagle

Ζεὺς ἀετὸν εἵλετο, Jupiter chose the eagle. Said when someone takes into his service distinguished people who are suited to his purposes. The poets have invented the idea that the eagle places the thunderbolt in Jupiter's hand because this bird flies higher than all others and cannot be harmed by a lightning strike.[1] He used the services of the same bird in abducting his catamite Ganymede.[2]

90 Aut minus animi aut plus potentiae
Less ambition or more strength

Ἦ φρονεῖν ἔλασσον ἢ δύνασθαι δεῖ μεῖζον, You must be either less ambitious or

* * * * *

4 From ἡμέρα 'day,' βίος 'life.' Pliny *Naturalis historia* 11.120; added in *1533*
5 Cicero *Tusculanae disputationes* 1.94, but see n2 above.

88 Apostolius 8.24
1 Last sentence added in *1515*

89 Apostolius 8.28
1 Cf *Adagia* III vii 1 (198 above with n127) and Eustathius 1351.23–6 on *Iliad* 24.292. This sentence was added in *1515*.
2 *Iliad* 20.231–6; Xenophon *Symposium* 8.29–30. This tongue-in-cheek addition (of *1517/18*) makes it clear that the ruler's 'purposes' may be nefarious as well as legitimate.

90 Apostolius 8.75

more capable. Suitable for high-spirited people whose pride is not matched by their strength. Or for someone who is not afraid to provoke people whom he may not be able to defeat. Φρονεῖν can be taken to mean 'to be sensitive': people who are of humble station have to be silent about many things because they cannot prevent the wrongs they see being done, and they cannot do what they feel should be done.[1] In the 'Sayings of Spartans' Plutarch attributes this saying to Archidamus the son of Zeuxidamus, seeing his son rushing too hastily and thoughtlessly to fight the Athenians: 'Either add to your strength or subtract from your courage.'[2]

91 Felicitas a Deo
Success comes from God

Θεοῦ δὲ δῶρόν ἐστιν εὐτυχεῖν βροτούς, Success comes to mortals as a gift of the gods.[1] The happy outcome of our affairs is not in us to determine, but depends on the will of the One above. It is for men to propose, but God disposes.[2]

92 Hystricis seta
A porcupine's spine

Θρὶξ ὑστριχος, A porcupine's bristle. This could be used to mean a biting sarcasm directed against someone. The expression derives from the animal that has the habit when provoked of shooting the sharp-pointed spines bristling on its back like darts[1] even to some distance, and it does this by drawing its skin tight. With these spines it transfixes the mouths of dogs that pursue it. The porcupine belongs to the same genus as hedgehogs though it has longer spines. India and Africa are the main places where porcupines breed, as Pliny tells us in book 8 chapter 35.[2]

* * * * *

1 This sentence was an addition of 1515.
2 Plutarch *Moralia* 218E; added in 1526

91 Apostolius 8.87
1 Aeschylus *Seven against Thebes* 625
2 This sentence added in 1528; cf Tilley M 298 Man proposes, God disposes.

92 Apostolius 8.92
1 'of shooting ... like darts' added in 1515
2 Pliny *Naturalis historia* 8.125 from whom all the information here is ultimately drawn, though from 'even to some distance' to the end was not added until 1517/18

93 Alter Ianus
Another Janus

Ἴανος ἄλλος, Another Janus. This will be suitable either for someone who is prudent and cautious or for someone who is two-faced and untrustworthy. Persius: 'O Janus, whom no stork ever pecked / From behind.'[1] The origin is the two-headed figure of Janus; the legend is too well known to be recounted here.[2]

94 Veste circumfers ignem
You are putting a cloak round a fire

Ἱματίῳ τὸ πῦρ περιστέλλεις, You are putting a cloak round a fire.[1] Used when something is thought to be absurd, or when someone promotes his own misfortune by favouring a prostitute or a flatterer or a false friend.[2]

95 Erinnys ex tragoedia
A Fury from tragedy

Ἐριννὺς ἐκ τραγῳδίας, A Fury from tragedy. A term for detestable old women. It comes from Aristophanes' *Plutus* where it is said of the figure of Poverty: 'But perhaps she is a Fury out of tragedy.'[1] In book 4 of his *Geography* Strabo reports that there are ten islands in the Gaditan ocean called the Cassiteridae, of which one is completely uninhabited, on the others live people who are dark in colour, wear tunics that come down to their heels

* * * * *

93 Apostolius 8.98. Otto 841. Tilley J 37 Like Janus two-faced
   1 Persius *Satires* 1.58. Also used in *Adagia* III iii 41 He has eyes in the back of his head, and IV i 78 A face behind your back (489 above)
   2 Varro *De lingua latina* 7.26; Virgil *Aeneid* 7.180; Ovid *Fasti* 1.95–144; Eustathius 1533.5 on *Odyssey* 5.249; Athenaeus 15.692D. Sentence added in *1515*

94 Apostolius 9.4. Socrates in Stobaeus *Eclogae* 3.6.14 Hense III 284, but see Estienne (n1 below).
   1 Estienne (LB II 1007) points out that περιστέλλω means *coöperio* 'cover completely,' or better still *circumtego, circumvolvo* 'wrap around.' 'The saying means "You are wrapping" or "hiding the fire in a cloak." Socrates himself told us how to explain the adage with this saying of his: "It is not possible to hide a fire with a cloak nor a shameful deed with time."'
   2 From 'or when someone' to the end added in *1515*

95 Apostolius 9.14
   1 Aristophanes *Plutus* 423

and a sword belt across their chests, and carry a staff in their hands[2] – in short, are very like the Furies of tragedy. From this it is clear this is the garb in which the Furies appeared in tragedies.

96 Aequalitas haud parit bellum
Equality never gives rise to war

Ἴσα πόλεμον οὐ ποιεῖ, Equality never gives rise to war. By equality we ensure peace; it is inequality that is the mother of discord. This is a maxim of Solon, as Plutarch writes in his life of Solon, informing us this saying was very popular: 'Equality never gives rise to war.'[1]

97 Piscis primum a capite foetet
The head of a fish is the first part to smell

Ἰχθὺς ἐκ τῆς κεφαλῆς ὄζειν ἄρχεται, The head of a fish begins to stink first. Used of bad rulers, whose contagion poisons the rest of the people. The expression seems to derive from the language of common people.[1]

98 Etiam baetylum devorares
You would eat even the *baetylus*

Καὶ βαίτυλον ἂν καταπίνοις, You would swallow even the *baetylus*. Used of a voracious person who puts everything into his stomach at once. The *baetylus* was the stone wrapped in swaddling clothes that Saturn swallowed, believing it to be Jupiter, as Hesychius tells us.[1]

* * * * *

2 Strabo *Geographica* 3.5.11 (not book 4); added in *1515*. The Gaditan ocean (from Gades, Cadiz) was the Atlantic; the Cassiterides, the 'Tin Islands,' are traditionally identified with Cornwall and the Scillies, though the name may be a generic one for any source of tin beyond the Mediterranean.

96 Apostolius 9.16
1 Plutarch *Solon* 14.2: Τὸ ἴσον πόλεμον οὐ ποιεῖ; sentence added in *1528*

97 Apostolius 9.18. Tilley F 304 A fish begins first to smell at the head
1 Suringar 172; another indication, added in *1515*, of Erasmus' suspicions of Apostolius

98 Apostolius 9.24
1 Hesychius B 103; added in *1517/18*. None of the classical sources of the story (eg Hesiod *Theogony* 485–6, Apollodorus 1.1.7, Pausanias 10.24.6, Lucretius

99 Malum vas non frangitur
A cheap jar is never broken

Κακὸν ἄγγος οὐ κλᾶται, A cheap jar is never broken. The inferior man is often the longer lived and safer in dangerous situations. A similar figure is used commonly nowadays: 'Weeds do not die.'[1]

100 Etiam quercus bacchatur
Even the oak dances for Bacchus

Καὶ δρῦς Μαινὰς ἐγένετο, Even the oak became a Maenad. An expression used of those who are not easily won over. It comes from the legend of Orpheus who charmed oak trees with his lute.[1] Maenads are women inspired by Bacchus.[2]

* * * * *

2.633–9) gives this name for the stone, though *baetylus* is named as a type of precious stone by Pliny *Naturalis historia* 37.135.

99 Apostolius 9.36. Tilley v 38 Ill vessels seldom miscarry
1 Suringar 112; added in *1515*

100 Apostolius 9.49
1 Following Apostolius
2 Sentence added in *1515*

WORKS FREQUENTLY CITED

This list provides bibliographical information for works referred to in short-title form in this volume.

Alexandrian Proverbs	See CPG 1 under 'Plutarchus'
Apostolius	See CPG 2
Appendix	See CPG 1
ASD	*Opera omnia Desiderii Erasmi Roterodami* (Amsterdam / Oxford 1969–)
Bergk	Th. Berg ed *Poetae lyrici Graeci* 4th edition (Leipzig 1900–15) 3 vols
CPG	E.L. Leutsch and F.G. Schneidewin eds *Corpus paroemiographorum Graecorum* 1: Zenobius. Diogenianus. Plutarchus (= Laurentianus 1). Gregorius Cyprianus cum appendice proverbiorum (Hildesheim 1961); 2: Diogenianus (Epitome). Gregorius Cyprianus. Macarius. Aesopus. Apostolius et Arsenius. Mantissa proverbiorum (Hildesheim 1961); 3: Supplementum: Crusius *Analecta*. Jungblut (= Laurentianus 2–5) (Hildesheim 1991)
Crusius *Analecta*	O. Crusius *Analecta critica ad paroemiographos Graecos* (Leipzig 1883) repr in CPG 3
CRF	O. Ribbeck ed *Comicorum Romanorum fragmenta* 3rd edition (Leipzig 1898)
CSEL	*Corpus scriptorum ecclesiasticorum Latinorum* (Vienna-Leipzig 1866–)
Diehl	E. Diehl ed *Anthologia lyrica Graeca* (Leipzig 1949–52) 3 vols
Diels-Kranz	H. Diels and W. Kranz *Die Fragmente der Vorsokratiker* (Berlin 1966–7) 3 vols
Diogenianus	See CPG 1
Dübner	Fr. Dübner *Scholia Graeca in Aristophanem* (Hildesheim 1969)

Erbse	H. Erbse *Untersuchungen zu den attizistischen Lexika* in *Abhandlungen der deutschen Akademie der Wissenschaften zu Berlin* (Berlin 1950)
Estienne	Henri Estienne [Henricus Stephanus] *Animadversiones in Erasmicas quorundam adagiorum expositiones* (Geneva 1558), printed as footnotes in LB
FGrHist	F. Jacoby ed *Die Fragmente der griechischen Historiker* (Leiden 1940–58)
FHG	C. Müller ed *Fragmenta historicorum Graecorum* (Paris 1841–70)
Jäkel	S. Jäkel ed *Menandri Sententiae* (Leipzig 1964)
Jungblut	H. Jungblut 'Über die Sprichwörtersammlungen des Laurentianus 80,13' in CPG 3
Kaibel	G. Kaibel ed *Comicorum Graecorum fragmenta* (Berlin 1975)
Kock	Th. Kock ed *Comicorum Atticorum fragmenta* (Utrecht 1976)
Körte-Thierfelder	Alfredus Körte ed *Menandri quae supersunt* ... addenda adiecit Andreas Thierfelder (Leipzig 1957)
Laurentianus	Ms Laurentianus 80.13. See Jungblut
LB	Erasmus *Opera omnia* ed Jean Leclerc (Leiden 1703–6; repr Hildesheim 1961–2) 10 vols
Lobel-Page	E. Lobel and D. Page eds *Poetarum Lesbiorum fragmenta* (Oxford 1963)
Mantissa	See CPG 2
Meineke	August Meineke ed *Stephani Byzantii ethnicorum quae supersunt* (Berlin 1849)
Nauck	A. Nauck ed *Tragicorum Graecorum fragmenta* (Leipzig 1889)
Otto	A. Otto *Die Sprichwörter und sprichwörtliche Redensarten der Römer* (Hildesheim 1962)
Otto *Nachträge*	A. Otto *Die Sprichwörter und sprichwörtliche Redensarten der Römer. Nachträge* R. Häussler ed (Darmstadt 1968); includes M.C. Sutphen *A Collection of Latin Proverbs supplementing*

	Otto's Sprichwörter und sprichtwörtliche Redensarten der Römer (Baltimore 1902)
PCG	R. Kassel and C. Austin eds *Poetae comici Graeci* (Berlin 1983–98)
PG	J.-P. Migne ed *Patrologia cursus completus, series Graeca* (Paris 1857–86)
PL	J.-P. Migne ed *Patrologia cursus completus, series Latina* (Paris 1844–64)
PMG	D.L. Page ed *Poetae melici Graeci* (Oxford 1962)
Poliziano *Miscellanea*	A. Politianus *Miscellanea centuria prima* (Florence 1489)
Rose	V. Rose ed *Aristotelis qui ferebantur librorum fragmenta* (Leipzig 1886)
Skutsch	Otto Skutsch *The Annals of Quintus Ennius* (Oxford 1985)
Suringar	W.H.D. Suringar *Erasmus over nederlandsche spreekwoorden en spreekwoordelijke uitdrukkingen van zijnen tijd* (Utrecht 1873)
Tilley	M.P. Tilley *A Dictionary of the Proverbs in England in the Sixteenth and Seventeenth Centuries* (Ann Arbor 1966)
TRF	O. Ribbeck ed *Tragicorum Romanorum fragmenta* 3rd edition (Leipzig 1897)
Walther	H. Walther *Proverbia sententiaeque Latinitatis medii aevi* (Göttingen 1963–67) 5 vols
Wehrli	Fritz Wehrli *Die Schule des Aristoteles* (Basle 1967–69)
West	M.L. West ed *Iambi et elegi Graeci ante Alexandrum cantati* (Oxford 1971) 2 vols
Zenobius	See CPG 1
Zenobius (Aldus)	'Collectio proverbiorum Tarrhaei, et Didymi, item eorum, quae apud Sudam, aliosque habentur per ordinem literarum' in *Habentur hoc volumine haec, videlicet: Vita et Fabellae Aesopi* ... published by Aldus (Venice 1505)
Zenobius (Athous)	Ζηνοβίου ἐπιτομὴ τῶν Ταρραίου καὶ Διδύμου παροιμιῶν in E. Miller, *Mélanges de littérature grecque* (Paris 1839) 341–84 (index in Crusius *Analecta*)

TABLE OF ADAGES

This book

was designed by

VAL COOKE

based on the series design by

ALLAN FLEMING

and was printed by

University

of Toronto

Press